BRUMBACK LIBRARY
VAN WERT, OH

3 3045 00036 5268

P9-AQC-164

11/89

FOR REFERENCE

Do not take from this room

DEC 1989

GREAT LIVES
FROM
HISTORY

GREAT LIVES FROM HISTORY

Renaissance to 1900 Series

Volume 5
Sche-Z

Edited by

FRANK N. MAGILL

SALEM PRESS

Pasadena, California   Englewood Cliffs, New Jersey

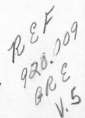

REF
920.009
GRE
V.5

Copyright © 1989, by FRANK N. MAGILL
All rights in this book are reserved. No part of this work
may be used or reproduced in any manner whatsoever or
transmitted in any form or by any means, electronic or
mechanical, including photocopy, recording, or any information storage and retrieval system, without written
permission from the copyright owner except in the case
of brief quotations embodied in critical articles and
reviews. For information address the publisher, Salem
Press, Inc., P. O. Box 50062, Pasadena, California 91105.

∞ The paper used in these volumes conforms to the
American National Standard for Permanence of Paper
for Printed Library Materials, Z39.48-1984.

Library of Congress Cataloging-in-Publication Data
Great lives from history. Renaissance to 1900 series /
edited by Frank N. Magill.

    p.   cm.
Includes bibliographical references.
Summary: This five-volume work examines the lives
of 495 individuals whose contributions greatly influenced the world's cultures that flourished from the Renaissance through 1900. An annotated bibliography ac-
companies each entry.
    1. Biography. 2. World history [1. Biography. 2. World
history.] I. Magill, Frank Northen, 1907-
CT104.G68   1989
920'.009'03—dc20
[B]
[920]   89-24039
ISBN 0-89356-551-2 (set)   CIP
ISBN 0-89356-556-3 (volume 5)   AC

PRINTED IN THE UNITED STATES OF AMERICA

LIST OF BIOGRAPHIES IN VOLUME FIVE

8904967

LIST OF BIOGRAPHIES IN VOLUME FIVE

GREAT LIVES
FROM
HISTORY

8904967

FRIEDRICH WILHELM JOSEPH SCHELLING

Born: January 27, 1775; Leonberg in Württemberg
Died: August 20, 1854; Bad Ragaz, Switzerland
Area of Achievement: Philosophy
Contribution: Schelling contributed to the development of German Idealism and to the rise of German Romanticism. His later ontological and mythological speculations, though unpopular among his contemporaries such as G. W. F. Hegel, have influenced modern existentialism and philosophical anthropology.

Early Life

Friedrich Wilhelm Joseph Schelling was born in Leonberg, Württemberg, where his father, Joseph Friedrich Schelling, was an erudite Lutheran pastor. In 1777, his family moved to Bebenhausen near Tübingen, where his father became a professor of Oriental languages at the theological seminary. Schelling was educated at the cloister school of Bebenhausen, apparently destined for the ministry by family tradition. A gifted child, he learned the classical languages by the age of eight. From 1790 to 1792, he attended the theological seminary at Tübingen, where he met Hegel and Friedrich Hölderlin, the great Romantic poet. The Tübingen Evangelical Theological Seminary, located in the buildings of an old Augustinian monastery, is idyllically set over the Neckar River on a cliff, ensconced in green hills, with a view of the snow-topped craggy Alps in the distance. Good friends while students at Tübingen, Schelling, Hegel, and Hölderlin were partisans of the French Revolution and spent many hours discussing philosophy: the pantheism of Baruch Spinoza, the pure concepts of Immanuel Kant, and the Idealist system of Johann Gottlieb Fichte.

For several years after finishing at Tübingen, Schelling was a tutor for the sons of a noble family in Leipzig. He was a precocious and passionate thinker and progressed more quickly in his career than the older Hegel. His first published philosophical work was *Über die Möglichkeit einer Form der Philosophie überhaupt* (1795; on the possibility and form of philosophy in general). This text was followed by *Vom Ich als Prinzip der Philosophie* (1795; of the ego as principle of philosophy) and the article "Philosophische Briefe über Dogmatismus und Kritizismus" (1796; philosophical letters on dogmatism and criticism). The basic theme of these works is the Absolute, which Schelling interpreted not as God but as the Absolute ego. This ego is transcendental and eternal and can be experienced through direct intuition, which Schelling defined as an intellectual process. In 1798, at the exceptionally young age of twenty-three, Schelling became a professor of philosophy at the University of Jena, where Hegel taught as an unsalaried lecturer between 1801 and 1807, and where in October, 1806, Napoleon I defeated the Prussian army and thus conquered Prussia, the most powerful state in Germany.

Life's Work

Schelling's life's work as a philosopher and teacher began at the University of Jena, the academic center of Germany. At Jena, he became a colleague and friend of the famous Fichte, at the time Germany's leading philosopher. Fichte, who had been one of Schelling's idols, had read and strongly approved of Schelling's early philosophical work. Schelling and Hegel, both Idealist philosophers, coedited the *Kritisches Journal der Philosophie*. Even though Hegel was five years older than Schelling, he at this time was thought of as Schelling's disciple; his first book compared the philosophies of Schelling and Fichte.

Jena at this time was also the center of German Romanticism, and in nearby Weimar Friedrich Schiller and Johann Wolfgang von Goethe, German dramatists and poets, were at the height of their careers. Schelling knew both and was profoundly influenced by the Romantic movement. German Romanticism, in turn, was influenced by Schelling's philosophy, which emphasized the importance of the individual and the values of art. German Romanticism and Schelling's Idealist philosophy are both characterized by the "inward path" to truth, the quest for the totality of experience, and the desire for unity and infinity. Schelling's career falls into two periods: the first, from 1795 to 1809, and the second, which was less productive but no less significant, from 1809 to 1854.

Schelling's peers at Jena—Goethe, Schiller, the Romanticists Friedrich and August Wilhelm Schlegel, the writer/critic Ludwig Tiech, and Hegel—constituted a close group of friends who strongly influenced one another's work. For convenience, Schelling's philosophy can be divided into four stages: the subjective Idealism or his work before Jena; the philosophy of nature; the philosophy of identity; and the philosophy of opposition between negative and positive. The two middle stages belong to his first period of productivity, while the fourth stage belongs to his final period. The second stage, his most famous and influential, began with his *Ideen zu einer Philosophie der Nature* (1797; partial translation as *Introduction to the Philosophy of Nature*, 1871). In opposition to Fichte's idea of the world as a product of ego, Schelling on the one hand argues that the world of nature is as important as the ego and on the other finds a common ground between the two in the essence of matter, which he defines as force. In his *Von der Weltseele, eine Hypothese der höheren Physik zur Erklärung des allgemeinen Organismus* (1798; on the world soul, a hypothesis of advanced physics for the interpretation of the general organism), Schelling argues that the interpretation of the unity of nature was the basic aim of science and thus that the object of scientific study was force, of which mechanical, chemical, electrical, and vital forces were merely different manifestations. This theory is similar to the unified field theory sought by Albert Einstein and now being convincingly proposed by modern physicists such as John Hagelin. In 1799, Schelling published another book on natural philosophy, defining force as pure activity. He believed that nature realized itself in finite matter through an infinite self-referral that never reached completion. This theory he considered parallel to Kant's idea of reason forever striving toward an unattainable absolute.

While in Jena, Schelling became engaged and eventually married under bizarre circumstances. Through his friendship with August Schlegel and his charming wife, Caroline, the daughter of a professor in Göttingen and one of the most intellectually gifted women in German Romanticism, Schelling became informally engaged to Auguste Böhmer, Caroline's sixteen-year-old daughter by a previous marriage. Auguste, however, died in 1800, and Schelling was later held partly responsible for having treated her illness on the basis of his amateur medical knowledge and his impetuous self-confidence— a common trait among the Romantics. This tragedy created a bond between Schelling and Caroline, who had already felt a mutual attraction. In 1803, through the aid of Goethe, Caroline obtained a divorce from Schlegel and married Schelling. The three remained friends in true Romantic style, but the intrigue surrounding the marriage renewed allegations of Schelling's role in Auguste's death, causing him to leave Jena and join the faculty at the University of Würzburg.

At the height of his second stage, Schelling published *System des transzendentalen Idealismus* (1800; *Introduction to Idealism*, 1871), his most mature and systematic philosophical statement, in which he attempts to unite his theory of nature with the theory of knowledge developed by Kant and Fichte. In defining human consciousness as pure self-activity in opposition to the not-self, Schelling built a theory involving three stages: a movement from sensation to perception, perception to reflection, and reflection to will. This movement connected knowledge and its object. Schelling believed that since concepts cannot exist without their objects, knowledge consists of a meeting of self, object, and process, or of knower, known, and process of knowing—a view also espoused by the Vedic philosophy of India. The transcendental idealism of this book was the one area in which Schelling influenced the mature philosophy of Hegel, especially his theory of the dialectic.

In 1806, Schelling was called to Munich to be an associate for the Academy of Sciences and the secretary of the Academy of Arts. Later, he became the secretary of the philosophical branch of the Academy of Sciences. These were government sinecure positions that gave Schelling extra time for research and allowed him to lecture in Stuttgart. Around this time, he became increasingly interested in aesthetic theory and lectures on the philosophy of art. He believed art to be an organic whole that was served by its parts and moved teleologically toward a specific purpose. This purpose was not pleasure, utility, knowledge, or morality but rather beauty, which Schelling defined as the infinite actualized within the finite. He held that human intelligence in philosophy is abstract and limited, whereas in art it awakens to itself and realizes its unbounded potential. Because it reconciles nature and history and is the aim of all intelligence, art is the highest philosophy.

Schelling's third stage of thought, the philosophy of identity, proposes that the production of reality arises not from the opposition of intelligence to nature but rather from the identity of all objects in the Absolute. The identity of nature and intelligence has its source in reason, defined as an infinite field. In describing Schelling's absolute theory of unity between subject and object, Hegel wittily compared it to the night, "in which all cows are black." Schelling's theory of absolute identity was a type of pantheism, holding nature to be inseparable, even if distinguishable, from God. Here Schelling derives from the mystic Jakob Böhme. Since the essence of God is will, He can be apprehended only by means of will—that is, in action—and not by means of mere rational comprehension.

During this period, Schelling published *Philosophische Untersuchungen über das Wesen der menschlichen Frieheit* (1809; *Of Human Freedom*, 1936), in which he distinguishes between two aspects of God: perfection and the ground of being. Evil is the ground which teaches mankind the difference between good and evil, and which is therefore a necessary stage in the development toward perfection.

In 1809, Caroline died prematurely. Schelling was so distraught he did not publish another book for the rest of his life and entered the final, existential phase of his career. He first propounded his positive philosophy of this period in *Die Weltalter* (1913, written in 1811-1813; partial translation as *The Ages of the World*, 1942), a work that consisted of three volumes, one of which is *Philosophie der Mythologie* (philosophy of mythology). In *The Ages of the World*, Schelling describes the history of God as the divine principle expressed in human history, especially in religion and myth. God is the eternal nothing, the ungrounded basis necessary for the ground to exist. By alienating Himself from Himself through His own oppositional nature, God the Absolute creates the possibility of His relative opposite, which Schelling defined as freedom. Freedom is both the cause of the fall from the Absolute and the trace of the Absolute after the fall. Whereas a negative philosophy developed the idea of God by means of reason alone, Schelling's positive philosophy developed this idea by reasoning backward from the existence of the created world to the existence of God as its creator.

Summary

The two phases of Friedrich Wilhelm Joseph Schelling's career were distinctly different. His second, more despondent, phase consisted of his last philosophical period, stretching across forty-five years from 1809 to 1854, in which he saw his significance as a German Idealist decline. Failing to revive his influence against Hegelianism in Berlin in 1841, he became melancholic and pessimistic, a condition he tried to surmount by developing a system of metaphysics based on Christian revelation and a personal God. Hegel's great philosophical influence was denied to Schelling, whose early and middle periods—his philosophy of nature and philosophy of identity—fell between Fichte's Idealism and Hegel's system of the Absolute spirit.

Nevertheless, over the past century Schelling's independence and importance to philosophy have become more apparent. In its concern not only with the nature of reality but also with the fact of its very existence, Schelling's philosophy bears a strong, if suggestive, resemblance to modern existentialism. In *Philosophie der Mythologie*, Schelling ventures into the field of philosophical anthropology by arguing that humanity, as the embodiment of freedom and creative intelligence, is the essence of the world, which finds expression in mythmaking and religion, humanity's most profound activities. He explored the moods of sadness associated with humanity's being in the world. Like Søren Kierkegaard, Friedrich Nietzsche, Martin Heidegger, and Jean-Paul Sartre, Schelling sought to express the ineffable poignancy of human existence, anticipating the notions of existential anxiety and psychoanalytic resistance to cure. Schelling, however, was convinced that despair was denied the last word on human existence by the revelation of God.

Bibliography
Brown, Robert F. *The Later Philosophy of Schelling: The Influence of Boehme on the Works of 1809-1815*. London: Associated University Presses, 1977. A comprehensive analysis of Schelling's ontology and doctrine of God as influenced by Jakob Böhme's mysticism. Deals with philosophical and theological problems, such as the immutability of God, and the stages in which Schelling incorporates Böhme's ideas. Contains bibliography of German and English secondary texts.

Esposito, Joseph L. *Schelling's Idealism and Philosophy of Nature*. London: Associated University Presses, 1977. Analysis of Schelling's philosophy of nature and its influence on nineteenth century science. Also traces the influence of Schelling's idealism in America and provides a modern vindication of objective idealism against those who criticize Schelling for the lack of a guiding vision. Contains selected bibliography of secondary sources, mainly in German.

Marx, Werner. *The Philosophy of F. W. J. Schelling: History, System, and Freedom*. Translated by Thomas Nenon, with a foreword by A. Hofstadter. Bloomington: Indiana University Press, 1984. Explores Schelling's conception of history as the relationship between freedom and necessity, then compares this conception with the contemporary theory of history developed by J. Habermas, showing how the latter first renounces and then proceeds to incorporate the categories of the former. Also treats Schelling's self-intuition compared to Hegel's phenomenology and interprets Schelling's notion of human freedom.

Schelling, F. W. J. *The Ages of the World*. Translated with an introduction by Frederick de Wolfe Bolman. New York: AMS Press, 1942. Schelling's text is preceded by a seventy-nine-page introduction, in which Bolman analyzes the twofold nature of Schelling's philosophy, discusses reality and nature in his development through 1812 and his interests after 1812, and then interprets *The Ages of the World*. Ends with a synoptic outline taken from the original manuscript.

_____. *System of Transcendental Idealism*. Translated by Peter Heath, with an introduction by M. Vater. Charlottesville: University Press of Virginia, 1978. Schelling's most mature and complete philosophical statements and one of his few works translated into English. Concerns the relation between self and object in his transcendental idealism. Good introduction that compares Schelling to Fichte, Hegel, and other philosophers and discusses the relationship between the self and consciousness.

White, Alan. *Schelling: An Introduction to the System of Freedom*. New Haven, Conn.: Yale University Press, 1983. White covers Schelling's entire fifty-year career in terms of the history of modern philosophy, lucidly arguing that Schelling attempts to produce a system of freedom. Schelling is shown to identify problems with freedom and evil not treated by Hegel. Contains selected annotated bibliography.

William S. Haney II

FRIEDRICH SCHILLER

Born: November 10, 1759; Marbach, Württemberg
Died: May 9, 1805; Weimar, Saxe-Weimar
Areas of Achievement: Drama, literature, historiography, and philosophy
Contribution: Schiller's main contribution to German literature was in the field of drama, especially historical drama. In philosophy, his contributions were mainly in the areas of ethics and aesthetics. Belonging to the school of German classicism, he was one of the leading contributors to German Idealism in literature and philosophy.

Early Life

Born at Marbach in Württemberg, the son of an army surgeon, Friedrich Schiller went to school in Ludwigsburg, the residence of the Dukes of Württemberg. Though Schiller wanted to become a Protestant minister, his father was ordered by Duke Karl Eugen of Württemberg to send his son to the Hohe Karlsschule, the newly established military academy, located near Ludwigsburg. At this academy, young men at an early age were prepared for the civil and military service of the state of Württemberg. Schiller studied first law and then medicine from 1773 until 1780. He was graduated with a degree in medicine and became regimental surgeon of a regiment stationed in Stuttgart. During his time at the academy, Schiller wrote poetry and his first drama, *Die Räuber* (*The Robbers*, 1792), written in 1777-1780 and published in 1781. This play is rightly regarded as the most representative drama of his *Sturm und Drang* (storm and stress) period. When Schiller attended the first performance of his play at the Mannheim National Theater in 1782 without leave of absence from his regiment in Stuttgart, he was reprimanded by Karl Eugen, his commander in chief, and forbidden to engage in any further writing with the exception of medical treatises. Rebelling against this punishment and the strict discipline of military life, Schiller deserted in 1782 and fled to Mannheim, where his first drama had been performed with great success, in order to pursue a career as a dramatist. For almost a year, the fugitive stayed in hiding in the small village of Bauerbach in Thuringia. In 1783, Schiller was appointed *Theaterdichter* (stage dramatist) of the Mannheim National Theater. During his stay in Mannheim, both his dramas *Die Verschwörung des Fiesko zu Genua* (1783; *Fiesco: Or, The Genoese Conspiracy*, 1796) and *Kabale und Liebe* (1784; *Cabal and Love*, 1795) were performed on the Mannheim stage. His drama *Don Carlos, Infant von Spanien* (1787; *Don Carlos, Infante of Spain*, 1798) remained a fragment during those years. In 1784, however, his contract in Mannheim was not renewed, so Schiller followed an invitation from his friend Christian Gottfried Körner to come to Leipzig and later to Dresden.

In 1787, Schiller went to Weimar, which had become the intellectual center of Germany, where he met Johann Gottfried Herder and Christoph Martin Wieland, while Johann Wolfgang von Goethe was in Italy. During the next year, Schiller stayed in the towns of Volksstädt and Rudolstadt, where he met Charlotte von Lengefeld, his future wife. During this time, he began his career as a historian and philosopher, concentrating in his philosophical studies on the major works of Immanuel Kant. These philosophical and historical preoccupations mark Schiller's transition from his *Sturm und Drang* subjectivity to the objective idealism of his classical period. His dramatic production came almost to a standstill during this time.

Life's Work

On the basis of his *Geschichte des Abfalls der vereinigten Niederlande von der spanischen Regierung* (1788; *The History of the Defection of the United Netherlands from the Spanish Empire*, 1844), Schiller was appointed professor of history at the University of Jena in 1789 upon the recommendation of Goethe. He was married to Charlotte von Lengefeld in 1790. After a serious illness in 1791, from which he never completely recovered and which led to his early death in 1805, Schiller visited Körner in Dresden and his homeland, Württemberg, in 1793. His friendship with Goethe, which began in 1794, led to a working relationship that became the basis of German classicism. Although their relationship was not without tensions, it proved to be stimulating and rewarding for both writers and gave direction to the course and development of German literature for the next ten years. Schiller continued to live in Jena until 1799. His correspondence with Goethe records their literary activities and their opinions and projections for the future of German and European culture. From 1795 to 1797, Schiller edited *Die Horen*, a literary journal, to which Goethe contributed a number of his writings. During his stay in Jena, Schiller returned to creative writing with his dramatic Wallenstein trilogy. In December, 1799, Schiller moved to Weimar, where he wrote the dramas *Maria Stuart* (1800; English translation, 1801), *Die Jungfrau von Orleans* (1801; *The Maid of Orleans*, 1835), *Die Braut von Messina: Oder, Die feindlichen Brüder* (1803; *The Bride of Messina*, 1837), and *Wilhelm Tell* (1804; *William Tell*, 1841). The work of this most productive period of his life, from 1794 to 1804, during which Schiller wrote his best dramas and poems, was largely a result of the stimulus of his relationship with Goethe. In 1802, Schiller was raised to the nobility, adding "von" to his last name.

During these years, most of Schiller's creative energies were devoted to the field of drama, especially historical drama. He succeeded in becoming the most important German dramatist second to Goethe at the end of the eighteenth century, and one of the most important of all European dramatists. All of his dramas deal with the concept of freedom. While in his early dramas of the *Sturm und Drang* period freedom is perceived mostly in terms of physical freedom, his dramas of the classical period center on ethical freedom. For his later plays, Schiller selected mostly historical plots, because he considered world history an ideal proving ground for the conflict between individual freedom and political necessity. His protagonists usually decide in favor of physical annihilation in order to preserve their moral freedom and integrity.

Schiller's principal contributions to lyric poetry consisted of philosophical poems and of historical ballads which demonstrate his talent for dramatic action and his awareness of philosophical problems. His poems include the philosophical poem "An die Freude" ("Ode to Joy," well known in its musical setting by Ludwig van Beethoven in his ninth symphony), "Die Götter Griechenlands," and the elegy "Der Spaziergang"; among his most famous ballads are "Der Ring des Polykrates," "Die Kraniche des Ibykus," and "Die Bürgschaft."

Schiller was not only a dramatist and poet but also a historian. *The History of the Defection of the United Netherlands from the Spanish Empire* and *Geschichte des dreissigjährigen Krieges* (1791-1793; *History of the Thirty Years' War*, 1799) are examples of his work in this area. Schiller's historical research influenced his dramatic works, supplying him with plots and background material for his dramas.

Schiller's philosophical essays fall mainly under the headings of ethics and aesthetics. His essays on dramatic theory deal with the function of tragic emotions and the use of the pathetic as well as the sublime in dramatic art. In his aesthetics as well as his ethics, Schiller was strongly influenced by Kant, whose moral rigidity Schiller tried to counterbalance by his concept of the *schöne Seele* (beautiful soul), in which duty and inclination are in harmony. In his poetics, Schiller established the so-called naïve attitude and sentimental, or reflective, attitude as two legitimate approaches to literature, while in his philosophical anthropology he projected a dialectic development beyond Enlightenment philosophy.

Summary

Together with Goethe, Friedrich Schiller is regarded as one of the representative national dramatists and poets of Germany. Historical drama, as he fashioned it at the end of the eighteenth century, became the dominant model for this genre during the nineteenth century. History was conceived in terms of Schillerian drama. Schiller's plays furnished the librettos for many of the operas from Gioacchino Rossini to Giuseppe Verdi. Only with the advent of naturalist drama did the predominance of Schiller's model of the historical drama come to an end.

In the nineteenth century, Schiller was celebrated in Germany as a liberal idealist until 1848, and, after the revolution had failed, as a German nationalist and a representative of German Idealism. This idealism became suspect after World War I and World War II, especially because of its lack of practical experience and its disregard of the realities of political life. Expressionist drama and the non-Aristotelian drama of Bertolt Brecht finally replaced the Schillerian model. Yet even in the 1960's, Rolf Hochhuth's controversial historical drama *Der Stellvertreter* (1963; *The Deputy,* 1963) followed the Schillerian model and became one of the outstanding works of the postwar years. Schiller's idealism is now considered as more complex and problematical than nineteenth century German ideology would admit. After William Shakespeare, Schiller is still one of the most widely performed dramatists on the German stage in East and West Germany.

In the relationship of Jews and Germans, Schiller played an important role. Many Jews considered Schiller to be the speaker of pure humanitarianism and the representative of the highest ideals of mankind. Before the Holocaust of World War II, Schiller personified to the Jews what they considered to be German. For many Austrian, German, Polish, and Russian Jews, the encounter with Schiller was much more real than with the actual Germany. Although Schiller had never addressed himself to the Jews or to Jewish problems, this fact did not affect the Jewish passion for his dramas and poetry. An example of this passion was the adoption of Schiller's name by many Russian Jews, among them famous Zionist leaders.

In Great Britain and the United States, Schiller was received as a representative of German Romanticism. While Thomas Carlyle, who wrote *The Life of Schiller* (1825), and the American Transcendentalists Ralph Waldo Emerson, Margaret Fuller, and Henry David Thoreau were highly appreciative of Schiller's achievements, George Bernard Shaw was negative in his criticism of Schiller's Romanticism in the preface to *Saint Joan,* his own Joan of Arc drama of 1923.

Bibliography

Garland, H. B. *Schiller, the Dramatic Writer: A Study of Style in the Plays.* Oxford, England: Clarendon Press, 1969. A study of individual dramas. Includes a two-page bibliography.

Graham, Ilse. *Schiller's Drama: Talent and Integrity.* London: Methuen, 1974. Includes individual readings of Schiller's dramas as well as some chapters on special issues raised by the plays as a whole. Includes extensive notes, a bibliography, and an index.

Mainland, William F. *Schiller and the Changing Past.* London: Heinemann, 1957. A study of Schiller's dramas in comparison to some of their sources. Not a systematic study. Includes a bibliography and an index.

Miller, R. D. *Schiller and the Ideal of Freedom: A Study of Schiller's Philosophical Works with Chapters on Kant.* Oxford, England: Clarendon Press, 1970. A study of Kant's concepts of moral and aesthetic freedom and Schiller's concept of freedom through harmony. Includes an index.

Simons, John D. *Friedrich Schiller*. Boston: Twayne, 1981. A later study of Schiller's life and work. Includes notes and references, a selected bibliography, and an index.

Stahl, Ernst L. *Friedrich Schiller's Dramas: Theory and Practice*. Oxford, England: Clarendon Press, 1954. A discussion of Schiller's dramas as well as his aesthetic doctrine and theory of tragedy. Includes a chronological table, a selected bibliography, and an index.

Thomas, Calvin. *The Life and Works of Friedrich Schiller*. New York: Henry Holt, 1901. Reprint. New York: AMS Press, 1970. A traditional but reliable biography which includes a brief summary of secondary literature, a general index, and an index of writings.

Witte, William. *Schiller*. Oxford, England: Basil Blackwell, 1949. A study of Schiller as letter-writer, poet, and playwright. Includes a bibliography and an index.

Ehrhard Bahr

FRIEDRICH SCHLEIERMACHER

Born: November 21, 1768; Breslau, Silesia
Died: February 12, 1834; Berlin, Prussia
Areas of Achievement: Theology and philosophy
Contribution: Schleiermacher helped Christian theology address the challenges and opportunities that were offered theological thought by modern historical consciousness. His most lasting contribution has been his theological system.

Early Life

Friedrich Daniel Ernst Schleiermacher was born in Breslau, Silesia. His parents entrusted his education to the Moravian Brethren at Niesky. This Moravian community espoused a form of Lutheran piety associated with Count Nikolaus Ludwig von Zinzendorf. They respected the primacy of the devotional life and particularly urged a devotion to Jesus over theological formulations. They also appreciated the disciplined life.

At Niesky, where the young Schleiermacher studied from 1783 to 1785, he followed a pietistic curriculum and also had his first taste of a humanistic education. First at Niesky and then at the Moravian theological school in Barby, he was engaged in the study of Latin and Greek. This Greek study was to prove to be the beginning of classical studies and eventually led to his great German translation of Plato. In these years, he came into contact with an impressive style of piety which continued to inform his life and thought. He withdrew from the seminary at Barby because he found little understanding among his teachers for his own honest struggles and doubts. His horizons were expanded beyond Moravian piety and his previous classical studies when, in 1787, he transferred to the University of Halle.

In Berlin in 1790, Schleiermacher passed his first theological examination, and shortly thereafter he accepted a position as a private tutor in the household of Count Dohna, in West Prussia. In 1793, he became a teacher in Berlin, and the following year he completed his second theological examination. In 1794, he also received ordination in the Reformed Church and entered its service as the assistant pastor in Landsberg. The tradition of Moravian piety, his classical studies, and his ordination for ministry in the Reformed Church all serve as the backdrop for Schleiermacher's life's work.

Life's Work

Schleiermacher's two most celebrated literary works are *Über die Religion: Reden an die Gebildten unter ihren Verächtern* (1799; *On Religion: Speeches to Its Cultured Despisers*, 1892) and *Der christliche Glaube nach den Grundsätzen der evangelischen Kirche im Zusammenhange dargestellt* (1821-1822; *The Christian Faith*, 1928). Both works have their geographic place of origin in Berlin, yet they were written in two different periods of Schleiermacher's life and are separated by two decades.

On Religion was written after several years' experience as a preacher and after having worked on several philosophical treatises. The Reformed clergyman had been called to the Charité Hospital in Berlin as a chaplain and preacher. Close to the turn of the century, Schleiermacher was enjoying the cultural milieu of the new Berlin society and a circle of Berlin's Romantics, to whom he had been introduced through his friendship with the poet Friedrich Schlegel. This was the beginning of the first creative period in his career. It was especially the speeches collected in *On Religion* which first made Schleiermacher famous. His audience was a circle of nontheological friends, the cultured despisers of religion, the literary and philosophical circles of society in the capital city. For them, piety had been displaced by aesthetic intuition.

In the first speech, which Schleiermacher calls an apology or a defense, he draws the distinction between religion's trappings and religion itself. The young chaplain asks his friends why they have only been concerned with shells of religion rather than going to the kernel of the matter. That kernel concerns the "pious exaltation of the mind [*Gemüt*] in which . . . the whole world is dissolved in an immediate feeling of the Infinite and the Eternal." The second and longest speech develops the nature or essence of religion. His concern was that religion be certain of its own roots and its independence in its relationship to philosophy and to morality. Religion is not only knowing or rationalism. It is not simply doing or moralism. Religion starts and ends with history. History is the most general and the most profound revelation of the deepest and the most holy. What is the finest and dearest in history can only be received in the feeling of the religious mind. Religion has to do with receptivity; it has its life in gaining perspective or intuition and feeling (*Anschauung und Gefühl*). Perspective is oriented toward the *Universum*, which has to do not only with the universe of space but also with the spiritual or intellectual world and with the historical context of relationships.

The third speech collected in *On Religion* is about the cultivation or formation of religion. Piety lies beyond teaching. A teachable religion itself would be absurd. Yet teaching can awaken piety in others. The fourth speech presents the relationship of religion and society and speaks of religious community, communication, and the church. The final speech discusses the God who became flesh, providing an overview of the phenomenological world of religion.

Following these speeches, in 1800 Schleiermacher published an ethical companion piece, *Monologen: Eine Neujahrsgabe* (*Schleiermacher's Soliloquies*, 1926). Taken together, *On Religion* and *Schleiermacher's Soliloquies* brought forth charges of pantheism. These charges, together with some concern about the young Schleiermacher's circle of friends in Berlin, led his elder and friend Friedrich Samuel Gottfried Sack to encourage a stay some distance from Berlin in Stolp. Schleiermacher thus left Berlin to serve as a court chaplain in Stolp from 1802 to 1804. He later accepted a call to Halle as preacher to the university, which included academic duties in a special appointment, which eventually became a regular appointment as professor. Schleiermacher's appointment made the theological faculty the first in Prussia to include both Lutheran and Reformed theologians.

When Schleiermacher returned to Berlin, he was a mature thinker, theologian, and philosopher. In 1809, he became preacher at Trinity Church, and in the same year he married Henriette von Willich, the widow of a friend who had died two years earlier. She brought two children into the marriage, and four other children issued from their union. By this time, the first edition of his translation of Plato's dialogues had appeared. The following fall he became a professor at the new university in Berlin, where he was to remain almost a quarter of a century. He was the first dean of the university's theological faculty, a position he occupied several times. He lectured in Christian ethics, church history, dogmatics, New Testament studies, and practical theology, as well as aesthetics, dialectics, ethics, hermeneutics, pedagogy, and psychology.

It was in the milieu of Berlin and his several responsibilities there that he conceived, composed, and published his major work, *The Christian Faith*. The two-volume work has a significant title, which translated reads, "the Christian faith systematically set forth according to the principles of the Evangelical church." The last part of the title suggests that Schleiermacher was a church theologian who took history seriously. In his introduction to his magnum opus, Schleiermacher gives an explanation of dogmatics and its methods. After the introduction, he divided his work into two major parts. The first concerns the development of religious self-consciousness as it is presupposed by but also contained in Christian piety. It treats creation and preservation and also the attributes of God and the states of the world which correspond to creation and preservation. The original divine attributes are God's eternity, omnipresence, omnipotence, and omniscience.

The second part of *The Christian Faith* develops self-consciousness as it is determined by the antithesis of sin and grace. This part appears to move from an understanding of sin to christology, through soteriology (theology dealing with salvation), ecclesiology, and eschatology (theology dealing with the Second Coming and Last Judgment). The theologies discussed in the second part are both more dialectical and more unified or coordinated than this simplified schema would suggest. For Schleiermacher, pious self-consciousness is determined by the consciousness of sin and grace. The consciousness of each person is developed within a system of three coordinates: the human being, the world, and God. Sin, both original and actual, is understood as the human condition. The state of the world is thus evil, while God's attributes are holiness and righteousness. The Christian is conscious of God's grace. The Holy Spirit is the means of grace, which arises out of God's love and wisdom.

Schleiermacher by and large held to the traditional dogmatic sequence of salvation history moving from creation to the Last Judgment. His one departure from this traditional order comes in his treatment of the doctrine of God. Along with the doctrine of God's attributes (love, wisdom, omniscience, and the like), the doctrine of God usually appears at the beginning of dogmatics. In Schleiermacher's dogmatics, the doctrine of God's attributes is treated in three sections over the whole of the work, but there appears to be no doctrine of God. The human experience of reality is thus called to serve in characterizing God's attributes. Rather than being omitted in Schleiermacher's dogmatics, God is described in relation to man's experience of reality.

According to Schleiermacher's method, each part of *The Christian Faith* consists of an ingenious tripartite arrangement which discusses pious self-consciousness, theology or divinity, and cosmology or the world; yet, in each section, the sequence of these topics is different. The self, God, and the world are therefore treated three times before Schleiermacher comes to the conclusion of his work. For the conclusion of the work, Schleiermacher transposed the doctrine of the Trinity, traditionally in dogmatic literature at the beginning with the doctrine of God, to the climax of his dogmatics.

Summary

Friedrich Schleiermacher is without a peer among modern theologians in the originality of his attempt to reconstruct the doctrine of God. His theology respects the fundamental distinctions between God and the world and between divinity and humanity, while affirming the interrelatedness of God, the self, and the world. In his life and thought, both piety and culture remained constant themes. He has rightly been recognized as the "father of modern theology."

Schleiermacher was not a theologian who disassociated himself from the preaching office of the church. Karl Barth has noted that Schleiermacher actively sought to present the most exposed, the most difficult and decisive theological position in the pulpit. That was true throughout his creative and mature life. Like Martin Luther and John Calvin before him, Schleiermacher gave himself year after year to the demands of both preaching and academic work.

Bibliography

Barth, Karl. "Schleiermacher." In *Protestant Theology in the Nineteenth Century: Its Background and History.* Valley Forge, Pa.: Judson Press, 1973. An appreciation and critique of Schleiermacher's theology from

Barth's own perspective as a theologian who provides an alternative to Schleiermacher. Contains a modest index of names.

Gadamer, Hans-Georg. *Truth and Method*. Edited and translated by Garrett Barden and John Cummings. New York: Continuum Publishing, 1975. This substantial work contains an analysis of Schleiermacher's hermeneutics and the questionableness of Romantic hermeneutics. Gadamer was a student of Martin Heidegger. Includes a helpful subject and name index.

Gerrish, B. A. "Continuity and Change: Friedrich Schleiermacher on the Task of Theology." In *Tradition and the Modern World: Reformed Theology in the Nineteenth Century*. Chicago: University of Chicago Press, 1978. Schleiermacher is discussed in the context of the Reformed tradition. Includes a good treatment of Emil Brunner's early work on Schleiermacher, which has never been translated.

_____. *A Prince of the Church: Schleiermacher and the Beginnings of Modern Theology*. Philadelphia: Fortress Press, 1984. A very brief introductory study that places Schleiermacher's theology in a broad context.

Niebuhr, Richard R. *Schleiermacher on Christ and Religion: A New Introduction*. New York: Charles Scribner's Sons, 1964. Treats the elements of Schleiermacher's style with fine discussions of his hermeneutical and historical background.

Redeker, Martin. *Schleiermacher: Life and Thought*. Translated by John Wallhausser. Philadelphia: Fortress Press, 1973. An excellent introduction by the editor of the German critical edition of *The Christian Faith*. Contains a good bibliography and a brief index of persons.

Arthur B. Holmes

HEINRICH SCHLIEMANN

Born: January 6, 1822; Neu Bockow, Mecklenburg-Schwerin
Died: December 26, 1890; Naples, Italy
Area of Achievement: Archaeology
Contribution: A stunningly successful merchant in his early years, Schliemann began a new career in his middle age as an archaeologist. Relying on an unwavering faith in Homer, he found and excavated Troy and unearthed the riches of Mycenae, and thus singlehandedly brought the splendors of the Greek Bronze Age to the attention of both amateurs and professionals.

Early Life

Heinrich Schliemann was born, the fifth of many children, in the small village of Neu Bockow, in Mecklenburg-Schwerin. His christened name was Julius, but he soon took the name of an older brother who had died ten weeks before Schliemann was born. Schliemann reports that by age seven he had already decided to find Troy upon seeing a woodcut of it in a history book that he received as a present from his father for Christmas in 1829. When Schliemann was nine years old, his mother died. It was also about this time that his father, Ernest, was disgraced for an affair with a maid and was temporarily suspended from his post as a Protestant clergyman. The scandal was an embarrassment and this, in addition to his mother's death, caused the family to break up.

Schliemann entered school, but in 1836 he was forced to leave to serve as an apprentice in a grocer's shop. It was during this period that he met a drunken miller, a former student, who recited Greek for Schliemann and intensified his love of Homer. Manual labor was difficult for Schliemann, who was of slight build and pale complexion. He soon departed to make his fortune in Venezuela, but a shipwreck caused him to land in Amsterdam, where he took a series of menial jobs. During this period, he began his lifelong habit of language study, based on a method of his own devising. He eventually learned some eighteen languages and claimed to learn them in periods ranging from six weeks to six months. In 1844, he joined a mercantile firm, and in 1846, his hard work and newly acquired fluency in Russian convinced the firm to send him as its representative to Russia. There, Schliemann flourished, trading many items, but especially indigo, from his base in St. Petersburg, where he quickly established his own business.

He was soon a millionaire, and in 1851 embarked for the United States, ostensibly to help settle the affairs of his dead brother Ludwig but also to make investments in the booming West. He established a bank dealing in gold dust in Sacramento and earned large profits. By 1852, he was back in St. Petersburg, where he married Ekaterina Petrovna Lyschin. He was to have two children, Sergei and Nadezhda, but little happiness from this union. He profited greatly from the Crimean War and the American Civil War, and in 1863, in his early forties and at a stage at which most men look forward to settling down, he liquidated his business and began the second phase of his life.

Life's Work

In 1866, after a two-year world tour which included the Far East and resulted in the first of his eleven books, Schliemann enrolled in the Sorbonne, finally able to complete his education. He soon traveled again and once more visited the southern United States; yet most important for his future work were visits to several Greek sites that he would later excavate, including Ithaca, Mycenae, Tiryns, and Troy. He even dug, without permission, in the area of Troy in 1868, trying to disprove the theory that Burnarbashi held the remains of Homer's Troy. Schliemann was convinced that his choice, Hissarlik, was the true site of Troy.

Upon returning to St. Petersburg to find his estranged wife gone, along with their children, Schliemann left that city, never to return. In 1869, he received a doctorate from the University of Rostock for his publications to date and then returned to the United States to divorce under the state of Indiana's liberal laws. It was during this trip that Schliemann received American citizenship, and not in 1850 as he often related. He was proud of his citizenship and often signed himself "Henry Schliemann."

Even before Schliemann left the United States, he wrote a former tutor, now a Greek archbishop, asking him to find a wife suitable to help him pursue his dream of finding Troy. The archbishop suggested his cousin, Sophia Engastromenos, whom Schliemann courted cautiously. Impressed by her beauty and love of ancient learning, he married her on September 23, 1869. She, along with Troy, was to be an overriding passion in his life. The couple had two children, Andromache and Agamemnon.

In 1870, Schliemann began to dig at Hissarlik, again illegally, as his permit from the Turks was slow in coming. By 1871, he began legal excavations, but his excavation techniques were unquestionably inferior. He chose speed over care and eliminated higher strata without proper documentation in his zeal to get to the lowest levels. At times, he employed up to 150 men, and his equipment included jackscrews, chains, and windlasses to tear down walls that hindered his progress. In 1873, he found the famed "gold of Troy," a hoard of gold jewelry, which he smuggled out of the country. One crown alone was said to consist of 16,353 individual pieces. Widely displayed in a photograph of Sophia wearing them, the jewels were lost when Allied forces invaded Berlin at the end of World War II. Schliemann ended excavations in 1873 and published *Troja und seine Ruinen* (1875; *Troy and Its Remains*, 1875), whose bold claims of having found Priam's city brought strong criticism. Denied a permit for Troy by Turkish officials bristling at the loss of the treasure, he turned his sights elsewhere.

In 1874, Schliemann was already at Mycenae, where he dug illegally for five days before being stopped. There, he hoped to find Homer's "Mycenae rich in gold," the home of Agamemnon, Greek leader at Troy. As he waited for permission from the Greeks, however, he was well occupied. He first settled a suit by the Turks for the loss of the treasure and then traveled again, as he always did when between projects. In 1876, he began at Mycenae and, with naïve faith in the ancient author Pausanias, excavated within the walls of the city, looking for the tombs of Agamemnon and Clytemnestra. He soon found five shaft graves that contained vast wealth (the gold alone weighed some thirty-three pounds). He was wrong in his dates, for these graves antedate the supposed dates of Agamemnon by some 250 to 300 years, but the excitement he caused was immense. Schliemann announced his finds in the media, and the public's imagination was immediately stirred. His subsequent book *Mycenæ* (1878) did not receive unanimous praise, since his tendency to make hasty judgments on incomplete evidence was antithetical to the staid approach of most classical scholars.

Never one to rest for long, Schliemann was off again for Troy, where he dug from 1879 to 1880. His book *Ilios* (1880) is more reasoned and careful than his previous works and shows a greater respect for proper archaeological technique. It also contains the autobiographical essay that is the sole source for information on Schliemann's early life. In 1881, he excavated at Orchomenus, another city important in Homer's writings, and visited the ongoing excavations by the Germans at Olympia, where he was impressed by the modern and careful techniques being used.

In 1882, Schliemann was back at Troy, trying to understand its confusing stratigraphy, this time with the help of Wilhelm Dörpfeld, a young architect whom Schliemann had met at the Olympia excavations. The publication that resulted from this dig, *Troja* (1884), was a great improvement on his earlier works.

At this time Schliemann began to take an interest in the island of Crete, where he was convinced that he would find further prehistoric remains. With his astonishing skill for finding the right places to dig, he located the future site of Knossos, home of the Minoan civilization. The businessman in him prevailed, however, as he never could agree to pay the asking price for the site. Later, this civilization would be unearthed by Sir Arthur Evans, a man who was much influenced by Schliemann and his finds.

Schliemann next turned to another site indicated by Homer, Tiryns. Just a few miles from Mycenae and the fabled home of Heracles, Tiryns was a strong citadel whose stone walls continue to be impressive. The publication of *Tiryns* (1885) served further to convince the world of the vibrancy of Bronze Age, or Mycenaean, culture. Schliemann traveled in 1886 and 1887, partly to rest and partly to recover his health which, never sound, had begun to deteriorate. In December of 1889, he returned to Troy in order to silence some of his critics. In 1890, on his way home to spend Christmas with his family in Greece, Schliemann's chronic earaches became worse. He underwent surgery in Halle in November, but in his haste to return to his family he left bed early, only to collapse on Christmas Day in Naples. Temporarily denied access to a hospital because of a lack of identification, Schliemann was taken instead to a police station. He died the next day, December 26, 1890, apparently as a result of the infection's spreading to his brain.

Summary

Heinrich Schliemann was an uncompromising businessman. He was also a passionate romantic who believed in Homer as others would believe in the Bible and who put a copy of Homer's *Iliad* to his son Agamemnon's forehead shortly after the child's birth. Schliemann was cold and arrogant with his critics but could be tender to his wife and children. His early excavation techniques were undoubtedly appalling, and he destroyed much that was of value. Yet it was he who found what others had failed to find, and he strove to improve his technique as he went along, often bringing experts such as Dörpfeld to his later excavations.

In some respects, it is Schliemann's energy that most impresses. He did not begin his archaeological career until he was in his forties, and he was largely self-taught. He financed his excavations himself, using profits from investments, which he continued to manage while he excavated and wrote ceaselessly.

While other scholars produced theories from behind their desks, Schliemann went to Asia Minor with Homer in hand and found the site generally accepted today as Troy. While others read Pausanias on Mycenae, Schliemann used his writings to unearth a civilization that had lain beneath the surface of the Greek soil for three thousand years. In the end, this was Schliemann's greatest accomplishment, for through his energy and excavations he changed forever the way the Western world viewed Homer and its own heritage.

Bibliography
Brackman, Arnold C. *The Dream of Troy.* New York: Mason and Lipscomb, 1974. A novelistic biography recounting Schliemann's discovery of Troy. Vivid but not scholarly. Poorly reproduced illustrations.
Calder, William M., and David A. Traill, eds. *Myth, Scandal, and History.* Detroit: Wayne State University Press, 1986. Consists of five essays demythologizing Schliemann through critical examination of his record. Also includes an edition of his Mycenaean diary.
Cottrell, Leonard. *The Bull of Minos.* New York: Facts on File, 1953. A

general book on Bronze Age Greece, with significant space devoted to Schliemann and his works. A good introduction for the reader who wants to learn something of the actual remains Schliemann unearthed as well as something about the man himself. Somewhat uncritical in its acceptance of Schliemann's versions of events.

Deuel, Leo. *Memoirs of Heinrich Schliemann*. New York: Harper & Row, 1977. Thorough analysis of Schliemann's life, with generous selections from his own works, letters, and diaries. Balanced, with careful criticism and analytical sections, full notes, and a bibliography.

Payne, Robert. *The Gold of Troy: The Story of Heinrich Schliemann and the Buried Cities of Ancient Greece*. New York: Funk & Wagnalls, 1959. A readable and enjoyable biography, flawed only by its tendency to accept much of what Schliemann wrote at face value.

Poole, Lynn, and Gray Poole. *One Passion, Two Loves: The Story of Heinrich and Sophia Schliemann, Discoverers of Troy*. New York: Thomas Y. Crowell, 1966. A very enjoyable study of the later part of Schliemann's life, using previously unpublished letters.

Stone, Irving. *The Greek Treasure: A Biographical Novel of Henry and Sophia Schliemann*. Garden City, N.Y.: Doubleday, 1975. A biographical novel, based on careful study of the available Schliemann material, some of it used here for the first time.

Kenneth F. Kitchell, Jr.

ARTHUR SCHOPENHAUER

Born: February 22, 1788; Danzig, Poland
Died: September 21, 1860; Frankfurt am Main
Area of Achievement: Philosophy
Contribution: In the tradition of Immanuel Kant, Schopenhauer developed a pessimistic system of philosophy based upon the primacy of will.

Early Life

Arthur Schopenhauer was born on February 22, 1788, in the Hanseatic city of Danzig (modern Gdańsk), then under nominal control of Poland. His father, Heinrich, was an affluent merchant of Dutch aristocratic lineage, cosmopolitan in outlook and republican in politics. After Danzig lost its freedom to Prussia in 1793, he moved his family and business to Hamburg. Schopenhauer's mother, Johanna, also of Dutch descent, later became a successful romantic novelist.

Since Heinrich Schopenhauer planned a mercantile career for his son, Arthur's education emphasized modern languages, which came easily to him. At age nine, he was sent to Le Havre to learn French, the first of six foreign languages he mastered. In return for agreeing to enter a merchant firm as an apprentice, his father rewarded him with an extended tour—lasting nearly a year and a half—of England, Scotland, France, Switzerland, Austria, and Germany, an experience that strengthened his own cosmopolitan perspective and further developed his facility with languages.

As an apprentice and later a clerk, Schopenhauer found the work tedious and boring, and after the death of his father by drowning, presumed a suicide, in 1805, he altered his life's goals. With an inheritance adequate to assure independence and with encouragement from his mother, he entered grammar school at Gotha and then studied under tutors in Weimar, mastering Latin and Greek. At age twenty-one, he enrolled as a medical student in the University of Göttingen, changing to philosophy in his second year. His first influential teacher, G. E. Schulze, advised him to concentrate on Plato and Kant—the two thinkers who would exert the strongest impact on his philosophy.

In 1811, Schopenhauer attended lectures at the University of Berlin by Johann Gottlieb Fichte and Friedrich Schleiermacher; scathing responses in his notes set the tone of his lifelong contempt for German academic philosophy. When revolution against Napoleonic rule flared in Berlin, Schopenhauer fled to the village of Rudolstadt, where he wrote his dissertation for a doctorate from the University of Jena. In *Über die vierfache Wurzel des Satzes vom zureichende Grunde* (1813; *On the Fourfold Root of the Principle of Sufficient Reason*, 1889), he explores types of causation—physical, logical, mathematical, and moral.

After receiving his doctorate, Schopenhauer returned to Weimar to live in his mother's house, but the two could not agree. She found him moody, surly, and sarcastic; he found her vain and shallow. Disagreements and quarrels led her to dismiss him, and he left to establish his residence in Dresden in 1814, there to begin his major philosophical work. For the remaining twenty-four years of Johanna Schopenhauer's life, mother and son did not meet.

Life's Work

In Dresden, after completing a brief treatise on the nature of color, Schopenhauer was ready to begin serious preparation of his greatest philosophical work, *Die Welt als Wille und Vorstellung* (1818; *The World as Will and Idea*, 1883-1886). Its four books, with an appendix on Kantian philosophy, include the conceptual ideas that Schopenhauer developed and elaborated throughout his career as an independent philosopher. Book 1 explains the world, everything that the mind perceives, as representation, a mental construct of the subject. Through perception, reasoning, and reflection and by placing external reality within the mental categories of time, space, and causality, one understands how the world operates. Yet one never understands reality as it exists, for the subjective remains an essential element of all perception.

The fundamental reality that eludes understanding is, as book 2 makes plain, the will, that Kantian thing-in-itself. Understood in its broadest sense, will exists in everything—as a life force and much more. In plants, it drives growth, change, and reproduction. In animals, it includes all of these as well as sensation, instinct, and limited intelligence. Only in man does the will become self-conscious, through reflection and analysis, though the will is by no means free in the usual sense. Every action is determined by motives—to Schopenhauer another name for causes—that predetermine one's choices. Thus, one may will to choose but not will to will. With its conscious and unconscious drives, will presses each person toward egoistic individualism; yet demands of the will, far from bringing peace, well-being, and gratification, lead only to additional struggle and exertion. As a consequence, unhappiness in life inevitably exceeds happiness.

As a respite from the imperious demands of the will, man finds solace in the beauty that exists in nature and art, and the awakening of the aesthetic sense serves to tame the will by leading it toward disinterested contemplation. To enter a room and discover a table filled with food is to anticipate involvement, consumption, and interaction with others. To look at a painting of the same scene invites simply reflection and appreciation, removing any practical considerations from the will, thereby suspending its feverish activity.

Yet the solace afforded by beauty is only temporary; in book 4, Schopenhauer explores saintliness, which implies denial and permanent taming of the will. By recognizing that others experience the same unrelenting strife that the will brings to himself, a person can develop compassion. Through the power of reflection, one can recognize one's own motives and, through studying motives, become aware of those previously unknown and unacknowledged. Thus, while he cannot achieve freedom of choice, man may acquire a negative capability of rejecting and taming the will. Renunciation, denial of the will, represents for Schopenhauer the path to Nirvana. The best attainable life is that followed by the Hindu *sanyasas* and the ascetic saints of early Christendom.

After publishing his magnum opus, Schopenhauer left for a vacation in Italy, confident that his work would be recognized as a true account of the philosophy foreshadowed by Kant and accepted as a solution to all outstanding problems of philosophy. Instead, the work was ignored both by the reading public and by academic philosophers. From Dresden, he moved to Berlin, where he expected to become a university professor. Appointed to lecture on philosophy at the university, he selected a schedule that competed with lectures by G. W. F. Hegel, then at the height of his popularity, whose optimistic system was the antithesis of Schopenhauer's. Unable to attract students, Schopenhauer spent more than a decade in reading and desultory wandering, though with Berlin as his primary residence. In 1833, he settled in Frankfurt, where he remained for the final years of his life.

There his life assumed a measure of regularity and simplicity. His modest wants were easily met on his inherited income. Although he gave serious consideration to marriage more than once during his lifetime, he rejected the idea, choosing casual relationships instead. He lived in a boardinghouse, took regular walks for exercise, and dined in company at the Englische Hof Hotel. His day began with work in the morning, followed by a brief diversion through playing the flute. In the afternoons, he stopped by the public library for reading and study; an omnivorous reader, he was widely knowledgeable in the arts and sciences and, like his father, read the London *Times* almost every day of his adult life. He was short of stature, with a thick neck—characteristics, he thought, of genius. His portraits show penetrating blue eyes; a lined, intelligent face; a prominent, forceful nose; and, in old age, two curled locks of white hair on either side of a bald head.

Schopenhauer produced a series of minor works as further elaboration of his system—an attack on academic philosophy, *Über den Willen in der Natur* (1836; *On the Will in Nature*, 1888), and *Die beiden Grundprobleme der Ethik* (1841; *The Basis of Morality*, 1903). After issuing a much-expanded second edition of his major work in 1844, he completed two volumes of essays and miscellaneous writings on a wide variety of subjects, *Parerga und Paralipomena* (1851; *Parerga and Paralipomena*, 1974). With its graceful if sometimes barbed style and its combination of brilliant insights and freely indulged speculation, it expanded the philosopher's reading public.

During his final decade, Schopenhauer experienced the fame and adulation he had long anticipated. A third edition of *The World as Will and Idea* appeared in 1859, this time owing to popular demand. His work was widely discussed and became the subject of university lectures throughout Europe. He began to attract followers, some drawn more by his lucid, jargon-free prose than by his ideas, and on his birthdays tributes poured in from admirers. Shortly before his death, he began to experience recurring chest pains; on the morning of September 21, 1860, he sat down to breakfast at his usual time. An hour later, his doctor, stopping by to check on him, found him still seated in the chair, dead.

Summary

A philosopher in the tradition of Kant, Arthur Schopenhauer modified Kantian terms and categories to accord primacy to will, regarding it as the inscrutable thing-in-itself. Far from an optimistic view, his alteration implies a largely blind force striving for individual advancement and doomed to frustration and defeat. Confronted with this pessimistic reality, the reflective person seeks to tame the will through asceticism. In the *Upanishads*, his favorite bedtime reading, Schopenhauer discovered that Eastern religious thinkers had anticipated important ideas of his system, and he himself helped popularize Hindu and Buddhist thought in Europe.

Schopenhauer's successors have generally accepted portions of his system while rejecting others, and his influence has been almost as varied as his system. Friedrich Nietzsche followed him in granting primacy to the will but envisioned will as a constructive force for progress. Eduard von Hartmann attempted a synthesis of Schopenhauer and Hegel in his *Philosophie des Unbewussten* (1869; *Philosophy of the Unconscious*, 1931). Scholars have discovered a profound debt to Schopenhauer in Hans Vaihinger's *Die Philosophie des Als-Ob* (1911; *The Philosophy of "As If,"* 1924); Ludwig Wittgenstein was influenced by Schopenhauer as well. Sigmund Freud acknowledged that, in large measure, his theory of the unconscious was anticipated by the philosopher.

Since Schopenhauer gives aesthetics a prominent and honorable place in his system, it is not surprising to discover that he has influenced artistic creation significantly. Richard Wagner enthusiastically embraced Schopenhauer's speculations on music, in part because he accorded music first place among the arts. Writers such as Leo Tolstoy in Russia; Thomas Mann in Germany; Guy de Maupassant, Émile Zola, and Marcel Proust in France; and Thomas Hardy, Joseph Conrad, and W. Somerset Maugham in Great Britain are, in varying degrees, indebted to Schopenhauer for their worldview and for their pessimistic depiction of human life and character. One should note, however, that the enthusiasm for blind will at the base of twen-

Great Lives from History

tieth century Fascism is a perversion of Schopenhauer's thought. Passages in Schopenhauer that reflect racism, anti-Semitism, and misogyny, attitudes undeniably present in his work, should be placed within the context of his overall pessimism concerning human nature.

Copleston, Frederick. *Arthur Schopenhauer, Philosopher of Pessimism*. London: Burns, Oates, and Washbourne, 1947. Examines Schopenhauer's system in the light of Roman Catholic and religious thought. Calls attention to inconsistencies and contradictions but at the same time provides insightful summary and analysis of Schopenhauer's major ideas.

Fox, Michael, ed. *Schopenhauer: His Philosophical Achievement*. Brighton, England: Harvester Press, 1980. A collection of essays by distinguished scholars. The book is divided into three sections: general articles, giving overviews of Schopenhauer, articles dealing with basic philosophical issues, and comparative studies that relate Schopenhauer's philosophy to others' and explore intellectual debts.

Gardiner, Patrick. *Schopenhauer*. Baltimore: Penguin Books, 1963. A general but penetrating analysis of Schopenhauer's life and philosophy. Gardiner offers a balanced assessment of the philosopher's strengths and weaknesses, clarifying the intellectual debt to Kant but providing only brief consideration of Schopenhauer's influence on others.

Hamlyn, D. W. *Schopenhauer*. Boston: Routledge & Kegan Paul, 1980. A general survey of Schopenhauer's philosophy. Clarifies his terms, explains his epistemology, and offers extensive analysis of his philosophical debt to Kant.

Magee, Bryan. *The Philosophy of Schopenhauer*. New York: Oxford University Press, 1983. A scholarly introduction to Schopenhauer's philosophical system. Explores the effects of his early life on his system and places his ideas in their philosophical tradition. Numerous appendices trace his influence on others.

Wallace, William. *Life of Arthur Schopenhauer*. London: Walter Scott, 1890. A comprehensive overview of Schopenhauer's life, philosophical system, and influence. Biographical information draws heavily upon previous studies in Germany and offers an illuminating account of his daily life.

Stanley Archer

FRANZ SCHUBERT

Born: January 31, 1797; Himmelpfortgrund, near Vienna, Austria
Died: November 19, 1828; Vienna, Austro-Hungarian Empire
Area of Achievement: Music
Contribution: Schubert created the *Lied* (art song) and set models for subsequent ones in his more than six hundred *Lieder.* His larger instrumental works, in their freedom of form and enhanced key relationships, became models for the lyrical Romantic sonatas and symphonies of the later nineteenth century. The expressively songful character of his shorter piano pieces was equally influential.

Early Life

Franz Schubert was born in a suburb of Vienna, the son of a schoolmaster and one of the five of his fourteen children to survive infancy. Though the Schubert family were in humble circumstances, they were highly musical, and Franz as a child learned violin from his father, piano from his older brother Ignaz, and singing and basic music theory from Michael Holzer, choirmaster of the parish church of Liechtenthal. At the age of nine, Franz was engaged as a boy soprano in the Imperial Chapel and was enrolled in its school, the Imperial and Royal Stadt-Konvikt (boarding school), where he was also a violinist in the student orchestra.

His earliest surviving compositions date from 1810. In 1811, he began keyboard studies with the court organist, Wenzel Ruzicka, and in the following year began studies in composition with Antonio Salieri, who had been Wolfgang Amadeus Mozart's rival and one of Ludwig van Beethoven's teachers. This year was critical in other ways for Schubert: His voice changed, thus preventing him from continuing in the chapel choir as a boy soprano, and his mother died. His father remarried in the following year.

Though Schubert's voice had changed, he remained a scholarship student at the Imperial and Royal Stadt-Konvikt. In 1813, he renounced his scholarship, probably because he would be required to devote his time to academic studies rather than to music, and instead entered the teacher training program at the St. Anna Normal School in 1814. He continued to participate in the Imperial and Royal Stadt-Konvikt's musical life and played in its orchestra, for which his first three symphonies were written. In 1814, he wrote string quartets for his family ensemble, in which he played viola, and his first major compositions. He set to music the poem "Gretchen am Spinnrade" (Gretchen at the spinning wheel) from Johann Wolfgang von Goethe's *Faust: Eine Tragödie* (1808; *The Tragedy of Faust*, 1823). He also wrote the Mass in F Major for the parish church in Liechtenthal.

After passing the examination for teacher certification in 1814, Schubert was a part-time assistant in his father's school, preferring to devote most of his time to composition. He was exempted from military service because he was barely five feet tall (thus below the army's minimum height requirement); his friends called him *Schwammerl* (little mushroom) because of his stocky build and short stature.

Schubert met Therese Grob, a skilled amateur soprano, in 1814 and fell in love with her. In 1816, the relationship was ended, since Schubert could not afford to marry her after he was rejected for a post as music teacher at the Normal School in Laibach (modern Ljubljana, in Yugoslavia). From then on he was indifferent to women, seeking rather the company of congenial friends, many of whom he had known since his days at the Imperial and Royal Stadt-Konvikt and who were extremely helpful in getting his music performed or in writing texts which he set as songs. From the year 1816 come the fourth and fifth symphonies, a string quartet, the Mass in C Major, and more than one hundred songs. The following two years were relatively fallow.

Life's Work

Two works from 1819 mark Schubert's full musical maturity: the Piano Quintet in A Major (called *Trout* because the fourth movement is a set of variations on his song "Die Forelle," which means "trout") and a remarkably concise three-movement Piano Sonata in A Major. He also finished the first of his operas, *Die Zwillingsbrüder* (the twin brothers), which received six performances in the following year. Schubert made several ventures into opera during the following four years, all of which were unsuccessful because of the lack of dramatic interest in the librettos.

The year 1823 was critical for Schubert in other respects. He became seriously ill; most writers consider the ailment to have been syphilis, from which he recovered although the secondary symptoms, especially headaches and gastritis, plagued him through the remainder of his life. Yet he completed *Die Schöne Müllerin* (the fair maid of the mill), his first song cycle, so called because he set to music a group of poems by the same author, Wilhelm Müller, which were written around the central theme of a miller's apprentice who falls in love with his employer's daughter when she prefers a huntsman.

Next, Schubert concentrated on writing chamber music and songs. His main chamber works of this period are two great string quartets, in A minor and D minor; an octet for clarinet, bassoon, French horn, string quartet, and string bass in six movements; and several piano duets, written for the daughters of the Esterházy family when he spent the summer as a music teacher on their country estate of Zselis in Hungary (he had been there earlier in 1818). Schubert's immediately succeeding works include the Symphony in C Major, finished in 1826; a large-scale String Quartet in G Major, also completed in that year; and a large-scale Concert Rondo in B Minor for violin and piano.

The year 1827 saw two piano trios and the gloomy song cycle *Winterreise* (winter journey), in which Schubert again used poems by Müller. In *Winterreise*, a young man, rejected by his beloved, undertakes a journey on foot in midwinter in a vain effort to forget her and risks losing his sanity. From this cycle comes one of Schubert's best-loved songs, "Der Lindenbaum" (the linden tree), which is virtually a folksong in German-speaking countries. The central theme of isolation and alienation displayed in this song cycle was a favorite one in Romantic literature.

The year 1828 saw Schubert's greatest achievement. Foreign journals were reviewing his music favorably, and foreign publishers were interested in his music. His public concert devoted entirely to his music was a great success. Many of his best compositions—the Fantasy in F Minor for piano duet, the String Quintet in C Major, the last three piano sonatas, the Mass in E-flat Major, and the group of songs published after his death as *Schwanengesang* (swan song)—stem from this, his final, year. He had even begun lessons in counterpoint with Simon Sechter, later to be the teacher of Anton Bruckner. In November, his health suddenly deteriorated; in slightly more than a week, he lapsed into a coma and died. His illness was diagnosed by his doctors as "nervous fever"; most modern scholars consider his fatal illness to have been typhoid fever, brought on by the unsanitary conditions of the suburb of Vienna where he was then living.

Many legends that have evolved about Schubert have been demolished by subsequent research. He was a prolific composer, but his supposed spontaneity was the result of much forethought and revision. For example, one of his most famous early songs, "Erlkönig" (the elf king), with a text by Goethe, was supposed to have been written in a single afternoon in 1815 and performed that evening. Schubert, however, revised "Erlkönig" six times before its publication as his Opus 1 in 1821. One of the tragedies of music is Schubert's abandonment of several major compositions before their completion. The most famous of these incomplete works is the "Unfinished" Symphony in B Minor (1822), in which Schubert wrote two outstanding symphonic movements and sketched a third movement as a scherzo, but not even sketches have survived for a finale.

Schubert's life of poverty has also been misunderstood. He rejected positions with regular hours, seeking one that would enable him to devote full time to composing. Such positions were bestowed on those with many years of musical achievement, and Schubert was passed over in favor of much older and more experienced men. He was relatively well paid by his publishers, but he spent money lavishly when he had it, not so much on himself as on the circle of friends with whom he lived and whom he accompanied on summer vacations in the mountains, where he did much of his composing. Social conditions had changed: The nobility, ruined by the Napoleonic Wars, could not support a composer in the manner that Joseph Haydn or Ludwig van Beethoven had been aided, and the middle-class public could not provide a steady income. Schubert's main audience consisted of the friends who attended the so-called Schubertiads—evenings when Schubert and others played the piano and sang for a mostly male audience, who did much drinking and stayed as late as 3:00 A.M. He was beginning to achieve a wide reputation as a composer of merit during the last year of his life.

Summary

Only a small amount of Franz Schubert's music was published during his lifetime—several songs and piano duets, but only one string quartet, four piano sonatas, and no orchestral music. His music was aimed more toward the middle-class drawing room than the concert hall, and Schubert himself was not a charismatic virtuoso performer such as Niccolò Paganini or Franz Liszt, who were able to attract well-paying crowds.

Schubert changed the course of music in many ways. Before him, composers who wrote songs undertook to provide a simple setting for a poem, with an almost rudimentary piano accompaniment that often was intended to be played by the singer, rather than to create an independent musical composition that would utilize the full resources of the piano and all the techniques of harmonic color and melodic expression in the way that Schubert did. In the sphere of the large instrumental work, Schubert provided an alternative to Beethoven, writing movements that were lyric and epic rather than heroic and dramatic. Schubert used the possibilities inherent in the widening of the tonal spectrum to expand the forms of his movements. The short, spontaneous piano piece was not original with Schubert, but he set the standard for subsequent works in this genre.

Schubert's influence on subsequent composers was not immediate but was especially strong on those who played major roles in making his music known throughout the nineteenth century: Robert Schumann, Franz Liszt, and Johannes Brahms. The full range of Schubert's genius has become appreciated only in modern times with the performance and recording of many of his large-scale works.

Bibliography

Brown, Maurice J. E. "Schubert." In *The New Grove Dictionary of Music and Musicians*, edited by Stanley Sadie. London: Macmillan, 1980. Brown's critical studies of Schubert's music are distilled in this comprehensive article embracing both the composer's life and music.

_____. *Schubert: A Critical Biography*. New York: St. Martin's Press, 1958. This is the standard scholarly study of Schubert's work, with the focus on his music. Written for the person with musical understanding.

Deutsch, Otto Erich, ed. *Schubert: Memoirs by His Friends*. Translated by Rosamond Ley and John Nowell. London: A. & C. Black, 1958. This volume contains many firsthand accounts by those who knew Schubert personally and intimately.

Deutsch, Otto Erich, with Donald R. Wakeling. *The Schubert Reader: A Life of Franz Schubert in Letters and Documents*. New York: W. W. Norton, 1947. This documentary biography consists of English translations of the documents directly pertaining to Schubert, thus providing direct insight into the composer's life and the circumstances surrounding his work.

Einstein, Alfred. *Schubert: A Musical Portrait*. New York: Oxford University Press, 1951. This sensitive appreciation of Schubert's music by one of the giants of early twentieth century musical scholarship is well worth reading because of its valuable and penetrating insights into Schubert's music.

Osborne, Charles. *Schubert and His Vienna*. New York: Alfred A. Knopf, 1985. This is a book on Schubert for the general reader, with the emphasis on his life and environment rather than on his music. Provides a very readable introduction to Schubert, though the musical information is mostly praise rather than critical analysis.

Reed, John. *Schubert*. London: J. M. Dent & Sons, 1987. Provides excellent discussion of Schubert's life, with the music important though subordinate. Written in a style suited more for the general music lover than for the specialist scholar. Some musical background is necessary for a full appreciation of this volume.

Solomon, Maynard. "Franz Schubert and the Peacocks of Benvenuto Cellini." *Nineteenth-Century Music* 12 (1989): 193-206. The author strives to show that Schubert and his circle of friends were part of Vienna's homosexual underground. In the absence of any direct evidence, he relies heavily on gossip, inference, implication, and code words in use 170 years ago.

Rey M. Longyear

ROBERT SCHUMANN

Born: June 8, 1810; Zwickau, Saxony
Died: July 29, 1856; Endenich, near Bonn, Prussia
Area of Achievement: Music
Contribution: Schumann was important not only as a composer of music
  during the Romantic period but also as an editor of *Neue Zeitschrift für
  Musik*, which did much to establish standards of musical criticism.

Early Life

Robert Alexander Schumann was born on June 8, 1810, at Zwickau in
Saxony. His father was a publisher of scholarly books, and his mother was
the daughter of a surgeon. Robert was the youngest of five children, four
sons and one daughter. August Schumann's publishing business was successful enough that Robert was able to enter a private preparatory school for his
early education. Already, at his father's instigation, he was studying the
piano, the instrument that would remain his favorite throughout his life. After the preparatory school, Schumann attended the Zwickau Lyceum, where
he studied the classics as well as the piano. Literature and music, then, were
both strong interests of the young Schumann and remained so throughout his
life.

At the lyceum, Schumann played the piano in concerts, read widely in
classical Greek and Roman authors, and studied such German writers as
Friedrich von Schiller and Johann Wolfgang von Goethe. He even wrote
some poetry, although when he attempted to recite from memory one of his
poems before the student body, his mind went blank, and he stood in silent
embarrassment on the stage. This incident may have contributed significantly
to Schumann's aversion to public speaking throughout his life.

Schumann spent his formative years if not in affluence at least at a comfortable material level. In 1826, however, tragedy struck when his elder
sister Emilie, who was afflicted with typhus fever and a terrible skin disease,
committed suicide. August Schumann was crushed by this event and himself
died a few weeks later. Schumann, too, was deeply affected by his sister's
death and from that time forward could never bring himself to attend a
funeral, not even his mother's. Schumann's mother, Johanna, and Gottlob
Rudel, the guardian appointed to look after Robert's share of August's estate, agreed that the boy should pursue a legal career. With no one to support
his own desires, Schumann acquiesced, although he knew that he would
never lose his love of music. In an 1828 letter to a friend describing his
feelings upon leaving the lyceum, he wrote, "Now the true inner man must
come forward and show who he is."

Enrolling first at the University of Leipzig, Schumann found the study of
law even more boring than he had feared. Influenced by a friend at Heidel-

berg, who wrote of the exciting university life there, Schumann persuaded his mother and Rudel that he should go to Heidelberg to continue his study. He was, however, anything but the model student, spending his time in taverns and restaurants instead of in the pursuit of his legal studies. He also spent much time with Anton Thibaut, a law professor much interested in music. Schumann spent many hours at Thibaut's home, making and enjoying music.

On July 30, 1830, Schumann wrote what he called the most important letter in his life: one to his mother, pleading that he be permitted to give up his legal studies and journey to Leipzig to study piano with Friedrich Wieck, who promised to turn the young Schumann into a great pianist. Johanna Schumann agreed, and at age twenty Robert Schumann began his musical career.

Life's Work

Schumann had met Wieck in Leipzig. A kind of self-made man, the latter's early life was the opposite of Schumann's. Poor, and often forced to rely on charity for food and for money to cover his education, he developed into an autocrat with a violent temper. Following his own system of instruction, he set himself up as a piano teacher. He saw the clear relationship between playing the piano and singing and trained his students to strive for a "singing touch" at the keyboard. His prize student was his own daughter Clara. Viewing her almost as an extension of himself, Wieck carefully molded and developed her talent to a level that made her something of a sensation across Europe. In 1832, when Schumann came to study with Wieck, Clara was thirteen years old. The relationship between them grew over the next several years from one of elder brother and younger sister to one of love.

On one occasion, when Wieck had taken Clara on a performing tour, Schumann, perhaps in an effort to find a technique to help him catch up with the talented Clara, fashioned a sling of sorts to keep one finger out of the way while the others were being exercised. Exactly what happened to his hand is not clear. Schumann himself only said that it was lamed. Some scholars suggest that no injury actually occurred and that Schumann may have suffered motor damage from an overdose of mercury, a substance then widely prescribed for syphilis. Whatever the cause, the effect was devastating to the young pianist. He tried numerous cures to no avail.

When Wieck discovered that the relationship between Schumann and Clara was becoming more than simply friendship, he flew into a rage, vowing that his daughter was destined to be a concert pianist, not a hausfrau. Love, however, was not to be daunted, and the two young people applied to the courts for permission to marry. The wedding took place on September 12, 1840, and the couple settled in Leipzig, an important musical center of the time.

An ardent admirer of Franz Schubert's piano music, Schumann, up to the time of his marriage, had written only for the piano. In 1840, however, he turned his creative efforts to *Lieder* (art songs), many of which were in celebration of his love for Clara. These *Lieder* show clearly Schumann's attention to form and reflect the same power of emotion and flow of melody as do Schubert's, although the harmonics are more complex. Schumann probably realized that such art songs gave him the opportunity to blend his feeling for poetry and his genius for melody. In these songs, as one might expect, the piano has a more significant role than it does in those of other composers of *Lieder*.

Schumann's gift with words was evidenced also in his editorship of *Neue Zeitschrift für Musik* (new journal for music), a magazine that served as an outlet for the writings of young Romantic musicians in Germany. Indeed, when Schumann first met Felix Mendelssohn in 1835, he was more noted for his work with this magazine than for his music, a situation that led Mendelssohn to see him first as a kind of dilettante. Schumann, on the other hand, had only the highest regard for Mendelssohn as a composer.

If 1840 could be called Schumann's year of songs, the next year could certainly be called the year of symphonies. Although he had flirted earlier with the idea of a symphony, he had never completed one. In 1841, he completed two. The First Symphony, whose initial idea came to Schumann from a poem about spring by Adolf Böttger, was completed in the remarkably short period of one month. Called the *Spring Symphony*, it is buoyant and fresh in its mood and is marked by a driving rhythmic energy. The Symphony in D Minor was also written in 1841, although it was not published until ten years later and is referred to as the Fourth Symphony. It was performed once in 1841, but because of the cold reception it received, Schumann withdrew it and put it aside until 1851, when he revised it. Schumann left no word as to what meaning lay behind the music of this symphony. It was no doubt Schumann's intention, according to Brian Schlotel, that it be received as absolute music.

Schumann spent the year 1842 working primarily on string quartets, three of which he dedicated to Mendelssohn. This same year, he accompanied Clara on a concert tour to Hamburg. Although her marriage no doubt limited her career as a concert pianist, Clara was ever ready to play her husband's compositions and to interpret them faithfully to her audiences. It was in a sense a perfect combination—Schumann's talent as a composer complemented by his wife's talent as a pianist.

In 1843, Schumann turned his efforts toward composing choral works, the most important of which was "Paradise and the Peri," a work for solo voices, chorus, and orchestra. Schumann conducted it himself December 4, 1843. Encouraged by the reception of this work, he composed a musical setting for Goethe's *Faust* (1790-1831). Also at about this time, Schumann suffered a second physical breakdown, the first, less serious, having occurred in 1842. This second breakdown was marked by constant trembling, a number of phobias, and auricular delusions, and it made serious work impossible. Hoping that a total change of scene would be helpful, the Schumanns moved to Dresden.

While at Dresden, Schumann completed the Piano Concerto in A Minor (1845), the famous C Major Symphony (1846), and his only opera, *Genoveva* (1848). The latter was an unsuccessful attempt to emulate Richard Wagner's German operas. In addition to composing, Schumann directed the Liedertafel, a male choral society. Neither of the Schumanns was particularly happy with the music scene in Dresden, and when the opportunity to become municipal director of music at Düsseldorf arrived, Schumann accepted. Unfortunately, Schumann did not exhibit the same level of talent in conducting as he did in composing, and he was encouraged in 1852 to resign. After some argument, he finally left in 1853.

In 1850, Schumann completed his Symphony No. 3, the *Rhenish*, and also his Concerto for Cello and Orchestra. In the former, Schumann attempted to put into music his feelings about the Rhine, a river rich in scenery and legend. The full score of the symphony was completed in somewhat more than one month, and Schumann himself conducted it in Düsseldorf on February 6, 1851. Although his artistic talents and creative powers are apparent in this symphony, time for Schumann was running out. Within three years, in a period of utter depression, he attempted suicide by jumping into the river that had stimulated his imagination to compose the *Rhenish*. Although the suicide attempt was thwarted by some fishermen, death came soon enough. Schumann's last years were spent at Endenich, a hospital for the insane. With his limbs in terrible convulsions and with the sounds of music filling his head, Schumann died on July 29, 1856.

Summary

Along with Frédéric Chopin, Felix Mendelssohn, Johannes Brahms, and Anton Bruckner, Robert Schumann composed works that reflect the artistic energies of the Romantic movement in music. Schumann was also instrumental in developing critical standards for music. His periodical *Neue Zeitschrift für Musik* served as an outlet for musical criticism and as a support for struggling composers of the time, including Chopin and Brahms.

Schumann's music itself reflects clearly the strong emotions and individualistic values of the Romantic period. Focusing early in his career on miniature pieces, Schumann exemplified the desire of Romantic composers to communicate directly and intensely with the listener. The year 1840 may be called Schumann's year of songs, many of which were inspired by his wife Clara. These beautiful flowing melodies testify to Schumann's love of poetry and his desire to meld the literary with the musical.

Alternating periods of intense creative productivity with periods of deep depression, Schumann moved from miniatures and songs to larger works— symphonies, choral works, chamber music, piano concerti, and an opera. His four symphonies are generally considered the most significant contributions to that genre since Ludwig van Beethoven's works. Although sometimes criticized for their somewhat heavy and unimaginative orchestrations, Schumann's symphonies show his desire to experiment with both themes and form.

In his chamber music, Schumann made great use of the piano, sometimes to the consternation of some musicologists. Nevertheless, as John Gardner and others have pointed out, Schumann's influence ranged widely among his contemporaries and successors in that genre. Once the piano took over from the harpsichord in the late eighteenth century, the door was open for a Schumann to give the former its deserved place in chamber music.

Except for the Piano Concerto in A Minor, some musicologists view Schumann's concerti as representing a falling off of his creativity. Others argue, however, that Schumann, like other composers of the period, faced the challenge of "getting out from under" Beethoven and that his concerti are justified efforts in new directions of form and theme. He saw the concerto as a great art form, one that was to be treated not casually but nobly— but one which had to evolve if it were to remain vital.

Schumann completed his first symphony at the age of thirty, after having heard Schubert's Symphony in C Major in 1839. Certainly influenced by Beethoven's work in the symphony, Schumann nevertheless sought new forms in his own symphonies. Not generally considered a giant of symphonic composition, Schumann must still be viewed as having considerable importance in symphonic history. The same may be said for his choral music. Often neglected, this music came late in Schumann's life, when his mental problems increasingly interfered with his creative powers. Still, as Louis Halsey has argued, much of this music is of high quality. A man of restless personality and strong creative spirit, Schumann has been called the typical Romantic. Not a revolutionary to the same degree as Beethoven, he nevertheless made a significant contribution to music of the Romantic period.

Bibliography

Bedford, Herbert. *Robert Schumann: His Life and Work.* New York: Harper & Brothers, 1925. A readable biography that traces Schumann's career. Focuses on cities in which Schumann lived and worked. Somewhat dated.

Brion, Marcel. *Schumann and the Romantic Age.* Translated by Geoffrey Sainsbury. New York: Macmillan, 1956. Places Schumann in the German Romantic tradition and examines his work against the background that influenced him. A good basic book on Schumann.

Niecks, Frederick. *Robert Schumann*. London: J. M. Dent and Sons, 1925. A standard biography that presents a meticulous and exhaustive record of Schumann as a man and as a composer.

Ostwald, Peter. *Schumann: The Inner Voices of a Musical Genius*. Boston: Northeastern University Press, 1985. Written by a psychiatrist, a fascinating study of the degenerative forces that brought Schumann to his death in a mental hospital. Relates Schumann's music to his states of mind.

Schumann, Robert. *The Musical World of Robert Schumann*. Edited and translated by Henry Pleasants. New York: St. Martin's Press, 1965. Presents a chronological arrangement of Schumann's own writings on various composers of his time. A good view of Schumann the critic. Good for insights into various composers and their music.

Walker, Alan, ed. *Robert Schumann: The Man and His Music*. New York: Barnes & Noble Books, 1972. A study of Schumann through thirteen essays by music scholars. Covers Schumann's background as well as the various kinds of music he composed.

Wilton Eckley

HEINRICH SCHÜTZ

Born: October, 1585; Köstritz, Reuss
Died: November 6, 1672; Dresden, Saxony
Area of Achievement: Music
Contribution: Heinrich Schütz was the most important German composer of his era, and his works and pupils had an immense influence on the subsequent development of music in Germany. He is especially noted for his combining of the German church music traditions with the newer Italian styles developing in the early seventeenth century.

Early Life

Heinrich Schütz was born in October of 1585 into a family of prosperous innkeepers in Köstritz, near Gera, the capital of the principality of Reuss. The exact day of Schütz's birth is disputed, but he was baptized on October 9. His father, Christoph, had been town clerk in Gera before taking over the Golden Crane Inn in Köstritz. Heinrich was the secondborn of eleven children in a close-knit family.

In the summer before Heinrich turned five, the family moved to Weissenfels, where his father had inherited an inn, the Golden Ring. Christoph provided a good religious and liberal arts education for his children, and Heinrich showed a special talent for music, becoming a fine singer. His voice attracted the attention of Langrave Moritz of Hessen-Kassel when this learned and musical nobleman stayed at the Schütz family inn. Moritz persuaded Schütz's parents to send Heinrich to his court in Kassel, where the lad served as a choirboy and studied at the Collegium Mauritianum, displaying a special gift for languages—Latin, Greek, and French—as well as music.

It was not the intention of Schütz or his parents that he take up music as a profession; therefore, in the fall of 1608, he entered the University of Marburg to study for a career in law. Once again, however, Moritz intervened in his life by offering to send Schütz to Venice to study music with the renowned Giovanni Gabrieli. This was an exciting prospect for Schütz, and it was not difficult to convince him to postpone his legal studies.

The rich musical life of Venice and the inspiration of Gabrieli and his compositions had a profound influence on Schütz. He acquired a thorough knowledge of contrapuntal writing and published a book of five-voice madrigals as a demonstration of his achievements at the end of his initial two-year stay. He received high praise for his madrigals and for his organ playing, even substituting as organist for Gabrieli on occasion. His study in Venice was extended for a third year and even beyond but was ended by the death of Gabrieli in August of 1612. A close relationship had developed between Schütz and his teacher; Gabrieli gave Schütz one of his rings on his deathbed, and Schütz spoke of Gabrieli only in terms of highest praise.

When Schütz returned to Germany, he assumed a position as second organist at Moritz's court. He also gave serious consideration to his family's urging to return to his legal studies. He would probably have done so but for a request from Johann Georg I, Elector of Saxony, for Schütz to come to Dresden to assist with the musical festivities in conjunction with the baptism of the elector's son. Schütz spent several weeks at the elector's court during the fall of 1614, and the next April the elector requested that Moritz lend him Schütz for a two-year period. Although Moritz protested and later tried to regain the services of the musician he had discovered and cultivated, Schütz left Kassel in August, 1615, for what turned out to be a lifetime position in the service of the Elector of Saxony.

Life's Work

Any remaining doubts that Schütz or his family had about his pursuing a musical career were now resolved by his appointment at one of the most important courts in Europe. When he arrived in Dresden in 1615, he took on the duties of Kapellmeister, even though he was not officially given that title until three or four years later.

As music director for the court, Schütz's responsibilities included directing the performances for important religious and political ceremonies, composing much of the music that was presented, and hiring and supervising the musicians of the court. Moreover, he instructed the choirboys, taking a special interest in those who showed promise in musical composition. Among his pupils were several who became well-known composers, Heinrich Albert, Christoph Bernhard, Johann Theile, and Matthias Weckmann.

In 1619, Schütz published the *Psalmen Davids* (Psalms of David) a collection of twenty-six psalm settings which, in their use of multiple choirs with eight to twenty voice parts and accompanying instruments, show the influence of Gabrieli and the Venetian style. At about the same time as the publication of the *Psalmen Davids*, Schütz married Magdalena Wildeck, the eighteen-year-old daughter of an electoral court official. Two daughters were born to the couple, but after only six years of an especially happy marriage Magdalena contracted smallpox and died on September 6, 1625. After his wife's death, Schütz spent more than a year making musical settings of the psalm paraphrases written by a Leipzig theologian, Cornelius Becker. Schütz derived great comfort from his work with these psalms and later (1628) published them as a collection known as the *Becker Psalter*.

In the spring of 1627, Schütz composed *Dafne*, the first opera written in German, set to an adaptation of a libretto by Ottavio Rinuccini. The score for this work, like most of Schütz's secular compositions, has not survived. Toward the end of the 1620's, economic conditions at the Saxon court deteriorated through the increasing financial drain of the Thirty Years' War.

Since no elaborate ceremonies requiring music would be likely in such troubled times, and since Schütz wished to learn more about current musical activities in Italy, he requested a leave to travel for a second time to Venice.

Schütz found the prevailing musical style of Venice in the late 1620's to be quite different from that which he had known there twenty years earlier. The famous Claudio Monteverdi was now the leading musical figure, and his perfection of the style of dramatic monody was of great interest to the German composer. Schütz wrote that he learned "how a comedy of diverse voices can be translated into declamatory style and be brought to the stage and enacted in song," a practice that was "still completely unknown in Germany." Schütz's stay was slightly over a year this time; before he left, he published a collection of Latin church music with instruments, *Symphoniae sacrae* (1629; sacred symphonies), which includes works showing the influence of the new monodic style he encountered during his stay in Venice.

When he returned to Dresden late in 1629, Schütz found conditions unimproved; any hope for betterment of the situation was ended by the official entry of Saxony into the Thirty Years' War in 1631. Over the next two years, musical activity declined to almost nothing, and Schütz spent extended periods of time during the next twelve years serving in other places. He served as director of music for the Danish court in Copenhagen from 1633 to 1635, and again from 1642 to 1644. In 1639 and 1640, he was in a similar position in Hanover and Hildesheim. Schütz continued to compose, whether he was away directing the music for a foreign court or at home in Saxony trying to do the best he could to preserve what was left of the musical establishment there. In 1636 and 1639, he published two books of *Kleine geistliche Concerte* (little sacred concerti), church music written for performance forces appropriate for the times—one to five solo voices and organ.

On May 21, 1645, Schütz wrote a letter to the elector, requesting retirement from active service as Kapellmeister so that he could devote himself to completing various musical compositions; however, Johann Georg did not permit his music director to retire at this time and persistently ignored or rejected similar requests from Schütz over the next eleven years. In 1647, Schütz published the second part of his *Symphoniae sacrae*, consisting of large-scale works that he had written earlier for performance in Copenhagen. In the next year, he published *Geistliche Chormusik* (sacred choral music), a very influential collection of twenty-nine motets in five to seven parts, vocal and instrumental, which emphasized independent polyphonic writing. The third book of *Symphoniae sacrae*, published in 1650, included works written for larger performing forces than Schütz had employed since *Psalmen Davids* of 1619.

Schütz's desire to retire from active direction of musical performances at the court was realized only when Johann Georg died in 1656; his son and successor, Johann Georg II, granted the seventy-one-year-old composer his pension and the retention of the title of Senior Kapellmeister. Even though Schütz retired to Weissenfels and wrote works for the new elector only on special occasions, he remained very active. He visited the Dresden court three or four times a year, traveled and assisted with music at other courts, revised and expanded his *Becker Psalter*, and continued to produce new compositions, including several important works of the oratorio type.

Two authentic portraits of Schütz exist, one a formal court pose, painted by Christoph Spetner when the composer was about sixty-five. The other is an anonymous miniature in oils, dated 1670, which shows the eighty-five-year-old composer with the lines of age clearly visible in his face but with a strong stance and intense gaze giving evidence of a still vital and forceful personality. At about the same time that this portrait was painted, Schütz returned to Dresden to spend his last days. On November 6, 1672, he suffered a fatal stroke. His funeral was held on November 17 at the Frauenkirche, with members of the court chapel performing some of his compositions. He was buried in a place of honor near the chancel of the church.

Summary

Henrich Schütz was both the greatest German composer of the seventeenth century and one of the most important and influential figures in the musical development of the entire Baroque era. He firmly established a musical style which combined German seriousness and sensitive treatment of text with Italian ideas of dramatic monody and the Venetian concerted and polychoral style. By so doing he shaped the direction that German Baroque music would take for the next one hundred years.

Over a long and active career, he composed in all of the genres of music used in his time except independent instrumental music. Unfortunately, many of Schütz's works have not survived; major eighteenth century fires in both Dresden and Copenhagen as well as the usual ravages of time were responsible for the destruction of many of his manuscripts, including the opera and ballet scores he is known to have produced. Despite the evidence of his composition of secular music, it is clear that his greatest interest and contribution was in the field of church music.

Approximately five hundred works by Schütz are extant, most of them included in the fourteen collections that were published during his lifetime. Among these collections, all but the first, his book of madrigals, consist of religious pieces, mainly settings of biblical texts. Although he did set Latin texts, German was the language that Schütz used in the vast majority of his compositions, and scholars credit the skillful utilization of this language for much of the incisive strength and feeling of urgency contained in Schütz's music.

The period from the beginning of the seventeenth century until the middle of the eighteenth century is an important time in German Protestant music, sometimes described as the golden age of Lutheran church music. It is clear that Schütz stands as the dominant figure at the beginning of this major development in Baroque music.

Bibliography

Moser, Hans Joachim. *Heinrich Schütz: His Life and Work*. Translated by Carl F. Pfatteicher. St. Louis: Concordia Publishing House, 1959. A monumental biography of the composer which treats both his life and his compositions in great detail. This is the standard work in an excellent English translation; includes illustrations, lists of works, and extensive musical examples.

_____. *Heinrich Schütz: A Short Account of His Life and Works*. Edited and translated by Derek McCulloch. New York: St. Martin's Press, 1967. A concise version of the author's definitive study. Gives a clear account of Schütz's life and brief discussions of his major works with some musical examples.

Petzoldt, Richard, and D. Berke. *Heinrich Schütz und seine Zeit in Bildern*. Kassel: Barenreiter, 1972. A most interesting and helpful collection of pictures and reproductions related to Schütz and his time. Arranged chronologically and accompanied by a commentary in both German and English.

Rifkin, Joshua, and Colin Timms. "Heinrich Schütz." In *The New Grove North European Baroque Masters*, by Joshua Rifkin et al. New York: W. W. Norton, 1985. An important and authoritative survey of Schütz's life and works. Incorporates research undertaken since the publication of Moser's books. Includes a comprehensive list of Schütz's compositions and an excellent bibliography.

Schütz, Heinrich. *The Letters and Documents of Heinrich Schütz, 1656-1672: An Annotated Translation*. Edited by Gina Spagnoli. Ann Arbor, Mich.: UMI Research Press, 1989. Presents letters and documents from the second half of Schütz's life in the original German with English translations and critical commentary.

Skei, Allen B. *Heinrich Schütz: A Guide to Research*. New York: Garland, 1981. A valuable source for finding further information about Schütz and the times in which he lived. The main part of this work is a 632-item annotated and classified bibliography which covers not only Schütz's life and works but also the general and musical background of his time and his reputation and performance of his works since his death.

Byron A. Wolverton

IGNAZ PHILIPP SEMMELWEIS

Born: July 1, 1818; Buda, Hungary, Austrian Empire
Died: August 13, 1865; Vienna, Austrian Empire
Area of Achievement: Medicine
Contribution: Semmelweis, a Hungarian physician, was the first to recognize the infectious nature of puerperal fever (childbed fever). His use of antiseptic techniques in obstetric practice greatly reduced deaths from the fever and paved the way for the development of modern surgery.

Early Life

Ignaz Philipp Semmelweis was born in 1818 in Buda, Hungary, the fifth of ten children born to József Semmelweis, a prosperous grocer, and Terézia Müller, the daughter of a coach manufacturer, one of the richest men in Buda. Semmelweis' father belonged to a German ethnic group and had moved to Buda from Kismarton, becoming a citizen in 1806. In the early nineteenth century, the influence of the German and Serbian elements was so great in Buda that the busy center of commerce had lost much of its Hungarian, Magyar, character. The trading class, including the Semmelweis family, spoke a German dialect, Buda Swabian, at home and in commerce. Although most people in this class spoke Hungarian fluently, few were able to read and write it correctly. The teaching of Hungarian was compulsory in the secondary schools, but formal instruction was still, for the most part, in Latin and German. Consequently, Semmelweis experienced language difficulties throughout his lifetime. His clumsy German dialect made him the butt of jokes in Vienna, where he was to spend the most important part of his life, and his confessed antipathy to writing made him reluctant to publish his discoveries and respond to his critics.

Little is known about Semmelweis' childhood. Described by his contemporaries as a happy, honest, and industrious child, Semmelweis attended the Royal University Catholic Grammar School, one of the best schools in Hungary, where he placed second in a class of sixty. After a two-year arts course at the University of Pest, he began the study of law in 1837 in Vienna. The University of Vienna and its affiliating general hospital, the Allgemeines Krankenhaus, were world centers for the study of medicine. After attending an autopsy with friends who were medical students, Semmelweis abandoned the study of law for medicine. He studied medicine in Vienna for a year, continued his studies from 1839 to 1840 at the University of Pest, and returned to Vienna to complete his studies and receive his medical degree in 1844 at the age of twenty-six.

Three rising young professors who were to make medical history befriended and influenced Semmelweis: Josef Škoda, professor of internal medicine, Karl von Rokitansky, the pathologist who directed the Institute for

Pathological Anatomy of the medical school, and Ferdinand von Hebra, the first professor of dermatology at the University of Vienna. Under these professors, the carefree young Semmelweis became a serious and disciplined doctor.

Life's Work

Semmelweis decided to specialize in obstetrics and gynecology, working in the obstetric and surgical clinics of the Allgemeines Krankenhaus. During the two years he had to wait for the position that he had been promised, he obtained his master's degree in obstetrics and doctor's degree in surgery, visited the obstetric clinic daily, frequented Škoda's lectures, and dissected with Rokitansky. Semmelweis was appointed first assistant lecturer to Professor Johann Klein in July of 1846.

The obstetric clinic was divided into ward 1, where medical students were instructed, and ward 2, where midwives were taught. Semmelweis was assigned to ward 1, where Klein was in charge. Before going to the clinic each day, Semmelweis performed autopsies on obstetric and gynecological cases. Postmortem dissection followed every death in the hospital. Ward duties included examining every patient in labor, conducting daily teaching rounds, assisting with operations, and instructing the medical students through autopsies and clinical practice.

Sensitive and compassionate by nature, Semmelweis was appalled by the mortality rate from childbed fever, or puerperal fever (from puerperium, the six weeks following childbirth), which ranged as high as 25 to 30 percent. Although the disease had been known since ancient times, it did not become a scourge until the beginning of the seventeenth century, when lying-in hospitals were established to care for the poor. It rarely occurred outside the hospitals. Between 1653 and 1863, there were two hundred so-called epidemics of puerperal fever in Europe.

The disease was variously attributed to atmospheric influences, overcrowding, poor ventilation, the onset of lactation, anxiety, bowel inflammation, deterioration of the blood, suppression of the discharge from the uterus, and a host of other causes. By the end of the eighteenth century, many English physicians had come to believe it was a specific acute infectious disease peculiar to pregnant women, transmitted in the same way as smallpox or scarlet fever, through direct or indirect contact. To prevent epidemics, doctors isolated the patient, used disinfectants, and maintained clean and well-ventilated wards. Thus, they were able to prevent the spread of the disease, while not completely understanding its nature. Oliver Wendell Holmes, Harvard anatomist and professor, subscribed to this contagion theory and in 1843 was the first to discuss the danger of attending women in labor after performing autopsies.

Although most obstetricians in Europe believed that puerperal fever was unpreventable, Semmelweis was obsessed by the desire to discover the cause of the disease. He systematically eliminated each hypothesis. Except for the fact that medical students were taught in ward 1 and midwifery students were taught in ward 2, the two wards were identical; they were both filthy, poorly ventilated, and crowded. Admissions to each ward occurred on alternate days. Yet the death rate in ward 1 was two to three times higher than in ward 2. Semmelweis concluded that puerperal fever could not be an epidemic of infectious disease because an epidemic would affect the two wards indiscriminately, occur outside the hospital, and exhibit seasonal variations. Through careful analysis of statistical data from 1789 on, he determined that the fatality rate was lower during periods when there was less interference with the birth process, fewer examinations, or fewer dissections. Gradually he came to suspect a connection between puerperal fever and the students' common practice of examining patients without careful handwashing after dissection. Unfortunately, his preoccupation with a problem that Klein considered inevitable and the collection of statistics which put the clinic in a bad light, alienated his superior, and on October 20, 1846, Semmelweis' appointment was discontinued.

Semmelweis was reinstated in his position on March 20, 1847, and returned to work from a holiday, only to learn that his friend Jakob Kolletschka had died in his absence from blood poisoning from a septic wound incurred during an autopsy. The findings at Kolletschka's autopsy were identical to those of the puerperal patients and their babies. By May, 1847, Semmelweis was sure that matter from the cadavers caused puerperal fever. The mortality in the second ward was low because midwifery students did not do postmortem examinations. Semmelweis decided that hands could only be considered clean if they no longer smelled of the cadavers. He instituted a strict policy of handwashing in chlorinated lime and using a nailbrush before each examination. Mortality rates in his ward dropped from 18.27 in April, 1847, to 0.19 by the end of the year. There were no deaths in March and August of 1848, but mortality rates increased when students were careless and when a woman with cancer of the uterus and another woman with an infected knee were admitted. Semmelweis now realized that infection could be airborne and transmitted from any infected source as well as from the examining hand soiled from cadavers. He prescribed handwashing between examination of individual patients.

Semmelweis encountered resistance to his methods. Klein did not understand him, resented his innovations, and became his bitter enemy. Medical students and nurses resented having to wash their hands. The rest of the world misunderstood his theory. Since he refused to publish, his friend Hebra published an editorial in December, 1847, in the journal of the Medical Society of Vienna about Semmelweis' discovery. Hebra clearly indicated that discharge from living organisms as well as cadaveric infection could cause puerperal fever but, unfortunately, called it an epidemic disease. A second article by Hebra, stressing the spread of puerperal infection from postmortem dissection, appeared in the journal in April, 1848, but this time he failed to allude to Semmelweis' discovery that the disease could be transmitted by material from living bodies as well as from cadavers. This created a serious misunderstanding of Semmelweis' theory. Physicians who did not practice postmortem dissection rejected the theory outright.

Meanwhile, Europe was in political turmoil and Semmelweis' Hungarian patriotism further offended Klein. When his appointment ended in March, 1849, Klein refused to renew it. Semmelweis tried to regain his post. When it was finally offered to him, there were restrictions he believed too degrading to accept. Before leaving Vienna for the last time, in May, 1850, he presented his discovery to the Medical Society of Vienna in a lecture, "The Origin of Puerperal Fever."

For the following six years, Semmelweis was in charge of the obstetrics department at the St. Rochus Hospital in Pest. There, he reduced the mortality rate from puerperal fever to less than 1 percent, compared with 10 to 15 percent in Vienna during the same period. He became professor of obstetrics at the University of Pest in 1855, developed a successful private practice, married in 1857, and had five children. His theory was accepted in Budapest, but the hostility of Vienna and the world community of obstetricians filled him with agony and bitterness.

In 1861, he finally published his life's work, *Die Ätiologie, der Begriff, und die Prophylaxis des Kindbettfiebers* (*The Cause, Concept, and Prophylaxis of Childbed Fever*, 1941). Prominent obstetricians and medical societies ignored or rejected his work, and he responded in scathing open letters which alienated even his friends. In 1865, fifteen years after leaving Vienna, Semmelweis developed signs of mental illness, and on August 13, died in a mental home in Vienna. Ironically, the cause of death was blood poisoning from an injury sustained during an operation he had performed. The truth of his doctrine was not accepted in Europe for at least two decades after his death.

Summary

It is difficult to appreciate Ignaz Philipp Semmelweis' contribution to medical science from the perspective of the twentieth century. So many advances have become commonplace; so many truths that were bitterly resisted have become self-evident. Working before Louis Pasteur's research in 1857 led to the germ theory and laid the foundation for advances in modern medicine, Semmelweis recognized the infectious nature of puerperal fever and realized that it was not a specific disease per se but could be caused by contact with any infected material through either direct or indirect means. Many physicians of his day working in different countries recognized aspects of the truth about puerperal fever. There are similarities in the work of Semmelweis, Holmes, and Joseph Lister, so the debate about who deserves the most credit in the history of antisepsis may never be resolved. Semmelweis, however, was the first to recognize that the disease was a form of blood poisoning, and he applied antisepsis in surgery as well as in obstetrics fifteen years before Lister.

Semmelweis was a great scientist who combined the powers of clinical observation, expert knowledge of pathology and obstetrics, and scientific honesty. He refused to accept the prevailing dogma of his day but persevered in his determination to understand the cause of the disease and the means of preventing it. He developed a theory about the cause of puerperal fever, tested it, and developed a means of preventing the disease. He was the first person in medical science to prove his theory using statistics.

It was Semmelweis' great misfortune that all but a few of his contemporaries rejected his theory, which resulted in the needless sacrifice of countless lives. Great discoveries have seldom been accepted without a struggle, but there can be no doubt that he contributed to his own tragedy. He antagonized his critics by his abrasive manner, and he refused to publish. If he had published when he was in Vienna with the help of Škoda and Hebra, his ideas might have been received more favorably.

Bibliography
Antall, József, and Géza Szebellédy. *Pictures from the History of Medicine: The Semmelweis Medical Historical Museum, Budapest*. Budapest, Hungary: Corvina Press, 1973. A collection of color photographs of portraits and artifacts from the Semmelweis Museum. Narrative includes a brief overview of Semmelweis' life and contributions and a history of the museum, which is the house where he was born.
Céline, Louis-Ferdinand. *Mea Culpa and The Life and Work of Semmelweis*. Translated by Robert Allerton Parker. Boston: Little, Brown, 1937. Reprint. New York: Howard Fertig, 1979. A subjective, romantic, and passionate tribute to Semmelweis, written by a French novelist.
Gortvay, György, and Imre Zoltán. *Semmelweis: His Life and Work*. Translated by Eva Rona. Budapest, Hungary: Akademiai Kiadó, 1968. A comprehensive and definitive biography, translated from Hungarian for the Federation of Hungarian Medical Societies' celebration of Semmelweis' birth. Incorporates the latest research to correct errors in previous biographies and includes a chronological list of events in the life of Semmelweis, along with numerous illustrations.
Semmelweis, Ignaz. *The Etiology, Concept, and Prophylaxis of Childbed Fever*. Translated by K. Codell Carter. Madison: University of Wisconsin Press, 1983. Semmelweis' classic contribution to medical literature. Includes statistical proofs and logical arguments. Redundant, awkward style.

Slaughter, Frank G. *Semmelweis, the Conqueror of Childbed Fever.* Reprint. New York: Collier Books, 1961. The most readily available and beautifully written biography of Semmelweis, with imaginative speculations. Helpful orientation to historical and scientific context of Semmelweis' life and work. Contains a few insignificant errors from previous biographers.

Thompson, Morton. *The Cry and the Covenant.* Garden City, N.Y.: Doubleday, 1954. A moving, dramatic, fictional biography, more concerned with fact than fiction. Contains both graphic details and a description of the broad social and cultural context in which Semmelweis conducted his research.

Edna B. Quinn

MICHAEL SERVETUS

Born: 1511; Villanova, Spain
Died: October 27, 1553; Geneva
Areas of Achievement: Religion and medicine
Contribution: Servetus was the first to provide a systematic account of Unitarian ideas. As a doctor, Servetus' greatest achievement was the discovery of the pulmonary circulation of the blood.

Early Life

Michael Servetus was born in 1511 in Villanova, Spain. His parents, Antonio Serveto, alias Reves, and Catalina Conesa, were locally prominent; his father was raised to the nobility in 1529. Little, however, is known about Servetus' childhood. It is evident, however, that the young Michael was given a good education. During the years of his youth, Spain was in a period of relative toleration and admiration of Renaissance learning. The works of Humanists such as Thomas More and Desiderius Erasmus were in circulation. The mixed heritage of Spain meant that both Jewish and Islamic literatures were also available, and Servetus had become well acquainted with the Koran before reaching maturity. His writing suggests that Jewish and Muslim criticisms of the Trinity as polytheistic influenced his own opinion.

Upon completing his primary education, Servetus studied law at Toulouse in 1528-1529. It was here, in all probability, that he first saw a complete copy of the Bible (the Catholic tradition was that priests studied the Bible and then told communicants about it). Eagerly perusing the scriptures, he concluded that there was no biblical basis for the doctrine of the Trinity.

Meanwhile, his academic talents led to a position in the service of Juan de Quintana, confessor to Charles V, King of Spain and Holy Roman Emperor. As a servant of Quintana, Servetus was taken to Italy, where emperor and pope were meeting to settle their differences. His observation of the veneration and obeisance paid to the pope and other church officials during the ceremony in Bologna left a deeply negative impression on the young Servetus.

After leaving Quintana's employ in late 1529 or early 1530, Servetus visited Johannes Oecolampadius in Basel. Although Servetus was inclined toward the Protestant movement, Reformers such as Oecolampadius, fighting desperately to establish their own sects, were little more tolerant of deviation than were papal authorities. The newcomer's forthrightness about his Unitarian beliefs led to agreement among the leading Reformers in Switzerland—including Huldrych Zwingli, Martin Bucer, and Oecolampadius—that if he would not convert to the true faith, he should be suppressed.

Life's Work

During his time in Switzerland, Servetus wrote his first book, *De Trini-*

tatis Erroribus Libri Septem (1531). Although his Latin was crude, Servetus' discussion of the Trinity was erudite, and the work's publication marked his emergence from obscurity. Later, wishing to respond to some of his critics, Servetus revised and expanded his views in *Dialogorum de Trinitate libri duo, de justicia regni Christi capitual quatuor* (1532).

Trinitarian doctrine, which the Church had adopted as orthodox, was far from simple. God, it stated, had a single essence but existed in three co-equal, eternal forms: Father, Word or Son, and Holy Spirit. The Son had both human and divine natures, each of which had all the properties of the other. Despite all of these forms and natures, God—that is, the single essence—was One.

Servetus, who believed that the Church's teachings should be understandable to all the faithful, regarded Trinitarian thought as a disguised polytheism with no scriptural warrant. Father, Son, and Holy Spirit, according to Servetus, were simply the various manifestations of God and not separate entities at all. The Holy Spirit was God's spirit, which enters all men and has no independent existence. The biblical Jesus was purely human, though specially infused with the Holy Spirit, as shown by his supernatural origins. He was sent by God, as the prophets had been. Although Servetus never made a clear distinction between the human Jesus and Logos, the Word (he applied the term "Christ" to both), some might judge his Unitarian doctrine simpler and easier to understand than Trinitarian orthodoxy.

Although some Protestants of Servetus' time were apparently troubled by Trinitarian ideas, they preferred to avoid debate on that point, and Servetus' assertion that God as the Holy Spirit was in all things sounded too much like pantheism. Accordingly, in 1532 Oecolampadius and Bucer repudiated him, and he fled to France. He was welcomed to his new country by an arrest order from the Inquisition. Warned of the danger, he flirted with the idea of emigrating to the New World, but instead enrolled at the University of Paris as Michel de Villeneuve. Though he made himself unpopular with his haughty behavior and even challenged John Calvin, himself a fugitive, to a debate (Servetus did not appear), Villeneuve was not unmasked. Increasing hostility toward heretics, however, made discretion the better part of valor, and in 1534, still as Villeneuve, Servetus moved to Vienne, just outside Lyons.

Many people around Lyons favored religious reform, and the leading cleric, Archbishop Pierre Palmier, was as liberal as any ecclesiastic of the time. Publishing flourished in the area, and Servetus was quickly employed as editor and corrector for the firm of Trechsel. His first project was a new edition of Ptolemy's study of geography; he was to correct errors made by previous editors and to update the work, incorporating new discoveries. The 1535 edition was so successful that he was commissioned to do an even more completely revised version that was published in 1541.

Servetus quickly developed a friendship with Symphorien Champier, a local Humanist and doctor. In 1537, presumably on Champier's advice, Servetus returned to the University of Paris to study medicine. He supported himself by publishing medical pamphlets and lecturing on geography, but when he added astrology, he was soon in trouble. Because of a remark by Saint Augustine that the stars influence the body but not the will, the Church had permitted the use of astrology in medical treatment. It did, however, condemn efforts to foretell the future. Although apparently moderate in his espousal of astrological influence, Servetus was greatly annoyed by criticism of his ideas and wrote *Apologetica Disceptatio pro Astrologia* (1538) in response. He was brought before the Parlement of Paris to answer charges that included heresy. Although the court ordered confiscation of all copies of his apology for astrological study, it went no further than to read him a lecture on respect for his university's faculty. Soon Servetus left Paris, apparently without taking a degree.

Although he did not publish the information until 1553, it was probably in Paris that Servetus made the medical discovery that is most commonly associated with his name: the concept of the pulmonary circulation of the blood. Galen, the second century Greek physician whose ideas still dominated Western medicine, had asserted that blood was created in the liver and consumed as part of the body's nutritive process. Servetus accepted these ideas but also recognized the blood's purification in the lungs and return to the heart. The fact that this discovery was published in a theological tract is explained by Servetus' adoption of the idea that the soul is in the blood. Galen spoke of a vital spirit that flowed through and vivified humans; for Servetus, that spirit was clearly the Holy Spirit. Although Matteo Realdo Colombo is known to have made the same discovery during this period, an unpublished manuscript of Servetus seems to predate Colombo's work, and it is certain that Servetus published first.

After two or three years at Charlieu, in late 1540 or early 1541 Servetus returned to Vienne; he spent the next twelve years working as physician and editor. He had the patronage of Palmier and aristocratic friends and patients. His second edition on Ptolemy appeared in 1541. The next four years were spent editing the Bible.

Perhaps hoping that Calvin might still be induced to reconsider his doctrine, Servetus initiated a correspondence, but he was haughty and didactic. He enclosed copies of his earlier works on theology, and in 1546, a draft of what would become *Christianismi restitutio* (1553). Calvin, increasingly exasperated, eventually stopped replying and, despite requests, did not return the books and manuscripts to their author. He did send a copy of his own book, *Christianae Religionis Institutio* (1536; *Institutes of the Christian Religion*, 1561), which Servetus inscribed with sarcastic and critical annotations and returned. Whether out of rage at being ignored or simply out of excessive zeal, Servetus drifted off into apocalyptic prophecy.

In *Christianismi restitutio*, Servetus attempts to restore the Church to its original nature—a common theme for him and most Christian Reformers. Although the Protestants had made a beginning on one of the central tenets that had to be reformed—the means of redemption—they had done nothing to improve church doctrine concerning the Incarnation. Servetus expanded his earlier idea that God is manifest in all things, skirting but not quite embracing pantheism. He called for adult baptism, suggesting that the ritual represented a process of redemption and spiritual rebirth that could not occur until the individual was mature in his knowledge of good and evil; such maturity was not possible before age twenty. After all, Servetus noted, Jesus deferred baptism until the age of thirty. His position on baptism was much like that of the Anabaptists, but he rejected the social radicalism that marked that group.

Soon after the anonymous publication of *Christianismi restitutio* in January, 1553, Servetus was betrayed to the Inquisition. Although he did not write the letters of betrayal, Calvin supplied evidence from the correspondence of a few years earlier. Arrested and questioned, Servetus escaped. His whereabouts were unknown until he was arrested by Genevan authorities in August.

Calvin, who argued that Protestants should be no less ruthless than Catholics in the fight against heresy, worked to have Servetus prosecuted. The trial, which was highlighted by direct, though mostly written, confrontation between the two theologians, was also a battleground in the confrontation between Calvin and the Libertine Party for control of the city. The outcome was a triumph for Calvin. Servetus was condemned for heresy and sentenced to the stake. He was burned, dying in agony, on October 27, 1553. Two months later, the Catholic authorities in Vienne burned his effigy. Calvin was never again challenged for control of Geneva.

Summary

Michael Servetus is an example of the Renaissance man, for his intellect penetrated divergent areas of thought. Servetus knew classical and modern languages, theology, mathematics, and medical science. His discovery of the pulmonary circulation of the blood was a significant advance in physiology, and he practiced successfully as a physician. Although not the first to advance a Unitarian theory, Servetus was a key figure in pulling such ideas together and stating them systematically. As such, he is an important forerunner of modern Unitarianism.

Servetus' failures came in the areas of politics and human relations. He was so convinced that his views were correct that he had no patience with those who disagreed. He died a martyr not only to his faith but also to tolerance and free speech, yet he probably could have avoided that martyrdom by leaving Calvin alone. His ego drove him to proselytize and to become infuriated when his ideas were rejected. His career, then, reflects the best and worst of the Renaissance and Reformation era. As Humanist and scientist, he had great breadth and depth of knowledge. His condemnation to a hideous death by both Protestants and Catholics exemplifies the tension and fear produced by the zealously held religious convictions of the Reformation.

Bibliography
Bainton, Roland H. *Hunted Heretic: The Life and Death of Michael Servetus, 1511-1553*. Boston: Beacon Press, 1953. Reprint. Gloucester, Mass.: Peter Smith, 1978. A valuable biography, containing a thorough description of Servetus' life as well as an analysis of his theology. The account is balanced, well documented, and easy to read. An extensive bibliography is also included.
_____. "Michael Servetus and the Pulmonary Transit." *Bulletin of the History of Medicine* 7 (1938): 1-7. A short but helpful discussion of the major medical discovery made by Servetus. This article will be most useful for those interested in Servetus as a doctor.
Durant, Will. *The Story of Civilization*. Vol. 6, *The Reformation*. New York: Simon & Schuster, 1957. Colorful writing and effective storytelling are the hallmarks of Durant's monumental series about civilization. This volume and its concise biography of Servetus are no exceptions. For the general reader seeking information about Servetus and his era, Durant is a delight. Unfortunately, his work is marked by rather too-frequent factual errors and should be used with care.
Friedman, Jerome. *Michael Servetus: A Case Study in Total Heresy*. Geneva: Droz, 1978. A biography with an emphasis on the religious elements in Servetus' career and a tendency to be hostile toward its subject. The analysis of Servetus' theology and his problems with the Church is interesting but not always convincing.
Fulton, John F., and Madeline E. Stanton. *Michael Servetus: Humanist and Martyr*. New York: H. Reichner, 1953. A biography that is rather favorable to Servetus. The authors make an effort to establish Servetus' place in Renaissance Humanism, and the book is most useful for setting that context.
Wilbur, Earl Morse. *A History of Unitarianism*. Vol. 1, *Socinianism and Its Antecedents*. Cambridge, Mass.: Harvard University Press, 1947. This standard work on Unitarianism devotes five chapters to the career of Servetus. The focus is on theology and Servetus' importance in the development of the Unitarian position. Much biographical information is included.
Wilcox, Donald J. *In Search of God and Self: Renaissance and Reformation Thought*. Boston: Houghton Mifflin, 1975. Although Servetus is discussed

at length in this book, it provides an excellent background for an understanding of his life and theology. The emphasis is on intellectual history,
particularly religion, and the major themes of the era are clearly presented.

Fred R. van Hartesveldt

SESSHŪ

Born: 1420; Akahama, Bitchu Province, Japan
Died: 1506; Yamaguchi, Suho Province, Japan
Area of Achievement: Art
Contribution: Sesshū is considered the greatest of Japanese landscape paint-
ers and a major ink painter whose genius pushed Japanese art toward its
apex at the beginning of the sixteenth century.

Early Life

Sesshū was born in a rural village, Akahama on the Inland Sea, and was
placed while very young in the Hofukuji, a large temple in the city of Soja
nearby, to undergo religious training. Still in his early years, Sesshū entered
the Shokokuji monastery in Kyōto as a novice. He acted as attendant to a
priest, Shunrin Shuto, who eventually became chief abbot. He also studied
painting with the monk-painter Tensho Shubun, who later was welcomed by
the Ashikaga Shogunate as a master of the official academy. Both Shunrin
and Shubun had a tremendous influence on Sesshū's life. Sesshū became a
monk and practiced Zen discipline under the tutelage of the Zen master
Shunrin, who was highly respected for his piety and truthfulness. Sesshū's
career was determined by Shubun, whom Sesshū called "my painting master," and who was the first Japanese artist to rise to the full power and grasp
of Chinese art.

Already enjoying great renown as a painter and past the age of forty,
Sesshū left the Shokukuji in 1462, for nothing could satisfy him short of
studying in China. He moved west in the hope of making his way to China
and established himself in a studio in Yamaguchi, which was under the
control and patronage of the Ouchi family. Japan was going through a time
of civil disturbance which culminated in the Onin Wars (1467-1477), which
devastated Kyōto and dispersed its culture to the provinces; Yamaguchi
thrived as a "Little Kyōto." In 1467, Sesshū traveled to China with a sho-
gunal commercial fleet to study Chinese ink painting at first hand. His trip,
which took him by land from Ningpo to Peking, gave him numerous opportunities to see not only some famous Chinese scenery but also many Chinese
paintings, including those by Ming Dynasty painters still unknown in Japan.
Sesshū had gone to China in search of a good painting master and found only
mediocre ones who were weighed down with academic formalism. The grandiose landscape of the continent, however, revealed to him the secret composition in Chinese painting. Wherever he went, he drew landscapes and
scenes of popular life which display the essential qualities of his art: solid
construction and concise brushwork. He traveled especially to all the famous
scenes where the great Sung landscapists had painted from nature. His style
of sketching was so rapid and incisive that he brought back to Japan in 1469

thousands of fresh impressions of all the most noted places in Chinese scenery and history, along with accurate studies of costumes worn by famous individuals and of portrait types.

Life's Work

After returning to Japan in 1469 with his invaluable raw materials from China, Sesshū moved from place to place in northern Kyushu in order to avoid the disorder of civil war. He finally settled in Oita, under the patronage of the Otomo family. There he opened a studio which he named "Tenkai Togaro" and which was situated high on the side of a hill overlooking town, water, and mountains. Sesshū would often begin his work by gazing out upon the beautiful broad landscape that lay beneath his window. After a drink of sake, he would pick up his bamboo flute and play a sonorous, lingering melody to establish the right mood. Only then would he take up his brush and begin to paint. He was truly prolific; his floor was constantly covered with scattered pieces of used and unused paper. His monk friend Bofu Ryoshin, after visiting him in 1476, commented that everyone in the town, from the nobility to the common people, admired Sesshū's art and asked for a piece of his work. It seems that Sesshū never grew weary of depicting his private world, communing from time to time with the great world of nature outstretched beneath his balcony.

His practice of *zazen* (meditation) and his custom of making leisurely pilgrimages to various Buddhist temples and monasteries seem to have given him a strong body and robust health; he was able to travel on foot to various parts of the country, painting realistic pictures of the places he visited along the way. Sesshū always kept his clerical name and his Buddhist robe, which allowed him to travel through districts that were dangerous or that were barred to others.

Between 1481 and 1484, Sesshū made a long journey throughout Japan, making landscape drawings along the way. This artistic pilgrimage deepened his ability to capture the essential features of Japanese landscapes in his wash drawings. The Sung tradition of Chinese wash drawing had been fully assimilated in Japan, thanks to Shubun's talents and common sense, but it was Sesshū who first succeeded in giving a deeply personal and national expression to the new technique. Moreover, Sesshū's style is remarkable for its clear departure from the lyrical mode associated with his teacher Shubun. Dynamic brushwork and structured composition dominate Sesshū's works. He thoroughly developed and perfected a style of his own, and throughout his career he pushed back the limits of expression. Sesshū was completely wrapped up in his art. Upon returning to the west, he set up his Tenkai Togaro studio in Yamaguchi.

Sesshū was extraordinarily prolific. His studio became a place of pilgrimage as people requested a token from his brush. He painted the walls of many monasteries (unfortunately long-since destroyed) and hundreds of six-fold screens, of which many have moldered away or been burned. An enormous amount of his work remains, however, though it is so zealously prized and guarded that few have seen many of his great masterpieces.

Among his compositions that are available to public view and representative of his work are *Autumn and Winter Landscapes*, a pair of hanging scrolls which must have belonged to a sequence of four seasons, a traditional theme for a set of landscapes, and *Landscapes of the Four Seasons* (1486), a long picture sequence illustrating the transition from spring to winter, done in a horizontal hand scroll format and representing the synthesis of his art. *Haboku Landscape* (1495), his best-known work, is a landscape in cursive style. It was given to his disciple Josui Soen, a painter-monk of the En-kakuji, when he took leave of Sesshū to return to Kamakura after a long course of study in his studio. The landscape, with a few rapid wash strokes accentuated with dark black lines, skillfully represents a tiny segment of nature lacking neither grandeur nor stability. *Amanohashidate* (1502-1505; bridge of heaven), drawn on the spot during a visit to the famous place on the Sea of Japan, represents the climax of his art. In this panoramic view of a pilgrimage site, all the details are represented with clean-cut lines, accompanied even by the names of the localities. Sesshū succeeded in capturing the innermost qualities of the famous place; to the technique of wash painting, he gave a highly personal expression.

Sesshū's versatility extended to other genres such as bird and flower painting—numerous sets of screens on this subject have been attributed to him. Moreover, noteworthy examples of portraits and other figure subjects including *Huike Severing His Arm*, a large, deeply moving composition executed in 1496 in which Huike (Hui-k'o) is cutting off his arm to show his will power to Bodhidharma.

Sesshū died shortly after painting *Amanohashidate*; he was vigorously healthy right up to the end of his life. During his lifetime, Sesshū was the host of many pupils, mostly Zen priests, of whom the greatest is Sesson Shukei. Among other acknowledged masters of this Sesshū school were Shugetsu Tokan, Umpo Toetsu, Kaiho Yusho, and Soga Chokuan. The Sesshū school continued on into the seventeenth century before melding with other schools. Its decline and death was not surprising, for no school of Japanese pictorial art so entirely depended on the skill of its delineator.

Summary

The style of Sesshū is central in the whole range of Asian art. Its primary vigor lies in its line—Sesshū's conceptions are thought out in terms of dominant lines. The line is hard, rough, and splintery, as if his brush were intentionally made of hog bristles irregularly set. Sesshū is a great master of straight line and angle. Moreover, he perfected the Chinese *suiboku* style of painting, making it typically Japanese by using the *haboku* technique, literally "flung ink," which employs a freely handled wash. *Suiboku* was monochrome work using black ink on a brush, which emphasized skilled brushwork in place of a balance of color. Sesshū was the master of this style.

Sesshū loved painting landscapes because the landscape remains personal. It is the man who selects its elements, stamps them with his seal, infuses them with his strength, his will, his impetus. The genius clings throughout to human values, imposes them on the world, and victoriously refashions a world of his own. Sesshū's primary achievements can be easily categorized. He was preeminently skillful in landscape and figure painting. He excelled in the portrayal of birds, animals, and flowers. His manner was distinguished by the rapidity and certainty of its brushwork. He cultivated the habit of capturing as much of the subject as possible with one stroke. The effects of details such as leaves, feathers, and the like were almost invariably done at the single application of the brush, controlled by an unerring but perfectly free hand.

Many of the finest artists of the sixteenth century claimed to be his successor. The competition became so fierce that Unkoku Togan and Hasegawa Tohaku became embroiled in a legal dispute over the right to claim artistic descent from Sesshū.

Bibliography

Akiyama, Terukaza. *Japanese Painting*. Cleveland: World Publishing, 1961. A beautiful volume with illustrations covering the whole range of Japanese painting according to their genre. Chapter 6 emphasizes the influence of Chinese art and the development of monochrome painting, at the heart of which is Sesshū.

Binyon, Laurence. *Painting in the Far East*. 3d rev. ed. London: Edward Arnold, 1923. An interesting analysis of Sesshū's paintings appears in chapter 11.

Fenollosa, Ernest F. *Epochs of Chinese and Japanese Art*. New York: Frederick A. Stokes, 1912. One of the first interpreters of note on Japanese and Chinese art. Reviews Sesshū's accomplishments and their significance. Provides a unique perspective of Sesshū.

Paine, Robert Treat, and Alexander Soper. *The Art and Architecture of Japan*. Baltimore: Penguin Books, 1955. Part 1 deals with the broad sweep of Japanese painting through history. Chapters 9 and 10 emphasize Sesshū, his compatriots, and his influence on successors. The 1981 revised third edition contains an updated, invaluable bibliography by W. D. Waterhouse.

Tanaka, Ichimatsu. *Japanese Ink Painting: Shubun to Sesshū*. Translated by Bruce Darling. New York: Weatherhill, 1972. A standard work on Sesshū and his master Shubun which places them in historic perspective in the development of Japanese painting. Chapter 4 is devoted exclusively to Sesshū.

Warner, Langdon. *The Enduring Art of Japan.* New York: Grove Press, 1952. A classic analysis of Japanese art trends in a historical perspective. Chapter 5 emphasizes the Ashikaga period, into which fit Sesshū and ink painting.

Edwin L. Neville, Jr.

GEORGES SEURAT

Born: December 2, 1859; Paris, France
Died: March 29, 1891; Paris, France
Area of Achievement: Art
Contribution: Seurat became one of the most perceptive imagists of the
modern city and its inhabitants in the late nineteenth century. His great
curiosity about new developments in technology and the sciences transformed his art into one based increasingly upon scientific and pseudo-
scientific theories, something valued highly by twentieth century modern
movements. His work may be seen also as a prophecy of surface abstrac-
tion and grand decoration.

Early Life

Georges Seurat was born in Paris in 1859. His father, Chrysostome-
Antoine Seurat, a legal official, retired at age forty-two and lived apart from
his wife, Ernestine, and their three children. Seurat saw his father each week
at dinner at his mother's apartment on the boulevard de Magenta in Paris.
His parents' marriage has been described as advantageous, respectably bourgeois, and comfortable but dreary.

Seurat shared his mother's strong and regular features as well as the precision and diligence with which she applied herself undemonstratively to tasks
at hand. With his father, Seurat shared a quiet, serious, even distant mien.
Very little is known of Seurat's childhood, and he was difficult to get to
know as a man. Most reminiscences from his friends or colleagues are consistent in their inability to penetrate the artist's personality. It is debatable,
however, whether Seurat's private nature was abnormal. In his dedication
to work, he was serious to the point of humorlessness, touchy, and even
irritable.

Seurat, who drew well as a child, was encouraged in art especially by a
maternal uncle, Paul Hausmonte-Faivre. The novice artist drew objects from
his environment that caught his interest; by age fifteen, Seurat's interest in
art had become an obsession, and he withdrew from a regular school to
enroll in a local drawing school. At this municipal school from 1875 to
1877, he moved through a demanding and classically based curriculum,
which stressed endless hours of drawing human anatomy from engravings,
from casts of antique sculpture, and from live models. Seurat's academy
drawings reveal that he apparently preferred disciplined and sober images
from symmetrically ordered compositions with a minimum of gesture and
dramatic movement. He thus studied the work of Jean-Auguste-Dominique
Ingres and Hans Holbein, the Younger.

Seurat's next stage of training came on entering the prestigious École des
Beaux Arts in 1878; he was admitted to the painting class of Henri Leh-

mann, a disciple of Ingres. Seurat may have appreciated Lehmann's disciplined drawings more than his paintings, and Seurat's academic training may have failed to stimulate a healthy interest in color. The years 1875-1879 witnessed Seurat's growth primarily in draftsmanship, careful techniques, sophisticated design, and an identification with imagery carrying moral overtones, all lessons carried over into his mature work.

Life's Work

Following a year of compulsory military service, Seurat returned to Paris in November of 1880 and in a short time settled into a studio not far from the site where he had studied with Lehmann. Seurat left the École des Beaux Arts after barely a year for reasons still unclear, but by 1880-1883 he was again submitting work to the salon. During this same period, Seurat devoted himself to challenges in drawing and in so doing developed a mature style. His drawing and painting methods became parallel manifestations of a desire to regularize Impressionist painting methods and record everyday urban life with the nobility of classical art in the museums. With Impressionism as a starting point, Seurat restricted himself to drawing in black and white, usually with charcoal, chalk, or conte crayons, moving away from an emphasis on line and contour toward softer, broader marks that acknowledged mass, the subtleties of atmosphere, and a concentration upon light. This approach yielded effects both academic and vanguard. The drawings reveal by 1883 a strong traditional handling of form through tonal contrast. Yet the regularized all-over treatment, the neutral stance toward imagery, and the increasing concern with scientific theory had little in common with accepted academic practices at the time.

A masterful approach was evident by 1883 in Seurat's drawings; at that time, he felt sufficiently confident to develop a major painting, one upon which he hoped to establish a reputation. His confidence was based upon intense practice in drawing over three years plus much exploration in painting methods and in color theory. A thorough familiarity with Eugène Chevreul's theories of simultaneous complementary contrasts of colors and a reading of Ogden Rood's *Modern Chromatics* (1879) helped him immeasurably to realize optical mixing in both painting studies and finished drawings.

The first painting to benefit from this theoretical and technical input was the large work *A Bathing Place, Asnieres* (1883-1884). In the preparatory works and the final painting, French citizens swim, go boating, or rest as they enjoy a noon-hour break from work in the industries of a northern Paris suburb. Here the artist calculated and toiled to synthesize the variables and immediacy of Impressionist works by Claude Monet, Pierre-Auguste Renoir, and others.

The salon jury of 1884 did not find *A Bathing Place, Asnieres* museum-worthy, but fortunately for Seurat a number of other rejected artists that year formed the Société des Artistes Indépendants, which sponsored uncensored, unjuried shows and accepted Seurat's painting. Seurat was encouraged but remained frustrated and threw himself into an even more ambitious painting, *A Sunday on the Grand Jatte*, painted 1884-1886, and with dimensions nearly the same as *A Bathing Place, Asnieres*.

The monumental painting depicts nearly life-size middle-class Parisians enjoying a work-free day on a slender island in the river Seine, where, dressed in current fashions, many promenade or sit quietly. Compositionally speaking, the lengthening shadows of mid-afternoon help unify the complex placement of figures. Many of the strollers are arranged in silhouetted profile and almost no figures venture a spontaneous movement. Thus, there is a sense of the illogical leisure of mannequins instead of humans occupying a charmed environment. This mechanical aesthetic was no accident. In *A Sunday on the Grande Jatte*, Seurat methodically constructed a painting which extends the Impressionist treatment of subject but does not emulate the Impressionists' pursuit of transitory effects. It became a landmark work because it necessitated a new critical language and, as it happened, a new movement. Upon viewing the painting at the last Impressionist group show in 1886, art critic and friend to Seurat Félix Fénéon proposed the term Neoimpressionism.

Furthermore, *A Sunday on the Grande Jatte* possessed a radical appearance, composed as it was of thousands and perhaps millions of tiny dots painted with impressive control and evenness. The technique employed became known as pointillism because of the use of points or dots of unmixed pigments. Yet pointillism, arresting in its own right, was not the most important part of Seurat's program. The artist was investigating new quasi-scientific painting theories devised by critics Chevreul, Charles Blanc, and John Ruskin, as well as developments in commercial printing. That intense study resulted in the concept of divisionism, a theory that advocated breaking down colors into separate components and applying them almost mechanically to a primed canvas in almost microscopic amounts, whereupon an optical mix occurred for spectators. The resultant optical mix was thought to be superior in luminosity to effects possible from traditional palettes wherein colors were mixed as tints or hues before application to a canvas. The immediate difference for Seurat was a painted approximation of the vibrating subtleties of reflected light, for example, as found in the partial tones of shadows in nature.

Not to be overlooked too was a concurrent advancement in color printing—the chromotypogravure, which intrigued Seurat, already fascinated by technology. The chromotypogravure replicated colors via screens or regular systems of dots and, as in Seurat's pointillism, produced an atmospheric mass and subtle gradations instead of lines or sharp contrasts of form.

Pointillism and divisionism, which regularized the painted effects of Impressionism, would have been satisfying accomplishments in themselves for some progressive painters of the 1880's, but not for Seurat. Upon finishing *A Sunday on the Grande Jatte*, which was also rejected at the Paris Salon, he took up a different challenge, that of systematizing the means of expressing emotional effects in paintings through carefully predetermined amounts of colors and types of light. Regularizing emotions in paintings was not new in France. There were plenty of precedents from Nicolas Poussin in the 1600's to Jacques-Louis David in the late 1700's. Seurat's new preoccupation, though, was based mostly on the publications of Charles Henry, a contemporary psychologist and aesthetician. Henry sought a scientific way to regularize connections between the formal elements of painting—colors, tones, or lines—and their impact upon viewers' emotional responses.

Such formulas appeared in Seurat's next well-planned painting, *Une Parade de cirque* of 1888. Known generally as *La Parade* (the side show), it focused on the midway of an urban circus. The scene, lit by gas jets, may be a nocturne, but more is dark in *La Parade* than the atmosphere. This entertainment scene is not joyous, despite a milling crowd and performing musicians. Solemnity and dutiful actions seem the rule and are reinforced by a muted surface system of dark blue and red dots. The painting is a balanced geometrical artifice underscored by the application of the ancient Greek guide, called the golden section, believed to establish beautiful proportions.

A number of marine subjects painted at or near Honfleur, Grandcamp, Port-en-Bessin, and Gravelines represent the artist's other painting interests from 1885 to 1891. These paintings parallel the works discussed in this essay technically and compositionally, and, though perhaps less provocative, they are no less brilliant in conception or execution.

Only days before the Salon des Indépendants opened in 1891, Seurat became ill, possibly from infectious angina or acute meningitis. Quickly moved from inadequate lodging to his mother's apartment, also in Paris, he lapsed into delirium and died there on March 29.

Summary

Precocious as a youth, Georges Seurat was the master of his intentions for art by 1880. He could not know it at the time, but his career would be over in only eleven years. Deliberate in technique and a theoretician besides, his mature oeuvre included fewer than twenty major paintings, yet Seurat is considered one of the most influential of the late nineteenth century painters in France.

He modernized classical configurations and exhausted orthodox formulas, after which he ventured into uncharted waters and speculated upon radical approaches to picture-making. Indeed, art viewers during his life and since usually imagine that technique or process was his dominant concern. Yet much of Seurat's conceptual direction was governed by careful reading of art theory, literature, physics, and pioneering works in psychology. Furthermore, despite the appearance of Cartesian order and asymmetrical balance invoked through the golden section of the ancient Greeks, Seurat's paintings by 1886 reflect an exploration of the new Symbolist movement, a movement decidedly subjective.

Seurat's primary subject, interwoven among fields of dots, was the modern city and the activities of its various classes of people, in particular the middle-class at its leisure. In so doing, he transformed pedestrian information into a dignified and clarified expression, befitting the traditional art of the museums while simultaneously reflecting an enthusiasm for science and technology.

Bibliography

Broude, Norma. "New Light on Seurat's 'Dot': Its Relation to Photomechanical Color Printing in France in the 1880's." *Art Bulletin* 56 (December, 1974): 581-589. In a valuable piece of scholarship, Broude explores the parameters of the pointillist technique. In doing so, she draws quite helpful connections between Seurat's method, begun about 1885, and a new commercial printing technique involving chromotypogravure. There are also connections to an equally new attempt at color photography called the autochrome process. Those technologies fascinated Seurat because he was searching for an optically induced half-tone value system.

Dorra, Henri, and John Rewald. *Seurat.* Paris: Les Beaux-arts, 1959. Noteworthy are letters between Seurat and the Symbolist art theorist Fénéon, a perceptive and well-documented chapter titled "The Evolution of Seurat's Style," a chronological list of exhibitions in which Seurat's paintings have been shown, a lengthy bibliography, plus indexes of patrons and collectors as well as Seurat's art listed by title and subject.

Goldwater, Robert J. "Some Aspects of the Development of Seurat's Style." *Art Bulletin* 23 (March, 1941): 117-130. Concentrates upon stylistic developments in the last five years of the artist's career, plus relationships between Seurat's career and those of his contemporaries. Goldwater emphasis that Seurat was highly interested in various currents of his time, both in art and in other professions to the degree that he was as much influenced by contemporary developments as he influenced others.

Prak, Niels Luning. "Seurat's Surface Pattern and Subject Matter." *Art Bulletin* 53 (September, 1971): 367-378. This fine article addresses some of Seurat's intentions for the surface characteristics of his mature style, chief among which were the transformation of observed fact into rigorous abstract pattern. That, according to Prak, was achieved eventually by the painter through continual simplification of figures, continuity of forms (either defined or suggested), and the application of Blanc's theories to painting.

Thomson, Richard. *Seurat*. Salem, N.H.: Salem House, 1985. A good monograph which benefits from international research. Its standard chronological approach is enriched by rarely seen drawings and painted studies and a penetrating text, which correctly explores Seurat's absorption in current art and scientific theory.

Tom Dewey II

LUDOVICO SFORZA

Born: July 27, 1452; Vigevano, Republic of Milan
Died: May 27, 1508; Loches, Toubrenne, France
Areas of Achievement: Government and patronage of the arts
Contribution: One of the most spectacular and significant statesmen and
political manipulators of the High Renaissance in Italy, Sforza directed
the Duchy of Milan during a crucial period of European history. His
political maneuvers determined the following century of Italian affairs.

Early Life
The fourth legitimate son of Francesco Sforza, first Sforza Duke of Milan,
and Bianca Maria Visconti, Ludovico Sforza was born into two of the most
powerful families of the fourteenth century. At birth, his mother gave him
the surname Maurus, which she later changed to Maria. By that time, however, "Maurus" had evolved into the nickname "Il Moro" (the Moor),
which Ludovico liked, not only because it suited his dark complexion but
also because it conjured up images of romance and adventure. Thereafter,
the name stuck; Ludovico even used puns on that name to provide the meta-
phorical basis of some of his favorite personal devices and symbols, a
Moor's head (*moro*) and a mulberry tree (*mora*). He became his mother's
favorite while still young, remaining devoted to her his entire life. Discover-
ing that he was bright, she directed his early education and eventually hired
the Humanist Francesco Filelfo as his tutor. Sforza received a thorough
grounding in the new learning of the Renaissance, becoming adept in both
ancient languages and literature and the intellectual and technical innovations of the time. As a result of this background, he would later take his
responsibilities as patron of the arts and literature and as commissioner of
public buildings seriously, though he apparently had little confidence in the
consistency or accuracy of his taste and judgment.

When the twenty-four-year-old Sforza was visiting France, his brother
Galeazzo Maria, who had succeeded their father as Duke of Milan ten years
earlier, was assassinated on December 24, 1476, leaving the seven-year-old
Gian Galeazzo as heir. The child's mother, Bona of Savoy, assumed the
regency, with Cicco Simonetta as principal adviser. Intrigues seemed to occur overnight, prompted chiefly by older Sforza relatives. When a plot impli-
cated Ludovico and his brothers, all three were exiled. Eventually, however,
Ludovico persuaded Bona to pardon him. On his return to Milan, he learned
that Bona had taken a young servant, Tamino, as her lover. He used both his
privileged position and his inside knowledge to gain control, having Simonetta murdered, driving Tamino away, discrediting Bona, and getting the
nominal duke to appoint him chief counselor. From that time—November,
1780—he was virtual duke.

Life's Work

Sforza's life was the governing of Milan. At first, that meant making his rule legitimate, but eventually it would mean making it both legitimate and secure; neither was easy. Sforza's opening move was to ally himself with Ferdinand I, King of Naples. This eventually led to a marriage arrangement between Isabella of Aragon, granddaughter of Ferdinand, and the teenage Gian Galeazzo; in confirming the marriage, Sforza probably outsmarted himself, failing to realize that this articulate and ambitious woman would not accept the title of duchess without the power. At any rate, he refused to relinquish control after the wedding, thereby precipitating his ultimate downfall. Isabella immediately began conspiring to turn her Aragonese kinsmen against him, especially after January, 1791, when he married the young and equally spirited Beatrice d'Este of Ferrara, who was also of the family of Aragon. The Aragonese listened to Isabella.

Desperate for allies, Sforza turned to Charles VIII of France, establishing a mutual defense compact with him in 1492. Later that year, Alexander VI became pope with the support of Sforza's brother, the Cardinal Ascanio; this gave Sforza hope of papal support. Temporarily safe, Sforza attempted to maintain security by constructing a tenuous web of secret alliances and counteralliances. Once again he was too subtle for his own good: Charles VIII, who claimed the throne of Naples in his own right, and who had become obsessed with establishing a base in Italy for mounting a crusade, seized upon a pretext of perceived danger to invade Italy in 1494. During this campaign, Charles visited Gian Galeazzo at Pavia; the next day, the young man became ill and died, in circumstances that looked suspiciously like poison.

Meanwhile, Sforza was also carrying on surreptitious negotiations with the Emperor Maximilian I, who needed both money and a wife. In exchange for accepting a well-dowried niece of Sforza, Maximilian agreed to legitimate him as Duke of Milan. Gian Galeazzo's death occurred before this could happen. To divert public accusation, Sforza immediately summoned the Milanese Council, proposing that the duke's infant son be named his successor. Since he had packed the council, he knew in advance that its recommendation would be in favor of strength and experience, not rule by children. Thus, Sforza finally became Duke of Milan in name as well as in fact.

In the meantime, Charles pushed on through Italy and subjugated Naples. His success unsettled the states of Italy; Sforza feared that he had given Charles a foothold from which he would not budge—a fear intensified by the presence in Charles's army of the Duc d'Orléans, himself a claimant to the throne of Milan through his mother. Quickly Sforza withdrew his troops from the alliance and opened talks with Venice. The various Italian states joined forces to trap Charles in the peninsula, but he evaded them, withdrawing from Italy in October, 1495. Sforza took credit for forcing the retreat; he bragged at the time that the pope was his chaplain, the emperor his *condotierre* (military commander), Venice his chamberlain, and the King of France his courier. This was at best wishful thinking; Sforza was more likely a master in the art of self-deception.

He did not have much leisure to indulge such delusions. Maximilian came for a visit but proved too poor and vacillating to provide any real assistance. Shortly thereafter, the pope changed his strategy, Venice asserted its independence, the Aragonese recovered Naples, and Charles VIII died, to be succeeded by Sforza's antagonist, the Duc d'Orléans, now Louis XII, who had himself crowned both King of France and Duke of Milan. Far from manipulating his enemies, Sforza was now hemmed in on all sides. Sforza tried the desperate expedient of urging the Turks to invade Venice. Instead, Maximilian abandoned him, and the pope, France, and Venice formed a common league. Louis XII invaded the outlying districts, seizing the mountain strongholds. Sforza had no recourse but to flee. With his fortress at Milan in the hands of his chosen commandant, he packed his treasury in an immense mule train and escaped to Maximilian's court at Innsbruck. The emperor had probably never dreamed of such a windfall; Sforza's coffers went a long way toward solving Maximilian's financial problems.

In the meantime, rather than defending the castle to the death as instructed, in September, 1499, Sforza's commandant surrendered it to the French for 150,000 ducats. Sforza's cause was almost lost. He used what remained of his treasure to hire an army of Swiss and Burgundian mercenaries. At first, his campaign was successful; the people rallied behind him, since the high-handed methods of the French had alienated them. Yet Sforza did not have the opportunity to bring his opponents to battle. The Swiss were bribed to surrender him to the French, which they did on April 5, 1500. Taken to France as a prisoner, he was confined to the fortress at Loches in Touraine, where he remained in captivity until his death eight years later.

Sforza's lifetime marked the high point of Italy's greatness. At the beginning of his life, Italy was the paragon of Europe, the leader in the new civilization of the Renaissance, setting the pace of innovation in painting, music, sculpture, literature, philosophy, and all the arts of civilization. At the beginning of Sforza's career, Italy was considered a superior civilization, impregnable, almost sacrosanct, a region populated by a higher race. By his end, it had become a playground for petty princes and their mercenaries, stamped with fraud, corruption, greed, and venality. Worse, its vulnerability to external aggression had been exposed. Henceforth, it would become merely a collection of victims for plundering.

Summary

Like many other notable Renaissance princes, Ludovico Sforza has not been given the attention by contemporary historians that he received from previous generations.

Yet Sforza was celebrated in his time for the splendor of his court and his patronage of the arts. He set a standard of living that has rarely been equaled for style and taste. His center lacked the strenuous intellectualism and the learned grace of his great predecessor, Federigo da Montefeltro of Urbino; yet that gathering of learning, beauty, and wit, the fantasy of all academics since, could never be duplicated, and Sforza did not try. He wanted to build not a haven for intellectuals but a model of harmonious living for all of his citizens. This did not mean conspicuous consumption of luxury for the sake of ostentation, though there was plenty of that. It did mean that general prosperity and enlightened regulation were fundamental to his plan—ideals which unfortunately often conflicted with his political and military operations. Along these lines, he built a model farm to test new agricultural methods; for it and others near it, he devised a new system of irrigation by canal. He had his hometown and favorite retreat of Vigevano completely rebuilt. He promoted art, literature, science, and trade.

Yet his reputation for courtly living derived more from his dreams and plans than from what he actually was able to bring into being. Sympathetic contemporary biographers contributed largely to his legend. Thus Sforza is widely credited with patronage of Leonardo da Vinci and Donato Bramante. Yet the encouragement he gave them was often more verbal than financial. Ludovico commissioned the astonishing *Last Supper* (1495), which he also had almost completely reconstructed; he also did much to make both art and learning more available to the community. The final judgment on his patronage is aptly symbolized in the fate of the great statue of Francesco Sforza, which, like so many of Ludovico's dreams, never materialized. The brass for its casting was diverted during the French invasion to be made into cannons, and the model itself was shattered by French soldiers, who used it for target practice, after the fall of the castle.

Finally, Sforza is perhaps best seen as a man who dreamed grandly but could not control the forces, social and political, in which he found himself. It is hard to imagine what might have happened had he not seized power when he did. He failed to accomplish what he intended. The temporary security he provided made the destruction following him seem that much more devastating. In his subtlety he outmaneuvered himself. His extravagance was financed by increasing and unpopular taxation. Yet for his time he was magnificent. If he, with his intensity, intelligence, and force, failed, what would have happened under Gian Galeazzo? He has been blamed for the dissolution of Italian self-rule that followed him, but it is likely that it would have taken place anyway. His career is ultimately tragic, for he tried much and failed grandly. His attempt remains impressive.

Bibliography

Breisach, Ernst. *Caterina Sforza: A Renaissance Virago.* Chicago: University of Chicago Press, 1967. In this scholarly biography of one of the most remarkable women of the fifteenth century, Breisach includes much incidental information about Sforza since his focus is properly on his subject. He does emphasize the interrelationship of the two, which was not of primary importance for Sforza. The bibliography is helpful in locating material on Sforza, most of which is in Italian.

Burckhardt, Jacob. *The Civilization of the Renaissance in Italy.* Translated by S. G. C. Middlemore. 2 vols. New York: Harper & Row, 1958. In this classic study, Burckhardt may be said to have invented the idea of the Renaissance as a cultural entity. Since one of his focal points is the development of the individual personality, he shows insight into all the major personalities of the period, as he does with Sforza. His material is dated, however, and he does not present a unified treatment.

Larner, Joseph. *The Lords of Romagna: Romagnol Society and the Origins of the Signorie.* Ithaca, N.Y.: Cornell University Press, 1965. Larner presents a balanced view of Sforza with extensive information and provocative points of view. His portrait is somewhat revisionist, in that he rejects the once-conventional notion that Sforza was simply a subtle schemer with dreams of glory. He presents Sforza as a progressive for his time, concerned with the welfare of the state as a whole.

Plumb, J. H. *The Italian Renaissance: A Concise Survey of Its History and Culture.* New York: Harper & Row, 1965. Though not known as an authority on the Italian Renaissance, Plumb here presents a brilliant synthesis of the basis of that culture. His account of Sforza is lucid, readable, and packed with detail. This is easily the best source for the general reader.

Potter, G. R., ed. *The New Cambridge Modern History.* Vol. 1, *The Renaissance.* Cambridge: Cambridge University Press, 1967. Includes a general account of Sforza in relation to the historical events of his time.

James Livingston

SHAKA

Born: c. 1787; Mtetwa Empire
Died: September 22, 1828; Zulu Empire
Areas of Achievement: Monarchy and the military
Contribution: Shaka revolutionized the military and political organization of the Zulus and their neighboring peoples, transforming the systems from the traditional to what might have developed into a modern nation-state, had not colonialism intervened. His achievements enabled the Zulus to resist European conquest until the late nineteenth century and preserved Zulu national identity.

Early Life

Shaka was the illegitimate child of a young Zulu chieftain and a woman from a clan with whom his father ordinarily could not have chosen a wife because of kinship restrictions. His parents attempted unsuccessfully a contrived marriage, but Shaka and his mother were shortly exiled from his father's *kraal* (homestead). They went to live with his mother's clan, a branch of the Mtetwa people, but there Shaka found himself ostracized and humiliated by the boys in his age group.

Even before attaining puberty, Shaka displayed the personality that was to mold his career. He was a reclusive, brooding child, deeply attached to his mother, prone to outbursts of consuming violence. It has been reported that he once nearly killed two older boys who had taunted him. When his father's *kraal* offered reconciliation and membership in his adolescent age group, Shaka angrily rejected the offer in public, embarrassing his father and deepening the feud between the two clans of Shaka's parents.

There is nothing to indicate that Shaka received any more than the traditional education provided for all Zulu youths in adolescence. That would have amounted to indoctrination into tribal customs and pragmatic knowledge of the environment. Oral tradition depicts Shaka as a youth driven to reckless bravery, a superior athlete and warrior whose talents only fed the jealousy of his peers.

Life's Work

At the age of twenty-one, Shaka joined the fighting ranks of the great Mtetwa chief, Dingiswayo. A remarkable leader in his own right, Dingiswayo had conquered some thirty tribes, including the Zulu, and had attempted to discourage the incessant feuding among his subjects, much of it caused by the food and land shortages resulting from a prolonged drought in the region in the late eighteenth century. Dingiswayo organized trading expeditions to the tiny European outpost on the coast of southern Africa and formulated the beginnings of a centralized kingdom.

Life as a soldier offered Shaka the opportunity to display his genius for military innovation. Traditionally, combat in southern Africa had been decided by the two opposing groups deploying themselves some fifty yards apart and hurling javelins and spears across the intervening distance until one side or the other retired. Shaka, dissatisfied with these tactics, adopted the *assegai*, a short stabbing sword, as his weapon, thus requiring hand-to-hand combat with enemies. There is some evidence that Shaka was familiar enough with advanced forms of iron-smelting technology to comprehend that, properly forged, these blades could be made much harder and more destructive than the less elaborate iron weapons normally used by his people.

Shaka also developed more disciplined tactics than previously used in the region. He disdained the loose array of warriors characteristic of javelin combat in favor of a close-order deployment, wherein a solid line of animal-skin shields confronted the enemy. Two "horns" of infantry extended from this central formation to outflank enemy forces. Reserves to the rear of the formation stood ready to rush into any weakness created in the enemy lines. Shaka's regiment won victory after victory against confused opponents. His new tactics changed warfare from limited skirmishing to a modern bloodletting that often terrorized potential opponents into submission.

Shaka's father, meanwhile, had maneuvered himself into the Zulu chieftancy. Upon his death in 1816, a grateful Dingiswayo had Shaka installed as the Zulu leader. Two years later, Zwide, the chief of a rival tribe and would-be usurper, assassinated Dingiswayo, and Shaka set out to wreak vengeance. Luring Zwide's much larger force into a valley where no provisions could be found and foregoing the final battle until his opponents were weak from hunger, Shaka's men devastated Zwide's forces.

Shaka now displayed an insight even more remarkable than those which punctuated his military career. He dispatched the survivors of Zwide's army to his rear guard and, following their retraining in Zulu military tactics, incorporated them into his army. The lands vacated by Zwide's fighters and their families were colonized by Zulu. Shaka evidently perceived that, in order to build a large army and empire, the tribal structure of southern Africa had to be broken down. The notion of awarding land to successful and loyal soldiers, in a country where most land had been held more or less in common, carried the seeds of social and economic revolution.

Within six years after the death of Dingiswayo, Shaka's empire embraced tens of thousands of square miles. He could muster an army of 100,000 men. From the giant *kraal* at Bulawayo, Shaka ruled over an entity without precedent in southern Africa. European traders and diplomats made their way to Bulawayo to seek alliances and privileges.

It was a fleeting moment. Shaka's military regimen was harsh beyond reason, a product of his own troubled mind. He demanded celibacy of his troops, granting the right to marry only to those who excelled in battle. His officers clubbed to death any recruit too faint-hearted to bear the pain and deprivation of forced marches and ordeals. His new military tactics were like a plague loosed on the land, virtually depopulating the country around Bulawayo and forcing his columns to march hundreds of miles for new recruits and conquests. Shaka ruled as an absolute monarch, and a tyrannical one at that. His periodic fits of rage often led to the execution of hundreds of innocent bystanders. Soldiers who were only suspected of cowardice were killed at once. European guests at Bulawayo reported that Shaka almost daily chose soldiers or courtiers, at whim, for execution.

Throughout Shaka's career, his penchant for violence seems to have been most pronounced in connection with the original injustice meted out to his mother. Shortly after becoming chief of the Zulus, Shaka hunted down those who had ostracized him and his mother and had them impaled on stakes. The occasion of his mother's death—by natural causes—caused a violent outburst. In Bulawayo alone, seven thousand people were killed over the next two days. Shaka's officers summarily butchered anyone who did not meet arbitrary standards for adequate display of grief. Shaka ordered his empire into a bizarre year of mourning for his mother. Under pain of death, married couples were to abstain from sexual relations. No cows or goats were to be milked, no crops planted. Shaka's army embarked on a new round of conquests, in some cases hundreds of miles from Bulawayo.

Such demands pushed even the most loyal of Shaka's followers beyond their limits. Food shortages and disease quickly began to take their toll. In 1828, when Shaka ordered his army to attack the Portuguese settlement at Delagoa Bay, his brothers, Dingane and Mhlangane, assassinated him. Dingane then killed Mhlangane, assumed the throne, recalled the exhausted army, and revoked Shaka's irrational edicts.

Summary

Given Shaka's extraordinary behavior, especially in the last years of his life, historians have been prone to characterize him in psychological terms. Shaka has been labeled a psychotic and a manic-depressive. Because he left no male heir—he often observed that a son would try to kill him for the throne—and because he demanded nudity and celibacy among his soldiers, some historians suspect latent homosexuality. Perhaps any leader of Shaka's dimensions might be cast in psychological types. Preferably, however, one should understand Shaka as a true innovator, perhaps a genius, let loose in a society and environment typified by violence, natural upheaval, and the beginnings of contact with the outside world.

Most historians concur that Shaka lived in a South Africa wherein the population was approaching the limits of agricultural productivity; land, therefore, was already coming to be viewed as a scarce resource and a basis of political power. The great droughts and famines which seem to have ravaged south Africa in the eighteenth century, together with the more limited but still novel sociopolitical achievements of his predecessor Dingiswayo, made Shaka's world one of turbulence and frayed traditions. As is evident from the frequent appearance of potential usurpers and ambitious chiefs among Shaka's opponents, there were many who might have undertaken the task of building an empire. Shaka succeeded because of his unique mentality.

Shaka's achievement also passes a crucial historical test: It survived and flourished long after the death of its creator. Despite the level of violence which seems to have attended it, Shaka created a Zulu protostate which remained intact for the rest of the nineteenth century. Only the British, using the latest in automatic weapons, finally managed to subdue the Zulus in 1879. Consciousness of a Zulu national identity remains a strong mobilizing force in the struggle for authority and land in the modern Republic of South Africa.

Bibliography

Ballard, Charles. "Drought and Economic Distress: South Africa in the 1800's." *Journal of Interdisciplinary History* 17 (1986): 359-378. Discusses how favorable conditions in the eighteenth century fostered growth of Nguni population and herds, while drought in the early nineteenth century forced rapid migration and accelerated development of the absolutist state of Shaka by forcing Zulus into military service.

Gluckman, Max. "The Rise of a Zulu Empire." *Scientific American* 202 (April, 1960): 157-168. Gives an excellent summary of major events, and speculates on Shaka's possible psychological condition.

Guy, J. J. "A Note on Firearms in the Zulu Kingdom with Special Reference to the Anglo-Zulu War, 1879." *Journal of African History* 12 (1971): 557-570. Although it deals with events later than the Shaka period, this valuable study criticizes both British and Zulu use of firearms and their frequent failure to deploy them to full advantage.

Inskeep, R. R. *The Peopling of Southern Africa.* New York: Barnes & Noble Books, 1979. A study of the factors influencing population movements in southern Africa and methods of reconstructing these patterns.

Lamar, Howard, and Leonard Thompson, eds. *The Frontier in History: North America and South Africa Compared.* New Haven, Conn.: Yale University Press, 1981. Demonstrates how comparative frontier studies can lead to hypotheses concerning the emergence of military leadership in such diverse cultures as North American Indians and southern African tribes. An important methodological experiment.

Marks, Shula. "Firearms in Southern Africa: A Survey." *Journal of African History* 12 (1971): 517-530. Suggests that, although the Zulus acquired firearms early in the eighteenth century, they were little used for military purposes until it became necessary to defend against the British. Underscores the importance of Shaka's military innovations in using indigenous weapons and tactics.

Ogunbesan, K. "A King for All Seasons: Chaka in African Literature." *Présence Africaine* 88 (1973): 197-217. Examines the role of Shaka as a pan-African cultural hero and his exemplary role as seen by writers and intellectuals.

Ritter, E. A. *Shaka Zulu: The Rise of a Zulu Empire*. New York: G. P. Putnam's Sons, 1955. A classic account of the career of Shaka. Some passages take the style of a historical novel, but the work is essentially accurate.

Roberts, Brian. *The Zulu Kings*. New York: Charles Scribner's Sons, 1975. A popular but useful and innovative account of the rise of Shaka. Stresses Shaka's concept of a territorial power base as a revolutionary development in African political thought.

Selby, John. *Shaka's Heirs*. London: George Allen & Unwin, 1971. Provides an extended discussion of Shaka's career and of those who attempted to emulate him in the Zulu environment which the warrior king had altered forever.

Ronald W. Davis

THE SIEMENS FAMILY

Ernst Werner Siemens

Born: December 13, 1816; Lenthe, Prussia
Died: December 6, 1892; Berlin, Germany

Sir William Siemens

Born: April 4, 1823; Lenthe, Prussia
Died: November 19, 1883; London, England

Friedrich Siemens

Born: December 8, 1826; Lübeck, Prussia
Died: May 24, 1904; Berlin, Germany

Karl Siemens

Born: March 3, 1829; Lübeck, Prussia
Died: March 21, 1906; St. Petersburg, Russia
Areas of Achievement: Invention and technology
Contribution: The four Siemens brothers were notable for their many contributions to applied technology in nineteenth century electrical and steel industries, including telegraphy, the electric dynamo, and the open-hearth steel furnace.

Early Lives

Four brothers among the thirteen children of Christian Ferdinand and Eleonore Deichmann Siemens and many of the brothers' sons became famous as inventors, scientists, and engineers, whose applied technology led to the creation of significant advances in electrical and steel industries, especially in telegraphy, the dynamo, the electric railways, and in the open-hearth steel furnace. Their father was a farm manager of large Prussian estates; he died in 1840, only a year after their mother had died.

The eldest son, Ernst Werner, while serving in the Prussian artillery at the age of twenty-three, assumed the guardianship of his seven younger brothers and successfully guided them into technological schools and profitable positions across nineteenth century Europe. Two brothers and one sister died in childhood; one brother became a farmer; and another became a glass manufacturer. Werner, William (earlier named Karl Wilhelm), Friedrich, and Karl were all born in Prussia (modern West Germany). These four made enormous contributions to modern technology and manufacturing in their lifetimes.

Werner and some of his brothers attended St. Catherine's School in Lübeck. Upon completion of grammar school there, Werner enlisted in the Prussian army in order to enter the Berlin Artillery and Engineering School. Upon graduation in 1837, he was promoted from ensign to second lieutenant in the Third Artillery Brigade and was stationed at Magdeburg. He took William along to study at the Trade and Commerce School there while he continued in the military service. Transferred to Wittenberg in 1840, Werner experimented with electrolysis and succeeded in developing a process for gold plating by galvanic current and was granted a five-year patent for it in 1842. By selling his rights to a jewelry firm, he began a lifelong income from his inventions.

William Siemens emigrated to England in 1843 and became a naturalized citizen in 1859. A prolific inventor, he was granted 113 English patents; as a shrewd businessman, moreover, he accumulated a large fortune. Karl Siemens had studied at Lübeck and at Berlin before joining his brother Werner in his endeavors. He became the most cultivated and diplomatic member of the family, having a keen sense of business management. Werner wrote of him: "Karl was the true connecting link between us four brothers, who indeed differed radically from one another, but were bound together for lifelong common work by an all-abiding fraternal love." Friedrich Siemens had gone to sea from Lübeck in sailing ships but returned to work with Werner and then with William in England. Werner declared him "the born inventor" with a "characteristic of steady, spontaneous, uninfluenced thinking and self-training [which] gave him a peculiarly meditative air and his performances a pronounced originality."

Life's Work

One of the great technological achievements of the Siemens brothers was the development of instruments and the establishment of international firms under their control for the European and Asian telegraph systems. First to utilize the substance called gutta-percha for covering underground telegraph wires, Werner created a screw press that extruded the substance around the wire while hot and cooled it into a seamless insulated covering that could carry electrical current underground or underwater. Then, he joined forces with a young physical mechanic, Johann Georg Halske, forming the firm of Siemens and Halske in Berlin, to perfect his invention of a self-interrupting dial telegraph instrument. Werner resigned from the military service in 1847, the year of his dial invention, and began manufacturing telegraph cable and equipment to fulfill contracts from Prussia and Russia to lay long lines between key cities, which soon outmoded all optical semaphore systems along military or railroad routes.

By the 1850's, Werner's firm had constructed the line from Berlin to Frankfurt am Main, and that success led to contracts with his brother William to lay submarine cables across the Atlantic, with his brother Karl to lay lines out of St. Petersburg for Russia and to connect the famous London to Calcutta, or Indo-European, telegraph line that opened in 1870. The rare combination of inventive skill, manufacturing capability, and useful diplomatic-political connections enriched the firms of the Siemens brothers and their shareholders.

As the London agent for his brothers' European firm of Siemens and Halske, William spent much of his career advancing the realm of the electric telegraph. In 1874, he laid the first Atlantic cable from England to the United States from a special ship he designed, the *Faraday*. For his distinguished achievements, he won medals at industrial exhibitions and the presidency of many English engineering and metals associations. In 1862, he was elected a Fellow of the Royal Society of London, the oldest scientific society, founded in 1662. In 1883, seven months before his death, he was knighted by Queen Victoria for his services. He had married Anna Gordon in 1859; they had no children, and she died in 1901.

Karl developed the Russian branch of the German firm and directed most of the construction of the international telegraph lines and cables that the family firms won contracts to build. Later, he became a Finnish-Russian citizen in order to do business in Russia; he married and lived in St. Petersburg for many years and was raised to the hereditary Russian nobility in 1895. After Werner's death, Karl became head of Siemens and Halske (Johann Georg Halske withdrew from the partnership in 1867).

Perhaps the most significant invention of the Siemens brothers was the construction of the regenerative furnace for the emerging steel industry. Friedrich pioneered the work of the firm on the application of the regenerative principle into the smelting of steel in conjunction with the French engineer Pierre-Émile Martin to create the famous Siemens-Martin open-hearth furnace. In England in 1856, Sir Henry Bessemer had patented a forced-air process for the smelting of steel; in the United States, William Kelly had devised a "pneumatic process" as early as 1849 but belatedly received an American patent in 1857. Friedrich and William applied their regenerative principle to the smelting furnaces with much larger capacities for molten metal, glass, and special materials. In 1864, in cooperation with Martin, they developed the so-called Siemens-Martin process, which works on the heat-storage principle.

In conventional furnaces, air and the combustible gases are introduced cold into the furnace, and the hot waste gases escape via smokestacks. In the regenerative process, the heat of the waste gases is captured for use in preheating the air and the combustible gases. Two or four refractory brick chambers are next to the smelting unit, and, in alternating fashion, the hot waste gases are passed through the chambers, which have large thermal-storage capacity. Then, valves close and new air and gases are preheated as they are introduced through the hot chambers and fed into the furnace. This process creates much higher temperatures for smelting, permits the use of low-grade gases, and saves on fuel costs.

For twelve years, from 1847 to 1859, William, in England, had tried unsuccessfully to apply this regenerative principle to steam engines. In 1856, Friedrich obtained a patent for the idea of using a waste heat condenser for industrial furnaces. In France, Martin had made steel by wrought iron, or cast iron, in a similar regenerative open-hearth furnace. Martin and the Siemenses combined their efforts in the Siemens-Martin process, which utilized iron ore directly from the mines. Eventually, the open-hearth process became immensely profitable as the recycling of scrap iron was implemented. First adopted for commercial steel manufacture in 1865, by 1896 the tonnage of steel from England's Siemens-Martin furnaces had surpassed the production of all Bessemer furnaces.

A third field of invention and manufacture evolved from Werner's invention of the "dynamo-electric machine," which he demonstrated in 1866. Almost at the same time, Charles Wheatstone in England and Samuel Alfred Varley in France had exhibited similar apparatuses and contested the priority of Werner's claim. Eventually Werner gained recognition when he demonstrated his invention and published an account of the principle behind it. Again, it was the firm of Siemens and Halske that was quickly able to apply the new dynamo into practical applications and then manufacture the electrical apparatus.

Nearly 250 dynamos were manufactured each year by Siemens and Halske in the 1880's. The number reached five hundred by 1892, as street and home lighting came of age, as did electrical motors for streetcars, railways, and factories. Siemens and Halske proceeded to develop the first electric tramway in 1881 in Lichterfelde with an overhead bow collector touching the trolley line. Siemens' arc lamps illuminated the Berlin Potsdamer Platz in 1882; the brothers demonstrated their first electric lift or elevator at the Mannheim Industrial Exhibition in 1880 and in 1892 produced their first electricity meter, called a "saber meter."

Summary

Werner and Sir William Siemens were the outstanding geniuses among the Siemens brothers; Friedrich and Karl Siemens extended the technology developed by the firm of Siemens and Halske into telegraph and electric systems sold, installed, and maintained by the company across the Western world. The family was instrumental in advancing the theoretical and technological fields of nineteenth century electronics with hundreds of patents granted to them and to members of their pioneering firm.

The Siemens brothers were significant leaders in German, English, and Russian enterprises of telegraphy, telephones, and electrical systems that served to promote the advancement of knowledge, the speedy transmission of information, and the shipment of people and material via electrical railways across Europe and Asia. Their several contributions to the manufacturing of steel, copper, and glass into less expensive materials for modern life immensely contributed to the Industrial Revolution after the great Crystal Palace Exposition of London in 1851, when Siemens and Halske were awarded the Council Medal, the first of hundreds to be won by the brothers.

Bibliography

Derry, T. K., and Trevor I. Williams. *A Short History of Technology from the Earliest Times to A.D. 1900.* New York: Oxford University Press, 1961. This text is a sequel to the five-volume *A History of Technology*, begun by Charles Singer. Good coverage of the Industrial Revolution. A chapter entitled "Coal and the Metals" covers developments in the making of inexpensive steel. Comparative tables showing the chronological events of technological achievements in Great Britain, Europe, and the United States along with bibliographies for each chapter enhance this introductory study.

Pole, William. *The Life of Sir William Siemens.* London: John Murray, 1888. The authorized biography of the Siemens brother who had made England his home. It was produced by a popular biographer of that era with the help of family and friends, who provided personal papers and recollections.

Siemens, Charles William. *The Scientific Works of C. William Siemens.* 3 vols. Edited by E. F. Bamber. London: John Murray, 1889. These papers, including his addresses, lectures, and papers read before scientific societies, provide closer detail of his inventions and business ventures.

Siemens, Georg. *History of the House of Siemens.* 2 vols. Freiberg, Germany: Karl Alber, 1957. This set describes the development of inventions by the various Siemens brothers and the practical applications of them via the business enterprises in Europe and elsewhere. Much of the business story relates the efforts of William and Werner (volume 1). The tragic chapters on the two world wars include the technological advancements in telephony, telegraphy, and electrical fields to the year 1945 (volume 2).

Siemens, Werner von. *Inventor and Entrepreneur: Recollections of Werner von Siemens.* Translated by W. C. Coupland. 2d ed. London: Lund Humphries, 1966. This autobiographical work provides one of the best stories of the gifted Siemens family and modestly relates Werner's own great achievements as inventor and businessman. His story centers on the telegraph and electrical systems that his firm, Siemens and Halske, had established in many nations.

Singer, Charles, et al., eds. *A History of Technology.* Vol. 5, *The Late Nineteenth Century, 1850 to 1900.* Oxford, England: Clarendon Press, 1954-1958. Although the Bessemer process had pioneered the making of steel, the Siemens-Martin open-hearth method ultimately outproduced it in the twentieth century. This volume presents the most readable introduction of both means of steel manufacturing.

Paul F. Erwin

DIEGO DE SILOÉ

Born: c. 1495; near Burgos, Spain
Died: October 22, 1563; Granada, Spain
Areas of Achievement: Architecture and art
Contribution: Siloé ranks as one of Spain's greatest architects for his exquisite translations and combinations of Roman, Moorish, and High Renaissance Italian style into a Spanish idiom, most evident, despite his many other works, in the great Cathedral of Granada.

Early Life

While the artistic and intellectual achievements of fifteenth and sixteenth century Renaissance figures are often well documented, this is rarely true of their early lives. Of Diego de Siloé, it is known that about 1495 he was born in Old Castile in or near Burgos, Spain. Founded in the eighth century, Burgos had served as an important commercial center, as the seat of the monarch for many years, and more important for Siloé, as a town famed for its architects and architecture, all markedly influenced by northern Gothic styles and very little by those of Mediterranean origins.

Burgos was also the home of the wealthy and cultivated Bartholome Ordóñez, who, breaking with local tradition, between 1490 and 1500 studied with the great Florentine and Neapolitan sculptors and artists, absorbing the best of his Italian masters and becoming familiar with Michelangelo's work. In Naples, Ordóñez befriended Diego, the son of Gil de Siloé. Apparently a migrant from Orléans, France, to Burgos, Gil had earned esteem in his adopted town as a specialist in late Gothic carving. Diego and Ordóñez collaborated to perfect their craftsmanship. Given his Catholic artistic convictions, Ordóñez, like Siloé, was a devotee of Michelangelo's Florentine style and a spiritual disciple of Donatello. Each man's influence upon the other was beneficial. Siloé's sculpture of *Saint George Slaying the Dragon* (c. 1514-1515) for the renowned Caraccioli Altar and his *Virgin and Child*, a relief for a chapel of the Naples Cathedral, amply demonstrate this stylistic affinity.

Returning to Burgos in 1519, Siloé immediately was selected by the cathedral to design an alabaster monument to a bishop. With restrained, High Renaissance, three-dimensional realism, the monument's face was made from the bishop's death mask and was soon recognized as the most convincing of Spain's integrated effigies, even exceeding similar works by Ordóñez. Only twenty-four years old, Siloé next designed a masterpiece in the Escalera Dorado's iron balustrade, with painted and gilded bas-reliefs, varied grotesques, and delightful nudes. Between 1523 and 1526, he collaborated on the Constable Chapel at Burgos Cathedral. There his mastery of polychrome wood sculpture, the *Presentation* in particular, as well as his *Pietà* at Saint

Anne's Altar, represented the best of Renaissance elements, establishing him as Burgos' undisputed master of his field.

Such creativity led in 1528 to his completion of an unfinished church in Granada, marking it with traditional heraldic devices evocative of proud Spanish lineages and with heroic figures, both ancient and biblical. For a Granadan bishop he designed a monument of Almería marble, while in the late 1520's he carved for San Jeronimo the choir stalls and the prior's seat. In that same church, the bust of the Virgin and Child beneath a bust of God is comparable to the finest Italian Renaissance work of its genre.

Collectively, such commissions expressed the maturing characteristics of Siloé's youthful style: joyous and passionate yet restrained Catholicity; meticulous and imaginative execution; lively and gently rhythmic lines. With remarkable chasteness and clarity, Siloé combined the vestiges of Spanish Gothic with *mudéjar*, a style developed during the Moors' domination of Spain. These stylistic signatures, and his eclecticism, uniquely identified him with the best of High Renaissance art.

Life's Work

Siloé's crowning efforts were invested from approximately 1528 until the late 1530's in the design, erection, and embellishment of the great Cathedral of Granada. Siloé's role in the cathedral's origins for years divided architectural and art historians, blurring an accurate understanding of the cathedral's architectural evolution and a full appreciation of Siloé's contributions. Modern scholarship generally acknowledges that the credit for the cathedral belongs more to Siloé than to anyone else. He did employ the peripheral walls of the original foundations, but within that arc the foundations for the chevet (the apse or termination of the apse—that upper portion of a church, which usually consists of several smaller, secondary apses radiating from the main apse) were of Siloé's design. Moreover, the nave's proportions are solely attributable to him.

Contrary to allegations that he enclosed the cathedral's rotunda sanctuary by copying a fashion common in other Spanish churches, Siloé opened it not only to the transept but also to the ambulatory. Most such criticisms reflected efforts to place the cathedral's development entirely within the Spanish architectural tradition, while in fact, Siloé's experiences were broader. Because of his years of working in Italy, more of his inspiration and stylistic conceptions flowed from the Tuscan-Roman Italy of the High Renaissance than from northern Europe. Siloé, however, did not employ pure Italian Renaissance architecture in the vocabulary of the Cathedral of Granada. No Italian church featured a prototype of the rotunda of the Granada Cathedral. Granada's dome roofed a high, cylindrical shaft of space, opened by tunnels at its base. The normal Latin cross that characterized Italian churches was replaced by Siloé's siting the choir in the central aisle as well as by a cruciform arrangement of the nave around a central lantern. Unlike Italian architectural idioms, the Granadan dome did not dominate. Siloé's conjunction of a domed rotunda with a basilican nave was unprecedented in medieval Europe.

Though Siloé's design was always under the scrutiny of communal and church officials and though it was without traditional models, whether from the Gothic, *mudéjar*, or Italian Renaissance, Siloé's cathedral was very much a distinctive hybrid. It owes perhaps more to ancient Roman architecture and Vitruvius than to the modern Roman style, which he imitated in many other designs.

Siloé's combination of the mausoleum with the cathedral's ambulatory was also novel. Other Renaissance churches had been planned to include the mausoleum with ambulatory, but they were never constructed. Nor did earlier European models of the apse have such central openness as Siloé's did. The cathedral's huge rotunda rises from two stages of Corinthian columns with a Roman grandeur, but it is well proportioned to its space. Siloé made the chevet, the cathedral's spiritual center, the cynosure of his design.

As Siloé designed the cathedral, he planned to have more than one hundred windows and whitewashed walls to create a luminous interior; the church was to be capped by a lantern of glass located over the nave's central bay. Such a light-flooded interior comported fully with a general Renaissance ideal. Unfortunately, this effect was never achieved.

In 1559, Siloé carefully designed a floor plan in which each section of the pavement was to be distinguished from other units by different colors and patterns. This practice was as ancient as buildings in Pompeii and Herculaneum and was even relatively common in classical households. It remained spectacularly effective. Black-and-white marble squares were to cover the sanctuary; black marble would floor the transept; and white marble was to cover the ambulatory pavement. Siloé probably also sought to accentuate the central aisle with a cross of black marble within the white flooring of the square nave, emphasizing the cruciform shape dramatically.

The cathedral's upper structure was supported by multiple cruciform piers: Gothic vaults with well-proportioned Roman ribs rose from Roman piers. Construction of basilican churches during the Renaissance—structures consisting of naves and aisles with a clerestory and a large, high transept from which an apse projected—had presented previous architects with almost insurmountable problems. Siloé managed with his combination of ancient orders of columns with barrel vaults to resolve these problems with great ingenuity. No less ingenuity was demonstrated in his distinctive styling and decoration of the cathedral's four portals. A finishing touch, a twin-towered façade that was to rise above the roof, was never completed. Nevertheless, the Cathedral of Granada stands as one of Renaissance Europe's great processional churches.

Summary

The liberation of Spain following centuries of Moorish domination, along with the restoration of both secular and Christian authority, lent special inspiration to national religious celebration. This fact helps to explain the communal and religious support that drew Diego de Siloé and other artists, sculptors, and architects to Granada as well as to numerous other Spanish communities during the first sixty years of the sixteenth century. His association with Ordóñez in Italy and his collaboration with him and others in Spain as well as his many commissions filled a substantial catalog by the time he had reached his mid-twenties, establishing him as a master who seems to have been in constant demand.

Despite years of confusion and critical debate about his role in designing, building, and embellishing the Cathedral of Granada, modern scholarship appears to confirm that while he deserves less credit than once was accorded him on minor points, the great cathedral is nevertheless his premier achievement. Siloé ingeniously, joyously hybridized elements of Gothic, Moorish, and Renaissance architecture with the essentials of ancient Roman structures. Siloé's extraordinary, versatile talent produced what has since been exalted as a unique architectural-artistic monument. Principal elements of its design and construction reached across to Spain's overseas empire and cultural enclaves in the sixteenth and seventeenth centuries.

Bibliography

Byne, Arthur, and Mildred Stapley. *Spanish Architecture in the Sixteenth Century.* New York: G. P. Putnam's Sons, 1917. An informative work. Though somewhat technical, the writing is clear and sufficiently authoritative to inform lay readers. It has good photographs, schematics, and plates. There are notes, a bibliography, and an index.

Hamlin, Talbot. *Architecture Through the Ages.* New York: G. P. Putnam's Sons, 1940. A well-written, richly illustrated survey for the lay reader. Superb photographs and numerous schematic drawings. Possesses an extensive, useful index.

Kubler, George, and Martin Soria. *Art and Architecture in Spain and Portugal and Their American Dominions, 1500 to 1800.* Harmondsworth, England: Penguin Books, 1959. This authoritative and ambitious work is superb for an understanding of Siloé's achievements. The writing is scholarly and somewhat uncompromising, but there are extensive chapter notes and scores of excellent photographs, schematics, and plates. Also includes a superb index.

Rosenthal, Earl. *The Cathedral of Granada: A Study in the Spanish Renaissance.* Princeton, N.J.: Princeton University Press, 1961. This is perhaps the definitive work on the cathedral. Covers all that is known about Siloé, his colleagues, the debates about the evolution of the cathedral, its technical construction, its setting, and its meaning. The terminology is scholarly, but the work is immensely informative. There are hundreds of photographs, illustrations, schematics, and plates. Contains a lengthy appendix, a very extensive bibliography, and an excellent index.

_____. "Changing Interpretations of the Renaissance in Art History." In *The Renaissance: A Reconsideration of Theories and Interpretations of the Age*, edited by Tinsley Helton. Madison: University of Wisconsin Press, 1961. Rosenthal is a preeminent authority on Spanish Renaissance architecture, particularly on Ordóñez, Siloé, and the Cathedral of Granada. Essential reading for an understanding of Siloé. The book has plates, notes, and a useful index.

Clifton K. Yearley

ŚIVAJĪ

Born: April 6, 1627; Poona, India
Died: April 3, 1680; Rajgarh, India
Areas of Achievement: Government and politics
Contribution: The founder of an independent Marāthā kingdom, Śivajī was a pioneer of guerrilla warfare, a great general, and a fiery Hindu nationalist. He became a symbol of Hindu statesmanship for twentieth century Indians.

Early Life
Śivajī Bhonsle was born in the city of Poona, in west India, on April 6, 1627, the son of parents from two prominent Marāthā families. His mother, Jija Bai, was the daughter of Lukhji Jadhava of Devagiri, and his father was Shanji Bhonsle. The Marāthās, a resourceful and self-reliant hill people, successfully resisted Muslim rule for three generations and also held the later British invaders at bay. Śivajī's father virtually abandoned him and his mother shortly after his birth. Consequently, Śivajī was reared largely by his mother and his guardian Dadaji Kondadev, a clever former official of the neighboring Muslim sultanate of Bijapur.

During the first nine years of his life, Śivajī experienced constant peril. He and his mother were forced to stay on the move, wandering from place to place to escape capture by attacking Mughal armies. Eventually, they settled in Poona in 1636 and lived there for ten years. Then they moved to a newly built mountain fortress, Rajgarh, which in time became the capital of his Marāthā empire.

Three major forces molded Śivajī's character. His mother wielded the paramount influence. This spirited woman was proud of her Kshatriya (warrior caste) heritage and centered her ambition on her son, developing in him traits of defiance and self-assertion. A devout Hindu, she imparted her love of religion to him and provided an education focused on the great epics the *Rāmāyana* and the *Mahābhārata*. He became fond of devotional music and attended the sermons of various Hindu teachers in the Poona vicinity. He never lost his love of Hinduism, later introducing compulsory recitations of the war chapters of the *Rāmāyana* by all his troops. The second great influence on his character was his guardian, Dadaji. Not merely a clerk or accountant, Dadaji was a strict disciplinarian, a shrewd tactician, and a fierce Hindu nationalist as well. He hated Muslim domination and felt a deep affection for the peasantry. His skill in politics and his passion for justice deeply influenced Śivajī. The third influence was Mahārāshtra itself. He spent much of his boyhood roaming the secluded hills west of Poona, where he was exposed to nature's demands and learned to cope with deprivation. He developed methods of guerrilla warfare and gained firsthand knowledge of the needs of the common people by constantly moving among them as a youth. Before he reached the age of twenty, Śivajī gained control of several districts west of Poona and began to raise his own army. He repaired and garrisoned forts and improved the local administrative machinery. He thus earned the reputation of an able and upright ruler.

Life's Work

When Dadaji died in 1647, Śivajī embarked upon a vigorous policy of territorial expansion. Politics of the western Deccan were dominated by two independent but corrupt Muslim sultanates, Bijapur and Golconda, and languid Mughal armies interested more in personal gain than in imperial conquest. Śivajī took advantage of the absence of aggressive Mughal generals to expand. Intensely pragmatic, he employed any and all means to attain his ends. He had two main objectives in mind as he launched his expansion. First, he wanted to secure the welfare of the Marāthās under his control. Second, he sought to create well-defined frontiers which were easily defended against the Mughals. Between 1648 and 1653, he managed to organize a small, cohesive state encompassing the region around Poona. In addition to forming a formidable army, Śivajī also built naval forts and created a powerful navy backed by shipbuilding yards and arsenals. By the mid-1650's, Śivajī was clearly the outstanding Marāthā statesman and a threat to the surrounding Muslim principalities.

Bijapur reacted to the threat in 1659 by raising a well-equipped army under the control of Afzal Khan to send against Śivajī. Afzal Khan swept into Śivajī's domains in September, 1659, plundering and destroying as he went. Śivajī could not defeat Afzal Khan's forces in open combat and so decided to attack him by deception instead. After complicated negotiations, the two opponents met for a conference on November 10, 1659. Śivajī, a short, wiry adventurer of only five feet in height, seemed to pose no personal danger to the powerfully built Bijapur general. Śivajī, however, took advantage of the situation by wearing an iron vest and a metal skull cap under his turban and by carrying a concealed dagger in one hand and tiger claws in the other. While the exact details of the khan's encounter with Śivajī may be lost in legend, the Marāthās claim that when Śivajī came into the conference tent the khan attempted to kill him with a dagger. Śivajī parried the blow and ripped open the khan's bowels with the tiger claws, killing him nearly instantly. The death of the khan demoralized the Bijapur troops, who left the field without a battle. Bijapur no longer threatened the new Marāthā state.

This success, in addition to Śivajī's general expansion in the western Deccan, alarmed the Mughal emperor, Aurangzeb, who had spent many years in the Deccan as a prince and was intimately familiar with the politics there. Determined to quell the Marāthās, Aurangzeb sent a powerful force against Śivajī in January, 1660, under the direction of Shaista Khan. The khan seized Poona and for three years hunted Śivajī in all directions. Only Śivajī's intimate knowledge of Mahārāshtran geography and guerrilla tactics prevented his capture.

Once again, Śivajī resorted to a stratagem to save himself. Through secret agents, he learned the details of the khan's schedule and the arrangements of his command center. On the evening of April 15, 1663, Śivajī launched a surprise attack on the khan's personal quarters, killing nearly fifty people and wounding the khan. That forced the Mughals to relax the pressure on Śivajī for a time. He took advantage of the lull to plunder the rich port city of Surat, one of the most highly prized Mughal possessions. This direct attack on the Mughal Empire's power and prestige incensed Aurangzeb, who sent a huge new army under the Rajput Jai Singh to deal with the Marāthā "mountain rats."

Jai Singh's powerful force arrived in Poona in March, 1665. Śivajī, unaware of his coming, was campaigning in the South. When he heard of the new danger, he returned immediately to Rajgarh, but Jai Singh established a firm hold on the regions north of Poona and Śivajī could not hope to defeat him. Accordingly, he signed a treaty with Jai Singh on June 12, 1665, agreeing to hand over twenty-three of his important forts, keeping only twelve minor ones for himself. Śivajī then proceeded to Āgra to attend Aurangzeb's formal accession to the Mughal throne on May 12, 1666.

Aurangzeb then made the single greatest mistake of his life. In return for giving up his forts, Śivajī expected to be made a full ally of the Mughals and to be appointed as a first-class *mansabdar* (commander of horse). Instead, Aurangzeb made him a third-class officer with no title or presents. Śivajī was so insulted that he fussed and fumed and eventually fainted. He was carried from the court and put under house arrest. Instead of making an indispensable ally in the Deccan, Aurangzeb created a bitter enemy. While Aurangzeb debated what to do with him, Śivajī planned a clever escape and fled Āgra on August 19, 1666. Following a circuitous route, he arrived back at Rajgarh on September 12. His daring escape buttressed his already considerable national reputation and he was welcomed back to the Deccan as a returning monarch.

Thereafter, the persistent Marāthā gnats tried to sting the iron Mughal bull to death. By 1670, Śivajī had recaptured most of the fortresses he had ceded to the Mughals in 1666. He felt strong enough to launch a second, even more successful attack on Surat, plundering it for three full days in October, 1670. In 1674, after thirty years of struggle, Śivajī decided to confirm his conquests by having himself crowned *Chatrapati* (lord of the universe) in a traditional Hindu coronation in which some eleven thousand Brahmans chanted sacred Vedic mantras and more than fifty thousand of his followers pledged their allegiance to the great Hindu king, the reincarnation of the great god Siva.

This coronation, however, did not confirm Śivajī as ruler of all Mahārāshtra and the surrounding regions. Aurangzeb could not move against the Marāthās because he was occupied with campaigns against the Afghans in the northwest. Within the Deccan, however, Bijapur and Golconda remained unreconciled to Marāthā expansion, and Śivajī waged several campaigns against them over the next four years. Despite his considerable successes, Śivajī never controlled a very sizeable domain or incorporated all Marāthās into his empire.

Śivajī died of a fever on April 3, 1680, at his capital of Rajgarh. His death did not bring an end to Mahārāshtra's struggle for independence, however, for he bequeathed to his sons and fellow Marāthās his fierce spirit of Hindu nationalism. They continued his battle against Mughal power, preventing Aurangzeb from ever gaining full control of the Deccan.

Summary

Śivajī was hailed by his followers as the founding father of the Marāthā nation but was reviled by the Mughals as a "mountain rat." There is little doubt that his exploits made him a savior to the Hindus, a protector of the *tilak*, the ritual paint on Hindu foreheads. Charismatic and shrewd, Śivajī inspired his people to become a nation, rallying Hindus to a sense of their own worth and power. Twentieth century Hindu nationalists have eulogized him as the earliest of the modern Hindus who struggled against foreign oppressors for India's national survival.

Śivajī was a fierce warrior who campaigned relentlessly for Marāthā independence. He sought self-rule and the freedom to practice his own religion. He mastered guerrilla tactics in fighting both Mughal and Bijapur armies. He and his "mountain rats" would wait for the heavily laden armies to enter the hill country and then swoop down to plunder whatever they could use. They employed hit-and-run tactics against numerically superior enemies and chose to fight only when it was to their advantage. He secured mountaintop fortresses to which he could retreat to escape the pursuit of more powerful forces. Using his intimate knowledge of his homeland to the best advantage, he well deserves to be labeled one of the founders of modern guerrilla warfare.

His commitment to Hinduism and religious freedom was genuine. In some respects, he appears to have cared more for religious freedom than for political dominion. At the same time, however, he realized that religious freedom for Hindus could not be achieved without political freedom. In that respect, he articulated a political philosophy in common with the leaders of the twentieth century independence movement. He thus became a symbolic hero to Hindus in the political climate of the early twentieth century. In their minds, Śivajī began the work that Mohandas Gandhi would complete. Even as he welded the scattered Marāthā people into a political and military unit with a powerful new sense of identity, so did Śivajī create a Hindu national identity. His colorful life and his ruthlessness tinged with fantasy provided the perfect raw material for a legendary hero. Thus, Śivajī was an important historical figure in his own right, as he united the Marāthās as a people and prevented Mughal domination of the Deccan. He is also important as a symbol of the new India, of a people united in a quest for political independence and a new national identity.

Bibliography
Gascoigne, Bamber. *The Great Moghuls*. New York: Harper & Row, 1971. This well-written, general history of the Mughals chronicles the rise and fall of the empire from the founder, Bābur, through Aurangzeb. Profusely illustrated, it provides a handy guide to the complex history of the major emperors and their rivals. Presents a compelling portrait of Śivajī's struggles against Aurangzeb.

Hansen, Waldemar. *The Peacock Throne*. New York: Holt, Rinehart and Winston, 1972. A detailed history of the Mughal period. Provides many insights into the Deccan problem as it was perceived by both Śivajī and Aurangzeb. Hansen's explication of the relationship betweeen Śivajī and Arangzeb is especially useful.

Ikram, S. M. *Muslim Civilization in India*. Edited by Ainslie T. Embree. New York: Columbia University Press, 1964. Provides a comprehensive summary of the role of Muslims in India from 712 to 1857. Ikram assesses the role of Śivajī and provides a basic chronicle of his military and political exploits from a Muslim perspective.

Majumdar, R. C., et al. *An Advanced History of India*. 2d ed. London: Macmillan, 1961. The most detailed history of India by Indian scholars that is readily available in the West. Strikes a balanced view of Śivajī leadership style and explains both his successes and his failures. Provides a useful appraisal of Śivajī's position in the history of the Indian nationalist movement.

Pearson, M. N. "Shivaji and the Decline of the Mughal Empire." *The Journal of Asian Studies* 35 (February, 1976): 221-236. Focuses on the relationship between Śivajī's persistent independence in the Deccan and the decline of Mughal power. Although Śivajī played a major role in the weakening of the Mughals, other causes also were at work.

Sardesai, G. S. "Shivaji." In *The Mughal Empire*, edited by R. C. Majumdar. Bombay, India: Bharatiya Vidya Bhavan, 1974. Sardesai presents a condensed version of his lifelong scholarly investigation of Śivajī. While he takes a favorable position on Śivajī, he presents a basically balanced view. This is perhaps the most convenient source for Śivajī's biography.

Wolpert, Stanley. *A New History of India*. New York: Oxford University Press, 1982. This general history of India provides the broad historical context for understanding Śivajī's role during the Mughal period. Contains a helpful bibliography of secondary sources.

Loren W. Crabtree

SŌTATSU

Born: Date unknown; Noto Province, Japan
Died: c. 1643; Kanagawa, Kaga Province, Japan
Area of Achievement: Art
Contribution: In collaboration with the artist and calligrapher Honami Kō-etsu, Sōtatsu founded the Rimpa school of painting. This style, characterized by the use of traditional Japanese themes, bold colors, and innovative paint and ink techniques, would influence Japanese art for nearly two hundred years.

Early Life

Sōtatsu's early life is so cloaked in obscurity that art historians can scarcely agree on such elementary information as the year of his birth, his family name, or formative influences on his art. There is general agreement that he was born in Noto Province, perhaps in the early 1570's. His father is believed to have been a wealthy merchant named Tawaraya, and Sōtatsu is often referred to as Tawaraya Sōtatsu, although his paintings were usually signed with the honorific title *hokkyō* or with the seals *Taiseiken, Taisei,* or *Inen.* His family name is considered to be Kitagawa or possibly Nonomura, and scholars have linked him by marriage to a distinguished line of artisans, including Ogata Dōhaku, the great-grandfather of Rimpa painters Ogata Kōrin and Ogata Kenzan. He is also believed to be related though his wife's sister to Kōetsu.

Little is known of Sōtatsu's formal education, but his painting teacher, Kaihō Yūshō, an artist renowned for his eclectic blend of Chinese and Tosa style influences, appears to have been instrumental in directing Sōtatsu's art toward the native themes of Zen Buddhism and classical literature favored by the Imperial court, rather than the Kano style popular with the shogunate.

Sōtatsu's first official notice seems to have come around 1600, but it was the result of his skill as a craftsman rather than through an original work. Probably on the recommendation of Yūshō, who visited the Itsukushima shrine in 1598, Sōtatsu was commissioned by the Taira family to restore three medieval Buddhist sutra scrolls there, finishing them in 1602. His talent for matching the highly cultivated style of the Heian period (784-1185) and his love of the Buddhist themes which predominate in much of his early work resulted in his receiving the honorific Buddhist title of *hokkyō* around 1621. These qualities also provided the bond which joined him to his most important collaborator, Kōetsu.

Life's Work

Though Sōtatsu's career spanned more than forty years, from 1600 to 1643, his decade of work with Kōetsu, from 1605 to 1615, is often considered to be his most productive period. During this time, the artist developed his mature style and pursued those themes from Japanese classical literature, music, dance, and mythology that were to have a lasting impact on succeeding generations of Rimpa painters. The collaborative aspect of their relationship is considered to have enhanced many of the aspects of their work, as Kōetsu was an acknowledged master of calligraphy as well as a fine painter. The similarity in the styles of both men and the ambiguous nature of their division of labor on many projects have long vexed art scholars in their efforts to establish the authorship of certain works.

Kōetsu had established a workshop at Takagamine, near Kyoto, which attracted artists and craftsmen in such diverse media as painting, pottery, papermaking, landscape gardening, and calligraphy. Sōtatsu undoubtedly frequented the studio but seems to have remained independent of it. He maintained his own establishment, called Tawaraya, in Kyoto, where he did a brisk business selling fans, scrolls, and decorative items. Starting about 1605, the two men began producing hand scrolls with calligraphy by Kōetsu over woodblock prints by Sōtatsu on paper manufactured by the papermaster Sōji. A fine early example of this work is the so-called deer scroll. Here the deceptively simple, cartoonlike deer charm the viewer with their sprightly gait and their sly, haughty smiles.

Far more complex and ambitious were Sōtatsu's screen paintings. It is in these that he was able to bring his skill as a craftsman to bear on the classical themes favored by Kyoto aesthetes to create works of startling originality. The *yamato-e* style of painting, characterized by the use of themes from Japanese literature and mythology, and represented by the Tosa school, had declined in popularity by the late 1500's. A more vulgar style featuring the use of vivid color and favored by many of the feudal lords increasingly contended with a muted, Chinese inspired, approach (Kano) favored by the Tokugawa shogunate and the samurai class. The Chinese style, pioneered by Sung Dynasty painter Mu-Ch'i Fa-ch'ang, sought to evoke the inner feeling or spirit of the subject rather than to emphasize strictly representational aspects.

Sōtatsu's special genius lay in reviving the particularly Japanese themes of *yamato-e* and combining them with decorative techniques—inkwashes, paint puddling, the use of bright colors, finely executed detail, and grandiose scale—to create art of startling boldness and subtlety. By the later years of Sōtatsu's life, not only the artistocrats of Kyoto but also the court of the shogun at Edo, its attendant daimyo, and large numbers of wealthy merchants eagerly sought his work.

One of the keys to Sōtatsu's skill lies in the enormously varied scope of his works. The Rimpa school is sometimes referred to as the decorative school, and the huge volume of purely decorative work done by Sōtatsu on fans, tea bowls, scrolls, and screens—some are as large as six panels—

provided invaluable experience both in the execution of fine detail and in the development of innovative ways of utilizing space.

Both of these elements may be found in Sōtatsu's illustrative works based on the *Tales of Ise* (ninth century) and *The Tale of Genji* (1001-1015). In the *Sekiya* screen, which illustrates a favorite *yamato-e* theme from *The Tale of Genji*, the scene is fraught with anticipation and tension: Genji encounters his former lover in a closed oxcart stopped at the Sekiya gate. The facial expressions of all the participants betray their relationship to the story, but the focus of the picture is on the unseen and unrequited lover. The details on this large three-panel screen are as finely wrought as those on any of the artist's miniature fans.

The *Bugaku Dancers* reveals a similar love of detail. Additionally, Sōtatsu's simple, almost abstract approach to the use of space in the painting achieves a harmonious balance despite the lack of background. The effect on the viewer is not unlike that of being an eavesdropper on the performance.

Another hallmark of the mature Sōtatsu style is his innovative use of ink and paint, often inverting the standard techniques of both mediums. His painting *The Cormorants*, for example, utilizes a background of heavy ink, added like pigment. Several paintings, notably *The Wind and Thunder Gods* and the *Sekiya* and *Bugaku* screens, feature bold use of gold and silver pigments, reflecting his growing taste for striking color.

Perhaps Sōtatsu's most innovative bending of technical norms was the development of the *tarashikomi*, or boneless method of painting. There is no inked outline of the subject. Instead, as in the screen painting *The Poppies*, wet colors are applied in successive layers, each before the previous one had dried. The subtle blending of all colors creates the effect of flowers emerging from a mist. A similar effect, this time using gold and silver pigment, may be found in the scroll (done with Kōetsu) *Flowers and Grasses of the Four Seasons*.

So little is known of Sōtatsu's life that it is impossible to give a physical description of him as a mature man. There are no self-portraits, and with the exception of a 1630 copy of a Buddhist scroll, his works have proved tantalizingly difficult to date. His signature seals were often added years after paintings were completed. Indeed, in a number of cases, scholars are not even certain which works are his and which are Kōetsu's and must rely on subtle nuances of style to make their judgments. From the few details that have emerged of Sōtatsu's later life, it is generally accepted that he moved to Kanagawa sometime around 1640. There he spent his last years in the service of the Maeda family of Kaga Province, where he died about 1643.

Summary

If precious little of Sōtatsu's life is accessible to historians, it is almost impossible to overestimate the impact of the Rimpa school on Japanese art.

In a very real sense, Sōtatsu and Kōetsu reflect in art the spirit of the Tokugawa age. Maturing during a period of robust political dynamism and foreign adventure in the 1590's, followed by the concerted effort of the Tokugawas to cultivate Japanese values in an environment free from foreign influences, their art reflects the harmonious synthesis of traditional values and bold, vibrant technique. In the aesthetic hothouse of Edo Japan, the ability of Rimpa painters and artisans continually to develop original personal styles while drawing from centuries of native models ensured their popularity for generations of demanding patrons.

The style of the Sōtatsu-Kōetsu school continued after the passing of both men. Some scholars have argued that it reached its greatest refinement with the Ogata brothers, Kōrin and Kenzan, in the late seventeenth century. Both Sōtatsu's and Kōetsu's sons continued the artistic tradition, and it is probable that the Ogatas received their training from them. Most scholars believe that, following the deaths of the Ogatas in the early eighteenth century, the quality of Rimpa productions declined to a certain extent. The spirit, if not the technical quality of the school, would reappear during the Meiji period (1868-1912), another age of self-conscious Japanese national feeling, in the form of the Nihonga or modernist school of painting.

Sōtatsu's style may be seen as one of the highest expressions of formalism in Japanese art. While he exhibited considerable skill in the depiction of detail, as well as in evoking emotion, his main emphasis is on bold tonal experiments, eye-pleasing color, and the asymmetrical but harmonious use of space. As Shuichi Kato writes, Sōtatsu "was indeed a perfect visual expression of the traditional Japanese mind and sensitivity, manifest through ages also in other cultural spheres: in architecture, in literature, and, in a sense, even in social and political life."

Bibliography

Grilli, Elise. *Tawaraya Sōtatsu*. Rutland, Vt.: C. E. Tuttle, 1956. Though dated, this work contains the most complete account of Sōtatsu's life and work available to the general reader in English. Grilli provides a well-balanced examination of Rimpa art with an emphasis on the influences of the Tosa, *yamato-e*, and Kano styles. Illustrated.

Kato, Shuichi. "Notes on Sōtatsu." In *Form, Style, Tradition: Reflections on Japanese Art and Society.* Translated by John Bester. Berkeley: University of California Press, 1971. A capable translation that places Sōtatsu's work in *yamato-e* context. Contains a good analysis of class tastes and their relation to the Rimpa school. The author contends that Sōtatsu represents the best of traditional Japanese eclecticism. Illustrated.

Paine, Robert Treat, and Alexander Soper. "The Return to Native Traditions: Edo Period, 1615-1867." In *The Art and Architecture of Japan.* Baltimore: Penguin Books, 1955, rev. ed. 1975. Perhaps the most comprehensive treatment of Japanese art, especially in the Edo period, available in one volume. Provides considerably detailed biographical information on Sōtatsu's early years and his relationship with Kōetsu. The authors see in the Rimpa school a truly original Japanese art tradition. Illustrated.

Rosenfield, John J., and Shūjirō Shimada. "Kōetsu, Sōtatsu, and Their Tradition." in *Traditions of Japanese Art: Selections from the Kimiko and John Powers Collection*. Cambridge, Mass.: Fogg Art Museum, Harvard University, 1970. A large, beautifully executed selection from the Fogg Art Museum's holdings. Each chapter contains a concise overview of the period, and each illustration is highlighted by detailed explanatory text. There is an in-depth examination of Kōetsu's Takagamine salon and perceptive and sensitive explorations of calligraphic technique. Illustrated.

Stanley-Baker, Joan. "Azuchi-Muromachi and Edo (1573-1868)." In *Japanese Art*. London: Thames & Hudson, 1984. A brief, well-informed look at Sōtatsu, Kōetsu, and Kōrin within a broad context of three millennia of Japanese art. Especially effective in placing the Rimpa school within broader political and artistic developments of the Hideyoshi and Tokugawa eras. Illustrated.

Charles A. Desnoyers

LAZZARO SPALLANZANI

Born: January 12, 1729; Scandiano, Duchy of Modena
Died: February 11, 1799; Pavia, Cisalpine Republic
Areas of Achievement: Biology, physiology, chemistry, geology, and natural history
Contribution: Spallanzani is famous for his acute scientific observation and experimentation. Although he tackled problems in geology, volcanology, meteorology, chemistry, and physics, Spallanzani's studies of infusoria, circulation of the blood, as well as biological reproduction, digestion, and respiration are of great scientific significance.

Early Life

Lazzaro Spallanzani was born in Scandiano, northeast of the Apennines, where his father, Gianniccolò, was a prominent lawyer. During his early schooling there, his interest in astronomy earned for him the nickname "the astrologer." When fifteen, Spallanzani was sent to the Jesuit seminary in Reggio Emilia, where he pursued rhetoric, philosophy, and languages. In 1749, he started law studies at the University of Bologna. Spallanzani's cousin, Laura Bassi, professor of physics and mathematics there, supervised his study of the sciences, natural history, Greek, Latin, French, and antiquities. Nature intrigued Spallanzani, and after three years his father permitted him to devote himself to the sciences.

In 1753 or 1754, Spallanzani received his doctorate in philosophy. After taking minor orders in the Roman Catholic church, he returned to the seminary to teach logic, metaphysics, and Greek in 1755. In 1757, he was ordained and, retaining his seminary post, became a lecturer in mathematics at the University of Reggio Emilia. The following year, he also began teaching Greek and French at Nuovo Collegio, which replaced the seminary. During these years, Spallanzani released his first publications, *Theses philosophicae . . .* (1757) and *Riflessioni intorno alla traduzione dell' "Iliade" del Salvini . . .* (1760; internal reflections on Salvini's translation of the *Iliad . . .*). By 1760, he had acquired a scholarly reputation and the epithet "the Abbé Spallanzani." Paying minimal attention to his religious duties, he devoted his time, church income, and university salary to scientific research.

Physically, Spallanzani was of medium height and robust build. He had black eyes, an aquiline nose, a high forehead, a dark complexion, and a resonant voice. Athletic when young, he later enjoyed hunting, fishing, and playing chess. On the one hand, Spallanzani has been described as frugal, self-assured, sociable, and magnetic. On the other, this man of science has been called arrogant, intolerant, obstinate, and ambitious. Resenting criticism, he could be vengeful, ruthless, and violent when crossed.

Life's Work

In 1761, Spallanzani began his biological research after reading works of Georges-Louis Leclerc, Comte de Buffon, and John Turberville Needham. By 1762, he was a professor of mathematics at the university and of Greek at Nuovo Collegio. In 1763, Spallanzani became a professor of philosophy at the university and at the College of Nobles in Modena.

In Modena, Spallanzani attacked the theory of spontaneous generation, which asserted that living things could come into being without a living predecessor, an idea that was championed by Buffon and Needham. In his *Saggio di osservazioni microsopiche concernenti il sistema della generazione de' signori di Needham e Buffon* (1765; account of microscopic observations concerning Needham and Buffon's system of generation), Spallanzani reported hundreds of beautifully executed experiments on infusoria, which refuted Buffon and Needham's views and confirmed that infusoria were living organisms that did not arise spontaneously in strongly heated infusions protected from contamination by air. Many considered Spallanzani's experiments conclusive evidence against spontaneous generation.

Next, Spallanzani turned to regeneration and transplantation and then to circulation of the blood. His conclusions that lower animals have greater regenerative power than higher ones, that organisms generally regenerate only superficial organs, and that an individual organism's ability to regenerate varies inversely with age were published in *Prodromo di un opera da imprimersi sopra le riproduzioni animali . . .* (1768; *An Essay on Animal Reproductions*, 1769). The first of Spallanzani's works to appear in English, *An Essay on Animal Reproductions* received mixed reviews. In *Dell' azione del cuore ne' vasi sanguigni* (1768; on the action of the heart on the blood vessels), he described the effect of the systolic action of the heart upon blood flow in salamanders, extending and occasionally correcting Albrecht von Haller's studies.

In 1769, Spallanzani moved to the University of Pavia, in Lombardy, where he spent his remaining years as a popular and famous professor of natural history. In addition, Spallanzani assumed direction of the university's Natural History Cabinet (museum). There, Spallanzani assailed spontaneous generation in his inaugural address, *Prolusio* (1770), then expanded his examination of circulation of the blood. This work culminated in *De' fenomeni della circolazione . . .* (1773; *Experiments Upon the Circulation of the Blood . . .* , 1801), which presented a physico-mechanical explanation of the heart's action and the circulation of the blood and reported the first observation of blood passing through the capillaries of warmblooded animals.

The results of Spallanzani's continued investigation of infusoria appeared in *Opuscoli di fisica animale e vegetabile . . .* (1776; *Tracts on Animals and Vegetables*, 1784, 1786). Here, Spallanzani dispelled Needham's objection that no infusoria grew in Spallanzani's containers because heat had destroyed the vegetative force by showing that loosely corked infusions boiled longer and showed better growth than those boiled for shorter periods of time. He also refuted Buffon's theory that spermatozoa developed in decomposing semen and demonstrated that they were components of living animals.

In the late 1770's, Spallanzani's popularity as a teacher swelled. He continued improving the museum, and he investigated animal digestion, biological reproduction, and artificial fecundation. In *Dissertazioni di fisica animale e vegetabile* (1780; *Dissertations Relative to the Natural History of Animals and Vegetables*, 1784, 1789), Spallanzani described his experiments on gastric digestion. Observing the solvent action of human and animal "gastric juices"—a term he coined for saliva, bile, stomach, and other secretions—he determined that digestion occurs primarily in the stomach and is a chemical, rather than mechanical, putrefying, or fermenting process. In addition, Spallanzani recounted experiments on animal sexual behavior, fertilization, and embryological development. Seeking to discover how animal eggs are fertilized, he examined the role played by semen in fecundation. Spallanzani attempted artificial inseminations of several animals and was successful with a spaniel. His experiments demonstrated that contact between semen and egg is essential for fertilization, but he concluded that the solid parts of semen, not spermatozoa, were the fertilizing elements. In *Dissertations Relative to the Natural History of Animals and Vegetables*, Spallanzani argued for the embryological theory of preformation, contending that the preformed plant or embryo awaits fertilization within the egg and, after fertilization, expands according to a plan established by God. In his final section, he maintained that embryos exist in all plant seeds and develop with or without fertilization.

In this period, Spallanzani traveled in Europe, collecting museum specimens and indulging his passion for natural history. In 1784, Spallanzani was offered a professorship at the prestigious University of Padua. Enticed to stay at Pavia by a year's leave, a salary increase, and an ecclesiastical benefice, Spallanzani began his leave in August, 1785, by sailing to Istanbul, where he stayed for eleven months. His account of the journey describes the natural history and other aspects of Istanbul and Eastern Europe.

In 1788, Spallanzani visited the kingdom of The Two Sicilies, collecting for the museum and recording volcanic, geological, and other observations. While studying the active volcanoes Vesuvius, Stromboli, Vulcano, and Etna, he concluded that their eruptions result from gaseous explosions. Returning to Pavia, he performed chemical experiments on lava. These observations and investigations appeared as *Viaggi alle due Sicilie e in alcune parti dell' Appennino . . .* (1792-1797; *Travels in the Two Sicilies and Some Parts of the Apennines*, 1798).

During the early 1790's, Spallanzani conducted zoological research, most important on the flight of bats he had blinded, for example, by burning out their eyes. Led to reject the theory that flying bats avoid collisions by relying on touch, taste, smell, or hearing, his *Lettere sopra il sospetto di un nuovo senso nei pipistrelli . . .* (1794; *Letters on a Supposed New Sense in Bats*, 1941) suggested that a sixth sense or some unidentified organ in the head was responsible. Subsequently, however, Spallanzani accepted Louis Jurine's theory, connecting bats' flight with their hearing.

Then, Spallanzani's research assumed a more chemical air. Johann Friedrich August Göttling's erroneous description of the combustion of phosphorus prompted Spallanzani to examine that topic, and he published his results in *Chimico esame degli esperimenti del Sig. Göttling, professor a Jena, sopra la luce del fostoro di Kunkel . . .* (1796). Turning to respiration, he investigated gases emitted by plants enclosed in vessels of water or air, which were then placed in sunlight or shade. Part of a 1798 article, his last publication, stated his conclusions. Later, in *Mémoires sur la respiration* (1803; *Memoirs on Respiration*, 1804), some of Spallanzani's papers on animal respiration were printed. In these papers, Spallanzani showed that oxidation occurs neither in the lungs nor in the blood, as had been argued, but in the tissues. Moreover, he demonstrated that during oxidation animal tissues emit carbon dioxide, which the blood then carries away—a discovery often attributed to nineteenth century chemist Justus von Liebig.

Throughout his life, Spallanzani enjoyed good health, although he experienced minor digestive disorders. In early February, 1799, complications from an enlarged prostate and chronic bladder infection sent him into a coma; he died a week later, one of the most famous contemporary scientists in the West.

Summary

Lazzaro Spallanzani possessed broad scientific interests and throughout his life published many reports and letters in scientific periodicals, in addition to his monographs. His treatises appeared in French, English, and German and were recognized for their literary style as well as their substance. Although Spallanzani's conclusions often were debated by his peers and although some of his experiments are considered inhumane today, he remains known for an experimental skill that hardly was equaled for a century afterward. Most important, Spallanzani furthered the development of scientific thought in many fields.

Spallanzani's experimentation on spontaneous generation added to evidence mounting against that theory. His experiments on infusoria contributed to the foundation of bacteriology, and his studies of their mortality when subjected to intense heat played a seminal role in the invention of food canning. Spallanzani's experiments on animal sexual behavior, fecundation, semen, and spermatozoa led to the modern understanding of animal reproduction; his pioneering work on artificial fecundation and his successful artificial insemination of a viviparous animal—the first recorded—mark the beginning of modern work in that field.

Spallanzani achieved the first in vitro demonstration of animal digestion and established the basic theory of digestion held today. His ideas were not accepted immediately, but his work paved the way for nineteenth century biochemical studies of digestion. Spallanzani also laid the foundation for modern studies of animal and plant respiration. His research had little impact until the 1830's, however, and was not continued until the late nineteenth century. Finally, among Spallanzani's geological observations are notable contributions to mineralogy, and his work on volcanic eruptions is considered fundamental to modern volcanology.

Bibliography
Adams, A. Elizabeth. "Lazzaro Spallanzani (1729-1799)." *The Scientific Monthly* 29 (1929): 529-537. Presents a reasonably accurate chronology of Spallanzani's life and a well-documented assessment of his scientific method and contributions. Adams' inclusion of translations from Spallanzani's works and correspondence elevates this above other readily available biographical articles.
Bulloch, William. *The History of Bacteriology.* London: Oxford University Press, 1938. Chapter 4 includes a detailed account of the controversial theory of spontaneous generation, Spallanzani's experimentation on infusoria, and his role in the theory's demise.
Foster, Michael. *Lectures on the History of Physiology During the Sixteenth, Seventeenth, and Eighteenth Centuries.* Cambridge, England: Cambridge University Press, 1924. Lecture 8 describes Spallanzani's experimental work on digestion and relates it to that of his contemporaries.
Galambos, Robert. "The Avoidance of Obstacles by Flying Bats: Spallanzani's Ideas (1794) and Later Theories." *Isis* 34 (1942): 132-140. This well-researched article provides detailed information on Spallanzani's ingenious experiments and contains translated excerpts from his correspondence on the subject.
Gasking, Elizabeth B. *Investigations into Generation, 1651-1828.* Baltimore: Johns Hopkins University Press, 1967. Chapter 11, devoted to Spallanzani, concentrates on his experiments and conclusions on animal sexual reproduction and fecundation, particularly the role of semen in fertilization, and places Spallanzani's work within the context of the history of preformation.
Meyer, Arthur William. *The Rise of Embryology.* Stanford, Calif.: Stanford University Press, 1939. Offers illuminating accounts of Spallanzani's investigation of spontaneous generation, animal reproduction, artificial insemination, hybridization, and his preformationist views. Meyer's exten-

sive excerpts from Spallanzani's publications and correspondence are also enormously valuable.

Martha Ellen Webb

MIKHAIL MIKHAYLOVICH SPERANSKY

Born: January 12, 1772; Cherkutino, Russia
Died: February 23, 1839; St. Petersburg, Russia
Areas of Achievement: Government and law
Contribution: A career bureaucrat, Speransky sought to liberalize and modernize the Russian government by limiting the power of the autocracy, reforming local government, and codifying Russian law.

Early Life

Mikhail Mikhaylovich Speransky was born on January 12, 1772, of peasant origins, in Cherkutino, a small provincial village to the northeast of Moscow. His family was impoverished and poorly educated and lacked even a family surname. In fact, Speransky did not acquire his name until he began his formal education at the age of twelve, when he entered the ecclesiastical academy at the provincial capital of Vladimir. He was already a promising student, and his intellectual skills and academic accomplishments brought him immediate recognition. In 1790, Speransky was accepted for advanced study at the prestigious Alexander-Nevsky Seminary in St. Petersburg, once more distinguishing himself in his academic pursuits. In addition to the traditional seminary curriculum, Speransky acquired a thorough foundation in the rationalist and materialist thought of the Enlightenment and philosophe writers, which would influence him for the rest of his life. Following his graduation in 1792, Speransky was offered a part-time teaching post at the academy, and in 1795 he was appointed instructor of philosophy and prefect (dean). After rejecting the proffered appointment, Speransky entered the service of Prince A. B. Kuratin, an influential member of the imperial court. For the next year, Speransky continued his study of French Enlightenment thought and encountered the philosophy of Immanuel Kant as well. In 1796, Kuratin was appointed by Emperor Paul I as procurator-general of the senate, which was similar to being prime minister of the government. Kuratin then used his influence to secure for Speransky a position in the government bureaucracy at the beginning of 1797.

By the end of 1798, Speransky had ascended into the upper levels of the bureaucratic Table of Ranks. In the process, he acquired increased responsibilities and hereditary noble status, both of which reflected his growing importance and influence within the bureaucracy and St. Petersburg society. He became acquainted with the concepts of English political philosophy and its emphasis on conservative social corporateness and institutional reform, which now attracted the previously Francophile nobility following the excesses of the French Revolution. It was at one of these encounters that Speransky met his future wife, Elizabeth Stephens. They were married in 1798 and in 1799 produced a daughter, also Elizabeth. His wife died shortly after their daughter's birth. Speransky, already aloof and introverted by nature, became even more withdrawn as he used his career as a means to overcome his personal grief.

Life's Work

In 1801, a new czar, Alexander I, ascended the Russian throne. With him came the hope on the part of many younger Russians that his vague sympathies toward liberalism and reform could be translated into reality. For Speransky, it brought the notice of the new czar and his appointment to the newly formed Ministry of Interior. Attaching himself to the fringes of the "unofficial committee," Speransky spent the years between 1802 and 1808 creating the intellectual foundations required for the restructuring of the Russian political and social order. In his deliberations, he drew upon the philosophical ideals of the Enlightenment, the political concepts of the English system, and his own understanding of Russian historical development.

From the outset, Speransky recognized that the key to any broad reform within Russia was the reform of the autocracy itself. As constituted by the reforms of Peter I and consolidated by Catherine II in the previous century, the autocracy was the only legitimate source of authority within the Russian political system and could not be prevented from exercising that authority in a capricious and arbitrary manner. To Speransky, this represented the epitome of political lawlessness, which could not be tolerated in a rational and enlightened society. Not only was such lawlessness destructive to the stability, cohesion, and order of the society in general, but also in Russia's case it was the primary cause of her political, economic, and social backwardness. Moreover, it prevented Russia from throwing off the burdens of that backwardness by obstructing modernization through meaningful reforms. The only enlightened means to overcome this lawlessness on the part of the ruler, Speransky argued, was the establishment of the rule of law to which all within the society were subject. In this way, rules could be established to govern the relationship between the ruler and the ruled, while also formulating the context in which authority would be exercised by the ruler.

Although Speransky formulated the essential elements of his rule of law concept in 1801-1802 and 1803 for "Mémoire sur la legislation fondamentale en général," summarized by V. I. Semevskii as "Pervi politicheskii traktat Speranskogo" (1907; on the fundamental laws of the state) and "Zapiska ob ustroistve sudebnykhi i pravitel' stvennykh uchrezhdenii v Rossii" (1905; report on the establishment of judiciary and government institutions in Russia), the opportunity to present his formulations to Alexander did not occur until 1809. By the time it did, Alexander's earlier sympathies had dissipated. He rejected Speransky's constitutional plan (known also as the Plan of 1809) as an unacceptable limitation of authority of the autocracy. Speransky's influence at the imperial court began to wane. By 1812, a variety of factors conspired to drive him from power. The cruelest blow, however, came from Alexander himself, who sent his former administrative secretary and assistant into exile, first at Nizhni Novgorod on the upper Volga River and then to Perm in western Siberia near the Ural Mountains. He remained there in disgrace until 1816.

In 1816, the exiled Speransky was permitted to return to government service as a provincial official in the remote province of Penza, near Perm. There he began the difficult task of reforming the chaotic Siberian local government. Pleased with his success, Alexander then appointed Speransky governor-general of Penza in 1819 so that he could implement his Penza reforms throughout Siberia. In 1821, Alexander recalled Speransky to St. Petersburg and appointed him to the State Council for the purpose of reorganizing the system of local government in Russia along the Siberian model. By 1825, Speransky succeeded in establishing a system that would serve Russia for the remainder of the nineteenth century.

Speransky now turned his attention to judicial and legal reform. All agreed that the Russian judicial system, like that of local government previously, was in shambles. The obvious solution was a new codification of Russian laws to replace the Sobornoye Ulozheniye 1649 (code of 1649), which had never been effectively updated. By 1832, Speransky published the *Plonoye sobraniye zakanov Rossiyskoy imperii* or PSZ (1830; complete collection of the laws of the Russian Empire), which represented the codification of all laws enacted between 1649 and 1832. Speransky also compiled and published the *Svod Zakanov* (1832-1839; digest of laws), incorporating all legislation still in force in 1832. Together they served as the ultimate source of legal authority in Russia until 1917. When Speransky died in 1839, he was a much honored and respected statesman.

Summary

Ironically, the impact of Mikhail Mikhaylovich Speransky's career as a reformer is twofold. His early reforms demonstrated that there were individuals in Russia who were concerned about the direction of Russian development during the first half of the nineteenth century. Many of them, like Speransky, concluded that Russia's only hope for future salvation was through the dissolution of the autocracy and the establishment of some form of constitutional government. The fact that Speransky's own constitutional proposals foundered on the rock of autocracy and were thus stillborn did not alter that outlook. Others soon emerged to assume the mantle of leadership in the struggle against the autocracy. One such group, the Decembrists, incorporated many of the ideas from Speransky's Plan of 1809 into their political programs for reform in 1825. While they also failed in the attainment of their goals, it became very clear that the struggle against the autocracy would continue until it accepted the end of its absolutism. Had the autocracy been willing to implement the constitutional reforms put forth by Speransky in 1809, limited as they were, it might have survived the challenges against it after 1870. That it did not do so only postponed the fate which it suffered in 1917.

This leads to the second aspect of Speransky's reforms that must be considered. For the most part, it involves the nature of his work after 1816, which significantly enhanced the efficiency and effectiveness of government administration in Russia. The great irony is that while Speransky's earlier reforms contributed to efforts to reform the autocracy, his later reforms made it possible for the autocracy to resist those efforts and to survive during the remainder of the nineteenth century.

Bibliography
Christian, David. "The Political Ideals of Michael Speransky." *The Slavonic and East European Review* 54 (1976): 192-213. A scholarly and historiographical examination of Speransky's political ideals. Belongs to the school of interpretation which argues that Speransky was a radical liberal reformer and thus rejects Marc Raeff's *Rechtstadt* interpretation (see below). Excellent footnotes incorporating considerable bibliographical material.
Gooding, John. "The Liberalism of Michael Speransky." *The Slavonic and East European Review* 64 (1986): 401-424. Through criticism of Speransky's writings, Gooding supports the conclusions of Christian's article. Includes extensive footnotes which encompasses a wide range of bibliographical materials.
Jenkins, Michael. "Mikhail Speransky." *History Today* 20 (1970): 404-409. A short and popularized account of Speransky's career designed primarily for high school students.
Raeff, Marc. *Michael Speransky: Statesman of Imperial Russia, 1772-1839.* The Hague: Martinus Nijhoff, 1957. The most comprehensive, analytic, and scholarly biographical treatment of Speransky in the English language. Contains exhaustive notes, a bibliography, and indexes that guide the student into every facet of Speransky's life and activities as well as that of general Russian history between 1772 and 1839.
_____. *Plans for Political Reform in Imperial Russia, 1730-1905.* Englewood Cliffs, N.J.: Prentice-Hall, 1966. This collection of original sources includes documents on government reform (1802) and the codification of state law by Speransky (1809).
_____. *Siberia and the Reformers of 1822.* Seattle: University of Washington Press, 1956. A comprehensive and scholarly treatment of Speransky's Siberian reforms of 1816-1821 and their impact on the shaping of his reform of local government in Russia after 1822. Extensive notes, a bibliography, and indexes.

David K. McQuilkin

BARUCH SPINOZA

Born: November 24, 1632; Amsterdam, United Provinces
Died: February 21, 1677; The Hague, United Provinces
Area of Achievement: Philosophy
Contribution: Spinoza was a major figure among seventeenth century philosophers. Though he inspired few open disciples, Spinoza helped to lay
the groundwork for future developments in philosophy and letters. He
also contributed much to the emergence of political and religious tolerance. He is one of a handful of philosophers who can be said to have lived
an exemplary life.

Early Life
Baruch Spinoza was born November 24, 1632, in Amsterdam, in the
United Provinces. His parents, Michael and Hanna Deborah, were Spanish-
Portuguese Jews who had emigrated to Holland to escape religious persecution. This persecution was relatively recent in origin. Jews living in Spain
during the late Middle Ages had experienced a period of tolerance under the
Moors, who were Islamic. The return of Christian rule utterly reversed this
trend. Subject to all manner of plunder and murder during the Spanish Inquisition, many Jews decided to convert to Christianity. A large number of
these converts, however, continued to practice Judaism in private. That led
to a new round of persecution and finally to the expulsion of Jews from
Spain in 1492. Some converted Jews (or *marranos,* as they were called)
sought refuge in Portugal. Over time, persecution arose there as well. Holland became a logical next step for Jews who desired the freedom to practice
their religion and pursue fruitful commerce. Spinoza's parents are believed
to have been *marranos* who had sought refuge in *Jodenburt,* the Jewish
quarter of Amsterdam. There they could practice Judaism openly, enjoying
the fruits of religious tolerance unmatched in all Christendom. They were
also free to pursue a broad range of commercial opportunities.

This relatively self-contained community first nurtured Spinoza, providing
him with material comforts and an extensive education in Jewish religion
and philosophy. Ultimately, however, Spinoza was cast out. How and why
that came about is pivotal to an understanding of Spinoza's early life as well
as to his subsequent career.

Spinoza's father was in the import-export business and is believed to have
been highly successful. Spinoza helped in the family business but at some
point became far more interested in his studies than he was in commerce. He
wished, moreover, to broaden his studies beyond the usual fare, exploring
the less orthodox canons within Jewish thought and acquainting himself with
non-Jewish sources of learning. This, in itself, was not unusual. Many members of the Jewish community had opened themselves to the world around

them. As a result, Spinoza's father was agreeable, arranging for Spinoza to study Latin outside the *Jodenburt* in the home of Francis Van den Ende, a freethinker and something of a political radical. The study of Latin enabled Spinoza to explore the rationalist philosophy of René Descartes. Though Descartes did not openly disparage traditional religion, his philosophy was an attempt to understand the world through reason rather than faith. Spinoza also launched into what was, for a Jew, even more controversial, a study of the New Testament.

The result of these unorthodox studies was that Spinoza moved irretrievably beyond the dominant beliefs of the community into which he had been born, rejecting its commercialism as well as the exclusiveness of the Jewish faith. Indeed, it appeared to some that he was rejecting religion altogether. As Spinoza's beliefs became known, the leaders of the *Jodenburt* responded first by attempting to bribe Spinoza with a generous monetary allowance in return for his outward compliance with orthodox beliefs. Spinoza refused this offer. Shortly thereafter, he was tried and found guilty of what amounted to a charge of heresy. In 1656, Spinoza was excommunicated.

Why Spinoza's accusers acted is not as self-evident as it might seem. The Jewish community in Amsterdam permitted a fair amount of diversity, and Spinoza was outwardly quiet about his dissenting opinions in theological matters. He was not, so far as is known, a gadfly in the image of Socrates. These circumstances have led some scholars to explain Spinoza's excommunication as a response by Jewish leaders to their fear of renewed persecution by Christians flowing either from Spinoza's apparent atheism or from his association with Dutch political radicals. The fact that Spinoza had already begun to divorce himself from the Jewish community (he was no longer living in the *Jodenburt* at the time of his excommunication) supports such an interpretation. Another theory is that Spinoza was thought dangerous because of his opposition to wealth and privilege within the Jewish community. Whatever the motivation, Spinoza was excommunicated at the age of twenty-four. Shortly afterward, he was forced by Dutch authorities to leave Amsterdam's city boundaries—this, too, at the urging of the Jewish leaders.

Life's Work

Though Spinoza's excommunication was of great symbolic importance, it did little to change the way he actually conducted his life. Spinoza left behind his Hebrew name, Baruch, substituting for it the Latin equivalent, Benedict (both mean "blessed"). Yet he did not become a Christian. Nor did he marry. He lived quietly, first in Rhijnsburg, later in Voorburg, accumulating only so much money as he needed to pay his bills. A good neighbor and well loved by friends, he devoted the rest of his life to his studies.

What income Spinoza did have may have come from his knowledge of optics and skills as a lens grinder. That, at least, has become part of the Spinoza legend. There is no evidence, however, that Spinoza actually earned a living in this way. It has, therefore, been hypothesized that, in order to sustain himself, Spinoza accepted moderate amounts of money from friends, though here, too, the evidence allows for little more than an educated guess. What is known is that Spinoza repeatedly rejected large gifts from wealthy friends and also that he refused a professor's chair at the University of Heidelberg.

Two reasons have been advanced for this behavior: Spinoza's humble tastes and, most important, his devotion to writing what he thought was true, regardless of who might be offended. Such candor required thoroughgoing independence. This is not to say that Spinoza led an entirely isolated existence. He exchanged ideas with numerous intellectuals, religious reformers, and political activists until the end of his life. The outcome of this combination of lively discourse and independence of thought was a body of work which drew immediate attention from avid supporters as well as critics and which has stood the test of time.

Spinoza's earliest work of note was his *Renati des Cartes principiorum philosophiae pars I et II, more geometrico demonstratae, per Benedictum de Spinoza* (1663). Though the essay is little more than an exegesis, it demonstrates Spinoza's profound grasp of the system he spent much time criticizing. The appeal of Descartes for Spinoza lies in Descartes' stated goal of explaining the world through the use of reason alone, thus taking a giant step beyond medieval Scholasticism, which, at best, gave reason status nearly equal to that of revelation. Spinoza's central criticism of Descartes was that he continued to take much on faith.

In 1670, Spinoza's *Tractatus theologico-politicus* (*A Theologico-Political Treatise*, 1862) was published anonymously. In this work, Spinoza broke new ground, writing perhaps the most eloquent defense ever of religious freedom. The treatise includes a critical essay on the Bible which points out its rather haphazard assembly of very different works from different eras into a single text. It also distinguishes the role of reason, which is to discern truth, from that of religion, which is to foster piety. While these points may seem innocent enough to modern readers, the treatise was greeted with a chorus of criticism from a variety of clerics, many of whom branded its author an atheist, and the Catholic church, which banned it. Spinoza's circle of friends and supporters, on the other hand, deeply appreciated his achievement.

The rancor with which *A Theologico-Political Treatise* was received may well have persuaded Spinoza that it would be neither wise nor prudent to publish again during his lifetime. While prudence in this matter is easily understood, it is likely that wisdom also played a role in Spinoza's decision. Throughout his life, Spinoza demonstrated a high regard for the atmosphere of tolerance in the United Provinces, which permitted the Jewish people to worship and he himself to think freely. To publish controversial works openly might risk the habits of tolerance which were just then taking root. His other major works remained unpublished until after his death in 1677, and even then remained anonymous (actually, authorship was designated by the use of Spinoza's initials). These include his unfinished *Tractatus politicus* (1677; *A Political Treatise*, 1883), which, beginning from Hobbesian premises about human nature, ends up with a very un-Hobbesian defense of democratic principles, and *Ethica* (1677; *Ethics*, 1870), Spinoza's most substantial and most famous work.

In *Ethics*, Spinoza borrows the language of Descartes (including such notions as "substance," what might be called matter, and "extension," what might be called form) to finish the interpretation of the world as it is known through reason. While God plays a central role in Spinoza's worldview, it is not the role to which one is accustomed by traditional religion. Instead, God is depersonalized and indifferent. For many readers, this translated into atheism; for others, it is a form of pantheism. Whatever one's interpretation, the distinctiveness of *Ethics* lies in the direct connection of this metaphysical framework with a theory of how human beings should seek to do what is right and also achieve happiness in the absence of divine commandments. Ethical conduct and happiness flow from the proper combination of emotion (or passions) and reason, neither being completely dominant over the other.

Ethics is clearly not designed to be edifying or stylish. It is argued through what Spinoza thought to be the philosophical equivalent of geometric proofs. These, quite frankly, seem tedious at first glance. Yet, for those who were not busy condemning Spinoza's godlessness, the book conveyed (and for many readers still conveys) breathtaking beauty and insight, giving off a special aura that is not strictly intellectual, literary, or spiritual, but that somehow partakes of all three.

In addition to his formal writing, Spinoza left behind a large body of correspondence which is indispensable to an understanding of his life and thought. These letters not only provide a running commentary on Spinoza's philosophical works but also indicate the considerable interest his ideas inspired and the affection in which he was held by many friends. These friends mourned deeply when Spinoza died suddenly and, if reports are correct, peacefully, on February 21, 1677, at the age of forty-four.

Summary

During his lifetime, Baruch Spinoza established an underground reputation as one of the greatest philosophers of his day. Even those such as Gottfried Leibniz who openly disparaged him could not ignore the forcefulness of his thought. In addition to his purely intellectual achievements, Spinoza served as an inspirational figure for the circle of freethinkers with whom he was in contact. For them, Spinoza's devotion to truth, defense of tolerance, and humility made him a rallying point in their attempts to bring about further progress. At the same time, however, in the eyes of many observers, Spinoza's name was synonymous with atheism, which was widely held to be nothing less than diabolical.

Over time, the viewpoint of Spinoza's supporters has easily outdistanced that of his critics. It is true that the triumph of analytic philosophy in Anglo-American universities has tended to devalue the broad synthetic enterprise in which Spinoza was engaged, and there is an archaic quality to Spinoza's terminology. Nevertheless, Spinoza's stature as one of the three great rationalist philosophers (along with Descartes and Leibniz) and his influence on later philosophers such as G. W. F. Hegel, who themselves became seminal thinkers, is well established.

Yet Spinoza's influence goes beyond the discipline of philosophy. Literary figures such as Gotthold Ephraim Lessing and Johann Wolfgang von Goethe were profoundly influenced by the beauty, if not the logic, of Spinoza's worldview. Psychologists continue to debate Spinoza's treatment of emotion and its relation to knowledge. Libertarians still celebrate his quest for religious freedom and free expression. Intellectual historians look to Spinoza in their search for a bridge between Oriental and Western values or for the roots of modern democracy. There are others who read Spinoza's work or study his life simply for insight into their own lives. In short, Spinoza remains an inspirational figure for those who take the time to learn about him. Paradoxical as it may seem, there is something deeply spiritual about this man who was excommunicated by Jews for heresy and repeatedly condemned by Christians as an atheist.

Bibliography
Browne, Lewis. *Blessed Spinoza: A Biography of the Philosopher.* New York: Macmillan, 1932. A lively, well-written account of Spinoza's life by a professional biographer. A good introduction to Spinoza the man. Should be augmented by more current research.
Feuer, Lewis Samuel. *Spinoza and the Rise of Liberalism.* Boston: Beacon Press, 1958. Uses historical, psychological, and philosophical analysis to link Spinoza's excommunication to his political orientation. Feuer portrays Spinoza as the first in a long line of politically radical Jewish intellectuals.
Hampshire, Stuart. *Spinoza.* London: Faber & Faber, 1956. A highly accessible introduction to Spinoza's philosophical system. Places Spinoza's thought into a clear historical context and discusses the relationship between Spinoza's metaphysics and other aspects of his philosophy.
Kayser, Rudolf. *Spinoza: Portrait of a Spiritual Hero.* Translated by Amy Allen and Maxim Newmark. New York: Philosophical Library, 1946. As

the subtitle suggests, an inspirational and highly sympathetic account of Spinoza's life. Albert Einstein provides a brief introduction.

McShea, Robert J. *The Political Philosophy of Spinoza*. New York: Columbia University Press, 1968. Fits Spinoza into the tradition of political philosophy from Plato and Aristotle to the present, offering particularly cogent comparisons of Spinoza's thought to that of Niccolò Machiavelli and Thomas Hobbes. Provides a lengthy bibliography.

Spinoza, Baruch. *The Ethics and Selected Letters*. Edited by Seymour Feldman. Translated by Samuel Shirley. Indianapolis: Hackett Publishing, 1982. A compact, accessible edition of Spinoza's most extensive philosophical piece, together with some of his more philosophically revealing letters. Also provides a fairly recent selected bibliography of works by and about Spinoza.

—————. *Spinoza: Dictionary*. Edited by Dagobert D. Runes. New York: Philosophical Library, 1951. Presents extracts from Spinoza's philosophical works and correspondence, arranged alphabetically according to subject. The result is a handy guide to key concepts in Spinoza's thought. Albert Einstein provides a brief foreword.

Ira Smolensky

MADAME DE STAËL

Born: April 22, 1766; Paris, France
Died: July 14, 1817; Paris, France
Areas of Achievement: Literature, philosophy, government, and politics
Contribution: Madame de Staël publicly articulated the liberal, rational opposition to the injustices and corruption of the French government during the Revolution and under Napoleon I. Her social and literary criticism, as well as her colorful personal life, placed her in the vanguard of the Romantic movement, and her two major novels constitute early treatments of the concerns of women.

Early Life
Madame de Staël was born Anne-Louise-Germaine Necker in Paris on April 22, 1766, the only child of Suzanne Curchod Necker, the beautiful and highly educated daughter of a Swiss clergyman, and the Genevese financier Jacques Necker, who was to achieve fame as minister to Louis XVI. Despite her learning, Madame Necker was considered a rather narrow woman by the urbane Parisians, and her relations with her daughter were always rigid and distant. Though not without critics of his own, the stodgy Jacques Necker was widely esteemed as a man of public and private virtue. Germaine's natural love for her father was intensified by her childhood awareness of the public acclaim he enjoyed. As an adult, Germaine's consciousness of her place in the prominent Necker family helped to form her notions of social criticism and political activism and her sense of personal destiny.

A precocious child, Germaine was educated at home in imagined accordance with *Émile: Ou, De l'éducation* (1762; *Emilius and Sophia: Or, A New System of Education*, 1762-1763), Jean-Jacques Rousseau's radical exposition on childhood education. Madame Necker stalwartly maintained one of the literary salons for which Paris was celebrated during the eighteenth century, and Germaine grew up on familiar terms with such people as Denis Diderot, Jean Le Rond d'Alembert, Comte de Buffon, and Abbé Raynal. In this rarefied environment, she absorbed the liberal politics and morals of the Enlightenment.

On January 14, 1786, after years of negotiation, Germaine Necker married a Swedish aristocrat, Eric Magnus, Baron de Staël-Holstein, a favorite of Gustav III and—in accordance with the marriage negotiations—Swedish ambassador to the French court. De Staël may have felt some affection for Germaine (and some, certainly, for her dowry of 650,000 pounds), but she apparently felt none for him, and their first child, Edwige-Gustavine, was probably the only one of their four children actually fathered by de Staël. More important, however, Germaine gained a measure of social and economic independence from the marriage. In the embassy residence in Paris, she established a salon of her own, which soon became the gathering place for such liberal members of the aristocracy as Mathieu de Montmorency, Talleyrand, and Louis, Vicomte de Narbonne Lara. In the early days of her marriage, she used her husband's court connections to try to advance the position of her father, and she took advantage of de Staël's frequent absences to lead the relatively independent life that was possible for women of her station in eighteenth century Paris.

Life's Work

Madame de Staël's residence at the Swedish embassy in Paris was one of the more attractive features of her marriage agreement, for Jacques Necker had been dismissed by Louis XVI in 1781 and had moved his family to Saint-Ouen, where Germaine had sorely missed the intellectual life of Paris. Necker was recalled by Louis XVI in 1788, and was then dismissed and recalled once again at the fall of the Bastille. He continued at his post through the march on Versailles in September, 1789, and the massive nationalization effected by the Assembly under Comte de Mirabeau. Necker finally resigned in September, 1790, and repaired to the family estate of Coppet, near Geneva.

During her father's interrupted tenure at court, Germaine attempted to elicit support among her influential friends of the liberal aristocracy for a constitution and a bicameral government, as a compromise between the continued abuses of the Bourbon dynasty and the inevitable triumph of the Third Estate. On August 31, 1790, she gave birth to a son, Auguste, fathered by Narbonne, with whom she had been involved for about a year and a half. Determined that Narbonne should be the leader of the new government, Madame de Staël became further embroiled in intrigues at court until Narbonne was appointed war minister at the request of Marie Antoinette; he was dismissed, however, in March 1792. At about the same time, de Staël was recalled to Sweden when Louis and Marie Antoinette were arrested attempting to escape Paris in a maneuver arranged by Gustav III. Gustav was assassinated in March, 1792, however, and de Staël returned to Paris, where Madame de Staël continued to encourage the constitutionalists and agitated for the restoration of Narbonne. She finally fled Paris for Coppet the day before the September massacres began in 1793.

Madame de Staël's relationship with Narbonne—which followed a similar liaison with Talleyrand and coincided with a profound friendship with Montmorency—was characteristic of her lifelong attraction to the heroes of her political and intellectual causes. Much of her own appeal resided in her power as a fascinating conversationalist, and even those who were prepared to be intimidated by her were often won over by her exuberance and lack of pretension. Possessing none of her mother's conventional beauty, she was nevertheless a woman of imposing physical appearance. Her wide, luminous eyes were considered her most attractive feature. A woman of Junoesque proportions, Madame de Staël continued to dress in the revealing diaphanous fabrics and décolleté lines of empire fashion even after she had grown heavy in middle age. Her frank display of her ample bosom and legs, and her continuance of the eighteenth century custom of the *levée*, amazed younger, more conservative Parisians and provoked the derision of her enemies. She customarily wore a turban, which undoubtedly lent a Byronic dash to her overall appearance.

During the Terror, Madame de Staël lived much of the time at Coppet, spending considerable money and energy smuggling refugees from the liberal aristocracy out of Paris. She gave birth to her son Albert, also the child of Narbonne, on November 20, 1792, and left shortly thereafter for England, where Narbonne had sought refuge from the Terror. Rumors of her complicity in the Revolution and in the Terror were circulated by aristocratic French émigrés living in England until she was no longer received by members of the upper class. Disappointed by the conservatism of the British, her relationship with Narbonne strained, she returned in June, 1793, to her husband near Coppet, where Narbonne finally joined her in August, 1794.

In 1794, the year of her mother's death, Madame de Staël met Benjamin Constant, with whom she would be involved in a passionate and embattled relationship for the next fourteen years. With the fall of Robespierre in 1794, she returned to Paris and reopened her salon. At this time, she worked to encourage support for the positive changes wrought by the Revolution; the degree of influence she wielded is measured by the fact that she was expelled from the city alternately by both royalists and republicans. Her only daughter, Albertine, probably the child of Constant, was born in Paris on June 8, 1796. In 1797, Madame de Staël formally separated from her husband; debilitated by a stroke suffered in 1801, he died the following year en route to Coppet.

In 1795, Madame de Staël published *Essai sur les fictions* (*Essay on Fiction*, 1795), in 1796, *De l'influence des passions sur le bonheur des individus et des nations* (*A Treatise on the Influence of the Passions upon the Happiness of Individuals and Nations*, 1798), and, in 1800, *De la littérature considérée dans ses rapports avec les institutions sociales* (*A Treatise on Ancient and Modern Literature*, 1803). In these and later writings, her examination of the concept of perfectibility—the idea that scientific progress would lead humankind toward moral perfection—and her contention that critical judgment must be relative and historically oriented earned for her a place near Chateaubriand as a precursor of Romanticism. In 1802, she published the novel *Delphine* (English translation, 1803), which explores the role of the intellectual woman.

One of the most significant factors in Madame de Staël's life was her relationship with Napoleon, whom she first met in 1797. She early admired him as a republican hero: His successful coup of 18 Brumaire seemed to actualize the liberal abstractions of revolutionary politics. Napoleon, thoroughly conventional in his attitude toward women, however, could not approve of the highly vocal, public role that Madame de Staël had assumed; moreover, he resented the free discussion of his government that was encouraged at her salon, to which even his own brothers were frequent visitors. As he became more tyrannical, she became increasingly critical, eventually labeling him an "ideophobe." He expelled her from France in 1803 and crowned himself emperor the following year.

Her eleven years in exile from France during the reign of Napoleon seemed a spiritual and intellectual death sentence to Madame de Staël. Immediately upon her expulsion, she visited Germany, where she was welcomed as the author of *Delphine*. She met with the great thinkers and writers of Weimar and Berlin, including Johann Wolfgang von Goethe, Friedrich Schiller, and August Wilhelm von Schlegel, with whom she formed a long-lasting attachment. In April, 1804, Constant brought her news of her father's death. Prostrate with grief, she returned to Coppet.

From 1804 to 1810, Madame de Staël officially resided at Coppet, where she gathered around her a group of loyal and intellectually stimulating friends, including Schlegel and Jeanne Récamier. She spent much of her time away from the estate, however, venturing into France and traveling to Italy until she was confined to Coppet as a result of the machinations of the French and Genevese police. The Romantic and feminist concerns of her 1807 novel *Corinne: Ou L'Italie* (*Corinne: Or, Italy*, 1807) brought her renewed fame, and in 1810 she completed *De l'Allemagne* (*Germany*, 1813), a thinly disguised critique of contemporary France, which was suppressed by Napoleon; it was published in England in 1813.

In 1811, she took another lover, John Rocca, a young Genevese sportsman who had been wounded in military action and was now tubercular. Rocca fathered her last child, Alphonse, and in 1816 they were married. Shortly after the birth of Alphonse, she fled Coppet and traveled throughout Europe, involving herself in Russian and Swedish political intrigues directed toward overthrowing Napoleon. Napoleon's abdication in 1814 brought Madame de Staël the freedom to reestablish herself in Paris, where she died on Bastille Day, in 1817.

Summary

Madame de Staël was a brilliant and unconventional woman whose circumstances of birth allowed her to witness some of the most significant events of Western history and whose intelligence and moral courage led her to participate. In the face of serious opposition, she lived with great enthusiasm and energy, balancing the exercise of intellect and creativity with the pursuit of a passionate personal life.

Madame de Staël tended the flame of the Enlightenment through the darkest days following the French Revolution. The rational tenor of her criticism of oppression and her defense of freedom provided a constant corrective not only to political tyranny but also to the social and cultural constraints that bound her as a woman. In her nonfictional prose, she sought support for her philosophical stance in the individualistic spirit of English and German Romanticism and in the cultural relativism afforded by her experiences in Germany, Italy, and Russia. Her examination, in *Delphine* and *Corinne*, of the difficulties encountered in the personal lives of gifted and creative women has gained new attention from feminist critics. Madame de Staël thus continues to assert her vivacious presence.

Bibliography
Gutwirth, Madelyn. *Madame de Staël, Novelist: The Emergence of the Artist as Woman.* Urbana: University of Illinois Press, 1978. This book is a feminist analysis of the biographical, cultural, and social sources of the novels *Corinne* and *Delphine*, especially in their focus on the complications created by talent and love in women's lives. Includes notes, a bibliography, and an index.

_____. "Madame de Staël, Rousseau, and the Woman Question." *PMLA* 86 (January, 1971): 100-109. Gutwirth discusses Madame de Staël's attempted resolution of the conflict between the conservative ideals of feminine behavior endorsed by Rousseau and the more radical example of achievement provided by her own life.

Herold, J. Christopher. *Mistress to an Age: A Life of Madame de Staël.* Indianapolis: Bobbs-Merrill, 1958. This standard biography is eminently readable and sympathetic, although slightly ironic in tone. Herold treats Madame de Staël's life in its entirety, emphasizing the effects of her relationship with her parents and focusing on her prodigious literary accomplishment and her unconventional personal life. Informed by an easy familiarity with French politics and culture, the book includes illustrations, an extensive annotated bibliography, and an index.

Hogsett, Charlotte. *The Literary Existence of Germaine de Staël.* Carbondale: Southern Illinois University Press, 1987. Writing from a feminist standpoint, Hogsett provides a critical analysis of Madame de Staël's writings as they reveal her development as a woman writer struggling to define herself in a male-dominated tradition. Contains notes, a bibliography, and an index.

Levaillant, Maurice. *The Passionate Exiles: Madame de Staël and Madame Récamier.* Translated by Malcolm Barnes. New York: Farrar, Straus & Cudahy, 1958. Levaillant examines Madame de Staël's life in exile at Coppet, with particular focus on her friendship with Jeanne Récamier. The book quotes extensively from the two women's correspondence.

Moers, Ellen. "Madame de Staël and the Woman of Genius." *American Scholar* 44 (Spring, 1975): 225-241. A discussion of Madame de Staël's view of the gifted woman in terms of the cultural liberation provided by the Italian setting of *Corinne*.

West, Rebecca. "Madame de Staël." *Encounter* 13 (July, 1959): 66-73. This article is a perceptive review of Herold's biography, supplementing his depiction of Madame de Staël with an intelligent assessment of circumstances mitigating some of the more eccentric aspects of her life.

Diane Prenatt Stevens

GEORG ERNST STAHL

Born: October 21, 1660; Ansbach, Franconia
Died: May 14, 1734; Berlin, Prussia
Areas of Achievement: Chemistry and medicine
Contribution: Stahl was a physician who developed the phlogiston theory, modern chemistry's first great explanatory system. It provided chemists with a deeper understanding of such reactions as combustion and the smelting of metal ores, and it guided research into such productive discoveries as new gases and the composition of the chemical molecule.

Early Life

Georg Ernst Stahl was born on October 21, 1660, in St. John's parish in Ansbach, then part of Franconia, a duchy in southern Germany. His father was a Protestant minister, and he grew up heavily influenced by Pietism, a seventeenth century movement in the Lutheran church to infuse new spirit into an increasingly dogmatic Protestantism. Pietism stressed the moral, devotional, and mystical aspects of Christianity, and this doctrine helped to shape Stahl's view of the world, which was sensitive to the presence of the spiritual. As an adolescent, he developed an interest in chemistry through reading a manuscript of lectures given by Jacob Barner, a professor of medicine at Padua. In the same period, he read a study of metals and minerals by Johann Kunckel von Löwenstjern, a court alchemist and apothecary who would later help to instigate Stahl's development of the phlogiston theory. Stahl once said that he knew these works by Barner and Kunckel von Löwenstjern practically by heart. They stimulated him, under the practical guidance of an enameler, to begin doing chemical experiments.

In the late 1670's, Stahl traveled to Thuringia in central Germany to study medicine at the University of Jena. One of his teachers, Georg Wolfgang Wedel, was a proponent of iatrochemistry, a discipline which held that diseases originate in the imbalance of chemical elements in the body, and that the physician's task is to restore the body's chemical equilibrium. Stahl later wrote against the iatrochemists, for he could not understand how such a great variety of human illnesses could be attributed to such a small range of chemical causes, for example, acidity and alkalinity. Although he disagreed with the iatrochemists, some of their ideas, such as explaining physiological processes in terms of chemical composition, did inform his medical theory and practice. During his years of study at Jena, Stahl formed a close friendship with Friedrich Hoffman, a fellow student who shared Stahl's fascination with chemistry and medicine. Even while he was a medical student, Stahl showed great ability as a chemist, and in 1683, around the time that he received his M.D. degree, he began to teach chemistry at Jena.

As a young teacher, he wrestled with many of the ideas that had fashioned the classical and modern doctrines of chemistry and medicine. He studied alchemy, and in 1684 he expressed his belief in the possibility of transmuting such metals as lead into gold (his mature attitude toward transmutation was much more cautious). He read the works of such natural philosophers as René Descartes and Robert Boyle, and he grew skeptical of their claim that all chemical phenomena could be explained in terms of mechanical interactions between variously shaped particles of homogeneous matter (this mechanical view of nature also conflicted with his Pietism). The courses that Stahl taught at Jena in chemistry and medicine gained for him such renown that in 1687 he was invited to become personal physician to Duke Johann Ernst of Sachsen-Weimar, a position he accepted and held for seven years.

In 1693, the Elector of Brandenburg, Frederick III (who later became King Frederick I of Prussia), founded a new university at Halle. He gave Hoffmann the duty of establishing the faculty of medicine, and Hoffmann invited his friend Stahl to join him. Halle was a center of the Pietist movement, and, when Stahl found that he would be able to teach medicine and chemistry in association with his friend, he agreed to go. In 1694, the year the University of Halle was officially inaugurated, Stahl took his post, one he would hold for twenty-two years.

Life's Work

As second professor in medicine at Halle, Stahl lectured on theoretical medicine, physiology, pathology, pharmacology, and botany, whereas Hoffmann, as first professor, lectured on practical medicine, anatomy, physics, and chemistry. Through the efforts of these talented and hardworking professors, Halle became a leading medical school. Unfortunately, as time went on, Stahl and Hoffmann became rivals instead of friends. Temperamentally, they had always been different, though there is little evidence to support the traditional contrast of Stahl as misanthropic and intolerant, and Hoffmann as congenial and open-minded; however, there is evidence that their differences were the result of increasingly divergent views on intellectual issues. In particular, Hoffmann became a dedicated iatrochemist who saw living organisms as machines, whereas Stahl, though he interpreted physiological processes through chemical changes, insisted that neither mechanical nor chemical laws were able to account fully for the mystery of life.

In addition to his problems with Hoffmann, Stahl encountered troubles in his personal life. He had married after he had come to Halle, but in 1696 his wife died of puerperal fever, which, despite his best medical efforts, he failed to cure. In 1706, his second wife died of the same disease, and in 1708 a daughter died. Although Stahl married a total of four times, little else is known of his family life. He did have a son who became interested in chemistry and who popularized a method of making silver sulfate from silver nitrate and potassium sulfate.

Despite these misfortunes in his personal and professional relationships, Stahl's years at Halle were extremely productive. He worked prodigiously. His lectures in medicine and chemistry were very popular, and they became the bases of the books that issued from his pen in a steady stream, many of them in Latin, some in German, and some in a mixture of Latin and German. His subjects were wide-ranging: medical theory, pharmacology, physiological chemistry, chemical theory, experimental chemistry, fermentation, metallurgy, and many others. His style was convoluted and confusing, and many scholars believe that he wrote both too much and too quickly and that his awkward sentences indicate not complexity of thought but a lack of clear thinking.

His greatest medical work was *Theoria medica vera* (1708; the true theory of medicine), which presents in massive detail his doctrines of physiology and pathology as well as his animistic medical philosophy. Paramount among Stahl's basic ideas, in his medicine and in his chemistry, is a sharp distinction between the living and nonliving. Stahl was influenced in his views about this distinction by Johann Joachim Becher, who would also influence his ideas on phlogiston. Like Stahl, Becher was the son of a Protestant pastor, and he also went on to become a university professor of medicine, though, unlike Stahl, he converted to Roman Catholicism rather than Pietism. Like Becher, Stahl argued that living things cannot be reduced to a conglomerate of mechanical effects. He did not deny that nonliving things functioned mechanically or that living things, in certain activities, could be interpreted mechanically (for example, the arm as a lever in lifting an object), but the mechanism is always an instrument in the control of a directing agent or anima. Stahl used the Latin word anima, usually translated— though with loss of meaning—as soul or spirit, to capture his belief that every bodily response was rooted in an indivisible vital principle, but anima was not a mystical idea for him, since he arrived at it through rational analysis.

Some scholars have misunderstood Stahl's animism and antimechanism. He was not a reactionary, trying to revive a defunct religious or ancient Greek worldview. In fact, he was extremely critical of Aristotle's and Galen's theories, which he found conflicted with experience. The mechanical philosophy, too, had failed to produce much medical progress because mechanists failed to grasp that it was the soul, not physics and chemistry, that rules the body. The mind clearly acts on the body through voluntary actions, but even involuntary bodily effects have psychic causes. For example, mental perturbations such as anger and fear can change the pulse rate and upset the digestion. Therefore mental changes do regulate the materials of the body according to certain goals.

In contrast to Stahl's medical ideas, which did little to advance the field, his chemical ideas had great influence. His best work in chemistry was done during his Halle professorship, and this work was as antimechanist as his medical work. He deeply believed that simple machine models could not adequately explain chemical phenomena. Although he accepted the existence of atoms, he regarded the corpuscularian viewpoint as deficient, since, as he put it, atomic theories scratch the surface of things and leave their kernel untouched. He could not see how arranging and moving inert and homogeneous particles around could generate such qualities as color and reactivity.

Stahl defined chemistry as the art of resolving compound bodies into their principles and recombining these again. Since, in his view, atoms never exist by themselves, elements are formed when these indivisible particles join chemically to form what he called "mixts," and these mixts unite with other mixts in a hierarchy of increasing complexity. Though the highly reactive original elements could never be isolated, they could leave one mixt and enter another. Stahl believed that, for chemists to do meaningful work, they had to assume chemically distinct kinds of matter. For example, he defined metals in terms of their visual and tactile properties, more specifically, their luster and malleability. He defined acids in terms of their reactions with color indicators such as the syrup of violets. Mechanistic explanations of these qualities were clever but speculative and untestable, whereas Stahl preferred to take a direct, empirical approach to the practical problems of chemistry.

In his attempts to find convincing chemical explanations of phenomena, Stahl relied heavily on the doctrines of Becher. In 1703, he brought out an edition of Becher's *Physica subterranea* (1669; geological physics), and in the same year he wrote an analysis of Becher's ideas. Stahl disagreed with Becher's contention that metals grow like plants in the earth and that lead changes into gold with time, but he found much to admire in Becher's ideas about minerals. Germany was then the center of a thriving mining industry, and many studies were being done on metallurgical processes. In *Physica subterranea*, Becher stated that the world's nonliving substances were composed of three different types of earth: a glasslike earth (*terra lapidea*), endowed with substantiality which rendered bodies solid and difficult to change; an oily earth (*terra pinguis*) was primarily responsible for combustibility, but it also accounted for odor, taste, and color; and a fluid or mercurial earth (*terra mercurialis*) supplied ductility, fusibility, and volatility. Stahl took Becher's second earth and gave it the name "phlogiston." The word had been used earlier, in different contexts and in different senses, and the idea of combustibility as a general principle had been used since antiquity (in the medieval period it surfaced as the alchemical principle sulfur). Stahl's great accomplishment was to take phlogiston and make it into the organizing idea for chemistry. Becher gave almost no experimental support for his theories, whereas Stahl collected numerous observations and experimental facts to confirm his views. His theory also stimulated chemists to do many new experiments.

The explanation of combustion was a central feature of the phlogiston theory. When a substance burned, phlogiston was expelled, and so burning was a decomposition. Stahl saw phlogiston as the principle of fire but not fire itself. Other chemists called phlogiston the food of fire or the inflammable principle. Since phlogiston was an elementary principle, its nature could be known only from its effects. Like the elementary atoms, phlogiston was impossible to isolate, and like the reactions of the mixts, phlogiston could only be transferred from one substance to another. In combustion, phlogiston went out of the flame to combine with the air, but since air had only a limited capacity to absorb phlogiston, this transfer reaction eventually lessened. Furthermore, Stahl noted that a flame could blacken a pane of glass, and this showed that phlogiston was responsible for color.

In an important extension of the phlogiston theory, Stahl recognized that the rusting of metals was similar to the burning of wood, since phlogiston was emitted in both processes. When Stahl heated a metal strongly, the process of rusting was accelerated and what he called an ash appeared (later phlogistonists called this a calx, and the process of making this powdery material from the metal was called calcination). More poetically, the calx was the dead body of the metal, from which the soul of phlogiston had been removed by fire. From his studies, Stahl deduced that a metal was really a compound of a calx and phlogiston. He could reverse the process by heating the calx with charcoal, a rich source of phlogiston. This brought about a transfer of phlogiston from the charcoal to the calx, re-creating the metal.

One thing that troubled later chemists about the phlogiston theory was an observation, known to the medieval Arabs and to many chemists of the sixteenth and seventeenth centuries, that calcined metals actually increased in weight. At first glance, this observation contradicts the phlogiston theory's analysis of calcination as a decomposition. Therefore metals should lose weight when they are calcined (because they lose phlogiston), and the calx should gain weight when reconverted to the metal. In fact, the reverse is true, as Stahl knew. Nevertheless, this did not shake his confidence in his theory, because he thought of phlogiston not as an isolable substance but as a weightless, perhaps buoyant, fluidlike heat that could flow from one body to another. Since phlogiston was like light and electricity rather than like air and water, it made no more sense to weigh metals and ores to discover the loss or gain of phlogiston than it would to weigh a piece of paper to measure its whiteness.

Stahl first conceived the phlogiston theory at the end of the seventeenth century, and he developed its implications for combustion, calcination, and the smelting of ores during the first decade of the eighteenth century, when he also applied his theory to such biological phenomena as fermentation and respiration. The theory's spread throughout Europe augmented Stahl's fame, but it aggravated rather than improved his relationship with Hoffmann. The atmosphere between them was so poisoned that Stahl welcomed an invitation in 1716 to become personal physician to the King of Prussia, Frederick William I, in Berlin. While at the Prussian court, Stahl continued to write, do research, and teach students. Among his most important publications during this period was *Fundamenta chymiae dogmaticae et experimentalis* (1723; the fundamentals of dogmatic and experimental chemistry), a work prepared for publication by Johann Samuel Carl, whom Stahl regarded as his best pupil. Depictions of Stahl from this period show a man in a large dark-haired wig surrounding a face with strong features and a melancholic bearing. Stahl, contented with his new life in Berlin, never returned to Halle but held his court appointment until his death on May 14, 1734.

Summary

Georg Ernst Stahl's life bridged two ages, and his phlogiston theory is often seen as a bridge from alchemy to modern chemistry. His personality, which many have interpreted as a combination of opposites, suited him for this linking role. He was deeply attracted to the devotional and penitential rigors of Pietism, but his penetrating intelligence also found satisfaction in constructing a highly rational system of chemistry. In his youth, he had been fascinated by alchemy, and he continued to use alchemical symbols throughout his career, but in his developed theories these symbols stood for a new explanation of the composition of chemical substances.

Today, most people associate Stahl with the phlogiston theory that dominated chemistry for nearly a century, and many scientists have the impression that this domination retarded chemical progress; however, modern historians of science, though they recognize Stahl's theory as false, find much to praise in it. Some even see it as a great landmark in the history of chemistry, because it was the first logical theory to encompass most important chemical transformations. It rejected the confusing ideas of alchemy, established chemistry as an independent discipline, and constituted a paradigm within which experimental work could be planned, practiced, and related to other discoveries.

Through the eyes of an early eighteenth century chemist, the phlogiston theory was a liberation from enervating scientific concepts of the past, and the most intelligent and creative chemists of the period accepted Stahl's theory with enthusiasm. In England, Joseph Priestley, Henry Cavendish, and Joseph Black were phlogistonists; in Germany, Caspar Neumann, Johann Pott, and Andreas Marggraf; in Sweden, Torbern Bergman and Carl Wilhelm Scheele; in Russia, Mikhail Vasilyevich Lomonosov; and in France, Pierre-Joseph Macquer and even Antoine Lavoisier, until he developed his oxygen theory. These scientists found Stahl's ideas extraordinarily useful in making such important discoveries as new gases and inorganic solids.

Bibliography
Crosland, Maurice P. *Historical Studies in the Language of Chemistry.* Cambridge, Mass.: Harvard University Press, 1962. This book, which derives from a doctoral dissertation that Crosland wrote for the University of London, traces the evolution of chemistry, through a study of its language and nomenclature, from the period of alchemy to the end of the nineteenth century. Though intended for scientists and historians of science, Crosland's book should lead the general reader to a better appreciation of the history of chemistry, including Stahl's contributions, when it is seen from this new perspective.

Donovan, Arthur, ed. *The Chemical Revolution: Essays in Reinterpretation. Osiris* 4 (1988). This entire issue centers on new views of the chemical revolution. Though intended for historians of science, the essays deal with a time period and subject matter that make the material accessible to a wider audience.

Ihde, Aaron J. *The Development of Modern Chemistry.* Reprint. Mineola, N.Y.: Dover, 1983. Though the book's emphasis is on the period of chemistry since the chemical revolution, Stahl's work is discussed in the initial section on the foundations of chemistry. Contains useful bibliographic notes.

Leicester, Henry M. *The Historical Background of Chemistry.* New York: John Wiley & Sons, 1956. Although he discusses how some important chemical ideas have influenced world history, Leicester's emphasis in this book is on the evolution and interrelations of chemical concepts within the history of science. Unlike Ihde above, he devotes considerable attention to the earlier periods of chemistry. Contains a good discussion of Stahl's views. Accessible to readers with little or no chemical background.

Partington, J. R. *A History of Chemistry.* Vol. 2. London: Macmillan, 1961. This volume of Partington's monumental history of chemistry (which he failed to complete before his death) contains two chapters on the phlogiston theory, one devoted to Becher, the other to Stahl. Contains a selected bibliography of Stahl's writings.

Weeks, Mary Elvira. *Discovery of the Elements.* 7th ed. Easton, Pa.: Journal of Chemical Education, 1968. Because the phlogiston theory was important in the discovery of such elemental gases as hydrogen, oxygen, and nitrogen, this book has many references to Stahl's work. The book was originally intended to acquaint chemists with the great achievements of their science, but there is much in these densely packed pages to interest more casual readers.

Robert J. Paradowski

FREIHERR VOM STEIN

Born: October 26, 1757; Nassau, Holy Roman Empire
Died: June 29, 1831; Cappenberg, Prussia
Areas of Achievement: Government, politics, and social reform
Contribution: Stein was the architect of the reform movement in Prussia,
   during the period from 1806 to 1808, that altered the authoritarian nature
   of the Prussian state in the direction of modern liberalism and resulted in
   fundamental changes in Prussian institutions.

Early Life

Heinrich Friedrich Karl, Freiherr vom und zum Stein was the ninth of ten
children born to Karl Philipp Freiherr vom Stein and Langwerth vom Stein
(née von Simmern). The vom Stein family was of the Imperial Knighthood
and had been independent proprietors within the Holy Roman Empire for
more than seven hundred years when Karl (as he was called by his family
and friends) was born in his ancestral home at Nassau on October 26, 1757.
His father had entered the bureaucracy of the neighboring state of Mainz,
where he eventually rose to the rank of privy councillor.

Stein's parents impressed upon him that as a representative of his caste he
had the patriotic duty to devote his life to the service of the community. With
that end in mind, he was matriculated at age sixteen at the University of
Göttingen to study law and political science preparatory to entering government service. Although Göttingen was experiencing perhaps its most dynamic era of literary ferment during Stein's stay there, he was relatively
unaffected by it. He concentrated on the study of history and of constitutional and legal theory, which apparently deepened the patriotic feelings
imbued in him by his parents and strengthened his determination to enter
government service.

Stein's original inclination was to enter the still-extant but ineffective
government machinery of the Holy Roman Empire. After leaving Göttingen,
he traveled to the Imperial Chamber at Wetzlar, the Imperial Court Council
in Vienna, and the Imperial Diet at Regensburg in order to gain an understanding of the political and administrative structure of the empire.

Apparently disillusioned by the largely figurehead nature of imperial administration, Stein accepted an appointment to the Prussian bureaucracy under Frederick William II in 1780 at the age of twenty-three. Some of his
biographers have suggested that even at this early age, Stein had already
concluded that the best hope of unifying all the German people into a strong
political entity, with liberal institutions and a constitution, lay with Prussia.

Life's Work

For the next sixteen years, Stein held progressively more responsible positions within the Prussian government, primarily in mining operations and in the provincial administration in Prussian Westphalia. This experience gave him an intimate knowledge of the workings of local government and led to his appointment in 1796 as head of all the Prussian Rhenish and Westphalian administrative districts. His success in this capacity and other endeavors resulted in his appointment in 1804 as minister of economic affairs for the royal government in Berlin. There Stein rapidly developed the conviction that the Prussian governmental and social systems would have to be drastically reformed and modernized if Prussia were to survive what Stein perceived as an inevitable clash with the burgeoning Napoleonic empire. Stein's vocal insistence on reform resulted, in 1807, in his dismissal by Frederick William III shortly after the disastrous Prussian defeat by Napoleon I at the Battles of Jena and Auerstedt.

Stein's forced retirement to his family estate at Nassau gave him time to systematize and set down on paper his ideas concerning the reforms necessary to modernize and rejuvenate the Prussian state. In his famous *Nassauer Denkschrift* (1807; Nassau memorandum), Stein argued that if the Prussian state was to survive, its citizens must be allowed to participate in the management of its affairs. He further suggested in his memorandum that only self-government could instill into the Prussian people the patriotism and community spirit which would allow Prussia to survive in an increasingly dangerous world. Stein's lifelong study of British history and his admiration for the British parliamentary system undoubtedly contributed to his advocacy of the establishment of a similar system in Prussia.

During Stein's unwilling retirement, Napoleon forced Frederick William to sign the Treaty of Tilsit. The terms of the treaty considerably diminished the size and autonomy of the Prussian state and convinced many Prussians in the bureaucracy and the army of the necessity of sweeping reforms in the governmental apparatus. Napoleon insisted on the dismissal of Frederick William's foreign minister, Karl von Hardenberg, and the appointment of Stein in his place. Frederick William confirmed Stein as Prime Minister of Prussia on October 4, 1807.

Stein took advantage of a wave of patriotism and widespread demand for reform engendered by the twin debacles of Jena and Tilsit to force Frederick William to accede to the first of the great changes in Prussian government, administration, and society later known collectively as the Prussian Reform movement. The first, and in many ways the most far-reaching, of the reforms was promulgated on October 19, 1807, as the Law Concerning the Emancipated Possession and the Free Use of Landed Property and the Personal Relationships of the Inhabitants of the Land. This law emancipated the Prussian serfs from feudal obligations and enabled the Prussian aristocracy to sell their land to non-nobles. In addition, the law enabled all Prussians to follow the vocation of their choice. The law was a decisive step toward the destruction of the old caste relationships of Prussian society and the creation of civic and legal equality.

One year later, Stein was responsible for the creation of effective local self-government for the towns and cities of Germany through the issuance of the *Städteordnung* (municipal ordinances). He then turned his attention to modernizing the national government. He replaced the old, secretive councillor administration with departmental ministries of foreign affairs, internal affairs, finance, justice, and war, each with responsibility and authority for the whole of the Prussian kingdom. He also reorganized provincial administration along more efficient lines. Whether Stein would have succeeded in introducing in Prussia the national parliament, which he so admired in the English system, will never be known. Napoleon forced Frederick William to dismiss him from office on November 24, 1808, after French spies intercepted a letter Stein sent to a friend criticizing the French emperor and his policies toward Prussia.

Stein took refuge until 1812 in Austria, where he continued to correspond with his successor Hardenberg and with other men in the bureaucracy and the army of Prussia who were carrying the banner of reform. In 1812, he answered a summons by Alexander I of Russia to come to St. Petersburg as a political adviser. He was instrumental in that capacity in negotiating the Russo-Prussian alliance in 1813, after Napoleon's 1812 invasion of Russia ended in catastrophe. He then provided moral leadership for the German states during the war of liberation, which ended with Napoleon's final defeat and exile in 1815. During that period, Stein also continued to influence those men in Prussia who pursued progressive reform, men such as Johann Gottlieb Fichte, August von Gneisenau, Ernst Arndt, Heinrich von Kleist, and Wilhelm and Alexander von Humboldt. At the Congress of Vienna, Stein championed the cause of the political unification of the German states but was not satisfied with the final form that unification took. He regarded the Germanic Confederation that resulted from the deliberations at Vienna as little more than the ghost of the recently deceased Holy Roman Empire.

After the Congress of Vienna, Stein retired to his estate of Cappenberg, Westphalia, where he devoted the remainder of his life to the writing of history and to the publication of the works of other historians on the subject of German history. He died in his home on June 29, 1831.

Summary

Freiherr vom Stein was a pivotal figure in the transformation of Prussian government from an absolute monarchy toward liberalism and constitutionalism. He was, along with Hardenberg, one of the champions of the concept that such changes must be instituted peacefully and slowly from above, or else they will be brought about violently and quickly, and with unforeseeable consequences, from below, as in the French Revolution. His conviction that the reforms must be made was based less on a concern for individual liberty and human rights than on a desire to prevent German institutions from being overwhelmed by the French. He realized that the powerful forces of nationalism and liberalism unleashed by the French Revolution of 1789 could not be withstood without unleashing similar forces in Germany. He hoped to control those forces while retaining the virtues of older Prussian society.

The unfinished nature of his reforms had far-reaching consequences for the development of Prussian and German society: The serfs were freed, but without land; the former serfs were reduced to the status of migrant agricultural laborers, many of whom migrated to the cities and became the nucleus of the proletariat, which turned to Marxism and trade-unionism in later decades and caused much turmoil in imperial Germany. Equality before the law was established, but without constitutional guarantees; the widespread and unsatisfied desire among the Prussian intellectual community and the bourgeoisie for a constitution and a parliament culminated with the Revolution of 1848. The principle of participatory government was established, but without a medium through which it could be practiced. The essentially conservative approach to reform adopted by Stein created a tradition in Prussia of expecting the government to effect necessary reform in societal institutions that prevailed into the twentieth century.

Bibliography
Gray, M. W. "Prussia in Transition—Society and Politics Under the Stein Reform Ministry of 1808." *Transactions of the American Philosophical Society* 76 (1986): 1-175. Gray's article is primarily concerned with the milieu in which Stein's reforms took place and the effects of the reforms on Prussian society, rather than with Stein himself. An excellent introduction to the era of the Prussian Reform movement.
Holborn, Hajo. *A History of Modern Germany, 1648-1840.* New York: Alfred A. Knopf, 1964. Holborn's book contains several chapters on the Prussian Reform movement and provides sketches of the most important of the leaders of the movement, including Stein. The book places the reform movement and the reformers in their proper perspective in German history.
Meinecke, Friedrich. *The Age of German Liberation, 1795-1815.* Translated by Peter Peret and Helmuth Fischer. Berkeley: University of California Press, 1977. One of the best accounts of the period, Meinecke's book provides a good account of Stein's life and work. Meinecke argues that Stein and the other reformers successfully provided the transition between absolutism and representative government that made possible the unification of Germany half a century later.
Seeley, John Robert. *Life and Times of Stein: Or, Germany and Prussia in the Napoleonic Age.* New York: Greenwood Press, 1968. Seeley's book is

the only full-length biography of Stein in English. It is perhaps overly laudatory. In the main, it agrees with Meinecke's evaluation of Stein and his reforms.

Simon, Walter. *The Failure of the Prussian Reform Movement*. Ithaca, N.Y.: Cornell University Press, 1955. Simon is critical of both the reforms and the reformers, including Stein, of whom he writes at great length. Simon argues that the failure of the reforms to establish a unified German state with a constitutional, parliamentary form of government led directly to the development of the authoritarianism of the German empire after 1871 and ultimately to the Third Reich.

Paul Madden

JAKOB STEINER

Born: March 18, 1796; near Utzendorf, Canton of Bern, Switzerland
Died: April 1, 1863; Bern, Switzerland
Area of Achievement: Mathematics
Contribution: Steiner was one of the greatest geometers of the first half of
the nineteenth century. His major geometrical books and dozens of articles
established him as a chief authority on isoperimetric geometry and as the
founder of modern synthetic geometry in Germany.

Early Life

Jakob Steiner was born into a family of thrifty, humble, and hardworking
Swiss farmers, near the village of Utzendorf, Canton of Bern, Switzerland,
on March 18, 1796. Though the youngest of five children, he contributed
from a very early age to the family income, the family expecting nothing
more than the most modest intellectual development. Consequently, he remained illiterate until he was fourteen and continued farmwork until he was
nineteen. According to his later recollections, before he had any formal
education he developed an astounding capacity for spatial conceptualization.
Contrary to the desires of his father, Jakob entered the school of the Swiss
educational reformer Johann Pestalozzi at Yverdon. Out of conformity with
Swiss educational precepts, Pestalozzi continued stressing the pedagogical
importance of individual training and direct experience for his students. Before Pestalozzi's institution failed, Steiner had become a teaching assistant.
Thereafter, Steiner entered Heidelberg University, where he pursued numeri-
cal perceptions in connection with imaginative spatial concepts. From 1818
until 1821, while earning a living as a teacher, Steiner worked with one of
the institution's leading geometers, whose lectures and ideas he profoundly
disdained. Notwithstanding, Steiner obtained his doctorate from Heidelberg,
thereafter accepting a teaching position as a tutor at a private school.

Fortunately, the eldest son of the famed German statesman and philologist
Wilhelm von Humboldt was one of his pupils. Steiner's acquaintance with
the distinguished Humboldt family altered his fortunes. The Humboldts introduced him to Berlin's premier mathematicians, and Steiner was encouraged to accept a teaching post at a Berlin vocational institution during the
next decade.

Eventually the University of Berlin created an endowed chair, which
Steiner was to fill—indeed, he had, since 1834, been a member of the
Berlin Academy on the basis of his previous mathematical, or geometrical,
writings.

Life's Work

Steiner's mathematical publications commenced in 1826, while he still tutored at his vocational school. This creative production coincided with the founding by August Leopold Crelle of what became one of the nineteenth century's most famous mathematical publications, *Journal für die reine und angewandte Mathematik* (the journal for pure and applied mathematics). Professionally, Steiner expanded his reputation in 1832 with his *Systematische Entwicklung der Abhängigkeit Geometrischer Gestalten* (systematic evolution of the mutual dependence of geometrical forms), a planned introduction to a five-part series never to be completed.

Steiner's work does not readily reduce to layman's terms. It is projective geometry, built upon synthetic constructions. Geometry's basic forms are based on planes. Projective geometry moves from the fundamental plane to lines, planar pencils of lines to pencils of planes, bundles of lines, bundles of planes—and then into space itself, steadily generating higher geometric forms. For Steiner, one form in this projective hierarchy related with the others.

It was not the originality of Steiner's work that was dominant, although the questions he raised were then novel considering geometers' principal preoccupations. Steiner's own view was that "the writings of the present day have tried to reveal the organism by which the sundry phenomena of the external world are bound to one another." What he sought to determine was how "order enters into chaos," how all parts of the external world fit naturally into one another, and how related parts join to form well-defined groups. Specifically, it was the brilliantly stated and systematic treatment Steiner lent to his inquiries that gained for him his reputation.

The unique and justly famed French École Polytechnique, with its unparalleled training of France's intellectual elite and special concentration of intensive mathematical training had long before Steiner's day divided geometry into two branches: the analytical and the synthetic, or projective. In the early seventeenth century, René Descartes had explained how numbers could be utilized to describe points in a plane or in space algebraically. Steiner, however, concentrated on the other branch: projective geometry, which did not usually resort to the measurements or lengths of angles.

Steiner learned something from Johann Pestalozzi and his eccentric preoccupation with right triangles, and as a pedagogue Steiner, like Pestalozzi, encouraged his students' independent and rigorously logical search for learning. As might be expected, Steiner avoided figures to illustrate his lectures. His own intuitions were so much a part of his character, he sought both in teaching and writing to use them. Nor did he neglect his own disciplined scholarship. He read exhaustively the works of his European counterparts, staying on the cutting edge of his investigations.

Mathematical authorities agree that in midcareer Steiner still fell short of his goals by rejecting the achievements of some of his predecessors and contemporaries. For example, he lost the chance to employ signs drawn from

Karl August Möbius' synthetic geometry and therefore the opportunity for the full deployment of his imagination. It is small wonder that Steiner sometimes wrote of "the shadow land of geometry."

Steiner's practical ambitions, related to, but lying near or on the margin of his geometrical scholarship, were not as shadowy. Perhaps this was understandable, for in class-conscious Berlin and the German academic world, his social origins were not advantageous. His special professorship or chair created for him at Berlin University was partly an effort to avoid this implicit embarrassment. Moreover, the timing of his publications was partly calculated to advance him toward the directorship of Berlin's planned Polytechnic Institute. Hence, in 1833 he published a short work, *Die geometrischen Konstructionen, ausgeführt mittelst der geraden Linie und eines festen Kreises* (*Geometrical Constructions with a Ruler, Given a Fixed Circle with Its Center*, 1950), which was intended for high schools and for practical purposes. Indeed, following his appointment to his Berlin chair, he never completed what he promised would be a comprehensive work.

Steiner apparently was not surprised when analytical geometricians discovered that his own results could often be verified analytically. It was not so much that Steiner disdained others' analyses. Rather, he was headed in a different direction of inquiry, and he believed that analysis prevented geometricians from seeing things as they actually are. Like other projective geometers, he thought that because projective geometry could advance so swiftly from a few fundamental concepts to significant statements, he, like them, eschewed the formidable axiomatic studies that were the hallmark of Euclidean geometry. Most mathematicians argued against him, however, that despite Steiner's disclaimers, there was no royal road to a new geometry. No matter how logical, clear, and intuitive Steiner's projective geometry was, most geometricians actually wanted to see—metrically and analytically—what the projectivists were describing. Geometry was, for its nineteenth century scholars, simply too full of irrationals to make its results completely tenable.

Summary

Jakob Steiner was not the originator of projective or synthetic geometry. Nevertheless, his contributions were substantial and significant in the revival and advancement of synthetic geometry. This was the result of his clearly presented intuitions and his marvelous systematization of his projections. Before the close of his career, moreover, he had both trained others through the clarity of his lectures and writings and encouraged other geometricians such as Julius Plücker, Karl Weierstrass, and Karl von Staudt to resolve problems which had eluded or defeated him. These geometricians, through their own citations and references to his work, spread his name further throughout the European mathematical community. In addition, Steiner left a substantial body of published works.

By the 1850's, his health declined and the eccentricities of an always contentious character increased. He journeyed from spa to spa seeking the rejuvenation of his health. He died on April 1, 1863, at such a spa in Bern, Switzerland. Yet his repute and the respect of geometricians for his revitalization of synthetic geometry and its conundrums outlasted him.

Bibliography

Klein, Felix. *Development of Mathematics in the Nineteenth Century*. Translated by M. Ackerman. Brookline, Mass.: Math-Sci Press, 1979. Klein's work is indispensable, as very little of Steiner's writing has been translated into English. Filled with technical mathematical signs, symbols, and equations, it nevertheless contains much that is understandable by laymen. His expositions include biographical material on all mathematicians treated, with Steiner prominently among them, as well as good contextual explanations of their objectives, problems, and results. Contains ample illustrations.

Kline, Morris. *Mathematical Thought from Ancient to Modern Times*. New York: Oxford University Press, 1972. A layman's survey, which while largely ignoring Steiner, nevertheless places his work in a broad comprehensible framework. Contains illustrations, a good select bibliography, and an index.

Newman, James R., ed. *The World of Mathematics: A Small Library of the Literature of Mathematics from A'h-mosé, the Scribe, to Albert Einstein*. 4 vols. New York: Simon & Schuster, 1956. Volume 2 of this work is pertinent to Steiner's context and to defining aspects of his work. Illustrations help nonspecialists appreciate the nature of some synthetic, isoperimetric geometrical problems and their attempted solutions. A fine explication of certain projective geometrical investigations. There are bibliographical citations scattered throughout and a select bibliography and usable index at the end of the second volume.

Porter, Thomas Isaac. "A History of the Classical Isoperimetric Problem." In *Contributions to the Calculus of Variations, 1931-1932: Theses Submitted to the Department of Mathematics of the University of Chicago*. Chicago: University of Chicago Press, 1933. Rather than a raw thesis, this essay is an excellent survey of the synthetic geometrical problems Steiner, among others, tackled. Illustrated and readily understandable for those lacking special math training. Includes a substantial, if somewhat dated, bibliography.

Torretti, Roberto. *Philosophy of Geometry from Riemann to Poincaré*. Boston: Reidel, 1978. This important study is critical for a sound understanding by specialists as well as nonspecialists of a creative period in the development of both German and French mathematics, once again placing

Steiner in a somewhat different historical context from that of the works cited above. It has some illustrations, a select bibliography, and an index.

Clifton K. Yearley

STENDHAL
Marie-Henri Beyle

Born: January 23, 1783; Grenoble, France
Died: March 23, 1842; Paris, France
Area of Achievement: Literature
Contribution: Stendhal combined the themes of Romanticism with the style of realism. His insistence on telling the truth about emotions in simple, stark terms resulted in novels that, although not very popular during his lifetime, have become classics.

Early Life
Information about the life of Marie-Henri Beyle (who wrote as Stendhal) is voluminous and almost all suspect. Too much of it comes from his own autobiographical works—*Vie de Henry Brulard* (1890, 1949; *The Life of Henry Brulard*, 1925) and *Souvenirs d'égotisme* (1892, 1950; *Memoirs of Egotism*, 1949)—which are faithful accounts of Stendhal's feelings about the events of his life but not necessarily faithful accounts of the events themselves. His father, Chérubin Beyle, was a lawyer and, according to Stendhal, acquisitive and stern. His mother, Henriette Gagnon Beyle, to whom he was exceptionally close, was gay and urbane. The loss of his mother in 1790 was a devastating blow. His Aunt Séraphie Gagnon took over the task of rearing the seven-year-old Marie-Henri, but he found her a sour-tempered disciplinarian. Their relationship was never warm. His grandfather, Henri Gagnon, provided not only a cheerful refuge from his father and Aunt Séraphie but also an introduction to the intellectual world of the Enlightenment. The young Marie-Henri found little companionship outside his family. He was kept away from the other children of the community, whom his father and aunt regarded as common. His tutor, the Abbé Jean-François Raillane, was cold and old-fashioned. One of the many things Beyle liked about the French Revolution was that in 1794 Raillane had to flee from it.

One of the many reforms generated by the Revolution was the creation of local schools. Such an institution opened in Grenoble in 1796, and Beyle was enrolled. It was his first opportunity to mix freely with people his own age. His performance was poor during his first year. He soon fell head over heels in love with a theater performer, Virginie Kubly, and although they never actually met, she was his first passion. Romantic turmoil would never again be long absent from his life. By 1799, he had the opportunity to study mathematics at the École Polytechnique in Paris.

Beyle, however, never enrolled at the school. With the fascination of a small-town boy in the big city, he began to explore Paris. Within a month, he was seriously ill and was rescued by cousins named Daru, who gave him a place to stay and an introduction to society. Later, they obtained for him a position as clerk at the Ministry of War. Although Beyle's health returned, his illness caused him to lose much of his hair. From this time on, he wore a wig, and as he was stout, with short legs and a large head, he always felt physically inadequate. His luminous eyes were his only striking feature.

His position as a clerk proved depressing, but in May, 1800, Beyle was invited to join his cousins in Italy. En route, he visited Jean-Jacques Rousseau's birthplace in Geneva and then joined Napoleon I's army, which was passing through the St. Bernard Pass to surprise the Austrians. Milan entranced Beyle. He began learning Italian and was smitten by Angela Pietragrua, whose bureaucrat husband tolerated her many liaisons. Sexually uninitiated and still very shy, he was unsuccessful with Angela but contracted syphilis from a prostitute. Symptoms, apparently from this disease, recurred for the remainder of his life. In September, Pierre Daru was able to get his young cousin a provisional commission as sublieutenant in the cavalry. His posts in small rural villages proved boring, and Beyle soon finagled a staff position. Daru was angered because his name was used without his permission, and after a few months Beyle was ordered back to his regiment. He returned on October 26, 1801, only to fall ill; taking a medical leave, he set out for Grenoble.

He enjoyed his new status in his hometown and prolonged his leave, occupying his time by studying the philosophy of the Sensationalists. Beyle came to deny that man was rational, but although he rejected free will, he did conclude that the self-aware human could change his fate by living deliberately. Intellectually, he was growing up, and his long yearning for action was giving way to analysis. He resigned his commission and resolved to pursue a career of letters. Following yet another unrequited infatuation, he set off for Paris in April, 1802, to become a playwright.

Life's Work

For the next two years Beyle lived the life of a scholar in Paris, reading William Shakespeare, John Locke, Thomas Hobbes, and especially Antoine Destutt de Tracy, whose rationalism he found appealing. He tried unsuccessfully to write drama in verse and lived on a small allowance from his father, who was glad to have his son out of the army.

While taking acting lessons, Beyle fell in love with Mélanie Guilbert, a starlet of twenty-four and an unwed mother. In April, 1805, he agreed to accompany her to Marseilles, where she had a job and he had an opportunity to go into business with his friend Fortuné Mante. These plans soon fell apart. In the spring of 1806, he returned to Grenoble and began to seek the favor of Pierre Daru again. In October, he went to Brunswick with Pierre's brother Martial, who was to be intendant there. Beyle spent the next two years as a civil servant in Brunswick, bored but successful.

Beyle was now a favorite of Pierre Daru and a good friend of his wife,

Alexandrine, who with good grace and no ill will rebuffed a clumsy effort at seduction. On August 1, 1810, Beyle was appointed auditor of the Council of State. He was soon living sumptuously and beyond his means. He also began an affair with Angélina Bereyter, a member of the Opéra-Bouffe of the Théâtre Italien. Although the two remained together until 1814, the attraction for him was essentially physical.

After a leave in 1811, during which he toured his beloved Italy and renewed his courtship of Angélina Bereyter—successfully this time—Beyle asked to be reassigned to active military duty. He was sent off as a courier in the summer of 1812 and found himself following the army to Moscow. When Napoleon ordered retreat, Beyle was appointed commissioner of war supplies and ordered to organize supplies at Smolensk, Mohilar, and Vitebsk. With the retreat becoming little more than a rout, he could not continue his mission beyond the first city, and after much hardship and danger as he joined the flight, he got back to Paris on January 31, 1813. He was justly proud of his conduct but ready to be done with war.

In the spring, however, he was ordered back to duty and, surprisingly revitalized, was a witness to the Battle of Bautzen in May. He then fell ill, probably from typhus, but recuperated and was back in Milan in early September. His military experiences proved invaluable for later writing, when he became one of the first to portray battle realistically from the individual's perspective. At the end of the year, he returned to Paris, hoping to write comic plays and find a permanent situation in Italy. Instead, he was ordered to help prepare for the defense of Dauphiné. The strain was too much, and he was soon ill again. He took leave but, lacking income, had to give up his luxurious life-style. Eager to establish himself as an author, he published, at his own expense, a biographical study of the composers Joseph Haydn, Wolfgang Amadeus Mozart, and Pietro Metastasio in 1814, but the book was mostly plagiarized. He was fortunate that his love of secrecy and aliases had led him not to use his own name.

Unable to find a job, Beyle returned to Milan, where he tried to live on his army pension and renewed his relationship with Angela Pietragrua. Needing money, he devoted himself to writing, publishing two books in 1817, *Histoire de la peinture de Italie* (1817) and *Rome, Naples, et Florence en 1817* (1817, 1826; *Rome, Naples, and Florence in 1817*, 1818). The former was in part plagiarized, and the original parts were personal, emotional reactions to the work of various painters. The latter was a sort of travelog with commentary and was a minor success. It was also his first use of the name "Stendhal," taken from a small German town and used to obscure the identity of an author critical of the handling of Italy at the Congress of Vienna. It was to become Beyle's most common pseudonym and the one under which he became famous. Pleased by having had some success, Stendhal started the first of two efforts to write a study of Napoleon. Neither of these was ever finished, and the manuscripts were published only after his death. They do make clear the author's view of the young Napoleon as the heir of the Revolution, of the Empire as a betrayal of the revolutionary ideals, and of the restored Bourbon government as contemptible.

On March 4, 1818, Stendhal met Mathilde, Viscontini Dembowski, whom he always called Métilde. Wildly in love, he pursued her for three years, only to be repeatedly rejected. In 1821, penniless and again suffering from venereal disease, he returned to Paris. The relationship with Métilde resulted in *De l'amour* (1822; *Maxims of Love*, 1906), in which he offered a combination of objective analysis and confession. He was developing his characteristic style, combining the rationalism of the Enlightenment with the emotional outpourings of the Romantics.

Stendhal made his home in Paris for the next decade, visiting England twice and Italy once during those years. In 1823, he published part 1 of *Racine et Shakespare* (1823, 1825; *Racine and Shakespeare*, 1962). This work catapulted Stendhal from the rank of minor author into a prominent place among those battling over aesthetic standards. Stendhal's firm assertion that there are no permanent criteria for beauty put him clearly in the ranks of the Romantics. Shakespeare was his example of a playwright who rejected the traditions and took his art into glorious new realms. Stendhal continued his role of Romanticism's champion with *Vie de Rossini* (1823; *Memoirs of Rossini*, 1924), which defends Romantic music. As Stendhal's fame grew, so did his acquaintances among the literati of Paris; among his associates were Honoré de Balzac, Benjamin Constant, Alfred de Musset, Alphonse de Lamartine, and Adolphe Thiers. His love in the mid-1820's was Countess Clémentine (Menti) Curial, but though they remained friends, she ended the affair in 1826. Stendhal responded by writing *Armance* (1827; English translation, 1928), his first novel. Although generally regarded as a failure, *Armance*, which concerned the frustrations of love dampened by impotence, allowed Stendhal to express his sense of alienation and launched him on a career of writing fiction.

At the end of the decade, Stendhal, realizing that his greatest success had come with travel books, added *Promenades dans Rome* (1829; *A Roman Journal*, 1957), which became a popular guidebook to the city. He also had several brief love affairs. Suddenly, in 1830, Stendhal's years of struggle culminated in a work of genius. *Le Rouge et le noir* (*The Red and the Black*, 1898) was a brilliant blending of styles: first- and third-person perspectives, Romantic self-revelation, and classical external analysis. Stendhal achieved a remarkable shifting of perspectives among characters and narrator without losing simplicity or sacrificing the clarity of the story.

Even as Stendhal was producing *The Red and the Black*, France was undergoing the July Revolution, and with the establishment of the more liberal government of Louis-Philippe, the author hoped that he might again find a place in government service. He requested a job as consul in Italy and was posted to Trieste, only to be rejected by the Austrian government, which controlled that city, as a radical—his political comments in his travel books had not been forgotten. In February, 1831, he was named consul at Civitavecchia on the Tyrrhenian Sea, near Rome.

During his service at Civitavecchia, Stendhal wrote his two previously mentioned autobiographical pieces and the unfinished novel *Lucien Leuwen* (1855, 1894, 1926-1927; English translation, 1950). His writing was interrupted by intermittent ill health, and in March, 1836, he returned to Paris, where he remained for three very productive years. His most important work of this period was *La Chartreuse de Parme* (1839; *The Charterhouse of Parma*, 1895), which he expanded from one of his Italian short stories in about two months. The hero, Fabrice del Dongo, is more like the youthful Stendhal in being innocent and idealistic than was Julien Sorel of *The Red and the Black*, who is crafty and self-serving. Both characters, however, are examples of men who rise from relatively obscure beginnings and whose careers conclude on the executioner's scaffold.

In June of 1839, Stendhal reluctantly began his return to Civitavecchia, taking three months to make the trip. In the fall, he began a new novel, *Lamiel* (1889, 1971; English translation, 1950). Although typically Stendhalian in describing the struggle of an ambitious youth to find success and love, it is unusual in that the youth is, in this case, female. As a result of increasing problems with vertigo and, in March, 1841, an attack of apoplexy, Stendhal could not complete this novel. On October 21, 1841, he left for France, where, after attending a rally, he died of a stroke during a walk on March 23, 1842.

Summary

As a novelist, Stendhal broke new ground by his skillful combination of classical style and Romantic themes. All of his important works are consciously autobiographical, though they are much more concerned with accurate descriptions of feeling than of events. Despite the emphasis on the personal, the prose style remains simple and analytical, much more like that of the philosophes than the Romantics. With his ability to tell a story from shifting points of view, displaying the emotions of various characters, Stendhal was establishing a new novel form that would be a hallmark of the twentieth century.

Stendhal also contributed to social history. His travel works, such as *Mémoires d'un touriste* (1838; partial translation in *Memoirs of a Tourist*, 1962), offer not only travel notes but also social and political commentary. Such eyewitness accounts are always valuable, but when the witness has the sensitivity of a Stendhal, their value is much enhanced. Thus, his writings are still read as both history and literature.

Bibliography
Alter, Robert, with Carol Cosman. *A Lion for Love: A Critical Biography of Stendhal*. New York: Basic Books, 1979. The emphasis of this volume is criticism, and its authors do an excellent job of presenting their analysis of Stendhal in a historical context. Not the book to read, however, for a clear chronological description of his life.
Atherton, John. *Stendhal*. London: Bowes & Bowes, 1965. A short but effectively done biography. Atherton's comments are insightful and well grounded in research.
Brombert, Victor H. *Stendhal: Fiction and the Themes of Freedom*. New York: Random House, 1968. Although a work of criticism, this book contains much biographical information, and it gives a useful analysis of the themes in Stendhal's fiction. Ties his work into what is known of the nineteenth century novel.
May, Gita. *Stendhal and the Age of Napoleon*. New York: Columbia University Press, 1977. An excellent, full biography that provides a detailed chronological account of Stendhal's life. The best straightforward biography available.
Strickland, Geoffrey. *Stendhal: The Education of a Novelist*. New York: Cambridge University Press, 1974. An attempt to analyze the forces that shaped Stendhal and to show how those forces influenced his work. It is both biographical and critical, and although it could not replace a traditional biography, it does provide much useful analysis with a biographical foundation.

Fred R. van Hartesveldt

ANTONIO STRADIVARI

Born: 1644?; Cremona?, Duchy of Milan
Died: December 18, 1737; Duchy of Milan
Area of Achievement: Music
Contribution: Stradivari, the most famous violin maker in history, modified the traditional design of the violin as it had developed for one hundred years in Cremona. He created instruments during his lifetime that are renowned for their superb tonal quality and have been the models for violin making ever since.

Early Life

Antonio Stradivari was born into a family whose name can be traced in Cremona to the twelfth century; however, no record of his birth has been found in the various archives of Cremona, despite repeated efforts on the part of researchers. It is known that he was the son of Alessandro Stradivari, and his birth date has been tentatively established as 1644, based on notations of his age written on labels in violins that he made near the end of his life. The Latin form of his name, Stradivarius, is also found on the labels of his violins; this spelling is often used to refer to an instrument made by Stradivari.

The early years of Stradivari remain a mystery; he may have been apprenticed first as a wood-carver; beginning no later than the early 1660's, however, he studied the art of violin making with Niccolò Amati in Cremona. Amati, the leading violin maker of his day, represented the third generation of the Cremonese family who had created and developed the modern form of the instrument.

By 1666, if not earlier, Stradivari began to make violins on his own, and in the next year he established his own household and shop when he married Francesca Feraboschi. Six children were born to this marriage including two, Francesco and Omobono, who became violin makers and worked with their father.

The number of violins Stradivari produced before 1680 was not large; his reputation at this point did not extend far beyond Cremona, so the demand for his violins was not great. It is believed that during this time he designed and constructed a number of other instruments, especially plucked-string instruments such as guitars, harps, lutes, and mandolins. It is also clear that he continued to assist in his teacher's workshop for several years after he established his own shop, possibly up to the time of Amati's death in 1684. The few instruments that survive from this early period show that Stradivari was already a master craftsman who, although following the basic pattern of Amati, was cultivating his own ideas about the best tonal and artistic designs for the violin.

Life's Work

In 1680, Stradivari purchased a house at No. 2, Piazza San Domenico (later redesignated Piazza Roma), which was to be both home and workshop for the rest of his life. That he was able to purchase this three-story structure with a ground-floor shop at the front and ample living space for his family is good evidence of the financial success he was already enjoying. This new house had an attic and loft in which Stradivari is reported to have worked, leaving his varnished instruments to dry there during good weather.

From this house, Stradivari produced most of his stringed instruments, the most important and valuable such instruments ever made. Of an estimated output of eleven hundred instruments, approximately 650 are extant, some preserved in collections and museums but many of them in active use by some of the great string players of the present time. In addition to his celebrated violins, Stradivari also made other instruments of the violin family, violas and cellos.

In the 1680's, Stradivari built instruments that show an increasing independence from the models of Amati; he created violins with a more solid and robust appearance and a more powerful tone than those of his teacher. The color of the varnish on these instruments still shows the typical yellowish tint of Amati's workshop, but sometimes Stradivari added a darker reddish accent. The number of violins produced during this time increased as his fame spread beyond Cremona, and Amati's death in 1684 left him with no serious rival as the greatest violin maker of that city.

One of the remarkable qualities of Stradivari was his continuing search for any means which would produce a better instrument. The 1690's saw him working with a newly proportioned instrument known as the "long pattern," or "long Strad." In this design, he added 5/16 of an inch to the length of the violin without increasing the width. At the same time, he made subtle alterations in the design to keep the symmetry of the instrument intact. The effect of this new design was to produce a richer, darker tonal quality reminiscent of the sound produced by violins made in Brescia, the only other Italian city to rival Cremona in violin making.

In 1698, Stradivari's wife died and was given an elaborate funeral, and in August of the next year the fifty-five-year-old craftsman married Antonia Maria Zambelli. Five children, none of whom followed in the father's profession, came from this union. The years from 1700 to 1720 represent the peak of Stradivari's illustrious career and are often called the "golden period." His violin designs of this time moved away from the long pattern, and the tonal qualities of the instruments demonstrate a marvelous combination of the darker, richer tone of the previous era and the lighter, sweeter tone from the Cremonese tradition. In these years, Stradivari used the best materials that he (or anyone else) ever put into a violin; especially noteworthy are the magnificent maple backs of many instruments. The varnish now reached the orange-brown tint that is regarded as the typical Stradivari color.

Because of the great value and importance of individual instruments produced by Stradivari, names are used to identify them, names of owners or names associated with some story connected with the particular instrument. Many of the violins made during the golden period are among the most famous: the "Betts" of 1704, now in Washington, D.C., at the Library of Congress; the "Alard" of 1715, which some experts regard as the finest extant Stradivarius; the "Messiah" or "Salabue" of 1716, which was never sold by Stradivari and has been preserved in the best condition of any of his violins, now on display in the Ashmolean Museum in Oxford, England.

It was also during the period from 1700 to 1720 that Stradivari became especially interested in the development of the smaller cellos that were being sought by performers who were evolving the solo capabilities of this instrument. Earlier cellos were larger in size, designed to be an accompanying bass instrument. Stradivari had built a few of these larger instruments, but from 1707 through 1710 he produced a series of the smaller cellos that set the modern standard for the design of that instrument, an achievement no less significant than what he accomplished for the violin.

After 1720, when he was seventy-six years old, Stradivari might have been expected to turn most of the work over to his sons, Francesco and Omobono, who had assisted him through the years, but such was not the case. During the decade of the 1720's, he remained very active in the production of violins. The tonal quality of these instruments is very high, even though the wood he used is not as beautiful as that of the previous period, and there are occasional signs of old age in details of workmanship.

The number of instruments produced after 1730 dwindles considerably, but it is clear that Stradivari continued to make violins by himself up to the last year of his life. While in these very late instruments the workmanship shows clear signs of failing hand and eye, the basic design and execution remain those of a master. There are also a number of instruments from this time that were made jointly by Stradivari, his sons, and his pupil Carlo Bergonzi. These instruments are labeled as made "under the discipline of Antonio Stradivari."

That this man was still actively engaged in his profession at the age of ninety-three is indicative of the remarkable constitution that he must have enjoyed. There are no authentic portraits of Stradivari; a contemporary described him as tall and thin, always to be seen wearing a white cap and a white leather apron—his work clothes. On December 18, 1737, Stradivari died; his second wife had preceded him in death by nine months. They were buried in a tomb located in the Chapel of the Rosary in the Church of San Domenico just across from the Stradivari house. Other members of the family were buried there through 1781, but in the nineteenth century the church was neglected, falling into such disrepair that in 1869 it was demolished and a public park was laid out on the site. Only the name stone of the tomb is preserved in the Civic Museum in Cremona, where there are to be found also drawings, patterns for instruments, and other artifacts of Antonio Stradivari.

Summary
Antonio Stradivari brought the art of violin making to its highest level, unsurpassed even to the present day. He patiently and persistently explored the possibilities of the instrument that had been passed on to him by the master builders of his era. At the same time he was constantly searching for better ways of creating the greatest tonal and artistic beauty in these instruments.

During his lifetime, Stradivari was certainly highly regarded and widely known for his skill as a violin maker, for he received commissions for his instruments from many affluent individuals and royal courts. Many of the performers of this time, however, still preferred the designs of Amati and those of Jakob Steiner, the Austrian violin maker who produced fine instruments with a smaller but more brilliant tone. By the end of the eighteenth century, with changing musical styles and the need for a greater volume of sound from musical instruments, Stradivari's designs for the violin became the clearly favored pattern and have remained so up to the present time.

The fact that these instruments, made several hundred years ago, not only are the best instruments made up to that time, but are also acclaimed as unsurpassed since that time, has led many to search for some special secret possessed by Stradivari that explains the dominance of his instruments. The particular characteristics of the wood that he used and the varnish on his instruments have been the subject of intense study and speculation for years. Certainly the choice of materials is important, as is the varnish (not only the recipe but also the manner of application), but most authorities agree that Stradivari's secret was his genius in combining all of the various materials, design, and execution in a way that makes a Stradivarius the ultimate of the violin maker's art.

Bibliography
Balfoort, Dirk J. *Antonius Stradivarius*. Translated by W. A. G. Doyle-Davidson. Stockholm: Continental Book Co., 1947. A concise account of Stradivari's life, interwoven with good descriptions of the different periods of instrument making. Also included are a number of photographs not to be found in other sources.
Doring, Ernest N. *How Many Strads? Our Heritage from the Master*. Chicago: William Lewis & Son, 1945. A listing and description of the instruments produced by Stradivari, divided into eight periods. Doring tabulates 509 instruments in this work with detailed ownership histories for many of them, while others can be identified only very briefly. Photographs of

more than one hundred instruments are included, and there is also a chapter on Stradivari's two violin-making sons.

Goodkind, Herbert K. *Violin Iconography of Antonio Stradivari, 1644-1737.* Larchmont, N.Y.: Herbert K. Goodkind, 1972. A large deluxe volume which has as its main purpose a complete inventory of all known Stradivari instruments; seven hundred such string instruments are listed and described here. Photographs of four hundred instruments are a major part of this work, and there is a valuable index of thirty-five hundred names of owners. Some essays on Stradivari and certain aspects of his violins and an extensive bibliography of more than 150 items are included.

Henley, William. *Antonio Stradivari, Master Luthier, Cremona, Italy, 1644-1737: His Life and Instruments.* Edited by C. Woodcock. Sussex, England: Amati, 1961. The bulk of this small volume is devoted to a chronological listing with brief descriptions of 455 Stradivari violins, violas, and cellos. Short chapters on Stradivari's life and periods of work and an editor's foreword dealing with fake instruments are included.

Hill, W. Henry, Arthur F. Hill, and Alfred E. Hill. *Antonio Stradivari: His Life and Work (1644-1737).* London: William E. Hill and Sons, 1902. Reprint. New York: Dover, 1963. The standard work on Stradivari's life and instruments, written by three brothers who were violin experts and devoted much of their lives to the study of Stradivari and other string instrument makers of the seventeenth and eighteenth centuries. Incorporates unpublished research of A. Mandelli of Cremona.

Byron A. Wolverton

JOHANN STRAUSS

Born: October 25, 1825; Vienna, Austria
Died: June 3, 1899; Vienna, Austria
Area of Achievement: Music
Contribution: Strauss built upon the musical achievements of his father and
Austrian dance composer Joseph Lanner to raise the waltz to its highest
level of development, a point at which it passed from dance music to
symphonic music. His achievements in the operetta were less dramatic,
for only two of his operettas have received lasting acclaim.

Early Life

Johann Strauss was born in Vienna, Austria, the eldest child of Johann
and Anna (Streim) Strauss, both of whom were musically accomplished.
Indeed, the father's reputation as a composer, performer, and conductor of
waltzes was already established when the younger Strauss was born. The
younger Strauss early demonstrated his musical gift when, at the age of six,
he played a waltz tune on the piano. Despite the considerable musical talent
of all of his sons, the elder Strauss forbade them to pursue their interests,
allowing them to play only the piano, not the violin, the instrument essential
to waltz composition. Strauss's mother, however, not only preserved his first
composition but also successfully circumvented her husband's prohibition
against the violin lessons. The conspiracy between son and mother, who
provided one of her husband's violins and the money for the lessons, was
eventually discovered by the elder Strauss, who destroyed the violin and beat
his son.

Although his father had enrolled him in the prestigious Schottengym-
nasium for four years and the Polytechnikum, where he studied business, for
an additional two years, Strauss was able to escape the banking career that
his father intended for him when the elder Strauss left his family for Emily
Trampusch in 1842. Strauss had secretly studied the violin under Franz
Amon, whose position as conductor of one of the Strauss orchestras made
him familiar with the elder Strauss's gestures and mannerisms, which the
younger Strauss imitated. When Strauss could openly pursue his musical
career, he continued his violin studies with Anton Kohlmann, ballet master
and violinist at the Kärnthnertortheater, and studied music theory with
Joseph Drechsler, organist and composer of church music. Under Drechsler's
tutelage and prodding, Strauss composed a church cantata, though Strauss's
real interest was in waltz composition.

Because of his father's stubborn opposition, Strauss encountered many
obstacles when he attempted to stage his first concert. The elder Strauss, by
suggesting that he would musically boycott any ballroom allowing his son to
perform, effectively closed the Viennese musical world to his son. Strauss

accordingly went outside the inner city and staged his first concert at Dommayer's Casino at Heitzing, a suburb of Vienna, on October 15, 1844. Despite the somewhat hostile crowd—his father's business manager, Carl Hirsche, had provided tickets to rowdies to disrupt the concert, which consisted of Strauss's own waltz compositions—the *Sinngedichte* (poems of the senses) earned nineteen encores. One reviewer wrote, "Good evening, Father Strauss! Good morning to you, Strauss Junior!"

After his son's triumphant debut, the elder Strauss offered his son a position as concertmaster and assistant conductor, but the offer was refused. The two men effected a reconciliation of sorts, but their essential differences surfaced in 1848, when civil war erupted. The conservative elder Strauss sided with the Royalists, and his son sided with the rebels. Though neither Strauss's political commitment was strong, the change from waltzes to marches did produce some notable music. When the revolt was brutally crushed and Francis Joseph became emperor, the younger Strauss incurred royal displeasure, but his father's fate was worse: a decline in personal popularity, unprofitable tours, depression, and in 1849 death from scarlet fever. With his father's death, the son began a career that would establish him as "the Waltz King."

Life's Work

After his father's death, Strauss assumed control of his father's orchestra and at his first concert, October 11, 1849, played Mozart's *Requiem*, thereby winning the loyalty of the Viennese, some of whom had resented his challenge to his father. He also partly atoned for his political "error" of 1848 by his 1854 performance of his popular *Annen-Polka* at the ball prior to Francis Joseph's marriage to Elisabeth von Wittelsbach. In the 1850's, the waltz craze captivated Vienna, and the prolific Strauss produced scores of new waltzes to meet the increasing demand. While many of the compositions were named for professional associations and societies—the astute Strauss knew how to market his product—only one, the *Acceleration Waltz* (written for the students of the Vienna engineering school), involved a marriage of title and music.

So popular were Strauss's waltzes and so exhausting was his conducting schedule (he conducted daily, and often more than one of his orchestras) that in 1853 he had to convalesce in the Alps. It was this hectic pace that resulted in his drafting his brother Joseph, who was an engineer, as a conductor. (Strauss later persuaded his brother Eduard to assume a similar role.) Because he had been freed from sole responsibility for the family business, Strauss could tour and perform abroad as his father had done. In 1854, he signed a contract to perform yearly in Russia at the resort of Pavlovsk, and he toured Europe with an orchestra between 1856 and 1886.

Aside from his abortive relation- ;; with Olga Smirnitzki, whom he had met in Pavlovsk, Strauss had only casual liaisons with women until 1862, when he met and married Jetty Treffz, an older woman who had been mistress to Baron Moritz Todesco. In a sense, Jetty replaced Anna Strauss. Released in 1864 from all contractual obligations as conductor of the family orchestral business, Strauss turned to composition at the mansion he and Jetty had bought at Heitzing. The 1860's were marked by Strauss's greatest waltzes, *Tales from the Vienna Woods* and *The Blue Danube*, though the latter, which was originally written for performance with a choral group, was initially a failure, primarily because of the lyrics. When it was later played in Paris as a purely orchestral performance, it was so well received that it became the musical motif of the International Exhibition of 1867.

Strauss's triumph in Paris resulted in an invitation to England in 1867, where he won more critical acclaim. His most notable tour, however, occurred in 1872, when he was paid $100,000 to appear at the World's Peace Jubilee in Boston. There, before an outdoor audience of 100,000 people, he conducted, with the help of many assistant conductors, an orchestra of 1,087 instruments. This musical extravaganza, later repeated on a more modest scale in New York, appalled Strauss, who nevertheless thereby became the richest musician of his time.

Even though the waltz was virtually synonymous with Strauss and Vienna, another musical form began gaining favor among the Viennese. Jacques Offenbach had popularized the operetta, a kind of parodic opera with a socially subversive message. Jetty and Maximilian Steiner, impresario of the Theatre an der Wien, convinced Strauss to apply his talent to the operetta. Had he remembered the fate of *The Blue Danube*, Strauss might well have foreseen that music without a suitable libretto was doomed to failure. In addition, Strauss seemed an unlikely composer for operetta because he had had practically no exposure to theater and consequently knew little about dramatic composition; he was simply more comfortable with music than with language. On the other hand, he already had found the constraints of the waltz formats incompatible with his developing symphonic interests.

The first operetta was not staged because of casting problems; the next two, with mediocre librettos, were comparative failures with brief runs. Yet *Die Fledermaus* (1874; the bat), his third effort, proved to be an enormous success, though its farcical content was at odds with a depressed Vienna, which had just suffered a stock market crash. The operetta, involving a masked ball and a confusion of characters, was adapted from a play and had a good plot; the libretto by Richard Genée and Karl Hafner was exceptional. In fact, *Die Fledermaus* marked the zenith of Strauss's career in operetta, and, though he wrote several more, he did not return to the form until 1885, when *Der Zigeunerbaron* (the gypsy baron) was staged. Like *Die Fledermaus*, *Der Zigeunerbaron* succeeded because the music and the libretto, which was by Ignaz Schnitzer, were complementary rather than at odds.

During the eleven years between his operetta successes, Strauss's life changed dramatically. Jetty, the inspiration for his more serious music and his operetta efforts, died in 1877. After a disastrous five-year marriage to Angelica Dietrich, who was thirty-three years his junior, he married in 1887 Adele Deutsch Strauss, a young widow, with whom he spent his remaining years. In order to divorce Angelica and marry Adele, he had to become a Protestant, surrender his Austrian citizenship, and become a citizen of the Duchy of Saxe-Coburg-Gotha.

His marriage and his developing friendship with Johannes Brahms made Strauss's last years contented ones. He continued to write operettas, as well as some orchestral waltzes. One of his most notable waltzes was the *Kaiser-waltzer* (1888; emperor waltz), written in celebration of Francis Joseph's forty-year reign. This piece is both waltz and march, suggesting the emperor's glory, and has been regarded as more tone poem than dance. Such was the identification between "the Waltz King" and Francis Joseph that Strauss's death on June 3, 1899, was regarded as the end of a political as well as a musical era.

Summary

The Strauss family's virtual control of the music business in Vienna paralleled the dominance of the Habsburg dynasty, which in the nineteenth century enjoyed one of its most opulent and successful periods. The waltz and the beauty and harmony it represented became a kind of opium of the people, and the Habsburg prosperity created a mood receptive to it. The acknowledged "Waltz King" was the younger Johann Strauss, arguably one of the most Viennese of composers.

Strauss found in the waltz the almost perfect vehicle for his own personality, which had its dark side. Beneath the sweeping vitality and lush sweetness of the waltz was a wistful melancholy especially suited to Strauss. The waltz, however, became a prison for him as he attempted to force his musical inspiration into the tyranny of monotonous three-quarter time. As he developed, absorbing not only the waltz influence from his father and Joseph Lanner but also the more liberating influence of Franz Liszt and Richard Wagner, he was inevitably drawn toward the symphonic and away from the demands of the dance industry. His waltzes accordingly changed; the introduction and coda became almost as long as the waltz proper.

For his operettas, Strauss used the work of Jacques Offenbach and Franz von Suppé as the foundation for his own efforts. In his *Der Zigeunerbaron*, however, he transcended his predecessors and actually gave the operetta a new direction that was followed by others, including Franz Lehár. Strauss, in effect, brought both nineteenth century music forms to their artistic heights, but neither form was to survive the cultural and political upheaval that also accounted for the Habsburgs' demise. Strauss embodied the nineteenth century, and his grave, opposite Schubert's and next to Brahms's in the Central Cemetery in Vienna, testifies to his stature not only in Austria but also in the universal world of music.

Bibliography
Fantel, Hans. *The Waltz Kings: Johann Strauss, Father and Son, and Their Romantic Age*. New York: William Morrow, 1972. While Fantel provides biographies of the two Strausses, he stresses the relationship of music to politics so that the reader has a broad cultural and political context for tracing the evolution of the waltz. The well-written, informal text is well indexed, and Fantel provides a good bibliography, particularly of the extramusical context, and a list of the compositions of father and son.
Gartenberg, Egon. *Johann Strauss: The End of an Era*. University Park: Pennsylvania State University Press, 1974. Places Austria in a broader European political context and provides an interesting account of the predecessors of the waltz. Gartenberg analyzes *Die Fledermaus* in detail and explains why Strauss's operettas, with two exceptions, did not succeed critically. Profusely illustrated, well indexed, and documented—contains bibliographies concerning the Strauss family, as well as the literature and music of the period, the Habsburg dynasty, and the political context.
Jacob, Heinrich E. *Johann Strauss, Father and Son: A Century of Light Music*. Translated by Marguerite Wolff with an introduction by Pitts Sanborn. Freeport, N.Y.: Books for Libraries Press, 1939. Jacob stresses the conditions in Vienna that facilitated the development of the waltz, relates Strauss's waltzes to other contemporary music, and devotes much attention to the operettas. Although the focus is on the Strauss family, Jacob does discuss the heirs, notably Franz Lehár, to the Strauss tradition.
Pastene, Jerome. *Three-Quarter Time: The Life and Music of the Strauss Family of Vienna*. Westport, Conn.: Greenwood Press, 1971. Pastene divides his book into three parts: Johann Strauss, the father; Johann Strauss, the son; and the other Strauss sons and Lehár. Pastene, himself a conductor, provides lengthy analyses of several major works and also includes a catalog by opus numbers and the works by the four members of the Strauss musical dynasty.
Wechsberg, Joseph. *The Waltz Emperors: The Life and Times and Music of the Strauss Family*. New York: G. P. Putnam's Sons, 1973. Wechsberg discusses the origins of the waltz, defines the era of the waltz as beginning with Joseph Lanner and ending with Strauss's death in 1899, finds Strauss's best waltzes really symphonic music, and explores the psychological side of his subject. The book is profusely illustrated (many of the illustrations are in color) with memorabilia and lithographs.

Thomas L. Erskine

SÜLEYMAN THE MAGNIFICENT

Born: 1494 or 1495; probably in İstanbul, Ottoman Empire
Died: September 5 or 6, 1566; near Sziget, Hungary
Areas of Achievement: Government, politics, and law
Contribution: Süleyman I was undoubtedly the best-known Ottoman Turkish
sultan: He extended the domains of the Ottoman Empire eastward, establishing a long-lasting border between the Sunni Turks and the Shi'ite
realm under the Safavid shahs. His reign marked a period of internal
stability, primarily through an ordered system of laws.

Early Life

Süleyman I, tenth in the line of Ottoman Turkish sultans, was the son of
Sultan Selim I (ruled 1512-1520) by his wife Aisha Sultan. Aisha Sultan was
herself the daughter of a prestigious Islamic ruler, Menghli Giray, the head
of the Black Sea Crimean khanate. Little is known about Süleyman's early
education in the palace environment of İstanbul. The young prince received
practical training, first as governor of the district, or *sancak*, of Kaffa,
during the sultanate of his grandfather Bayezid II, and later, under Selim, as
governor of the province of Manisa (ancient Lydia, in Asia Minor).

Possibly because Selim was such a dominant sultanic authority, his son's
succession at the time of Selim's death seems to have come automatically,
without the necessity of advance preparation to avert internal intrigues between rival pretenders. Once on the Ottoman throne, Süleyman proved that
he was more than worthy of Selim's confidence in his administrative as well
as his military capacities.

Life's Work

The Ottoman sultan whose reputation is symbolized by the Western epithet, "the Magnificent," carried a different title in Ottoman tradition. The
nearly half-century rule of Süleyman (from 1520 to 1566) earned for him the
Ottoman epithet *Qanuni*, or law giver. This honor resulted largely from the
fact that he systematized imperial Turkish rule over diverse provinces conquered by his predecessors in Christian Europe and in the Arab Islamic zone.
Süleyman's reign was also marked by repeatedly spectacular demonstrations
of Turkish strength. Süleyman personally commanded thirteen major Ottoman military campaigns, ten against European adversaries and three in Asia
against Islamic rivals.

Süleyman's reputation for military leadership began in the first two years
of his reign, when he captured the city of Belgrade (1521) and the island
fortress of Rhodes (1522). From then on, Ottoman armies would play an
important role in the international game of influence between the French
Valois king Francis I and the Austrian Habsburg emperor and Spanish king

Charles V. The latter was a natural rival of Süleyman because the Habsburg and Ottoman empires were both tempted to expand claims over the territory of weaker Danubian neighbors.

First, at the battle of Mohács in 1526, when the Ottomans toppled the last medieval Hungarian dynasty, killing King Louis II, and again in the spectacular campaign of 1529, the future of Hungary was the object of Habsburg-Ottoman struggles. These ended, at least temporarily, when Süleyman laid siege to Vienna itself in September, 1529. After this extraordinary show of force, Süleyman was able to ensure recognition of his protégé-king John Zápolya in Buda.

From the Danubian valley, the focus of Ottoman imperial pretensions spread to North Africa. Here again, despite Habsburg efforts to stop the sultan's expansionist diplomacy, Ottoman domination would become increasingly imminent in the 1530's. An important sign of Süleyman's intention to bring the North African areas into closer dependence on the Ottoman Empire was his appointment of Khayr ad-Dīn (known in the West as Barbarossa), perhaps the dominant renegade corsair leader along the North African coast, to the post of *kapudan pasha* (Ottoman high admiral) in 1533.

In 1534, Süleyman also succeeded in annexing Iraq to the empire— defeating the Safavid Persian shah's claims. From their southernmost bases in Iraq, the Ottoman navy could proceed to dominate the Persian Gulf, entering the Indian Ocean at the height of Süleyman's reign. Süleyman took great interest in the newly annexed Ottoman province of Iraq. He built an important mausoleum in Baghdad for Abu Hanifah, founder of the Hanifite school of Islamic law (the "official" school followed by the Ottomans). He also personally visited the most important Islamic shrines of Iraq, including the holy Shi'a sites of Nedjef and Karbala.

By the 1540's and 1550's, it was quite clear that, with the exception of the westernmost area of North Africa (the independent sultanate of Morocco), all major Arab zones of the eastern and southern Mediterranean would fall under the suzerainty of Süleyman or his immediate successors. Only the borders of the Danubian west and eastern Anatolia, where the struggle with the Safavid shah went on until the Treaty of Amasia in 1555, were still in question. It might have been possible to gain a comparable treaty with Süleyman's Habsburg rival, Emperor Ferdinand I, who had never abandoned hopes of dominating Hungary. Apparently Süleyman's Grand Vizier Rustem (who was also his son-in-law) made this impossible until his death in 1561. No sooner had Süleyman signed a treaty (1561) than, with the advent of a new Habsburg monarch (Emperor Maximilian), new hostilities erupted.

The last five years of Süleyman's long reign seemed to be marked with signs of both personal and political decline. The death of his wife Khurram demoralized the sultan. Two of his sons, Princes Bayezid and Selim, began a bitter rivalry. The tragic outcome of this split, which ended with the execution of Bayezid, not only shook the sultanic family itself but also affected the interests of contending political groups who could no longer be certain how to organize support for the future sultan, Selim II. Nevertheless, Süleyman's visible strength was enhanced by his choice of a new grand vizier, Mehmed Sokollu. Süleyman accompanied his armies, now virtually under Sokollu's command, one more time, to the Hungarian battlefield of Szigetköz. Although the Ottomans were successful in this confrontation with their perennial Christian enemies, Süleyman died during the campaign, presumably without knowledge of his army's victory.

Summary

The reign of Süleyman the Magnificent can be considered representative of the golden age of the Ottoman Empire, which ran roughly from 1450 to about 1600: The empire at that time was politically, militarily, and culturally strong. Probably the outstanding example of the strength of Ottoman political and military organization was the Janissary (literally, new army) corps. Although this military corps had arisen at least a century before Süleyman's sultanate, it seems to have reached the zenith of its efficiency in the first half of the sixteenth century. What the Janissaries represented militarily was characteristic of the entire structure of Ottoman rule under Süleyman: absolute loyalty and individual subservience to the sultan.

Süleyman was careful to maintain and control the Ottoman institution that could provide for such a system of unquestionable loyalty; this was the *devshirme*, or levy of non-Turkish conscripts, who were mainly Christian youths "contributed" by subject populations in the Balkan zone or raided areas beyond Ottoman frontiers. Such conscripts, called *kapi kullar* (slaves of the imperial gate), were brought into the special schools of İstanbul and given special training to prepare them for very select service, either as military elites or bureaucratic officials—such high-ranking officers as the grand vizier could be drawn from these men. Since their sole source of sponsorship was the palace at İstanbul, such elites could be sent to any area of the empire at the sultan's will.

In Süleyman's time, the practical results of such centralization were still quite visible: There were very few acts of insubordination, either within the formal imperial administration or on the part of provincial populations under Ottoman rule. In this respect, Ottoman governing institutions under Süleyman represented a considerably more efficient substructure for monarchical authority than could be found anywhere else, either in Europe or in the immediately adjacent areas of western Asia under the Ottomans' neighbors, the Safavid shahs of Iran. The unquestioned authority of the sultanate probably contributed to other symbols of self-assurance in the Ottoman Empire under Süleyman I. There are suggestions, in the form of the great *ganunnahmes*, or "books of law" prepared under the sultan's supervision for each major province of the empire, of a pervading sense of social and economic order that would have affected not only elite but also all classes of governed populations, whether Christian, Jewish, or Islamic. One may still observe, in the splendid architectural monuments (especially mosques and schools, or *medreses*) erected by Süleyman's chief architect, Sinan Pasha, models of structural support and harmony which, in purely aesthetic terms, reflected the assurance of imperial supremacy.

Bibliography

Fisher, Sydney N. *The Middle East: A History*. New York: Alfred A. Knopf, 1968. Chapter 17 of this well-known general history is entitled "The Ottoman Empire as a World Power." In addition to providing a comprehensive review of the major events of Süleyman's reign, Fisher covers a number of cultural topics including Ottoman literature and architecture of the period.

Gibb, H. A. R., and Harold Bowen. *Islamic Society and the West: A Study of the Impact of Western Civilization on Moslem Culture in the Near East*. Vol. 1, *Islamic Society in the Eighteenth Century*. New York: Oxford University Press, 1960. Although the joint authors of this work dedicate the majority of their analysis to Islamic society in the eighteenth century, chapters 2 and 3 ("Caliphate and Sultanate" and "The Ruling Institution") provide essential details of the internal organization of the Ottoman Empire in the age of Süleyman I. These include discussions of the army and central administration, both originally recruited by means of the *devshirme* system.

Hodgson, Marshall G. S. *The Venture of Islam: Conscience and History in a World Civilization*. Vol. 2, *The Gunpowder Empires and Modern Times*. Chicago: University of Chicago Press, 1974. Chapter 3 of this volume is entitled "The Ottoman Empire: *Shari'ah*—Military Alliance, 1517-1718." In this section dealing with the strongest period of Ottoman history, the author provides an analytical framework for comparing prototypes of government and society in several geographical areas of Islamic civilization. The Ottoman model represented by Süleyman is compared with that of the Safavid shahs in Iran and the "Indo-Timuri" (Mughal) empire of India.

Inalcik, Halil. "The Heyday and Decline of the Ottoman Empire." In *The Further Islamic Lands, Islamic Society and Civilizations*. Vol. 2 in *The Cambridge History of Islam*, edited by P. M. Holt, Ann K. S. Lambton, and Bernard Lewis. Cambridge: Cambridge University Press, 1970. This is the most concise history of the Ottoman Empire in the age of Süleyman. Like most other political histories dealing with the reign of Süleyman, it turns very quickly to a discussion of decline under his immediate successors, particularly under Selim.

Lybyer, Albert H. *The Government of the Ottoman Empire in the Time of Suleiman the Magnificent.* Cambridge, Mass.: Harvard University Press, 1913. This is one of the earliest attempts by a Western historian to provide a comprehensive history of Süleyman's reign. Nevertheless it provides basic facts and the beginnings of an analytical framework for discussing the structures of the Ottoman "ruling institution," a term and concept taken over and developed in much greater detail by H. A. R. Gibb and Harold Bowen in the 1950's.

Byron D. Cannon

BERTHA VON SUTTNER

Born: June 9, 1843; Prague, Austro-Hungarian Empire
Died: June 21, 1914; Vienna, Austro-Hungarian Empire
Areas of Achievement: Literature and social reform
Contribution: Suttner inspired and organized peace movements and was instrumental in persuading Alfred Nobel to establish the Peace Prize named for him. Her novel *Die Waffen nieder!* (1889; *Lay Down Your Arms*, 1892) was a clarion call for disarmament.

Early Life

Bertha von Suttner, née Countess Kinsky, was born in Prague into an old noble family with a long and distinguished military tradition. Her father, Field Marshal Count Joseph Kinsky, died before she was born. On her mother's side, Kinsky was related to the poet Joseph von Korner. In her teens, she dreamed of a career as an opera singer; she was encouraged in this, but, after a short while, she realized that her talent was insufficient. A precocious child, she read Plato's works and those of Alexander von Humboldt, a great German scientist, before she was sixteen. From her governesses she learned French and English. Later, she taught herself Italian. Kinsky must have been a beautiful girl. When she was only thirteen years old, a prince wanted to marry her, and in letters she is invariably mentioned as a very lovely girl. She was an only and very lonely child, and until the age of twelve she had no playmates. This experience reinforced her inclination to live in a world of dreams and fantasies.

After her father's death, her mother was left with a modest income, but the expenses of Kinsky's singing lessons and her mother's compulsive gambling at the fashionable casinos diminished their limited funds. At the age of thirty, Kinsky took a job as a governess with the family of Baron and Baroness von Suttner. Though their youngest son, Arthur, at twenty-three years of age, was seven years younger than Kinsky, the two fell in love. Their romance was eagerly fostered by the girls of the family; they were very fond of Bertha and were fascinated by the development of romantic love. It was quite otherwise with the parents. When the romance was discovered the highly incensed baroness did not lose any time in finding a new, distant position for Kinsky.

This new position was with Alfed Nobel, the inventor of dynamite, who lived, at the time, in Paris. A bachelor at age forty-three, he was looking for a secretary-housekeeper who was also familiar with languages. In his advertisement he wrote, "A very wealthy, cultured, elderly gentleman, living in Paris, desires to find a lady, also of mature years, familiar with languages, as secretary and manager of his household." Despite her youth, Kinsky undoubtedly fit all the other requirements, for she was hired right away. A week later Nobel had to return to Sweden; the king had summoned him. Kinsky too was called away from Paris. Upon receipt of a telegram from Arthur confessing that he could not live without her, Kinsky hurried to Vienna. There, in great secrecy, they married.

For their honeymoon, which according to Kinsky lasted nine years, they went to the Caucasus in Russia. The invitation had come from a prince, who was one of their friends. Their stay was a curious blend of being both guests and employees of their hosts. At first the prince had hopes of finding employment for Arthur. When that failed, Arthur was employed as an architect and overseer while Bertha gave music and language lessons. When the day's work was done, they changed their workclothes for evening dresses and tuxedos and mingled on equal footing with the local aristocracy. Arthur started to write articles that were published in the Austrian newspapers. Whether out of envy or the desire to imitate—she herself wrote that she could not decide which—Bertha too began to write. Her first published work was a light piece, an essay of the type known as a feuilleton, and it was signed with a pseudonym, but still it gave her confidence. Filled with the assurance that they could make a living as writers, they were ready to return home. In May, 1885, after nine years, they said farewell to the Caucasus.

Life's Work

Upon their return, Bertha and Arthur were forgiven for their secret marriage, and they rejoined Arthur's family. Published two years before their return, Bertha's book *Inventarium einer Seele* (1883; inventory of a soul) gave her entrée into literary circles. She soon added two important works to her oeuvre. *Daniela Dormes* (1886) and *Das Maschinenzeitalter: Zukunftsvorlesungen über unsere Zeit* (1889). *Daniela Dormes* in many ways is more a discussion than a novel. In it, however, one can discern Saltner's philosophical and moral views: She is sympathetic to the plight of the Jews, and she believes in Darwinism as a social force. *Das Maschinenzeitalter* is a look into the future. Suttner commented that she wrote the book to rid herself of the gloom with which the present filled her. The book was replete with scientific and philosophical themes; in scientific circles there was so much prejudice against the capacity of women as thinkers that a book signed with a woman's name would not have been read, so Suttner used the pseudonym "Jemand" (anyone).

The turning point of Suttner's life was approaching. With the money earned by *Das Maschinenzeitalter*, she and her husband decided to go to Paris. There they again met Nobel, and through him they also met the intellectual and social elite of the city. It was in Paris that Suttner first heard about the existence in London of a society called the International Peace and Arbitration Society. From that moment, she decided to promote it with all her efforts. She realized that her talent lay in writing; she also realized that in order to reach as many people as possible, the novel form would be best. As a published author, she assumed that the publication of *Lay Down Your Arms* would not be a problem. The topic, however, was considered so dangerous that many publishers refused it. Suttner would have liked to have had the book run as a serial in a periodical, but this was refused. A publisher finally accepted the work but demanded that certain parts be cut and others be rewritten. The publisher also wanted to change the title to a less provocative one. Suttner refused. To the astonishment of the publisher, *Lay Down Your Arms* became a best-seller; it was translated into dozens of languages. She received plaudits from Nobel and Leo Tolstoy, among others. Tolstoy compared the book to Harriet Beecher Stowe's *Uncle Tom's Cabin* (1852) and commented that he hoped that just as Stowe's work had influenced the abolition of slavery so should *Lay Down Your Arms* influence the abolition of war.

The success of the book soon engulfed Suttner in a series of peace activities. In 1891, she was elected president of the Austrian Peace Society, and she represented her country at a congress of international peace movements in Rome. The same year, she met a journalist, Alfred Hermann Fried, who also was later to receive a Nobel Peace Prize. The two founded a monthly periodical that bore the same title as that of Suttner's book. During the next eight years, this monthly was a powerful instrument in keeping the peace movement before the eyes of the world. Suttner also was occupied with the preparations for the First Hague Peace Conference. The conference aroused great expectations. The Czar of Russia, Nicholas II, had called upon world leaders to discuss efforts toward universal peace. This call was hailed by the champions of peace as a gigantic step toward its achievement. Until that time, pacifists had been considered as dreamers and utopians. This condescending attitude hurt their cause as much as the hostile attitude of the militarists. Jean-Henri Dunant, the founder of the Red Cross, commented that now, "whatever may happen, the world will not shriek, 'Utopia!'" "Utopians," as Suttner noted, was the favorite circumlocution for "crazy fellows." At the conference, France was represented by a former prime minister and Great Britain by Julian Pauncefote, the British ambassador to the United States. One of the honorary presidents of the conference was Andrew D. White, the American ambassador to Germany. Among all these glittering personalities, Suttner was feted, admired, and listened to. Ivan Bloch, a Russian journalist, was instrumental in the endeavor to change world opinion to accept disarmament and peace as a real possibility and not merely as a utopian dream. Bloch's book *Budushchaia voina* (1898; partial translation as *The Future of War, in Its Technical, Economic, and Political Relations*, 1899) was widely regarded as being partially responsible for the idea of a peace conference. His thesis was that with the advanced technology of arms and armies the idea that one could wage war without destroying society was "utopian." Before going to the conference, Bloch had a long interview with the czar.

Suttner also fought against anti-Semitism. Her husband perhaps played a more important role in this fight, but she was his coworker. Anti-Semitism was virulent in the Austro-Hungarian Empire. Indeed, one of Adolf Hitler's chief idols was the anti-Semitic mayor of Vienna. Arthur founded the Union to Combat Anti-Semitism.

In December, 1902, Arthur died. In order to bear her grief, Suttner threw herself into furthering the cause of peace. She wrote, she attended meetings, and she went to conferences. In 1904, she went on a speaking tour in the United States. She met President Theodore Roosevelt, who assured her that universal peace was coming. She was impressed by Philadelphia and its Quaker inhabitants, friends of peace. On her return to Europe, she was greatly encouraged by the way many dominions of the British Empire were about to be given Commonwealth status. She saw a promising future for other states, particularly for her homeland, where the old age of the emperor made people aware of inevitable changes that would follow his death. In 1905, she received the Nobel Peace Prize.

In the summer of 1914, an International Peace Conference was scheduled to be held in Vienna. In the last week of June of that year, however, a shot rang in a provincial city in an obscure province of the Austro-Hungarian Empire. It killed the heir to the throne of the Empire as well as his wife. Soon there were millions and millions of other victims; World War I had erupted. Suttner was spared the knowledge of war—she died of stomach cancer a week before the assassinations in Sarajevo.

Summary

Bertha von Suttner united in herself two traits that are rarely found together: idealism and realism. It was her idealism that led to her faith in a world without war. Hundreds before her had that same dream, but Suttner also had the clear-sightedness, the practical sense, and the knowledge of the way the world is directed by statesmen and leaders. In her work she was helped by her husband, who shared her ideas and was also a writer of some note. Even greater help came to her in the form of the zeitgeist. At the turn of the century, a host of great writers, philosophers, and statesmen were advocating the idea of a peaceful world. The idea was there—in search of a leader. Suttner took the role. The peace conferences she organized, the speaking tours she embarked upon, her book with its noble challenge, and the periodical she helped found all had the effect of making and keeping the world aware that the fight for peace can be as vigorous as its opposite. When Suttner was received by the crowned heads of Great Britain, Sweden, Norway, and the Netherlands, when she conferred with a former president and the President of the United States, it was not only a personal triumph, but also a victory for the cause of peace. The Nobel Peace Prize and the annual peace conferences that followed the First Hague Peace Conference are testimony to her influence.

Bibliography

Davis, Calvin DeArmond. *The United States and the First Hague Peace Conference*. Ithaca, N.Y.: Cornell University Press, 1962. An excellent account of the First Hague Peace Conference with particular emphasis on the American role in it. Offers a scholarly, lucid presentation of the problems of establishing a Permanent Court of Arbitration.

Kemp, Beatrix. *Woman for Peace: The Life of Bertha von Suttner*. Translated by R. W. Last. London: Oswald Wolff, 1972. Kemp had access to the Library of the United Nations in Geneva, where most of the material pertaining to Suttner's work is now collected. Occasionally laudatory, this nevertheless critical work provides an illuminating look at Suttner's life and work. Except for Suttner's own memoirs, it is the best work about her. The accounts of her lecture tours and the text of her speech in San Francisco in 1912 are valuable. Complete bibliography and index.

Playne, Caroline E. *Bertha von Suttner and the Struggle to Avert the World War*. London: Allen & Unwin, 1936. The author knew Suttner personally and participated with her in two International Peace Conferences. Contains good anecdotal material. The style is somewhat pedestrian, but the eyewitness accounts are useful. Index, no bibliography.

Suttner, Bertha von. *Memoirs of Bertha von Suttner: The Records of an Eventful Life*. Boston: Ginn, 1910. Because Suttner kept a diary, her memoirs are quite detailed. She gives outstanding sketches of statesmen, writers, and leaders of nations. Index.

Wiener, P. B. "Bertha von Suttner and the Political Novel." In *Essays in German Language, Culture, and Society*, edited by Siegbert S. Prawer et al. London: University of London, 1969. A useful and enlightening essay on the essence of the political novel, with special regard to the difference between the political novel and the social novel. Provides a good analysis of Suttner's main work, *Lay Down Your Arms*, and compares it to other antiwar novels. The notes following the articles are alone more valuable than many a longer article.

George Javor

ALEKSANDR VASILYEVICH SUVOROV

Born: November 24, 1729; near Moscow, Russia
Died: May 18, 1800; his estate, Kobrin, near St. Petersburg, Russia
Area of Achievement: The military
Contribution: By abandoning the defensive tactics of the period, Suvorov created a new type of army in which speed, mobility, and independence of judgment by junior officers were valued more than drills and sieges.

Early Life

Aleksandr Vasilyevich Suvorov was born on his parents' estate southwest of Moscow. His paternal grandfather, Ivan, had been an aide to Czar Peter the Great, while his father, Vasili, entered the military service as an administrator, achieving the rank of *generalanshef*, between lieutenant general and field marshal. Vasili married Avodita Theodeyevna Manukova, daughter of the governor of St. Petersburg.

At birth Suvorov was underweight and colicky. As he matured, he remained puny and sickly. Limited in physical activities, he turned to his father's library, where he enjoyed reading military history. With the aid of tutors, he learned Russian, French, German, Latin, Greek, and eventually Turkish and Italian. Because of his intuitive understanding of military tactics, in October, 1742, he was enrolled in a guards regiment but did not join that regiment until 1745.

Young Suvorov slowly rose in rank, becoming a lieutenant in 1754. He then spent a year at the War College with his father. After that, he joined the Kurinski Regiment and was promoted to major. During this period, he wrote two fictional dialogues which contain the seeds of his later innovative ideas. Russia became involved in the Seven Years' War, and Suvorov was given command of three battalions stationed in and around Memel. Seeking action, he transferred to the main army fighting Frederick the Great and was present at the Battle of Kunersdorf in August, 1759. He openly criticized the failure of imperial forces to exploit their victory by seizing Berlin. In July, 1761, he was given command of a detachment of cavalry in western Poland and won a series of victories over the Prussians. At Golnau, he received a slight chest wound and went home.

The imperial commander in chief, Pyotr Aleksandrovich Rumyantsev, suggested to the new emperor, Peter III, that Suvorov be rewarded, but Peter rejected the idea and pulled Russia out of the war, surrendering all gains and forcing Russia's allies to capitulate. Many Russians resented that action; they seized Peter and proclaimed his wife, Catherine, empress. Catherine became fond of the urbane Suvorov and agreed to follow Rumyantsev's suggestion by appointing young Suvorov colonel of first the Astrakhan and then the Suzdal Regiment.

Life's Work

Suvorov wrote the regimental regulations detailing his orders: The army must constantly drill—not parade, but simulate battle. Walls were built to be scaled; moats dug to be crossed; men and horses charged with guns ablazing. His troops never received the order to retreat, only to advance to a new position. He reduced the size of the military square and abandoned the long line of musketeers. The smaller squares were spread apart; the musketeers became marksmen. Speed, mobility, and individual initiative replaced detailed commands. Discipline was essential, but so was health and spirit. In 1765, when the regiment was sent to the forest around Lake Ladoga, he ordered a church, two schools, and gardens built. Suvorov was loved by his troops, and they would follow him to the ends of Europe.

In May, 1771, he learned that a Franco-Polish army was near Kraków; Suvorov reached the enemy at Landskron. The French general thought that the Russians would rest, but Suvorov's army was trained to march into battle. The enemy was destroyed. In September, Suvorov learned that three thousand Poles were advancing. He attacked them at dawn. By 11:00 A.M., the Polish force was routed.

Turkey declared war, and Catherine sent Suvorov into the Balkans. On the night of May 9, 1773, he led his men across the Danube River and destroyed a Turkish force of five thousand at Turtukai. The Turks sent a new army to Turtukai, and, although severely wounded, Suvorov commanded another assault. The Turks were again routed. In July, the still weak hero was transferred to the army under the command of Catherine's lover, Grigory Aleksandrovich Potemkin. Suvorov made it clear that he did not like Potemkin and was sent to Hison on the lower Danube.

Still weak, he returned home to marry Princess Varvara Ivanovna Prozorovskaya. By the time their daughter was born, he was back at the front. In the spring of 1774, he trained a detachment and took them across the Danube. On June 10, his eight thousand troops routed sixty thousand Turks at Kozludj. The Turks willingly ended the war on July 10.

For the next few years, Suvorov saw little military action. In August, 1787, however, Turkey again declared war, and Suvorov was entrusted with the defense of the south. He went to Kinburn. On the night of October 2, he destroyed a Turkish armada. All but five hundred of the five thousand Turks were killed, and seven of their ships were sunk. The Russians lost only 227 men, with a similar number of wounded. One of the wounded was Suvorov, who was shot in the arm.

The following spring, Potemkin arrived to besiege Ochakov. Suvorov was asked to command part of the besieging force, but he wrote, "You cannot capture a fortress by looking at it." Potemkin sent him to Moldavia. He went to Jassy, where he was instructed to link up with an Austrian force. On July 20, 1789, he crushed the Turks at Fokshany. On September 7, the

Austrians reported that they were about to be overwhelmed by the Turks. Suvorov's troops covered sixty miles in thirty-six hours to attack the Turks along the Rymnik River. For his victory, Catherine rewarded Suvorov with a title and money; the Austrians made him a Count of the Holy Roman Empire. Catherine wanted a quick victory to end the war. Potemkin, entrusted with the siege of the Turkish fortress at Ismail, summoned Suvorov, who arrived on December 2 and began to train the troops. Between dawn and afternoon on December 11, a Turkish army of forty thousand was annihilated. Potemkin congratulated the victor; Suvorov responded with a barb. Catherine and her lover were furious, and Suvorov was transferred to Finland, while Catherine showered honors on Potemkin.

After Potemkin died and the Turks agreed to a peace, Catherine allowed Suvorov to return to his command in the south, but, when trouble began in Poland, she gave the command to Rumyantsev. The latter summoned Suvorov. On September 6, 1794, Suvorov defeated a Polish force at Krupshchitze and then gathered forces to attack the Polish citadel at Praga. The attack on October 24 was over in three hours. Suvorov negotiated lenient terms for the Poles, but Catherine abrogated all the surrender terms. Furious, Suvorov went to Kobrin, the estate Catherine had awarded him.

The sixty-five-year-old field marshal authorized his aide, Lieutenant Colonel Friedrich Anthing, to write and publish a history of his exploits up to 1794. He also began to write and circulate a manuscript, *Nauka Pobezhdat* (1806; the knowledge of victory, but usually called the art of victory), detailing his theories. "Train hard, fight easy. Train easy, and you will have hard fighting," became his motto. In language that a peasant could understand, Suvorov revealed his theories. Because of the nature of cannon and rifles, it was better to charge a battery with saber and bayonet than to march slowly forward. Because of the death toll caused by disease, cleanliness was important and a quick storming was less costly than a long siege; because mobility and speed were the secret to victory, junior officers must be capable of assuming responsibility. Because the army needed the support of the local population, the army must always respect that population. Because spirit was essential, religion was essential.

In November, 1796, Paul I came to the throne. He exiled Suvorov to his estate at Konchansk, south of St. Petersburg, where he spent his time studying the tactics of Napoleon Bonaparte, the only general he considered his equal. In December, 1798, Russia, Austria, and England united against France. The imperial fleet was sent into the Mediterranean and Adriatic seas, while Russian armies were sent to the Netherlands, Switzerland, and Italy. The Austrians requested that Suvorov be sent to Italy. The seventy-year-old warrior arrived in Italy in April, 1799, and was appointed commander in chief of the Austrian army, even though the Austrians disliked his battle plan. Suvorov and the commander of the imperial fleet complained to Paul that their allies restricted their freedom. Suvorov entered Turin on May 14. He secured local cooperation only to have his arrangements countermanded. Suvorov was in a bind: Logistic support was provided by the Austrians, and they vetoed his actions. When word arrived of an approaching French army, Suvorov left the Austrians and crushed the French at the Trebbia River. When word of that victory spread, isolated French citadels capitulated.

Paul demanded that Emperor Francis II of Austria give Suvorov a free hand, but Francis refused. Word came that the last French force in Italy was approaching, and Suvorov met and destroyed it at Novi. He then demanded permission to invade France, but Francis again refused and ordered him to join the Russians in Switzerland. Learning of Suvorov's intent to join Russian forces led by Aleksandr Rimsky-Korsakov in Switzerland, the French fortified St. Gotthard Pass and planned to destroy the Russians at Zurich. Suvorov reached Taverne on September 15, but the Austrians had not delivered the promised supplies. Suvorov awaited the supplies for four days. On September 21-22, the Russians cleared the French from St. Gotthard Pass and then defeated another French force at Kinzig Pass. The four-day delay at Taverne was fatal, however, for the French had destroyed the Russian army in Switzerland. When Suvorov learned of the disaster, he decided to go to Glarus via the Pragel Pass. A French force blocked him, while the victorious French army attacked the rear, but Suvorov's army defeated both. By this time, Suvorov was coughing and had a high fever. Word arrived of the failure of the Anglo-Russian campaign in the Netherlands, and Paul informed Francis that all Russian troops were ordered home. Paul promoted Suvorov to the unprecedented rank of generalissimo. By March, 1800, the sick hero was at his Kobrin estate.

Paul received a full report and decided that the allies had to be punished. He began to plan to send Russian troops to India to help the Indians oust the British. He became furious at Suvorov, who had won all the victories while breaking his specific military instructions and dress codes. Suvorov was stripped of his honors. Sick and broken in spirit, Suvorov died on the afternoon of May 18, 1800, regretting that he had not had the opportunity to face Napoleon.

Summary

Until the mid-nineteenth century, European historians tended to dismiss Suvorov as an eccentric who could not possibly have won so many victories. In Russia, historians paid scant attention to his exploits until after the disaster of the Crimean War. While military technology, altered by the Industrial Revolution, made Suvorov's use of the saber and bayonet obsolete, his vision of speed and mobility became increasingly popular. As World War II approached, Suvorov's writings were published and studied. In the dark days of 1941-1942, his victories over the superior forces of France and Turkey raised him to the level of national hero and medals were given in his honor. As Russian sources began to be studied by non-Russian historians, Suvorov's achievements began to be understood and appreciated. While many of his tactics are irrelevant in modern times, the spirit he imparted to his troops, which allowed them to perform exactly as he wished, is still envied.

Bibliography

Alexander, John T. *Catherine The Great: Life and Legend.* New York: Oxford University Press, 1989. Making extensive use of Catherine's writings as well as other primary documents and unpublished material, the author stresses the personal side of Catherine's court. Excellent for understanding other Russian generals such as Potemkin and Rumyantsev.

Blease, W. Lyon. *Suvorof.* London: Constable, 1920. The author, an army doctor who spoke Russian, wrote the first biography in English that attempted to deal with Suvorov's personal life. Blease understood the charismatic nature of Suvorov's leadership but did not appreciate his generalship.

De Madariaga, Isabel. *Russia in the Age of Catherine the Great.* New Haven, Conn.: Yale University Press, 1981. Making extensive use of Russian sources, the author integrates Suvorov's military activity with the whole of Russian foreign policy. An excellent study of Russia's response to the Enlightenment emerges.

Duffy, Christopher. *Russia's Military Way to the West: Origins and Nature of Russian Military Power, 1700-1800.* London: Routledge & Kegan Paul, 1981. This is an excellent study of the growth of Russia's military power in the eighteenth century. The last chapters concentrate on Suvorov's exploits.

Longworth, Philip. *The Art of Victory: The Life and Achievement of Generalissimo Suvorov (1729-1800).* New York: Holt, Rinehart and Winston, 1965. Making extensive use of Russian sources, the author has written an excellent biography. While little is mentioned of Suvorov's personal life, there are extensive quotations from his military writings and a useful summary of Suvorov's role in military history.

Osipov, K. *Alexander Suvorov.* Translated by Edith Bone. London: Hutchinson, 1941. This is an English translation of one of the many Soviet editions which appeared almost annually between 1940 and 1950. While much of the work is uncritical hero-worship, it is useful in understanding Suvorov's growing reputation, especially during the war years.

Saul, Norman E. *Russia and the Mediterranean, 1797-1807.* Chicago: University of Chicago Press, 1970. Despite the title, the work details the growing Russo-English conflict in the Mediterranean from the 1780's. It was as a result of English policy that Catherine and Paul were unable to use the Baltic fleet to help Suvorov and the fleet commander in the

Mediterranean/Balkan region.

Soloveytchik, George. *Potemkin: A Picture of Catherine's Russia*. Rev. ed. London: Percival Marshall, 1949. While lacking footnotes and a bibliography, this is still a useful study of the relationship between Catherine, Potemkin, and Suvorov.

Waliszewski, Kazimierz. *Paul the First of Russia: The Son of Catherine the Great*. Philadelphia: J. B. Lippincott, 1913. This is an excellent translation from a French work that made extensive use of Russian sources, especially the letters from Suvorov to Paul. It should be noted, however, that all footnotes from the original edition are omitted.

J. Lee Shneidman

EMANUEL SWEDENBORG

Born: January 29, 1688; Stockholm, Sweden
Died: March 29, 1772; London, England
Areas of Achievement: Invention, physiology, and religion
Contribution: Swedenborg was first a mechanical prodigy, then a scientist and philosopher, then an anatomist, and finally a theologian. Recognition of his achievements has followed a similar time line. His peers saw him as a genius in science and invention, but it was much later before his anatomical studies were appreciated. His many contributions to Christian religious thought are still not widely known.

Early Life

When Emanuel Swedenborg, the third child of Jesper and Sara Swedberg, was born, his father was court chaplain in Stockholm and was later appointed Bishop of Skara. In 1719, the family was ennobled and took the name Swedenborg. Very little is known of Swedenborg's childhood. In 1699, he entered the University of Uppsala and ten years later read his graduation essay. Shortly afterward, he began extensive travels in England and on the Continent. Although there is no evidence that Swedenborg actually met Isaac Newton, he studied Newton's works avidly. Swedenborg did work with both Edmond Halley and John Flamsteed.

Throughout his travels in France, Germany, the Netherlands, Denmark, Bohemia, and Italy, Swedenborg searched insatiably for scientific knowledge, lodging when possible with scientists, craftsmen, and mathematicians. In 1714, he drafted papers on fourteen mechanical inventions, some of which he soon published in the *Daedalus Hyperboreus*, the first Swedish scientific journal, since recognized by the Society of Science of Uppsala as the first of its proceedings. He was appointed to the Swedish Board of Mines in 1716 and devised a number of mechanical devices to increase the efficiency of mining operations. In 1721, he published a Latin treatise on chemistry.

Life's Work

The work that established Swedenborg's reputation as a scientist of note was a massive three-volume set published in 1734. The two volumes on copper and iron smelting were translated into several languages and became standard reference works. Next, his attention turned to physiological studies, his avowed motivation being a search for the human soul. These studies, which include several large volumes, are significant not because they rival in any sense later research using far more refined equipment but because of the remarkably intelligent way in which Swedenborg analyzed and interpreted the phenomena he was able to observe. In 1901, when Max Neuburger noted certain anticipations of modern medical views made by Swedenborg, the

University of Vienna ordered a complete set of Swedenborg's treatises from
the Royal Swedish Academy. These studies showed, 150 years before the
work of any other scientist, that the motion of the brain was synchronous
with respiration and not with the motion of the heart. His views on the
physiological functions of the spinal cord agreed with recent research, and
he anticipated much later studies on the functions of the ductless glands.

It is curious that Swedenborg, a man of such astonishing achievement in
physics and biology, is almost completely ignored in the annals of science.
One reason for his obscurity is that between 1749 and 1756 he published
anonymously, in eight large volumes, a work entitled *Arcana coelestia quae
in scriptura sacra seu verbo Domini sunt detecta* (*The Heavenly Arcana*,
1951-1956). This monumental work signaled the beginning of Swedenborg's
work as a theologian. The last twenty-three years of his life were devoted to
writing and publishing the works that identify him as a religious reformer
and Bible interpreter.

Swedenborg's biblical interpretations did not earn for him widespread recognition, because he used visions as the basis for his interpretations. In an
autobiographical letter to his friend the Reverend Thomas Hartley, written in
1769, Swedenborg stated, ". . . I have been called to a holy office by the
Lord himself . . . , when he opened my sight into the spiritual world and
enabled me to converse with spirits and angels. . . . From that time I began
to print and publish the various *arcana* that were seen by me. . . ." To his
contemporaries, influenced by the intellectual climate of the eighteenth century, with its materialistic conception of the universe, Swedenborg was an
enigma, sacrificing a brilliant career as an esteemed scientist to pursue religious studies.

Swedenborg, nevertheless, continued his theological publications, publishing these works anonymously and distributing them at his own expense
until the last three years of his life. In the first and largest of these, *The
Heavenly Arcana*, Swedenborg does an intensive interpretation of the first
two books of the Bible, Genesis and Exodus, claiming that these books,
along with most of the text of the Bible, have an inner, spiritual sense. The
story of Creation, for example, becomes a symbolic story of the birth or
creation of spirituality in every human being. Once this spirituality is recognized, the Bible can be used as a personal psychological guide to life.

In addition to the detailed critique of Scriptural spiritual meaning, Swedenborg introduced between chapters lengthy articles on his otherworldly
experiences, not only relating actual conditions he says he observed in
Heaven, Hell, and an intermediate world of spirits but also chronicling his
encounters with spirits he believed had previously lived on other inhabited
planets.

The concept of the nature of God found in these writings is clearly Christian in intent and belief, but at the same time it deals constructively and

logically with the concept of a trinity in God. According to this teaching, the being called God the Father in Scripture is a symbolic name for the essence or essential nature of God, a perfect merging of divine love and wisdom, corresponding to what has traditionally been called the soul in any human being. The Son of God, the Christ of the New Testament, is the earthly manifestation of the one God, corresponding to the human body through which the soul of every human being expresses itself. The enigmatic Holy Spirit is, on one hand, the operation or influence of God in creation and, on the other, the discernible nature or personality of God, corresponding to the nature or personality of any human being. These three areas of thought—the concept that there is a continuous and connected inner sense in the Word, that there is a real and knowable life after death, and that God is one in essence and in person, with three distinguishable aspects—are the primary distinctive beliefs of Swedenborgianism.

Immanuel Kant may have introduced the most enduring negative attitude toward the worth of studying Swedenborg. For reasons not clearly known, Kant published a strange work in 1766, *Träume eines Geistersehers erläutert durch Träume der Metaphysik* (*Dreams of a Spirit-Seer, Illustrated by Dreams of Metaphysics*, 1900), which ridiculed Swedenborg and his theological writings. Kant described Swedenborg's magnum opus as eight volumes of sheer nonsense; because in his later years Kant became so influential on the Continent, this ridicule became a curse that led to Swedenborg's being largely ignored by scholars for generations.

The charges made during his lifetime that Swedenborg was a writer of nonsense and the related charge that he was insane were completely insupportable. He was too well known for his scholarly, methodical, and highly respected scientific works to be dismissed in such cavalier fashion. The religious writings of Swedenborg were taken so seriously by his own people that in 1769 heresy charges were leveled against two of his prestigious disciples at Gothenburg, a sad affair that lasted two or three years before it was quietly dropped for lack of evidence.

Just before Swedenborg left for his last trip to London to publish *Vera Christiana religio* (1771; *True Christian Religion*, 1781), his final summary work, he met with King Adolf Frederick, who is reported to have said, "The consistories have kept silent on the subject of my letters and your writings. We may conclude, then, that they have not found anything reprehensible in them and that you have written in conformity with the truth."

Summary

During his lifetime, Emanuel Swedenborg made no effort to found a new religious movement, contenting himself with publishing his works and distributing them at his own expense to leading clergymen and scholars. It was not until fifteen years after his death that the first movement to found a new church organization began in London among readers of his works. That modest beginning has led to the present numerically small but worldwide following of Swedenborgians, including both those who are members of a Swedenborgian church organization and those who are simply readers of Swedenborg's works.

In particular, interest in Swedenborg has been kindled by an ongoing reassessment of eighteenth century thought. Rejecting the traditional, positivistic view of the Enlightenment, scholars in many disciplines have shown that the contrast between the rational and the irrational in the Age of Reason cannot be neatly demarcated. Swedenborg, scientist and visionary, is a significant case in point.

Bibliography

Block, Marguerite B. *The New Church in the New World: A Study of Swedenborgianism in America.* Introduction and epilogue by Robert H. Kirven. New York: Swedenborg Publishing Association, 1984. With Kirven's updating, this work, based on Block's Ph.D. thesis, is a thorough and reliable standard reference work.

Jonsson, Inge. *Emanuel Swedenborg.* Boston: Twayne, 1971. Only the first chapter of this work is, strictly speaking, a biography. The major part of the book focuses on the thought content of Swedenborg's writings. The keenest assessment by the author is of Swedenborg's scientific and philosophical works.

Sigstedt, Cyriel O. *The Swedenborg Epic: The Life and Works of Emanuel Swedenborg.* New York: Bookman, 1952. Reprint. London: Swedenborg Society, 1981. This is the most complete and thoroughly documented biography of Swedenborg. The reprint edition has an errata sheet correcting a number of minor errors.

Söderberg, Henry. *Swedenborg's 1714 Airplane: A Machine to Fly in the Air.* Edited by George F. Dole. New York: Swedenborg Foundation, 1988. The author, a retired vice president of Scandinavian Airlines, discovered Swedenborg's invention while researching a book on the history of flight. He notes that a model of Swedenborg's craft is the first sight that greets visitors to the Smithsonian's Early Flight Room.

Woofenden, William Ross. *Swedenborg Researcher's Manual.* Bryn Athyn, Pa.: Swedenborg Scientific Association, 1988. This work combines for the first time an annotated bibliography of all Swedenborg's works, an extensive annotated bibliography of collateral literature on Swedenborg's thought, a glossary of special terms, summaries of key concepts found in Swedenborg, and a section giving locations and descriptions of major documentary collections of Swedenborgiana worldwide.

William Ross Woofenden

HIPPOLYTE-ADOLPHE TAINE

Born: April 21, 1828; Vouziers, France
Died: March 5, 1893; Paris, France
Areas of Achievement: Art, literature, historiography, and philosophy
Contribution: As a critic and historian of the arts and society, Taine dominated much of the intellectual life in France in the last half of the nineteenth century. Influential in England and the United States, much of his history and literary theory has fallen into disrepute in this century. Yet his method and his appreciation of literary works continue to engage critics and historians.

Early Life

Hippolyte-Adolphe Taine was twelve years old when his father, an established attorney, died. Left with a modest inheritance and scholarly inclinations, the young man was sent to a boarding school in Paris. He loved learning and soon revealed a mind superior to both his fellow students and his teachers. Deeply influenced by the philosopher Baruch Spinoza, Taine had lost his religious faith by the age of fifteen. He took a naturalistic view of the world, in which the human intellect and nature are viewed as parts of a single process. History, if it was examined carefully, revealed a total structure that functioned on the same principles as nature. Consequently, societies grew and declined in an organic manner as did natural phenomena, and the historian or philosopher could find the laws of society, history, literature, or any human endeavor in the same way that scientists found such laws to operate in nature.

It was Taine's devotion to Spinoza that led to his failing the *agrégation* (a series of examinations at the École Normale Supérieure) in 1851. His conservative examiners found his elucidation of Spinoza's moral system to be "absurd." In effect, Taine was flouting their most fundamental conceptions about free will and morality, for he argued that human beings were largely the products of their race, their time, and their environment. Taine seemed to attack the concept of individuality and of moral responsibility, apparently abandoning the notion that human beings created their own world in favor of a belief in determinism.

If Taine's early academic career was hampered by his unorthodox views, his lectures on literature and art soon brought him attention both in France and abroad. He was the harbinger of the great naturalistic novelists of the nineteenth century such as Émile Zola, who took as their subject matter the way a culture shapes human character. Taine was one of the first men of letters to study science rigorously and to develop a human psychology based on his courses in physiology, botany, zoology, and anatomy. His work was greeted with enormous enthusiasm, since it promised to put the study of history, literature, and culture as a whole on an objective basis and free it from the arbitrary prejudices of the critic.

Life's Work

The publication of Taine's *Histoire de la littérature anglaise* (1863-1864; *History of English Literature*, 1871) solidified his reputation as the leading philosophical critic of his age. Rather than simply present summary descriptions of the great English authors' lives and works, Taine propounded the notion that English literary history was not solely the record of individual achievements. Rather, it had a shape and a structure that could be elucidated, so that each author became a part of a tradition and could be seen as the product of his environment and his age. Literature was no more an accident, or merely the manifestation of an individual mind, than were the elements of nature.

In collections of essays and lectures in the next ten years and in his travels across Europe, Taine promoted a methodology based, he believed, on the rigor of scientific principles. In a lecture on the nature of art (first given in Paris in 1864 and published in English translation in 1875), Taine established the rules of his method. According to Taine, one must first study the artist's body of work and become familiar with the artist's characteristic themes and techniques. Then one must examine the artistic tradition out of which the artist develops, taking note of how his work is illustrative of that tradition. Finally, it is necessary to explore the social climate, the intellectual influences, the race, the language, and the customs of the world the artist inhabits. Taken in total, this method, in Taine's view, yields a comprehensive, unbiased view of art.

Taine's view of art is historical: "Arts appear and disappear along with certain accompanying social and intellectual conditions," he asserts in his lecture on the nature of art. The implication of his argument is that artistic genius is an intensified example of environmental influences. The artist is the finest expression of the whole culture but not a creation unto himself. All that makes William Shakespeare distinctive can be found in his contemporaries, Taine argues, but only Shakespeare expresses the exquisite combination and modulation of those elements that make a great artist. Returning to science as his guiding principle, Taine concludes: "The productions of the human mind, like those of animated nature, can only be explained by their *milieu.*" Such a statement, in his estimation, was a law he had discovered in his study of art, not an idea he foisted upon it. He offers his readers "facts," for science "imposes no precepts, but ascertains and verifies laws."

It must be remembered that Taine was writing at a time when eminent Victorian figures such as Thomas Carlyle were advancing a great man theory of history. The legacy of Romanticism had been to exult in individualism and to see society coalescing about the figures of extraordinary men. On the contrary, Taine contends, a writer such as Honoré de Balzac is great precisely because he creates a literature of characters who typify their times, their culture, and their race. Balzac's *La Comédie humaine* (1829-1848; *The Human Comedy*, 1885-1893, 1896), his series of novels on French life, are the best history of his era because he is so attuned to the way in which his characters are manifestations of their society. Similarly, Stendhal repays study because he is so intimately aware of how individual psychology is linked to the history of his times. His characters are motivated by historical conditions; there is a logic to their imaginations that springs from their milieu.

In the last twenty years of his life, Taine shifted from an interest in art and philosophy to the writing of a history of contemporary France. Never deeply engaged by political issues, he nevertheless felt the need (given his historical frame of mind) to discover the roots of his culture. Because he believed that societies grow organically, and thus that individuals and events are all connected to one another, he devised a multivolume history beginning with the *ancien régime* (the era before the Revolution) and ending in his own day.

The French Revolution bothered Taine because it seemed more like a disruption than a continuation of history. The year 1789 was when France was radically changed from a society that evolved from a tradition to a new country that established a government according to universal, abstract principles. Taine did not believe that such principles existed, except insofar as they might be seen evolving in history. His profoundly conservative cast of mind could not allow for a catastrophic event that suddenly transforms the structure of a society. In his view, such an upheaval is doomed to failure.

Taine is not nostalgic about the past. Indeed his history of France documents the desperate situation of the people in the twenty-five years preceding the Revolution. He does not deny the need for change, but he deplores the anarchy and violence of the Revolution. Napoleon I restored order but at the cost of destroying liberty among various social classes. Having to deal with the failed revolutions of his own time (the upheaval of 1848, the Paris Commune of 1871), Taine was not sanguine about the way his countrymen effected change. His rather vague solution was to counsel a sympathetic understanding of the place of all classes and elements of society.

Summary

Except for his literary essays, Hippolyte-Adolphe Taine is not read much today. His notions of science are outdated and suspect, and he is unable to see that the vaunted objectivity of his methodology is no such thing. When Taine's history of France is examined, it is clear that it is as subjective and determined by his biases as any other history would be. Taine would not have been very surprised by this judgment, since he believed that human beings were the products of their times. Yet he did fail to see the contradictions in his own methodology, that his brand of conservatism was temperamental and could not be explained only in terms of his time, place, and tradition.

It has been noted that Taine's reputation since his death has steadily declined. Yet subsequent critics and historians owe Taine an enormous debt. For example, Taine reversed the excesses of Romanticism, with its lionizing of the individual, and perceived important facts about the relationship between the individual and society that naturalistic novelists explored with considerable brilliance. Nearly every critic who has covered the subjects and the periods that were at Taine's command has felt compelled to deal with his ideas—if only to refute them. Finally, Taine merits study as one of the last men of letters who tried to integrate his insights into many different fields of study: psychology, literary criticism, aesthetics, art, philosophy, and history. In an era of specialization, his work is still an admirable example of the effort to grasp intellectual life in its entirety.

Bibliography
Eustis, Alvin A. *Hippolyte Taine and the Classical Genius.* Berkeley: University of California Press, 1951. A well-written scholarly monograph that concentrates on Taine's debt to classical writers and scholarship. Information is presented succinctly and judiciously. The bibliography is still useful.
Gargan, Edward T., ed. Introduction to *The Origins of Contemporary France,* by Hippolyte-Adolphe Taine. Chicago: University of Chicago Press, 1974. Gargan's long introduction provides important biographical information on Taine and a shrewd analysis of his position as a historian.
Kahn, Sholom J. *Science and Aesthetic Judgement: A Study in Taine's Critical Method.* London: Routledge & Kegan Paul, 1953. An important monograph for specialists, this book will prove somewhat difficult for students not already familiar with several of Taine's texts. Nevertheless, this is an essential study of Taine's philosophy and methodology.
Weinstein, Leo. *Hippolyte Taine.* Boston: Twayne, 1972. The only comprehensive introduction in English to Taine's life and work. Chapters on his life, philosophy, method, and psychology, career as a literary and art critic, and role as a historian of France give a thorough summary and critique of Taine's achievements and influence. Notes, an annotated bibliography, and an index make this an indispensable study.
Wellek, René. *A History of Modern Criticism, 1750-1950.* Vol. 4. New Haven, Conn.: Yale University Press, 1965. One of the most important sources for tracing the history of literary criticism and Taine's place within it. Wellek discusses the significance of Taine's *History of English Literature* and the way the critic deals with matters of style.

Carl Rollyson

TALLEYRAND

Born: February 2, 1754; Paris, France
Died: May 17, 1838; Paris, France
Area of Achievement: Politics
Contribution: Talleyrand directed the foreign relations of his country in a
time of changing principles and changing regimes—the Directory, the
Consulate, the Empire, and the Restoration Monarchy—trying to adjust
his French patriotism with the establishment of a viable balance of power
that formed the basis of European relations for a century.

Early Life

Talleyrand's family came from an old and highly distinguished line of
sovereign counts, but at the time he was born the family had lost a considerable amount of its former importance. His parents were courtiers whose
business, attending the offspring of Louis XV, gave them little time to spend
with their most recent addition. Talleyrand was sent to a wet nurse, a poor
woman who lived in the Saint-Jacques district. Although such surrogate
mothering was a common practice, with Talleyrand it was excessive: The
parents did not see their son for the next four years. While in his nurse's care
only several months, he fell from a chest of drawers, breaking his right foot.
The injury did not receive proper medical attention and the bones knit badly,
leaving him with a club foot. For the rest of his life he was unable to walk
without a cane or a brace.

When Talleyrand was three, his older brother died, leaving him heir to the
family title and estates. He would have become a soldier, but his injury made
this impossible. The family therefore decided to have him forfeit his rights in
favor of his younger brother, Archambaud, and become a churchman. After
elementary school, he attended the seminary of Saint Sulpice. From there,
he went to the Sorbonne receiving, in 1774, a degree in theology. He took
his first vows in April, 1775. Several months later, as the Abbé de Périgord,
he attended the royal coronation of Louis XVI at the Cathedral of Rheims.

Talleyrand's noble lineage gave him entrée to the court and its opportunities. In September, 1775, he was confirmed as the Abbot of Saint-Rémy
in Rheims, a sinecure that paid him eighteen thousand livres a year. Henceforth, his rise in the church hierarchy was rapid: In 1779, he became a
deacon and a priest; in 1880, he became an agent-general of the Assembly of
the Clergy to manage ecclesiastical property; in 1789, he became the Bishop
of Autun. He also managed to pick up other properties in Champagne and
Poitou. All of his benefices combined gave the thirty-four-year-old prelate a
personal income of about 100,000 livres a year. With such resources he
could now live the good life, far from ecclesiastical duties in provincial
cities.

In church matters he had a reputation as a defender of tradition and privilege, but his private life was otherwise. He preferred to spend his time in Paris, frequenting the salons, conversing with such men as Voltaire, Comte de Mirabeau, and Charles Alexandre de Calonne, and seducing women. His sexual successes were the subject of much gossip, admiration, and amusement. Despite absenteeism from his official obligations—he only visited his bishopric once for a period of thirty days—he became Autun's clerical delegate to the meeting of the Estates-General held at Versailles in May, 1789. The petition of grievance, or cahier, which he brought with him, and which he helped to write, called for the establishment of local representative government, for the abolition of feudal privilege, and for the creation of a national assembly to curb the power of royal despotism. He favored putting the estates of the Church at the disposition of the nation; when the time came, he provided the rationale for reconciling such expropriation with the sacredness of private property. Talleyrand argued that these church lands had been the property of the nation all along, maintaining the entire body of the faithful in a Catholic land could be the nation itself. His knowledge of Church administration was invaluable in helping to destroy the organization's power.

He also gave legitimacy to the civil constitution of the clergy by celebrating Mass on the Feast of the Federation, July 14, 1790, at the Champ de Mars on the first anniversary of the taking of the Bastille. He helped consecrate recently elected bishops to replace those who had refused to pledge their loyalty to the new order. Shortly afterward, in February, 1791, he renounced his priestly vows and returned to the status of layman, whereupon he was excommunicated by the pope.

Life's Work

Talleyrand's first attempt at national diplomacy, a métier that became his main profession the rest of his life, came in 1792. Because of the self-denying ordinance, he was unable to run for election to the new parliament created by the old constituent assembly. Instead, he managed to be sent on a mission to London to try to secure British neutrality in the event of the outbreak of hostilities between France and Austria. The mission was not succesful; the British wanted to maintain their free hand as the holder of the balance of power and rejected any commitments. Talleyrand nevertheless continued his diplomatic efforts. He returned to London on two other occasions—in January and May of 1792—but the results were equally disappointing.

At home Talleyrand watched with dismay the increasingly radical direction of politics. During his third visit to the British capital, France was at war with both Austria and Prussia. The early defeats led to the outbreak of domestic violence which led to the September Massacres, which made life dangerous for all men of Talleyrand's antecedents. With the coming of the Reign of Terror, he fled to Great Britain then was forced to leave for the United States, where for a time he lived in Philadelphia. He did not like American hospitality. In his opinion the climate was too hot or too cold, there was a dreadful lack of culture, and the food was inedible.

Not until 1796 did he return to France, the new government of the Directory giving him permission. He found that in his absence he had been elected to the newly formed Institute of Arts and Sciences. He renewed old acquaintances through which he came to the attention of the powerful director, Vicomte Paul de Barras, who had him named minister of foreign affairs in July, 1797. At this time France was in an expansionist mood, believing its destiny lay in extending its boundaries to the Alps and the Rhine and in liberating Europe's suppressed peoples from the yoke of feudalism and despotism. Its mission was to carry out a crusade for universal freedom.

Such ambitions did not seem unreasonable to nationalists, even though, as long as France was committed to such goals, there would be constant war. None who held high office at this time could have publicly believed otherwise, least of all a minister of foreign affairs. Talleyrand wanted to make France respected and feared, but he believed war to be wasteful and absurd. He wanted to end the current hostilities with Austria and Great Britain, but the victory had to contribute to the stabilization of Europe by not destroying the balance of power. It must also contribute to French prosperity.

To these ends Talleyrand put forth a scheme to establish French preponderance in the eastern Mediterranean by mounting an expedition to Egypt. The Turkish Empire was in dissolution and, by seizing its choicest parts, France could expand its commercial interests and hold bargaining counters to . bring about peace with the British. Ever mindful of his own interests, Talleyrand began cultivating a friendship with Napoleon I, who also favored the Egyptian campaign. Both were contemptuous of the current political system which they believed was contributing to French defeat and weakness.

In July, 1799, sensing that the end of the Directory was near, Talleyrand resigned his post and retired to private life. When Napoleon returned from Egypt in October of that year, Talleyrand joined a conspiracy to bring the general to power. For his support, Napoleon made Talleyrand foreign minister. The two seemed to agree on the essentials of French foreign policy and upon the necessity of creating a European equilibrium which could assure the security and prestige of France.

Talleyrand presided over the reorganization of Germany. He helped to arrange compensation for princes dispossessed of their territories on the west bank of the Rhine by giving them church lands in other parts of Germany. These transactions satisfied the time-honored principle of compensations, but they also made Talleyrand tremendously wealthy. In fact, the foreign minister was one of the greediest men of France in an age renowned for corruption. He saw nothing wrong in demanding kickbacks for his services to enable him to live in the style befitting his station. Such venality often made it difficult to ascertain the dividing line between personal and public advantage.

The height of his professionalism undoubtedly came with the signature of the Peace of Amiens, on March 25, 1802. In this treaty the British had to acknowledge effective French control of the Netherlands, Belgium, the left bank of the Rhine, and northern Italy. The British, especially in recognizing French power in the lowlands, abandoned a policy which they once regarded as essential for their security. Thus, after a decade of wars, France emerged as the most powerful state in Europe. Talleyrand boasted that his country now enjoyed such power, glory, and influence that even the most ambitious person could desire nothing more for his country.

Napoleon, however, was not the sort of master ever to be satisfied. While his foreign minister struggled to make the Peace of Amiens the basis of a new European equilibrium, Napoleon was planning ever larger conquests. Relations between the two men began to chill, but Talleyrand continued to share in Napoleon's glory. He could be an embarrassingly servile sycophant when it suited his purposes. When it at last became obvious that Talleyrand could no longer reconcile his sense of moderation and longing for personal survival with such a willful conqueror, he resigned. This event occurred in 1807, after the signing of the Treaty of Tilsit with Russia that recognized the division of Europe into two spheres: the Russian in the East and the French in the West. Talleyrand, having accumulated sufficient worldly goods to live in royal style—he was the master of the vast feudal estate of Valençay and of a superb townhouse in Paris on the Place de la Concorde—became the reigning prince of Benevento but again left before the inevitable fall of a regime.

Napoleon was vexed at his minister's desertion but continued to use him for special tasks. In these tasks Talleyrand proved less than reliable. At the summit conference at Erfurt with Alexander I, Talleyrand secretly urged the Russian czar to stand firm and not let Napoleon destroy Austria. After helping Napoleon arrange the overthrow of the Spanish Bourbons, Talleyrand turned against the venture and conspired with Police Minister Joseph Fouché to have Napoleon overthrown, replacing him with Napoleon's brother-in-law, Joachim Murat. Napoleon discovered who was behind the scheme and denounced Talleyrand, on January 28, 1809, before a restricted meeting of the council of state.

Talleyrand lived in retirement until 1814, when, with the Napoleonic Empire in ruins, he helped arrange the Bourbon Restoration. Talleyrand insisted that this be conditional upon the establishment of constitutional government. Talleyrand again became minister of foreign affairs. He was largely responsible for the Treaty of Paris, which concluded peace between France and the allies. He was also the principal French representative at the Congress of Vienna—arranged by the British, Russians, Prussians, and Austrians—which restored an equilibrium to a Europe ravaged by a quarter of a century of war.

Talleyrand retired once more, this time unwillingly, in September, 1815. Fifteen years later, however, with the advent of the July Monarchy, he was again offered the foreign ministry. He chose instead to go to London as an ambassador. He stayed in this post the next four years, participating in the negotiations which established an independent Belgium. In his long career he had served under seven different regimes and had intrigued against more than half of them; as he later noted, however, these betrayals had the support of a majority of his fellow countrymen. Upon his deathbed, he insisted that he receive extreme unction on the knuckles of his clenched fists rather than on his palms as befitting a bishop of the Roman Catholic church.

Summary

Talleyrand embraced the assumptions existent since the Treaty of Westphalia (1648) that foreign policy was essentially nonideological and that states could preserve their independence by preserving a proper balance of power. This moderate approach made him favor creating an entente with the entrenched powers against the revisionist powers, which meant assisting Great Britain and Austria curb Russia and Prussia, as he did at the Congress of Vienna. He characteristically exaggerated his role at that summit meeting, but his performance there was consistent with the principles by which he believed the affairs of nations should be conducted. "The first need of Europe," he told the representatives of the great powers, "is to banish forever the opinion that right can be acquired by conquest alone, and to cause the revival of that sacred principle of legitimacy from which all order and stability spring." Through skillful exploitation of the differences between the allies, he managed to put France on a more equal footing with them, helping to increase the respectability of the French monarchy as a force for order, moderation, and conservatism.

Although frequently vilified for his material and sexual avarice—he is a Freudian's delight with his loveless mother, his disinheritance, and his love-hate relationship with Catholicism—Talleyrand stands forth as the quintessential diplomat—one who realized that international politics is the art of the possible. He realized, too, that national security is not dependent on the survival of the fittest but on the mutual acceptance by great powers of their limitations and on the need to temper their rivalries and ambitions to preserve the security of one another.

Bibliography
Brinton, Crane. *The Lives of Talleyrand*. New York: W. W. Norton, 1936. If

Brinton's biography were not so engaging, intelligent, and analytically erudite, it would be dismissed as a rank apology. Indeed, Brinton seems to go out of his way to make allowances for Talleyrand, but his presentation of Talleyrand as the consummate moderate diplomat is nevertheless convincing.

Cooper, Duff. *Talleyrand*. New York: Harper & Row, 1932. This Tory politician makes no great discourse on Talleyrand's skills or vices, presenting him simply as an eminently sensible Frenchman, a practical, peace-loving man free from the vice of nationalism and horrified by the spirit of conquest. In a sense one of the first Europeans.

Ferrero, Guglielmo. *The Reconstruction of Europe: Talleyrand and the Congress of Vienna, 1814-1815*. Translated by Theodore R. Jaeckel. New York: G. P. Putnam's Sons, 1941. Ferrero credits three men with the creation of a new and stable order out of the ruins of the Napoleonic Empire: Czar Alexander I, King Louis XVIII, and Talleyrand, who "seems to have the right of precedence over all the statesmen who have appeared in the Western world since the Revolution." Ferrero attributes Talleyrand's predisposition to revolt against all regimes and powers to the childhood accident that left him a cripple.

Greenbaum, Louis S. *Talleyrand, Statesman and Priest: The Agent-General of the Clergy and the Church of France at the End of the Old Regime*. Washington, D.C.: Catholic University of America Press, 1970. Primarily an examination of the administrative history of the French Catholic church in the last third of the eighteenth century. Greenbaum also shows how such an organization became the school for statesmanship in forging the political career of Talleyrand.

Orieux, Jean. *Talleyrand: The Art of Survival*. Translated by Patricia Wolf. New York: Alfred A. Knopf, 1974. Comprehensive treatment which borrows heavily from the definitive biography by Georges Lacour-Gayet. Written in a catechistic style, the work portrays Talleyrand as a great custodian and transmitter of civilization, one "ever willing to meet the demands of the future for the sake of survival and the preservation of mankind's achievement."

Talleyrand-Périgord, Charles Maurice de. *Memoirs of the Prince de Talleyrand*. Edited by the Duc de Broglie. Translated by Raphaël Ledos de Beaufort and Mrs. Angus Hall. 5 vols. New York: G. P. Putnam's Sons, 1891-1892. A standard primary source. The first two volumes are somewhat sketchy in documentation. There is some compensation in the fullness of the official correspondence concerning the Congress of Vienna and the London Conference.

Wm. Laird Kleine-Ahlbrandt

TORQUATO TASSO

Born: March 11, 1544; Sorrento, Kingdom of Naples
Died: April 25, 1595; Rome
Area of Achievement: Literature
Contribution: Tasso—considered to be one of the greatest Italian poets—reflects the crisis of his age, and his writings seek to reconcile classical ideals with the renewed religious fervor arising from the Counter-Reformation. In this attempt to synthesize the vision of perfection and human dignity of the classics with Christian spiritual values lies the significance of his major works.

Early Life

Torquato Tasso was born in the coastal village of Sorrento, just south of Naples. His mother came from a noble Neapolitan family, while his father, originally from the northern town of Bergamo, was a diplomat and an accomplished man of letters who wrote a well-known chivalric poem entitled *Amadigi* in 1560. Although Tasso's first years were spent in the serene and idyllic atmosphere of the Mediterranean Sea, they were soon disturbed by a sudden and unexpected turbulence: His father, caught in the political misfortunes of his protector, the Prince of Salerno, was forced into exile, and all of his goods were confiscated. At the age of ten, Tasso was taken from the Jesuit school in Naples, where for two years he had studied Latin and Greek and had received a thorough religious training, and sent to Rome to be with his father. Thus began the agitated and roaming existence that was to mark his entire life, first by necessity and later as a tormented vocation. This abrupt separation from his mother, whom he was never to see again (she died prematurely a year later in 1556), left in the young Tasso an indelible impression that was to influence his lyrical production and reinforce his pessimistic view of the human condition. In 1557, he was at the court of Urbino; his father had just entered in the service of the duke, who was aware of Torquato's penchant for poetry and wanted the precocious young man to be a study companion to his own son. It was at Urbino that Torquato first came into contact with the splendid yet treacherous courtly environment that was to influence his life and writings deeply. At the age of fifteen, he relocated to Venice, and it was there, where the presence of the Turks was most felt and feared, that he began a rough draft of his famous epic poem on the First Crusade. The next five years were spent studying at the University of Padua, first law, according to his father's wishes, and then his own chosen fields of philosophy and letters. There, he met and frequented one of the most celebrated literary figures of the Renaissance, Sperone Speroni, and other famous scholars who stirred in him the ardent desire for lyrical expression.

At Padua, Tasso joined the Accademia degli Eterei and in 1562 published a chivalric poem in octaves, *Rinaldo* (English translation, 1792). This is a significant work in that it contains many of the themes that were to characterize his later production: the thirst for glory, adventure, and love and the yearning for chivalric ideals. It was during this time that Tasso's first doubts on religious matters surfaced—a lifelong spiritual struggle that would culminate in his later years in a complete revision of his famous epic using orthodox religious teachings and a dedication of the final years of his life to religious didactic works. Finally, it was at Padua that his love for Lucrezia Bendidio blossomed, and it was to her that many of his love poems would be dedicated.

Life's Work

In 1565, Tasso entered the service of Cardinal Luigi d'Este at the court of Ferrara and began the happiest and most fruitful period of his career; for the next ten years, he lived the ideal life of the man of letters for which he had longed. In 1567, he was given a literary stipend by Duke Alfonso II, and in this serene and refined courtly environment he was able to cultivate his genius and produce his most important works. Ferrara had been the home of the famous Renaissance poet, Ludovico Ariosto, and this for Tasso was both a source of inspiration and a spur to competition. Although the court of Ferrara was flourishing only in appearance and in reality was following Italy toward its political downfall, Tasso saw in its pomp and false grandeur the last vestiges of the ideals of the Renaissance, and he felt compelled to sing its praises.

Even though he composed many of his most beautiful poems during this period, dedicated to the ladies of the court, it was with the *Aminta* (1573; English translation, 1591) that Tasso established his reputation as a poet and playwright. This pastoral drama in five acts was first represented in the presence of Alfonso II on the island of Belvedere, the lovely summer residence of the Estensi, and was an immediate success. In his depiction of the world of the classical shepherd-poets, so rich in literary tradition, Tasso projected his ideals of a genteel and serene existence devoid in its primordial innocence of the sense of evil and sin. It also becomes for the poet an allegory of courtly life seen as a point of encounter for poets, sensitive souls, and fervent lovers. Although there are elements of tragedy in *Aminta*, all negativism is dissolved in the atmosphere of myth in which the drama evolves, and Tasso arrives at a perfect Renaissance unity of tone, rhythm, and style.

Only two years later, Tasso completed his most famous work and the one that established his poetic immortality, *Gerusalemme liberata* (1581; *Jerusalem Delivered*, 1600). The poem is divided into twenty cantos, in octaves, and follows the traditional hendecasyllabic scheme. While the subject matter is the historical conquest of Jerusalem by the First Crusade and therefore conforms to the rules of the epic, which Tasso had intended to follow as he states in *Discorsi del poema eroico* (1594; *Discourses on the Heroic Poem*, 1973), within the narration there are numerous secondary episodes that betray the poet's ambivalent feelings. It is in *Jerusalem Delivered* that the crisis of the Counter-Reformation is most strongly reflected. It is clear, especially in the love stories of Erminia, Clorinda, and Tancredi, that Tasso tries to recuperate the ideals of the Renaissance. Yet in the depiction of the struggle between good and evil, in the veiled sensuality and the sense of guilt found in the description of the garden of Armida, and in the tragic deaths of Solimano and Clorinda, a melancholy and pessimistic mood becomes apparent that reflects the crisis of the Baroque era.

Technically, *Jerusalem Delivered* tries to solve the debate concerning the relative merits of the chivalric and epic traditions. To the multiform variety of Ludovico Ariosto's chivalric poem, Tasso opposes the Aristotelian unity of action, and to the use of classical mythology he opposes the Christian supernatural. Yet the true value of the work lies in its depiction of the human condition; the main characters appear to be victims of a cruel fate that places them in utter solitude and renders them incapable of appeasing their desires. Even the surroundings are arid and desolate and seem to symbolize mankind's frailty and impotence.

This sense of tragic isolation was also felt in Tasso's personal experiences. Immediately after the completion of the epic, Tasso was haunted by religious scruples and personal self-doubt. On a literary plane, he revised the work along orthodox lines, culminating in the appearance of *Gerusalemme conquistata* (1593; *Jerusalem Conquered*, 1907), and he dedicated the rest of his life to religious writings such as *Le sette giornate del mondo creato* (1607; *Creation of the World*, 1982), in which he was able to meditate on Christian mysteries. On a personal level, he began a life of roaming marked by bizarre behavior and psychic disequilibrium. Torn by religious doubts (on more than one occasion he asked to be examined by the Inquisition) and haunted by a sense of persecution, he traveled throughout Italy only to return to Ferrara in 1579 on the occasion of the duke's marriage. Believing that he was slighted since little note was taken of his return, Tasso provoked a scandal by criticizing the duke, was declared mad, and was incarcerated in Sant' Anna.

After seven years of incarceration (much has been written concerning his presumed madness during this period), Tasso was freed through the intercession of the Prince of Mantua, but he could not find peace and continued to wander throughout Italy until his death on April 25, 1595.

Summary

Torquato Tasso is a prime example of the man of genius caught up in a period of transition, of change and upheaval. His major works reflect the conflict of the age of the Counter-Reformation and betray a nostalgic homage to the splendid literary revival of the Renaissance. Critics disagree as to whether Tasso was the last major poet of the Renaissance or the first great poet of the Baroque. Many consider him to be a transitional figure between the two periods, and indeed characteristic elements of both can be found in his writings. There is no disagreement, however, that Tasso belongs on the list of the world's greatest poets—from John Milton to Voltaire, from Lord Byron to T. S. Eliot, the poetry of Tasso has been praised and imitated, contemplated and enjoyed.

The melancholy and pessimistic mood that pervades much of his literary production can be attributed to the rapid changes that were taking place during his lifetime in the areas of religion, science, and politics. Amid such changes, Tasso attempted to reconcile the classical ideals that he cherished with contemporary reality. It is not surprising, therefore, that he was a favorite of the Romantic poets and still has much to offer to the contemporary reader.

Bibliography
Boulting, William. *Tasso and His Times*. London: Methuen, 1907. The classic biography of Tasso. Details the life of the author from both a factual and, at times, romantic point of view, with little critical analysis of his works. Although later scholarship has rejected its romanticized view of Tasso's life, Boulting's book is still fascinating reading and offers valuable insights into the author's age and the courtly environment that influenced his writings. Includes illustrations.
Brand, C. P. *Torquato Tasso*. Cambridge: Cambridge University Press, 1965. The standard English biographical and critical work on Tasso. Discusses the author's use of historical sources, gives a detailed account of his life, and analyzes his major works. Includes an interesting essay on the legend of Tasso's life and presumed madness, and ends with a lengthy chapter on the poet's contribution to English literature. Bibliographic references are included in the notes.
Cody, Richard. *The Landscape of the Mind*. Oxford, England: Clarendon Press, 1969. The first half of the book discusses the pastoral and Platonic theories in Tasso's *Aminta*. Also studies the play from the point of view of theater and makes references to it in the second half, where William Shakespeare's early comedies are analyzed.
Giamatti, A. Bartlett. *The Earthly Paradise and the Renaissance Epic*. Princeton, N.J.: Princeton University Press, 1966. Contains an interesting chapter on Armida's garden, with references to classical antecedents. Argues that *Jerusalem Delivered* was one of the most concentrated efforts of the sixteenth century to incorporate classical and chivalric materials into a Christian view of the world.

Greene, Thomas. *The Descent from Heaven: A Study in Epic Continuity.* New Haven, Conn.: Yale University Press, 1963. Presents a concise introduction to the epic from Homer to Vergil to Ludovico Ariosto's failed attempt. Proposes that Tasso does not produce a true epic since *Jerusalem Delivered* is too close to the romance tradition and much of the tragic potential is subordinated to the calls of the Counter-Reformation. Work includes a thorough bibliography.

Kates, Judith A. *Tasso and Milton: The Problem of Christian Epic.* Lewisburg, Pa.: Bucknell University Press, 1983. Following a discussion of the critical content of *Jerusalem Delivered*, this work analyzes *Discorsi dell'arte poetica* (1587), which is seen as a primer for the epic poem. The central chapter discusses *Jerusalem Delivered* in terms of the classical heroic and the modern romance. Concludes with Tasso's influence on John Milton's *Paradise Lost* (1667) and a lengthy bibliography.

Saez, Richard. *Theodicy in Baroque Literature.* New York: Garland, 1985. Places Tasso's work within a Baroque framework and uses religion as a critical guide. Of major importance is the bibliography that follows.

Tasso, Torquato. *Jerusalem Delivered.* Translated and edited by Ralph Nash. Detroit: Wayne State University Press, 1987. Easily the most readable translation in prose of *Gerusalemme liberata*. Includes a very useful glossary of names and places and an index of characters.

Victor A. Santi

PETER ILICH TCHAIKOVSKY

Born: May 7, 1840; Votkinsk (Vyatka district), Russia
Died: November 6, 1893; St. Petersburg, Russia
Area of achievement: Music
Contribution: Tchaikovsky is one of the most popular Western composers. His soaring melodies, expressive supporting harmonies, and lush orchestration have made his concertos and later symphonies the epitome of late Romantic musical opulence.

Early Life

Peter Ilich Tchaikovsky, the son of a mining engineer, received a good education as a child through his French governess, Fanny Dürbach, and his piano teacher, Mariya Palchikova. In 1848, his father retired and moved to St. Petersburg, where Tchaikovsky entered the preparatory program of the School of Jurisprudence in 1850, graduating nine years later. His mother, from whom he inherited his sensitivity, died in 1854. Tchaikovsky remained close to his father and siblings, five brothers and a sister, especially to his younger twin brothers, Anatoly and Modest.

Tchaikovsky accepted a position as a clerk in the Ministry of Justice in 1859, and in 1861 he began studies at the Russian Musical Society, which was transformed into the St. Petersburg Conservatory in 1862 under Anton Rubinstein. Tchaikovsky resigned his government position in the following year to become a full-time student at the conservatory, studying composition and orchestration with Rubinstein. He was graduated, with a silver medal in composition, in 1865. In the following year, he began his duties as a teacher of harmony at the newly founded conservatory in Moscow, headed by Anton Rubinstein's brother Nikolay.

Life's Work

Tchaikovsky's musical development was late in comparison to that of such composers as Ludwig van Beethoven, Franz Schubert, Robert Schumann, or Frédéric Chopin: The main compositions from his twenties are the song "None but the Lonely Heart," which contains the quintessential Tchaikovskyan melody in accompaniment to a text written by Johann Wolfgang von Goethe, and the uneven First Symphony in G Minor, subtitled *Winter Daydreams*. The first version of *Romeo and Juliet*, a fantasy overture based on William Shakespeare's tragedy, was finished in 1869, although the final version was not completed until 1880; this is the first of his orchestral works to be part of the standard repertory.

The works of Tchaikovsky's thirties include the second, third, and fourth symphonies; three string quartets (the first contains the famous "Andante cantabile," based on a Ukranian folk song that Tchaikovsky collected on a summer holiday in Kamenka in 1865); the first piano concerto (the introduction to the first movement is perhaps Tchaikovsky's best-known melody); and a violin concerto. The piano concerto received its premiere in the United States. Also from these years is his finest opera, *Yevgeny Onyegin* (Eugene Onegin), based on the poem by Alexander Pushkin; it is a psychological drama rather than a grand opera or mythological drama and showed that there was an alternative path to Richard Wagner's music dramas in the serious musical theater. Other major works include his orchestral fantasy *Francesca da Rimini* and the ballet *Swan Lake*.

The 1870's were the years in which Tchaikovsky began to establish his international musical reputation, but they were tragic for him personally. In 1868, he met the Belgian soprano Désirée Artôt, four years his senior, and began a courtship which was terminated first by his doubts about marriage and then by her sudden marriage to another singer in the touring opera company of which she was a member. In 1877, he married Antonina Milyukova, a young woman whom he scarcely knew; biographers have speculated that his real reason for his marriage was to quiet the rumors of homosexuality, which may have been manifested during his student days at the School of Jurisprudence. The marriage to Milyukova was a disaster, never consummated, and it eventually ended in divorce in 1881 after she bore another man an illegitimate child.

Further rumors about homosexual affairs at the Moscow Conservatory may have caused Tchaikovsky to resign his professorship there at the end of 1878. A more likely explanation is that Tchaikovsky came increasingly to resent the demands that teaching made on the time he wished to devote to composition. The advent of a mysterious patroness, Nadezhda von Meck, who provided him with a generous subsidy on the condition that they never meet (although they exchanged a voluminous correspondence), gave Tchaikovsky financial independence for twelve years.

The six years afterward were less productive ones for the composer. The main works of this relatively fallow period were the opera *Orleanskaya Dyeva*, after Friedrich Schiller's drama *Die Jungfrau von Orleans* (1801; *The Maid of Orleans*, 1835), a fanciful historical drama about Joan of Arc; the Piano Trio in A Minor, an elegy for Nikolay Rubinstein; and the serenade for string orchestra.

Tchaikovsky was not a member of the circle of composers around Mili Balakirev, the *Moguchkaya Kuchka* (mighty handful), which included Modest Mussorgsky and Nikolay Rimsky-Korsakov, but he did receive advice from Balakirev on *Romeo and Juliet* and on the work marking Tchaikovsky's creative renewal, the program symphony *Manfred*, based on a poem by George Gordon, Lord Byron, featuring the wanderings and unfulfilled love of an alienated outsider. Tchaikovsky finished the work in 1885; it belongs to that small group of literary program symphonies that includes Hector Berlioz's *Symphonie fantastique* and *Harold in Italy* and Franz Liszt's *Faust Symphony*. The four movements depict, respectively, Manfred's wanderings and his memories of his beloved Astarte; Manfred's encounter with the witch of the Alps; a pastoral slow movement where Manfred encounters the inhabitants of the Swiss mountains; and a final movement first depicting the court of the demon Ahriman, then featuring Manfred's forgiveness by Astarte and his peaceful death. The work is Tchaikovsky's orchestral masterpiece, but it is not performed frequently because of its length and technical difficulty.

Among the other works marking Tchaikovsky's creative renewal are the Fifth Symphony, his most popular work, in which he follows the technique of *Manfred* in having a "motto theme" appear in all four movements of the work in various transformations; the pleasant string sextet "Souvenir of Florence"; and his other major opera, *Pikovaya Dama* (*The Queen of Spades*), based on a story by Alexander Pushkin as adapted by Tchaikovsky's brother Modest. Despite its macabre topic, the opera has been one of Tchaikovsky's most popular.

Tchaikovsky's last few years were marked by outward success and constant travel, but deep inner conflicts. He was the first major composer to visit the United States, conducting his music in April and May of 1891 (especially the first piano concerto) in New York, Baltimore, and Philadelphia and visiting Washington, D.C., and Niagara Falls. He was very pleased at the acclaim and hospitality he received, but he was torn with homesickness for Russia. In the following year, he received an honorary doctor of music degree from the University of Cambridge in England. His outward honors were canceled in his mind by fits of despair, fears that his creativity was exhausted and that he was repeating himself musically, and compulsive travel marked by spells of homesickness during which he would cancel concerts to return to Russia. His two main last works, however, reveal the disparity in his creative impulses: the Sixth Symphony (called, after his death, the *Pathétique* by his brother Modest), with its unusual form, ends with a despairing slow movement; while the ballet *Shchelkunchik* (*The Nutcracker*, based on a tale by E. T. A. Hoffmann), has delighted children at Christmas for decades—the suite extracted from the ballet is Tchaikovsky's most frequently performed composition.

The circumstances of Tchaikovsky's death in November, 1893, shortly after the first performance of the Sixth Symphony, are still a matter of controversy. The traditional account is that either by accident or by design (if one accepts the "suicidal" thoughts expressed in the last movement of the Sixth Symphony) the composer drank a glass of unboiled water during a cholera epidemic in St. Petersburg in late 1893. Alexandra Orlova brought to the West the story that she had heard from an elderly member of the Russian Museum staff, who claimed that the drink was actually poison and was taken to escape the possibility of a scandal brought on by a homosexual encounter.

More recently a less lurid theory has been advanced: Tchaikovsky did ingest contaminated food or water during the cholera epidemic, but his doctor misdiagnosed his ailment until it was too late to institute a regimen of proper treatment.

Summary

Tchaikovsky composed effectively in virtually every musical genre of the late nineteenth century: symphony, opera, ballet, art song, concerto, chamber music, and even church music (his Russian Orthodox church music, especially the Vespers of 1882, includes some of the finest examples of the genre), though his solo piano music is the least effective of his works. He worshiped Wolfgang Amadeus Mozart's music and esteemed his French contemporaries—such as Georges Bizet, Léo Delibes, and Camille Saint-Saëns—over such German composers as Richard Wagner and Johannes Brahms, whose music he particularly disliked (Brahms reciprocated this feeling).

Tchaikovsky's musical development is more comparable to the spiral (as his brother Modest suggested) than to the straight-line development of a Beethoven or Schubert. Particularly striking elements of his style are his soaring melodies, his effective use of the orchestra, his rich supporting harmony (which in many respects recalls the devices of Liszt), and his experiments with musical form. Though not particularly close to the Russian nationalist composers, he could use Russian folk songs as effectively as any of them, as best seen in the finale of his Second Symphony.

His extensive travels in the West and his formal training in Western compositional techniques at the St. Petersburg Conservatory have given rise to the mistaken idea that he was Western rather than Russian in his musical orientation: yet he considered himself Russian above all, and he is still honored as a national treasure in the Soviet Union. Tchaikovsky has been faulted by critics for his piling of climax upon climax in an almost frenzied and hysterical manner (the development section of the first movement of the Fourth Symphony, for example), his compositional technique of seeming to stitch blocks of music together, and an almost blatant vulgarity (the finale of the Fifth Symphony), but Beethoven, Giuseppe Verdi, and Gustav Mahler have been accused of vulgarity also.

Tchaikovsky set the standard for the large-scale epic symphony, bravura concerto, and dramatic ballet among Russian and Soviet composers, and he is often the composer through whom many young persons are first attracted to art music. He remains one of the few composers for whom programs devoted entirely to his music attract a sizable audience. His popularity among the general musical audience shows no sign of waning, and recent critical studies have elevated his stature to that of one of the major composers of the late nineteenth century.

Bibliography
Abraham, Gerald, ed. *The Music of Tchaikovsky.* New York: W. W. Norton, 1946. A series of ten essays by specialists on various aspects of Tchaikovsky's life and work. Edward Lockspeiser's account of "Tchaikovsky the Man" is of special interest for the general reader, though all the essays are oriented more toward music lovers than musical scholars.

Brown, David. "Pyotr Il'yich Tchaikovsky." In *Russian Masters 1: Glinka, Borodin, Balakirev, Musorgsky, Tchaikovsky.* New York: W. W. Norton, 1986. The entry is essentially Brown's article on Tchaikovsky's life and works in *The New Grove* dictionary with additions. The article provides the best short survey of the composer's life and works, though it is flawed by the author's uncritical acceptance of Orlova's lurid account of Tchaikovsky's suicide. The list of works and bibliography are especially complete.

_____. *Tchaikovsky: A Biographical and Critical Study.* Vol. 1, *The Early Years (1840-1874).* New York: W. W. Norton, 1978. The most complete account of the composer's boyhood and youth, with critical discussions of his works of the period. The graphic analyses provide easy-to-grasp diagrams of the musical structure of these compositions.

_____. *Tchaikovsky: A Biographical and Critical Study.* Vol. 2, *The Crisis Years (1874-1878).* New York: W. W. Norton, 1983. The turbulent years of the composer's first compositions to gain international acceptance, coupled with the crucial events of his life during this period, are extensively discussed. The analyses of his music are not quite as detailed in Brown's other works and are flawed by some forced and unconvincing attempts to find thematic interrelationships. Two additional volumes are in preparation.

Orlova, Alexandra. "Tchaikovsky: The Last Chapter." *Music and Letters* 62 (1981): 125. This article contains the basic statement (though the author has since modified some of her arguments) of the sensational account of Tchaikovsky's supposed suicide after his trial by a court of honor composed of alumni of the School of Jurisprudence.

Poznansky, Alexander. "Tchaikovsky's Suicide: Myth and Reality." *Nineteenth-Century Music* 11 (1988). In an extensively documented study, the author refutes Orlova's argument that Tchaikovsky committed suicide and posits the thesis that the composer's death was the result of his doctor's misdiagnosis and that proper treatment was begun too late.

Wiley, Roland John. *Tchaikovsky's Ballets.* New York: Oxford University Press, 1985. This study examines the music of Tchaikovsky's three grand ballets—*Swan Lake*, *Sleeping Beauty*, and *The Nutcracker*—and also investigates the circumstances surrounding their composition, their original and subsequent productions, and the audiences for these ballets.

Yoffe, Elkhonon, ed. *Tchaikovsky in America: The Composer's Visit in*

1891. Translated by Lidya Yoffe. New York: Oxford University Press, 1986. Copious excerpts from Tchaikovsky's diaries, correspondence, and news accounts of the time of Tchaikovsky's visits to New York, Baltimore, and Philadelphia in 1891, and the abortive ventures to bring him to the United States for subsequent tours.

Rey M. Longyear

GEORG PHILIPP TELEMANN

Born: March 14, 1681; Magdeburg, Brandenburg
Died: June 25, 1767; Hamburg
Area of Achievement: Music
Contribution: In addition to creating a vast quantity of beautiful music, Telemann championed the development of simpler, more readily accessible forms of composition, expanded the control of the composer over his works, and paved the way for the transition from the Baroque to the classical style.

Early Life

Georg Philipp Telemann was the younger of two sons born to Heinrich Telemann, a minister at the Church of the Holy Ghost at Magdeburg. Both of Telemann's grandfathers had been clergymen, and nearly all of his known ancestors had been university educated. It was therefore natural that Telemann would be expected to follow in their footsteps. He was sent to local schools to study Latin, rhetoric, and dialectic (logical reasoning) but immediately demonstrated a great talent for music, too. Without any formal instruction, Telemann taught himself to play the violin, flute, zither, and keyboard instruments, as well as the rudiments of composition, by the age of ten. He was soon writing operatic arias, motets, short instrumental pieces, and, by the time he was twelve, his first opera.

Telemann's interest in music greatly alarmed his mother, who wanted him to become a minister. She prohibited him from engaging in any further musical activity, took away his instruments, and sent him away to school at the town of Zellerstadt. There, she hoped, the superintendent would guide the young man back to the true path. Ironically, however, the superintendent was an expert in theoretical music studies; instead of discouraging Telemann, he taught his pupil the relationships between music and mathematics and helped him hone his expertise in composition.

After completing his elementary schooling, Telemann continued his education at Hildesheim, where he was once again blessed with a mentor who encouraged his musical interests. For the next four years, Telemann wrote incidental songs for school plays (performed in Latin) and joined his fellow students in performances of German cantatas at a local church. He also traveled to Hannover and Brunswick, where he attended performances of French instrumental music and Italian opera. Fired with enthusiasm, he began writing compositions modeled on these popular styles.

In autumn, 1701, Telemann was matriculated at the University of Leipzig. Since he had displayed no interest in theology, his mother decided that he should study law. Telemann dutifully left all of his music and instruments at home in Magdeburg and even attempted to conceal his musical talent from the other students. He could not stop composing, however, and one day his roommate discovered a cantata Telemann had written and arranged to have it performed at the Thomaskirche, a famous Leipzig church. The mayor of Leipzig, who heard the performance, was so impressed that he commissioned Telemann to write a new cantata for the church every other week. From that point on, Telemann's future as a composer was firmly set.

Life's Work

From the very beginning of his career, Telemann was a pioneer of new musical styles. Throughout the seventeenth century, the dominant Baroque style had become increasingly complex, employing layers of counterpoint and polyphony in densely magnificent musical structures. By the early 1700's, however, younger composers were seeking new, simpler forms of musical expression that could be understood and enjoyed by a wider public than the highly educated and cultured upper classes. Composers such as Telemann, George Frideric Handel, and Gottfried Stoelzel were in the vanguard of this movement.

Telemann threw himself into his new profession with furious energy. In 1702, he organized a student collegium musicum (music society), which began giving regular public concerts. Since many of the music students earned a little extra money singing in local opera houses, Telemann's leadership of the collegium thus led him into a position as Kapellmeister (music director) of the new Leipzig Opera, where he composed numerous operas and employed students as both singers and instrumentalists. Two years later, in 1704, he added even more to his responsibilities by winning the position of organist and music director at the Neukirche, the university church. There he led his collegium musicum in concerts of sacred music, much of which he himself composed.

Inevitably, perhaps, older, more traditional composers resisted what they perceived in the new music as a decline of standards. Leipzig's music director, Johann Kuhnau, was in charge of music production for all of the city's churches, and he resented the instant popularity of the young newcomer. He complained to the city fathers that Telemann's new commission infringed on his rights and characterized Telemann as nothing but an "opera musician" who was stealing all the students away from the city churches to the Neukirche. Telemann's reputation had grown so much and so quickly, however, that Kuhnau's complaints were ignored.

So popular had Telemann become, in fact, that, in 1705, he was appointed Kapellmeister to the court of the Count of Promnitz at Sorau in Lower Lusatia (part of modern Poland). In eighteenth century Germany, an aspiring composer had two possible career paths: He could obtain a position as a choir or music director for a city in one or more of its local churches; or, if lucky, he might win employment as Kappellmeister or Konzertmeister (orchestra leader) at the court of a nobleman. With his appointment to the court of Promnitz, Telemann started his climb to the heights of the eighteenth century composer's world.

Like many German noblemen of the time, the count had acquired a taste for French instrumental music. Telemann was therefore required to churn out French-style overtures as well as other instrumental and operatic music, but, at least at first, he looked upon such "assembly-line" composing as an opportunity to sharpen his command of music theory. Traveling with the count to Upper Silesia, Telemann also became acquainted with Polish folk music, many of whose themes he later incorporated into his own works.

Though he was happy in his position, Telemann resigned in 1707, apparently because of unsettled political conditions in eastern Germany, which was being invaded by King Charles XII of Sweden. When the battlefront reached the lands of the count, his court was dispersed. Telemann had few regrets, however, for not only had he recently become engaged to one of the ladies-in-waiting to the countess of Promnitz but also he had received an even better appointment. On Christmas Eve, 1708, he arrived in the city of Eisenach to take charge of the newly formed musical establishment of the Duke of Saxe-Eisenach, one of the great noblemen of Germany.

As Konzertmeister of the duke's orchestra, Telemann continued to produce a constant stream of overtures, concerti, and chamber music. When the duke completed the construction of a new palace chapel, Telemann added church cantatas, oratorios, and ceremonial music to his output, in addition to supervising the training of choristers. During this busy period, he was only allowed to take a leave of absence for a few months in 1709, in order to return to Sorau to collect his new bride (but not until he had solemnly promised not to accept any other position).

In January, 1711, however, Telemann's life was shattered by the death of his wife following the birth of a daughter. It has been suggested by some historians that this experience drove him to leave Eisenach, while others assert that Telemann was simply tired of producing reams of music tailored to the tastes of his noble patrons. In any case, in February, 1712, he accepted an invitation to become music director for the city of Frankfurt, where he was more at liberty to compose as his inspiration led him. In addition, he had the opportunity to influence and develop the musical life of the city: Once again, he organized a collegium musicum, and he led it in weekly public concerts. He composed several cycles of cantatas and oratorios for the churches, orchestral and chamber works for the collegium, and special pieces for civic celebrations. He also remarried, in 1714, and somehow managed to find time to father ten more children (none of whom became a musician).

Though relatively content at Frankfurt, Telemann was disappointed by the lack of an outlet for his operatic talents. When the city of Hamburg offered him the position of city music director there in July, 1721, he quickly accepted, apparently because Hamburg had an opera house. For the rest of his life, Telemann provided the city with unprecedented quantities of church and civic music, trained and led choirs, organized yet another collegium musicum, and led its concerts. At the same time, as music director of the Hamburg Opera from 1722 until it closed in 1738, he wrote and directed more than twenty operas of his own, also producing those of other composers, including Handel. Not satisfied with all these accomplishments, Telemann became his own publisher, personally engraving the printing press plates, writing his own advertising copy, and arranging for distribution in cities all over Europe.

In 1740, he decided to retire from independent composing in order to devote the rest of his life to writing books on musical theory, though he continued to meet his civic obligations as Hamburg's music director. For fifteen years, he kept to this decision, but, in 1755, possibly influenced by his old friend Handel, he once again, at age seventy-four, began to write oratorios, and many of these were performed long after his death in 1767. In an age when popular music came and went almost as quickly as the latest hits of modern times, this was a remarkable testament to the genius of this most prolific of composers.

Summary

Georg Philipp Telemann was not a physically remarkable man, despite his prodigious energy and unusual longevity. Portraits of him reveal a stolid, serious, workmanlike demeanor; he could easily be taken for a banker. Until recently, this image reflected critical opinion of Telemann's music, too: It was considered pleasant and craftsmanlike, but not at all in the same class as that of Johann Sebastian Bach. Telemann was regarded as a hack who had turned out masses of superficial music (more than three thousand pieces) on demand. Only in the last half-century have his achievements begun to be adequately appreciated.

Telemann was part—and often the leader—of a movement that brought great changes in German music. Until the beginning of the eighteenth century, a composer's music was dictated by the position he held: Music directors were not allowed to write operas, and court composers had to satisfy the tastes of their patrons. Telemann, however, refused to be bound by such restrictions: He took his music out of the churches and the noble courts and into the newly constructed opera houses and concert halls. In his public concerts, he might combine a program of church music, instrumental works, and operatic excerpts, thus giving music lovers an opportunity to hear and enjoy many varieties of music. By aggressively promoting the publication of his music, he assured that it would be available to anyone who wanted it, and, by making many of his works as simple as possible, he encouraged musicians of all levels of ability to play it, whether professionally or simply at home for pleasure. Insisting that the composer had the right to do with his works whatever he saw fit, Telemann helped to establish a new tradition of the artist as an independent agent, rather than simply the servant or employee of someone else.

Through his tremendous energy and his interest in teaching others, Telemann influenced an entire generation of German composers. The collegia he established became the training ground of younger men such as Johann Friedrich Fasch and Gottfried Stoelzel, who modeled their compositions after his. The texts he wrote were used and praised many decades after his death. His music, however, was buried in obscurity at the beginning of the nineteenth century. The Bach revival of the 1840's fostered an image of Baroque composition sharply at odds with the simpler kind of music that Telemann wrote, and it was not until the twentieth century that scholars such as Max Schneider and Romain Rolland argued that Telemann and Bach were simply not comparable: Bach, they asserted, looked backward to a style that was already obsolete, while Telemann was a forerunner of the classical period. It is only recently, through the growing number and popularity of Telemann recordings, that his primary goal of making music for everyone is finally being met.

Bibliography
Abraham, Gerald. *The Concise Oxford History of Music*. London: Oxford University Press, 1979. An outstanding general history of music. Groups types of music topically, rather than by composer, with a broad chronological framework. Thus, references to Telemann are scattered about the text, according to the type of music being discussed (such as Italian opera, French overtures, and so on). Extensive bibliography.
Borroff, Edith. *The Music of the Baroque*. Dubuque, Iowa: William C. Brown, 1970. An excellent, if brief, introduction to Baroque music for students with minimal musical background. Musical examples are explained sufficiently to allow beginning students to learn a substantial amount of music theory relatively painlessly. Includes excellent, entertaining, and well-arranged illustrations. An outstanding feature is the inclusion of brief discographies for each type and area of music discussed.
Bukofzer, Manfred F. *Music in the Baroque Era, from Monteverdi to Bach*. New York: W. W. Norton, 1947. A classic text on the Baroque era. Although highly readable, this is definitely an academic work for the serious student and requires substantial music background. Contains useful chapters for the nonspecialist on "Musical Thought of the Baroque Era" and "Sociology of Baroque Music," which illuminate the social, political, and intellectual milieu in which Baroque composers worked. A massive bibliography, and lists of published editions of composers' works are included.

Maczewsky, A. "Georg Philipp Telemann." In *Grove's Dictionary of Music and Musicians*, edited by Eric Blom, vol. 8. London: Macmillan, 1954. Maczewsky's article was the standard biography of Telemann at the beginning of the post-World War II revival of interest in the composer. Well-written, solidly researched, but not superseded by Martin Ruhnke's work, cited below.

Petzoldt, Richard. *Georg Philipp Telemann*. Translated by Horace Fitzpatrick. New York: Oxford University Press, 1974. The only modern book-length biography of Telemann in English. Full of fascinating anecdotes as well as a thorough analysis of Telemann's music. While a knowledge of music theory would be helpful, almost any reader can enjoy this enthusiastic work. Includes a comprehensive bibliography.

Rolland, Romain. *A Musical Tour Through the Lands of the Past*. Translated by Bernard Miall. London: Oxford University Press, 1922. As one of the greatest twentieth century music historians, Rolland was largely responsible for the reevaluation of Telemann. Rolland insisted that Telemann was an unappreciated genius whose energy, fertile imagination, and unselfish desire to give music to the whole world inspired his followers and helped bring about the classical era.

Ruhnke, Martin. "Georg Philipp Telemann." In *North European Baroque Masters*. New York: W. W. Norton, 1985. A concise biography, one of six included in this volume, all by noted musical scholars. Contains an excellent, up-to-date catalog of Telemann's works, as well as a comprehensive bibliography.

_____. "Relationships Between the Life and Work of Georg Philipp Telemann." *The Consort* no. 24 (1967): 271-279. One of the few specialized studies of Telemann in English. Useful even for those without extensive musical background, since it focuses on the events of Telemann's life and how they appear to have influenced his work. Ruhnke presents evidence to refute many older views of Telemann and analyzes and compares the three autobiographies Telemann wrote.

Thomas C. Schunk

SAINT TERESA OF ÁVILA

Born: March 28, 1515; Ávila, Spain
Died: October 4, 1582; Alba, Spain
Areas of Achievement: Church reform and theology
Contribution: This patron saint of Spain and doctor of the Church was active in reforming monasticism in Spain. She is also known for her mystic writings, which describe how mental prayer can bring the soul through successive stages to union with God.

Early Life

In the sixteenth century, in the aftermath of the victory over the Muslims and of the expulsion of the Jews, religious fervor, controversy, and fanaticism dominated Spain. The Inquisition was established to impose purity of thought on the peninsula. In this atmosphere of religious zeal, the Inquisition forced Teresa de Cepeda y Ahumada's Jewish grandfather, Juan Sánchez, and his two sons (including Teresa's father) to accept public humiliation to prove that they were sincere converts to Christanity. Such demonstrations did not necessarily preserve converted Jews from future abuse, so Sánchez took his wife's name, de Cepeda, and left his home in Toledo to begin a new life free from the scrutiny of the Inquisition. Teresa's father, Alonso de Cepeda, settled in Ávila, where he worked as a merchant and tax collector. There he married his second wife, Beatriz Ahumada, Teresa's mother.

Teresa was born on March 28, 1515, in Ávila. She was a cheerful, vivacious child who loved friends and conversation. She was very pretty, plump with white skin and curly black hair. Her looks and personality made her a favorite of her father and her nine siblings, and throughout her life she continued to charm all who knew her. As a child, she enjoyed reading, from her father's serious books to her mother's light romances.

The carefree childhood years ended when Teresa was thirteen and her mother died. For three years, Teresa indulged in behavior that she recalled could have damaged her reputation. Her father removed her from danger by sending her to study at the Augustinian convent. In 1536, she overcame her father's objections and entered the Carmelite Convent of the Incarnation in Ávila, where she took her vows the following year.

The Convent of the Incarnation observed a mitigated Rule of Mount Carmel, which meant that it was not very strict. For almost twenty years in the convent, Teresa was torn between her conflicting desires. She yearned for a spiritual life, reading mystic books and practicing mental prayer. At the same time, she desired a secular life, enjoying the admiration of her many visitors. In later years, Teresa wrote against lax convents that permitted nuns to indulge in such vanities, and her experience as a young nun shaped her reform movement. During this time, perhaps partly because of her internal turmoil, she became ill and suffered pain and temporary partial paralysis. For the rest of her life, she endured recurring illness. When she was thirty-nine years old, she had a vision of Christ and then began to have other mystic experiences that finally let her free herself from her worldly temptations and begin her spiritual life as a mystic and church reformer.

Life's Work

Teresa's first visible manifestations of spirituality were raptures, during which she became rigid and cold with no discernible pulse. During these raptures, Teresa also was reputed to have experienced levitation, floating up uncontrollably, much to her embarrassment. These external manifestations of her spiritual state did not end her struggles with the Spanish hierarchy. Her grandfather's Jewish past was not forgotten, and it made some religious leaders look at her experiences with suspicion.

By 1557, the Catholic Reformation was well under way. The Council of Trent was meeting to defend doctrine against the challenge of Protestants. Spanish Catholics such as Teresa seemed to fear Lutherans as much as they feared appearances of the Devil. As part of the Church's rigorous reform, Pope Paul IV issued a new Index of forbidden books that censored many of the mystical writings that had guided Teresa's mental prayers. Religious authorities searched convents and confiscated books. In 1559, the Inquisition increased its efforts to protect the peninsula from unorthodox thought, often focusing on converted Jews, whom they believed were susceptible to secret nonconformity often expressed through mystic theology. Church authorities assigned Teresa a series of confessors to examine her raptures, and her confessors' doubts caused her much turmoil. In 1559, she received her most famous vision, seeing and feeling an angel piercing her heart with a spear. This vision settled her doubts; she no longer feared confessors or inquisitors. Thus spiritually at ease, she began her active life as a reformer of the Carmelite Order.

In 1560, Teresa and a small group of nuns at the Convent of the Incarnation made a vow to follow the more rigorous unmitigated rule of the original Carmelites. Her desire to move out of her unreformed convent into a new one in Ávila raised an outcry. Many monks and nuns objected to Teresa's dedication, because such a reform represented an implicit criticism of their own lives. Further objection came from the population of Ávila. In the mid-sixteenth century, almost one-fourth of the population in Spain was ecclesiastical, either clerical or monastic. The lay public had to finance this religious population, and the people of Ávila were reluctant to support another convent within their city walls. Opposition from both of these groups, monastic and lay, plagued the reform movement that represented much of Teresa's life's work.

Two years after Teresa began her efforts at reform, she received permission to establish a new convent in Ávila. In August of 1562, she founded the reform convent of San José, and became its prioress the following year. As a symbolic gesture of her new reform, she and the novices removed their shoes to wear rough sandals. This act gave her reform movement the name Discalced (without shoes), and writers describe the subsequent struggles within the Carmelite movement as between the Calced and Discalced groups.

Teresa's notoriety brought her again to the attention of the Inquisition, which ordered her to write an account of her life for its review. In 1562, Teresa completed the first version of her autobiography, which she later expanded. The Inquisition found this *Libro de su vida* (wr. 1565, pb. 1611; *The Life of the Mother Teresa of Jesus*, 1611) acceptable. This work is a major source of information about the saint's early life. It also opens a new and influential side of Teresa's active life, her writings. In addition to her autobiography, Teresa wrote four books, six shorter works (including a collection of verses), and many letters, of which 458 survive. Her most famous mystical works are *El camino de perfección* (wr. 1565, pb. 1583; *The Way of Perfection*, 1852), written to guide the nuns in her newly reformed convents, and *El castillo interior: O, Tratado de las moradas* (wr. 1577, pb. 1588; *The Interior Castle: Or, The Mansions*, 1852). In these and other works, Teresa described her techniques of mental prayer, which had been so important in her own spiritual growth.

From 1567 to 1576, Teresa expanded the Discalced Reform by establishing new convents throughout most of Spain. Teresa, frequently ill, traveled throughout the countryside to bring enclosed convents, erected in poverty, to many parts of the kingdom. The indefatigable founder overcame problems of opposition and financing to found seventeen reform convents for women. During her travels, Teresa met John of the Cross, a Carmelite and priest, who became her confessor, friend, and supporter in establishing two Discalced monasteries for men.

Between 1576 and 1578, the expansion of the reform movement was stopped by increasing pressure from the opposition. The Calced Carmelites kidnapped leaders of the Discalceds to force them back into observance of the Mitigated Rule of Carmel. Calced monks imprisoned John of the Cross in Toledo for eight months during these times of troubles. The turmoil reached Teresa herself; once again, the Inquisition summoned her to respond to its interrogations. Throughout this period, Teresa wrote many letters to gather support for her movement and was able to win the support of influential patrons, including King Philip II of Spain.

Finally, in 1580, her reform movement was victorious. Pope Gregory XIII officially separated the Calced from the Discalced Carmelites, sanctioning the reform and creating its independent administration. Teresa's favorite, Jerome Gracián, was made the first leader of the Discalceds, and John of the Cross became an administrator of the movement. Teresa was content that papal authority had safeguarded her reform, and she spent the last two years of her life establishing three more foundations and writing many letters. She became ill as she journeyed to the reform convent in Alba and died there on October 4, 1582. (The day after her death, the Gregorian reform calendar was adopted, and her feast day is celebrated on October 15 because of the changed calendar.)

Summary

Nine months after Teresa of Ávila's death, her followers exhumed her body and allegedly found that it had not decayed. Her supporters used this discovery to forward her cause for sanctity, and her immediate popularity led to repeated dismemberments of the body and distribution of her relics to many churches. In 1614, Pope Paul V declared her blessed, and the Spanish parliament proclaimed her the patroness of Spain in 1617. In 1622, Pope Gregory XV pronounced Teresa a saint.

One of Teresa's enduring accomplishments was her reform of Spanish monasticism, which was part of the Catholic Reformation's response to the growth of Protestantism. The Discalced Reform she began continued and spread after her death to remain a force in Spanish life. Teresa is probably most widely remembered for her mystical experiences and for her written articulation of spiritual doctrine. The sculptor Gian Lorenzo Bernini popularized the piercing of Teresa's heart in his statue, *The Ecstasy of Saint Teresa*, made in 1645 for the Church of Santa Maria della Vittoria in Rome. Reverence for this ecstasy grew in the eighteenth century, when churchmen examined Teresa's heart and discovered that it bore a hole as evidence of the angel's piercing arrow. In 1726, Pope Benedict XIII instituted the Feast of the Transverberation of Teresa's heart to commemorate this mystical event.

In 1970, Pope Paul VI declared Teresa to be a doctor of the Church and her works worthy of study. All Teresa's major spiritual writings include discussions of her mystic theology, but the most sophisticated expression of her theology is found in *The Interior Castle*. Teresa wrote this book while in a trance, and it discusses the soul's capacity to move progressively through the rooms of itself to reach God, who dwells at the center. By locating God at the center of the soul, Teresa expressed God's presence and accessibility to searching believers.

The Interior Castle mirrors the life of the saint herself. Teresa had to cut herself off from her past, which in Counter-Reformation Spain marked her as a converted Jew; she called herself Teresa of Jesus, renouncing her family name. She had to transcend the temptations that bound her for twenty years in feelings of sin, and she fought against a monastic system that she believed had grown too lax for spiritual safety. She did all of these things by retreating to a strength inside herself, where she found God. Through this strength, she changed her world and wrote to tell others how to change theirs.

Bibliography

Clissold, Stephen. *St. Teresa of Ávila*. New York: Harper & Row, 1982. A fine, easy-to-read short biography that brings Teresa's world and accomplishments to life. Provides a sensitive balance between the reputation of the saint, with her raptures and levitations, and the woman, who worked hard in her reform movement. Contains an index.

Lincoln, Victoria. *Teresa: A Woman*. Albany: State University of New York Press, 1984. A thorough, well-researched, and readable biography of Teresa with details on all aspects of her life and work. Stresses the woman rather than the saint. Contains a useful index and a brief bibliography.

O'Brien, Kate. *Teresa of Ávila*. London: Max Parrish, 1951. A short book describing Teresa's life and work. Rambling at times, but provides background on the Carmelite Order and Teresa's reform work.

Peers, E. Allison. *Saint Teresa of Jesus, and Other Essays and Addresses*. London: Faber & Faber, 1953. A collection of essays by the preeminent Teresan scholar. Contains an index.

Sackville-West, Victoria. *The Eagle and the Dove*. Garden City, N.Y.: Doubleday, Doran, 1944. A comparison of the life of Saint Teresa with that of Thérèse de Lisieux. The section on Teresa of Ávila offers a short account of her mystic experiences, written from within the Catholic tradition.

Whalen, James. *The Spiritual Teachings of Teresa of Ávila and Adrian Van Kaam: Formative Spirituality*. New York: University Press of America, 1984. Offers a sophisticated description of Teresa's theology and compares it with a twentieth century existential philosopher. Useful for those who want to explore the complexities of Teresa's thought and its relevance for modern times, but it is too complicated for the casual reader. Contains a full annotated bibliography.

Joyce E. Salisbury

ADOLPHE THIERS

Born: April 15, 1797; Marseilles, France
Died: September 3, 1877; Saint-Germaine-en-Laye, near Paris, France
Areas of Achievement: Government, politics, and historiography
Contribution: Thiers was a central figure among the moderate politicians who in the early nineteenth century created the July Monarchy and, forty years later, the Third Republic. He also wrote important multivolume histories of the revolutionary and Napoleonic eras.

Early Life

Marie-Joseph-Louis-Adolphe Thiers was born a month before his parents married. Four months later his ne'er-do-well father, Louis, disappeared and was not heard from again until his son was successful enough to provide financial support. Adolphe was reared in poverty by his mother, Marie-Madeleine (née Amic), and her mother. The experience left him with a lifelong inclination to seek some support and approval of his actions from older women.

With the help of relatives, Thiers received a proper education, and in November, 1815, he began a three-year tenure in law school at Aix-en-Provence. Thiers became a member of the bar in November, 1818, but times were hard for young lawyers. Thiers, short, almost gnomish, with a reedy voice, lacked the presence to get even his share of cases. He filled his time and pockets by competing for literary prizes offered by regional academies, but his real livelihood was provided by his mother. Prospects were few, and, urged by his friend François Mignet, Thiers decided to try his hand as a writer in Paris. He left his family and a woman who seems to have expected marriage.

In November, 1821, after a brief stint in a secretarial position, Thiers joined the staff of the liberal newspaper the *Constitutionnel*; three months later, he signed a contract to write a history of the French Revolution. Bourbon Royalism was in the political ascendancy, and the liberals were happy to have new recruits, so Thiers rose quickly.

By the mid-1820's, Thiers's reputation as a journalist was established, and the ten-volume *Histoire de la révolution française* (1823-1827; *The History of the French Revolution*, 1838) proved him to be a historian of note. He was moving in prominent circles, such as that of the banker Jacques Laffitte, where, along with his future rival François Guizot, he met the legendary Talleyrand. Political discussion was intense, and Thiers's hostility to the Bourbons and the aristocracy was growing. Although, like most liberals of the era, Thiers embraced the Enlightenment's faith in reason, commitment to civil rights, and religious skepticism, he still favored constitutional monarchy rather than a republic.

Life's Work

In January, 1830, Thiers, Mignet, and Armand Carrel inaugurated the *National*, which became Thiers's chief organ of persuasion for a number of years. The paper was a leading voice in the criticisms of the government of Charles X, and when the king's efforts to strengthen royal authority provoked open resistance in July, its offices were a center of revolutionary activity. Although he had spoken for moderation, faced with revolt, Thiers helped to write a proclamation claiming credit for the *National* in calling France to arms. He worked diligently to get a constitutional monarchy created under Louis-Philippe, the Duke of Orléans. That was formally accomplished on August 9.

In the first month of the new regime, Thiers was given several senior-level government appointments and resigned from his journalistic connections. He would serve in six governments over the next decade. Thiers, however, had too little property to qualify. The Dosne family sold him a house in Paris on good terms, and Thiers was elected deputy for Aix-en-Provence and appointed Parliamentary Undersecretary for the Ministry of Finance.

Practical experience influenced Thiers's views of government, and by the spring of 1832 he had shifted from the Party of Movement to the Party of Resistance. The death of the premier, Casimir Périer, led to a new government with Thiers as minister of the interior. His delicate task was to control the Duchess of Berry, who was leading efforts for a legitimist uprising in the name of her dead husband. She was interned without trial and, conveniently for Thiers, proved to be illegitimately pregnant. The duchess was allowed to leave the country quietly. In January, 1833, Thiers shifted to the Ministry of Commerce and Public Works, and in June he was elected to the French Academy.

The next November, the thirty-six-year-old Thiers married Élise Dosne, who had turned fifteen the day before the wedding. The dowry was 300,000 francs plus, unofficially, the money remaining due on his house, which was simply never paid. The relationship between Thiers and Élise was never very close, but Thiers became part of his wife's family, who gained political and economic influence from the connection. Madame Dosne, Thiers's mother-in-law, served for many years as the older woman Thiers needed for emotional support.

Thiers's political influence continued to grow, and by early 1834 he and Guizot were the dominant figures in the government. In the spring, unrest among workers, encouraged by the left-wing press, led to efforts at censorship and arrests for union activities. On April 13, barricades were erected in Paris, and Thiers, as minister of the interior, sent troops that crushed the uprising. Thiers's reputation was marred for the rest of his career, however, because of deaths that became known as the Massacre in the Rue Transnonain. The Left never forgot Thiers's involvement.

Elections in June resulted in extended political infighting among the leading politicians, but Thiers remained at the Ministry of the Interior. In February, 1836, the government, then under the Duke of Broglie, was defeated, and on February 22 Thiers became the premier. Knowing that his majority was undependable, he kept the chamber busy with noncontroversial internal improvements, while he pursued an active foreign policy in hopes of boosting his standing. After clashing with the king about support for a pro-French liberal government in Spain, Thiers was out of office in September.

Thiers was active in opposition until January, 1840, when, having organized the defeat of the current government, he left Louis-Philippe little choice but to ask him to form a government. Drawing in the Left with patronage and winning the support of the moderate conservatives who were eager for stability, Thiers had what appeared to be a solid administration. He had, however, inherited Middle Eastern trouble. A territorial dispute dating to the Greek revolt of the 1820's had been simmering between Muhammad 'Alī of Egypt and his overlord, the sultan. Thiers, the historian, tied Egypt's troubles to Napoleon I and also was interested in French expansion in North Africa. Thiers backed the Egyptian against all the other powers, believing that Mehemet could get hereditary possession of Egypt and life possession of Syria as a minimum concession. Eventually, the other powers acted without consulting France, and the Egyptians collapsed in the face of a token force. Anti-French feeling spread all over Europe, and by October, 1840, Louis-Philippe, who had never been willing to do more than talk to help Mehemet, replaced Thiers with a government run by Guizot. Although he did not suspect it at the time, Thiers was beginning thirty years as a member of the opposition.

Although he remained active in the chamber, Thiers devoted much time to writing. In 1839, he had signed a contract for a history of the consulate and the empire, receiving 500,000 francs for the first ten volumes. He traveled to Napoleonic battle sites and worked in French archives as he began to write this history. In December of 1840, he was elected to the Académie des Sciences, Morales, et Politiques.

In 1842 and 1846, Guizot was reelected, but there was more and more unrest. In February, 1848, a campaign of protest banquets came to a head when the government attempted to block one scheduled for a working-class district in Paris. Frightened by the ensuing demonstration, Guizot resigned. Frantic maneuvering to reestablish government led to a brief attempt by Thiers to take control, but, when told he was too unpopular, he stepped aside. In the end, the king abdicated in favor of his grandson. That proved unacceptable—Thiers made no effort to support the arrangement—and the Second Republic emerged. Openly reluctant about participating, Thiers was defeated in the first series of elections for the new National Assembly. In May, however, he won in four separate by-elections.

Once in office, Thiers began to fight for a bicameral legislature, which was rejected, and in opposition to the right to work. He argued that the country could not afford the national workshops, employing 1.5 to 2 million workers, started by the revolutionaries. He established his economic ideas in *Du droit de propriété* (1848). He grudgingly approved the election of Louis-Napoleon Bonaparte as president, but refused, out of loyalty to the Orleanist family and reluctance to face the many problems of the new government, to preside at the first cabinet. In the next few years, he devoted himself to conservative party politics, helping with a successful election campaign in the spring of 1849. He helped develop the very conservative Falloux Law, reforming education and a new electoral law reducing the electorate by almost one third. In debating the latter, he spoke of the dangers of the "vile mob," a phrase that would haunt him. Thiers openly broke with Louis-Napoleon in 1851 over control of the military, but a prosperous economy and a reputation for stable government kept the prince-president's popularity high. When in December, 1851, Louis-Napoleon made himself Emperor Napoleon III, Thiers and seventeen other deputies were among ten thousand opponents exiled or transported. Thiers settled in Switzerland until August, 1852, when the exile was lifted, and worked on his history of the consulate and empire. Over his life, Thiers produced some thirty volumes of political history. He also wrote his memoirs.

By 1863, Thiers had finished the last volume of his twenty-volume *Histoire du consulat et de l'empire* (1845-1862; *History of the Consulate and the Empire of France Under Napoleon*, 1845-1862) and was open for new employment. Napoleon's popularity was in decline and the republicans were gaining popularity. Thiers was persuaded to run in the following year's elections. He won a Parisian seat, getting workers' votes despite his anti-Left reputation. He promptly embarked on a campaign, championing individual freedoms. With the emperor seeking to regain lost support, liberalization was steadily achieved.

The July, 1870, confrontation with Prussia over the question of a Hohenzollern (a royal German family) candidate for the Spanish throne found Thiers arguing for peace. Although he was the subject of jeers when the Franco-Prussian War erupted, the rapid and overwhelming Prussian victory—Napoleon was captured at Sedan, and Paris was besieged by mid-September—vindicated him. Thiers refused to be in the government of national defense, but he accepted a diplomatic mission, visiting London, St. Petersburg, Vienna, and Florence in a vain quest for support. He did manage to arrange for armistice talks.

Thiers's goal was to hold elections and, having established a new government, to make peace on the best possible terms, though France was not in a very good bargaining position. He was opposed by Léon Gambetta, leader of the republican Left. Thiers prevailed, and elections were held February 8,

1871, with Thiers's supporters winning a clear victory. The new assembly elected Thiers, almost unanimously, as chief of the executive power of the French republic. In the peace treaty with Prussia, France lost Alsace-Lorraine and was saddled with a 5,000-million-franc indemnity. One of Thiers's biggest successes as head of the new Third Republic was raising two large loans and getting that indemnity paid without undermining the national economy.

The withdrawal of the Prussians had left left-wing militants in control of Paris. When the new national government tried to assert control, civil war erupted. Thiers had to raise an army and defeat the Paris Commune, keep the Prussians from taking advantage of the trouble, and hold public support. Although the city had to be shelled and brutality was common, the city was recaptured, and, because the action was prompt and uncompromising, the Prussians found little opportunity to fish in troubled waters. There was left-wing sentiment especially in the cities, but few were willing to chance a renewal of the horrors of 1793. In the end, Thiers triumphed.

In August, 1871, Thiers was appointed President of the Republic, a post he held until May, 1873. During his tenure, he presided over the establishment of a conservative republic. He fought unsuccessfully for protectionism and blocked efforts to establish an income tax. He also resisted the adoption of the Prussian system of universal military service. Thiers had become convinced that a republic was the only workable system for a conservative France. His loss of power was largely the result of urging the right to abandon its dream of monarchy and accept the republic. This cost him support, and he was unable to control a confrontation between conservatives and radicals. He had to resign. Thiers spent his last four years active in opposition politics and, on September 3, 1877, after a choking fit at lunch, lapsed into a coma and died.

Summary

Adolphe Thiers's life can hardly be separated from nineteenth century French politics. He devoted his energies to public service, political journalism, and political history. His biography is really the political history of nineteenth century France, for he was intimately involved in all the major changes of that century. He had made his name in time to influence the Revolution of 1830—he produced more than one hundred articles for the *National* in the first six months of that year—and became part of the new government. Thiers's skills, however, were most effective in opposition—as practical politician, journalist, or historian. Thiers spent almost his entire career out of power. The conversational debating style he developed to overcome his naturally weak voice was very effective, and he was a formidable parliamentary foe.

During the middle of the century, Thiers wrote history and championed political moderation in the chambers, his reputation for knowledge and stability growing. In retrospect, his rise to power in the crisis of 1870 seems almost inevitable. Not only was he already respected, but also his resistance to the wave of nationalism that led to the war won for him even more kudos. Not only did he deal effectively with making peace but also he proceeded to oversee the creation of a conservative republican regime that lasted until it was destroyed by the Nazi conquest of World War II.

Bibliography

Albrecht-Carrié, Rene. *Adolphe Thiers: Or, The Triumph of the Bourgeoisie.* New York: Twayne, 1977. A short, straightforward biography by a very good historian. Does a good job of showing Thiers to be a part of the rise of the middle class to dominance during the nineteenth century.

Allison, John M. S. *Thiers and the French Monarchy.* Boston: Houghton Mifflin, 1926. A major study involving Thiers's career. The main theme is the monarchy, but, given Thiers's intimate involvement with that institution, he plays a major part in the book.

Bury, J. P. T. *France, 1814-1940.* London: Methuen, 1949. A classic survey introduction to French political history. An excellent source for brief accounts of Thiers's activities, but more important for providing context in which those activities must be seen to be understood.

Bury, J. P. T., and R. P. Tombs. *Thiers, 1797-1877: A Political Life.* London: Allen & Unwin, 1986. Excellent biography with the emphasis on Thiers's public life. The authors portray their subject as a centrist who evolved from constitutional monarchist to republican over the course of his career.

Horne, Alistair. *The Fall of Paris: The Siege and the Commune, 1870-71.* New York: St. Martin's Press, 1965. A superbly written account of the collapse of the Second Empire and the emergence of the Third Republic. The author's treatment of these events as part of the same larger development is effective and informative. Both the style and the approach lend themselves to the nonspecialist.

Fred R. van Hartesveldt

GIOVANNI BATTISTA TIEPOLO

Born: March 5, 1696; Venice
Died: March 27, 1770; Madrid, Spain
Area of Achievement: Art
Contribution: The last important painter of the Venetian school, Tiepolo was the most versatile of the Italian ceiling painters. Although he worked primarily in the Baroque tradition, his work shares some qualities of the rococo.

Early Life

Giovanni Battista Tiepolo was born in Venice on March 5, 1696, the son of a wealthy merchant. When his father died, Tiepolo's mother apprenticed him to Gregorio Lazzarini, a minor painter, from whom Tiepolo received his first instruction in painting. Later, Tiepolo became familiar with the Venetian decorative tradition. His first work, *The Sacrifice of Isaac* (1716), is noteworthy for its strong contrasts of light and shade. This early work reflects the influence of Giovanni Battista Piazetta, a member of the Bolognese and Roman Baroque school of painting.

Tiepolo's career as an independent artist actually began in 1717, at which time his name first appears on the lists of the Venetian painters' guild. His studio was so successful at this time that he married Cecilia Guardi, the seventeen-year-old sister of the painters Giovanni Antonio and Francesco Guardi. Despite his success, Tiepolo continued to learn, employing techniques from both Venetian and foreign painters of the eighteenth century in his prolific outpouring of etchings after sixteenth century subjects. Tiepolo's *Madonna of Carmelo and the Souls of Purgatory* (1720) clearly demonstrates the influence of Piazetta. His tendency to create large masses in violent contrasts of light and dark on a diagonal is evident in another early work, *Repudiation of Hagar*, which he painted when he was twenty.

The works that Tiepolo entered for the competitions of 1716 and 1717, *Crossing the Red Sea* and *Martyrdom of Saint Bartholomew*, respectively, led to several commissions. His first important commission was *Glory of Saint Teresa*, which he painted for the vault of the side chapel in the Church of the Scalzi. This work was followed by four paintings of mythological subjects, *Diana and Callistro, Diana and Actaeon, Apollo and Marsyas*, and the *Rape of Europa*. Church commissions were followed by commissions from such private persons as Doge Cornaro, who assigned him to paint the canvases and frescoes for his palace in 1722. The paintings that he did for the Palazzo Sandi a Corte dell'Alberto, while foreshadowing the heroic subjects of his later works, still possess the qualities of his early works, such as figures with popping round eyes and contorted limbs. During this time, Tiepolo was still looking for a style and a medium that suited him. He was still imitating the style of the non-rococo painters, and the prosaic way in which he treated his historical and religious subjects testified to the fact that he was an unlearned painter.

Life's Work

Tiepolo reached his full maturity of expression in his frescoes. The promise that was displayed in his first frescoes, the *Power of Eloquence* and the *Glory of Saint Teresa*, which were painted for the Palazzo Sandi a Corte dell'Alberto in 1725, was fully realized in the frescoes of the Archiepiscopal Palace in Udine. Between 1725 and 1728, he frescoed the *Fall of the Rebel Angels* in the ceiling above the main staircase and painted several episodes from the Book of Job in the gallery with the help of his longtime assistant, Mengozzi Colonna, who did the framings. In these paintings, which feature Abraham and his descendants dressed in sixteenth century costumes, he replaced the gloominess that had characterized his early works with dazzling colors. These paintings are distinguished from those of his contemporaries in their credibility. For example, the central figure in *Angel Appealing to Sarah* is a nearly toothless old woman, not a beautiful noblewoman. When he was finished, Tiepolo returned to Venice and his family.

Tiepolo was still developing as an artist when, at age thirty-five, two important commissions took him to Milan in 1731. At the Palazzo Archinto, which was destroyed by bombings during World War II, he painted the *Triumph of the Arts* and mythological scenes in four ceilings, the most successful of which was *Phaethon Begging Apollo to Allow Him to Drive the Chariot of the Sun*. As in most of his ceiling frescoes, the ceiling becomes the sky. Some of the scenes still survive in *modelletti*, pen-and-ink watercolor sketches which he usually submitted to his patrons before starting work. Working with his characteristic speed, Tiepolo completed the *Story of Scipio* frescoes, historical paintings in Baroque settings, in only a few months for the Palazzo Casati-Dugnani. Unlike the Udine frescoes, which are witty and dashing, the subjects of these scenes are much more serious and elevated.

Tiepolo spent the next two years, 1732-1733, at Bergamo, where he frescoed four allegorical figures and some scenes in the life of John the Baptist in Colleoni Chapel. The airy landscapes of these paintings represent an innovation in his style. The *modelletti* and two small pictures, *The Last Communion of Saint Jerome* and the *Death of Saint Jerome*, are characterized by a grainy texture. The clear-cut contours of the figures illustrate the progress that he had made since the sketches of the Udine period. During this same period, Tiepolo painted three large canvases depicting an episode from Roman history for the main saloon of the Villa Grimani-Valmara. To the Bergamo period may also be assigned the altarpiece in the parish church of Rovetta Sopra Bergamo. In this painting, *The Virgin in Glory Adored by the*

Apostles and Saints, he eliminated all traces of Piazetta, abandoning the dark tonality, heaviness of color, and agitated undulation in his line. Tiepolo closed the 1730's with the frescoing of the ceiling of the Palazzo Clerici in Milan, which ranks as one of the most fascinating pictorial creations of the century and introduced a new compositional principle: the creation of a centrifugal effect by concentrating a group of figures along the edge of the ceiling.

In the decade between 1740 and 1750, Tiepolo experimented with forms of the great luminosity that had been rediscovered by Piazetta and Guardi and reached full maturity as an artist. By this time, the most prestigious families of the republic were vying for his works. He only left Venice once during this period, and that was to decorate the Villa Cordellina at Montecchio Maggiore. The works produced in this period, many of which have secular themes, reflect a decorative balance and a greater fusion and transparency. He also became closer to the classical tastes of the time through his long relationship with Count Francesco Algarotti. Algarotti's insistence that Tiepolo strive for extreme delicacy and refinement manifests itself in the *Banquet of Antony and Cleopatra*, which Tiepolo created for the central saloon of the Palazzo Labia. Not only is this one of Tiepolo's greatest frescoes, but also it is one of the most beautiful examples of pictorial illusionism ever painted. This effect was achieved with the help of Mengozzi Colonna, who turned each of the end walls into a façade with a tall central archway leading into the fresco itself. Tiepolo's fascination with the classic world is still evident between 1745 and 1750, when he painted *Neptune Offering to Venice the Riches of the Sea*. At the end of the decade, he collaborated with his son Domenico to paint the *Consilium in Arena*, which commemorated the Council of the Order of Malta.

In 1750, Tiepolo and his two sons, Domenico, age twenty-three, and Lorenzo, age fourteen, were summoned to Würzburg to decorate the newly built Residenz of the prince-bishop. During his three-year stay at Würzburg, Tiepolo painted two masterpieces which rank among the greatest creations of pictorial art. Tiepolo began with the ceiling of the saloon, where he painted *Apollo Conducting Barbarossa's Bride, Beatrice of Burgundy*. The frescoes on the walls, which glorified several episodes in the life of the Emperor Frederick I (Barbarossa) are much less imaginative. He then turned his attention to the staircase ceiling, the most monumental undertaking of his career until that time. The staircase ceiling, on which Tiepolo depicted Olympus and the four parts of the known world, has been called Tiepolo's Sistine Chapel. The influence of Peter Paul Rubens, whose work Tiepolo saw in Germany, is apparent in the ceiling. Before leaving Germany, Tiepolo also found time to execute numerous works on canvas. The romantic, poetic themes that now preoccupied him culminated in four charming canvases depicting the story of Rinaldo and Armida. He also ventured outside Würzburg to paint one of his finest religious works, the altarpiece of the *Adoration of the Magi*, for the Church of the Benedictines of Schwarzach. While in Germany, he was assisted by Domenico and by a group of pupils from his school.

Tiepolo returned to Venice in 1753, confident that he had succeeded in promoting Venetian painting outside Italy. Instead of simply basking in his fame, Tiepolo continued to build his reputation in Venice. Two years after his return, he was elected president of the Venetian Academy. In 1757, he and Domenico frescoed the hall and four downstairs rooms for the Villa Valmarana. By this time, Tiepolo had completely abandoned the diagonal perspective of his youth; instead, the figures move in planes parallel to the wall. He returned to the influence of Paolo Veronese, one of Italy's greatest ceiling painters, in the relationships of the figures in *Sacrifice of Iphigenia*. That same year, Tiepolo also frescoed four circular panels with allegories of the Arts, Music, Science, and History on the ceiling of the grand saloon in the Palazzo Valmarana-Trenta in Vincenza, which was destroyed in the bombardments of 1945. His Catholic sensibilities once again surfaced in the great altarpiece of Saint Thecla, which he painted for the Church of the Grazie at Este in 1759.

While working at the Villa Pisani, Tiepolo was invited by Charles III of Spain to decorate the royal palace. Without his faithful assistant Mengozzi Colonna, who was now seventy-four years old and feeble, or his two sons, Tiepolo arrived at Madrid after two months of traveling by land. After recovering from fatigue, the sixty-six-year-old painter began painting the *Apotheosis of Spain* in the throne room in 1762. In this fresco, Spain is surrounded by symbolic and mythological figures in the skies. In 1764, Tiepolo painted two ceilings of lesser importance in the same palace. After completing the frescoes, Tiepolo remained in the service of the king, painting seven altarpieces at Aranjuez. He had no sooner finished them than the king replaced them with works by Anton Raphael Mengs, Francisco Bayeu, and others, leaving Tiepolo a disappointed and bitter man. Though damaged, the surviving altarpieces reflect a new intensity; no longer are the subjects excuses for grand displays of celestial pageants. The last three years of his life were occupied by feverish activity. He executed many works for the court of Russia, which were sent from Spain, as well as a series of small canvases of religious subjects, such as the *Flight into Egypt*. On March 27, 1770, Tiepolo died suddenly in Spain. He was buried in his parish church of Saint Martin, but both the church and his tomb have been destroyed.

Summary

Giovanni Battista Tiepolo will be remembered not only as one of the greatest decorative painters of eighteenth century Europe but also as the man who revived Venetian painting. A tireless and prolific worker, he achieved success at an early age, first displaying his formidable talent in the Church of the Ospedaletto at the age of nineteen. As his fame spread, he helped to free Venetian art from the chiaroscuro style with its strong contrasts of light and shade. Tiepolo also stands apart from his contemporaries in his mastery of linear perspective, which is exhibited in the weightless qualities that the figures in his ceiling frescoes seem to possess. Above all, Tiepolo raised the status of fresco painting from that of a secondary, decorative role to the high artistic rank that it had held in the golden age of the Cinquecento. Like his predecessor, Bonifazio Veronese, Tiepolo was skilled in the art of setting angels and gods in a seemingly limitless space. His dramatic imagination populated his frescoes with subjects drawn from both mythology and religion who are painted as flesh and blood human beings instead of mere puppets. His frescoes were, in a sense, the definitive complement to the rococo churches and palaces of his day.

Tiepolo's work has suffered the same critical fate as that of other artists who achieved considerable wealth and fame in their lifetime. The hostile response of the Spanish court toward his work foreshadowed the nineteenth century's hostile reception of his work, especially in France and England. Even at the height of his success, he was the victim of shifting tastes, being popular primarily in northern Italy. Modern taste, though, seems to have accepted his work without reservation.

Bibliography

Barcham, William L. *The Religious Paintings of Giambattista Tiepolo: Piety and Tradition in Eighteenth-Century Venice.* New York: Oxford University Press, 1989. Barcham's study, the first to concentrate on Tiepolo's religious paintings, treats its subject as an expression of the values of the Venetian Republic. Illustrated with four line drawings, 133 halftones, and nine color plates.

"Giovanni Battista Tiepolo." In *Encyclopædia Britannica: Macropædia*, vol. 18. 15th rev. ed. Chicago: Encyclopædia Britannica, 1983. Relies heavily on Morassi's work. This lengthy article concentrates on Tiepolo's major works.

Levey, Michael. *Painting in XVIII Century Venice.* New York: Phaidon Press, 1959. Not primarily a biography, although the chapter on Tiepolo discusses his major works in chronological order and demonstrates how they typify each stage of his development as an artist. This chapter does a fine job of showing how Tiepolo's work either followed or strayed from the artistic trends of his day. Illustrated with several plates.

Morassi, Antonio. *G. B. Tiepolo: His Life and Work.* Translated by Mr. and Mrs. Peter Murray. New York: Phaidon Press, 1955. A standard biography, providing details of Tiepolo's life along with descriptions and critical assessments of the works from each period in his life. Beautifully illustrated with both black-and-white and color plates, the book covers most of Tiepolo's works.

Alan Brown

TINTORETTO
Jacopo Robusti

Born: c. 1518-1519; Venice
Died: May 31, 1594; Venice
Area of Achievement: Art
Contribution: Tintoretto was a leading exponent of the mannerist movement in painting, a style which parted with the rational symmetry of the Renaissance and moved toward dramatic imbalance and tension and the creation of mysterious moods by means of chiaroscuro, radical foreshortening, and unorthodox brushwork.

Early Life

Jacopo Robusti derived his artistic pseudonym, "Tintoretto," from his father's trade as a dyer (*tintore*). He left Venice only once or twice in his lifetime, for a visit to Mantua and the Gonzaga court in 1580 and a probable trip to Rome in 1547. His marriage at age thirty-six produced eight children, of whom four, most notably Domenico and Marietta, were painters.

Tintoretto may have studied under Bonifazio de' Pitati (Bonifazio Veronese). Almost uniquely among Renaissance artists, however, he was largely self-taught, copying available models of Michelangelo's works and devising his own clay or wax models, dressing them, arranging them in different attitudes in cardboard houses, and introducing light through tiny windows in order to study the effect of lights and shadow on the figures. He also suspended the models from above to learn their chiaroscuro effects and foreshortenings when seen from below. As early as 1545, the letters of Pietro Aretino, Tintoretto's first important patron (for whom he painted *Apollo and Marsyas* in 1545), criticize his arrogance and apparent hasty sketchiness (which stemmed from the artist's early work in fresco but was also a genuine factor in his inventive style).

In his own lifetime, Tintoretto's biography was written by Giorgio Vasari. In 1642, Carlo Ridolfi's adulatory biography reported that Tintoretto had served an apprenticeship with Titian which ended within days because of Titian's jealousy of his pupil's talent coupled with Tintoretto's youthful pride. The real reason for the dismissal, however, may have been Tintoretto's careless style. The combined judgment of Titian and Aretino were, in any case, costly in terms of artistic patronage, as they were the arbiters of taste in Venice. Nevertheless, Tintoretto reputedly hung in his studio the motto (coined by Paolo Pino in his *Dialogo della pittura*, 1548), "The drawing of Michelangelo, the color of Titian."

As Tintoretto began his career, however, the Tuscano-Roman style and the colorful, horizontal Venetian style of these two masters were locked in a losing struggle with the new mannerist impulse throughout Italy; in Venice, the carriers were Andrea Schiavone, Veronese, and, eventually, Tintoretto.

Tintoretto's earliest works (1539-1540) are standard *sacre conversazioni* (Virgin and Child with saints), in the warm reds, golds, and whites expected of a painter of a Venice dominated by Titian. They contain almost nothing of the conscious artificialities of emergent mannerism. His early *Last Supper* (1545-1547) is marked by emotional restraint and horizontal symmetry; only the violent foreshortening of the floor is a mannerist device.

Tintoretto's reputed visit to Rome and his first masterpiece culminate this early period of laborious experimentation. His *Saint Mark Rescuing a Slave* (1548) indeed evinces the muscular forms of Michelangelo and the rich color of Titian. The large monument forecasts the dramatic use of light so prominent in Tintoretto's narrative style.

Life's Work

During the 1550's, the chief elements of Tintoretto's unique style found their place in his voluminous output. *Susanna and the Elders* (1550) manifests the use of strong diagonals. In the Genesis scenes for the Scuola della Trinitá (1550-1553), the colors are less brilliant as Tintoretto first joined color, light, and form to create the mood dictated by the subject matter. The Old Testament scenes (1554-1555) brought to Madrid by Diego Velázquez mark an important moment in Tintoretto's evolving mannerism: The six ceiling paintings feature color that is subtle but sparkling with light and an almost improvisational sketchiness. In the later 1550's, the artist began to use crowds in procession to accentuate space. In *Saint Ursula and Her Virgins* and the *Miracle of the Loaves and Fishes*, the processions fade away into the depths of the paintings, dissolving in the distance in a *non finito* (unfinished) diaphanous sketchiness.

Between 1552 and 1562, Tintoretto contributed, for the cost of materials alone (he was disliked in the artistic community for frequently underpricing his art or working free), several paintings to his beloved parish church, Madonna dell' Orto. One was his famous *Presentation of the Virgin in the Temple*. On either side of the high altar, his *Laws and Golden Calf* and *Last Judgment* rose fifty feet high.

During the 1560's, Tintoretto's work became increasingly dramatic, psychological, and artistically sophisticated. He achieved these effects by using a less diffuse, more immediate light source allowing more pronounced chiaroscuro, increased use of diagonal composition, and vast panoramic scenes. He continued to be prolific. In the *Finding of the Body of Saint Mark*, the radically oblique, sharply receding vault of the church and the stark chiaroscuro enhance the miraculous event taking place in the foreground. Similarly, the ominous storm lightening the edge of the clouds is the focus of the *Translation of the Body of Saint Mark* (both were painted for the Scuola di S. Marco in 1562-1566). Tintoretto concurrently painted for S. Trovaso

Church a *Crucifixion* with massive diagonals and a *Last Supper.*

In 1564, Tintoretto started his work in the Scuola di S. Rocco, which was to span twenty-three years. The Scuola was an asymmetrical building, worthy of Tintoretto's bold designs. There followed a series of large scenes of Christ's Passion, including an immense and profoundly moving *Crucifixion,* which John Ruskin pronounced "above all praise." Tintoretto was made a member of the Scuola, a sort of civic-service lodge, and later a lifetime officer.

Contemporaneously (1564-1568), Tintoretto produced a *Crucifixion,* a *Resurrection,* and a *Descent of Christ into Limbo* for S. Cassiano Church, a *Last Judgment* for the Sala del Scrutinio in the Doges' Palace, and for the Church of S. Rocco, a great *Saint Roche in Prison.* Between 1576 and 1581, Tintoretto resumed his work in the upper hall of the Scuola di S. Rocco. There, the ceiling received twenty-one Old Testament scenes, while the walls were decorated with ten events from the life of Christ, of which the *Baptism* and *Ascension* are noteworthy.

Meanwhile, Tintoretto's trip to Mantua in 1580 bore fruit in the eight battle scenes completed with the help of assistants. From 1577 to 1584, too, the artist painted, with less enthusiasm, the four small allegories of classical mythology in the Sala del' Anticollegio of the Doges' Palace. He also executed important scenes from Venice's history in the Sala del Senato, and in the imposing Sala del Maggior Consiglio, an enormous *Paradise* occupying the years 1584-1587. It was the largest oil painting ever done until that time.

In 1583, Tintoretto returned to the Scuola di S. Rocco, this time producing scenes from the life of the Madonna in the lower hall. His conception was consummate: His space opens out dynamically in all directions and his perspectives are limitless; light dominates and dissolves volume and color, rendering his figures incorporeal and unfinished. The entire project in Scuola di S. Rocco has been compared to the Sistine Chapel and the Raphael stanze. Tintoretto finally put down his brush in 1587 and painted no more for the Scuola di S. Rocco.

Among Tintoretto's approximately three hundred paintings are dozens of portraits. In these, he aimed to capture the inner spirit or personality of the subject more than his clothing or background. Notable is his self-portrait at age seventy. Additionally, about one hundred drawings survive; they are mainly practice sets by which Tintoretto perfected his chiaroscuro and foreshortening skills and cartoons for mosaics in San Marco Church.

His last works include two large oils for the presbytery of S. Giorgio Maggiore. Of these, the *Last Supper* epitomized all of his earlier achievements and effects and attained a new level of psychological impact: The darkened room is lit by a lamp striking the disciples from behind and by an unnatural glow radiating from the halo of Christ, who intently administers communion; the table thrusts diagonally into the canvas; angels hovering above add their mystical presence. All of this is in stark contrast to the realism of the Venetian pitchers on the table, a cat drinking from the water cistern, and the everyday activities of servants taking place in the same room.

Tintoretto's last work, the *Entombment* for the chapel of S. Giorgio Maggiore (1594), also employs a double illumination, one the natural sunset, the other artificial, or rather spiritual, which divides the groups of figures by their separate lighting.

Summary

The legendary rivalry between the older Titian and Tintoretto has occasioned an ongoing division among art critics. Both are truly representative of Venetian artistic tradition, but Titian had known the glorious time of Venice; his art reflects the sensuous richness of the city. Tintoretto, however, was born in a Venice humbled by the League of Cambrai (1508); he grew up in a Counter-Reformation atmosphere of religious revival. Thus, a religious mysticism pervades his art.

Contemporaries also took sides. Vasari and Aretino favored Titian. In the seventeenth century, the age of the Baroque, the tide moved to Tintoretto, who was much admired by El Greco and Ridolfi. The eighteenth century saw Tintoretto unfavorably, through the neoclassical eyes of the Age of Reason. Ruskin represents the nineteenth century preference for Tintoretto over Titian and even over Michelangelo. Jakob Burckhardt, however, regarded Tintoretto as crude, barbaric, and artistically immoral, "abandoning himself to the most shameless superficiality."

To the twentieth century, Tintoretto is a giant; he has been regarded variously as one who succeeded in spiritualizing reality, a forerunner of modern illusionism or of German Expressionism. The theatrical quality of his later works comports well with modern artistic sensibilities, which share his delight in foreshortening, his artificial use of lighting to emphasize action or suggest spirituality, his penchant for oblique composition, his use of subdued subaqueous color, his *non finito* sketchiness, and his preoccupation with the human body caught unfolding and poised in mid-action.

Bibliography

Berenson, Bernhard. *Italian Pictures of the Renaissance: A List of the Principal Artists and Their Works, with an Index of Places, Venetian School.* 2 vols. London: Phaidon Press, 1957. Volume 1 includes a complete list of Tintoretto's works and their locations; volume 2 contains seventy-six black-and-white plates. These volumes present a list of all the principal Venetian artists, their works and their locations, and 1,334 representative plates.

Honour, Hugh. *The Companion Guide to Venice.* London: Fontana Books,

1970. Tintoretto's art is affectionately discussed as discovered by the visitor to the churches and galleries of Venice. En route, the reader is exposed to the cultural and political history of Venice in its living stones and works of art and in its relationship to the rest of Italy. Street plans and museum layouts bring the world of Tintoretto into clarity.

Newton, Eric. *Tintoretto*. New York: Longmans, Green, 1952. A superlative biography with details not found elsewhere. Throughout, Newton draws from Ridolfi and urges caution in accepting Ridolfi's interpretations. Includes a chronological list of Tintoretto's paintings and seventy-six black-and-white plates.

Tintoretto. *Tintoretto: The Paintings and Drawings*. Edited by Hans Tietze. London: Phaidon Press, 1948. A short biography and appreciation of Tintoretto. Especially useful for its three hundred black-and-white illustrations and excellent detailed commentary on each plate.

Daniel C. Scavone

TITIAN
Tiziano Vecellio

Born: c. 1490; Pieve di Cadore, Venetian Republic
Died: August 27, 1576; Venice
Area of Achievement: Art
Contribution: Titian is considered one of the greatest artists of the Italian High Renaissance. During his long and prolific career, he developed an oil-painting technique of successive glazes and broad paint application which influenced generations of future artists.

Early Life

Titian was born Tiziano Vecellio in the northern Italian town of Pieve di Cadore. Over the centuries, there has been considerable confusion concerning his birth date, as a result of a misprint in his biography by sixteenth century art historian Giorgio Vasari, who recorded it as 1480. The progress of Titian's career, along with other documentary evidence, indicates instead that Titian was born sometime between 1488 and 1490.

According to the 1557 biography of Titian's life written by his friend Lodovico Dolce, it is known that Titian arrived in Venice, in the company of his brother Francesco, when he was only eight years old. He first worked for the mosaicist Sebastiano Zuccato but soon entered the workshop of the aging painter Gentile Bellini. Unhappy with Gentile's old-fashioned style, he moved to the studio of Gentile's brother, Giovanni, and it is there that Titian learned the current Venetian style and techniques. He also met the short-lived but magnificent painter Giorgione. By 1508, Titian had left Bellini's studio and was working with Giorgione, perhaps as his assistant, on exterior frescoes for the Fondaco dei Tedeschi (German Commercial Headquarters) in Venice.

Until around 1515, Titian's style would remain very close to that of Giorgione. In fact, scholars have difficulty distinguishing between the two hands when their paintings from this period are unsigned. The most famous example of this attribution problem is the so-called *Fête Champêtre* of around 1510, now in the Louvre. The lush pastoral setting, soft lighting, and strong atmospheric qualities characterize the styles of both artists at this time.

In 1511, Titian completed his first dated work, a series of three frescoes in the Scuola di San Antonio at Padua. This commission established his career. Within the next decade, his independent, mature style found expression.

Life's Work

In 1518, Titian's *Assumption of the Virgin* was unveiled at the Church of the Frari in Venice. In this dynamic, monumental composition, Titian seemed suddenly to assimilate the achievements of the Roman High Renaissance style. Since there is no evidence that he had yet traveled beyond the region near Venice, it is assumed that he learned these stylistic lessons through visiting artists, drawings, and reproductive engravings. The painting reflects the harmony and delineation of forms typical of High Renaissance classicism, and an energetic movement similar to that found in Raphael's Vatican murals and Michelangelo's Sistine Chapel ceiling. To this Titian added his distinctive brilliant colors, unified by successive layers of glazes.

During the succeeding decades, Titian's reputation grew until he was, along with Michelangelo, the most famous artist in Europe. His patrons included some of the most powerful men and families of the age. For Alfonso I d'Este of Ferrara he created, among other works, three famous mythological paintings, *The Bacchanal of the Andrians* (c. 1520), *The Worship of Venus* (1518-1519), and *Bacchus and Ariadne* (1522-1523), which were installed in Alfonso's alabaster *studiolo*. He also worked for the Gonzaga of Mantua and several popes. His most important patrons, however, were the Spanish Habsburgs. In 1533, Titian was summoned to Bologna for the first of several meetings with the emperor Charles V, who became one of his greatest admirers. The emperor made him a count and brought him to Augsburg two times as court painter. When Charles died in 1558, his son Philip II continued the relationship.

These prestigious patrons brought Titian fame, wealth, and social position. A shrewd businessman, he invested wisely and by the 1530's was living in luxury. Sometime in the early 1520's he began a relationship with a woman named Cecilia, by whom he had four children, two before they married in 1525. Cecilia died in 1530, and the next year Titian moved his family to a palace which came to be known as the Casa Grande. There he lived a princely existence far removed from the craftsmen status which artists had held only one hundred years earlier.

Titian's compositions were often revolutionary as he freed Renaissance classicism from its planar symmetry. He exploited the dramatic possibilities of diagonal placings and perspectives, and set up unusual spectator viewpoints. In this way he could give traditional subjects a fresh look. This predisposition to creative compositions was evident very early in his career. *The Gypsy Madonna* (1510-1515) is a variation of the half-length Madonna and Child popular with Giovanni Bellini. Yet Titian has moved all the major forms off center and encouraged the viewer to look diagonally into a landscape to the left of the Madonna. *The Madonna of the Pesaro Family* (1519-1526) shows a more radical alteration of a traditional subject. The pyramidal grouping of figures, with the enthroned Madonna at the apex, has been shifted so that it is placed diagonally to the frontal plane.

Titian's style never stagnated. Over the years, his brushwork loosened and forms were increasingly defined by color and light instead of line. In 1546, he returned from an eight-month visit to Rome, and from this point on his broad handling of paint increased. The result was a type of optical realism, in which the structures of objects were built up through a free application of paint. Details that the human eye does not see without close inspection were not delineated with precise drawing but rather indicated with freely manipulated color and light. In the hands of a master such as Titian, the result was one of startling reality since he had essentially reproduced with paint the reality which the human eye actually absorbs. An example of this loosely painted style was *The Rape of Europa* (1559-1562), in which textures of fur, skin, cloth, and water were faithfully rendered through broad relationships of color and light. Titian's development of this technique, which would influence artists throughout forthcoming centuries, played no small part in his fame.

Toward the end of his long career, Titian's technique loosened still further, and a certain dematerialization of form took place in his paintings. Especially in his religious works, which reflected his own growing awareness of mortality, physicality was overcome by mystical light and emotional expression. Like the late works of Michelangelo, Titian's final paintings seemed more concerned with spirituality than with the substance of the natural world.

Summary

Titian's career was a watershed in the evolution of artistic status within society. Well traveled and well respected, he was a friend of princes and intellectuals. Collectors clamored for his works and, despite a large workshop and numerous assistants, he could not satisfy them all. The laws of supply and demand were in his favor and provided a degree of freedom for artistic development rarely seen before. He became the first artist to achieve the status of gentleman.

As early as the middle of the sixteenth century, artists and intellectuals argued over whether Titian or Michelangelo was the greater painter. At the center of this discussion was Titian's emphasis on color, versus Michelangelo's preference for line, in creating forms. Some art historians see a dualism of technique and expression beginning with these two artists which can be traced through Baroque art to the theories and practices of the later European art academies. To be sure, sixteenth century Italian painters formulated a tradition which would serve as a reference point for art until the middle of the nineteenth century. Titian's style was an essential option within that tradition.

Bibliography

Freedberg, Sidney J. *Painting in Italy: 1500-1600*. Baltimore: Penguin Books, 1975. An extensive chronological survey of painting in sixteenth century Italy, this volume discusses the various stages of Titian's career as they relate to contemporary artistic developments in Venice and the rest of Italy. A solid introduction to Titian's art, with an emphasis on stylistic issues. Contains limited but pertinent photographs and a basic bibliography.

Panofsky, Erwin. *Problems in Titian, Mostly Iconographic.* New York: New York University Press, 1969. Examines the subjects of a number of Titian's paintings and how they connect with medieval and Renaissance iconographic traditions. Shows how Titian drew upon both popular imagery and high philosophical ideas in devising his symbolism. Contains numerous photographs. There is no bibliography, but as with all Panofsky's work, the extensive citations in the footnotes serve as the equivalent.

Rosand, David. *Painting in Cinquecento Venice: Titian, Veronese, Tintoretto.* New Haven, Conn.: Yale University Press, 1982. Contains several innovative articles which place Titian's compositions within the pictorial and theatrical traditions of Venice. Lengthy analysis of *The Madonna of the Pesaro Family* and *The Presentation of the Virgin.* Contains excellent illustrations, photographs, and bibliography.

Rosand, David, and Michelangelo Muraro. *Titian and the Venetian Woodcut.* Washington, D.C.: International Exhibitions Foundation, 1976. Discusses Titian's involvement with the graphic media, especially woodcuts. Extensive illustrations of woodcuts by Titian and other artists influenced by his imagery or technique. Expansive catalog entries on the prints, with excellent illustrations and insightful art historical analysis. Includes a topically limited bibliography.

Wethey, Harold E. *The Paintings of Titian.* 3 vols. New York: Phaidon, 1969-1975. The standard reference in English and the most recent catalogue raisonné of Titian's paintings. Each volume contains general essays surveying the artist's biography, chronology, stylistic development, and handling of themes. Extensive catalog entries on every known or attributed painting, with photographic reproductions (black-and-white) of the complete works. Wethey's attributions of some early and minor works are not universally accepted, and his analysis of influence can at times be narrow-minded; yet this still remains the most complete source on Titian.

Madeline Cirillo Archer

ALEXIS DE TOCQUEVILLE

Born: July 29, 1805; Verneuil, France
Died: April 16, 1859; Cannes, France
Areas of Achievement: Political science and sociology
Contribution: A political and social analyst, Tocqueville was the earliest, the
greatest, and surely the most percipient observer of the initial growth and
increasing persuasiveness of democracy in all areas of American culture.

Early Life

Alexis-Henri-Charles-Maurice Clérel, Comte de Tocqueville, was born in
the Paris suburb of Verneuil on July 29, 1805, a few years after his aristocratic parents had been released from their imprisonment by revolutionary
forces for their close relations with the collapsed monarchy of Louis XVI
and for their outspoken support of it before revolutionary tribunals. Alexis'
father, Hervé, subsequently became a prefect (governor) in various states
under the restored monarchy of Charles X. His mother never fully recovered
from her treatment during the Revolution. Living on family properties
at Verneuil, Tocqueville was first tutored by Abbé Lesueur, the Catholic
priest who had taught his father and a man whom Tocqueville would re-
member affectionately for having instilled in him a belief in the Christian
principles that he would abandon for a time but would return to in later life.

In his adolescence, the young Tocqueville spent six years in Metz and
completed his studies brilliantly at the local *lycée*. A perceptive, if not an
omnivorous, reader profoundly impressed by the writings of René Descartes,
Tocqueville gave up his strict Catholicism for a more critical Christian De-
ism, that is, a belief in human reason, rather than God, as the operative force
in man's affairs. Emotionally and intellectually more at ease with tangible
matters that were susceptible to precise analysis than with theories, Tocqueville embarked on law studies, which he completed in 1825. Almost immediately, he and his brother Edward took an extended tour of Italy and Sicily,
the importance of which emerged in the voluminous and detailed journals he
kept. What he perceived was not so much the invariable landscapes as evidences of social structure, the shape of which he deduced by the structure of
the applicable political systems and laws. Perhaps because he was only
twenty-two years old, he imaginatively compared his keen observations on
the Italian scene with his knowledge of French and British institutions.

Meanwhile, in 1827, he was offered a career which both his family background and his own predilections seemed to favor. By royal patent from
Charles X, Tocqueville was appointed to a Versailles judgeship in the department of Seine and Oise, literally within the shadow of the king's residence. Fearful that the routines of his office might render him incapable of
judging great movements or of guiding great undertakings, Tocqueville, nev-

ertheless, devoted himself to his duties. Later, Charles X, the king who had appointed him, chose abdication in the face of the Revolution of 1830. At war with himself for having to swear allegiance to the new monarch, Louis-Philippe, whose values he repudiated, Tocqueville still remained in service long enough to request from the minister of interior in 1831 leave to investigate the penal system in the United States.

Life's Work

Accompanied by another French magistrate who was both a colleague and a friend, Gustave de Beaumont, a man who later served as a deputy to the National Assembly and as the French ambassador to London and Vienna and was a writer-scholar of distinction in his own right, Tocqueville invented the pretext of studying the American penal system in order to tackle the larger task that he had set for himself—a thorough, on-site investigation of what then was the world's first and only completely democratic society: the United States. Only twenty-six years old, Tocqueville appeared less robust than the country that would absorb his attention. Portraits accent long arms and a short, thin, and frail body. Beneath locks of brown hair, his delicate, aristocratic face was dominated by large, intelligent brown eyes. He and Beaumont embarked for New York in April, 1831.

Returning to France in 1832, Tocqueville and Beaumont finished their study of the American penal system. It was published in 1833 as *Du système pénitentiaire aux États-Unis et de son application en France* (*On the Penitentiary System in the United States and Its Application in France*, 1833). This official obligation resolved, Tocqueville left his judicial post, moved into a modest Paris apartment, and began what he later described as the happiest two years of his life, writing his two-volume *De la démocratie en Amérique* (1835, 1840; *Democracy in America*, 1835, 1840). This work was proclaimed the classic treatment of its subject throughout the Western world and assured Tocqueville's fame as a political observer and political philosopher, and, later, as a sociologist.

While writing the third volume of *Democracy in America*, Tocqueville in 1837 sought election as a deputy from his native constituency, La Manche. Failing in 1837, he succeeded in 1839, serving in the Chamber of Deputies continuously until 1851 and almost always in opposition to the government of Louis-Philippe. From 1842 to 1848, practicing his belief that a healthy state was founded upon vigorous local government, he served on the local general council. Although he never perceived himself as a political leader, he nevertheless reinforced his convictions by public service.

Meanwhile, he was among the few who prophesied the coming of the Revolution of 1848, which ended the Second Republic, replacing it with the plebiscite government of Louis Napoleon, who was soon to proclaim the Second Empire and his rule as Napoleon III. Though he had voted against

Napoleon, Tocqueville was reelected to a new national assembly and on June 2, 1849, was appointed France's foreign minister. Once again, his acceptance of the post was intended to keep the republican spirit alive, certain as he was that Napoleon intended to bury it. Over the next few months as foreign minister—he resigned on October 31, 1849—he dealt with the Austrian-Piedmontese conflict, the Turkish question, problems with the Roman Catholic church, and Swiss rights of asylum, each an important problem at the time.

Exhausted when he left office, he served on yet another parliamentary commission studying the question of Napoleon's reeligibility as president— an issue resolved dramatically by the president's own *coup d'état* of December 2, 1851. It was amid such events, the latter of which shocked Tocqueville as well as most of Europe's informed opinion, that he began writing *Souvenirs de Alexis de Tocqueville* (1893; *The Recollections of Alexis de Tocqueville*, 1896, 1949) in June, 1850. Although many scholars regard it as his greatest book, a classic historical, sociological, and political analysis of the antecedents, personalities, and events of the Revolution of 1848 in France, Tocqueville had not intended it for publication.

With the completion of *The Recollections of Alexis de Tocqueville*, Tocqueville was already embarked on his *L'Ancien Régime et la révolution* (1856; *The Old Régime and the Revolution*, 1856), in which, after five years of exhaustive archival research, he demonstrated that the centralization of power in France was not a consequence of the Revolution of 1789 but rather had been proceeding for centuries. This extension of power, pursued by an alienated and obsolete aristocracy and running counter to gains in popular power and popular enthusiasm for equality and freedom, helped make revolution inevitable. This was Tocqueville's last work. Lying ill for several weeks at his family estate at Cannes, he confessed, regretted that he had not been a more ardent disciple of Catholicism, and died on April 16, 1859.

Summary

Alexis de Tocqueville's principal moral and intellectual concern was with freedom. He was not a liberal, however, any more than he was a democrat. Liberalism skirted on unbridled individualism, democracy on an egalitarian reductionism, a tendency to put everyone on an equal, but low level. Rather, in Tocqueville's view, all freedom begins with recognition that man is the creature of a larger collectivity, a creature of God. Lacking this appreciation, no one can really call himself free. From that basic premise—and it suffuses all of Tocqueville's major works—he strove through his extraordinary powers of observation and research to develop a political philosophy that struck a balance between men's rights and their duties. While capable of dealing in abstractions in these matters, he nevertheless felt comfortable only when fitting them into historical and substantive cultural contexts, whether his immediate interests were structural, that is, sociological, or lay in the measurement and movement of power, that is, political.

Being neither a liberal nor a democrat but a French aristocrat who recognized that the authority of aristocracies in France and Great Britain had been shattered—and in the United States, he believed, had never existed—lent Tocqueville's work its much-admired objectivity. His major studies were offered primarily for the consideration of Frenchmen. While democratization had proceeded much further in the United States, France, he believed, also confronted the same conditions. While manifested dramatically in political upheavals and revolutions, both historical tendencies (toward popular power and toward centralized power), he believed, were centuries in the making. The question for his day was, Would the age-old centralizing process that he discerned, when joined with the inevitable centralizing power of majoritarian and egalitarian democracy, lead to tyranny—though a tyranny of, or in the name of, the masses? Tocqueville sensed what the twentieth century has proved—most authoritarian states have justified themselves as being democratic, as governing in the name of the people. Democrats, it seemed on his evidence, were assuming the political and administrative roles of aristocracies. In the face of the egalitarian surge, however, the centralization of power was broadening, not declining, hence the interference of the state increasingly menaced the integrity of the individual's freedom.

Thirteen years older than Karl Marx, Tocqueville wrote of the importance of classes in history, while utterly rejecting what later became Marx's determinism respecting their roles. Unearthing the interrelations among a people's perceived and historical experiences, their manners and mores, and the configuration of their political institutions, his works place him among the other great men who analyzed the nature of society, beginning with Aristotle and proceeding through modern times.

Bibliography

Herr, Richard. *Tocqueville and the Old Regime*. Princeton, N.J.: Princeton University Press, 1962. The author, a specialist in modern French history, deals with the incompleteness and apparent inconsistencies of Tocqueville's *The Old Régime and the Revolution*. An informative and well-written work with a selective bibliography and a useful index.

Laski, Harold J. "Alexis de Tocqueville and Democracy." In *The Social and Political Ideas of Some Representative Thinkers of the Victorian Age*, edited by F. J. C. Hearnshaw. London: G. G. Harrap, 1933. Laski, a distinguished British liberal-left political analyst and a force behind the extension of the British welfare state, cogently examines Tocqueville's views on social democracy and their relevance to modern democracies. No notes, bibliography, or index. Generally available.

Mayer, Jacob Peter. *Alexis de Tocqueville: A Biographical Study in Political*

Science. New York: Harper & Brothers, 1960. Mayer is one of the foremost authorities on Tocqueville, having researched, translated, revised, and completed many of Tocqueville's works. This is a delightfully informative and clearly written overview intended for general readers. There is one portrait, an appendix assessing Tocqueville's influences after a century, endnotes, a useful bibliography, and a reliable index. Generally available.

Mayer, Jacob Peter, and A. P. Kerr. Introduction to *Recollections*, by Alexis de Tocqueville. Translated by George Lawrence. Garden City, N.Y.: Doubleday, 1970. This is the best edition of what many regard as Tocqueville's finest work. Mayer and Kerr, experts on Tocqueville, provide an informative introductory essay, many footnotes, a select bibliography, and an extensive index. Available in good bookstores as well as major college and university libraries.

Pierson, George W. *Tocqueville and Beaumont in America*. New York: Oxford University Press, 1938. This remains the definitive study of Tocqueville's months in the United States. A thorough evaluation of the settings through which these two friends passed, of the people they met, and of the sources that they employed for their study of the American penal system and, in Tocqueville's case, for his great study of democracy. Traces Tocqueville's intellectual development with an eye to clarifying all of his writings. Clearly written and understandable by general readers. There are footnotes, a good bibliography, and a valuable index.

Tocqueville, Alexis de. *Democracy in America by Alexis de Tocqueville*. Edited by Phillips Bradley. 2 vols. New York: Alfred A. Knopf, 1945. This is a revised version of the first English translation and includes informative notes, historical essays, useful bibliographies, and extensive indexes in each volume. The author claims that Tocqueville's work remains one of the most magisterial analyses ever produced on the principle of the sovereignty of the people, its cultural roots, and its evolving political effects.

Zetterbaum, Marvin. *Tocqueville and the Problem of Democracy*. Stanford, Calif.: Stanford University Press, 1967. An examination of Tocqueville's proposition that democracy was inevitable and therefore that democracy had to be made safe for the world. The author's view is that the "inevitability thesis" distracted readers from Tocqueville's central concern about perfecting democracy and of harmonizing the demands of justice with those of excellence. However brief, this is an enlightening study, clearly written and intended for the general reader. There are footnotes throughout, a useful bibliography, and a valuable index.

Clifton K. Yearley

TOKUGAWA IEYASU
Matsudaira Takechiyo

Born: January 31, 1543; Okazaki, Mikawa Province, Japan
Died: April 17, 1616; Sumpu, Suruga Province, Japan
Areas of Achievement: Government, politics, and the military
Contribution: Ieyasu united Japan under a feudal administration and brought
it to the height of its cultural tradition in a closed society which lasted for
more than two centuries.

Early Life

Tokugawa Ieyasu was born Matsudaira Takechiyo in Okazaki Castle, the
son of a minor warrior chieftain, Matsudaira Hirotada, whose lands lay
between the domains of the Imagawa and the Oda families on the Pacific Ocean. To cement an alliance with Imagawa Yoshimoto, Hirotada dispatched Ieyasu as a hostage in 1547. Ieyasu, however, was seized by Oda
Nobuhide, who held him hostage for two years. A truce between Yoshimoto
and Nobuhide allowed Ieyasu, whose father had died in the meantime, to be
taken as hostage to Sumpu, the castle town of Yoshimoto. His grandmother,
Keyoin, a nun in Sumpu, started Ieyasu's education by teaching him calligraphy and arranging for a Zen monk, Tagen Sufu, adviser and kin of
Yoshimoto, to educate him further. Sufu, an expert in the principles and
practice of warfare and well versed in tactics and strategy, taught Ieyasu the
relationship of warfare to government and administration. Ieyasu's education
in both military and civil affairs, continually internalized through practical
application, eventually refined him into the greatest political and military
figure in the history of Japan.

As early as the age of ten, Ieyasu began to participate in military duties,
initially in noncombatant positions, such as commander of the castle guard.
At age twelve, he became an adult and took the name Motonobu. The following year, in 1556, he returned to Okazaki as head of the family to find his
Matsudaira retainers awaiting him, although the Imagawa family continued
to garrison the castle. In 1558, at the age of fifteen, he made his first sortie,
an assault on a peripheral fortress of Oda Nobunaga, who had succeeded his
father, Nobuhide. Ieyasu destroyed the fort, raided the area, and before
withdrawing smashed a pursuit force dispatched by Nobunaga. When Yoshimoto refused to recall the Imagawa garrison at Okazaki, Ieyasu changed his
name to Motoyasu. For two more years, he served Yoshimoto until Yoshimoto was killed in battle by Nobunaga forces at Okehazama in 1560. Although Ieyasu had successfully overrun a Nobunaga frontier fortress, he
realized that Nobunaga had been victorious and that Yoshimoto's heir was
incompetent. Ieyasu thus returned to Okazaki, reclaimed the domain for his
family, forced the Imagawa garrison out, and established himself as an inde-

pendent lord at the age of seventeen.

In 1561, he joined hands with Nobunaga and took the name Ieyasu. Little by little, he encroached on Imagawa holdings until he controlled both Mikawa and Totomi provinces. In 1567, an imperial order pronounced him Lord Tokugawa Ieyasu, and, as an ally of Nobunaga, he extended his holdings eastward along the seacoast. Fighting much of the time against the Takeda family, he added Suruga Province to his holdings.

When Nobunaga was murdered in 1582, his chief general, Toyotomi Hideyoshi, began taking over his domains and alliances. In 1583, to offset Hideyoshi's power, Ieyasu made an alliance with Hojo Ujimasa in Odawara and split the eastern Takeda domains, taking the Kai and Southern Shinano Provinces. When Hideyoshi became *Kampaku* (regent to the emperor) in 1585, some Tokugawa allies went over to his side, and Ieyasu, to maintain peace on his western borders, struck a deal with Hideyoshi in 1586 and swore loyalty to him in 1588. Thus, when Ujimasa refused to submit to Hideyoshi, Hideyoshi attacked, using Ieyasu as his point man. When Odawara fell in 1590, the Hojo leaders were ordered to disembowel themselves, and the Kanto Plain, with its six provinces of Izu, Sagami, Musashi, Kozuke, Kazusa, and Shimosa, was given to Ieyasu along with 110,000 *koku* (one *koku* is equivalent to an area which would harvest five bushels of rice) of land in the Omi and Ise Provinces not far from Kyoto in exchange for Ieyasu's lands in the Mikawa, Totomi, and Suruga provinces. It provided Ieyasu with a one-million-*koku* increase in land, separated him further from Hideyoshi, and made him point man for further expansion of Hideyoshi's control to the east. Ieyasu now established his castle in Edo, which is the modern Imperial Palace in Tokyo, and began a promising future.

Life's Work

The 1590's was a decade of preparation. The policies Ieyasu followed in consolidating his control in the Kanto Plain were later successfully pursued to unify and administer Japan for two and a half centuries of peace following the Battle of Sekigahara in 1600 and the subsequent subordination of all the feudal lords under Ieyasu's control.

Ieyasu believed that good government consisted of keeping the goodwill of the governed. Consequently, he immediately lightened taxation, punished or got rid of administrators who exploited or abused the collection of taxes, tightened administrative regulations to restrict the authority of district administrators, and established mechanisms of inspection to audit their performance. It is not surprising that peasants from other domains began filtering into Tokugawa holdings to escape high taxes and harsh rule.

Ieyasu regarded religion as one of the instruments of government and guaranteed the lands of temples and shrines that accepted his leadership. He issued sets of regulations to guide abbots in administering the temples and priestly behavior and made religious controversy against the law. Eventually, everyone had to carry an identification card which stipulated to which Shinto shrine and Buddhist temple he belonged. Ieyasu adroitly used nuptial services in politics, marrying his daughters and granddaughters to important feudal lords. These marriages eventually related Ieyasu to almost every major feudal lord in the country, thus consolidating his relations with the strategic feudal houses. Moreover, he soon began arranging marriages among feudal houses, thus strengthening his political infrastructure.

Ieyasu was the perfect specimen of a type that Japanese nationality and training tends to produce. With a powerful physique, he ensured his own physical health with a frugal diet, the avoidance of any excess, a fondness for all kinds of exercise, and an outdoor, active life. Hawking was his real interest, although he was skilled in archery, fencing, and horsemanship and excelled at shooting.

A disciplined man with great self-control, Ieyasu kept his powder dry during Hideyoshi's two Korean campaigns between 1592 and 1598 and after Hideyoshi's death was in a position to consolidate his strength and establish an administration that covered all Japan. Ieyasu was appointed shogun by the Imperial Court in 1603 and reconstituted the *Bakufu* (shogunate), which both Nobunaga and Hideyoshi had ignored.

In patterning his shogunate on the previous Kamakura and Ashikaga shogunates, Ieyasu studied the basic codes of those regimes in the *Azuma Kagami* (mirror of the east) and *Kenmoku Shikimoku* (code of the Kenmu year period), respectively. The *Azuma Kagami* particularly provided historical justification for his regime. As a history of the founding of the Kamakura shogunate, its lessons are clear. A shogun rules through his vassal bands. He rules justly, punishing insurgents and rewarding loyal followers. He keeps the peace and, through the action of a grateful and cooperative court, receives and at the same time passes on to his heir and descendants the title of shogun. Consequently, Ieyasu took care to ensure that no person or institution should be able to interfere with Tokugawa rule and that the military class under his family should be the ruling power. To protect his family position, he retired in 1605 and had his son Tokugawa Hidetada appointed shogun, although he continued to rule. He also saw to it that his grandson Iemitsu would succeed his father, Hidetada, when Ieyasu died.

In a strategic distribution of fiefs following the Battle of Sekigahara, Ieyasu placed *fudai* lords (hereditary lieges) in key domains throughout Japan to keep an eye on the *tozama* (outside lords) with whom he had no hereditary ties. In order to reduce their wealth and thus limit their military strength, Ieyasu imposed upon the feudal lords obligations such as rebuilding castles, expanding the Imperial Palace in 1611, and building roads.

Ieyasu was devoted to the accumulation of wealth, but he did not spend it. Instead, he repeatedly advised vassals to live frugally and in his own daily habits tried to serve as a model. This is one of the reasons why the pursuit of profitable foreign trade was inimicable to his interests. Ieyasu had taken the English captain Will Adams into his service in 1601, sanctioned the visits of the Dutch in 1606 and the English in 1613, and approved Japanese trading ventures to Southeast Asia. Profits on a six-month round-trip voyage to Southeast Asia, for example, ranged from 35 percent to 110 percent, averaging 50 percent per voyage. Once Toyotomi power had been eliminated once and for all by the capture of Osaka Castle in 1616, however, two other factors came into play discouraging foreign trade. One was the persecution of Christians, who were regarded as the advance guard of foreign invasion. The other and most important was the domestic policy of Ieyasu, which brought all the feudal lords under his control. Foreign trade could only help the western *tozama* lords to become wealthy, and that caused gradual foreign restrictions until the country was closed off completely in 1640 under Ie-mitsu.

Summary

In his early years and all through his life, Tokugawa Ieyasu was a good fighter and a born strategist. He fought more than forty-five battles. He did not win them all, but at Mikatagahara he defeated a force led by Takeda Shingen twice as great as his own. Later, he defeated Hideyoshi twice at Komakiyama and Nagakute before submitting himself as a vassal. The Battle of Sekigahara showed his true mettle as a general. He smashed a combined force larger than his own and settled once and for all his military supremacy over all the other feudal lords.

In his later years after 1590, when he took over the Kanto Plain, he showed his genius as an administrator. Ieyasu made no effort to create a systematic government. He gave direct orders rather than governing by legislation. What legislation there was was neither bulky nor particularly original. It carried on the codes of the Kamakura and Ashikaga shogunates with the purpose of keeping the Tokugawa family in a position of complete and unassailable domination. It included terms of the oath to be taken by all *daimyo* (feudal lords) and laws to be observed by the imperial house and court nobles and by the feudal lords and their samurai retainers. Ieyasu exacted unconditional obedience of the whole military class. Moreover, the court could do nothing without the consent of the shogunate, restricting itself to ceremony and aesthetics.

Bibliography

Boxer, C. R. *The Christian Century in Japan, 1549-1650*. Berkeley: University of California Press, 1951. This is a classic examination of the century of foreign trade prior to the closing of the country in 1640. The changing attitude of Ieyasu toward Christians is examined.

Murdoch, James, and Isoh Yamagata. *A History of Japan During the Century of Early Foreign Intercourse, 1542-1651*. Kobe, Japan: Japan Chronicle, 1903. Chronicles the Christian century in Japan. Includes an account of the establishment of the Tokugawa shogunate under Ieyasu.

Sadler, A. L. *The Maker of Modern Japan: The Life of Tokugawa Ieyasu*. London: Allen & Unwin, 1937. The first major effort to capture the life and times of Ieyasu and the meaning of his life.

Sansom, George. *A History of Japan, 1334-1615*. Stanford, Calif.: Stanford University Press, 1961. Contains two excellent chapters on Ieyasu's life and the early years of the Tokugawa shogunate, respectively. See also the chapter on the Tokugawa government in volume 3.

_____. *The Western World and Japan*. New York: Alfred A. Knopf, 1950. An important work on Japan in the international scene. Chapter 9 is particularly relevant to the Tokugawa attitude toward foreign trade.

Totman, Conrad. *Tokugawa Ieyasu: Shogun*. San Francisco: Heian International, 1983. A well-written, in-depth biography of Ieyasu which employs flashbacks to heighten interest.

Edwin L. Neville, Jr.

LEO TOLSTOY

Born: September 9, 1828; Yasnaya Polyana, Russia
Died: November 20, 1910; Astapovo, Russia
Areas of Achievement: Literature and social reform
Contribution: During the first half of his long and active life, Tolstoy brought universal fame to Russian literature through his fiction. In later years, he achieved worldwide renown as a pacifist, social activist, and moralist. He is equally significant as a novelist and moral philosopher.

Early Life
Leo Tolstoy traces his aristocratic origins back to the founding of the Russian state in the ninth century. His ancestors, at times faithful servants, at times opponents of the Crown, amassed fame as well as respectable wealth over the centuries. Thus Tolstoy, though orphaned at age eight, grew up in comfort under the care of relatives at the various Tolstoy residences. He subsequently shaped a vague memory of his mother, who died when he was two, into an idealized portrait of the perfect woman and featured such a paragon in many of his major works. His first published narrative, *Detstvo* (1852; *Childhood*, 1862), re-creates a boy's tender relationship with and painful loss of his mother.

A flamboyant life-style, filled with carousing and gambling, prevented Tolstoy from completing university study, but he revealed an early talent for writing and meticulously recorded daily details, from purest thoughts to debauched acts, in his diaries. He continued keeping such journals until old age, providing future literary historians with rich source material for every stage of his life. His elder siblings and relations, dismayed at the young count's irresolution and wantonness, sent him in 1851 to the Caucasus, where Russia was engaged in sporadic military operations with hostile natives.

Tolstoy's subsequent participation in the Crimean War put an end to the unstable years of his youth. Active service during the siege of Sevastopol motivated him to set down his impressions of the carnage in a series of sketches, "Sevastopol v dekabre," "Sevastopol v maye," and "Sevastopol v avguste" (1854-1856; collected in translation as *Sebastopol*, 1887). His original and above all truthful accounts pleased a public that had grown tired of the prevailing vainglorious, deceitful war reports. So convincingly did Tolstoy chronicle the horror of battlefield life and communicate his disillusionment with war that czarist censors moved to alter his exposés. Tolstoy's later devotion to nonviolence stems from these experiences. His perceptions about the ineptitude of military commanders juxtaposed to the courage and common sense of foot soldiers resurface in his major work, *Voyna i mir* (1865-1869; *War and Peace*, 1886). Moreover, his dispute with the authorities over his forthright reporting set the stage for a lifelong confrontation with the imperial autocracy.

Life's Work

Tolstoy's long literary career followed several distinct directions. The labors of his younger years belong to the field of aesthetic literature, though he embarked on that course only after lengthy deliberation. When he returned to St. Petersburg in 1855 following military service, high society lionized the young hero and for a time drew him back into the swirl of its carefree amusements. His strong didactic bent and quarrelsome nature did not, however, endear him to the literary establishment. He soon antagonized writers on all sides of the social and political spectrum and in the end thought it best to develop his talents without the help of contemporaries. The deaths of two brothers and an execution witnessed in Paris in 1857 led him to approach life in a more serious vein. He opened and directed a school for peasant children on his estate, using pedagogical methods which he himself established, and entered into lively journalistic polemics with other educators over his scheme of placing moral teachings above the acquisition of knowledge. These and other controversial public exchanges brought renewed government interference which impelled Tolstoy to turn to less antagonistic activity. In 1862, he married Sophia Behrs, sixteen years his junior, became a country gentleman, and settled down to a life of writing.

The 1860's were almost wholly devoted to the composition of the epic *War and Peace*, which went through so many revisions and changes of focus, even as it was being serialized, that no clearly definitive version of the novel exists. Among the diverse issues embedded in the finished product are Tolstoy's own interpretation of the Napoleonic Wars, a richly drawn panorama of early nineteenth century Russian upper-class society supplemented by many biographical details, a firm conviction that the values of close-knit family life are far superior to social rituals, and a wealth of sundry philosophical observations. *War and Peace* owes its immense success to the author's vast descriptive talents, which manage to neutralize his lifelong tendency to sermonize.

Reflections on the importance of stable domestic existence also dominate Tolstoy's second major work, *Anna Karenina* (1875-1878; English translation, 1886), in which he chronicles the fates of three aristocratic families and demonstrates that the title figure's insistence on personal happiness to the detriment of family duty engenders tragedy for all concerned. The novel also develops Tolstoy's pet notion that Russian peasant mores are morally superior to high society's ideals. Ideas about the meaning of death and the validity of suicide also represent an important strain in *Anna Karenina*, reflecting Tolstoy's own frequent contact with death, as he lost several children and other close relatives in the 1870's during the composition of the novel. The themes of these two major works are echoed in the many shorter pieces produced by the prolific Tolstoy during the same period.

The late 1870's represent a watershed for Tolstoy, a time when a prolonged spiritual crisis forced him to evaluate both his privileged life and his literary endeavors. A drastic reorientation evolved from this period of introspection. No longer able to justify his considerable wealth in the face of millions of illiterate, destitute peasants and laborers, Tolstoy resolved to make amends by placing his talent and means at the disposal of the poor. In consequence, he actively challenged what he perceived to be the hypocrisy of Russia's ruling institutions. Since the Russian Orthodox church worked closely with the conservative czarist government to maintain the status quo, it too became a target of Tolstoy's dissatisfactions. After publication of the strongly anticlerical *Voskreseniye* (1899; *Resurrection*, 1899), Tolstoy found himself excommunicated, an action he dismissed lightly, having over the years developed a personal Christianity which became the basis of much of his nonfictional writing. His spiritual anxieties and search for an acceptable faith are chronicled in *Ispoved* (1884; *A Confession*, 1885). Both Tolstoy's literary style and his subject matter underwent extreme changes during this time. The works became shorter, using more succinct and simpler language, and became decidedly more opinionated. Fiction largely gave way to social and philosophical commentary, and even the remaining fictional pieces were intricately shaped to transmit Tolstoy's moral messages. Thus, *Smert Ivana Ilicha* (1886; *The Death of Ivan Ilich*, 1887) presents Tolstoy's view of the proper attitude toward death and dying, and the play *Vlast tmy* (1887; *The Power of Darkness*, 1888) warns of the grim consequences engendered by evil thoughts and deeds. Tolstoy justified the political nature of this type of fiction by challenging the very morality of aesthetic detachment. Since even his polemical commentaries adhered to respectable literary standards, he never lost his readership. On the contrary, people of all persuasions debated his works with interest, even fascination.

Tolstoy's efforts to use his name and fortune in support of favorite causes gave rise to severe disharmony within the Tolstoy family. For long years, the spouses battled over property and copyright privileges. These quarrels led Tolstoy to replace his earlier emphasis on family unity with issues of personal salvation and questions of ethics. He returned to the theme of family in one of his most controversial narratives, *Kreytserova sonata* (1891; *The Kreutzer Sonata*, 1890). In this work he denies that marriage is a valid social institution by defining its main purpose as the gratification of lust, detrimental to women and destructive of personal integrity. The major character, Pozdnyshev, murders his wife in a bout of jealousy and proposes the abolition of all sexual acts, even at the expense of humanity's extinction.

Not all Tolstoy's later views express such absolute negatives, but most of his mature output was disputatious in nature. For example, his treatise *Chto takoye iskusstvo?* (1898; *What Is Art?*, 1898) sets forth his revised opinion on the nature and role of literature. He dismisses most art, including his own earlier writings, as immoral and undemocratic, suggesting instead that all art forms be morally instructive and executed in simple, guileless fashion accessible to the multitudes.

Throughout his long life, Tolstoy continued to espouse peaceful settlement of international conflicts. In time, his advocacy of nonresistance made him into a prominent spokesman against war and the death penalty. His regard for the impoverished masses and his many controversial stands brought him worldwide fame. The image of the revered, bearded, aged "repentant nobleman," holding court and expounding his position on national and global topics while dressed in homemade rural attire, drew diverse crowds from far and wide. His very renown prevented an angry czarist government from treating him harshly. To prevent the total dissolution of his domestic bonds, Tolstoy permitted the family to remain at the imposing country estate, but he himself withdrew to a humble corner of it to observe a rigorously modest life-style. At the age of eighty-two, he decided to cut even these ties and secretly left home to live henceforth entirely according to his convictions. Illness almost immediately forced him to abandon the train journey, and he died at the station master's house a week later, surrounded by dignitaries and reporters. He lies buried in a distant corner of his estate. His simple, unadorned grave and the mansion, converted into a Tolstoy museum after the Russian Revolution, are a favorite stop for countless visitors and tourists.

Summary

Leo Tolstoy's impact as both artist and moralist continues undiminished. His fictional works, especially his earlier ones, retain a charm that is proof of his enormous descriptive powers. Yet even these works express personal preferences and values, which the author elucidates at every opportunity. Thus it is, in the final analysis, Tolstoy the teacher, moralist, and public commentator who dominates. Through his doctrine of nonresistance, which he based on the words of Jesus and through which he resisted many inequities of the state, he set examples for similar movements in India under Mohandas Gandhi and the United States under Martin Luther King, Jr. While his pronouncements on behalf of the poor often assume an overly shrill tone, he backed these convictions with solid action. Not only did his income and efforts facilitate great humanitarian projects, from famine relief to resettlement of religious dissenters, but also he himself found no peace until he had adjusted his life-style to fit the humblest. His deliberations on death and ideas on how to cope with it cut through the stilted social conventions of his time to find universal appreciation and application in the twentieth century.

Closely linked to Tolstoy's thoughts about death and dying was his quest for a new religious attitude. By examining the doctrines and practices of the

Russian Orthodox church as well as other religions and finding them incompatible with Jesus' words, he pointed to alternative approaches, advocating a way of life based on the Gospels, not church dogma. In this, too, he anticipated certain twentieth century movements toward a personal fundamentalism.

Tolstoy also generated opposition. His dogmatic and frequently cantankerous method of conveying his beliefs alienated many potential adherents. In the manner of all prophets, he brooked no contradiction of his scheme of universal ethical improvement. Even so, his many achievements and contributions as major writer, social activist, and moral philosopher remain universally acknowledged.

Bibliography

Benson, Ruth Crego. *Women in Tolstoy: The Ideal and the Erotic*. Urbana: University of Illinois Press, 1973. Concentrates on Tolstoy's changing vision of the role and importance of family life. Suggests that Tolstoy struggled most of his life with a dichotomous view of women, regarding them in strictly black-and-white terms, as saints or sinners. Analyzes the female characters in the major and several minor works in terms of such a double view. An interesting and provocative piece of feminist criticism.

Bloom, Harold, ed. *Leo Tolstoy*. New York: Chelsea House, 1986. A collection of critical essays, encompassing the years 1920-1983. The views expressed give a very good sampling of the wide range of opinions about Tolstoy prevalent among Western critics. Many of these critics assign a prominent place in literary history to Tolstoy, comparing him to, among others, Homer and Johann Wolfgang von Goethe. Some of the articles deal with specific works; others define Tolstoy's contributions to nineteenth century European intellectual movements. Limited bibliography.

De Courcel, Martine. *Tolstoy: The Ultimate Reconciliation*. Translated by Peter Levi. New York: Charles Scribner's Sons, 1987. A detailed biography, annotated with selected bibliography, which relies heavily on the notebooks and diaries of Tolstoy and those of his wife, Sophia. Concentrates on Tolstoy's domestic life but has extensive references to his general public activity. Posits the unique notion that Tolstoy left home at the end of his life in order to return to aesthetic literature.

Greenwood, E. B. *Tolstoy: The Comprehensive Vision*. New York: St. Martin's Press, 1975. For Greenwood, Tolstoy's diverse strivings were attributable to his belief that art and life could be brought together under one philosophical tenet. Greenwood detects a search for such a unified vision in most of the major writings. Stresses Tolstoy's contribution to philosophy and religion.

Rowe, William W. *Leo Tolstoy*. Boston: Twayne, 1986. Concise introduction to Tolstoy's life and work, with special emphasis on the major novels and later didactic writings. Discusses, briefly, most of Tolstoy's major concerns. Excellent treatment of individual characters in the major novels. Selected bibliography.

Simmons, Ernest J. *Tolstoy.* London: Routledge & Kegan Paul, 1973. Extensive chronological account of Tolstoy's public activities. Includes social and cultural background on Russia during Tolstoy's time and discusses the importance of Tolstoy's theories on religion, society, morality, and literature. Adds comments on Tolstoy's relevance to the twentieth century and on his international stature. Selected bibliography.

Tolstaia, Andreevna S. *The Diaries of Sophia Tolstoy.* Edited by O. A. Golinenko et al. Translated by Cathy Porter with an introduction by R. F. Christian. New York: Random House, 1985. Illustrated. This massive personal record of Tolstoy's wife, detailing their life together, spans the years 1862-1910. Sophia Tolstoy kept an almost daily account of her husband's opinions, doubts, and plans concerning his literary activity and social ventures as well as of his relationship with other writers and thinkers. The diaries often portray Tolstoy in an unfavorable light, since the spouses were temperamentally incompatible, and she chafed under his domination. She collaborated closely with Tolstoy for many decades, however, and her notes give a fascinating and intimate view of the Tolstoy family and of the extent to which this family served as background for many of the literary episodes.

Wilson, A. N. *Tolstoy.* New York: W.W. Norton, 1988. A long but immensely readable biography, breezy, insightful, and opinionated, by a prolific and highly regarded British novelist. Illustrated; includes a useful chronology of Tolstoy's life and times as well as notes, bibliography, and index.

Margot K. Frank

EVANGELISTA TORRICELLI

Born: October 15, 1608; Modigliano
Died: October 25, 1647; Florence
Areas of Achievement: Physics, mathematics, invention, and technology
Contribution: Torricelli extended Galileo's system of mechanics to fluids, developed Torricelli's theorem, which mathematically calculates the velocity of liquid emerging from an opening in a vessel, and invented the barometer. He also stands among the founders of modern integral and differential calculus.

Early Life

Evangelista Torricelli was the eldest of three children born to Gaspare Torricelli, a textile artisan, and his wife, Caterina Angetti. Possessing only moderate income, Torricelli sent his talented young son to his uncle, who directed his education. After covering the humanities, the young Torricelli studied mathematics and philosophy with the Jesuits in Faenza from 1625 to 1626, displaying remarkable talent. Consequently, in 1626, Torricelli's uncle sent him to study with mathematician and hydraulic engineer Benedetto Castelli in Rome. Castelli recognized his student's outstanding scientific ability and soon appointed Torricelli his secretary.

While serving in this capacity in September, 1632, Torricelli replied for Castelli to a letter from Castelli's former teacher, the great Italian astronomer and physicist Galileo. Torricelli introduced himself to Galileo as a mathematician who had studied classical Greek geometry. In astronomy, Torricelli declared that he had studied both traditional Aristotelian astronomy and the new astronomy but was convinced of the superiority of the Copernican system. Noting that he had studied Galileo's recent book, *Dialogo sopra i due massimi sistemi del mondo, tolemaico e copernicano* (1632; *Dialogue Concerning the Two Chief World Systems, Ptolemaic and Copernican*, 1661), Torricelli proclaimed himself a member of the "Galilean sect."

Historians today are unsure of Torricelli's whereabouts, activities, or studies between late 1632 and 1640. It is likely, however, that during those years Torricelli was secretary to Galileo's friend Giovanni Ciampoli, governor of various cities in the Marches and Umbria.

Life's Work

During these years, Torricelli's interest in mathematics and physics grew, and many of the propositions published in *Opera geometrica* (1644; geometric works) were formulated around 1640 or 1641. For example, about 1640 Torricelli rectified a section of the logarithmic spiral and thus completed the first mathematical rectification of a curved line other than the circle. Before returning to Rome in 1641, Torricelli presented Castelli a treatise he had written extending Galileo's theory of the parabolic motion of projectiles. Castelli praised the paper, and in April of 1641 delivered it to Galileo. During his visit, Castelli recommended Torricelli to help Galileo with his scientific work.

On October 10, 1641, Torricelli joined Galileo and physicist Vincenzo Viviani in Galileo's home at Arcetri. There he was Galileo's assistant and secretary until Galileo's death in January, 1642. Torricelli then succeeded Galileo as mathematician and philosopher to Ferdinand II. For the remaining five years of his life, Torricelli flourished at the ducal court. Charming, witty, and well liked, Torricelli wrote comedies, lectured (sometimes on scientific topics), and continued his scientific work.

In 1644, Torricelli published *Opera geometrica*. The first of its three sections, entitled *De sphaera et solidis sphaeralibus libri duo* (two books concerning the sphere and spherical solids), has two parts. The first, written around 1641, concerns figures produced by the rotation of a regular polygon inscribed in or circumscribed around a circle on one of its axes of symmetry. In the second part, Torricelli considered the motion of projectiles.

The second section of Torricelli's *Opera geometrica* contains his 1641 treatise *De motu gravium naturaliter descendentium et proiectorum libri duo* (two books concerning falling bodies and projectiles). In it, Torricelli continued Galileo's mathematical study of falling bodies and the motion of projectiles, broached topics in differential calculus, and extended Galileo's mechanics to fluid flow. Torricelli sought a dynamic explanation, which Galileo had not, and, although he employed medieval impetus theory, Torricelli obtained mathematical conclusions still accepted in the twentieth century. It was also in this treatise that Torricelli first formally stated Torricelli's principle, that a rigid system of bodies can move spontaneously on the earth's surface only if its center of gravity descends. Examination of the tangents of the trajectories of projectiles led him to the fundamental problem of differential calculus, to determine the tangent of a given curve at a given point. His unpublished notes contain an implicit recognition of the inverse character of differentiation and integration, the fundamental theorem of the calculus. In another historic passage, Torricelli treated jets of liquids as falling bodies and projectiles and arrived at Torricelli's theorem. This theorem, formulated in 1643, states that the speed v of a liquid at the point of efflux from an orifice in a container is equal to that which a single drop of the liquid would have if it were falling freely in a vacuum the vertical distance h, from the top of the liquid to the orifice, that is, $v = \sqrt{2gh}$, where g is the acceleration caused by gravity. He furthermore demonstrated that liquid issuing from an orifice in the side of a vessel assumes a parabolic trajectory.

The third section of Torricelli's *Opera geometrica* contains his *De dimensione parabolae, solidique hyperbolici problemata duo* (two problems concerning the dimension of the parabola and the hyperbolic solid). Among its

most notable features is Torricelli's quadrature of the cycloid, the first publication of a mathematical determination of the area of this important new
curve. The treatise also includes the first publication of a method to determine the tangent of any point of the cycloid.

In *Opera geometrica*, Torricelli employed and extended the newly developed "method of indivisibles" of Bonaventura Cavalieri. Viewing the
area of plane figures and the volume of solid figures as the sum of infinitely
small chords or planes, respectively, Cavalieri formulated the basic principle
of integration. By 1641, Torricelli had developed a method of indivisibles
utilizing curved chords and planes, and numerous theorems derived by it
appear in *Opera geometrica*. The most notable one calculates the finite volume of a solid generated by the rotation of an infinite section of an equi-
lateral hyperbola.

Opera geometrica spread Torricelli's fame as a geometer and physicist
across Europe. It was the only work Torricelli published in his lifetime; the
remainder of his scientific achievements were communicated through letters
in which he penned noteworthy contributions to analytic geometry, the development of integral and differential calculus, and physics. For example, in
1646 he proposed his universal theorem for determining the center of gravity
of any geometrical figure through the relation between two integrals. His
correspondence also contains arguments on priority of discovery, particularly
with Gilles Personne de Roberval. In 1646, Roberval accused Torricelli of
plagiarizing his discoveries, made in 1634-1638, of the quadrature of the
cycloid and the measurement of the solid generated by the rotation of the
cycloid around its base.

In addition to his mathematical research, Torricelli contributed to the field
of meteorology. Abandoning the accepted theory that wind is generated by
the evaporation of exhalations from the earth, Torricelli posed the modern
theory that winds occur because of differences in the temperature and density
of atmospheric air. Observation of the temperature and density of atmospheric air thus interested Torricelli, and he developed new devices for this
task. Some historians claim that Torricelli transformed an air thermoscope
(an air-filled, uncalibrated glass bulb with its open end submerged in water)
developed by Galileo into a thermoscope or thermometer containing water
and later alcohol, but this seems dubious.

There is little doubt, however, that Torricelli invented the mercury barometer while attempting to determine why water rose to only approximately
thirty-four feet in pumps and why siphons would not draw water over hills
greater in height. To find an answer, in 1644 Torricelli devised an experiment involving a four-foot-long, mercury-filled glass tube, sealed at the top
and inverted in a dish, which it appears Viviani first executed. Observing
that the weight of the air was able to push mercury (fourteen times heavier
than water) to a height of only twenty-nine inches in the tube (one-fourteenth

the height it could push water), Torricelli concluded in a June 11 letter that the force maintaining the mercury was not an internal suctional "force of vacuum" in the tube but was the weight of the external air pressing on the mercury in the bowl. Torricelli also remarked that he was striving to construct an instrument to show changes in atmospheric pressure—the first barometer. Torricelli's work was praised by Ferdinand II, and after October, 1644, news of Torricelli's barometric experiments traveled quickly across Europe.

In astronomy, Torricelli developed exceptional technical ability in manufacturing telescope lenses. By 1643, he was selecting high-quality glass, accurately grinding the lenses, and following Hieronymus Sirturi's suggestion to avoid pitch and fire in fastening the lenses to produce lenses equaling or surpassing those of the best contemporary Italian telescope maker. In 1644, the duke presented Torricelli a gold collar and medallion in recognition of his expertise.

In October, 1647, Torricelli contracted a brief and violent fever, probably typhoid. After dictating his memoirs, he died on October 25, at age thirty-nine. He was buried in Florence in the Church of San Lorenzo.

Summary

Evangelista Torricelli was one of the most prominent mathematicians of the seventeenth century. His quadrature of the cycloid, development of curved indivisibles, and work on solids of rotation moved mathematics toward modern integral calculus. Torricelli's *Opera geometrica* possesses added historical significance because it clearly presented Cavalieri's methods, thus paving the way for the diffusion of the geometry of indivisibles, from which integral calculus stemmed, throughout Europe. Torricelli's successful attempts to determine the tangents of curves and his work on maxima and minima assisted in the foundation of differential calculus. In his treatment of the parabolic motion of projectiles, Torricelli implicitly recognized the inverse character of differentiation and integration, which forms the fundamental theorem of the calculus. Consequently, when Isaac Barrow published that theorem in 1670 he recognized Torricelli's contribution to its development. Torricelli's work in hydrodynamics was considered so fundamentally important that the twentieth century physicist Ernst Mach awarded Torricelli the title of "the founder of hydrodynamics."

The seventeenth century saw the development of radically new optical and physical instruments that greatly affected scientific research, among them the thermometer and Torricelli's barometer (called the "Torricelli tube" until Robert Boyle gave it the name barometer in 1667). Even today, the space above the liquid is known as the "Torricelli vacuum." Although the barometer was not widely used until long afterward, Torricelli's invention and his barometric experiments provoked a rash of experimental work and theoretical speculation. More important, these experiments discredited the ancient Aristotelian idea that "nature abhors a vacuum," forced scientists to reevaluate their worldview in the light of the existence of a vacuum, and assisted in the establishment of the mechanical philosophy in the scientific revolution.

Bibliography

Boyer, Carl B. *A History of Mathematics*. New York: John Wiley & Sons, 1968. In the best treatment of Torricelli in any English-language history of mathematics, Boyer presents a thorough and illuminating discussion of Torricelli's mathematical contributions, relates him to the seventeenth century mathematical community, and places his work within the general context of the development of mathematics.

Middleton, W. E. Knowles. *The History of the Barometer*. Baltimore: Johns Hopkins University Press, 1964. Chapter 2 of this excellently researched book discusses Torricelli's barometer and barometric experiments and includes translations of Torricelli's letters describing them.

——————. *A History of the Thermometer and Its Use in Meteorology*. Baltimore: Johns Hopkins University Press, 1966. This authoritative history of the thermometer does not support the view that Torricelli made major improvements in that instrument.

Nemenyi, Paul F. "The Main Concepts and Ideas of Fluid Dynamics in Their Historical Development." *Archive for History of Exact Sciences* 2 (1962): 52-86. One of the few works available on pre-Eulerian fluid dynamics, this article describes Torricelli's work in hydrodynamics and places it within the historical development of ideas in the field.

Westfall, Richard S. *The Construction of Modern Science: Mechanisms and Mechanics*. New York: John Wiley & Sons, 1971. Reprint. New York: Cambridge University Press, 1977. Part of the Cambridge History of Science series, this work contains a concise discussion of Torricelli's barometric experiments and his theories of free-fall and impact, placing them within the context of the scientific revolution.

Martha Ellen Webb

LENNART TORSTENSON

Born: August 17, 1603; Torstena, Vastergotland, Sweden
Died: April 7, 1651, Stockholm, Sweden
Area of Achievement: The military
Contribution: Torstenson has been called the "father of field artillery." He
ably advanced the reforms in artillery introduced by King Gustavus II
Adolphus of Sweden and made standardized, mobile, rapid-firing field
artillery the decisive factor in several Swedish victories of the Thirty
Years' War, thereby introducing these reforms to the rest of Europe.

Early Life

Lennart Torstenson began his service to the Swedish crown as a page in
1618. From 1621 to 1623, he accompanied the king on the Livonian Campaign. During that service, he impressed the king sufficiently to be sent to
study for two years in the Netherlands under Maurice of Nassau, Prince of
Orange. Maurice was one of the first to recognize fully the potential of
artillery, and he was a pioneer in developing professional, regularly paid,
and rigidly trained and disciplined armies. He developed a dependable supply system for the army, which provided well-stocked commissariats wherever the army moved. He introduced the concept of well-coordinated, combined use of infantry and cavalry, to which he now added artillery. He also
began to standardize artillery calibers. Maurice, however, still envisioned a
rather static role for artillery in siege work as well as on the battlefield.
Students from all over Europe, especially from the Protestant countries, were
introduced by him to these military reforms, and nowhere were these reforms more effectively adopted and advanced than in Sweden.

Following this training, the young Torstenson served in the campaign
against Prussia during the early part of the Thirty Years' War. Gustavus II
Adolphus, himself a pioneer in the modernization and standardization of
field artillery, put Torstenson, age twenty-seven, in command of the first
field artillery regiment organized in Europe. By that time, Gustavus had
carried out impressive modifications of the formerly unwieldy and unreliable
artillery. He had reduced the former sixteen types of guns to three—the 3- ,
12- , and 24-pounders. The latter was now the heaviest gun, replacing the
former 48-pounder. Only the 3-pounders (in British sources frequently referred to as 4-pounders) and 12-pounders, however, were classed as field
artillery. The comparatively light 3-pounder (weighing five hundred pounds)
could be moved and operated in the field by one or two horses and two or
three men, thus making it possible to employ artillery in fluid battlefield
situations. For the first time, artillery was an effective antipersonnel weapon,
usually firing canister or grapeshot, having almost the effect of an automatic
weapon. These new guns could also provide more rapid fire than older guns,

since the shot was attached by straps to the bag holding the powder charge, enabling rapid loading. Newer technology also made possible the construction of lighter and shorter gun barrels. The development of a more standard and safer gunpowder helped to maintain and even improve consistency in range and accuracy, despite the lighter weight and the shorter barrels. Science and technology were rapidly becoming integral elements of modern warfare. Another aspect of these reforms was the substantial increase in the number of artillery pieces in the Swedish army, made possible in part by Sweden's ample supply of copper, until the ratio between guns and men was an unprecedented 9.4 guns for every one thousand men. Gustavus attached two of the light and mobile 3-pounder field guns to every infantry and cavalry regiment. Torstenson inherited these reforms and continued to build on them.

Life's Work

Torstenson's first major achievement came during the Swedish phase of the Thirty Years' War, in the Battle of Breitenfeld near Leipzig (September, 1631), when his gunners were able to deliver a rate of fire three times that of their German imperial opponents. (The 3-pounders could also fire eight rounds for every six fired by the musketeers.) He was also able to exploit his artillery's greater mobility and move the guns up with the advancing infantry during the decisive counterattack, thus cinching a clear Swedish victory, the Protestants' first major success. While the Swedes lost 4,000 of the 40,000 men engaged, the imperial forces lost a total of 21,600 of the 32,000 men involved. Swedish artillery, which outnumbered imperial artillery fifty-four to twenty-six played a major role in achieving this uneven casualty ratio. This battle also marked the victory of Sweden's new linear formations (originally introduced by Maurice of Nassau) over the old massive formations (the "Spanish square"), which, in one form or another, had dominated European military tactics for centuries. The Swedish linear formation was usually five men deep, thus putting every man in direct contact with the enemy during the melee. Mobility had won over mass. The best commentary on these new tactics is the fact that the imperial forces now attempted to imitate these methods, though they were initially not very successful. As a result of the Breitenfeld victory, Sweden was recognized as a major European military power, and northern Germany remained Protestant. Torstenson's reward was a promotion to general in 1632. If Breitenfeld pointed to the end of the old "Spanish square," the Battle of Rocroi in northeastern France in 1643 (won by the dynamic French commander Condé the Great over the Spanish) sealed its fate.

In April, 1632, Torstenson's artillery again provided the decisive difference in the Battle of Lech, in which his artillery covered the Swedish army's crossing of that river and enabled the Swedish forces to penetrate into

Bavarian territory. Torstenson, however, was captured by imperial forces in the Battle of Alte Feste later that year. Significantly, this battle, which turned into a Swedish defeat, was primarily lost because the terrain was so rough that the Swedes were unable to maneuver their field guns during the engagement. As a result of his capture, Torstenson was not present at the fateful Battle of Lützen (November 16, 1632), a victory which was diminished by the death of Gustavus. Torstenson was exchanged a year later. After serving as chief of staff to Johan Banér in 1635 in eastern and central Germany, and after Banér's death, he was put in command of the Swedish army in Germany, having been promoted to field marshal. Torstenson was still in Sweden at the time of his appointment and arrived in Germany to assume command in time to prevent a mutiny against the temporary commander, General Karl Gustav Wrangel. The troops had not been paid for some time and threatened to quit, leaving Sweden without an army in Germany. Torstenson proved his worth in this command position as well, turning an undisciplined rabble (to which most armies had deteriorated during the latter stage of the Thirty Years' War) again into an effective field force, soon winning a series of victories. Torstenson regained control over the mutinous rabble by legalizing and formalizing the practice of looting occupied territory by which soldiers compensated themselves for their service. At the same time, Torstenson enforced a rigid and brutal discipline against all who went against his orders—against his own soldiers and the civilian population alike. Hangings of disobedient soldiers and uncooperative civilians were the order of the day. His men hated him, but he brought them victories and hence plunder. The unspeakable brutality of the soldiers during this final phase of the Thirty Years' War, and especially of the Swedish troops, still haunts German folklore.

In 1642, Torstenson advanced the Swedish forces to within twenty-five miles of Vienna and later that year won another decisive victory in the Second Battle of Breitenfeld, which effectively eliminated the imperial army as a viable military force in Germany. In the 1645 campaign, Torstenson again drove deep into Habsburg territory and, in the Battle of Jankow (March 15, 1645), about forty miles south of Prague, won yet another brilliant Swedish victory. This victory was an outstanding and decisive example of Torstenson's artillery's mobility, which was shifted from sector to sector as needed, making Jankow the hitherto most dramatic example of artillery's flexibility. Following this battle, the Swedes conquered all Moravia and again threatened Vienna.

Early in 1646, following repeated pleas by Torstenson, he was permitted to retire from military service because of ill health. Wrangel succeeded him. A year later, Torstenson was made Count of Ortala. Torstenson had suffered from gout for some time, being restricted to a bed or a litter during much of the last campaign, his hands so gnarled that he was at times unable even to sign orders. His last service was that of general-governor of Sweden's western border province of Westgotland.

Summary

Though the "military revolution" was already under way when Lennart Torstenson appeared on the scene, he can properly be called the father of field artillery. Building on the work of Maurice of Nassau and Gustavus, Torstenson converted the reforms of those two men to full reality on the battlefield.

Under the military reforms, the musketeers (firing ordered volleys, introduced by Gustavus, rather than scattered individual fire) had the task of opening a path for the pikemen, who were still the force to clinch the victory in the melee, or hand-to-hand combat. The light, mobile regimental artillery, able to move with the advancing infantry, assisted the musketeers in providing a breech in the enemy formation in a more massive and decisive fashion through its rapid, coordinated, and concentrated fire. That is also true of cavalry charges, which increased their shock effect through the use of their own regimental guns. Though these reforms gradually spread to other countries, most armies during the Thirty Years' War still employed artillery in a static role, even on the battlefield. In fact, during the period of pre-French revolutionary "neoclassical" warfare, European armies experienced regressive developments in artillery employment as well as in other reforms introduced during the early seventeenth century. In the French army, artillery officers did not hold military rank until 1732, and drivers in many armies continued to be civilians. The use of contract artillery with privately owned horses substantially reduced the potential of mobility on the battlefield, since the contractors removed their valuable horses from harm's way during the battle, restricting the ability to move the guns to the limits of human muscle power. King Frederick the Great introduced the use of army horses in the Prussian army during the middle of the century.

The Battles of Breitenfeld and Jankow demonstrate Torstenson's innovations most dramatically and completed the conversion of field artillery from a purely static function on the battlefield to its modern role as part of the combined arms of infantry, cavalry, and artillery. At least some of the credit that is frequently attributed to Gustavus has to be shared with Torstenson.

Bibliography
Montgomery of Alamein, Viscount. *A History of Warfare.* Cleveland, Ohio: World Publishing, 1968. A general history of warfare which places the Thirty Years' War and Sweden's role in a broader perspective. Contains illustrations, maps, an index, and a short bibliography.

Ogg, David. *Europe in the Seventeenth Century.* 6th ed. London: Adam and Charles Black, 1952. A general history that is old but still of great value.

Has extensive section on the Thirty Years' War and Sweden's role. Contains an extensive, though somewhat outdated, bibliography, and maps.

Roberts, Michael. *Essays in Swedish History.* Minneapolis: University of Minnesota Press, 1967. Essay 3, "Gustav Adolf and the Art of War," is excellent on the overall and extensive military reforms of the early seventeenth century, with an emphasis on Gustavus' contributions. Includes six pages of footnotes that provide excellent bibliographical information.

Scott, Franklin D. *Sweden: The Nation's History.* Minneapolis: University of Minnesota Press, 1977. A general history of Sweden, with Chapter 7, "Sweden's Age of Greatness," devoted to the period from 1611 to 1654. Includes maps and illustrations.

Wedgwood, C. V. *The Thirty Years' War.* New Haven, Conn.: Yale University Press, 1939. A standard work of the war with excellent overall discussions of Sweden's role. Includes maps, illustrations, an index, and an extensive bibliography.

Frederick Dumin

HENRI DE TOULOUSE-LAUTREC

Born: November 24, 1864; Albi, France
Died: September 9, 1901; Château de Malromé, France
Area of Achievement: Art
Contribution: By means of more than seven hundred paintings, sketches, lithographs, and posters, Toulouse-Lautrec recorded vividly the people and activities of Paris in the last decades of the nineteenth century. He elevated color lithography and the poster to major art forms.

Early Life

Henri Marie Raymond de Toulouse-Lautrec Monfa was born into an aristocratic family whose lineage went back to the time of Charlemagne. In separate falls in 1878 and 1879, he broke the femurs of both legs. Throughout his life his legs remained small, while his upper body grew normally. He always required a cane to support his four-foot, six-inch frame. After these accidents, he was not able to dance or to ride, the usual activities of his social class. During his convalesence, his mother and a family friend, René Princeteau, a deaf-mute artist of equestrian scenes, encouraged him to paint.

Though tentative in technique, his early pictures, *Soldier Saddling His Horse*, *Trotting Horseman*, *Amazon*, and *White Horse Gazelle*, are full of life and quite accomplished. They manifest an unfiltered naïveté and are all the more striking for their deliberate use of bold color combinations.

In 1882, Toulouse-Lautrec became a pupil of Léon-Joseph-Florentin Bonnat and, in 1883-1887, of Fernand Cormon. Both academicists, they taught Toulouse-Lautrec the principles of composition. His work was thenceforth more controlled. A visit home in 1883 produced the somewhat Impressionistic oil *The Artist's Mother at Breakfast*.

In 1885, twenty-one years of age and financially independent, Toulouse-Lautrec opened a studio in Montmarte in the building where Edgar Degas had his studio. Degas became his artistic idol, though in 1894 Degas would harshly accuse Toulouse-Lautrec of imitation. His first lithograph was a song-sheet cover in 1887 for Aristide Bruant, who gave Toulouse-Lautrec his first public showing on the walls of his café, Le Mirliton. Toulouse-Lautrec's pastel portrait of Vincent van Gogh, whom he had met at Cormon's in 1886, belongs to the same year.

In 1887, Toulouse-Lautrec painted *Portrait of the Artist's Mother Reading*. At first it seems Impressionistic, but, in fact, the subject is not treated as the focus of light; thrust in the foreground, her presence dominates the painting. For Toulouse-Lautrec, "Nothing exists but the figure. . . . Landscape is only accessory."

Life's Work

Toulouse-Lautrec's art is set against the period known as *fin de siècle* or *la belle époque.* Toulouse-Lautrec, who saw beauty in the ugly and heroism in the underside of Paris, reflects both terms. He called himself a historian of life, which he viewed without pity, false moralizing, or self-righteousness. His pictures are precious historical documents and rival novels and histories in describing the life and moral outlook of his generation.

Impressionism influenced Toulouse-Lautrec's work; yet he more precisely falls in the French drawing tradition of Jacques-Louis David, Jean August Dominique Ingres, and Degas. He did not use shimmering, all-enveloping light as did the Impressionists. He emphasized line, pattern, and pure, unmodeled color without chiaroscuro, as in Japanese art and the then-current Nabi movement. His colors, as are his subjects, are theatrical and often harsh. In his love of line, he differed from other Postimpressionists, such as van Gogh and Paul Gauguin, who stressed mass and solidity. By a few deft strokes of line, he penetrated his subjects' essential character. Toulouse-Lautrec's gift, as was Degas', was to capture figures from contemporary scenes in characteristic poses at unguarded moments, always with some caricature. As his friends noted, he would passionately pursue his subjects in the prime of their careers, then drop them.

In 1888, under the spell of Degas, Toulouse-Lautrec began to illustrate the lowlife of Paris. Montmartre was its focus since the opening of the café Le Chat Noir in 1881. His first important painting was *Le Cirque Fernando: Circus Rider,* done in the flat style of the Japanese prints he collected. Like Gauguin, whom he had recently met, he preferred a bold distortion of perspective to the Impressionists' sense of light.

By this time, Toulouse-Lautrec drew for the leading illustrated journals, *Courrier Français, Paris Illustré, Figaro Illustré,* and *Rire.* He did this not for money—Toulouse-Lautrec never needed art to make a living—but for recognition. In 1888, too, Toulouse-Lautrec first submitted work for the annual Brussels exhibition of the avant garde XX (the twenty) group. The next year saw his major oils, *Au bal du Moulin de la Galette* and *The Girl with Red Hair.* The Moulin de la Galette was one of Toulouse-Lautrec's café haunts.

The Moulin Rouge's opening ushered the gay nineties into Paris. This café became the in place for Paris society, including Toulouse-Lautrec and his cousin and companion, Gabriel Tapié de Céleyran. It was the venue of his best-known pieces. His painting, *Au Moulin Rouge: La Danse* (1890), graced the foyer of the café. It is his first depiction of the dancer La Goulue (the glutton: the stage name of Louise Weber) and her partner, Valentin le Désossé. In 1891, the Moulin Rouge commissioned Toulouse-Lautrec's first poster to advertise the same dancers. He created a sensation by flaunting La Goulue's scandalous white muslin drawers. The poster both launched her career and gave the artist wider recognition. Désossé dominates the foreground in stark profile, while Toulouse-Lautrec and his friends are silhouetted in back. In the same year, *La Goulue au Moulin Rouge* featured her famous deep décolletage.

Toulouse-Lautrec's thirty-one posters are consciously flat, asymmetrical, and decorative; figures are often cropped at the border. His "line, flair, and daring layout" were immediately praised in the press. Jules Chéret, the greatest poster artist of his day, named Toulouse-Lautrec as his successor. Toulouse-Lautrec's prints were better for his painting skills, but the fluidity and economy of stroke of the lithographic medium added to the descriptive capability of his paintings. He did many identical pictures in both mediums.

Toulouse-Lautrec's friendship with the rising star Jane Avril is marked by numerous representations of her over several years. Avril admired his art and may have been in love with him. *Jane Avril Entering Moulin Rouge*, *Jane Avril Leaving Moulin Rouge*, and *Jane Avril Dancing at Moulin Rouge* appeared in 1892. In the last, Toulouse-Lautrec used oils in a sketchy manner to render the dancer's movements. Avril is absorbed in her dancing, her isolation emphasized by the couple in the background who pay her no attention.

In 1892 came a masterpiece, *Au Moulin Rouge*. In a framework of diagonals appear the artist himself, his cousin Tapié de Céleyran, La Goulue, other friends at the table in the foreground, and the mysterious green-faced lady partially cropped off at the right. In 1892, two posters of Bruant in his familiar black coat and red scarf made the entrepreneur's profile known throughout Paris.

A Corner of the Moulin de la Galette of the same year is a minor masterpiece. Human forms are set in overlapping planes. The isolation of these denizens of the demimonde is established by the fact that no one's gaze engages that of another person.

In 1893, Toulouse-Lautrec's poster *Jane Avril at the Jardin de Paris* again "put her in the limelight," said the journal *Fin de Siècle* on September 3. Another poster, *Jane Avril at Divan Japonais*, announced a new café which opened auspiciously, attracting crowds to hear the songs of Yvette Guilbert, but closed soon after. Avril is in the foreground while Guilbert is shown performing but with her head cropped out of the frame. Toulouse-Lautrec's frequent use of cropping as well as his ability to focus on one area, allowing all else to appear marginal or distorted, reflects his awareness of the new medium of photography, which was then influencing the art world. On the psychological level, too, Toulouse-Lautrec recorded his subjects as a camera, with emotional detachment.

Also in 1893, Toulouse-Lautrec did a painting and poster, *Loie Fuller at the Folies Bergère*, of an American to whom he was briefly attracted for her whirling, serpentine "fire dance." His paintings won the approval of Degas and an invitation to join and exhibit for the Independents, a prestigious society of engravers.

Around 1893, Toulouse-Lautrec's interest turned to faces, especially as highlighted by the gas-flares of theaters, rather than the human form as a whole (now often merely sketched in). In this year, his theater prints for *L'Escarmouche* appeared as did eleven litho-portraits of Paris show-people for a *Café-Concert* album and a poster for the book *Au pied de l'échafaud* (1893; at the foot of the scaffold), which was the memoir of Abbé Jean-Baptiste Faure, the chaplain to thirty-eight condemned men. The silhouetted spectators behind the condemned man's harshly lit face are reminiscent of the first Moulin Rouge poster.

Already in 1892, Toulouse-Lautrec had painted prostitutes, most notably *Woman with Black Boa*, whose hard smile betrayed a calculating coldness. Two years later, he set up his studio in the newest and finest brothel, remained there for several months, and produced fifty oils and hundreds of drawings. The last and unquestioned masterpiece of this group names the brothel: *The Salon des Moulins*. Early in that year, Toulouse-Lautrec's poster for a new book, *Babylone d'Allemagne*, "papered every wall in Paris," according to *Fin de Siècle* of February 18, 1894. He also did lithographs for the *Revue Blanche*. His chief occupation for nine months, however, was the album of sixteen lithographs of Guilbert performing her risqué half-spoken chansons. The album had caused a scandal for its deification of a mere café diva. Critics called Guilbert the ugly made uglier. She herself complained at Toulouse-Lautrec's unflattering caricatures of her red hair, uptilted nose, and thin lips but still autographed the hundred copies. In addition, a charcoal and an oil of Guilbert displayed her odd, angular appearance and her trademarks: a low-cut gown and long black gloves.

In London in 1895, Toulouse-Lautrec sketched Oscar Wilde at his celebrated trial. In Paris, his large (five-foot square) oil entitled *Marcelle Lender Dancing the Boléro in "Chilperic"* and several drawings of her back reveal his then current female interest. An album, *Thirty Lithographs*, contained bust-only studies of Jeanne Granier, Lucien Guitry, Jeanne Hading, Sarah Bernhardt, and other stars of the stage. In this same year came his oil of *La Clownesse, Cha-U-Kao*, whose name derives from *chahut-chaos*, a wild dance popular at the Moulin Rouge; *La Danse de La Goulue*; and a portrait of cabaret singer May Belfort. The girl in *La Toilette* (1896) may have belonged to the dancers at Les Moulins. Herein Toulouse-Lautrec returned to a more modeled style. Important works in this year include an oil and a poster *Mademoiselle Eglantine's Troupe* dancing the can-can. Eleven prints of life in the brothels appeared in the women's journal *Elles*. Toulouse-Lautrec showed that these girls, portrayed conversing with clients and serving them camomile tea, were not uniformly lewd but had "exquisite feelings unknown to virtuous women."

An exhibition of lithographs at Maurice Joyant's Paris gallery first engendered a still-prevalent pejorative interpretation of Toulouse-Lautrec's life and art. The critic A. Hepp wrote, "The odd, deformed and limping man was evident in the works." Edmond Goncourt added, "All his drawings seem to reflect his own caricature-like deformity."

Certainly, Toulouse-Lautrec's deformity inevitably affected his outlook. An alternative view, however, recognizes that Honoré Daumier, Édouard Manet, Degas, and others had already established the lowlife as a subject of art. Thus, though Toulouse-Lautrec often joked about his appearance, was sensitive to others' comments, and felt less exceptional in the rough society which he portrayed, he was not morbidly alone in drawing on that society for his work. Rather, he was accepted in that company for his coarse wit and generosity as a congenial, nonthreatening presence.

Toulouse-Lautrec's drawings of lesbians in 1897 raised the forbidden to the level of art by their compassionate detachment. He was drinking heavily and reached a nadir early in 1899. On March 17, an alcoholic and suffering from venereal disease, he entered St. James Clinic at Neuilly-sur-Seine, on the outskirts of Paris, where he remained until May 20. While in the clinic, he nevertheless contributed twenty-two animal prints to the *Histoires Naturelles* of his friend Jules Renard and did a series of circus scenes from memory. After his release he recuperated by the sea, traveled, and painted *The Englishwoman at the "Star," Le Havre* in 1899. There then followed (1899-1901) a series of lithographs on the world of the racetracks, of which the best known is *The Jockey*, in color. He painted *La Modiste* in 1900.

After seven months with his mother at Malromé in 1900, he returned to Paris in 1901. His last painting is the unfinished *Examination Board*, in which the figures are not outlined but solidly modeled. The examinee is his cousin Tapié de Céleyran. His last months were spent at Malromé, where he died in September, 1901.

Summary

Henri de Toulouse-Lautrec was a post-Impressionist who, in altering what he saw in order to increase its impact on the observer, presaged the more subjective twentieth century German expressionism. His influence can be seen in the work of Edvard Munch, Pablo Picasso, and Henri Matisse. Amid the emergence of new movements in art such as pointillism, symbolism, and primitivism, he ascribed to no school. His most original achievements were in color lithography and poster art. Toulouse-Lautrec preeminently lived the French writers' slogan, that an artist must be of his time.

Bibliography

Canaday, John. *Mainstreams of Modern Art*. 2d ed. New York: Holt, Rinehart and Winston, 1981. Chapter 22 contains a brilliant appreciation of Toulouse-Lautrec, placing him in the larger context of *fin de siècle* art.
Cooper, Douglas. *Henri de Toulouse-Lautrec*. N. Y.: Harry N. Abrams,

1952. A short biography. Includes twenty-six illustrations, ten in color; available in most museum shops.

Fermigier, André. *Toulouse-Lautrec*. Translated by Paul Stevenson. N. Y.: Frederick A. Praeger, 1969. The best and most accessible biography; includes more than two hundred illustrations.

Toulouse-Lautrec, Henri de. *The Posters of Toulouse-Lautrec*. Edited with an introduction by Edouard Julien. Boston: Boston Book and Art Shop, 1966. A short text, but fine color copies of all thirty-one posters.

——————————. *Toulouse-Lautrec*. Text by John Nash. New York: Funk & Wagnalls, 1978. A volume in the Great Artists series, this concise biography rebuts the theory that Toulouse-Lautrec's deformity embittered his life and influenced his choice of subjects. Sixteen color illustrations with excellent commentaries.

——————————. *Toulouse-Lautrec: His Complete Lithographs and Dry Points*. Edited by Jean Adhémar. New York: Harry N. Abrams, 1965. A thorough biography emphasizing his lithography and posters. Complete in its reproduction of 350 lithographs.

Daniel C. Scavone

TOUSSAINT-LOUVERTURE

Born: May 20, 1743; near Cap Français, Saint-Domingue
Died: April 7, 1803; Fort-de-Joux, France
Areas of Achievement: Government, politics, and the military
Contribution: Toussaint-Louverture seized leadership of a chaotic revolution and transformed it into a successful struggle that ended slavery in Saint-Domingue, politically united the island of Hispaniola (modern Haiti and the Dominican Republic), and brought France's richest colony one step away from independence.

Early Life

Born in slavery to African parents, François Dominique Toussaint Bréda was reared in unique circumstances. His father, who claimed to be a prince, taught him the Arada language and lore, including herbalism. A solicitous godfather arranged for Toussaint to work in the refectory of a Catholic hospital, and the priests there provided instructions in religion and French. By the time Toussaint had to work full time on the plantation, he wrote French with difficulty, but he read easily and widely. Throughout his life, he retained a deep attachment to the Catholic church and an admiration for French culture.

The plantation overseer, Bayon de Libertad, made good use of Toussaint's broad education. Because of the boy's healing skills, de Libertad placed Toussaint in charge of the Bréda livestock. Toussaint developed special skills with horses and so mastered the equestrian arts that he was called the "centaur of the savannas." De Libertad later promoted Toussaint to coachman and plantation steward. Toussaint made Bréda one of the best administered, most productive plantations in northern Saint-Domingue, and "wise as Toussaint" was a regional expression among all races.

In 1777, at age thirty-four, Toussaint was given *liberté de savane*—virtual but not legal freedom. He continued to run Bréda and began a family. He married Suzanne Simone Baptiste, adopted her child by a mulatto lover, and fathered two sons himself. By 1789, when Toussaint was forty-six, he led perhaps as idyllic a life possible to one of African parentage in Saint-Domingue. He wielded authority on a plantation, enjoyed the respect of whites and slaves, headed a stable family, had a savings of 650,000 francs, and owned a sizable library.

Life's Work

On Toussaint's shelves were books by the French philosophes, including the study of the Indies by Abbot Guillaume Raynal. Raynal condemned slavery and predicted that in Saint-Domingue a black hero would arise and lead his fellow slaves out of bondage. Raynal's antislavery writings found a voice in the revolutionary National Assembly that convened in Paris in 1789. Not numerous enough to end slavery, the abolitionists focused their efforts on securing equality for mulattoes. Offspring of planters and their slaves, mulattoes typically were educated then, at age twenty-four, given freedom, property, and slaves. The forty thousand mulattoes equaled the whites in population, owned more than one fourth of the colony's half million slaves, but were saddled with racially discriminatory laws.

When the National Assembly left the decision to the colonial legislature, the mulattoes were bitterly disappointed. Vincent Ogé, leader of the mulatto delegation in Paris, returned to Cap Français and organized a rebellion in October, 1790. Authorities quickly smashed the insurrection, but Ogé's execution did not bring peace to the troubled colony. Already, small but serious disturbances between whites and mulattoes had flared in 1789 and 1790, but in August, 1791, a massive slave rebellion erupted.

A voodoo priest called upon all blacks to avenge themselves against the whites, and in the night of August 22, thousands of slaves responded to a drumbeat signal and began burning plantations and murdering whites and mulattoes in the northern plains. As refugees and pursuing *congos*, as the rebels were called, converged on Cap Français, Toussaint escorted de Libertad and his family to safety before leading 150 blacks to rebel headquarters.

Toussaint was immediately made one of the chieftain's field secretaries and given the title Physician in Chief of the Armies of the King of France. Blacks from Africa came from societies governed by kings believed to be semidivine, and in Saint-Domingue many slaves believed—much as French peasants believed—that if Louis XVI knew of their sufferings he would intercede. Toussaint constantly added recruits to his own band of followers, and by mid-1792 he commanded nearly one thousand rebels.

In June, 1792, the fighting intensified. Republican commissioners arrived to negotiate an end to the bloodshed, but whites and mulattoes rejected the blacks' petitions for improved conditions for slaves. Toussaint, one of the rebuffed negotiators, then concentrated on disciplining his *congos* and forcing the French to change the slave system.

Colonial defense was the responsibility of General Étienne Maynard Laveaux, who remarked in frustration that no matter how he positioned his forces Toussaint always found an *ouverture*, or opening. When spies reported this comment to Toussaint, he changed his signature by replacing "Bréda" with "Louverture," sometimes "L'Ouverture."

The byname Louverture trumpeted his skill as a tactical commander and, coincidentally, suited his gap-toothed smile. Until then he had been known as a *frâtras baton* ("weedy stick" or, even more apt for the guerrilla leader, "thrashing stick"). Sickly as a child, he was always thin. He was only five feet, two inches tall, but he had a dignified, even imperious, demeanor that gave him an air of command. Taciturn even among his intimates, Toussaint sought advice from priests, politicians, planters, and soldiers, but he rarely commented on their suggestions, and few could discern his emotions or thoughts by his expression.

In September, 1792, a reinforced Laveaux launched a counteroffensive that gained momentum until February, 1793. News that Louis XVI had been executed complicated the rebellion. Royalist soldiers and rebels, including Toussaint, offered their services to Bourbon Spain. Royalist planters appealed to Great Britain for protection from the *congos* and for the preservation of slavery.

In 1793, Saint-Domingue turned into a kaleidoscope of horror. Spanish armies, including that of Toussaint, invaded from the northeastern corner; a British expeditionary force seized important ports in the west and moved inland. Meanwhile, dozens of black leaders led slave insurrections, and mulatto generals fought to retain slavery and to achieve equality with whites. Fearing that the colony would be overwhelmed by the Spaniards and British, Acting Governor Léger-Félicité Sonthonax abolished slavery by decree on August 29, 1793. Thousands of blacks rallied to the French tricolor and halted the Spanish offensive; at the same time, tropical diseases crippled the British. When news of France's confirmation of the abolition decree reached the island, Toussaint left the Spaniards. Furious with Spanish officers, including fellow blacks, for reenslaving prisoners, Toussaint announced his *volte face* by massacring the Spanish population of La Marmelade.

Welcomed by Laveaux, Toussaint was promoted very shortly to brigadier general. For the remainder of 1794, Toussaint drove the Spaniards out of Saint-Domingue in a series of brilliant campaigns. While pressing the British, Toussaint learned that a mulatto coup had imprisoned Laveaux, who now was acting governor. Toussaint's forces quickly crossed the island and rescued Laveaux, who gratefully appointed Toussaint lieutenant governor and proclaimed him to be the black Spartacus foreseen by Abbot Raynal.

With the establishment of the Directory, Toussaint maneuvered to have Laveaux and Sonthonax—who had returned as governor—elected to the legislature and returned to France by August, 1797. Now fifty-four, Toussaint was Acting Governor and Commander in Chief of Saint-Domingue. Virtually independent, Toussaint negotiated the evacuation of British forces and trade agreements with Great Britain and another French foe, the United States. Defying instructions from Napoleon I, Toussaint crushed the last mulatto insurgent, André Rigaud, and invaded Spanish Santo Domingo. On January 29, 1801, Toussaint abolished slavery in the former Spanish colony and promised to work for the prosperity of all the island's inhabitants.

With Hispaniola united, Toussaint tried to protect the successful slave rebellion by restoring Saint-Domingue to prosperity. He devised a constitution that kept Saint-Domingue a French colony but minimized the extent of French authority. Recognizing that he was surrounded by colonies that depended upon slave labor, Toussaint seemed to be trying to keep a powerful patron while demonstrating that laborers need not be slaves to be productive. His labor code required all inhabitants to settle permanently and work; planters were to pay wages and share profits with workers. He outlawed voodoo, built roads, supported a fully integrated school system, and reestablished the Catholic church. Formerly known as the "Pearl of the Antilles," Saint-Domingue once accounted for 40 percent of France's foreign trade and supplied almost half of the world's coffee and more than half of the world's sugar. By 1800, production levels had recovered to almost half of the 1789 yields.

Napoleon was not impressed with Toussaint's military or governmental skills. Referring contemptuously to Toussaint as a "gilded African," Napoleon sent his brother-in-law General Charles-Victor-Emmanuel Leclerc and twenty-one thousand soldiers to Hispaniola to restore slavery and keep the island in France's colonial orbit. Masking the expedition's true purpose, Leclerc professed that Napoleon merely wished to honor Toussaint and his army.

The fleet began debouching its troops on February 2, 1802, only five months after Toussaint had discovered a plot among his generals, who charged him with restoring slavery. Suppressing the revolt resulted in more than two thousand deaths. Leclerc profited from lingering resentments, for, as Toussaint prepared to repel the French, his generals began to offer their armies to Leclerc. Toussaint inflicted heavy casualties on the French, but the reduction of his own forces compelled him to surrender on May 1, 1802. Leclerc permitted Toussaint to retire to one of his four plantations for a few weeks, then had him arrested on June 7, 1802. Toussaint was immediately whisked aboard the ship *Héros* and exiled to France. Napoleon refused to grant Toussaint a hearing and had him imprisoned in Fort-de-Joux, where he died of exposure and malnutrition on April 7, 1803.

Summary

Toussaint-Louverture's influence did not end with his death. Enraged at the treatment of Toussaint and aware of the real purpose of the expedition, blacks rose spontaneously against Leclerc and France. Despite twelve thousand reinforcements, the French could not withstand the combined attacks of guerrilla bands and tropical diseases. Black generals proclaimed Saint-Domingue independent of France and gave the former colony the Indian name Haiti. On November 30, 1803, seven months after Toussaint's death, eight thousand French soldiers departed Cap Français, leaving behind forty thousand comrades in graves and a new republic, the second to arise in the Americas.

Toussaint was posthumously hailed as the liberator of Haiti, but he otherwise has had a controversial legacy. To many, he provided proof of the capacity of blacks for education and self-government. These admirers emphasized Toussaint's repeated acts of humanitarianism, particularly his willingness to unify all races. Detractors emphasize Toussaint's shifting loyalties and occasional acts of brutality as evidence of deep cynicism and personal ambition.

Bibliography

Alexis, Stephen. *Black Liberator: The Life of Toussaint Louverture.* Translated by William Stirling. New York: Macmillan, 1949. Portrays Toussaint as a mystic who was driven by visions into megalomania.

Geggus, David Patrick. *Slavery, War, and Revolution: The British Occupation of Saint-Domingue, 1793-1798.* New York: Oxford University Press, 1982. Applauds Toussaint's humanitarianism and regards his military genius as the principal reason for the expedition's failure.

Heinl, Robert D., Jr., and Nancy G. Heinl. *Written in Blood: The Story of the Haitian People, 1492-1971.* Boston: Houghton Mifflin, 1978. Devotes one hundred pages to the Haitian revolution in lively, detailed, and nonjudgmental fashion. Excellent summary of an excruciatingly complex period.

James, C. L. R. *The Black Jacobins: Toussaint Louverture and the San Domingo Revolution.* New York: Dial Press, 1938. Rev. ed. New York: Vintage Books, 1963. The classic English biography, James believes that Toussaint failed because he had no political philosophy—such as socialism—to consolidate his victories and because he was so reserved that people misunderstood and mistrusted him.

Korngold, Ralph. *Citizen Toussaint.* Boston: Little, Brown, 1944. Differing from others in several factual details, Korngold highlights Toussaint's failures and successes and concludes that he was one of the most remarkable men of his period.

Ott, Thomas O. *The Haitian Revolution, 1789-1804.* Knoxville: University of Tennessee Press, 1973. A remarkable job of chronologically sorting out a confusing period, Ott's work identifies Toussaint as the most able and admirable individual connected with the revolution.

Paul E. Kuhl

TOYOTOMI HIDEYOSHI

Born: February 6, 1537; Nakamura, Owari Province, Japan
Died: August 18, 1598; Fushimi, Yamashiro Prefecture, Japan
Areas of Achievement: Government, politics, and the military
Contribution: Hideyoshi was one of the pivotal figures in the unification of
Japan out of a welter of competing feudal domains at the end of the
sixteenth century. As an astute general and canny power broker and law-
giver, Hideyoshi was to go a long way toward establishing the political
foundations that brought Japan from the middle ages into its early modern
period.

Early Life
Toyotomi Hideyoshi was born on February 6, 1537, at Nakamura, Owari
Province, near what is the modern city of Nagoya. His father was a retired
foot soldier in the service of Oda Nobuhide, the father of Oda Nobunaga,
who was to be Hideyoshi's overlord during the early phases of his military
career. Legends surrounding Hideyoshi's birth recount that his mother
dreamed that a ray of sunshine entered her womb and he was thus conceived.
Hideyoshi perhaps himself perpetrated this fable to embellish his otherwise
humble beginnings. The only picture extant of Hideyoshi shows a deeply
lined, narrow, ascetic face with cold haughty eyes and a sour mouth set atop
a squat body. Singularly ugly, he was later jokingly referred to by Nobunaga
as a "bald rat" or a "monkey."

Hideyoshi came of age in the latter part of Japan's Warring States period,
during which local lords jockeyed constantly for advantage with growing
armies of samurai and musket-wielding foot soldiers. The Ashikaga family
of shoguns maintained only nominal sovereignty over this patchwork of local
power centers, able to exert influence only through shifting military alliances. It is small wonder, therefore, that Hideyoshi chose a military career.
A family tradition, it was also virtually the only means of advancement for
those of humble birth.

In 1558, Hideyoshi, having already served in the army of another lord,
presented himself to Nobunaga, a fast-rising star who was master of Hideyoshi's home area. Nobunaga quickly took a liking to Hideyoshi, whose
military talents began to bloom as Nobunaga began the campaigns that were
to conquer the heartland of Japan around the ancient imperial capital of
Kyoto. Through military conquest, Nobunaga was to set in motion the process of pacification of contending power blocs which is known in Japanese
history as the unification. Fundamentally more ruthless than Hideyoshi in his
approach to military matters, Nobunaga moved to defeat feudal coalitions in
central Japan and also besieged and laid waste to armed Buddhist monasteries with a cruelty reminiscent of Genghis Khan.

As Hideyoshi demonstrated his military talents, his position in Nobunaga's command structure rose. It was Hideyoshi who, in 1566-1567, secured a victory over Tatsuoki Saito at Inabayama by constructing at night a fortress facing the enemy. Hideyoshi was rewarded with lands seized from Nobunaga's enemies. In these lands, Hideyoshi exercised an enlightened administrative policy of easing taxation in order to encourage economic development.

In 1575, Nobunaga, with Hideyoshi leading one of two wings of his army, pushed westward to challenge the formidable Mōri clan. Hideyoshi here made siege craft his specialty by taking the massive and strategic Himeji Castle and two other fortresses by imaginative engineering (including flooding) and by clever psychological warfare. In 1582, Nobunaga was treacherously assassinated. Hideyoshi hastily made peace with the Mōri clan, then returned to confront and defeat Nobunaga's murderer. At the council of vassals, Hideyoshi successfully presented himself as Nobunaga's avenger and overrode opposition to sponsor the infant grandson of Nobunaga as heir. He thus became, at age forty-five, the master of five provinces and primary councillor at the head of the mightiest military coalition yet seen in Japan.

Life's Work

Hideyoshi had now inherited the mission of completing unification, and he embarked upon a carrot-and-stick strategy of combining massive attacks on those who actively opposed him with generous land rewards to win over potential rivals as well as keep faithful supporters. In 1582, he defeated the Shibata family, who had opposed him within the coalition, then used Shibata lands to reward his supporters. By 1584, he came to an uneasy settlement with Tokugawa Ieyasu (who was later to complete the unification after Hideyoshi's death). In 1587, he undertook a difficult campaign to subdue the southern island of Kyushu. The defeated were treated generously, but loyal supporters were placed strategically in the center, and his erstwhile opponents, the Mōri, were given generous tracts in the north. At the conclusion of the Kyushu campaign, he issued his famous eleven-point edict against Christianity, denouncing it as subversive and calling for expulsion of Jesuit missionaries. Although the edict was not enforced for some years, it was clear that Hideyoshi was interested in European contact only for trade. It is possible that he used this as a gesture in support of his hegemony, since he issued the ban on behalf of the entire nation.

Military force was not the only implement used by Hideyoshi in his creation of a national hegemony. Any combination of forces could always undo any purely military arrangement. Therefore, he started to build political power out of his military position. First, he amplified his status as military hegemon through oaths of allegiance and the requiring of hostages from nominal subordinates. In 1585, he secured an appointment from the figurehead emperor to the office of imperial regent as a means of bolstering his legitimacy as a national leader. Realizing that the most solid basis for national power was the capacity to control the right to land proprietorships, Hideyoshi undertook a systematic program of redistributing landholdings aimed at reducing the powers of some lords, placing trustworthy ones in strategic locations, and appeasing potential rivals. It was mainly the smaller lords who were moved around, but gradually the idea solidified that the lords held their land in trust and not absolutely. Acceptance of this growth of central power might have been difficult except that it was recognized that Hideyoshi was merely doing at a national level what the lords had to do locally to hold their territory. They were willing to give up some autonomy to safeguard their domains under Hideyoshi's seal of approval. Never again after 1590 could individual lords acquire land rights not permitted by a national hegemon.

Between 1587 and 1590, Hideyoshi instituted administrative measures that were to be his most far-reaching legacies. He ordered the land survey begun by Nobunaga to be extended and improved. Uniform units of measurement were used. For the first time, Japan's leadership, both local and national, had an accurate plot-by-plot estimate of the productive capacity. This allowed a tax base to be determined, and it revolutionized the tax structure by allowing the lords greater access to the taxable product and standardized accounting. Once Hideyoshi determined the feudal lord's status in relation to productive capacity, he could more easily shift the lords around, since they were tied more to status than to a particular geographic place. In 1588, he ordered a mass confiscation of all weapons from peasants. That had the double aim of reducing the likelihood of armed rebellion and of separating the warrior classes from all unarmed commoners. In 1590, an accurate population census froze the social classes into samurai, farmers, artisans, and merchants and bound peasants to their land. Samurai were gradually pulled into castle garrisons and, rather than collecting their own taxes, were paid by fixed stipends.

In 1590-1591, Hideyoshi crushed his final remaining challengers in the east of Japan. Now that he was the undisputed master of Japan, he considered the conquest of Korea and China. The first Korean expedition in 1592 ended in a draw after the Japanese encountered determined resistance from the Koreans. The second, in 1597, ended with Hideyoshi's death. Surrounded by magnificent gardens and artworks, pleading for loyalty to his heir from his coalition vassals, he died on August 18, 1598.

Summary

Toyotomi Hideyoshi's military unification of Japan represents only one facet of a diverse life. In his own time, his primary impact seemed to be that he, more than any other individual, acted the role of central figure. He restored the imperial dignity, rebuilt the capital and other cities, enforced peaceful symbols upon the popular mind by parades, theatricals, and tea ceremonies for thousands of commoners. He encouraged new building and patronized new, flamboyant, and colorful artistic fashions. Ostentation became a tool of statecraft. Even the megalomania of the Korean expeditions seemed to bring personal destiny together with national destiny.

Hideyoshi's last appeals for loyalty to his five-year-old son failed. His plans for succession were aborted by the wily Ieyasu, who asserted his supremacy in one final battle, took the title of shogun, and went on to complete Japan's unification by taming feudalism into a stable, peaceful system for the next 250 years. He did so by making full use of the existing legal and administrative structure of census roles, frozen class structure, surveys, and tax procedures and by shifting lords around, assuring loyalty through hostages, closing off Japan from the outside, and the like. That Ieyasu built upon the existing legal, political, and social foundations is proof of Hideyoshi's enduring legacy.

Bibliography

Berry, Mary Elizabeth. *Hideyoshi*. Cambridge, Mass.: Harvard University Press, 1982. Clearly the primary biographical source in English on Hideyoshi's life and a thoroughly modern treatment. Save for artistic matters, Berry is comprehensive in her coverage. Gives a complete background and then exhaustively analyzes developments in economics, military affairs, and administrative and political arrangements. Based almost entirely on Japanese sources but, surprisingly, lacks a bibliography.

Dening, Walter. *The Life of Toyotomi Hideyoshi*. 3d ed. Kobe, Japan: J. L. Thompson, 1930. The first edition of this biography was published in 1888 and not much was added in later editions. A classic Victorian biography, rich with anecdotes and extensive detail about Hideyoshi the man. Contains extensive quotes of conversations without footnote citation; while it is true that Hideyoshi left much correspondence, it is probable that most is the product of the imagination of an author overanxious to paint a vivid personal picture. There is not much analysis on Hideyoshi nor much about the period as a whole.

Elison, George. "Hideyoshi, the Bountiful Master." In *Warlords, Artists, and Commoners: Japan in the Sixteenth Century*, edited by George Elison and Bardwell Smith. Honolulu: University of Hawaii Press, 1981. This essay sheds some light on Hideyoshi's genealogy by focusing on his search for legitimacy as a leader. Elison draws a theoretical comparison between Hideyoshi as a charismatic leader—drawing legitimacy from his accomplishments and through invented mythology about a supernatural birth and miraculous deeds—and Hideyoshi as one who sought traditional legitimacy by inventing a conventional pedigree and taking on court titles.

Hall, John W. *Government and Local Power in Japan, 500 to 1700: A Study Based on Bizen Province.* Princeton, N.J.: Princeton University Press, 1966. Hall offers many general historical comments and insights. His powers of summary are acute, so the book is valuable as an overview. His treatment of Hideyoshi in chapters 9, 10, and 11 shows the impact of some of the central decisions on this one region in western Honshu.

Hall, John W., Nagahara Keiji, and Kozo Yamamura, eds. *Japan Before Tokugawa: Political Consolidation and Economic Growth, 1500-1650.* Princeton, N.J.: Princeton University Press, 1981. This collection is the product of a binational conference on the Warring States and gives an overview of the whole period, focusing on historiographical questions. Hall's chapter on Hideyoshi's domestic policies attempts to draw out his contribution to the political scene as Japan moved out of its middle ages into its early modern condition. Hall summarizes specific measures devised by Hideyoshi, most of which were to survive as the basis for government for the next 250 years.

Murdoch, James. *A History of Japan During the Century of Early Foreign Intercourse, 1542-1651.* Vol. 2. Maps by Isoh Yamagata. Kobe, Japan: Kobe Chronicle, 1903. The second of a massive three-volume history. Murdoch, a Scot who spent many years teaching in Japan, is rather stilted in his prose, idiosyncratic in his approach, and often opinionated. Still, this work is occasionally extremely valuable. Modern works seldom offer such lavish detail. Hideyoshi is covered in chapters 8, 9, 12, and 13. Murdoch, who is ordinarily disdainful of feudalism as such, is more positive in his treatment of Hideyoshi. Although he ignores economic considerations, he offers a fuller picture of the range of administrative problems addressed by Hideyoshi.

Sansom, George B. *A History of Japan, 1334-1615.* Stanford, Calif.: Stanford University Press, 1961. This is the second volume in a three-volume history of Japan which is arguably the most complete general history of premodern Japan available in English. This well-illustrated and readable work, based entirely on Japanese sources, is indispensable as a reference work. Hideyoshi's life and career are covered in chapters 19 through 24, including a chapter on the artistic scene. Although less adequate for economic matters than more modern works, Sansom's history as a whole comes close to striking the perfect balance between lively prose and a wealth of detail. His bibliography is annotated, his appendices pertinent, his index meticulous. This is a full-service history to which all students of pre-1867 Japan should come first.

Toyotomi, Hideyoshi. *101 Letters of Hideyoshi: The Private Correspondence of Toyotomi Hideyoshi.* Edited and translated by Adriana Boscaro. Tokyo: Sophia University Press, 1975. Boscaro gives an extensive introduction and then intersperses the graceful translations with editorial comment and explanation of the letters. She explains some of the problems of dealing with this kind of documentation. Contains appendices, a catalog of letters with a photoreproduction of a sample letter, and notes on people and places.

David G. Egler

MAARTEN TROMP and CORNELIS TROMP

Maarten Tromp

Born: April 23, 1598; Brielle, South Holland
Died: August 10, 1653; at sea, near Scheveningen, Holland

Cornelis Tromp

Born: September 9, 1629; Rotterdam, Holland
Died: May 29, 1691; Amsterdam, Holland
Area of Achievement: The military
Contribution: While the Tromps and other Dutch heroes such as Michiel Adriaanszoon de Ruyter were in command, the Netherlands came close to being the chief naval power in Europe. The competition between the elder Tromp and the English commanders resulted in a revolution in naval tactics.

Early Lives

Though both Tromps, father and son, had distinguished careers and rose to the position of lieutenant-admiral, their lives show some interesting contrasts. The early life of Maarten Tromp contained enough experience to last an ordinary mortal a lifetime. He first went to sea in a warship commanded by his father and took part in the Battle of Gibraltar (April 25, 1607), when Jacob van Heemskerck crushed a superior Spanish fleet under the guns of their own fortress. Several years later, he accompanied his father on a merchant voyage. The ship was attacked by an English pirate, Maarten's father was slain, and Maarten himself was compelled to endure a life of "the utmost abandonment and cruelty" as cabin boy to his father's slayer. Released or escaped, he made other voyages and was captured by the Barbary pirates; he was released either on the payment of a heavy ransom or by impressing the Bey of Tunis with his skill in gunnery and navigation. In 1627, he entered the Dutch navy. For some years, he was occupied either in reforming the Dutch marine establishment or in fighting the privateers of Dunkerque, then under Spanish rule and a menace to Dutch commerce. Maarten was, then, a "tarpaulin" officer, one who had lived his life at sea and made his way up through the ranks, in contrast to the English commanders, who were likely to be either gentlemen volunteers or converted army officers. Throughout life, he lived plainly, contenting himself with a pickled herring for breakfast.

Cornelis Tromp, Maarten's second son, was far less austere in his habits; in later life, he married into a family with money and was able to afford a country estate, De Trompenburgh. His portrait shows a handsome man, but one inclined to stoutness, while his father's portrait shows the elder Tromp as lean and sharp featured. Cornelis went to sea early, however, and at the age of nineteen commanded a squadron against the Barbary pirates.

Life's Work

Maarten's first and possibly greatest deed as lieutenant-admiral of the Dutch fleet was to counter a Spanish invasion. In September of 1639, he fought a series of engagements near the Straits of Dover in which the Spanish fleet was all but destroyed. The victory caused immense rejoicing in the Netherlands; the battle had been fought, however, on seas over which England claimed jurisdiction and against the express order of Charles I, King of England. There were other potential sources of friction with England: the herring fisheries; the navigation acts, limiting the right of Dutch ships to trade in English ports; England's claim to have her ships saluted in the "Narrow Seas"; and, after the outbreak of civil war in England, apparent Dutch sympathy with the Royalists (Maarten himself had escorted Queen Henrietta of England when she returned from the Continent with supplies for Charles). Still, there was no open breach until 1652. On May 29, English Admiral Robert Blake was in the Channel with an English fleet and Maarten was there with a Dutch one; somehow—the guilt was never established— the accumulated irritations erupted into a full-scale naval battle, at the end of which Maarten retired with the loss of two small ships. Though there was as yet no formal declaration of war, it was obvious that the English would strike at Dutch commerce, and Maarten had the job of protecting it (July and August). In the North Sea, he encountered terrible storms, which scattered his fleet; he was unable to save the herring fishermen but did see some Indiamen safely to port with their valuable cargoes. Though most of his scattered fleet eventually made port, Maarten was disgraced and forced to resign. Another officer, Witte de With, was appointed to the vacant command but was so unpopular with the fleet that he too was dismissed.

Maarten was now reinstated, and again his task was to protect commerce and specifically to see a convoy of three hundred outbound merchant ships through the Channel (December). This he performed with ease. Blake, with a much smaller fleet than that of Maarten, attacked but was beaten off with the loss of five ships. Legend has it that Maarten sailed up the Channel with a broom at his masthead as proof that he could sweep the seas.

The next action (February, 1653) was again a convoying operation, this time inbound. Maarten was bringing some 150 merchantmen up the Channel when Blake attacked with a force nearly equal to that of Maarten. The fight lasted three days, with heavy losses on both sides. In the end, Maarten brought most of the convoy and his warships to port. He did not do so well in the Battle of the Gabbard Shoal in June. The reorganized English fleet had much the advantage, and Maarten, with his lighter ships, had to take refuge among the sandbanks of his own coast.

The English now set up a blockade, with devastating effects on the Dutch economy. Maarten was ordered to break the blockade. By a masterful maneuver, he brought the scattered Dutch fleet together, and, on August 10, he confronted the English fleet, now commanded by General George Monck, who would later engineer the restoration of Charles II of England and become the first Duke of Albemarle. The battle began at seven in the morning, and by eleven Maarten was dead, struck down by a musket ball. After his death, many of the Dutch captains deserted, and the battle ended in disaster. The Dutch had to make their peace with Oliver Cromwell. Maarten was buried at Delft, where a lavish monument recalls his services.

Meanwhile, Cornelis Tromp was serving in the Mediterranean, rising to the rank of rear admiral (1653). It was in the second Anglo-Dutch War that he came into prominence, though in a rather controversial way. On June 13, 1665, an English fleet commanded by the Duke of York (later James II) encountered a Dutch fleet led by Jacob van Wassenaer, Lord of Obdam. Obdam was killed early in the action; Cornelis attempted to assume command, but another admiral had a better claim, and in the confusion the Dutch fleet was routed. In 1666, Cornelis had to serve under de Ruyter, a brilliant leader of whom he was intensely jealous. In the action of July 25, when the Dutch were again at a disadvantage, Cornelis disgraced himself by breaking the line of battle in order to fight an independent action against the English rear and lost his command.

In the complications of Dutch politics, Cornelis was wise enough, or lucky enough, to support the stadtholder William, Prince of Orange (later King William III of England), who reinstated him in the navy. He took part in the third Anglo-Dutch War, in which the Netherlands was forced to fight France as well as England and to neglect its fleet in favor of the army. Nevertheless, de Ruyter, with a depleted fleet and forced on the defensive, more than held his own. In August, 1673, there was a general action in which Cornelis again found himself fighting a detached action against the English rear. Apparently there was no disobedience of de Ruyter's orders, for he remained in favor; the battle, moreover, had a part in the decision of Charles II to make peace (1674). The naval war was nearly over, though the land war continued until 1678. Cornelis was sent with a squadron to help the Danes against the Swedes and won a great victory (1676). In the same year, Cornelis attained his father's rank of lieutenant-admiral. He died on May 29, 1691, and was buried at Delft.

Summary

During Maarten Tromp's and Cornelis Tromp's lifetimes and those of other Dutch heroes such as de Ruyter, the Netherlands came close to being the chief naval power in Europe. The Dutch completely defeated Spain and Portugal; they built warships for France; and they fought the English as equals and were sometimes the victors. Their naval operations extended from Denmark to Sicily. This was a brief glory, for later in the century they were forced to divert their resources to defend themselves on land against the French and had to accept an unequal alliance with England.

Some historians would see the Anglo-Dutch Wars as chiefly important for producing a revolution in naval tactics and discipline. Prior to these wars, fleets had gone into battle in no particular order and had fought in a confused mass; the commander could exercise little control once the fighting started. Individual captains could do almost as they pleased, even to the point of deserting the fight. The new tactics, which remained standard for more than one hundred years, required the ships to go into action in a line so that all the guns could be brought to bear; a system of signals was devised, so that the commander could exercise some control. This system was first put into effect by Blake, Monck, and Richard Deane, all of whom were former officers in Cromwell's army; Blake was also responsible for the fearsome Articles of War, which defined the duties of seamen and, even more important, those of their officers. Maarten's relationship to these reforms is uncertain. He is said to have been responsible for the idea of dividing a large fleet into squadrons, and he is supposed to have invented the line earlier but to have been unable to put it into practice; he did respond to the English line by putting his ships into a parallel formation. The Dutch indiscipline continued, however, and Maarten's own son was not innocent in this respect.

Bibliography

Boxer, C. R. *The Dutch Seaborne Empire, 1600-1800*. New York: Alfred A. Knopf, 1965. This book is chiefly useful for what it relates about the political atmosphere in the Tromps' time and the social condition of seafaring folk. Contains a chronology and a bibliography.

Geyl, Pieter. *History of the Low Countries: Episodes and Problems*. London: Macmillan, 1964. A series of lectures rather than a connected narrative. Useful for what it relates of the tangled diplomatic relations with England and the Tromps' part in them.

Haley, K. H. *The Dutch in the Seventeenth Century*. New York: Harcourt Brace Jovanovich, 1972. Chiefly useful for an account of the social and cultural life of the period during which the Tromps lived. Among the numerous illustrations are an eyewitness sketch of one of Maarten's victories and a photograph of his monument. Contains a bibliography and a chronology.

Howarth, David. *The Men-of-War*. Alexandria, Va.: Time-Life Books, 1978. In spite of its popular character, this well-illustrated account of the first two Anglo-Dutch Wars appears to be carefully researched; it has an extensive bibliography. Very thorough on technical matters as well as on the characters and careers of the chief commanders, including Maarten.

Landström, Björn. *The Ship: An Illustrated History.* Garden City, N.Y.: Doubleday, 1961. Another well-illustrated work. Useful for its comments on Dutch and English ship types of the period.

Mahan, Alfred Thayer. *The Influence of Sea Power upon History, 1660-1783.* New York: Sagamore Press, 1957. In order to develop his thesis concerning the influence of sea power, Mahan analyzes at some length the second and third Dutch Wars. Contains some material on Cornelis.

Mets, J. A. *Naval Heroes of Holland.* New York: Abbey Press, 1902. Flamboyant, ultrapatriotic, and containing much that one suspects is fiction, this book is nevertheless useful as a counterbalance to other sources available in English, which generally have an English point of view.

John C. Sherwood

TSENG KUO-FAN

Born: November 26, 1811; Hsiang-hsiang, Hunan, China
Died: March 12, 1872; Nanking, China
Areas of Achievement: Politics and the military
Contribution: Tseng directed the Ch'ing Dynasty's extraordinary suppression
of the Taiping Rebellion. His strategy used locally recruited but professional armies and required twelve years to succeed. He continued to serve
in high office and is recognized as a key figure in the Ch'ing restoration
that began in the 1860's. Renowned for his probity, Tseng recruited men
who became the dynasty's chief ministers after his death, but few approached his talents or his upright character.

Early Life

Tseng Kuo-fan came from a large landowning family striving to become
part of the scholar-official elite. In 1838, he passed the highest imperial
examination and became a member of the prestigious Hanlin Academy,
where he had considerable leisure to develop his theories of government. In
1849, he was appointed to an important post in the central civil bureaucracy.
Over the next three years, he acquired broad experience in the upper eche-
lons of government.

The teachings of T'ang Chien, a scholar-official who adhered to the orthodox school of Neo-Confucianism associated with Chu Hsi, had great influence on Tseng. T'ang advocated a combination of Neo-Confucian self-
cultivation and active service to the state. Chu Hsi had followed that pattern;
it was also to characterize Tseng's life.

Tseng was a thin, stern-looking man with a long beard, whose whole
demeanor reflected his lifelong practice of Puritan self-denial. Tseng is famous for having kept a daily diary reflecting his moral concerns and for
his regular practice of self-examination and self-improvement in the Neo-
Confucian mode.

Tseng's father and his four younger brothers all gained distinction in service against the Taipings. Following Chinese social practice, Tseng was married at age sixteen to a woman chosen by his parents. Tseng had a typically
large family, two sons and five daughters. One son became a distinguished
diplomat and his daughters married prominent men. Tseng's family life was
exemplary in terms of Neo-Confucian morality, because he avoided personal
corruption and family favoritism while still harnessing his family's talents to
the dynasty's service.

Tseng should be counted among Peking's intellectual elite before 1852.
His own ideas were eclectic and focused on questions of practical administration or statecraft. He believed that the Ch'ing Dynasty had been harmed
by too much autocratic power. His solutions stressed practical measures that

would decrease centralization while maintaining the emperor's role in the system. Thus, he was not a reformer but sought the regular practice of Neo-Confucian principles of good government by morally upright men. Tseng believed that if good officials, on the emperor's behalf, emphasized three matters—recruiting able subordinates, conducting careful financial management, and maintaining appropriate military strength—then the dynasty's future would be assured. These principles became the hallmarks of his career.

Life's Work

In 1852, Tseng returned to his home district as the tide of the Taiping Rebellion swept out of south China and across the Hunan Province in the central Yangtze valley region. Tseng Kuo-fan was in retirement to observe the proper mourning following his mother's death, but he nevertheless accepted an imperial appointment to lead local defense efforts. The Taiping siege of the Hunan provincial capital of Changsha had not succeeded, but the rebel forces, swollen to more than half a million, had taken other cities and were preparing to attack eastward into the richer economic regions along the lower Yangtze River. In April, 1853, the city of Nanking in Kiangsu Province fell to the Taipings, who ruled from there until July, 1864.

Using the somewhat vague authority of his post, Tseng raised a new-style military force, the Hunan Army. This command, which became the model for other regional armies, combined bands of mercenary fighters with local self-defense forces under the leadership of an officer corps dominated initially by local literati. Tseng insisted upon sound organization, professional fighting skills, and absolute loyalty to the Ch'ing Dynasty. He believed that the Hunan Army had transcended its origins as a local militia and often stressed the differences between it and the many unruly militia units that flourished in the 1850's and 1860's. His army numbered as many as 130,000 and contained both land and naval fighting forces, but it was not large in terms of the period. Such locally organized and led military units were anathema to the dynasty, which feared that they might turn upon the throne, but Tseng's loyal service in Peking and his reputation as a staunch orthodox Neo-Confucian won important backers at the court for his experiment.

Initially the Hunan Army operated as an adjunct to the regular Ch'ing armies. Although the Hunan Army had only limited success in the mid-1850's, it took pressure off the hard-pressed regular Ch'ing armies and became accepted as a part of the anti-Taiping forces. Command of the Ch'ing forces remained in the hands of regular generals, many of whom were Manchus or Mongols. They made their headquarters at the so-called Great Camp of Kiangnan near Nanking. In 1856, the Taiping movement underwent an internal crisis which weakened their cause for more than three years. During this time, the Ch'ing regular military could not subdue the rebellion; then, in 1859, a new prime minister revived the Taipings. A spring offensive by the Taiping armies overran the Ch'ing headquarters at the Great Camp of Kiangnan in May, 1860, killing several top Ch'ing generals and destroying their units.

This Taiping offensive of 1860 became the turning point of the war. At this juncture, the dynasty turned to Tseng, who was elevated to the position of viceroy in the lower Yangtze region and given overall command of the efforts against the Taipings. Tseng initiated a plan to capture the Yangtze river city of Anking, above Nanking, which he saw as the key to control of the whole region. He placed his brother Tseng Kuo-ch'uan in command and, after a carefully prepared siege, Anking fell in September, 1861, with a slaughter of most of the city's inhabitants.

Tseng's next move was to advance his protégés, Li Hung-chang and Tso Tsung-t'ang, to be governors of key provinces in the lower Yangtze valley. They led their own provincial armies and pressed inward from the coastal region toward Nanking, while Tseng's forces deployed eastward from Anking. By mid-1862, Tseng's combined forces had hemmed in the Taipings. Another two years of bloody fighting ensued before the Taiping emperor was killed and most of his forces were slaughtered or captured. Tseng had accomplished a great victory that revived the Ch'ing Dynasty's rule of China.

Tseng's victory marked a shift that gave increased power and importance to Han Chinese officials in the Ch'ing system. Also, Tseng's success realized some changes that he had advocated in Peking prior to 1852. The creation of provincial armies, still loyal to the dynasty, and their leadership by Han Chinese modified the autocratic, centralized rule that he had criticized. The armies themselves, partly armed with Western weapons, embodied his concern with appropriate military strength. The civil war was financed by new taxes which embodied both innovation and prudent fiscal measures. The most notable was an internal transit tax on shipments of goods known as *likin*. This tax itself produced a more decentralized financial administration, thus also lessening central control, but avoided a fiscal crisis for the dynasty. Finally, Tseng made every effort to select the best men to serve in his own headquarters. He did not initiate each of these measures, but they all fit into his approach to statecraft.

Tseng maintained his Neo-Confucian reliance on achieving good government through men of moral character, rather than upon laws or formal discipline. Yet he sometimes despaired at the corruption among his own military and civilian subordinates. He lived with their failings, but he was extremely severe toward the Taipings. On the battlefield or in defeat, soldiers and civilians alike received little mercy from Tseng or his armies.

Tseng began the task of reconstruction while still fighting. Again, his approach stressed careful plans and administration. As always, he looked to the matters of prudent defense measures, recruiting able officials, and sound fiscal management. Within months of defeating the Taipings, he began disbanding most of the Hunan Army, searched carefully for the men of highest character to fill official posts, and tried to return the tax system to a peacetime basis so that both farmers and the dynasty could prosper.

As the reconstruction was beginning, the court again called on Tseng for help against a major rebellion, the Nien. These rebels had operated from nests or lairs in Anhwei and Honan provinces since the early 1850's. Remnants of the Taiping forces joined the Nien in late 1864, and then in May, 1865, Nien cavalry killed the Ch'ing commander, the Mongol general Senggerinchin. Within days, the frightened court, which had no effective armies between themselves and the Nien, assigned Tseng to take command. Tseng's own forces were already disbanded, so he relied upon the available Ch'ing and local forces, stiffened by Li Hung-chang's Anhwei army. Tseng led the anti-Nien efforts until December, 1866, during which time he penetrated the Nien's home territory and broke up their links to the villages. Tseng's strategy then called for his armies, stationed at key points in large encampments, to attack the columns of Nien cavalry as they moved outward from their former base areas. After Li Hung-chang assumed command in 1867, he followed a variation of this strategy and defeated the Nien within a year.

In addition to his role in the suppression of the Taiping Rebellion, Tseng played a part in the so-called Self-strengthening movement, which promoted the use of Western technology. His association with this movement began in 1861, when he and his subordinates began employing foreign units, especially foreign artillery and ships, against the Taipings. These foreign-equipped and foreign-led units were mercenaries. The most famous was the "Ever Victorious Army," which was led after 1862 by Charles "Chinese" Gordon, a British Victorian adventurer and hero. The battlefield effectiveness of these foreign units was undeniable, and Tseng accepted the suggestions that the Ch'ing forces should acquire new foreign equipment. Tseng remained an advocate of such borrowing until the end of his life, but he always saw Westernization as a secondary element in making China strong. Western weapons and technology had practical uses, but for matters of principle Tseng never wavered in his Neo-Confucian orientation.

In 1867, Tseng was appointed to a top position in Peking, and in 1868 he became viceroy of the metropolitan region around Peking. There is evidence that Tseng's health was already in serious decline at this time, but he remained a hard-working administrator. In 1870, he was called upon to settle the difficult diplomatic situation arising out of the Tientsin massacre, when Catholic missionaries were murdered by mobs who believed that Catholic sisters were killing the foundling babies they took in. Tseng took a conciliatory approach to the foreign demands, which angered some belligerent officials, so his protégé Li Hung-chang again relieved him. Tseng was transferred to the viceroy's post in Nanking and died in March, 1872, shortly after arriving there.

Summary

The dynasty granted Tseng Kuo-fan the hereditary title of marquis for his extraordinary service, and this unprecedented honor for a Han Chinese official was fully deserved. Without his leadership, the Manchu rule of the Chinese Empire would have fallen to the mid-nineteenth century internal peasant rebellions.

Tseng, although never the most powerful or influential official during his lifetime, has come to symbolize the revival of Ch'ing fortunes in the mid-nineteenth century. He became a model particularly to those who wanted to find in recent history a Chinese figure who upheld the highest virtues of traditional Neo-Confucianism. Tseng's austere, frugal, serious life of self-improvement and service to the state was invoked by Chiang Kai-shek, in particular, between 1928 and 1949.

Tseng's legacy also has its detractors. His own high principles proved insufficient to wean others away from self-aggrandizement and personal enrichment while in government service. Self-strengthening began the difficult business of matching the burgeoning power of the Western industrial nations, but it stopped far short of the adaptations China needed to ensure its own territorial integrity and military strength. The T'ung-chih restoration was real, but the institutional and personal weaknesses that Tseng found rampant survived under the Kuang-hsu emperor and produced a great crisis following the dynasty's defeat in the First Sino-Japanese War. Ultimately, Tseng's approach rested on the service of upright men as loyal officials to the state. The standards of duty, sacrifice, and service that Tseng himself embodied proved, however, too lofty for even his most able followers to achieve. With their lesser stuff the dynasty's slide resumed after Tseng's death.

Bibliography

Kuhn, Philip A. "The Taiping Rebellion." In *The Cambridge History of China*, edited by John K. Fairbank, vol. 10. New York: Cambridge University Press, 1978. An excellent summary of Tseng's career and his ideas; places him in the historical context of his times. For more detailed treatment see Kuhn's *Rebellion and Its Enemies in Late Imperial China: Militarization and Social Structure, 1796-1864* (Cambridge, Mass.: Harvard University Press, 1970).

Kuo, Ting-yee, and Kwang-ching Liu. "Self-strengthening: The Pursuit of Western Technology." In *The Cambridge History of China*, edited by John K. Fairbank, vol. 10. A description of the late nineteenth century effort at modernization which explains Tseng's influence without over-emphasis on his role.

Liu, Kwang-ching. "The Ch'ing Restoration." In *The Cambridge History of China*, edited by John K. Fairbank, vol. 10. A reconsideration of the

T'ung-chih restoration and Tseng's place in it.

Shen, Han-yin Chen. "Tseng Kuo-fan in Peking, 1840-1852: His Ideas on Statecraft and Reform." *Journal of Asian Studies* 27 (November, 1967): 61-80. A discussion of Tseng before he became famous, with attention to his place in the intellectual milieu of mid-nineteenth century China.

Wright, Mary C. *The Last Stand of Chinese Conservatism: The T'ung-chih Restoration, 1862-1874*. Rev. ed. New York: Atheneum, 1966. This is the strongest presentation of the case for a mid-nineteenth century restoration inspired by Tseng's ideal.

David D. Buck

IVAN TURGENEV

Born: November 9, 1818; Orel, Russia
Died: September 3, 1883; Bougival, France
Area of Achievement: Literature
Contribution: Turgenev combined the lyrical with the realistic in fiction that
had a powerful influence on social conditions in his own time and on later
writers such as Anton Chekhov and Henry James, who truly ushered in
the modern period in literature.

Early Life

Ivan Turgenev was born November 9, 1818, in Orel, Russia, to Varvara
Petrovna, a wealthy landowner, and Sergey Turgenev, a cavalry officer. According to Turgenev's own comments, he was an enthusiastic reader at an
early age, reading not only the fiction and poetry of Russian writers but also
the English fiction of Charles Dickens.

His family moved to Moscow in 1827, and in 1833 Turgenev entered the
University of Moscow, which he attended for one year, when, upon another
family move to St. Petersburg, he entered the university there. He was
graduated in 1837 and went to Berlin, where he was enrolled at the University
of Berlin, studying philosophy for three years. Upon returning to St. Petersburg in 1841 and failing to find an academic position, he secured a minor
post with the Ministry of the Interior. While traveling in Europe in 1843, he
met Pauline Viardot, a French singer, who became his lifelong love and inspiration.

Turgenev retired from the civil service in 1845 and began to devote himself full-time to writing poetry. Because his mother disapproved of this decision as well as of his infatuation with Viardot, a married woman, she cut off
his allowance. Turgenev followed Viardot, who tolerated his infatuation, to
Europe to be near her. He returned to Russia in 1850 because of his mother's
serious illness. When she died, he was left the heir of a substantial fortune
and was thus able to follow his literary interests, which at this time he very
successfully shifted from poetry to fiction. In 1847, he had begun the writing
of the short stories which, in 1852, were to be published as one of his
greatest works, *Zapiski okhotnika* (*Russian Life in the Interior*, 1855; better
known as *A Sportsman's Sketches*, 1932).

Life's Work

When *A Sportsman's Sketches* were being published in periodical form,
they created a social uproar in Russia, for they presented the serf as more
than a mere slave and, in fact, as often more human and genuine than the
landowners themselves. Because the stories were seen as a protest against
the serf system, the authorities began to watch Turgenev closely. In 1852,

when he wrote an enthusiastic obituary notice on the death of his fellow writer Nikolai Gogol, he met further disapproval; the authorities banished him to his country estate, where he was forced to stay for a year and a half.

When he returned to St. Petersburg, after the publication of *A Sportsman's Sketches* in book form, he found himself to be the leading light of St. Petersburg literary culture. *A Sportsman's Sketches* has often been considered historically important for the influence it had on the abolition of the serf system in Russia; in fact, the book has even been compared in this regard to Harriet Beecher Stowe's *Uncle Tom's Cabin: Or, Life Among the Lowly* (1852). Yet the aesthetic and critical importance of the stories, the reason many of them continue to be read, lies in their unique blend of the lyrical and the realistic. Such stories as "Bezhin Meadow" and "The Country Doctor," two of the most familiar in the collection, create a dreamlike and sometimes surrealistic world, even as they manage to remain solidly grounded in phenomenal experience. As a short-story writer, Turgenev historically stands somewhere between the folktale fantasy of Nikolai Gogol and the nightmare reality of Franz Kafka.

For the next few years after the success of *A Sportsman's Sketches*, Turgenev, who felt inspired by travel, was forced to stay at home because of the Crimean War. Moreover, many biographers suggest that he was in a deep depression because of the impossibility of his tireless love for Viardot. As a result, he published little during this period, with the exception of his short novel *Rudin* (*Dmitri Roudine*, 1873; better known as *Rudin*, 1947), which appeared in 1856. In a drastic shift—which may have resulted partly from his freedom to travel and partly from his acceptance of the Viardot situation—within the next five years Turgenev alternated between traveling on the Continent and writing some of his most respected works, including the novels *Dvoryanskoye gnezdo* (1859; *Liza*, 1869; better known as *A House of Gentlefolk*, 1894) and *Nakanune* (1860; *On the Eve*, 1871), the novella *Pervaya lyubov* (1860; *First Love*, 1884), and the essay "Gamlet i Don Kikhot" (1860; "Hamlet and Don Quixote," 1930). He also finished his best-known novel, *Ottsy i deti* (*Fathers and Sons*, 1867), in 1861 and had it published the following year.

Fathers and Sons is built around what Turgenev perceived as an emerging type of man in Russia, a type which he named "nihilist," a term to which Turgenev's novel gave great currency at mid-century. The character Bazarov in Turgenev's novel is one who rejects religion, art, and the Russian class system and emphasizes instead scientific empiricism. Turgenev was vilified by Russian intellectuals and praised by the Russian secret police for this depiction, for the novel was misinterpreted as supporting the conservative "fathers," while casting doubt on the radical "sons." Turgenev, in a defense of his work, argued that by "nihilist" he really meant "revolutionary," and that his work was directed against the gentry as the leading class. As a result, Russian critics began to see the work as the herald of the coming revolution.

In addition to frequently coming in conflict with either the authorities or the radical dissenters, Turgenev's life was also often plagued by conflict with his literary relationships. He was friends with such great Russian writers as Ivan Goncharov and Leo Tolstoy but had bitter quarrels with both of them. Goncharov accused him of plagiarizing from an unpublished manuscript, and Tolstoy accused him of moral illness because of his liaison with Viardot. The quarrel with Tolstoy, which occurred at a dinner party and involved a disagreement about helping the poor, almost resulted in a duel and lasted for seventeen years. A few years later, he also had quarrels with Fyodor Dostoevski because of a debt Dostoevski owed Turgenev.

In 1863, when the Viardots went to live in Baden-Baden, Germany, Turgenev visited them there, where he was received as an old family friend, a role he seemed willing to play, if only for the opportunity to be near Pauline. Indeed, his desire to be near her was so great that he also moved to Baden-Baden. From all indications, his life there was happy and his health was good, in spite of the fact that his relationship with the beloved Pauline was less than he desired. Enjoying a life of hunting and social leisure, however, Turgenev did little work; *Dym* (1867; *Smoke*, 1868) is the only novel that he wrote during his eight years in the German resort.

Turgenev's life always seemed dominated by his attachment to Viardot; when she moved once again, Turgenev followed, first to London and then to Bougival, France, where Turgenev and the Viardots bought a summer home jointly in 1874. In France, Turgenev began a close relationship with several prominent writers, including Gustave Flaubert, George Sand, Émile Zola, Edmond de Goncourt, and others. Once more, Turgenev seemed preoccupied with matters that kept him from his writing. The only important works he published during this period were two novellas, one of which was *Veshniye vody* (1872; *Spring Floods*, 1874; better known as *The Torrents of Spring*, 1897).

Turgenev began working on his last, and his longest, novel, *Nov* (*Virgin Soil*, 1877), in 1876. This story of love and revolution, published in 1877, was not well received by Russian critics; conservative commentators thought it criticized Russia too much, while radical critics thought the revolutionary characters were not true-to-life. Yet the work was enthusiastically read outside Russia, being immediately translated into many different languages and receiving rave reviews from influential critics.

Turgenev fell ill in early 1882 and moved to the summer home he owned with the Viardots in Bougival in June of that year. Although he was in much pain, his illness was not properly diagnosed as spinal cancer, and Turgenev did not believe his life was in danger. On September 3, 1883, after having dictated a story critical of the Russian aristocracy, Turgenev died surrounded by his family and friends. In a funeral that amounted to national mourning, he was buried in St. Petersburg in Volkov cemetery.

Summary

Ivan Turgenev always declared himself a realist whose every line was inspired by something that he actually observed. When his works were published, their importance lay less in their artistic and aesthetic qualities than in their documentation of the social realities of Russian life. Indeed, such works as *A Sportsman's Sketches* were said to have been at least a partial cause for the abolition of the serf system, much as *Uncle Tom's Cabin* had an effect on the abolition of the system of slavery in the United States. Turgenev's later works are also remembered for their depiction of a world that was doomed to die with the Russian Revolution.

Yet when Turgenev is most studied today, it is not for his social realism, but rather for what has been termed his poetic realism. It is his stories and his novellas, in which reality is presented as often lyrical and dreamlike, rather than his novels, in which he sought to present reality concretely and socially, that have won for him a permanent place in the history of modern literature. The influence of his short-story style on those writers who ushered in the modern period, such as Anton Chekhov, Henry James, and later Sherwood Anderson and others, is his most important literary legacy.

Bibliography

Freeborn, Richard. *Turgenev: The Novelist's Novelist*. New York: Oxford University Press, 1960. A general study of Turgenev's novels, both in terms of their place in nineteenth century Russian literature and culture and in terms of Henry James's view that Turgenev was a "novelist's novelist." Freeborn primarily discusses Turgenev's four major novels: *Rudin*, *A House of Gentlefolk*, *On the Eve*, and *Fathers and Sons*.

Magarshack, David. *Turgenev: A Life*. London: Faber & Faber, 1954. A detailed but highly readable account of Turgenev's life. Along with Yarmolinsky's biography cited below, it is the most frequently referred work on Turgenev. The work attempts to account for the relationship of Turgenev's art to his life and is particularly helpful in discussing the role that Turgenev's dramas played in the development of his art.

Pritchett, V. S. *The Gentle Barbarian: The Life and Work of Turgenev*. New York: Random House, 1977. This popular study is quite accessible to the general reader, but it is largely based on the previous biographies of Magarshack and Yarmolinsky. Although little is new here, it is characterized by Pritchett's lucid style and his critical understanding of Turgenev's fiction. Pritchett's approach is to use details from Turgenev's life to increase the reader's understanding of his novels and short stories.

Ripp, Victor. *Turgenev's Russia: From "Notes of a Hunter" to "Fathers and*

Sons." Ithaca, N.Y.: Cornell University Press, 1980. This critical study deals only with Turgenev's fiction between *A Sportsman's Sketches* and *Fathers and Sons* and therefore does not deal with his drama. It is valuable, however, in clarifying Turgenev's place in nineteenth century Russian literature and thought and in delineating the important cultural issues which inform his fiction.

Schapiro, Leonard. *Turgenev: His Life and Times.* New York: Random House, 1978. This biography makes use of materials about Turgenev's life and work previously available only in Russian and materials about his relationship with Viardot previously available only in French. This is purely a biographical study and makes no efforts to analyze Turgenev's work.

Yarmolinsky, Avrahm. *Turgenev: The Man, His Art, and His Age.* Rev. ed. New York: Orion Press, 1959. This is a revision of Yarmolinsky's authoritative biography of 1926. Not only is it valuable in providing a detailed account of Turgenev's life and artistic development but also it discusses his intellectual and artistic development and his contribution to an understanding of nineteenth century Russian culture.

Charles E. May

ANNE-ROBERT-JACQUES TURGOT

Born: May 10, 1727; Paris, France
Died: March 18, 1781; Paris, France
Areas of Achievement: Government, politics, and economics
Contribution: Turgot was perhaps the most important reform-minded minister to serve the French monarchy in the last generation before the Revolution of 1789. He is best known as an economic theorist. He championed the laissez-faire precepts of the "classical" economic school and strove to remove obsolete or artificial barriers to the free flow of trade in prerevolutionary France.

Early Life

Anne-Robert-Jacques Turgot, Baron de l'Aulne, was born into a famous family that had served the kings of France in various high bureaucratic posts since the sixteenth century. The history of the family, which may have been Scandinavian in origin, goes back further, at least to Norman times (eleventh century). Turgot's father, who managed the family estate in Normandy, was Michel Étienne Turgot, himself the son of a royal *intendant* (tax collector and financial agent). Michel Étienne held the office of "provost of the market sellers of Paris," a title which included a wide variety of functions. As city planner, he was responsible for many major improvements, including the great Paris sewer system on the Right Bank of the Seine River and the construction of a number of famous monuments. The elder Turgot married a noble woman of high status. All of their sons became famous, one as a magistrate, another as a military officer who also pursued scientific interests in botany, and the youngest, Anne-Robert-Jacques, as a highly placed royal administrator equally interested in philosophical and theoretical economic questions.

The young Turgot's earliest education was at the Collège Duplessis in Paris, then at the Collège de Bourgogne. While at the latter institution, he became particularly interested in the work of two great English thinkers who would influence his future: Sir Isaac Newton and John Locke. The French intellectual traditions represented by Montesquieu and his near contemporary Voltaire were also important to Turgot at this early age. Somewhat unexpectedly, Turgot entered the theological seminary of Saint Sulpice in 1743, when he was sixteen years old. After a few years he went on (in 1749) to the Annexe de la Sorbonne, which then served as the theological faculty of the University of Paris. Then, equally unexpectedly, in 1751 he decided to abandon his preparation for an ecclesiastical career, entering the service of the French high administration at the age of twenty-four.

Life's Work

Turgot's first appointment was to a magisterial position in the Parlement (high court) de Paris, which was constituted by and, to a certain degree, for the noble peers of France. Specifically, his post between 1753 and 1761 was that of "master of requests." Turgot's service in this high judicial body came at a very critical time, since this period was characterized by a number of preliminary clashes between the French crown and the nobility. These would eventually be considered among the first tensions which led to the French Revolution.

In this early stage of his official career, Turgot frequented many intellectual and literary salons in and around the city of Paris. He devoted particular attention to the doctrines of the *économistes* (more commonly referred to as "physiocrats"), at that time led by François Quesnay. The physiocrats argued that the source of all wealth is to be found in land and its products, and supported the then-emergent economic philosophy of *laissez-faire, laissez-passer*. As a member of the recognized intellectual circles who gave the mid-eighteenth century its reputation for enlightenment, Turgot contributed to the famous encyclopedia edited by Denis Diderot. His earliest outline of his own economic and social reform ideas came in 1759 in the form of an elegy, the "Éloge de Gournay," dedicated to a deceased friend whose ideas on the subject had influenced his thinking.

Soon thereafter (in 1761), an important change in Turgot's administrative career came when he was appointed to the *intendance* of Limoges. When appointed, he called the change a misfortune, first because of his pending isolation from Paris and also because he was about to come face to face with the disturbing reality of France's fiscal and financial affairs. During the years of his service in Limoges (1761-1774), Turgot gained recognition both for the many basic reforms he instituted in the name of King Louis XV, and for his published writings on economic questions. These included his *Mémoire sur les mines et carrières* (1764; memoir on mines and quarries), *Valeurs et monnaies* (1769; on value and money), and *Lettres sur la liberté du commerce des grains* (1770; letters on the corn trade). Perhaps Turgot's most celebrated work, however, was his *Réflexions sur la formation et la distribution des richesses* (1766; *Reflections on the Formation and Distribution of Wealth*, 1793). It was reputedly written to provide an explanation of the workings of European economic forces to foreigners (Chinese) visiting in France. Its influence and longevity as a model of eighteenth century classical economic thought, however, went far beyond this presumed goal.

When Louis XV died in 1774, his successor, Louis XVI, apparently immediately recognized Turgot's extraordinary capacities and insights. After appointing him very briefly to the post of Minister of the Navy, the king called Turgot to the high royal position of controller general of finance. Before accepting this post, Turgot met with the king to discuss what he considered to be the major reform issues of the day. While in the controller general's position (from 1774 to 1776), Turgot prepared and passed the so-called Six Edicts which, it was hoped, would save France from its deepening financial and economic crisis. These decrees, promulgated early in 1776, may be summarized in two categories: four edicts involving the abolition of minor administrative or fiscal institutions, which Turgot identified as obstacles to improved economic conditions, and two edicts that aimed at much more substantial institutional changes. The first category suppressed certain types of antiquated controls over grain trade in Paris; equally antiquated bureaucratic offices connected with ports and market operations; special taxes on livestock sales; and the outmoded system of taxing and selling suet and tallow to the chandler industry. Much more significant when one considers the connections between Turgot's reform priorities and the inevitable drift toward revolution in France were one edict suppressing the *corvée* (conscription, among the peasants, of unpaid labor for public projects or service to the privileged classes) and another abolishing the majority of France's restrictive craft guilds.

Turgot insisted that the removal of artificial controls in trade and commerce would be absolutely necessary for the recovery of France's badly declining levels of productivity. The implications of this argument certainly went far beyond the areas affected by the Six Edicts; they potentially aimed at all forms of privilege hampering free economic flow, including many outmoded prerogatives of the nobility and the clergy. This helps explain the unpopularity of Turgot's reform program among those sectors of privileged French society who refused to see what was likely to happen if the status quo remained. Pressures brought to bear on Louis XVI by these refractory elements led to Turgot's removal from office in 1776 and his decision to retire to pursue his own intellectual and writing interests. In March of 1781, some seven and one-half years before the outbreak of the French Revolution, Turgot died in retirement.

Summary

The life of Anne-Robert-Jacques Turgot illustrates at least two essential points about the nature of French society and politics in the prerevolutionary period. First, Turgot is an example, certainly not a totally isolated one, of a representative of France's privileged noble class who demonstrated serious concern for reforming a number of obsolete institutions that were part of the *ancien régime*. In some cases (four out of the famous Six Edicts of 1776, for example), what Turgot identified as obsolete had little or no direct bearing on particular vested class interests. Many changes he supported were practical in nature, designed to facilitate an expansion in the volume of a variety of seemingly minor commercial exchanges—something that would eventually benefit almost all elements of French society. In other cases, practical reforms, although they could be justified as promising general benefits in the long run, had immediate implications for specific interest groups.

His recommendation that the *corvée*, or free-labor levy, be abolished obviously struck out at very privileged elements, mainly noble and royal. The hostility of the upper class to such reforms is therefore understandable and fits what one might call standard stereotypes of reactionism in prerevolutionary France.

As Turgot stands out as an example of an enlightened conscience within the ranks of the noble class, other societal elements who opposed other categories of reform that he supported illustrate a second point that should be kept in mind about the variety of causes and contradictions behind the eventual revolution. Widespread opposition to abolition of the craft guilds—institutions that mainly affected the vested interests of the middle class of prerevolutionary France—points out the fact that resistance to changes in the obsolete feudal system was not limited to the upper, privileged classes. Wherever change appeared to menace specific interests in the short run, the logic of longer-term benefits was rejected in prerevolutionary France. This was obvious in the case of the nobility, the Church, and the king. It was less obvious in the cases of less easily identifiable elements, including merchants, craftsmen, and even peasants. Turgot's gift of insight enabled him to see the multidimensional implications of these obstacles, but a variety of vested-interest groups thwarted his endeavor to represent the commonweal.

Bibliography
Cobban, Alfred. *A History of Modern France*. Vol. 1, *Old Régime and Revolution, 1715-1799*. Harmondsworth, England: Penguin Books, 1957. This volume is the first in a three-volume general history written by one of the best-known and respected British historians of France. Its value for the study of Turgot's life is mainly for its coverage of the general sweep of French history throughout the eighteenth century, and especially for its comparisons between several different high ministers of the French Crown, both before and after Turgot's brief term of office under Louis XVI.
Dakin, Douglas. *Turgot and the Ancien Régime in France*. London: Methuen, 1939. This may be the most thorough and scholarly biographical study of Turgot in English. Dakin undertook this study while a student at Birkbeck College, University of London, and based his writings on Turgot's own works as well as on a number of contemporary French documents and published periodicals.
Lodge, Eleanor C. *Sully, Colbert and Turgot: A Chapter in French Economic History*. Reprint. Port Washington, N.Y.: Kennikat Press, 1970. This collection of three biographies provides a very useful complement to Frank Manuel's work (see below). First, all three of these figures were high ministers of state, and Lodge's emphasis is on the significance of their contributions as government figures. Second, her three figures represent three different periods in French history: the sixteenth, seventeenth,

and eighteenth centuries. Each biography, including Turgot's, is placed within a general historical framework written for the layman rather than the specialist.

Manuel, Frank E. *The Prophets of Paris*. Cambridge, Mass.: Harvard University Press, 1962. Manuel chose Turgot as one of six major intellectual figures of France, both under the *ancien régime* and in the postrevolutionary period. Because his objective is to compare Turgot's contributions with those of other French thinkers (for example the Comte de Saint-Simon, the Marquis de Condorcet, Charles Fourier, and Auguste Comte), the emphasis here is on ideas, not on Turgot's actual achievements as an administrator.

Shepherd, Robert P. *Turgot and the Six Edicts*. New York: Columbia University Press, 1903. This is a specialized study of Turgot's famous 1776 plan for reforming key elements in France's administrative and fiscal system. Although the author enters into the details of each edict and its potential ramifications for the French economy, the work is only sparsely documented by contemporary historians' standards.

Byron D. Cannon

LORENZO VALLA

Born: 1407; Rome
Died: August 1, 1457; Rome
Areas of Achievement: Religion and philosophy
Contribution: By means of his careful scholarship, Valla helped to legitimize
Renaissance Humanism, reorganize philosophical methodology, and ex-
pose certain prevalent Roman Catholic beliefs and practices to critical
scrutiny, thus helping to prepare the way for the rise of Protestantism.

Early Life
Few important details have survived concerning the early life of Lorenzo
Valla, one of the greatest of the Italian Renaissance Humanists. It is known
that he was born in Rome in 1407, to a pious, upper-class family that traced
its roots back to Piacenza, in the Italian Alps. The advantages he enjoyed by
birth were magnified by his education, for Valla was extremely fortunate in
his instructors, sitting at the feet not only of Vittorino da Feltre, one of the
premier scholars at the University of Rome, but also Leonardo Bruni, who
taught Valla Latin, and Giovanni Aurispa, who taught him Greek. Under
their tutelage Valla became a superb linguist. He became so proficient, in
fact, that he often was commissioned by the pope for official translations.
Ironically, the same linguistic proficiency which brought him papal attention
and commendation would eventually call forth the pope's ire.

While still in his early twenties, Valla was appointed to the "chair of
eloquence" at the University of Pavia, an appointment that required him to
teach rhetoric, Latin, and Greek. It was during his tenure at Pavia that Valla,
in 1431, was ordained a Roman Catholic priest.

The same year he was ordained, Valla published *De voluptate* (1431),
later revised under the title *De vero bono* (1433; *On Pleasure*, 1977). In it,
he searches for the highest human good. This search is conducted as a
comparative exposition, in dialogue form, between Leonardus, Antonius,
and Nicolaus, Valla's imaginary representatives of Stoicism, Epicureanism,
and Christianity, respectively. According to Leonardus, the highest human
good is moral virtue, which must be pursued at all costs, even the cost of
one's life and happiness, if need be. Antonius counters this assertion by
identifying pleasure (which he closely ties to utility), as the highest good.
Nicolaus, whose views are probably to be seen as Valla's own, says that
Christanity is the highest good because it combines the best of Stoicism and
Epicureanism without any of their shortcomings. To him, whoever serves
God gladly does best (that is, has virtue) and is happiest (that is, has pleasure). To Nicolaus, Christianity is our glad service for God and, because it
is, it is the highest human good.

Valla's service at the University of Pavia lasted for about three years until, in 1433, his public letter attacking a notable local jurist aroused such a tempest that he was forced to resign his academic post. For the next three years, in true Renaissance fashion, he followed the ancient peripatetic model for scholars, moving from Pavia to Milan, to Genoa, and to Mantua, before settling finally in Naples, where he became private secretary to King Alfonso, a post from which he rose to public prominence.

Life's Work

At about the same time that Valla enlisted in the service of the king, he published *De libero arbitrio* (c. 1436; *On Free Will*, 1948), an influential work that examines the relationship between divine foreknowledge and election, on the one hand, and human free will and responsibility, on the other. It also examines the relationship between reason and religion. In it, Valla argues that human beings cannot shun their responsibility to do good and they cannot blame God for their shortcomings, as if He were the cause of their evil and not they themselves. To Valla, because God is omniscient, He knows what a person will do even before he does it. That person, nevertheless, cannot say that God caused his action, because prior knowledge is not a cause. The verb "to know" is an intransitive verb. That is, it has no external effect. Simply to know that one will deposit money in one's bank account will neither make one richer nor cause the deposit to occur. Only going to the bank and leaving money in the account can do that, and that is a human responsibility. It also is something one is free to do or to leave undone. The fact that God knows what will happen does not alter the action or relieve a person of the responsibility to get it done. Nor does it vitiate the freedom to do so. Thus, divine foreknowledge and human freedom are compatible concepts. Infallible prediction is not the same as predeterminism.

Valla goes on to explain that while the human mind can comprehend such difficult problems, and even offer plausible solutions to them, religion is not reducible merely to reason. Some things in religion exceed reason's grasp. As a pious Renaissance Humanist, Valla believed that religion, rhetoric, and reason form a hierarchy. Religion, so to speak, is king; rhetoric is queen, and reason is their servant. Thus, while good theology and good philosophy are complementary, religion takes precedence over reason. Valla is not opposed to philosophy. He is opposed to bad philosophy and to philosophy that does not keep to its proper place or role. God's revelation is understandable to reason, but it is not subject to reason. Reason is subject to it.

At about the same time that Valla published *On Free Will*, he began work on what was perhaps his most popular work, *Elegantiae linguae latinae* (1444). This book is Valla's effort to restore Latin usage to its ancient purity, a purity he believed was lost at the hands of medieval Latinists, whom he called "barbarians." This book, therefore, is a Humanist handbook on how to achieve graceful style and verbal precision. Because it was the first great effort at Humanistic philology, it was the first work to place the study of Latin usage on a somewhat scientific basis. It soon became the standard textbook for Humanists interested in verbal accuracy and verbal art.

Dialecticae disputationes (c. 1439) is Valla's attempt to restore and restructure medieval philosophy by rearranging its arguments. In this book, Valla tried to simplify logic and to rearrange it according to the discipline of rhetoric. By allying philosophical clarity with rhetorical flourish, Valla was trying to teach scholars not only how to speak sense (logic) but also how to speak sense beautifully and compellingly (rhetoric). Reason (ratio) must be combined with eloquence (oratio). Valla, in other words, tried to modify the prevailing Aristotelianism of his day by showing that metaphysical truth could be clarified by linguistic criticism, literary analysis, and rhetorical emphasis. To Valla, Aristotle's philosophical language was unsound. *Dialecticae disputationes* is Valla's effort to correct this shortcoming with a philosophy that was rhetorically a better description of reality.

Easily Valla's most sensational work, *De falso credita et ementita Constantini donatione declamatio* (1440; *The Treatise of Lorenzo Valla on the Donation of Constantine*, 1922), revealed the fraudulent nature of the document upon which medieval popes based their claim for political and military power. Written while he was still in the pay of King Alfonso (an adversary of the pope), and probably written at the king's suggestion, this book resulted in Valla's trial on charges of heresy, a trial that was stymied by the king's intervention. The spurious Donation of Constantine, supposedly written by the ancient Roman emperor himself, gave the entire western region of the Empire to Pope Sylvester because the pope allegedly had cured the emperor of leprosy. As a result, Constantine withdrew himself and his court from Rome to Constantinople because he did not feel worthy to live in the same city as such a holy man as Sylvester. In gratitude for his healing, the emperor granted the pope political and military charge over the West.

Valla's critical analysis, both linguistic and historical, overturned the integrity of the document. By means of his own philological expertise, Valla showed that this document could not have been written in the fourth century, as it purports to have been. Instead, by exposing many of its anachronisms, he showed it to be an eighth century forgery, perhaps from Paris. Thus, while he was not the first to question this document's authenticity—Dante and John Wyclif had done so before him—he was the first to establish his objection on the basis of sound historical and linguistic judgment.

Having to some extent debunked papal claims to civil power, Valla next took aim at traditional Roman Catholic piety. *De professione religiosorum* (1442; on monastic views) is his effort to prove that religious people, such as priests, monks, and nuns, are not necessarily the best. Ostensibly a dialogue between Frater, a traditional Roman Catholic, and Lorenzo, whose views represent Valla's own, this book is a courageous and outspoken challenge to prevalent views on Christian life. In it, Valla denies, as the Protestant reformers do later, that any special spiritual status attaches to members of the clergy or of the religious orders. To Valla, all Christians are on equal footing. One must not be called religious simply because one has taken vows. Vows, he believes, are worthless if one does not lead a godly life. If one can lead a godly life without vows, why are they necessary? True sanctity comes from being acceptable to God, not to one's ecclesiastical superiors. Vows, in fact, are inimical to spirituality because virtue begins with pious inner attitudes, not obedience to external rules. On this point Valla believed the laity actually to be superior because when they obey they do so out of their own goodwill, not because of pressure imposed upon them from the outside. In addition to vows, Valla opposes the exaltation of poverty. To be wealthy, he said, is not the same as being sinful, nor is being poor synonymous with being pious. Christ taught us to be poor in spirit, not poor in goods. The monkish practice of giving all one's money to the poor so that one too may become a beggar is, to Valla, a perversion of Christianity, which is faith in Christ and love to God and humanity.

In 1448, Valla left the service of King Alfonso in order to assume the dual role of apostolic secretary to Pope Nicholas V and professor at the University of Rome, tasks that allowed him plenty of time to engage in scholarly pursuit. That he was employed by the pope, even after the attack on the Donation of Constantine was published, is a tribute to the pope's tolerance, to his confidence in himself and his office, and to Valla's prestige and worth as a scholar.

Valla's final major work, one published posthumously by Desiderius Erasmus, was his *Adnotationes in Novum Testamentum* (1505). This book deals with the Latin translation of the Bible (the Vulgate) in the light of Valla's knowledge of Greek. In it, he attempts to correct some of the Vulgate's mistakes, which he evaluated on grammatical, stylistic, and philosophical grounds. The first assesses the strict accuracy of the Vulgate's vocabulary and syntax, the second how well the Vulgate captured the eloquence and power of the original, and the third how fully the philosophical and theological content have been preserved. It was by these tests, Valla believed, that one could best aid the cause of theological restoration and the recovery of the fundamentals of Christianity.

After nearly a decade in Rome, Valla died, in 1457, after suffering an unidentified illness.

Summary

Lorenzo Valla was one of the most original and influential scholars of the Italian Renaissance. His work demonstrates most clearly the effect that accurate historical perspective and careful literary analysis could have on the various fields of knowledge, especially theology and philosophy. In that light, he was one of the leading critical minds of his age. He succeeded in establishing the new study of philology as a respectable and useful academic discipline.

Thus, Valla was a groundbreaker and a pioneer. His work served as a guide and inspiration for later Humanists such as Erasmus, who also desired to restore theology by means of the humanities. Valla also enjoyed a measure of success in reorganizing philosophical inquiry by freeing it from the control of medieval Scholastic methods. In this he anticipated later European thinkers such as Peter Ramus. By Protestants such as Martin Luther, Valla was considered a theological forerunner and a kindred spirit. Like them, he believed that faith was the basis of Christian living, not any external actions. Like them, he also denied the spiritual superiority of the monastic life-style, and he attacked the validity of some papal claims to authority. It is wrong, nevertheless, to see Valla as a Protestant. Although he was a protesting Catholic, he was not a Protestant. He never thought of himself as outside the Roman fold. Whenever he differed from the Church, he considered himself not un-Catholic, but "more orthodox than the orthodox."

Bibliography

Cassirer, Ernst, Paul O. Kristeller, and John Herman Randall, Jr., eds. *The Renaissance Philosophy of Man*. Chicago: University of Chicago Press, 1948. Chapter 2, "Lorenzo Valla," contains the best available English translation of *On Free Will*. The introduction to this chapter, by Charles Trinkaus, although it contains very little biographical detail, is an excellent entry into Valla's beliefs and intellectual methods. This chapter is enhanced by a useful annotated bibliography.

Kristeller, Paul O. *Eight Philosophers of the Italian Renaissance*. Stanford, Calif.: Stanford University Press, 1964. Although it recounts the biographical details of Valla's life only briefly, chapter 2, "Valla," provides a succinct yet lucid introduction to his thought and its historical background. This chapter pays special attention to Valla's *On Free Will, On Pleasure*, and *Dialecticae disputationes*.

Spitz, Lewis W. *The Renaissance and Reformation Movements*. 2 vols. Skokie, Ill.: Rand McNally, 1971. One of the finest and most accessible introductions to the period, the first volume of this set describes the various intellectual elements of Renaissance Humanism. Each chapter is well organized, readable, and accurate. Chapter 6, "Renaissance Humanism," contains a brief but excellent introduction to the life, background, and contribution of Lorenzo Valla. Though each chapter contains bibliographical references throughout, and though each chapter concludes with a useful bibliography, the titles listed concerning Valla are few.

Trinkaus, Charles. *In Our Image and Likeness: Humanity and Divinity in Italian Humanist Thought*. 2 vols. Chicago: University of Chicago Press,

1970. Chapter 3, "Lorenzo Valla: Voluptas et Fruitio, Verba et Res," is a well-documented, closely argued, seventy-page account of Valla's moral and religious thought. Trinkaus traces several key motifs through Valla's most important books, from which, in his footnotes, he quotes at length in the original Latin.

Valla, Lorenzo. *On Pleasure: De Voluptate.* Edited and translated by A. Kent Hieatt and Maristella Lorch. New York: Abaris Books, 1977. This excellent volume contains both the Latin original of Valla's book and an accurate, readable English translation on facing pages. The book is prefaced by a forty-page introduction that describes Valla's personality, his polemics, his Humanist background, and his *On Pleasure*. The volume concludes with twenty-five pages of notes and appendices. Though many works are alluded to in the process, no separate bibliography is given.

Michael Bauman

GIORGIO VASARI

Born: July 30, 1511; Arezzo, Republic of Florence
Died: June 27, 1574; Florence
Areas of Achievement: Literature, art, and architecture
Contribution: Modern knowledge of the lives and works of the principal, as
well as a number of lesser, artists of the Renaissance derives almost exclusively from Vasari's *Lives of the Most Eminent Painters, Sculptors,
and Architects.* Vasari was also a minor painter and architect.

Early Life

Giorgio Vasari, from ancient Arezzo, a hill town dating from Etruscan
times and rich in mementos of the Middle Ages and the early Renaissance,
was born into a family numbering several local artists among its antecedents.
His father, Antonio, a tradesman, compensated for his own lack of creativity
and financial success by maintaining close contact with men of consequence
within the Church and in artistic circles and was particularly proud of his
kinship with Luca Signorelli, a major figure in mid-Renaissance art, who
provided the young Vasari with his first lessons in drawing. His formal
training, however, began under the guidance of a Frenchman resident in
Arezzo, Guglielmo di Marsillac, now remembered as a major stained-glass
artist. Yet it is likely that Vasari learned much more from his daily exposure
to local art treasures; he claimed, in fact, to have spent his early youth
copying "all the good pictures to be found in the churches of Arezzo."

At age fifteen, as a result of his father's splendid contacts, Vasari was
taken to Florence by Cardinal Silvio Passerini of Cortona, who brought him
to the studios of Andrea del Sarto and Michelangelo. This initial contact
with Michelangelo marked the beginning of a close relationship destined to
last for forty years, and no single artist in Vasari's vast knowledge of Renaissance creativity was more admired by him than Michelangelo: "I courted
Michelangelo assiduously and consulted him about all my affairs, and he
was good enough to show me great friendship."

Cardinal Passerini also introduced him to members of the Medici family,
in whose favor Vasari would remain for the duration of his career. At this
particular time, however, such contact was of little consequence, for the
Medicis were soon driven from the city, and Vasari, fearful for his own
safety in the ensuing anti-Medici atmosphere, fled back to Arezzo, only to
find his hometown ridden with a plague that had already taken his father's
life. His uncle, as guardian of the family, advised him not to go home and
expose himself to such peril and instead arranged for him to live in nearby
villages, where he made a meager living doing decorative work in small
churches. The following year, the plague having run its course, he joined his
family in Arezzo, once more relishing the opportunity to observe and copy

local artworks and also finishing his first commission, a painting for the Church of San Piero.

Yet, when Florence again appeared safe for a Medici protégé, he returned, this time in the hope of making a reasonable living for his family, whose welfare was now his responsibility. He entered into an apprenticeship with a goldsmith. Once more his plans were disrupted by political upheaval, now in the form of the 1529 siege of Florence. Vasari, never one to court danger, made his way to Pisa, where he abandoned his new craft and returned to painting, quickly making a name for himself as a reliable, competent, hard-working artist. His patrons were not Pisans but exiled Florentines, members of the distinguished Pitti and Guicciardini families.

Still not yet twenty years old and driven by the restlessness of youth, Vasari soon left Pisa, traveling a circuitous route via Modena and Bologna back to Arezzo, where he completed his first fresco, a representation of the four evangelists with God the Father and some life-size figures. From that time on, he was never lacking in distinguished patronage. Working on commissions for local rulers, princes of the Church, and the pope, he completed, always in record time, major fresco projects in Siena, Rome, Arezzo, and Florence. His works in this medium, most notably those in Rome's Palazza della Cancelleria, the interior of Filippo Brunelleschi's monumental dome in Florence's cathedral, and the splendidly reconstructed rooms in the Palazzo Vecchio were viewed as masterpieces in their day, and Vasari was richly rewarded. Yet despite their great contemporary appeal, posterity has dealt harshly with Vasari's decorative works, viewing his efforts as superficial and flamboyant, devoid of intellectual clarity and spiritual depth.

Life's Work

Although Vasari described himself as a painter and architect and clearly exerted a major portion of his time and energy on works in these fields, he made his principal contribution with *Le vite de' più eccellenti architetti, pittori, et scultori italiani, da cimabue insino a' tempi nostri* (1550; *Lives of the Most Eminent Painters, Sculptors, and Architects*, 1855-1885), a prodigious compendium of information on art and artists gradually accumulated throughout his mature years. Wherever he happened to be—and he traveled widely—and whatever the primary purpose of his journey, he always devoted a significant portion of his time to the observation of works by other artists, making sketches and taking notes and, whenever the opportunity was there, acquiring original sketches and drawings for his steadily mounting collection to which in his work he refers time and again and invariably with great pride.

It is quite possible that without the prodding of others, in particular his Rome patron Cardinal Farnese, the *Lives of the Most Eminent Painters, Sculptors, and Architects* would have remained the writer's private, unpublished notes on the arts of the Renaissance. The subject of compiling all of his material into a published account, Vasari reports, was brought up at a dinner party in the home of the cardinal in 1546, when Paolo Giovio, already a renowned collector of portraits and a biographer but not an artist, expressed the wish for having available "a treatise discussing all illustrious artists from the time of Cimabue to the present." Considering that the first manuscript was ready for the scribe in 1548, it stands to reason that Vasari must have had most of the material on hand by the time the subject of a book was broached, and that the two ensuing years must have been spent organizing the vast body of notes into a logical entity.

Not everything in the work represents the writer's original thoughts. Vasari borrowed liberally from all available sources—written observations by Brunelleschi, Lorenzo Ghiberti, Ghirlandajo, Raphael, and many others—as a rule acknowledging his indebtedness. Such secondary aspects of the work, however, are far less important than Vasari's own meticulous, often pedantic, descriptions of thousands of works of art in terms of structure, form, color, and purpose. To facilitate the reader's comprehension and establish a degree of unity in his flood of observations, he puts forth a set of criteria which in his opinion form the basis on which a work of art should be judged. First in this hierarchy of values is *disegno*, or word design, by which Vasari implies not only the total layout of a particular work but also the actual skill of drawing that must precede the finished product. With *natura*, true to the Renaissance spirit, he claims that excellence in art derives from careful observation and faithful re-creation of nature, or even, in the Neoplatonic consciousness so prevalent at the time, an improvement on nature. *Decoro* refers to the appropriateness, the decorum, or dignity, that should always be part of all visual creativity, stressing that the representation must befit the subject at hand. *Iudizio*, a less tangible term, is a criterion applied to the evaluation of an artist's sense of sound judgment relative to his combining all the separate elements that go into the evolvement and completion of his work. Last in Vasari's listing is *maniera*, an overall consideration referring either to a single artist's unique style and approach or to the style, the manner, of an entire school, for example, the Sienese or the Florentine.

Vasari's own style of writing ranges from the matter-of-fact listing of data and descriptive details to a florid gushing of superlatives. In his discussion of Masaccio, he describes the *Pisa Madonna* in this straightforward way:

> In the Carmelite church at Pisa, inside a chapel in the transept, there is a panel painting by Masaccio showing the Virgin and Child, and some little angels at her feet, who are playing instruments and one of whom is sounding a lute and inclining his ear very attentively to listen to the music he is making. Surrounding Our Lady are St. Peter, St. John the Baptist, St. Julian, St. Nicholas, all very vivacious and animated.

Entirely different and far more elevated are his comments on Leonardo da Vinci:

> The excellent productions of this divine artist had so greatly increased and extended his fame that all men who delighted in the arts (nay, the whole city of Florence) were anxious that he should leave behind him some memorial of himself; and there was much discussion everywhere in respect to some great and important work to be executed by him, to the end that the commonwealth might have glory, and the city the ornament, imparted by the genius, grace, and judgment of Leonardo to all that he did.

While the weight and importance placed on Vasari's descriptions and evaluations in subsequent times have shifted, his approach to artistic biography remained the unchallenged standard for the next three hundred years. Even in modern times any study of the artists of the Italian Renaissance tends to have Vasari's *Lives of the Most Eminent Painters, Sculptors, and Architects* as its point of departure. It is to a considerable extent to his particular credit that neglect was not to be the destiny of the multitude of artists active on the Italian peninsula in those two hundred years he designated as the Renaissance.

Summary

In *Lives of the Most Eminent Painters, Sculptors, and Architects*, Giorgio Vasari devotes much space to a detailed description of his own numerous works carried out on commission in various parts of Italy, and to the lofty sociocultural standings of the many who sought to employ his talent and fame. It is therefore quite evident that he would have preferred to be remembered as a significant painter. Even so, he never succeeded in making a lasting impact in that field. Even his major commission, the challenging decorations in the most auspicious rooms in the Palazzo Vacchio, did not in retrospect come up to the standards set by his Florentine predecessors in the art of fresco painting, let alone those by artists much closer to his own time, Michelangelo and Raphael, whom he so deeply admired and whose works he so eloquently described. In the final analysis, he failed by his own standards as well, for most of his frescos are hopelessly congested, pompously rhetorical, wearisome to the eye, and clearly lacking the visual mellowness, the decorum and sound judgment set forth in his work as prerequisites for true artistic accomplishment.

None of this detracts in the least from the pioneering importance of his written work. Modern research carried out under circumstances far more favorable than those under which Vasari labored may have brought to light certain inaccuracies in his findings, and some of his evaluations have not withstood the test of time. More often than not, however, new research has simply resulted in a validation of his findings and observations. Furthermore, his minute descriptions of works of art constitute not only the basis on which the field of art history has been built but also provide the pattern for the process of attribution of works of art of the past, so important for the development of collections, private and public.

Bibliography

Burckhardt, Jacob. *The Altarpiece in Renaissance Italy.* Edited and translated by Peter Humfrey. New York: Cambridge University Press, 1988. Swiss scholar Burckhardt's nineteenth century works on the Italian Renaissance are considered classics in the field. Originally published in 1894 with two other essays, "The Collectors" and "The Portrait," the original edition was entirely without illustrations, whereas in this first English edition the accompanying illustrations, in color and black and white, greatly enhance the discussion. While Burckhardt based his studies on personal probing of the subject, his principal doumentation is rooted in Vasari's *Lives of the Most Eminent Painters, Sculptors, and Architects.*

Decker, Heinrich. *The Renaissance in Italy: Architecture, Frescoes, Sculpture.* New York: Viking Press, 1969. A profusely illustrated volume containing meaningful references to Vasari. Although this and other statements tend to reinforce some of the negative criticism so often aimed at Vasari, Decker also stresses the importance of his contribution and actually judges his frescos more favorably than do other writers.

Robert, Carden W. *The Life of Giorgio Vasari: A Study of the Later Renaissance in Italy.* New York: Henry Holt, 1911. Drawing on Vasari's own accounts and on other sources, the author discusses Vasari's contribution as an artist and a writer in the perspective of the creative spirit of the waning years of the Renaissance and the early period of mannerism. Because Vasari's own detailed description of his life and activities has made it less urgent to write on that subject, Robert's work still remains the only comprehensive study available in English.

Wackernagel, Martin. *The World of the Florentine Renaissance Artist: Projects and Patrons, Workshop and Art Market.* Translated by Alison Luchs. Princeton, N.J.: Princeton University Press, 1980. Wackernagel's book, a pioneering study originally published in 1938, examines the relationship between the arts and the immediate sociopolitical and economic conditions under which artists worked. Vasari's documentations and judgment, as well as his relationship with patrons, receive good coverage.

Wittkower, Rudolf. *Idea and Image: Studies in the Italian Renaissance.* London: Thames & Hudson, 1978. The last volume in the author's collected essays contains extensive references to *Lives of the Most Eminent Painters, Sculptors, and Architects*, always cited with great respect for the authority of the document. Particularly interesting is Wittkower's discussion of the evolvement of Michelangelo's dome of St. Peter's in the Vatican, of which, Wittkower states, Vasari provided "detailed and reliable description," in turn totally ignored by subsequent builders. Equally positive is Wittkower's estimation of Vasari's perspicacity relative to the development of Raphael's talent.

Reidar Dittmann

SÉBASTIEN LE PRESTRE DE VAUBAN

Born: May 15, 1633; Saint-Léger de Foucherest, France
Died: March 30, 1707; Paris, France
Areas of Achievement: The military and engineering
Contribution: Vauban is chiefly remembered as Europe's best and most prolific military engineer at a time when siege works and fortifications were crucial to the art of military affairs.

Early Life

Sébastien Le Prestre de Vauban was born in Saint-Léger de-Foucherest, France, in 1633, the son of a family whose position in society lay between the lower nobility and the bourgeoisie. His education, completed at Semur-en-Auxois, consisted of drawing, mathematics, and history. In 1651, while still seventeen, Vauban enlisted as a cadet in a regiment that elected to fight on the side of the Fronde rebels against the very young King Louis XIV. Because of his education, Vauban was put to work as a military engineer, fortifying the town of Clermont-en-Argonne. Later, he participated in the siege of Sainte-Menehould. Both experiences were solid preparation for his life's work. Captured by the Royalists, Vauban was pardoned, converted to the cause of the king, and sent back to Sainte-Menehould, this time to lay siege to his former friends. At the end of the Fronde wars in 1653, Vauban was returned to Sainte-Menehould to repair much of what he had previously helped destroy. Vauban had been fortunate in 1653 to have entered the royal service under the Chevalier de Clerville, by reputation, if perhaps not in practice, France's best military engineer. The advent of gunpowder had ushered in the age of artillery and with it the decline of the castle in favor of less vulnerable, lower, bastioned fortifications. Transitional work had already begun, but the times were right for a man of meticulous genius such as Vauban. After conducting sieges on behalf of Louis XIV, Vauban was commissioned *ingénieur ordinaire du roi* within de Clerville's department, a position from which he could gain the increasing affection of the king.

Life's Work

Vauban traveled on the king's behalf from 1659 to 1667, repairing old or developing new frontier fortifications. It was a long peace in Louis' very long reign, a reign filled with wars of aggrandizement and expansion. In 1667, Louis attacked Spanish troops in Flanders, and the dedicated Vauban excelled in siege craft in the king's royal service. Vauban fortified the key strategic towns of Lille and Tournai. Vauban's work had by this time so surpassed de Clerville that Louis promoted him over de Clerville. Vauban became *commissaire général*, or virtual director of France's fortifications and siege works.

Louis' schedule of wars was formidable. From 1667 to 1668, France fought in the War of Devolution, from 1672 to 1678 in the Dutch War, from 1688 to 1697 in the War of the League of Augsburg, and from 1701 to 1714 in the War of the Spanish Succession. The average-looking, rugged Vauban worked diligently at his post, shunning the splendors of the Sun King's fabulous court at Versailles. His world was the dusty trail and the supervision of field work while staying at modest frontier inns. Even after 1675, when Louis granted him an estate, Vauban spent little time there or with his wife. In his old age, Vauban carried out his work from the back of his sedan chair, borne by horses. In 1706, Vauban was elevated to marshal of France before dying a year later of pneumonia. Throughout, Vauban was one of Louis' longest-serving and most trusted servants, compiling to his credit the construction of at least thirty-three new fortresses, the restoration of more than one hundred older fortresses, and the execution of fifty-three successful sieges.

Vauban's contributions were in his offensive siege craft and defensive fortifications. After the horrors of the Thirty Years' War (1618 to 1648), nations wanted to regulate the military art with certain established, recognized rules. Military operations were carried out along the lines of chessboard moves. The capture of fortifications became the chesslike pieces and the actions which determined the winner in the wider military and diplomatic context.

Good fortifications were situated to offer a high degree of enfilading fire and mutually supporting positions, and they were layered for defense in depth. Walls and bastions were thickened and lowered to cushion against the effect of artillery. Vauban was recognized as a master at overcoming defenses as well as of creating them. He was a legend in his own time; indeed, it was noted that "a town besieged by Vauban was a town taken." Vauban's method of siege was first to blockade a fortified town, then to determine the best single point in the defenses where he could effect a decisive breach. Earthworks would be built to provide protective cover for the artillery and engineers. Vauban would then build three trench systems progressively toward and parallel to the particular point to be breached. These trenches, which were connected by zig-zag communications trenches, were referred to as the first parallel, second parallel, and third parallel. Offensive artillery was divided into three functions; mortar batteries and ricocheting batteries which would suppress defensive musketry and artillery and the heavy or main breaching batteries. The entire system was geometrically calculated with Vauban's mathematical precision. Often, days in advance, Vauban could predict the exact hour of a defense's fall. Once a breach had been made and assuming no relieving force was in sight, the conventions of the day permitted a garrison to surrender honorably. In fact, a town that refused and had to be taken by storm could rightfully, by the same rules, be sacked.

Vauban was equally skilled in defensive fortification. His methods were based not only on mathematics but also on common sense and his experience in analyzing the advantages of terrain. Vauban looked upon his talent as the art of being able to build to suit a given location rather than as a systematic adventure into applied science. Nevertheless, his emulators categorized his methods into three systems. His first system represented little more than adaptations from previous French and Italian engineers. His early development also borrowed from Blaise François Comte de Pagan, who had retired from active French service in 1642. Greatly simplified, Vauban's fortifications were polygonal, with bastions at strategic points. As a starting point for calculations, a standard length of fortifications front was set at 360 yards. This measure could be reduced or extended depending on the size of area to be protected and the intervening terrain. The other architectural components of the fortification, the ditches, lunettes, ravelins, bonettes, curtain walls, crown work, and horn work, were constructed as fractional expressions of the basic measure. The overall geometrical designs took the effects of contemporary musketry and artillery into consideration in order to provide for the best possible defense. Vauban reintroduced the tenaille and orillon, or ear, onto the bastion. Vauban's second system detached the bastions from the main works and created tower bastions, both feats intended to improve the realities of defense during a siege. His third system was used only once, at Neuf-Brisach. The defense was again extended in depth and the tower bastions were modified. Completed in 1706, one year before his death, it was arguably his finest work.

Summary

During his lifetime, Sébastien Le Prestre de Vauban was appreciated as Europe's leading military engineer. He was, however, more than that, for he wrote on a wide and complex series of issues in his twelve volumes of unpublished memoirs. In 1699, he was elected to the Académie des Sciences for accomplishments in applied science and mathematics. Throughout his travels in the four corners of France, Vauban amassed volumes of economic and social details, and he espoused a concern for humanitarian ideals. In the arena of military affairs, he invented, among others, the ricochet firing technique for artillery and the first good bayonet. Voltaire was inspired to pronounce Vauban to be "the finest of citizens." Yet this well-rounded individual will be forever remembered primarily for his fortifications and siege craft, at which he enjoyed unparalleled success in the seventeenth century and unrivaled adulation in the eighteenth. Vauban's reputation has come to the twentieth century intact. Controversy still shrouds the originality of his work, but that is hardly surprising, for he labored under financial constraints, diplomatic restraints, and the whims of his monarch, and quite often he simply had to work from preexisting structures. The original elements of his second and third system, however, seem beyond dispute, as is the sheer proliferation and essence of his construction. The fortified town of Neuf-Brisach is usually considered his masterpiece. As late as 1870, this 164-year-old fort stood against modern Prussian artillery and siege craft for thirty-six days, so long did Vauban's skill outlive the man.

Bibliography

Britt, Albert Sidney, III, et al. *The Dawn of Modern Warfare*. Wayne, N.J.: Avery Publishing Group, 1984. The volume is at its best as a quick reference to show where Vauban fit into Louis' governmental system and as a handbook for the period wars and military particulars. The text contains a picture of Vauban's offensive strategy.

Chandler, David G. *Atlas of Military Strategy, 1618-1878*. London: Arms and Armour Press, 1980. Vauban is profiled in two oversize pages. There is a bust picture, contemporary sketches of the fortifications of Strasbourg, and explanations of how to breach a wall, as well as two modern cartographical depictions of Vauban's methods. Interesting is a photograph of a three-dimensional model of Strasbourg's fortifications; the model was constructed in the 1720's. Included is a timetable composed by Vauban for sieges. Surrounding period events are well described in word and illustration within the book.

De La Croix, Horst. *Military Considerations in City Planning: Fortifications*. New York: George Braziller, 1972. The author traces his subject from the primitive world to the seventeenth century, concluding with Vauban. More attention is devoted to his defensive rather than to his offensive techniques. Well researched and illustrated.

Duffy, Christopher. *Fire and Stone: The Science of Fortress Warfare, 1660-1860*. Newton Abbot, England: David and Charles, 1975. Vauban's methods and the terminology surrounding the period engineering are difficult for the modern reader to understand. Duffy takes a topical approach to complex subjects, explaining them methodically in simplified but comprehensive detail. Well-chosen illustrations illuminate the text. This work is complementary to Duffy's *Siege Warfare* (see below).

_____. *Siege Warfare: The Fortress in the Early Modern World, 1494-1660*. London: Routledge & Kegan Paul, 1979. An indispensable book for creating the overall setting under which Vauban would begin his early work. The milieu of siege and fortification work is excellently portrayed from the close of the medieval period through Blaise François Comte de Pagan and the Chevalier de Ville, both of whom influenced Vauban's work. This book therefore directly complements Duffy's work cited above.

Hogg, Ian V. *Fortress: A History of Military Defence*. London: Macdonald and Jane's, 1975. One and a half chapters are devoted to the era of

Vauban. The work and accompanying illustrations are the best available for demonstrating the geometrical angles in Vauban's work.

_____. *The History of Fortification*. London: Orbis Publishing, 1981. One chapter on classical fortification sets the stage for the succeeding chapter, "The Age of Vauban." Contained is a picture of Vauban and eighteen other illustrations which give adequate coverage of the military architecture and its terminology. One excellent illustration depicts Neuf-Brisach, rated as Vauban's crowning structural achievement.

Paret, Peter, ed., with Gordon A. Craig and Felix Gilbert. *Makers of Modern Strategy: From Machiavelli to the Nuclear Age*. Princeton, N.J.: Princeton University Press, 1986. The article by Henry Geurlac is probably the best single treatment of Vauban as a well-rounded individual. The article explores Vauban's contributions in mathematics and applied science while recognizing his most significant contributions as siege craft and in the science of fortifications. Vauban's writings are examined, as are controversies over his originality.

David L. Bullock

LOPE DE VEGA CARPIO

Born: November 25, 1562; Madrid, Spain
Died: August 27, 1635; Madrid, Spain
Areas of Achievement: Theater, drama, and literature
Contribution: Lope de Vega was the creator of the Spanish national theater of the Golden Age. He established the norms that would characterize Spanish theater until the late seventeenth century.

Early Life

Lope de Vega Carpio was of humble origins. His father, an embroiderer, died when Lope de Vega was still a boy. At an early age, Lope de Vega was taken to Seville for a brief period, but he spent most of his life in Madrid, at that time a highly stimulating city and cultural center. Juan Pérez de Montalbán, Lope de Vega's disciple and first biographer, relates that at five years of age, Lope de Vega could read in Spanish and in Latin. At seven, he was writing his first compositions, and at ten, his first plays. Lope de Vega continued his studies at the Colegio de la Compañía de Jesús. About 1576, he entered into the service of Jerónimo Manrique de Lara, Bishop of Ávila. He probably later attended the University of Alcalá. In 1580, he left for Salamanca, where he was a student at the university.

Lope de Vega was involved in many amorous relationships and participated in several military campaigns. In 1579, when he had just turned seventeen, he fell in love with María de Aragón, then fifteen. In 1583, he accompanied Alvaro de Bazán on a military campaign to Terceira Island. It was upon his return that he met Elena Osorio, then unhappily married to a comic actor, and became her lover. By this time, Lope de Vega's reputation as a writer was starting to grow, and Elena's father, who recognized the young man's potential, did not oppose the relationship, but Lope de Vega, fiercely jealous of Elena's husband, wrote some provocative verses that caused a scandal. Elena reacted violently to his behavior, and the playwright then responded by attacking Elena and her family, once more in verse. In 1587, Lope de Vega was detained by the authorities for libel, and the following year he was condemned to exile. He then ran away with Isabel de Urbina, whom he married before embarking on the ill-fated Spanish Armada.

After Isabel's death in 1595, Lope de Vega was permitted to return to Madrid. During the following years, he developed into the leading Spanish playwright. It was during this period that he became embroiled in a heated literary polemic with the poet Luis de Góngora, whose ornate style Lope de Vega disliked intensely. In 1598, Lope de Vega married Juana de Guardo, while continuing his amorous relationship with Micaela de Luján, called Camila Lucinda in his verses. During the fifteen years he was married to Juana, he engaged in numerous affairs. In 1605, he entered into the service of the Duke of Sessa, who became his patron. When Juana died in 1613, Lope de Vega took holy orders without diminishing either his involvement in love intrigues or his literary production. By this point in his life, he had become the model for all the playwrights of his generation.

Life's Work

Lope de Vega's active love life did not distract him from writing. He was one of the most prolific literary figures in Spanish history. He claimed to have written about fifteen hundred plays, although modern critics maintain that this figure is certainly an exaggeration. About 470 of his full-length plays survive. In addition, he wrote short, one-act religious plays known as *autos sacramentales*, as well as poetry and novels. Because of his almost superhuman talents and energy, he was called the "Phoenix of Geniuses" and the "Monster of Nature."

Following the lead of Lope de Rueda, Lope de Vega began early in his career to write for the masses. He chose themes that would interest the common man, often dramatizing well-known and popular legends or historical events. Many of his plays were based on episodes from chronicles or on folk songs. By selecting subjects that were familiar and popular, Lope de Vega created a theater that would hold the interest of his audience, and one that was distinctly Spanish in nature.

In *El arte nuevo de hacer comedias en este tiempo* (*The New Art of Writing Plays*, 1914), published in 1609, Lope de Vega explained his dramatic theory. He recommended that playwrights choose subjects, such as love and honor, that would elicit strong reactions from the audience. He abandoned many of the conventions that characterized earlier Spanish theater. For example, classical tradition dictated that dramatists respect the unities of time, place, and action, according to which a plot must take place within the period of a day, must occur in one specific location, and must not include subplots. Lope de Vega found these rules artificial and restrictive. He preferred a more natural approach that would allow events to take place wherever and whenever appropriate. In one of his most popular plays, *Fuenteovejuna* (1619; *The Sheep-Well*, 1936), written between 1611 and 1618, the first act begins in the palace of the Calatrava Order, in Almagro; moves to the plaza of the town of Fuenteovejuna; skips to the palace of the Catholic monarchs Ferdinand and Isabella; and ends in the countryside surrounding Fuenteovejuna.

Lope de Vega wrote tragedy and comedy and also developed the *tragicomedia*, a play that mixes elements of both. His purpose was to imitate nature, in which tragedy and comedy exist side by side. He defined the structure of the Spanish drama, fixing the number of acts at three. He wrote all of his plays in verse and fixed the function of each metric form. For example, the romance, a traditional ballad form, was to be used for narrations, while the *décima*, a ten-line stanza, was to be used for laments. Lope de Vega explored other dramatic genres as well: He wrote historical, mythological, religious, pastoral, and novelistic plays. He also wrote *comedias de capa y espada* (cape-and-sword plays), so called because they depicted contemporary situations, and the actors therefore wore street clothes, which included a cape and sword. These plays usually revolved around love and intrigues, misunderstandings, and tricks. The most famous are *El perro del hortelano* (wr. 1613-1616, pb. 1618; *The Gardener's Dog*, 1903), based on one of Aesop's fables about a dog that neither eats nor allows others to do so, and *La dama boba* (1617; *The Lady Nit-Wit*, 1958), based on the commonplace that love makes fools wise. Lope de Vega's best-known works deal with events in Spanish history; others are based on legends.

Throughout his career, Lope de Vega argued for simplicity and naturalness onstage. When, in the seventeenth century, complex productions with special effects and complicated stage devices came into fashion, he opposed them. He also resisted the trend toward ornate language that characterized baroque literature. Nevertheless, his later plays reflect the new tendencies. *El castigo sin venganza* (1635; *Justice Without Revenge*, 1936) contains many erudite passages that include allusions to history and mythology.

Although Lope de Vega is known primarily as a dramatist, he began his career as a poet and wrote much religious and secular poetry in his later years. He also wrote one of Spain's greatest pastoral novels, *La Arcadia* (1598). Lope de Vega received many honors, among them membership in the Order of Saint John of Jerusalem, which was conferred upon him in 1627. His funeral was a national event and is said to have lasted nine days.

Summary

Prior to Lope de Vega Carpio, Spanish theater was highly dependent on Italian themes and forms. Lope de Vega created a theater that was an authentic expression of the Spanish personality. Even when he depicted foreigners, his characters were always Spanish in essence. His objective was to entertain his audience rather than to instruct or edify. Unlike his best-known follower, Pedro Calderón de la Barca, who was a court dramatist, Lope de Vega wrote for an audience that was often rowdy. In order to please these undisciplined theatergoers, he wrote plays imbued with humor, wit, and action. Even his tragedies contain humor, usually introduced by the servants or *graciosos*. Although his plays are not particularly philosophical, they reveal a deep understanding of human nature. Lope de Vega introduced a psychological element into the theater of his time which was later developed by dramatists such as Tirso de Molina and Calderón. It is perhaps surprising to what degree Lope de Vega's followers respected the norms he established. The Spanish play maintained its three-act format until the end of the seventeenth century and beyond. The basic character types, themes, and devices that

Lope de Vega introduced were used by all the major Spanish playwrights of the Golden Age.

Bibliography

Fitzmaurice-Kelly, James. *Lope de Vega and the Spanish Drama.* London: R. B. Johnson, 1902. Reprint. Brooklyn, N.Y.: Haskell House, 1970. An overview of the state of the Spanish theater at the time of Lope de Vega and of his innovations.

Hayes, Francis C. *Lope de Vega.* Boston: Twayne, 1967. Contains historical and biographical information and an examination of the elements of Lope de Vega's comedy. Analyzes genre, style, and technique for the beginning student.

Larson, Donald R. *The Honor Plays of Lope de Vega.* Cambridge, Mass.: Harvard University Press, 1977. An in-depth study of the evolution of Lope de Vega's treatment of honor, starting with early plays, in which the characters adopt unconventional solutions, through the plays of the middle period, which include some of the most brutal scenes ever to appear on the Spanish stage, to the late plays, in which he tempers his approach.

Moir, Duncan, and Edward M. Wilson. *A Literary History of Spain.* Vol. 3, *The Golden Age Drama, 1492-1700.* London: Ernest Benn, 1971. An overview of the development of Spanish theater from early Spanish masterpieces until the decline of baroque drama at the end of the seventeenth century. Special attention paid to Lope de Vega, his innovations, his genius, and his influence.

Rennert, Hugo Albert. *The Spanish Stage in the Time of Lope de Vega.* Reprint. Mineola, N.Y.: Dover, 1963. An overview of the growth of Spanish theater, the development of the *corrales,* and Lope de Vega's contributions.

Shergold, N. D. *A History of the Spanish Stage from Medieval Times Until the End of the Seventeenth Century.* Oxford, England: Clarendon Press, 1967. Special attention is given to the *corrales* and Lope de Vega's contribution to the development of a national theater. Contains essential information about the physical facilities in which his plays were performed.

Wilson, Margaret. *Spanish Drama of the Golden Age.* Oxford, England: Pergamon Press, 1969. Describes the development and characteristics of the *corrales* and of Lope de Vega's craftsmanship. Discusses his themes and techniques as well as his influence on subsequent writers.

Zuckerman-Ingber, Alix. *El bien más alto: A Reconsideration of Lope de Vega's Honor Plays.* Gainesville: University Presses of Florida, 1984. Argues that critics have misjudged Lope de Vega's attitude toward honor. Contends that he does not condone the honor code but rather attacks it by showing the violent extremes to which the obsession with honor can lead. Explores Lope de Vega's use of irony and his techniques of characterization in the honor plays, and how these convey his true attitude toward honor.

Barbara Mujica

DIEGO VELÁZQUEZ

Born: June, 1599; Seville, Spain
Died: August 6, 1660; Madrid, Spain
Area of Achievement: Art
Contribution: In his role as court painter to King Philip IV, Velázquez produced a series of masterly works that made him the preeminent artist in his native Spain and one of the greatest painters of the entire Baroque era in Europe.

Early Life

Diego Velázquez was born in Seville, Spain, the eldest of the seven children of Juan Rodriguez de Silva and Jerónima Velázquez. The exact date of his birth is unknown, but he was baptized on June 6, undoubtedly shortly after his birth. As was commonplace among many Spaniards, Diego adopted his mother's surname. His family belonged to the hidalgo class, the lowest order of Spanish nobility.

A bright boy and an excellent student, Velázquez received the Humanistic education typical for boys of his class; yet he early demonstrated a proclivity for a career in painting, considered a respectable vocation for the scion of a hidalgo family. Seville had a flourishing community of painters, and his parents encouraged their son's aspirations. In 1611, they apprenticed him to Francisco Pacheco, one of Seville's leading artists, although his training had possibly begun a year earlier under Francisco de Herrera, the Elder. Pacheco agreed to provide his charge with room, board, and clothing and to train him as both a painter and a gentleman. Pacheco's workshop provided a fertile atmosphere for the development of Velázquez's talents. Pacheco had a strong interest in the humanities, and poets, scholars, and public officials often gathered at his workshop to discuss the arts. Pacheco provided rigorous instruction in drawing for all of his students, but he allowed the young Velázquez considerable freedom to develop his own unique style.

Having passed the qualifying examination, Velázquez gained admission to the local painters' guild on March 14, 1617. This authorized him to have his own studio and accept commissions. The following year, on April 23, 1618, he married Pacheco's daughter Juana. Within three years, the young couple had two daughters, but only the elder, Francisca, survived infancy.

Of the approximately twenty paintings by Velázquez that have survived from his early period (1617-1621), the most distinctive are *bodegones*, a unique form of Spanish still life depicting ordinary people engaged in mundane activities involving food and drink. These works demonstrated Velázquez's concern for careful attention to composition and detail and utilized dramatic lighting reminiscent of the Italian Baroque master Caravaggio.

Had Velázquez chosen to remain in Seville, he could undoubtedly have become the city's preeminent painter and enjoyed a lucrative career accepting commissions from local churches. Yet he already clearly preferred secular art to religious art and had ambitions for advancement that could be achieved only at the royal court in Madrid. In April, 1622, he left Seville for the capital, ostensibly to view the famous collection of art at El Escorial Palace; yet he also had aspirations to paint Spain's new sovereign, Philip IV.

Life's Work

The dominant figure at Philip's court for the first two decades of his reign was Gaspar de Guzmán y Pimental, the Count-Duke of Olivares, who had many close friends in Seville, including Pacheco. During his initial visit, Velázquez failed to win a commission to paint Philip, but he won favorable attention with his portrait of the poet Luis de Góngora y Argote. In the spring of 1623, following the death of the king's favorite painter, Olivares summoned Velázquez to Madrid. The young artist's subsequent portrait of the king's chaplain, Juan de Fonseca, won for him widespread praise at court and gained for him the opportunity to paint Philip. This royal portrait, now lost, was so favorably received that Olivares immediately invited Velázquez to move to Madrid permanently. He also decreed that in the future no one else would be permitted to paint the king. Velázquez formally entered royal service on October 6, 1623. For the remaining thirty-seven years of his life, his fortunes were closely tied to Philip and his court.

Velázquez's sudden rise aroused the jealousy of more established court painters, but he firmly entrenched his position by defeating three of his elder rivals in a 1627 competition for a painting based on the theme of the expulsion of the Moors from Spain. The king rewarded Velázquez with the post of Usher of the Chamber, the first of many such favors he bestowed on his favorite painter over the years.

In 1627, Philip permitted Velázquez to travel to Italy, still the paramount place for artistic education during the seventeenth century. After initial visits to Genoa, Milan, Venice, and certain other cities, Velázquez settled for nearly a year in Rome. While there, he eagerly studied and sketched many works of the great masters and also painted several canvases of his own, including *The Bloody Cloak of Joseph* (1630), his only known work on an Old Testament theme. This initial Italian sojourn influenced Velázquez's style by inducing him to use freer brushstrokes and lighter colors.

Upon his return to Madrid in January, 1631, Velázquez found many commissions awaiting him. Among the earliest was a portrait of the new heir to the throne, Prince Baltasar Carlos, born during Velázquez's absence in Italy. Among the major projects that occupied his time in the 1630's was his role in the decoration of the Buen Retiro, the newly built royal palace in Madrid. By late 1635, he had completed three masterful paintings for its Hall of Realms—equestrian portraits of Philip and Baltasar Carlos and *The Sur-*

render of Breda (1634-1635), a grand, life-size canvas that celebrated a Spanish military victory against the Dutch in 1625. Soon afterward, Veláz-quez became preoccupied with the redecoration of Philip's hunting lodge known as the Torre de la Parada. In addition to selecting paintings by other artists to hang in its rooms, Velázquez also painted six major works for the lodge, including life-size hunting portraits of Philip, Baltasar Carlos, and the king's brother Ferdinand.

Velázquez's works for the Buen Retiro and Torre de la Parada cemented his position as the nation's leading artist and resulted in his continued advancement at court. Throughout these years, he retained the king's favor and carefully avoided becoming entangled in the complex world of court politics. Philip expressed his confidence in his favorite artist by naming him a Gentleman of the Wardrobe in 1634 and promoting him to Gentleman of the Bedchamber in 1643. Later in the same year, he appointed Velázquez Assistant Superintendent of Works, which empowered Velázquez to oversee Philip's numerous building projects. Despite his royal offices and commissions, Velázquez's salary was frequently in arrears; yet throughout this period the king allowed him to supplement his wages by accepting commissions from private individuals.

In 1649, the king permitted Velázquez to make a second trip to Italy, principally to purchase paintings and sculptures for a new gallery in the Alcázar Palace. Velázquez arrived in Genoa in March, 1649, and remained in Italy for more than two years, stimulated by the artistic company and the freedom to paint whom he pleased. He again spent the majority of his time in Rome, where he was an honored guest at the papal court. His most famous painting from this period was a portrait of Pope Innocent X. In gratitude for this work, the pontiff presented Velázquez with a gold medallion bearing Innocent's portrait. Velázquez's fellow artists in Rome also honored him in January, 1650, by electing him to membership in the Academy of Saint Luke.

After returning to Madrid, Velázquez soon achieved a more exalted position at court when Philip chose him over several rivals in 1652 for the post of royal chamberlain. This office brought Velázquez a greatly augmented salary and rent-free apartments in the treasury house adjoining the Alcázar Palace. The post also entailed time-consuming responsibilities that decreased his opportunities to paint. He found himself in charge of the decoration of all royal palaces, the upkeep of their furnishings, and the supervision of all arrangements for the king's visits around the country.

During this final decade of his life, Velázquez continued to paint numerous portraits of the royal family, including the innovative *Las Meninas* (1656), considered by many to be his masterpiece. In 1658, the king nominated him for the Order of Santiago, one of the nation's three great orders of knighthood. After securing a papal brief waiving the necessity of proving noble ancestry on both sides, Velázquez was formally admitted to the order on November 28, 1659.

Velázquez's last known works were portraits of the aging monarch's two children by his second marriage, the Infanta Margarita and her sickly younger brother, Prince Philip Prospero. He devoted his last months to the time-consuming preparations for the marriage of the king's elder daughter Maria Teresa to Louis XIV of France, an event that occurred in April, 1660, on the Franco-Spanish border. Only three months after returning to Madrid from these festivities, Velázquez fell ill from a fever while attending his sovereign at court. Despite the efforts of royal physicians, he died within a week, on August 6, 1660. Clad in the costume of the Order of Santiago, the king's favorite painter was buried the following night at services attended by numerous nobles and court officials. His wife of forty-two years died a mere week after her husband.

Summary

During an active career spanning more than four decades, Diego Velázquez established himself as the premier artist of the Golden Age of Spanish painting, as well as one of the most significant painters of the Baroque era. Unlike contemporaries such as Rembrandt in the Netherlands, Velázquez very early in his life secured a generous lifelong patron who provided him with financial security and creative opportunities to demonstrate his genius. With the exception of Peter Paul Rubens, no other artist better personified the genre of aristocratic Baroque painting.

For such a long career, Velázquez's known output was relatively meager. Only some 120 of his 162 known paintings have survived. His output declined as his duties as a courtier increased. One of the great ironies of Velázquez's career is that the royal patronage that afforded him the opportunities to achieve lasting fame also demanded great amounts of his time for pursuits other than painting. Although best known for his penetrating royal portraits, Velázquez dealt with a wide variety of subjects in his paintings, including *bodegones*, religious works, mythological studies, and a moving series of works depicting royal dwarfs and jesters. He was the only significant Spanish painter of his era to devote himself mainly to secular subject matter.

Velázquez founded no great school of painters. His closest follower was his son-in-law, Juan Bautista del Mazo, who succeeded him as court painter but failed to achieve his greatness. Velázquez's works did have a significant impact on artists of subsequent centuries, especially the Romantic painter Francisco de Goya, the realist Gustave Courbet, and the Impressionist Édouard Manet.

Bibliography
Brown, Dale. *The World of Velázquez, 1599-1660*. New York: Time-Life Books, 1969. Particularly emphasizes Velázquez's life and career in relation to the Spain of Philip IV. Includes lavish color illustrations and a brief bibliography.
Harris, Enriqueta. *Velázquez*. Ithaca, N.Y.: Cornell University Press, 1982. Contains a well-written survey of Velázquez's life and works, and two valuable appendices. The first is a translation of Pacheco's study of his son-in-law's early career, found in his 1649 *Arte de la pintura*. The second is an eighteenth century biography by court painter Antonio Palomino de Castro y Velasco. Includes a thorough bibliography.
Kahr, Madlyn Millner. *Velázquez: The Art of Painting*. New York: Harper & Row, 1976. Discusses Velázquez's life with a particular emphasis on his masterpiece, *Las Meninas*. Includes nearly one hundred black-and-white illustrations and a useful bibliography.
López-Rey, José. *Velázquez: A Catalogue Raisonné of His Oeuvre, with an Introductory Study*. London: Faber & Faber, 1963. After initially surveying the artist's life, this lavishly illustrated book devotes chapters to the various types of paintings he produced during his lengthy career. Also useful for its illustrated chronological catalog of more than one hundred extant Velázquez works.
Sérullaz, Maurice. *Velázquez*. New York: Harry N. Abrams, 1985. A volume from the Library of Great Painters series, this study includes an interpretative introductory essay and a chapter on Velázquez's drawings. Particularly useful are the forty-eight color plates with accompanying explanations and a three-page chronological survey of the major events in Velázquez's life.

Tom L. Auffenberg

GIUSEPPE VERDI

Born: October 10, 1813; Le Roncole, Duchy of Parma
Died: January 27, 1901; Milan, Italy
Area of Achievement: Music
Contribution: Verdi, one of the giants of nineteenth century opera, was an innovator who during a long career evolved his own form of music drama and contributed at least half a dozen of the most enduringly popular operas in the international repertory.

Early Life

Giuseppe Verdi was born on October 10, 1813, in Le Roncole, a village in the Duchy of Parma. He was the son of Carlo Verdi and his wife, Luigia, who together eked out a modest living as owners of a wine and grocery store. Verdi's musical talent revealed itself early, and his father bought him an old spinet when Giuseppe was eight. When he was ten, he played the organ at the village church. His talent was noticed by Antonio Barezzi, a wealthy merchant in nearby Busseto, who arranged for Verdi to be tutored by Ferdinando Provesi, the director of the music school in Busseto. Provesi taught him to play the flute, the bass clarinet, the horn, and the piano. After finishing high school in Busseto, Verdi became Provesi's assistant. In 1833, Verdi traveled to Milan, hoping to win a place at the conservatory, but his application was refused because he was over the age limit.

Barezzi provided for him to stay in Milan and take private lessons from Vincenzo Lavigna, a conductor at La Scala. Verdi proved to be a diligent student, sometimes working fourteen hours a day. In 1834, Verdi returned to Busseto, hoping to fill the vacancy left by the death of Provesi. The post, however, had already gone to another candidate, and the slight to Verdi caused a storm in the small town. Eventually, after a public competition, Verdi was appointed Busseto Master of Music. This was in April, 1836; the next month, Verdi married Margherita Barezzi, the daughter of his benefactor.

Verdi began teaching, composing, and conducting, and his first opera, *Oberto, conte di San Bonifacio*, was performed at La Scala in November, 1839. It ran for only fourteen performances, but Verdi received a contract for three more operas. He began working on *Un giorno di regno*, which was performed in September, 1840, but it was withdrawn after the premiere. Shocked by this failure and the death of his wife in the same year—as well as the loss of his infant son the previous year—Verdi decided never to compose again. After some months, the director of La Scala persuaded him to read a libretto based on the biblical story of Nebuchadnezzar. As a result, Verdi wrote *Nabucco*, his first major work. Premiered at La Scala in March, 1842, it was an immediate success, and Verdi found himself being hailed throughout Italy as the successor to his fellow countrymen, Vincenzo Bellini and Gaetano Donizetti.

Life's Work

Verdi often referred to the next nine years of his life, during which he wrote fourteen operas, as his period "in the galleys." The Italian operagoing public was accustomed to a regular supply of new works, and Verdi gave them what they wanted. After *Nabucco* came *I Lombardi alla prima crociata* (1843); audiences were quick to apply the story, about the struggle of the Lombards to free Jerusalem from the Saracens, to the contemporary Italian struggle to throw off Austrian rule, and Verdi's music became a symbol of Italian nationalism. *I Lombardi alla prima crociata* was followed by *Ernani* (1844), *I due Foscari* (1844), and *Giovanna d'Arco* (1845). In 1845, dissatisfied with standards of production, Verdi broke his connection with La Scala and was not to return until 1869. His next two operas, *Alzira* (1845) and *Attila* (1846), were performed in Naples and Venice, respectively. Then came what is probably the best opera of his early period, *Macbeth*, based on William Shakespeare's tragedy. It premiered in Florence in March, 1847.

Verdi had by now gained an international reputation, and later in 1847 he was in London, producing *I masnadieri*. The successful premiere was attended by Queen Victoria. Verdi returned home via Paris, where he renewed his friendship with Giuseppina Strepponi, who had sung in the premiere of *Nabucco*. They began living together, in defiance of the rigid conventions of the period, and married twelve years later. In 1848, political events became more important than artistic ones in Verdi's life. It was a year of revolutions throughout Europe, and the Austrians were driven out of Milan. When Verdi, who was an enthusiastic patriot, heard the news in Paris, he left immediately for Milan. The freedom and unification of Italy was still in the future; republicans and monarchists quarreled among themselves, and in May Verdi returned to Paris. Milan was occupied by Austrian troops once more in August; the failure of the nationalist revolt depressed Verdi.

In 1849, Verdi and Strepponi moved back to Busseto, scandalizing the local people by their illicit liaison. Four operas followed over the next four years, including the patriotic *La battaglia di Legnano* (1849) and *Luisa Miller* (1849). Then within two years came three masterpieces. *Rigoletto*, first performed in March, 1851, and based on a play by Victor Hugo, was Verdi's first worldwide success. The heartbreaking story of the hunchback Rigoletto and his beautiful daughter Gilda includes one of Verdi's most popular melodies, "La donna e mobile," and the brilliant quartet "Bella figlia dell' amore." Over the next four years, *Rigoletto* was performed all over Europe and in the United States.

After Verdi and Strepponi moved to a new home in Sant' Agata, close to Busseto, Verdi began working simultaneously on *Il trovatore* and *La travi-*

ata. *Il trovatore*, based on a drama by the Spanish playwright Antonio Garcia Gutiérrez, premiered in January, 1853, in Rome. It was an immediate and brilliant success, its superb melodies weaving a compelling tale of passion and vengeance, tenderness and melancholy. Less than two months later came the premiere of *La traviata*, based on a novel by Alexandre, Dumas, *père*. For several reasons, however, the first performance was a failure: Verdi had discarded some old conventions, and the opera was performed in contemporary dress; it also featured a courtesan as heroine, which offended public taste. In 1854, the opera was performed again, this time successfully, at a different theater in Venice.

Verdi was now famous and wealthy, although he was not immune to failure: *Simone Boccanegra* (1857), which followed *Les Vêpres siciliennes* (1855), was not well received. Verdi was to revise it twenty-four years later. His next opera, *Un ballo in maschera*, which concerns the assassination of Gustavus III Adolphus of Sweden, premiered in Rome in 1859. Like a number of Verdi's previous operas, it was subject to censorship—the authorities were wary of having an assassination depicted on the stage.

In 1859, political events once more came to the fore. To Verdi's delight, Milan was liberated, and after Parma voted to join neighboring Modena, Verdi was elected as deputy to the new assembly. He led a delegation to Vittorio Emanuele, King of Piedmont, to request the union of Parma with Piedmont. In 1861, Verdi was reluctantly persuaded to stand for election to Italy's new national parliament, and he remained a member until 1865. He did not care for the day-to-day business of politics. In the 1860's Verdi wrote only two operas: *La forza del destino* (1862), which was first performed in St. Petersburg in the presence of Czar Alexander II, and *Don Carlos* (1867). The latter was based on Friedrich Schiller's verse drama of the same name, and the libretto was in French.

In the last twenty-two years of his life, Verdi entered yet another creative phase. *Aïda*, commissioned by the Khedive of Egypt to mark the opening of the Suez Canal, was first performed in Cairo in December, 1871. Verdi stayed in Italy preparing for the performance in Milan, which followed shortly afterward. Full of pageantry and spectacle, *Aïda* was his greatest success. It has been called the last grand opera, and yet in spite of its vastness—a performance can use up to five hundred extras—the tender emotions of the three main characters, caught in a love triangle, are intimately conveyed. After the success of *Aïda*, Verdi seemed to have reached the summit of his career. Yet three great works were still to come. The first of these was the *Messa da requiem* (1874), in memory of the Italian poet and patriot Alessandro Manzoni, which is notable for the dramatic rather than devotional quality of the music.

For more than a decade following this work, Verdi lived in virtual retirement on his estate at Sant' Agata. He only reluctantly agreed to write *Otello* when he was shown the outstanding libretto, based on Shakespeare's play and written by the Italian poet Arrigo Boito. *Otello* was first performed at La Scala in February, 1887. It was another triumph: the musical event of the decade and Verdi's finest tragic opera. Verdi's final great work, *Falstaff* (1893), was an astonishing feat for a man in his eightieth year. It was his first comic opera in fifty years, and the libretto was again written by Arrigo Boito, based on Shakespeare's *The Merry Wives of Windsor*, with some material from *Henry IV*. Full of warm humor, fast-paced, and subtle, *Falstaff* was first performed at La Scala, in February, 1893. Verdi's last works were religious and included *Te Deum* (1896) and *Stabat Mater* (1897). In 1897, his wife died, and in January, 1901, while in Milan, Verdi suffered a stroke. He died six days later, on January 27, at the age of eighty-seven.

Summary

In spite of the fact that a large number of Giuseppe Verdi's twenty-six operas were hugely successful in his lifetime and that many of them quickly became part of the international repertory, full critical appreciation of his work was slow in coming. For some years after his death, only *Otello* and *Falstaff* were considered worthy of serious praise. The situation began to change first in Germany in the 1920's, with the Verdi Renaissance. This was partly a reaction against Verdi's great contemporary, Richard Wagner; indeed, during this period, there were almost as many performances of Verdi's operas in Germany as there were of Wagner's and far more than those of any other composer. Since then Verdi's reputation has steadily grown throughout the world. At least six of his operas, *Rigoletto*, *Il trovatore*, *La traviata*, *Aïda*, *Otello*, and *Falstaff*, are universally acknowledged as masterpieces and are among the most frequently performed, and best loved, of all operas. In addition, the *Messa da requiem* has power to rouse those who do not normally respond to religious music.

Verdi revolutionized nineteenth century opera. As an innovator, he was second only to Wagner. He quickly outgrew the operatic conventions of the period, which valued beautiful melodies and demonstrations of vocal agility more than dramatic action. Particularly from *Aïda* onward, Verdi perfected a form of continuous music drama, quite distinct from that of Wagner, in which the music served as an expression of character and dramatic situation. In this he proved himself equal to the daunting task of putting Shakespeare, the dramatist he most revered, into operatic form. These final works of Verdi reveal his technical mastery, psychological insight, and that deep sympathy for humanity—its passions, sufferings, follies, and nobility—that pervades his work as a whole.

Bibliography

Budden, Julian. *The Operas of Verdi*. 3 vols. New York: Oxford University

Press, 1973-1981. Three of the most impressive volumes ever written on Verdi. Volume 1 covers Verdi's first seventeen operas and includes plot summaries and biographical background. Shows how Verdi outgrew the conventions of nineteenth century Italian opera. Volume 2 covers *Il trovatore* to *La forza del destino* and includes details of Verdi's revisions and alterations. Volume 3 analyzes the composition, structure, and first performances of *Don Carlos*, *Aïda*, *Otello*, and *Falstaff*. Also discusses the creative process, the relationship between composer and librettist, and Verdi's relationship to contemporary Italian composers.

Conati, Marcello, ed. *Encounters with Verdi*. Translated by Richard Stokes. Ithaca, N.Y.: Cornell University Press, 1984. A major contribution to Verdi studies. Contains fifty eyewitness accounts written by Verdi's contemporaries who knew him, including composers, artists, musicians, critics, and journalists. Covers the period 1845-1900. Much of the material is previously unpublished. Conati's excellent introductions and extensive notes further illuminate Verdi's life and music. Also includes bibliography and index.

Gatti, Carlo. *Verdi: The Man and His Music*. Translated by Elisabeth Abbott. New York: G. P. Putnam's Sons, 1955. One of the most important and enjoyable biographies. Originally published in 1931. Gatti, who as a young man knew Verdi, writes tenderly and affectionately about the man he admired.

Toye, Francis. *Giuseppe Verdi: His Life and Works*. London: William Heinemann, 1931. One of the first comprehensive studies of Verdi in English. Divided into two parts. The first is intended for the general reader and surveys Verdi's life and music; the second is more specialized, treating each opera in detail, including an account of the librettos and their origins.

Verdi, Giuseppe. *Letters of Giuseppe Verdi*. Edited, compiled, and translated by Charles Osborne. New York: Holt, Rinehart and Winston, 1972. Contains nearly three hundred letters written by Verdi between the ages of thirty and eighty-seven. Verdi did not expect these candid, down-to-earth, pithy letters to be published; they reveal his immense care for every detail of his craft and give insight into his dealings with theater directors, publishers, and librettists. Contains a biographical introduction.

Weaver, William, and Martin Chusid, eds. *The Verdi Companion*. New York: W. W. Norton, 1979. Ten short essays on various topics, including Verdi's relationship with the Risorgimento, with the city of Milan, and with librettists, as well as his attitude to operatic texts and his relationship to contemporary Italian opera. Includes a critical bibliography, a seventy-page chronological timetable of his life, and a list of major works by date of first performance.

Bryan Aubrey

JAN VERMEER

Born: October 31, 1632; Delft, United Provinces
Died: December, 1675; Delft, United Provinces
Area of Achievement: Art
Contribution: Although most scholars firmly attribute fewer than thirty-five
paintings to the hand of Vermeer, he is considered a master of seventeenth
century Dutch painting and a major artist of the Western world.

Early Life

The city of Delft was both a commercial center and a provincial place at
the time of Jan Vermeer's birth in 1632. The city's artistic traditions reflected the court of the House of Orange in The Hague, since the court had
once been in Delft and city-court ties remained strong. Little is known of
Vermeer's early life. His father was a silk weaver who was also an art dealer
and a member of the Guild of St. Luke, to which artists, dealers, and artisans belonged. He owned a large house, the "Mechelen," which contained
an inn in the market square of Delft. The young Vermeer may not have
inherited his father's role as innkeeper, but he apparently took over the art
dealership in 1652 and continued to buy and trade paintings until his death.
Since Vermeer painted very few works annually, he would have needed the
dealership to support his wife and the eight children who survived infancy.
In April, 1653, he married Catharina Bolnes and reared all of their children
in her faith, although Catholicism was not in favor in the United Provinces.
A master in the Delft Guild of St. Luke, Vermeer was elected to its governing board and twice was elevated to the highest office as dean.

Few documents remain to testify to Vermeer's training as an artist. Certainly he would have been influenced by the paintings which his father—and
later he himself—bought and traded. He would have visited the studios of
other artists in Delft. He may have studied with the Delft painter Leonaert
Bramer. Bramer served on the guild's governing board and was a witness for
Vermeer at the time of his betrothal to Catharina Bolnes. Bramer had traveled and knew the work of Michelangelo da Caravaggio and his followers,
the Haarlem Classicists, and Flemish artists. Vermeer's appreciation of these
works is known by the type of paintings he owned and also by his own
paintings. Vermeer was also influenced by one of Rembrandt's students,
Carel Fabritius, who settled in Delft around 1650. Both Vermeer and Fabritius shared a common interest in perspective and optics, the close interaction
of figure and environment, and light and shadow effects.

Vermeer's early work consisted of biblical and mythological subjects,
such as *Christ in the House of Martha and Mary* (c. 1654-1655) and *Diana
and Her Companions* (c. 1655-1656). *The Procuress* (1656), Vermeer's earliest dated painting, probably was intended to suggest an episode from the

story of the prodigal son, a common theme in Dutch art. Indeed, many of his subjects in both early and mature works correspond to well-established iconographic tradition. His unique talents did not depend on the types of scenes he portrayed but rather the way in which he depicted them.

Life's Work

Vermeer is known as a poetic painter whose mature work consists almost entirely of quiet, intimate interior scenes which contain one or, at most, two persons. The viewer almost has a sense of intruding on someone's privacy when studying the carefully composed scene, for example, a picture of a young woman going about her daily tasks. The subject matter is restricted and the environment consists of the same or similar rooms. The entire scene is captured in such a luminous, pearllike atmosphere that even the most commonplace task seems to take on extraordinary significance. A cool light envelops the forms, flowing smoothly over a soft patterned tablecloth, enhancing the crisp white linen of a woman's headdress, picking out three-dimensional highlights on a metallic bowl, and finally dissolving itself in the velvety darkness of a heavy curtain fold.

In many ways, Vermeer's approach to painting was not unlike that of other Dutch painters in the second half of the seventeenth century. They were interested in realism, in light and texture, and in an accurate depiction of three-dimensional space. Some were quite interested in their subjects' psychological response to the environment. These artists recorded in great detail the ordinary objects of daily life—the ever-popular maps and paintings with which they decorated their interior walls, the textures of clothing and curtains, the polished gleam of a chandelier, the cool black-and-white checkerboard patterning of floors, and the way sunlight spread across a room from an open window. Like them, Vermeer's apparent realism sometimes carries overtones of symbolism and reference with which viewers of the time could identify. Earlier Flemish artists, such as Robert Campin and Jan van Eyck, had used extensive symbolism in their religious paintings. A taste for allegorical content continued in seventeenth century Dutch art. Sometimes the symbolism was obvious. In *The Allegory of Painting* (1666-1667), for example, Vermeer depicts an artist, seated on a stool and with his back to the viewer, painting his young model who wears a crown of laurel and holds both a trumpet and a heavy volume of Thucydides. She represents Clio, the muse of history, and Vermeer seems to suggest that she should be the artist's inspiration and source of fame, since history painting was considered the highest category of art. The large map prominently displayed on the back wall implies that the country's fame will be enhanced by the artist's work. Vermeer's clientele probably was limited to the more intellectual and refined person who would immediately have recognized and appreciated the implications of the painting.

Emblem books, popular throughout Europe in the sixteenth and seventeenth centuries, contained a moral which often was abstrusely presented. Thus a letter or a musical instrument in a painting could often be identified with the emotion of love. In the same manner, Vermeer often included in his work a "painting within a painting"—a map or landscape or seascape on the wall which carried some reference to the main subject. Unlike many of his contemporaries, however, who delighted in lively narrative carrying a didactic theme, Vermeer seldom indulged in storytelling and his references are much more subtle. In Vermeer's famous *The Love Letter* (1669-1670), for example, in which the mistress has just received a letter given to her by a servant, the seascape on the back wall, showing a calm sea, was understood as an omen of good luck in love. This emotion is reinforced by the musical instrument held by the mistress.

Vermeer shared with others of his time a keen interest in the mirror and lens and optical devices, such as the camera obscura. By using this, an image could be focused on a surface opposite the light source. Thus the artist could experiment with heightened contrasts of light and dark, enhancement of color, variations of perspective, and halation of highlights. It would appear from his paintings that Vermeer did not trace directly from the image but instead used the camera obscura as but another means to explore expressive possibilities.

Realist that he was, Vermeer was nevertheless far from being merely an imitator of nature. More than his contemporaries, he is noted for his success in bringing a mood of intimacy to a scene, while at the same time setting up a psychological tension that compels the viewer to continued investigation of the canvas. Relatively recent theories of perspective fascinated Dutch artists of the time, but Vermeer utilized its expressive potential rather than a rigid formula. He also changed the scale of the same maps and wall paintings to fit a particular work. Sometimes his background is dark and sometimes quite light to fit a special artistic vision. No one is more successful than Vermeer in creating a psychological mood between subject and environment.

Scholars have often remarked on Vermeer's special quality of pearly light. It does not startle with sudden contrasts, as is seen in some of the great Italian masters. It is nevertheless equally dramatic in the subtle way in which it envelops and defines each form, sparkles in highlights, and creates an interlocking perfection within the composition. This quality of light is beautifully demonstrated in *View of Delft* (c. 1660-1661). Larger than most of Vermeer's works, the painting seems to draw the viewer into a crystal-clear atmosphere of a huge, cloud-filled sky and shimmering water against a background cluster of buildings. Although Vermeer adjusted perspective and scale in this scene, he followed a long Dutch tradition of topographic views of cities.

The Astronomer (1668) is one of the only two dated paintings by the artist and offers a good example of his mature style. It probably is a companion piece to *The Geographer*, and both show the rare male figure in Vermeer's work, engaged in scholarly pursuits. The facile handling of lights and darks and the typical air of preoccupation in the subject matter represent Vermeer at his best. The gloves and maps so carefully represented reflect the intense scientific interests of the period.

The exact chronology of Vermeer's works continues to cause lively debate among scholars, since only two paintings are dated. Generally, it can be ascertained that in the early works brushstrokes are not as free and expressive, planes of color are less sharply defined, there is a greater concentration on specific texture, and the focus of the composition is more centered. *The Guitar Player*, usually dated in the early 1670's, indicates Vermeer's greater freedom of technique in his later years.

Summary

The works of Jan Vermeer are extremely popular. Museums fortunate enough to hold works by this artist treasure them immensely, and it is rare for a Vermeer painting to come on the art market. Despite these facts, the artist's name was not widely known until the middle to late nineteenth century. Even though he was an official of St. Luke's Guild twice, little is known about commissioned work by Vermeer and no certain record of possible students he may have had has been located. The earliest principal source of information on seventeenth century Dutch artists was a book written by Arnold Houbraken, published around 1720. It only mentions Vermeer's name and birth date. Since the number of Vermeer paintings is so small and probably those who owned them were a select and sophisticated group of collectors, very little information about the artist and his contributions was widely disseminated.

In 1866, the French critic Théophile Thoré (the pseudonym of W. Bürger) wrote a series of articles praising Vermeer's work with much enthusiasm. Within a short while, Vermeer's popularity was such that his name was often mentioned in art-historical writing and many of his works that had heretofore been attributed to more fashionable artists were returned to him. His popularity also presented a fertile field for forgers; the famous trial, in 1945, of Hans van Meegeren on charges of forging Vermeer's work spotlighted the avid interest of both scholars and the public in this artist.

The Impressionists of the late nineteenth century were greatly affected by Vermeer's sensitivity to his subject and his handling of light and color. Several of the French Impressionists, including Pierre-Auguste Renoir, considered Vermeer one of the greatest artists. There is little doubt that art historians will continue to probe the enigma that is Vermeer. It is even more certain that an increasing number of art lovers will discover and respond favorably to the works of the great master of Delft.

Bibliography

Alpers, Svetlana. *The Art of Describing: Dutch Art in the Seventeenth Century.* Chicago: University of Chicago Press, 1983. Essential reading for all students of seventeenth century Dutch art. Alpers relates seventeenth century Dutch painting to the primacy of visual representation, which confirmed seeing and representing over reading and interpretation as the means of a new knowledge of the world. An excellent chapter on the works of Rembrandt and Vermeer.

Blankert, Albert. *Vermeer of Delft: Complete Edition of Paintings.* Oxford: Phaidon Press, 1978. Contains sections of Vermeer documents by Rob Ruurs and provenances of all Vermeer pictures by Willem van de Watering. Argues Vermeer's high reputation among eighteenth century connoisseurs even when his paintings are attributed to others of greater renown at that time. Best overall resource for general reader and student.

Koningsberger, Hans. *The World of Vermeer, 1632-1675.* New York: Time, 1967. An excellent overview of Vermeer within the context of his time, especially useful as an introduction to the artist. Discusses and illustrates works of earlier Dutch artists who pioneered in developing the Dutch golden age in art. Artistic tastes, influences of the time, and the contemporary art market are addressed in clear terms. Excellent color plates.

Slatkes, Leonard J. *Vermeer and His Contemporaries.* New York: Abbeville Press, 1981. Numerous full-color reproductions enhanced by solid discussion of individual works by a recognized scholar in seventeenth century Dutch art. Discusses many artists of the 1650's and 1660's who were influenced by Vermeer. A brief introduction outlines recent scholarship. Includes a comprehensive summary of iconography and Dutch art in general. Useful for the undergraduate and the general reader.

Vermeer, Johannes. *The Paintings: Complete Edition.* Introduction, catalog, and attribution by Ludwig Goldscheider. 2d ed. London: Phaidon Press, 1967. The notes to the plates are outstanding, referring to important iconological interpretations and suppositions on Vermeer's use of optical means to enhance reality. Summarizes almost all significant earlier publications. Many reproductions improved and rearranged from 1958 publication. Detailed information on important scholarship by P. T. A. Swillings, Hofstede de Groot, and others.

Wheelock, Arthur K., Jr. *Jan Vermeer.* New York: Harry N. Abrams, 1981. Excellent full-page color reproductions of Vermeer's paintings enhance this book, which is an excellent introduction to Vermeer for both the undergraduate and the general reader. A small but select bibliography covers recent scholarship on the artist. Each full-page plate has a facing page of interpretative text. The introductory section places Vermeer in context of his time.

Mary Sweeney Ellett

PAOLO VERONESE
Paolo Caliari

Born: 1528; Verona, Republic of Venice
Died: 1588; Venice
Area of Achievement: Art
Contribution: Veronese was one of the greatest painters in sixteenth century Venice and, along with Titian and Tintoretto, was responsible for the countermannerism which characterized the style of that school of art. His luminous colors and dynamic, decorative compositions foreshadow the artistic concerns of the next century's painters.

Early Life

Paolo Veronese was born Paolo Caliari in 1528 in Verona, Republic of Venice. His father, Gabriele di Piero Caliari, was a sculptor and stonecutter in that city, and in all likelihood Veronese received his earliest artistic instruction in his father's studio, perhaps learning to model in clay. Further training came in the painting workshop of his uncle, Antonio Badile, and he may also have worked for a time with the painter and architect Giovanni Caroto.

Veronese appears to have remained in Verona until around 1552, when he left to execute commissions in various north Italian cities, including Mantua, where he worked on an altarpiece for the cathedral with several other painters. It is not clear exactly when he first settled in Venice, but in 1553 he was given work at the Venetian Ducal Palace. This important commission, also a collaboration, involved painting the ceiling of the room where the Council of Ten met for deliberations (Sala del Consiglio dei Dieci).

Veronese's style during his earliest period was in line with the sophisticated mannerism popular in Italy during the middle of the sixteenth century. In particular, his early work shows the influence of Emilian artists such as Parmigianino. As he matured, however, his style evolved a more classical handling of space and form. A natural predisposition for pictorial compositions, along with the influence of Titian's style, seemed to account for this countermannerist development.

Life's Work

Veronese is generally considered, along with Titian and Tintoretto, one of the greatest painters of sixteenth century Venice. His paintings, frequently of immense size and crowded with figures, are like tapestries filled with color and light. The sumptuous textures, details, and colors create patterns which emphasize the decorative qualities of what is, emphatically, a joyful, aristocratic art. Veronese's colors are pure and clear, a combination of pale and vivid tones, unsubdued by shadows or glazes such as those of Titian and Tintoretto.

Within a few years of his arrival in Venice, Veronese was given a commission which, along with his work in the Ducal Palace, established his reputation as one of Venice's preeminent painters. For the Church of San Sebastiano, he executed, around 1556, a series of frescoed murals and canvas ceiling paintings. The ceiling paintings in particular demonstrate dramatic compositional arrangements. Exploiting the position of the paintings above the viewer's head, Veronese employed perspective to create the illusion that the ceiling had opened up and that the scenes being depicted were in fact happening while the viewer looked up from below. In *The Triumph of Mordecai*, horses shy at the edge of an abyss in which, spatially speaking, the viewer stands. Lords and ladies look directly down from a balcony. Veronese was not the first artist to use this illusionistic device (called *di sotto in su*). Andrea Mantegna had employed it in the fifteenth century, and Corregio had explored its possibilities. Veronese, however, developed its full pictorial and atmospheric potential and served as a reference for Baroque artists of the seventeenth century.

Veronese appears to have spent most of his mature career in and around Venice. He did visit Rome sometime between 1555 and 1560, where he saw the work of the High Renaissance masters, but most of his travels took him to cities near Venice. Around 1561, he executed a series of frescoes at the Villa Barbaro in Maser, and in 1575 he is documented as working in Padua on a *Martyrdom of Saint Justina* and *An Ascension of Christ*. In the late 1570's, Veronese received one of his most important commissions. A 1577 fire had destroyed the painted decorations in the Hall of the Great Council (Sala del Maggior Consiglio) of the Ducal Palace, and Veronese was hired to repaint the ceiling. His central allegorical scene, *The Triumph of Venice*, combines the illusionism of the San Sebastiano ceiling paintings with a new spatial expansiveness full of strong, almost unearthly highlights and pure color.

Veronese's personal life was fairly uneventful. He married Elena Badile, the daughter of his teacher, in 1566 and had two sons. By all accounts he was a religious, morally strict man. It is ironic, then, that his name has been immortalized not only for his art but also for the fact that he was called before the Inquisition to defend one of his paintings.

In April of 1573, Veronese completed a painting depicting the Last Supper for the refectory of Saints Giovanni and Paolo in Venice, to replace a work of the same subject by Titian which had been destroyed by fire in 1571. Three months later, he was summoned to appear before the Holy Tribunal, or Inquisition, to answer complaints against the work. Specifically, the church hierarchy was concerned by what it perceived as a lack of decorum in the composition. The crowded painting showed, in addition to the traditional Christ and apostles, dwarfs, buffoons, drunkards, and Germans. These superfluous figures, added for picturesque and decorative effects, violated the decrees of the Council of Trent, which, in its codification of the tenets of the Counter-Reformation, had stated that religious paintings should contain no distortions or distractions which might interfere with the moral message. The transcript of Veronese's interview with the tribunal survives and shows him deflecting the criticism with naïveté, claiming that he added the excess figures for compositional, or artistic, purposes. The tribunal decided that Veronese was to make corrections at his own expense. Instead, he changed the title of the painting to *The Feast in the House of Levi*, and left it as he had painted it with only the most minor alterations.

Summary

Paolo Veronese is sometimes described by art historians as a proto-Baroque artist. His essentially naturalistic and illusionistic handling of form and space was certainly not in keeping with the mannerist taste which dominated Italian painting during the middle of the sixteenth century. Some of his mature works do, in fact, demonstrate expansive views of space, theatrical compositions, and decorative arrangements of color and light which point to the styles of the next two centuries. At the same time, other of his paintings look back to the pictorial traditions of fifteenth century Venice. In particular, his use of the old tableau composition, with figures lined along a shallow plane before a descriptive Venetian backdrop, hark back to the works of Vittore Carpaccio and Gentile Bellini.

Of the three great masters of sixteenth century Venetian painting (Titian, Tintoretto, and Veronese), Veronese's reputation has suffered the most in recent centuries. Critics often find his decorative compositions lacking in profundity. The perceived deficiencies are not those of talent or technique, but rather in the area of expression. This attitude may say more about the expectations of art in the modern world than about Veronese's intentions and accomplishments.

Bibliography

Cocke, Richard. "The Development of Veronese's Critical Reputation." *Arte Veneta* 34 (1980): 96-111. Discusses the critical attitudes toward Veronese over the centuries and the extent of his influence in each period of art. Especially valuable in describing Veronese's influence on Baroque artists.

_____. *Veronese.* London: Jupiter Books, 1980. A monographic overview of Veronese's life and career, this book is a useful introduction to the artist. Particular emphasis is placed on stylistic issues, although biographic information is also included. Contains one hundred illustrations, with some in color, and a bibliography.

_____. *Veronese's Drawings, with a "Catalogue Raisonné."* Ithaca, N.Y.: Cornell University Press, 1984. A thorough analysis of Veronese's drawings and how they relate stylistically and programatically to their related paintings. Includes a chronology of documentable activities, a bibliography, and illustrations and catalog entries for each drawing. Useful as a supplement to Cocke's monograph cited above.

Fehl, Philipp. "Veronese and the Inquisition: A Study of the Subject Matter of the So-Called *Feast in the House of Levi.*" *Gazette des Beaux-Arts* 58 (1961): 325-354. Discusses the iconography of Veronese's famous painting and the events surrounding the confrontation with the Inquisition.

Goldwater, Robert, and Marco Treves, eds. *Artists on Art.* New York: Pantheon Books, 1972. A translation of the examination of Veronese by the Holy Tribunal regarding his *Last Supper*, later retitled *The Feast in the House of Levi.* The original record is preserved in the Archives in Venice. Most other anthologies of art-historical documents also include this transcript.

Rosand, David. *Painting in Cinquecento Venice: Titian, Veronese, Tintoretto.* New Haven, Conn.: Yale University Press, 1982. This work contains readable, scholarly articles investigating the sources and influences on Veronese's compositions, including fifteenth century traditions and contemporary theater designs. Also provides an analysis of Veronese's waning reputation and a synopsis of the examination by the Inquisition. Contains excellent black-and-white photographs and a bibliography.

Madeline Cirillo Archer

ANDREA DEL VERROCCHIO
Andrea di Michele Cione

Born: 1435; Florence
Died: October 7, 1488; Venice
Area of Achievement: Art
Contribution: Verrocchio was one of the best sculptors of the later part of the fifteenth century and a great favorite of the Medici family. He was able to work in silver, bronze, and terracotta as well as marble and was also active as a painter. It was in Verrocchio's workshop that Leonardo da Vinci received his first training.

Early Life

Andrea di Michele Cione, best known to his contemporaries by his nickname "Verrocchio," was the son of Michele Cione and his first wife, Gemma. He was born in Florence, where he grew up and where he spent most of his life. His father, who was in his fifties when Andrea, his first child, was born, worked as a tilemaker or brickmaker and was a member of the Stoneworkers' Guild. He owned a home on the Via dell'Angolo in the parish of San Ambrogio as well as some land outside the city. Andrea's mother evidently died while he was young, for his father remarried and Andrea was reared by his stepmother. In 1452, his father died. The following year, the eighteen-year-old Verrocchio was involved in an incident in which a man was killed in a scuffle outside the walls of the city. Verrocchio had thrown a stone which hit a young wool worker, who subsequently died of his injuries. Verrocchio was brought before the authorities and charged with homicide, but he was acquitted and the cause of the death was determined to be accidental.

According to his sixteenth century biographer, Giorgio Vasari, Verrocchio was largely self-taught; historians have no certain knowledge of when he received his early training or who his teachers may have been. From 1467 onward, his name appears in the surviving contemporary documents as "del Verrocchio," and while a seventeenth century source reports that he received his first training in the shop of a goldsmith named Giuliano da Verrocchi, it is now known that he owed his nickname to the fact that in his youth he was a protégé of an ecclesiastic named Verrocchio. In the tax return which he and his younger brother Tommaso filed for the year 1457, he does state that he has been working as a goldsmith but complains that there is no work in this craft and that he has been forced to abandon it. One early source implies that he was trained by Donatello, and while that is possible, modern critics have also suggested that he may have studied or worked with Desiderio da Settignano or Bernardo Rossellino. In 1461, Verrocchio was one of a number of Florentine artists who were asked to furnish designs for the construction of a chapel in the cathedral at Orvieto, but none of the Florentines received the commission.

Life's Work

Verrocchio emerges as an important artist only in the late 1460's. His earliest authenticated works are decorative or architectural, and two of them were commissioned by the Medicis, marking the beginning of his long association with that family. The marble, brass, and porphery tombstone for Cosimo de' Medici in the Church of S. Lorenzo, Florence, was completed in 1467. By 1472, the year in which he was listed as a painter and carver in the records of the Florentine artists' professional association, the Guild of Saint Luke, he had completed his first major work and one of his most important ones: the tomb of Piero and Giovanni de' Medici in the Church of S. Lorenzo. Verrocchio employed virtually no figural decoration and no Christian symbolism, but the tomb has a solemn majesty which derives from his characteristic combination of simplicity of design and great richness of detail.

Verrocchio's famous bronze *David* in the Museo Nazionale di Bargello in Florence was probably commissioned in the early 1470's and is certainly one of the earliest of his figural compositions. Like Donatello's bronze *David*, it was a Medici commission, but there is an embellishment of the forms that signals the change in Florentine taste toward the richer and more sumptuous taste that marks the late fifteenth century. At about the same time, Verrocchio completed his most popular work, the wonderful bronze *Putto with a Dolphin* that was part of a fountain in the Medici villa at Careggi. This is a work of great importance for the history of Renaissance sculpture, for it is the first sculpture since antiquity to present equally pleasing views from all sides.

In January of 1467, Verrocchio received the first payments for one of his finest works, the bronze group of *Christ and Saint Thomas* in the central niche on the east front of the Or San Michele in Florence. The niche had originally been designed for a single figure, and the creation of a two-figure, more than life-size group for the narrow space presented unusual difficulties. Verrocchio was able to solve these problems by making the figures very shallow, a fact of which the spectator is unaware, and by letting the figure of Saint Thomas extend out of the niche toward the viewer. It is possible that the creation and execution of these figures may have occupied him for as long as eighteen years, for they were not placed in the niche until June of 1483.

Verrocchio also carried out several important commissions in marble, of which one of his finest is the half-length *Portrait of a Woman*, a work that bears a strong resemblance to Leonardo's *Portrait of Ginevra dei Benci*. None of his monumental marble works, though, remains in its original condition. The earliest of these was the monument to Francesca Tornabuoni, which was set up in the Church of S. Maria sopra Minerva in Rome, where the Tornabuoni family of Florence had a chapel. It may have been executed in the late 1470's, but very little of it remains. Of the monument to Cardinal Niccolò Forteguerri, there are at least some substantial remains and the original appearance of the work can be partially reconstructed from the large terracotta sketch held in the Victoria and Albert Museum in London. In May of 1476, Verrocchio's model was chosen from among five competitors by the council of Pistoia, the cardinal's native city. The monument was to be erected in the Cathedral of Pistoia, but the execution dragged on and several figures and some of the architectural framework were still not finished when Verrocchio died. The monument was given its present form in the mid-eighteenth century. Verrocchio also was responsible for some of the decoration of the huge silver altar frontal for the altar in the Florentine Baptistery. This masterpiece of the goldsmith's art had been begun in the fourteenth century, and generations of artists had contributed to it. In 1480, Verrocchio completed the silver relief representing *The Beheading of Saint John the Baptist*, which was placed on the lower right side of the altar.

Verrocchio and his studio regularly produced paintings as well as sculpture, but very few paintings can now be identified as his with any certainty. Of the many half-length Madonnas which have been attributed to him, there is little agreement as to which, if any, may be actually by him. The *Madonna Enthroned with Saints John the Baptist and Donatus* was commissioned from Verrocchio not long before 1478, but much of the execution seems to be by Lorenzo di Credi, who worked with Verrocchio and often collaborated with him. Verrocchio's best painting, and the only one which is universally agreed to be his, is the *Baptism of Christ*, which probably dates from the mid-1470's. Vasari's statement that one of the kneeling angels is by Leonardo, who was in Verrocchio's studio in 1476, is generally accepted. What is clear is that Verrocchio depended heavily on pupils, members of his workshop, and collaborators to produce the paintings which were commissioned from him.

The last years of Verrocchio's life were devoted to the design of what was to become his masterpiece: the over life-size *Equestrian Statue of Colleoni* in Venice. The noted Renaissance soldier Bartolommeo Colleoni of Bergamo had died in 1475 and in his will left funds for a commemorative equestrian statue to be erected in his honor in Venice. Verrocchio's full-scale model was completed in the summer of 1481, and in 1483 Verrocchio moved to Venice, where he remained until his death in 1488. At the time of his death, no parts of the work had yet been cast and it was not until 1496 that the work was completed and installed on a high pedestal in the Piazza of SS. Giovanni e Paolo. Although he never lived to see its completion, it is in every way the supreme achievement of his artistic genius.

Summary

Andrea del Verrocchio's contribution to the development of monumental sculpture during the Renaissance is a major one. Only Donatello ranks with him. Verrocchio's workshop was one of the largest and most active in Florence, and in his mastery of all facets of the visual arts he provided a role model for his greatest pupil, Leonardo da Vinci. Leonardo's conception of the artist as a man of science, versed in all aspects of engineering and anatomy as well as design, owes much to Verrocchio's example. It would be unfair, however, to see Verrocchio's achievement primarily in terms of the accomplishments of his best pupil. In his own right, he is one of the most characteristic artists of the Florentine Renaissance. The naturalistic element in his work is very strong, and in this he reflects the dominant ideal of the Florentine artist of his day: fidelity to nature. All aspects of the natural were to be studied and understood, but for Verrocchio this naturalism was never an end in itself. Instead, it was the means by which he could create a perfect and untarnished world of forms and ideal types. Verrocchio's contemporaries fully appreciated this aspect of his work. One of them noted that his head of Christ in the group of *Christ and Saint Thomas* was thought to be "the most beautiful head of the Saviour that has yet been made."

His masterpiece, the monument to Colleoni, shows how effectively he was able to balance these two tendencies. It is a work of enormous power, and the violent and aggressive twist of the rider's body gives a sense of tremendous energy waiting to be unleashed. To achieve this effect, Verrocchio has twisted the figure to the limits of human possibility. Similarly, the brutal face is an unflinching delineation of a type, not an individual, but it is rendered so plausibly that it seems more vital than any portrait. No fifteenth century artist better exemplified the artistic ideals of the era.

Bibliography

Covi, Dario A. "Four New Documents Concerning Andrea del Verrocchio." *The Art Bulletin* 48 (1966): 97-103. New and important documents dealing with the life of the artist and his work.

Passavant, Günter. *Verrocchio: Sculptures, Paintings, and Drawings: Complete Edition*. Translated by Katherine Watson. London: Phaidon Press, 1969. The best general modern survey. The text covers all aspects of Verrocchio's work, and there is a catalog of the sculptures, paintings, and drawings, which the author believes to be authentic, as well as information on rejected works.

Pope-Hennessy, John. *Italian Renaissance Sculpture*. London: Phaidon Press, 1958. The best general introduction to the field of Italian Renaissance sculpture, with extensive coverage of the major masters. The short article on Verrocchio is an excellent summary of his work as a sculptor and there are catalog entries of his major works.

Seymour, Charles, Jr. *The Sculpture of Verrocchio*. Greenwich, Conn.: New York Graphic Society, 1971. The best catalog of Verrocchio's sculpture. Contains notes on the principal works, an appendix of documents with translations, and a partial translation, with some explanatory notes, of Vasari's 1568 biography of the artist.

Vasari, Giorgio. *Lives of the Most Eminent Painters, Sculptors, and Architects*. Translated by Gaston du C. de Vere. Vol. 3. London: Medici Society, 1912. The standard translation of the second edition of Vasari's biography of the artist, first published in 1568. This is the only nearly contemporary biography of the artist, written by a man who was born more than twenty years after Verrocchio died. While it is not a reliable source for dates or attributions, it contains a wealth of information available in no other source.

Wilder, Elizabeth. *The Unfinished Monument by Andrea del Verrocchio to the Cardinal Niccolò Forteguerri at Pistoia*. Vol. 7. Photographs by Clarence Kennedy and appendix of documents by Peleo Bacci. Florence, Italy: Printed by M. and S. Tyszkiewicz, 1932. The most thorough study of any of Verrocchio's works. Includes complete documentation and excellent photographs.

Eric Van Schaack

ANDREAS VESALIUS

Born: December 31, 1514; Brussels
Died: October 15, 1564; Zacynthus (modern Zante), Greece
Areas of Achievement: Medicine and physiology
Contribution: Vesalius, a physician and anatomist of the Renaissance, was one of the most important figures in the history of medicine. He published the first modern comprehensive text of human anatomy. His accurate description of the structure of the human body, the result of firsthand dissection, is the basis of the modern scientific study of human anatomy.

Early Life

Andreas Vesalius was descended from a long line of physicians, of whom he belonged to the fifth generation. The family combined scholarly and humanistic interests (several had written medical treatises or commentaries on Arabic and Hippocratic works) with medical ability and ambition, having served the courts of Burgundy and the Habsburgs. Although the family had long lived in Flanders, it had come originally from Wesel on the lower Rhine River, hence the family's name, of which Vesalius is the Latin form. Vesalius' father was apothecary to the court of the Habsburg Emperor Charles V. As a boy, Vesalius dissected dogs, cats, moles, mice, and rats. He attended the University of Louvain from 1529 to 1533, where he studied Latin and Greek. He then went to the University of Paris to study medicine, remaining there from 1533 to 1536. The medical faculty at Paris was under the influence of Galen, the great second century Greek medical writer, whose authority in anatomical matters was unchallenged. Vesalius found that there was little practical teaching of anatomy. Human corpses were dissected only twice a year, but Vesalius found the procedure disappointing. The professor of anatomy never performed the dissection himself but merely read passages from Galen as an assistant dissected the cadaver. In most cases pigs or dogs were dissected. Eager to obtain human skeletons, Vesalius sought them from cemeteries and gallows outside the city, where he obtained corpses of criminals in various states of decay. He became skilled at dissection and gained a firsthand knowledge of human anatomy. He began to acquire a reputation as an anatomist and even conducted a public dissection.

Vesalius left Paris in 1536 upon the outbreak of war between France and the Holy Roman Empire. He returned to Louvain, where he completed his baccalaureate degree in the following year. Thereupon he traveled to Italy and enrolled in the University of Padua, which enjoyed an outstanding reputation. On December 5, 1537, Vesalius received his medical degree with highest distinction. On the following day, he was appointed professor of surgery, which entailed the teaching of anatomy as well. He was only twenty-three years of age.

Life's Work

The young professor was enormously successful at Padua, where he lectured to some five hundred students, professors, and physicians. Dispensing with an assistant, he personally descended from his academic chair to dissect cadavers. He prepared four large anatomical charts to illustrate his lectures. In 1538, he published three of them and three skeletal views, which have come to be known as *Tabulae anatomicae sex* (*Six Anatomical Tables*, 1874). The publication of these accurate and detailed plates marked a major advance in anatomical illustration. In the same year, he published a dissection manual based on Galen, *Institutiones anatomicae* (1538), and in the following year he published *Epistola, docens venam axillarem dextri cubiti in dolore laterali secandam* (1539; *The Bloodletting Letter of 1539*, 1946), in which he argued for the importance of the direct observation of the body.

As a result of his publications and success in teaching, Vesalius began to acquire more than an ordinary reputation. He was reappointed to the medical faculty in 1539 at an increase in salary. In his lectures on anatomy, Vesalius had, as was then customary, expounded the views of Galen, whose authority was accepted in virtually every medical faculty in Europe. In dissections he performed, however, he began to notice discrepancies between what he observed and what Galen had described. At first, so few cadavers were available that there was only limited opportunity for dissection. Beginning in 1539, however, corpses of executed criminals were made available to him. Repeated dissections made it increasingly apparent to Vesalius that Galen's descriptions were erroneous and that Galen had based his descriptions on the anatomy of animals, primarily apes, pigs, and dogs. He expounded his discoveries first at Padua (in his fourth public dissection, at which he ceased to use Galen as a text), then, in 1540, at Bologna, where he was invited to lecture.

As early as 1538, Vesalius had apparently contemplated a major work on anatomy. As his dissections revealed many discrepancies between Galen's anatomy and his own discoveries, he recognized the need for a new and comprehensive text to replace Galen. After his return to Padua from Bologna, he commenced work on one in earnest. Vesalius had woodcut illustrations for the work prepared in Venice, probably in Titian's studio. To produce at least some of the illustrations, he chose a compatriot, Jan Stepfan van Calcar, who belonged to the school of Titian and had drawn the skeletal figures for the plates in *Six Anatomical Tables*. Other painters associated with the school of Titian almost certainly had a hand in the illustrations as well. Vesalius selected a firm in Basel to print the work, and the wood blocks for the illustrations were transported by donkey. In the summer of 1542, Vesalius went to Basel to oversee printing of *De humani corporis fabrica libri septem* (seven books on the structure of the human body; best known as *De fabrica*), which was published in August, 1543. *De fabrica* was one of the most outstanding examples of the bookmaker's art in the sixteenth century. Every detail had been personally supervised by Vesalius: the paper, woodcuts, typography, and famous frontispiece. The woodcuts, showing skeletons and flayed human figures, represented the culmination of Italian painting and the scientific study of human anatomy. They were meant to be studied closely with the text and were so successful that they were frequently plagiarized; they set the standard for all subsquent anatomical illustrators.

In *De fabrica*, Vesalius corrected more than two hundred errors of Galenic anatomy and described certain features that were either previously unknown or had been only partially described. He was not the first to find mistakes in Galen, but he went beyond mere correction by insisting that the only reliable basis of anatomical study was dissection and personal observation. *De fabrica* was the first modern treatise on human anatomy that was not based on Galen or drawn from dissected animals. The most extensive and accurate description of human anatomy that had yet appeared, it surpassed all previous books on the subject. Its publication revolutionized the study of anatomy, not least of all by its outstanding use of illustrations. Vesalius was only twenty-eight years of age when the book appeared, less than a week after the publication of Nicolaus Copernicus' *De revolutionibus orbium coelestium* (1543; *On the Revolutions of the Celestial Spheres*, 1939), which challenged the dominant geocentric theory of Ptolemy as *De fabrica* challenged the anatomy of Galen. Both books aroused violent controversy. Vesalius' fame spread rapidly, and many Italian physicians came to accept his views. Yet Galen's supporters reacted with strong attacks. Jacobus Sylvius, the leading authority on anatomy in Europe and Vesalius' former teacher, published a vitriolic pamphlet against Vesalius, perhaps angered at his attacks on the deficiencies of training in anatomy. Disappointed by the opposition of the Galenists, he abandoned his anatomical studies, burned all of his manuscripts, resigned his chair at Padua, and left Italy to accept the position of third court physician to the Holy Roman Emperor Charles V.

Vesalius was to spend some thirteen years in the service of the emperor, following a family tradition of service to titled houses. In 1544, his father, who had been an apothecary to Charles, died and left a substantial inheritance to Vesalius, who then was married to Anne van Hamme. About a year later, a daughter, his only child, was born. Vesalius spent much of his time traveling with the emperor, who suffered from gout and gastrointestinal disorders. He served as a military surgeon as well, during which time he introduced several new procedures, the most notable of which was the surgical drainage of the chest in empyema. Vesalius enjoyed the full confidence of the emperor, and his professional reputation continued to grow. Upon Charles's abdication from the Spanish throne in 1556 (he had abdicated as Holy Roman Emperor in 1555), he granted Vesalius a pension for life.

In 1546, Vesalius found time to write a short work, *Epistola, rationem modumque propinandi radicis Chynae* (China root letter), in response to a friend who sought his opinion of a fashionable remedy called the China root. In 1552, he began work on a second edition of *De fabrica*, which was issued a few months after Charles's abdication in 1555, though, like the first edition, it was dedicated to the emperor. The new edition was even more sumptuous than the first. Vesalius took the opportunity to revise and correct the text and make a number of additions. In 1556, he took up residence in Madrid as one of the physicians in the service of Philip II, who had succeeded his father, Charles, as King of Spain. Vesalius' reputation was sufficiently outstanding that in 1559, when King Henry II of France was severely wounded in the head during a tournament, he was summoned to Paris, where he joined the distinguished French surgeon Ambroise Paré in treating the king. The wound proved fatal, however, and the king died ten days later. Vesalius' reputation as one of the greatest physicians of the age was secure, and his opinion was repeatedly sought. In 1562, Don Carlos, heir to the throne of Spain, received a severe head injury as the result of a fall. As his condition grew worse, the king summoned Vesalius to join several Spanish physicians in attendance on the infante. Although they distrusted him from the beginning, the Spanish physicians eventually allowed Vesalius to administer a treatment that resulted in a rapid improvement of the prince, who recovered.

In the spring of 1564, Vesalius embarked on a trip to the Holy Land by way of Venice. There is reason to believe that he did not intend to return to Spain. He seems to have been regarded with hostility by the Spanish physicians at court. He was probably motivated as well by a desire to return to an academic position, inspired by reading Gabriello Fallopio's *Observationes anatomicae*, which had been published in 1561. He was offered the vacant chair at Padua of his pupil Fallopio, who had recently died, and he signified his intention to take the position upon his return. He proceeded to Palestine by way of Cyprus, but he became ill on the return journey and died on October 15, 1564. He was buried on the island of Zacynthus.

Summary

The product of a long line of distinguished physicians and Humanists, Andreas Vesalius received a fine Renaissance education, had an excellent Latin style, and excelled in philological scholarship. He was trained in the Galenic system, which was taught in all European medical faculties. Only gradually did he come to see why Galen's anatomical descriptions, based on the dissection of animals, needed correction. Even then he was not wholly able to escape Galen's influence, for he sometimes reproduced his errors. His great contribution to medicine was his insistence that anatomical study be based on repeated dissection and firsthand observation of the human body.

The personality of Vesalius remains somewhat enigmatic. He appears to have been a man of considerable dynastic and personal ambition, who possessed great energy and desire to succeed. A man of genius, he enjoyed an enviable reputation in his own time but was nevertheless sensitive; he resented the attacks that were made on him by former teachers and jealous colleagues. Independent, unafraid of challenging authority, and confident of his own opinions, he combined great powers of observation with a reputation for remarkably accurate prognosis. He defended himself and his opinions when attacked but was willing to accept correction of his own errors.

Vesalius may be called the founder of modern anatomy. The importance that he placed on the systematic investigation of the human body led to dissection's becoming a routine part of the medical curriculum. His *De fabrica* revolutionized the study of anatomy, and its anatomical illustrations became the model for subsequent medical illustrators. Its publication marked the beginning of modern observational science and encouraged the work of other anatomists. Vesalius' ideas spread rapidly throughout Italy and Europe and came to be widely accepted within a half-century, in spite of the continuing influence of Galen. In his remarkable genius and his influence, Vesalius deserves to be ranked among the most distinguished contributors to medical science.

Bibliography

Cushing, Harvey. *A Bio-Bibliography of Andreas Vesalius*. New York: Schuman's, 1943. 2d ed. Hamden, Conn.: Archon Books, 1962. Contains an excellent bibliography of the various editions of Vesalius' writings and secondary literature about him.

Lambert, Samuel W., Willy Wiegand, and William M. Ivins, Jr. *Three Vesalian Essays*. New York: Macmillan, 1952. These essays deal with aspects of the printing and illustrations of *De fabrica*.

O'Malley, C. D. *Andreas Vesalius of Brussels, 1514-1564*. Berkeley: University of California Press, 1964. The definitive biography of Vesalius, which replaces that of Moritz Roth (Berlin, 1892).

Singer, Charles, and C. Rabin. *A Prelude to Modern Science*. Cambridge, England: Cambridge University Press, 1946. A discussion of the history of *Six Anatomical Tables* and its sources.

Vesalius, Andreas. *The Illustrations from the Works of Andreas Vesalius of Brussels*. Introduction and annotations by J. B. de C. M. Saunders and Charles D. O'Malley. Cleveland: World Publishing, 1950. Contains a lengthy introduction describing the life and career of Vesalius and reproduces the woodcuts from *De fabrica* and other works of Vesalius.

Gary B. Ferngren

AMERIGO VESPUCCI

Born: March 14, 1454; Florence
Died: February 22, 1512; Seville, Spain
Areas of Achievement: Exploration and cartography
Contribution: The first European credited with persuading his contemporaries that what Christopher Columbus had discovered was a "New World," Vespucci revolutionized geographic thinking when he argued that this region now bearing his name was a continent distinct from Asia.

Early Life

Amerigo Vespucci was the third son of a Florentine family of five children. His father, Stagio Vespucci, was a modestly prosperous notary and a member of a respected and learned clan that cultivated good relations with Florence's intellectual and artistic elite. The fortunes of the family improved during Amerigo's lifetime, and his father would twice occupy positions of fiscal responsibility in the Florentine government.

Unlike his older brothers, who attended the University of Pisa, Amerigo received his education at home under the tutelage of a paternal uncle, Giorgio Antonio, a Dominican friar. The youth became proficient in Latin and developed an interest in mathematics and geography, an interest which he was able to indulge in his tutor's extensive library. In his uncle's circle, Amerigo also became acquainted with the theories of Paolo Toscanelli dal Pozzo, a Florentine physician and cosmographer who first suggested the possibility of a westward voyage as an alternative route to the Orient, an idea that Columbus and others eventually borrowed.

The study of geography was considered useful for anyone interested in a career in commerce, the profession chosen for Amerigo by his parents. Travel was also considered suitable training for businessmen, and Amerigo accepted the first opportunity when another uncle, Guido Antonio Vespucci, a lawyer, invited the twenty-four-year-old to Paris. The elder Vespucci had been appointed Florentine ambassador to the court of Louix XI in 1478 and had asked his young relative to join him as his private secretary.

In 1482, two years after Amerigo's return to Florence from France, his father died, making Amerigo responsible for the support of the family. The following year, Amerigo became manager of the household of one of the branches of the ruling Medici family, and he performed his task loyally for the next sixteen years. In this capacity, he traveled to Spain at least once to look after the financial interests of the Medicis. He was in Spain again toward the end of 1491 and settled permanently in the city of Seville, where he established financial relations with the city's active Italian merchant community. He would eventually marry María Cerezo, a native of Seville. The couple had no children. -

At the close of the fifteenth century, the port city of Seville was the hub of commercial activity and the center of overseas travel and exploration. The Portuguese had taken the lead in the search for a new route to India by reaching the Orient circumnavigating Africa. Confirmation of the accuracy of their vision came with news that Bartolomeu Dias' expedition had reached the Cape of Good Hope (the southernmost tip of Africa) in 1488. The Spanish lagged behind their Portuguese neighbors until Columbus' triumphant return from his first voyage. The Crown had paid Columbus' expenses, and he was expected to search for yet another alternate route to the East. Following the theories of Toscanelli, Columbus sailed in 1492 and returned to Spain early the following year.

Columbus' initial optimistic reports that he had found a new route to Asia ensured greater interest and opportunities for investment on the part of all who knew of his trip, and Vespucci would soon be involved in several of the many maritime enterprises that mushroomed in Seville in the wake of Columbus' success. Vespucci, as a subaltern of the Italian merchant Giannetto Berardi, assisted Columbus in financing and outfitting a second voyage of discovery, which sailed in 1493. Berardi died before the provisioning of the fleet was complete, and Vespucci assumed the task. It is highly likely that Vespucci and Columbus had many opportunities to meet during this period and that the Florentine's early interest in geography and cosmography was revived as a result of these contacts. The lure of the sea and the prospects of discovery would soon prove irresistible. By 1499, Vespucci had decided to change professions from businessman to explorer.

Life's Work

Much controversy surrounds certain facts about Vespucci's life between the years 1497 and 1499—the period immediately prior to his first generally acknowledged ocean voyage—especially because some of his biographers assert that he, not Columbus, was the first European to discover the American mainland along the coast of northern South America. In order for this assertion to be valid, Vespucci would have had to undertake this voyage before Columbus' third—during which Columbus sailed along the coast of Venezuela—that is, before June, 1498. Vespucci was an inveterate letter writer. The most compelling evidence that he might have gone on this trip appears in a document of dubious authenticity attributed to Vespucci himself, the *Lettera di Amerigo Vespucci delle isole nouvamente trovate in quattro suoi viaggi* (c. 1505; *The First Four Voyages of Amerigo Vespucci*, 1885). This long letter is addressed to the head of the Florentine republic, the gonfalonier Piero Soderini. In this document, the author purports to have made four voyages overseas, the first of which, circa 1497, took him along the Caribbean coast of the American mainland—that is, to Venezuela, Central America, the Yucatán Peninsula, and the Gulf of Mexico, well in advance of Columbus. Since there is little independent evidence to corroborate information about this voyage, many scholars dismiss this episode as a fiction propagated by the letter, which could have been a forgery published by an overzealous and unscrupulous printer eager to cash in on a reading public thirsty for news of and reports from the New World. The fourth voyage described in the letter is also believed to be apocryphal.

What is universally accepted is the fact that Vespucci sailed for the New World as a member of a three-ship expedition under the commmand of the Spaniard Alonso de Ojeda in the spring of 1499. Two of the ships had been outfitted by Vespucci, at his own expense, in the hope of reaching India. Vespucci's expectations were founded on a set of maps drawn from the calculations of Ptolemy, the Egyptian mathematician and astronomer of the second century, whose work *Geōgraphikē hyphēgēsis* (*Geography*) was the foremost authority to fifteenth century Europeans on matters related to the size and shape of the world.

Ptolemy had concluded that the world was made up of three continents: Europe, Africa, and Asia. When Vespucci set out on his voyage in 1499, he expected to reach the Cape of Cattigara, the southernmost point of Asia on Ptolemy's map. Instead, his expedition reached the northern coast of Brazil and the mouth of the Amazon River. From there, Vespucci's ship proceeded southward to the equatorial zone, after which it turned northward to the Caribbean, navigating along the northeastern coast of South America. Seeing houses on stilts that reminded the crew of Venice, they named the area "Venezuela" (little Venice). The entire expedition returned to Spain, with a cargo of pearls and slaves and not the hoped-for Asian spices.

Back in Seville, Vespucci planned a second expedition that would take him farther south along the Brazilian coastal route, but his license to travel was suddenly revoked, on the grounds that he was a foreigner, when the Spanish crown, in competition with the Portuguese, began to treat geographical knowledge as secrets of state. When the ships that made up the expedition sailed in August, 1500, they carried only Spaniards. A Portuguese explorer, Pedro Álvars Cabral, had already claimed Brazil for the Portuguese crown in 1500 and, perhaps because of this fact, Vespucci's knowledge of its northern coast might have been of interest to Portugal. He was summoned to appear before King Manuel I. The monarch commissioned the Florentine to undertake a new voyage of discovery along the coast of Brazil, following Cabral's and Vespucci's own original intentions. Vespucci sailed from Lisbon in the spring of 1501.

This second independently verifiable voyage of Vespucci followed the coast of Brazil, crossed the equator, and proceeded south to Patagonia. Experiences during this last stage convinced Vespucci that Ptolemy's calculations had been mistaken, that the Cape of Cattigara and Asia were not where they were expected to be, and that the landmass before his eyes was more likely a new continent, separate and distinct from Asia. Upon his return to Lisbon, Vespucci, along with geographers and mapmakers, began to redraw and redesign Ptolemy's world to accommodate this new insight. The Atlantic coast of this region began to be detailed in maps that circulated throughout Europe, the first of which appeared in 1502.

Vespucci's employment by the Portuguese did not last long. He returned to Seville in 1502, disappointed that his plans for the exploitation of the new lands were not accepted by Manuel. In Spain, Vespucci's efforts and considerable geographical and navigational knowledge were finally recognized, and in 1505 he was granted citizenship by King Ferdinand II, who appointed him pilot major of the country's board of trade, the Casa de Contratación de las Indias. Vespucci held this position until his death in 1512.

Vespucci is believed to have been short of stature, with an aquiline nose, brown eyes, and wavy hair. This description comes from a family portrait painted by the Florentine muralist Ghirlandajo. Vespucci has also been described as deceitful, self-promoting, and cunning. His reputation suffered after the publication of two letters attributed to him, *The First Four Voyages of Amerigo Vespucci*, mentioned earlier, and *Mundus Novus* (c. 1503; English translation, 1916), an account of Vespucci's 1501 expedition addressed to Lorenzo de' Medici, his Florentine employer. In this second letter, the author argues that the lands he had recently visited (the Atlantic coast of South America) could only be part of a new world.

The ideas contained in the disputed letters, published in many editions and languages shortly after their initial printing, inspired a German mapmaker, Martin Waldseemüller, at Saint-Dié in Lorraine, to draw a new map to accompany narrative descriptions of this new world. The map, which was published in 1507, more closely resembles the geography of the American continent than earlier efforts, separates America from Asia, and assigns to the new land the name America in honor of its presumed discoverer Americus (Amerigo). The feminine version of Amerigo was selected to be consistent with the feminine names of the other continents, Europe, Africa, and Asia. This is the first known example of the use of America as the name of the new continent. The word was quickly accepted by northern Europeans as the rightful name for South America, but it would take some fifty years before southern Europe adopted the name and applied it to the entire American landmass, north and south.

Vespucci's complicity in this matter has never been fully established; some believe that he contributed to his own mythology by making himself the center of attention in all of his correspondence, never mentioning others in his circle under whose direction he might have worked. He is accused of taking credit for the deeds of his collaborators. Defenders of Columbus, the bulk of Vespucci's critics, argue that the new continent should have been named for Columbus rather then for Vespucci the impostor. Columbus, however, was never quite convinced that the lands he had reached were not in Asia and did not live long enough to experience the historical slight in favor of Vespucci.

Summary

Amerigo Vespucci, in spite of the fact that he has been seriously criticized by a number of eminent and revered figures, deserves much of the credit for revolutionizing geographic thinking in Europe. His travels, especially his vain search for Asia following a Ptolemaic map, convinced him that the accepted authority on things geographical was mistaken. To challenge Ptolemy and a scientific tradition of such long standing in sixteenth century Europe was an act of great intellectual and moral courage. While Europeans were slow in accepting the full implications of Vespucci's discoveries, his insights nevertheless received much immediate publicity. Vespucci's ideas captivated the imagination of cartographers and publishers, and a steady stream of historical literature filled the minds of Europe's growing reading public. These accounts fired readers' imaginations. Vespucci's conclusions stimulated the growing community of cartographers, navigators, and geographers. He described his experiences in detail, kept careful records of astronomical, navigational, and geographical observations, and made it possible for his contemporaries to accept the idea of America long before additional eyewitness evidence would confirm the wisdom of his insights.

Bibliography

Arciniegas, Germán. *Amerigo and the New World: The Life and Times of Amerigo Vespucci*. New York: Alfred A. Knopf, 1955. A most admiring biography, which argues vehemently in favor of the authenticity of Vespucci's four voyages. The author dismisses some of the criticism of Vespucci as nationalistic propaganda.

Parry, J. H. *The Discovery of South America*. New York: Taplinger, 1979. An informative and panoramic account of European expansion in America by one of North America's most respected historians. This work is filled with replicas of contemporary maps and charts and is a serious and objective treatment of the period. Parry disputes the authenticity of *The First Four Voyages of Amerigo Vespucci* but credits Vespucci with having contributed to Europe's knowledge of geography and navigation.

Pohl, Frederick J. *Amerigo Vespucci, Pilot Major*. 2d ed. New York: Octagon Books, 1966. The author devotes much attention to Vespucci's mature years, the period of his life that coincides with his voyages overseas. Pohl believes that Vespucci was a most deserving individual and that his fame was legitimately earned. Contains a complete English version of two of Vespucci's letters and two informative appendices.

Vigneras, Louis-André. *The Discovery of South America and the Andalusian*

Voyages. Chicago: University of Chicago Press, 1976. A carefully constructed survey of the separate expeditions from Spain to America beginning with Columbus' first voyage in 1492. A separate appendix is devoted
to Vespucci's Portuguese voyage. The author's treatment of Vespucci
echoes the consensus of contemporary scholarship about him by doubting
the authenticity of two of the four voyages.

Zweig, Stefan. *Amerigo: A Comedy of Errors in History.* Translated by
Andrew St. James. New York: Viking Press, 1942. An account by the
popular Austrian writer who at one point resided in Brazil. Zweig believes
that America received its name because of an error, and he argues that Vespucci's letters are filled with serious factual mistakes and coincidences.
For Zweig, Vespucci's great fame rests on a false foundation.

Clara Estow

GIAMBATTISTA VICO

Born: June 23, 1668; Naples
Died: January 23, 1744; Naples
Areas of Achievement: Philosophy and historiography
Contribution: Vico founded the philosophical study of history and elaborated the theoretical basis for sociological study.

Early Life

Giambattista Vico was one of eight children born to a Neapolitan bookshop owner and his scarcely literate wife. Giambattista was an energetic and prodigious child, already enrolled in school at the age of seven, when a fall from the top of a ladder fractured his skull. The fracture gave rise to a large tumor, and his doctor predicted that the boy would either die of it or grow up an idiot. Although Vico's convalescence was prolonged, neither part of the doctor's prediction came true. Vico came to credit the injury, however, with engendering his lifelong melancholic temperament, the sort of temperament, Vico said, that belongs to all men of ingenuity and depth.

Vico's early formal education was classical, which at the time meant indoctrination into medieval Christian Aristotelianism, but he also spent a great part of his youth in solitary study, which was doubtless encouraged by living upstairs from the family bookshop. At seventeen, Vico went, at his father's urging, to the University of Naples to study law. He read philosophy in his spare time and wrote ornate, metaphysical poetry for relaxation. He quickly grew impatient with the incessant note-taking and memorization of legal cases and quit his university lectures, saying that there was no true learning to be obtained from them. He resumed his devotion to private study of the works of great writers and supported himself by tutoring the nephews of the Bishop of Ischia in Vatolla. He continued to develop his ideas largely by himself for the ensuing nine years and developed passing enthusiasms for the philosophy of Epicurus, Plato, Cornelius Tacitus, Pierre Gassendi, Roger Bacon, René Descartes, and Baruch Spinoza, among others. In 1695, Vico returned to his native city and was appointed four years later to the professorship of rhetoric at the university. This was actually a minor post with a modest stipend; Vico kept the post until shortly before his death.

Life's Work

Vico's ideas gained rudimentary expression in two of the first tracts he published. In a 1709 oration *De nostri temporis studiorum ratione* (*On the Study Methods of Our Times*, 1965), Vico denied the applicability of the Cartesian geometrical method of analysis to the human studies of practical wisdom, ethics, politics, and law. What he wanted to put in its place emerged in a 1710 publication entitled *De antiquissima Italorum sapientia* (partial translation in *Selected Writings*, 1982). Vico focused upon etymology as a source of clues to the truth about human development. The Linguistic analysis utilized a sort of *ingenium*, the power of connecting separate and diverse elements, that Vico thought was necessary for human self-understanding and practical wisdom. This early work of Vico was met with a mixed reception; his critics complained of its obscurity. Nevertheless, Vico submitted it with an application for the chair of civil law at Naples when the post fell vacant in 1723. His rejection was a bitter disappointment and proved to be only the beginning of the neglect he had to endure throughout his carer.

The first edition of Vico's magnum opus, *Principi di scienza nuova intorno alla natura delle nazioni per la quale si ritruovano i principi di altro sistema del diritto naturale delle genti* (*The New Science*, 1948), was published in 1725. Vico had hoped that this work would do for the study of man and culture what Isaac Newton's *Philosophiae naturalis principia mathematica* (1687) had done for mathematical physics. Dissatisfied with its reception, he recast it twice; subsequent editions were published in 1730 and (posthumously) in 1744.

The structure of the third edition of *The New Science* was quite unusual. It contained an elaborate allegorical drawing for a frontispiece, followed by a detailed explanation of the icon. A chronological table followed, which placed in parallel columns the major events in the histories of seven peoples. Next came a catalog of 114 axioms that summarized the assumptions and conclusions of the work. The three remaining sections developed a narrative of human history, the elaboration of Vico's theory that human history manifested three ages: the age of gods, the age of heroes, and the age of men.

According to Vico, history was the gradual process of the humanization of man. In prehistory, bestial giants roamed the endless forests of the earth. Their mental powers were dormant in their enormous bodies so that all thought was sensation. They lived strictly in the present, copulating at inclination and increasing in size by inhaling the vapors of their excrement. The first formation of thunder and lightning elicited a new emotion of fear in the giants; they trembled at the sky and named it Jove. Jove was the first thought. Thus began the age of gods. It is an age whose story was told by Herodotus, when men thought that everything either was a god or was made by gods. Religion brought forth primitive morality, which begot the "might makes right" age of heroes, as characterized by Homer. As human powers of reason were developed to control unruly passions, the age of men was born.

Vico saw these ages as continuing in a never-ending cycle, or *ricorso*, that manifested an ineluctable, providential pattern which he called the "ideal eternal history" of man. Every culture, he believed, passed through these identical stages; each age had a characteristic mode of expression, set of customs, kind of law, and type of religion.

Vico believed his discoveries about the evolution of human civilization to be scientific. The method of inquiry which yielded these results attended precisely to the aforementioned characteristic institutions of each group of people. One of Vico's deepest insights was that man may know himself in a way he can never know what is external to him (that is, nature). Whatever is of man's own making speaks truth about him; this includes cultural institutions, language, and even history itself. Vico expressed this principle by saying that the true (*verum*) and the made (*factum*) are convertible. Thus, a systematic, historical investigation of all the results of human will and contrivance would produce a true understanding of man. Vico believed that this was the only way for man to reach self-understanding.

According to Vico, language study plays a special role in human self-understanding. Vico's original and extraordinarily interesting views on linguistic interpretation were of a piece with his principle of *verum ipsum factum*. He believed that the terms people use, including abstract terms, could be traced to linguistic contrivances of the earliest humans. Etymology thus could illuminate earlier environmental conditions, psychological states, and commonplace activities of human ancestry. That was a result of the fact that language and thought were coextensive for Vico; language was a direct reflection of the development of thought, rather than a tool that was deliberately and artificially constructed. Vico theorized that poetic figures, such as metaphor, in the language of his contemporaries had more directly expressed the experience of humans in earlier ages. Earlier people thought strictly in pictorial images, analogies, and personifications, and these formed the currency of their communication, which involved only gesturing and picture drawing. Vico designated such figures "imaginative universals," and they had a property which third-age ratiocinating men can scarcely recapture: that of invoking a universal image by means of a particular. The abstractions employed in the age of men are the opposite of the imaginative universal. Abstractions hold only what many particulars have in common, but which the particular alone can no longer express (with the exception, perhaps, of particular images in poetic contexts). Similarly, what third-age men call the extravagant fiction of mythology in fact expresses the most fundamental postulates and cognitive associations of the first men. Vico referred to his own saga in *The New Science* as a myth in just this sense.

Although Vico occupied most of his mature years writing reincarnations of *The New Science* in the hope of satisfying his critics, he also penned in his fifty-seventh year an intellectual autobiography. This was a pioneering work of its genre and a fascinating philosophical document in its own right.

Vico gained a very limited fame in his time. He received the honorific recognition of royal historiographer from the sovereign Charles of Bourbon only after his memory was failing and he had been overcome by physical infirmity. After his death, a bizarre quarrel over who should have the honor of carrying his coffin to the grave erupted between the Royal University professors and the confraternity of Vico's parish. The intransigent confraternity took their leave, and as a result the coffin remained at the family home for quite some time. Vico's son finally had to enlist the services of the cathedral to conduct the body to the sepulcher.

Summary

Giambattista Vico's work was largely ignored by his contemporaries, most of whom were enthusiastic Cartesians. He was not without outspoken detractors, however, who ridiculed him as obscure, speculative, and slightly mad. It has been said by twentieth century thinkers, who have the benefit of hindsight, that Vico was simply too far ahead of his time to have had any immediate influence. Yet the relative neglect of Vico's work continued in posterity. A small group of later thinkers have remarked on the importance of Vico, including Karl Marx, Samuel Taylor Coleridge, William Butler Yeats, and Matthew Arnold, but their work did not reflect any direct and significant influence from Vician thought. A very few thinkers have based their thought on Vico's insights: Jules Michelet, Benedetto Croce, and to a certain extent, R. G. Collingwood and Ernst Cassirer. Even though Vico must be credited with being the father of the social sciences and the philosophy of history, his work has yet to join the vanguard of seminal philosophical texts.

Most twentieth century thinkers have come to know Vico through James Joyce. Joyce referred readers who had difficulty with his works to Vico's *The New Science*. Joyce claimed that his imagination grew when he read Vico in a way that it did not from reading Sigmund Freud or Carl Gustav Jung. Joycean texts are replete with references to Vico, and they palpably appropriate Vico's cyclical theory of history as well as his theories of language and myth. Consequently, Vico's thought has enjoyed something of an epiphany in the late twentieth century that may yet certify his status as a great contributor to Western thought.

Bibliography

Adams, H. P. *The Life and Writings of Giambattista Vico*. London: Allen & Unwin, 1935. This biography is one of few which attempt to integrate Vico's life and his thought. It is amusing and elegant, and includes translations of some of Vico's poems. Indexed.

Burke, Peter. *Vico*. New York: Oxford University Press, 1985. A concise treatment of Vico's intellectual development, his main work, and his influence. Indexed, with a helpful list for further reading.

Caponigri, A. Robert. *Time and Idea: The Theory of History in Giambattista Vico*. London: Routledge & Kegan Paul, 1953. An excellent exposition of the main Vician themes of ideal eternal history, *ricorsi*, and the natural law. Densely packed and well indexed.

Crease, Robert. *Vico in English: A Bibliography of Writings by and About Giambattista Vico*. Atlantic Highlands, N.J.: Humanities Press, 1978. Forty-eight pages of bibliographical entries, including a section of works which simply discuss or mention Vico.

Croce, Benedetto. *The Philosophy of Giambattista Vico*. Translated by R. G. Collingwood. London: Howard Latimer, 1913. This now-classic commentary on the totality of Vico's thought may be too complex to serve introductory students, but it is a solid and reliable secondary source for issues not covered in more general literature. Well indexed.

Pompa, Leon. *Vico: A Study of "The New Science."* New York: Cambridge University Press, 1975. A very close analysis of Vico's text is offered here; this work is laced with quotations and helpful interpretations of passages in their context. Indexed, with a short bibliography.

Tagliacozzo, Giorgio, ed. *Vico and Contemporary Thought*. Atlantic Highlands, N.J.: Humanities Press, 1979. This collection of essays is an excellent example of many such works now available which mark a resurgence of interest in Vico's thought. These essays focus on the relevance of Vician insights to urgent twentieth century practical and philosophical concerns. This also contains the first English translation of Vico's essay *De mente heroica* (1732; *On the Heroic Mind*). Well indexed; contributors come from a wide range of disciplines.

Verene, Donald Phillip, ed. *Vico and Joyce*. Albany: State University of New York Press, 1987. Essays discuss Vician themes not only in *Finnegans Wake* but also in *Ulysses* and *A Portrait of the Artist as a Young Man*. Accessible to beginning students of Joyce's literature and Vico's thought. Well indexed; contributors from many disciplines.

Vico, Giambattista. *The Autobiography of Giambattista Vico*. Translated by Max Harold Fisch and Thomas Goddard Bergin. Ithaca, N.Y.: Cornell University Press, 1963. The first one hundred pages of this edition are the translators' introduction to Vico's life and thought; this is perhaps the best one hundred pages on Vico that an introductory student could possibly read. The second one hundred pages are Vico's autobiography, a delightful and accessible work, although it also repays careful scholarly study. Indexed, with a chronological table of Vico's life.

Patricia Cook

ÉLISABETH VIGÉE-LEBRUN

Born: April 16, 1755; Paris, France
Died: March 30, 1842; Paris, France
Area of Achievement: Art
Contribution: Vigée-Lebrun was one of the most celebrated artists of her time and is ranked with the best portraitists of the late eighteenth and early nineteenth centuries. By concentrating on the personalities of her sitters, she broke with the tradition of the empty ceremonial portrait.

Early Life

Élisabeth Vigée-Lebrun, born in Paris on April 16, 1755, was the daughter of Louis Vigée, a pastel portraitist and teacher at the Academy of St. Luke. From ages six to eleven, she attended a convent school, where, as she later recorded in her memoirs, she was constantly drawing whenever and wherever she could. Although, as she stated, "my passion for painting was born in me," her father can be credited with nurturing her ambition to become an artist. During school holidays, the young Élisabeth received her first lessons in drawing and oils from her father and some of his artist friends, especially Gabriel Francis Doyen and P. Davesne, both of whom would encourage her after her father died in 1767. At this time, she also had a few drawing lessons from Gabriel Briard, whom she described as an indifferent painter but a very fine draftsman. While working in Briard's studio in the Louvre, she met the renowned academician Joseph Vernet, who advised her not to follow any system of schools but to study only the works of the great Italian and Flemish masters. Furthermore, he urged her to work as much as possible from nature, to avoid falling into mannerisms. Taking Vernet's advice, she studied the works of such masters as Peter Paul Rubens, Rembrandt, Sir Anthony Van Dyck, Raphael, and Domenichino in public and private collections in Paris, and she made her own studies from nature, using family and friends as models.

The Royal Academy in Paris excluded all women from its classes of instruction; therefore, it was no coincidence that most successful women artists of the time were daughters of artists, receiving their training in their fathers' studios, totally outside the system of academic apprenticeship. Because of her father's early death, Vigée-Lebrun was largely self-taught, having acquired her artistic education by virtue of her own willpower, discipline, and willingness to work long hours. By the time she was fifteen, she was a professional portraitist, earning barely enough money to support her mother and young brother. At age nineteen, she was licensed as a master painter by the Academy of St. Luke and was exhibiting works at the salon there.

Vigée-Lebrun's natural instinct for innovative poses and compositions, combined with her ability to produce a flattering likeness, soon brought her many influential clients. One of the first of these was the Russian nobleman Count Ivan Shuvaloff, whose patronage helped establish her among the aristocracy. It was in 1776 that she received her first royal commission for several portraits of the king's brother—and she also married the art dealer Jean-Baptiste-Pierre Lebrun. Her growing reputation as a painter, coupled with her own attractive personality, now drew the cream of Parisian society to the musical and literary entertainments held in her home.

Life's Work

In 1779, Vigée-Lebrun painted the first of many portraits from life of Marie Antoinette, with the result that her name and her art became closely associated, in the public's mind, with the queen. Royal patronage was responsible, in fact, for Vigée-Lebrun's election to membership in the Royal Academy. While excluding women from its classes, the Royal Academy admitted a few women as academicians, but without all the privileges given to male members. Essentially, academy membership gave a woman only two advantages: some prestige and the right to exhibit in the salons. Earlier, Vernet had proposed Vigée-Lebrun for membership, but it had been denied when Jean-Baptiste Pierre, first painter to the king, objected on the basis of her marriage to an art dealer. Her eventual acceptance in 1783 was said to be attributable to the direct intervention of the queen. Pierre, envious of both Vigée-Lebrun's talent and her obviously favorable standing with the king and queen, then attempted to discredit her, claiming that the painter François-Guillaume Ménageot had retouched her reception piece—an allegorical painting entitled *Peace Bringing Back Plenty*.

Between 1783 and 1789, Vigée-Lebrun exhibited some forty portraits and history paintings in the academy's salon, including the famous *Marie Antoinette and Her Children*, now in the National Museum at Versailles. Painted in 1787, this work is significant for two reasons: First, commissioned by the minister of fine arts to replace an unsatisfactorily casual portrait of the queen and her children by Adolf Wertmüller, it acknowledged Vigée-Lebrun as one of the leading artists in France. Second, it illustrates many of the most important characteristics of her mature style. Using the pyramidal composition of the Italian High Renaissance, she created a didactic work which presents the queen favorably as both ruler and mother. As she so often did, Vigée-Lebrun has translated human emotions—in this case, the love between a mother and her children—into dramatic facial expressions and gestures, while at the same time emphasizing the regal dignity of the queen. The painting illustrates the superiority of Vigée-Lebrun's artistic intellect and technical mastery, as all details of costume and setting combine harmoniously with expression and gesture to give meaning to the work as a whole. This was the painting which she herself considered her masterpiece. It had fortunately escaped destruction when the revolutionary mobs invaded the palace at Versailles because the queen—finding the painting a too-painful reminder after the death of the young prince—had ordered it removed to a storeroom. Near the end of her long career, Vigée-Lebrun arranged for the painting to be exhibited publicly in the Museum of the History of France at Versailles, as evidence of her artistic legacy to the nation.

Given her strong Royalist convictions, Vigée-Lebrun was forced to flee Paris on the eve of the Revolution. In her memoirs, she recorded the details of her flight by public coach—disguised in peasant dress and accompanied by her young daughter—on the very night the mobs dragged the king and queen from Versailles. For the next twelve years, Vigée-Lebrun worked in Italy, Austria, Germany, and Russia. Having already achieved an international reputation as a painter, she was welcomed into aristocratic circles and honored by membership in the local academy in each city she visited. Possessed of an enormous energy for work and never lacking for commissions—for which she demanded fees that no other portraitist could command—Vigée-Lebrun produced some of her best work during these years.

She continued to make her own original contributions to the art of portraiture and to the taste of the time. She retained the virtuoso, almost impressionistic, brushwork that had first appeared in the early portrait of Count Shuvaloff (1775), as well as the bold coloristic effects she had learned from studying Rubens. A good example of her work from this period is her own portrait (1790), which she was asked to add to the Grand-Ducal collection of artists' self-portraits in the Uffizi in Florence. First exhibited in Rome, this work received wide acclaim, with the director of the French Academy there declaring it to be one of the most beautiful things Vigée-Lebrun had ever done. Other noteworthy examples include the portraits she painted in Russia, which are especially remarkable in terms of the variety of their imagery and the originality of composition, reflecting something of the exoticism and melancholy of the country itself.

Returning finally to Paris in 1801, she was received warmly but stayed only a short time, having found the city too much changed from prerevolutionary days. She went on to London and remained there for three years. Again, she found many clients among the aristocracy, including the Prince of Wales. The quality, as well as the popularity, of her work aroused the jealousy of some English artists but brought praise from Sir Joshua Reynolds.

After spending a year in Switzerland, Vigée-Lebrun, now in her fifties, returned to Paris in 1805. She led a quieter life, dividing her time between Paris and her country home in Louveciennes. She painted less, apparently having lost much of the inspiration provided by her early struggles to achieve stature in the art world and the stimulus of her extensive travels, although she continued to exhibit at the salon until 1824. Her last years were spent writing her memoirs and entertaining old friends, as well as many of the leaders of the new Romantic movement. She died in Paris on March 30, 1842, at the age of eighty-six.

Summary

Élisabeth Vigée-Lebrun was one of the most successful women artists of all time, achieving an artistic acclaim during her own lifetime that remained unmatched by any other woman until modern times. She excelled in a field that was popular and very competitive, but her success was not without a price. As the monarchy became more and more unpopular in prerevolutionary France, her accomplishments as a court painter made her a figure of controversy, with both the liberal press and the yellow journals labeling her an immoral woman, the mistress of various court officials, who attained academy membership with a reception piece painted by one of her lovers. Much of the gossip and slander also centered on her well-attended salon and the extravagance of her entertaining. Far from being profligate, she was in fact victimized throughout her life by two men who exploited her talent and appropriated her money for their own ends. The first was her miserly stepfather and the second was her husband, whose gambling debts were a financial drain on her until his death in 1813. Yet she never allowed these problems to interfere with her work. In the more than eight hundred paintings she produced, optimism prevailed. Her work—and the pleasure she took in it—was the driving force of her life.

Bibliography

Baillio, Joseph. *Élisabeth Louise Vigée Le Brun: 1755-1842*. Fort Worth: Kimbell Art Museum, 1982. A catalog of the first twentieth century exhibition of Vigée-Lebrun's work. Contains a brief but informative account of her career, a listing of works exhibited in Paris during her lifetime, and complete notes and documentation of the paintings shown in this exhibition, which were selected from museums and private collections there and throughout Europe.

Harris, Ann Sutherland, and Linda Nochlin. *Women Artists, 1550-1950*. Los Angeles: Los Angeles County Museum of Art, 1976. The catalog of one of the first exhibitions devoted entirely to women artists, it includes a perceptive discussion of Vigée-Lebrun's career and the development of her style as seen in several works in the exhibition. Also, an enlightening account of restrictions endured by women artists, in their training, in relationships with the academies, and in conditions imposed by society.

Petersen, Karen, and J. Wilson. *Women Artists*. New York: Harper & Row, 1976. An appraisal of works by women artists from the Middle Ages to the present. Contains a discussion of Vigée-Lebrun's work, placing it in the context of the eighteenth century.

Vigée-Lebrun, Élisabeth. *The Memoirs of Mme. Élisabeth Louise Vigée-*

Le Brun, 1775-1789. Translated by Gerald Shelley. New York: George H. Doran, 1927. An abridged translation of her memoirs, published originally in 1835-1837. This volume, more widely available than the earlier translation (see below), also includes her previously untranslated notes and portraits of many of the leading figures in the arts and politics of her day, all of whom were personal friends or acquaintances of the artist.

_____. *Memoirs of Madame Vigée Lebrun.* Translated by Lionel Strachey. New York: Doubleday, Page, 1903. A less abridged English translation of Vigée-Lebrun's memoirs. Provides a fascinating account of European society at the time.

LouAnn Faris Culley

SAINT VINCENT DE PAUL

Born: April 24, 1581; Pouy, France
Died: September 27, 1660; Paris, France
Areas of Achievement: Education, religion, and social reform
Contribution: Most renowned for his charitable and educational work, Saint
  Vincent de Paul founded the Congregation of the Mission, the Confrater-
  nities of Charity, and, with Saint Louise de Marillac, the Daughters of
  Charity. He also helped in the revival of French Catholicism, and the Ro-
  man Catholic church has named him the universal patron of its charitable
  institutions.

Early Life

Saint Vincent de Paul was born on April 24, 1581, in Pouy, France. He
was the third of six children in a peasant family and spent his childhood in
poverty. His education, financed through the sacrifices of his parents and his
own work as a teacher, included studies in the humanities under Franciscan
teachers at Dax, France, from 1595 to 1597, and in theology at the University of Toulouse, where he earned the *baccalauréat* in 1604. He was ordained a Roman Catholic priest in 1600. There are unconfirmed stories about
his having been captured by Barbary pirates at sea in 1605 and enslaved in
Tunis for two years before escaping by ship in 1607.

From 1607 to 1608, Vincent was at Avignon and Rome, and at this time
his aspirations were not particularly saintly: He hoped to obtain an ecclesiastical benefice that would enable him to retire to his home and support his
mother. While in Rome, he attracted the attention of Pope Paul V, who sent
him on a mission to the French court of Henry IV. Arriving in Paris in 1608,
Vincent met Pierre de Bérulle, an eminent and otherworldly priest who became Vincent's confessor and spiritual guide and who influenced him profoundly. Between 1609 and 1620, Vincent gradually reoriented his life goals
from the material to the spiritual. Beginning in 1610, he served as almoner
to Queen Marguerite of Valois, the former wife of Henry IV, and in 1612 he
became pastor of the parish of Clichy, near Paris. He served in this position
until 1626, working, according to what he regarded as his special vocation,
among the poor peasantry of the countryside.

During this period, Vincent also served as chaplain (from 1613 to around
1625) to the family of Philippe-Emmanuel de Gondi, general of the French
galleys. This position afforded Vincent the opportunity to work among the
peasants on the Gondi estates, to begin organizing the charitable efforts of
women of means, and to alleviate the sufferings of galley slaves. He directed
the charitable works of Madame Gondi, who persuaded him to deliver, on
January 25, 1617, the sermon on general confession that he considered the
first sermon of his mission. For five months in 1617, Vincent ran the parish

of Chatillon-les-Dombes near Lyons, where he found his first Confraternity of Charity, an organization of pious laywomen who ministered to the sick and the poor. He returned to the Gondi estates late in 1617 with plans to evangelize all of their lands, preaching many missions and organizing charitable confraternities. He also worked to bring spiritual and physical comfort to convicts condemned to forced labor on galleys, and his work was so successful that King Louis XIII made him royal chaplain of the galleys, in charge of all other fleet chaplains, on February 8, 1619.

Vincent was frail in physique; he has been described as sunny, smiling, and humble in facial expression; accounts of his personality reveal a man of patience, kindness, prudence, energy, and courage. His friend and first biographer, Louis Abelly, reports that Vincent was deeply devoted to the divine presence and that each time he heard a clock strike he would make the sign of the cross and renew his awareness of God's presence.

Life's Work

Vincent's success on the Gondi territories led to his founding, on April 17, 1625, of the Congregation of the Mission (also known as Vincentians and Lazarists), with the help of a gift of forty-five thousand livres from the Gondi family. The purpose of the congregation was to preach missions to poor peasants. It was approved by the Archbishop of Paris in April, 1626, given legal existence by the King of France in May, 1627, and finally approved by the Holy See in Rome in 1633. On January 8, 1632, Vincent took over the priory of Saint-Lazare in Paris, and it was there that the congregation's activities were centered until the time of the French Revolution. From Saint-Lazare, 550 missions to the rural poor were organized before Vincent died in 1660. The congregation grew in size and influence; in 1642, a permanent house was opened in Rome, and soon thereafter the pope ordered that all those to be ordained in Rome must make a retreat with the Vincentians.

While he pursued his work among the poor, Vincent also began to make significant contributions as a clerical reformer. Realizing that such reform was necessary for the revitalization of religious life in France, he began giving ten-day retreats in Beauvais in 1626 for men about to be ordained into the priesthood.

In 1633, Vincent worked with Louise de Marillac, whom he had met in 1625, to found the religious congregation of the Daughters of Charity. It was an innovative undertaking: The Daughters of Charity was the first noncloistered religious institute of women devoted to active charitable works. It developed from the Confraternities of Charity, which Vincent had established in Paris and other towns. Vincent composed a rule of life for the daughters, gave them conferences, and governed as superior general of their order. At first, they nursed the poor at home but went on quickly to teach poor children, care for foundlings, and establish hospitals.

Vincent's work as a clerical reformer led him into the field of formal education. In 1636, at Bons-Enfants, he established a seminary for young boys. In 1642, he expanded it to include the first of eighteen seminaries of ordinands conducted by the Vincentians during his lifetime.

Beginning in the late 1630's, Vincent's work carried him more and more into high official circles of the French government. At the request of King Louis XIII, he sent fifteen priests to serve as chaplains with the French army in 1636 and drew up a rule of life and procedures for them. He organized a mission that was preached at court in 1638 and resulted in the formation of a Confraternity of Charity, composed of ladies of the court. He made appeals for peace in war-stricken Lorraine and organized charitable relief there and in other provinces during the Wars of Religion. In 1643, Vincent was called to assist at the bedside of Louis XIII, who was dying. After the king's death, Queen Anne asked Vincent to become her confessor. He also became a member of the Council of Conscience, the body in charge of ecclesiastical matters in France. The council was headed by Cardinal Jules Mazarin, the powerful chief minister who succeeded Cardinal de Richelieu during the regency of Queen Anne. Mazarin, an aggressive politician and worldly man, opposed and thwarted many of Vincent's efforts and ultimately forced him to quit the council in 1653.

One of Vincent's constant concerns during these years was the morals both of the members of the French court and of the public in general. He helped to secure the suppression of indecent plays and books, worked to curb licentious behavior during the Carnival and other festivals, and promoted bans on blasphemy and dueling. He warned the queen against the indecency of the comedies being produced at court.

As a member of the council, Vincent worked, not always successfully, to ensure that only the best candidates would be chosen for the bishopric, and he opposed appointments motivated by nepotism or hopes for political gain. Here again he ran into difficulties with Mazarin; nevertheless, his practical and spiritual guidance was frequently sought by new bishops. It was also sought by reformers within the monastic orders, and Vincent was active in promoting reforms among the Benedictines, Augustinians, and Dominicans.

An orthodox believer, Vincent actively opposed teachings that ran counter to traditional Roman Catholic dogma. He waged a lengthy struggle against Jansenism, a heterodox reform movement that asserted that human nature is essentially evil and that only a small number of humans are predestined to obtain grace and win eternal salvation. He also worked to prevent Jansenist doctrine from being taught at the Sorbonne and rallied the bishops of France to petition the pope to condemn Jansenist errors. Pope Innocent X did so in 1655, as did his successor, Pope Alexander VII, in 1657. Vincent completed writing the rules of his congregation in 1658, falling ill that same year. He died peacefully, his mental faculties intact, on September 27, 1660.

Summary

Vincent de Paul's contemporaries regarded him as a saint; the Roman Catholic church formally beatified him in 1729 and later canonized him on June 13, 1737, proclaiming July 19 as his feast day in the liturgical calendar. His missionary, educational, and charitable works were recognized throughout France and on the Continent during his lifetime, and these works continued to bear fruit after his death. He was one of the most influential social workers in world history; Vincent's own organizations have survived into the twentieth century.

Through his life and works, Vincent has come to epitomize Christian social action for succeeding generations. His example inspired Frédéric Ozanam, a French historian, lawyer, and scholar, to found the Society of Saint Vincent de Paul in the 1830's. This celebrated charitable organization had about two thousand centers in twenty-nine countries by the time of Ozanam's death in 1853 and continues to serve the poor throughout the world. In 1885, Pope Leo XIII declared Saint Vincent de Paul the universal Patron of Charity. He has been honored with the titles of "Father of the Poor" and "The Inspiration of the Clergy."

Bibliography

Coste, Pierre. *The Life and Works of Saint Vincent de Paul*. Translated by Joseph Leonard. 3 vols. Westminster, Maryland: Newman Press, 1952. This 1932 study, which received the French Academy's prestigious Grand Prix Gobert, is the standard biography of Vincent. Complete, methodical, and scholarly, it offers the fullest available account of Vincent's life and achievements. Includes footnotes, indexes, illustrations, and a bibliography.

Kovacs, Arpad F., ed. *St. Vincent de Paul*. Jamaica, New York: St. John's University Press, 1961. Seven essays addressing Vincent's background, life, and influence. They cover the spiritual climate of his century, the social work of Vincent, his relationship to Jansenism, and other topics.

Maynard, Abbé. *Virtues and Spiritual Doctrine of Saint Vincent de Paul*. Revised by Carlton A. Princeville. St. Louis: Vincentian Foreign Mission Press, 1961. Draws from the conferences, correspondence, and personal lives of Vincent and Louise de Marillac to present their ideas about Christian virtues and doctrine. The majority of this volume is devoted to Vincent.

Purcell, Mary. *The World of Monsieur Vincent*. New York: Charles Scribner's Sons, 1963. A sensible, clear, and lively narrative of Vincent's life and times. Provides an excellent introduction for the general reader. Purcell focuses on Vincent's social and historical milieus, drawing vivid portraits of persons and places important in his life. Illustrations, notes, a bibliography, and an index are included.

Saint Vincent de Paul: A Tercentenary Commemoration of His Death, 1660-1960. Jamaica, New York: St. John's University Press, 1960. Includes twelve Saint Vincent de Paul Annual Lectures delivered at St. John's University between 1948 and 1959. This collection of lectures addresses aspects of Vincent's personality and spiritual and social views, his educational and charitable endeavors, his dealings with other social reformers and with political figures, his historical context, and the process of his canonization as a saint.

Vincent de Paul, Saint. *The Conferences of St. Vincent de Paul to the Sisters of Charity*. Edited and translated by Joseph Leonard. 4 vols. London: Burns, Oates and Washbourne, 1938. These are the texts of 120 conferences given by Vincent to the Daughters of Charity between 1634 and 1660. They address the practical and spiritual lives of the sisters. Leonard includes an introduction, explanatory narrative, and footnotes.

_____. *Letters of St. Vincent de Paul*. Edited and translated by Joseph Leonard. London: Burns, Oates and Washbourne, 1937. Vincent reportedly wrote approximately thirty thousand letters, the majority of which were lost over the centuries. These letters (nearly 250) written between 1607 and 1659, cover all aspects of Vincent's life and work. Includes a biographical introduction by Henri Bremond, as well as copious notes, an index, and illustrations.

Eileen Tess Tyler

RUDOLF VIRCHOW

Born: October 13, 1821; Schivelbein, Pomerania
Died: September 5, 1902; Berlin, Germany
Areas of Achievement: Medicine, politics, and anthropology
Contribution: Virchow received worldwide recognition for his contribution
to medical science, anthropology, archaeology, and public health. His
greatest contribution to medical science was in establishing the principles
of cellular pathology.

Early Life

Rudolf Ludwig Karl Virchow was born in the small eastern Pomeranian
city of Schivelbein, the only child of a minor city official and farmer. He
began his formal education in the *Gymnasium* at Coslin, where he distinguished himself by his linguistic abilities; he soon mastered Latin, learned
Greek, English, and French, and was a good Hebrew scholar. In October,
1839, he entered the medical school of the Friedrich-Wilhelms-Institut, in
Berlin. Johannes Müller, a physiologist, anatomist, and pathologist, and
Johann Lucas Schönlein, an outstanding German clinician, influenced Virchow as he began his research activities while still an undergraduate. In
1843, he presented his thesis "De rheumate praesertim corneae" (rheumatic
disease, particularly of the cornea), received his doctorate in medicine, and
was given the position of assistant at the Charité Hospital. In the following
year, he obtained the post of prosector of anatomy to the Charité Hospital,
acting as assistant to Robert Froriep, whom he eventually succeeded only
three years later, in 1846.

Froriep assigned to his young assistant, as a theme for independent investigation, the study of phlebitis. Virchow's thorough and brilliant studies
outlining the principles of thrombosis and embolism formed a new chapter in
pathology. In addition, his observations on leukemia opened new points of
view on the origin and nature of white blood corpuscles. In 1847, at the age
of twenty-six, with Benno Reinhardt he started the *Archiv für pathologische
Anatomie und Physiologie, und für klinische Medizin* (archives for pathological anatomy and physiology and clinical medicine), a journal he continued
to edit alone after his colleague's death in 1852.

In 1848, a singular event occurred which Virchow, in later life, regarded
as the most decisive in his life. Sent on an official mission to study an
epidemic of "hunger typhus" (relapsing fever) in famine-ridden Upper Silesia, a Prussian province occupied by a Polish minority, he published a
scathing report indicting the government, insisting that the causes of the
epidemic were social as much as—if not more than—medical. His anti-
government stance, coupled with the fact that, on his return, he had allied
himself with the ultraradical party and founded a medico-political journal,

Die medizinische Reforme (medical reform), resulted in his dismissal from all professional posts in Berlin. His fame as a pathologist had spread, and the University of Würzburg seized the opportunity and offered Virchow the professorship of pathology and the directorship of the newly founded Pathological Institute, where Virchow dedicated himself to research work.

As a young man, Virchow presented a small professorial figure. He was short, thin, blond, dark-eyed, and was accorded the nickname *Der Kleine Doktor* (the little doctor). He was quick in mind and body, often transfixing inattention or incompetence with a flash of sarcasm. Yet he was approachable, hospitable, and particularly warm and friendly to the sick and poor.

Life's Work

As professor of pathology at the University of Würzburg, Virchow entered the most creative period of his life. For the next seven years, his systematic and methodical research culminated in outlining the fundamental principles of cellular pathology. For centuries before Virchow, the origin of life and the seat of disease were the subjects of many theories and controversies. Medieval anatomists localized disease to one of the larger regions or cavities of the body, such as the head, chest, or abdomen. In the mid- to late eighteenth century, anatomists, led by Giovanni Battista Morgagni, attempted to find the actual diseased organ, and Marie François Xavier Bichat showed that in the same organ, sometimes one and sometimes another tissue might be the seat of disease. In the third decade of the nineteenth century, the microscope had disclosed the existence of cells, and in the next decade the study of pathological anatomy was directed to their study. Research in this area was faced with two major hurdles: First, cells could not be demonstrated in several tissues, even in their most developed state; second, the origin of new cells was completely unknown. The answer to the latter question was heavily prejudiced by the so-called cell theory of Theodor Schwann, who asserted that new cells arose from unformed, amorphous matter, which he termed "cytoblastema."

When Virchow arrived at the University of Würzburg in 1849, he had already brought with him some ideas about the principles of cellular pathology. Here, he proceeded to demonstrate the existence of cells in bone and in connective tissue, where their existence had hitherto been doubtful. This discovery of cells of connective and other allied tissues offered him the possibility of finding a cellular matrix for many new growths. These studies led to his coining the aphorism *omnis cellula e cellula* (each cell stems from another cell), which became the recognized hallmark of the biological cell theory. Virchow's conception of disease rested on four main hypotheses: first, that all diseases are in essence active or passive disturbances of living cells; second, that all cells arise from parent cells; third, that functional capacities of the cells depended on intracellular physicochemical processes;

and finally, that all pathological formations are degenerations, transformations, or repetitions of normal structures.

Internationally famous for his research and teaching at Würzburg, Virchow was called back to the University of Berlin in 1856. Virchow agreed to return on the condition that a pathological institute be founded. The government agreed, and Virchow arrived to continue work with indefatigable zeal and published his *Die cellular Pathologie in ihrer Begründung auf physiologische und pathologische Gewebelehre* (1858; *Cellular Pathology as Based upon Physiological and Pathological Histology,* 1860), describing his work on the subject. Virchow's own aphorism *omnis cellula e cellula* is the basis for his work on tumors during 1863-1867, which treats these formations as physiologically independent new growths of cellular structure. He continued to write and edit his medical journal and enjoyed the satisfaction of celebrating its jubilee in December, 1897. Under his direction, the department of pathology at the Charité Hospital became a model for other institutions. He personally supervised the establishment of one of the best pathology museums in the world. In addition, he delivered lectures regularly, which were attended by an international audience. He was not a great orator; his voice was weak and his speech simple, but once on the platform the small man with the sharp dark eyes commanded attention.

He once again entered politics and was elected member of the municipal council; in 1862, he took his seat in the Prussian Diet, and by his sheer ability was recognized as leader of the opposition Radical Party. He led a desperate fight against Otto von Bismarck's dictatorship, and it is said that Bismarck became so annoyed with Virchow that he challenged him to a duel, which was averted by behind-the-scenes negotiations through Bismarck's intermediaries, who were determined to prevent it.

Virchow was also president of the German Geographical Society and the Society of Anthropology and Ethnology. He even had his own anthropological collection, mainly consisting of crania of the different human races. An accidental shelling of the Museum of Natural History in Paris during the war prompted the publication of an indignant pamphlet stating that the Prussians were not a Germanic but a barbaric race. That stirred Virchow's patriotism to the extent that he instigated a colossal public census of the color of the hair and eyes in six million German schoolchildren, concluding that there was no evidence of a predominant "German type" among them. He was interested in archaeology and worked in excavation sites of ancient Troy in Greece and Egypt; he also conducted his own fieldwork in the Caucasus in 1894.

Virchow remained at the forefront of international medicine and was showered with honors from scientific academies in Germany, France, and England. In 1891, his seventieth birthday was celebrated and a gold medal was presented to him by the emperor in recognition of the immense services

Virchow had rendered to science. On January 5, 1902, he fell when exiting a tram car but, although he fractured a leg in the accident, recovered and was able to move about on crutches. He then went to Harzburg to recuperate, but he became weaker. Three weeks prior to his death, his friends decided to take him back to Berlin; Virchow did not tolerate the journey well, lapsed into a coma from which he never recovered, and died on September 5, 1902. Virchow was given a public funeral with honors and laid to rest in the cemetery of St. Matthew.

Summary

Rudolf Virchow, one of the founders of modern biomedicine, was also a proponent of social reform. According to Virchow, medicine was to be reformed on the basis of four principles: First, the health of the people is a matter of direct social concern; second, social and economic conditions have important effects on health and disease; third, the measures taken to promote health and to combat disease must be social as well as medical; and fourth, medical statistics should be the standard of measurement. Virchow's contribution to the improvement of public health was monumental; his discovery of the pathophysiology of the parasitic disease trichinosis led a successful ten-year campaign to establish compulsory meat inspection in Germany. At the request of the Berlin city council, he designed and supervised a sewage-disposal system that set the pattern for similar systems in Germany and elsewhere. He organized the ambulance service for the army; and, recognizing the importance of nurses to medical care, he opened a nursing school.

While Virchow made significant contributions in many fields, he became world-famous for his work in cellular pathology. The fundamental principles of cellular pathology outlined by him, particularly the dictum *omnis cellula e cellula*, forever closed the last loophole for opponents of this system and secured a position of great importance in physiology. Virchow was the first to systematize the theory of cellular pathology and to give medicine a common denominator for all diseases. Virchow's success may be attributed to the quality of his research, his prolific publications, his single-minded determination, and the growth of his influence on medicine. His work on cellular pathology had far-reaching consequences, contributing to progress in medicine and in surgery. It is therefore a fitting tribute that cellular pathology has been hailed as one of the great events in the history of medicine.

Bibliography

Ackerknecht, Erwin H. *Rudolf Virchow: Doctor, Statesman, Anthropologist.* Madison: University of Wisconsin Press, 1953. This is the first full-length study of Virchow, covering 240 pages. Although the author introduces the book with a brief life history, this is primarily an analysis of Virchow's work in medicine, politics, and anthropology. An extensive bibliography, strictly confined to items quoted in the text, is supplemented by an exhaustive biographical glossary. This book contains one sketch and two portraits of Virchow, including the first published portrait of Virchow as a septuagenarian.

Carr, James G. *Rudolph Virchow.* Chicago, Ill.: Northwestern University Bulletin, 1938. This concise twenty-three-page biography of Virchow contains translated excerpts of letters from Virchow to his parents that shed light on his early years, family life, and customs. No bibliography or illustrations are provided.

Jacobi, Abraham. *Rudolf Virchow.* New York: Trow, 1881. This thirty-five-page booklet is packed with information. Emphasizes Virchow's work in pathology and the work leading to the establishment of the principles of cellular pathology. Bibliography is not provided.

Virchow, Rudolf. *Diseases, Life, and Man: Selected Essays.* Translated by Lelland Rather. Stanford, Calif.: Stanford University Press, 1958. This book contains selected essays by Virchow on a range of subjects, including cellular pathology, scientific medicine, and philosophy. An excellent introduction by the translator covers Virchow's place in history, and explores his role in the establishment of the principles of cellular pathology and the foundations of modern medicine. An appendix contains the German titles and sources of articles translated, including an extensive biographical glossary.

Welch, Henry. "Rudolph Virchow, Pathologist." *Boston Medical and Surgical Journal* 125 (1891): 453-457. An article written on the occasion of Virchow's seventieth birthday celebrations at The Johns Hopkins University. This essay gives a thorough and scholarly review of Virchow's work in the field of pathology.

Anand Karnad
Abraham Verghese

FRANCISCO DE VITORIA

Born: c. 1483; Vitoria, Álava, Spain
Died: August 12, 1546; Salamanca, Spain
Areas of Achievement: Philosophy, theology, and law
Contribution: Vitoria was a Spanish theologian and pioneer in the field of international law. He is principally associated with his idea that the nations of the world constitute a community based on natural law.

Early Life

Francisco de Vitoria was born in the small town of Vitoria in the Basque province of Álava. The exact date of his birth is uncertain, but scholars generally place it between 1480 and 1486, with 1483 being the year most often mentioned. When still very young, Vitoria entered the Dominican Order, of which his elder brother Diego was also a member. He went to San Pablo in Burgos for his education, and, because he showed promise as a scholar in the classics, he was sent to the College of the Dominicans in Paris for further study. While in Paris, he also attended classes at the Sorbonne. His education equipped him as a Humanist versed in Greek and Latin texts, and Vitoria is also said to have met the great Humanist Desiderius Erasmus during those years.

Vitoria arrived in Paris around 1506 and studied first at the Dominican College of Saint Jacques, becoming well versed in the classics before occupying the chair of theology there. He was influenced by nominalist teachers, who helped revive the study of the *Summa theologiae* (c. 1265-1273; *Summa Theologica*, 1911-1921) of Saint Thomas Aquinas in addition to, or sometimes instead of, the previous standard Dominican text, *Sententiarum libri IV* (1148-1151; four books of sentences) by Peter Lombard. He even became involved in the preparations of editions of Aquinas' work that appeared in the period of 1514-1519. Before returning to Spain, he completed his degree of licentiate in theology at the Sorbonne on March 24, 1522.

Life's Work

Vitoria embarked on his life's work upon his return to Spain after earning his degree in theology. He had attained a good reputation among his colleagues and was able to serve at the College of Saint Gregory in Valladolid from 1523 to 1526 before being appointed to the chair of theology at the University of Salamanca. He would remain at the university until his death.

Vitoria made his first mark on history as he lectured on theology. He impressed a new character on this field of study, as his discussions were full of ideas, and drew other areas of learning into the consideration of theological questions. Such questions were not to be considered intellectual exercises but rather areas of legitimate practical concern in the real world. That such discussions and proposed solutions could actually produce serious consequences was shown in many lectures: notably those discussions on the rights and treatment of Native Americans in the newly discovered hemisphere and those on the question of what constitutes a just war. His teaching incorporated a desire for justice in world affairs and a strong belief that moral questions have an impact on all phases of life.

One of the greatest influences on Vitoria was his contact with the great Humanists, including Erasmus. Vitoria's defense of the Indians and his humanitarian principles in relation to war bear the stamp of this influence. Vitoria distinguished himself as a professor and helped increase the reputation of the University of Salamanca. At first he was compelled to lecture on the *Sententiarum libri IV* of Peter Lombard while he preferred Saint Thomas Aquinas, but it later became the rule to discuss the *Summa Theologica* with references to Lombard—a practice which better suited Vitoria's thinking. His courses soon met with favorable reactions as he combined solid doctrine with a clear, elegant style of exposition. Among his students were Melchor Cano, Domingo Soto, and Bartolomé de Medina. Although Vitoria did not publish his lectures, his students gathered many of them and published them after his death, as a tribute to him. Vitoria's reputation for applying theology to practical matters and his broad knowledge were such that Charles V consulted him on a number of questions, including the arguments by Henry VIII of England for annulling his marriage to Catherine of Aragon.

In 1532, Vitoria discussed the justifications for Spanish domination in the New World. In 1539 and 1540, Charles V consulted him about several matters relating to the conquest of the Indies. Then, in 1541, Vitoria was consulted on the question of baptizing Native Americans without religious instruction, a question brought to the Council of the Indies by Bartolomé de las Casas, in whose favor Vitoria argued. In 1545, Vitoria was invited to attend the Council of Trent; however, because of illness, other representatives were sent instead.

Vitoria's tenure at Salamanca lasted from 1526 to 1546. The last two years of his life, he suffered from rheumatic pain, and a substitute lecturer, Juan Gil Fernández de Nava, had to be called in. Vitoria died on August 12, 1546. The efforts of his students assured that his influence continued long after that.

Some of Vitoria's lectures were collected for publication by his former students in *Relectiones theologicae* (1557; English translation, 1934). Vitoria's guiding premise was that theology or questions of morality extend over the entire field of human activity. He particularly believed that the question of the treatment of the Native Americans as a barbarian race, not subject to an established human law, must be viewed from the point of view of divine law. The Native Americans had been reduced to servitude on the large land-holdings or to slavery in the mines. Compulsory labor and separation of families was the norm. Bartolomé de las Casas became a famous defender of the Native Americans at this time, and Vitoria himself defended a humanitarian view. Using his considerable skill in reasoning and argumentation, he contradicted proposed theories that allowed for the subjugation of Native Americans based on the right to convert them to Christianity, on the right to punish idolatry, or on the (supposed) superiority of Christians over so-called barbarians.

Vitoria also refuted the argument that Spain had title to the land based on discovery. He resorted to the Law of Nations, which allows such title only if the regions are uninhabited—which these clearly were not. He also argued that Spaniards could travel in these new lands on condition that they did not harm the inhabitants and that, where there was common property, Spaniards might also profit. Vitoria's concept of a just war included the idea that it was lawful for the Spaniards to defend themselves against Native American attacks, while always showing generosity and moderation to the defeated. If the Native Americans persisted with their attacks, however, the Spaniards were allowed recourse to the rights of war, including plunder and captivity, which were seen as the right to punish wrongdoing according to law.

Because of his many students and his participation in the important discussions of his time, Vitoria's influence was widespread. With the publication of his lectures, that influence continued after his death.

Summary

During the period when the rules of international law were being formulated, the two main schools of thought included positivists and naturalists. Hugo Grotius, the leading Dutch naturalist writer, is often regarded as the founder of modern international law. For other scholars, however, this title should go to Vitoria, who based his arguments as well on natural law. Vitoria's argument was that the basic principles of all laws are derived from principles of justice with universal validity. He believed that such principles were part of a natural, divine law, not a man-made one.

Vitoria spoke often on the question of war. To Vitoria, war was justified to assure free trade and communication when other means of persuasion had failed. The violation of a right was the essential condition for a just war. Defensive wars protected the individual or nation from tyranny; offensive wars might punish a nation guilty of injustice. In any case, he believed that the defeated should always be treated with moderation once the purpose has been achieved. Furthermore, a just war must always promote the common good of the world community over the advantage of an individual state.

When Vitoria has been called the founder of modern international law by scholars, it has been based particularly on *De Indis* and *De jure belli relectiones*, lectures given in 1532, published in 1557, and translated into English in 1917. In *De Indis*, he first defined international law as a natural law binding all states of the world, and he applied it to the treatment of the Native Americans in the New World. In visualizing an international society, he applied Saint Thomas Aquinas' principles to the concept of state and built a theory of international society as well on his principles. His guiding principle was that an international society was based on a natural association of equal states. In the areas of philosophy and theology, his contributions were recognized within his lifetime; Vitoria's contribution in the area of law, especially international law, are equally indisputable.

Bibliography

Benkert, Gerald Francis. *The Thomistic Conception of an International Society.* Washington, D.C.: Catholic University of America Press, 1942. Examines the writings of Thomas Aquinas and from his philosophical principles delineates the basis for constructing an international society. Particular emphasis is given to the views of Vitoria in the Spanish revival of Thomistic thought. Includes an extensive bibliography.

Delos, Joseph Thomas. *International Relations from a Catholic Standpoint.* Edited and translated by Stephen J. Brown. Dublin, Ireland: Browne and Nolan, 1932. Contains a discussion of the Catholic viewpoint on natural law and international relations. Particularly useful in defining the Catholic attitude and contributions to peaceful international relations throughout history and particularly the contributions of various theologians, Vitoria among them.

Francisco de Vitoria. *Francisci de Victoria De Indis et De Ivre Belli Relectiones*, edited by Ernest Nys. Vol. 7, *The Classics of International Law*, edited by James Brown Scott. Washington, D.C.: Carnegie Institution of Washington, 1917. Includes a translation by John Pawley Bate of the two *Relectiones theologicae* by Vitoria, along with the full Latin text. Marginal notes and summary of the major points are maintained from the original. Helpful introduction by Ernest Nys includes biographical information and a discussion of some of Vitoria's principal arguments.

Hamilton, Bernice. *Political Thought in Sixteenth Century Spain: A Study of the Political Ideas of Vitoria, De Soto, Suárez, and Molina.* Oxford, England: Clarendon Press, 1963. A discussion of the political ideas of four Spanish thinkers on natural-law theory, political communities, war, New World colonization, law of nations, and relative powers of Church and state. Contains bibliographies.

Reidy, Stephen J. *Civil Authority According to Francis de Vitoria.* River Forest, Ill.: The Aquinas Library, 1959. A specialized study of Vitoria's teaching on the nature and causes of civil authority with a discussion of his position on the ancient scholastic teaching. Contains a bibliography of books and periodicals in several languages.

Scott, James Brown. *The Spanish Origin of International Law: Francisco de*

Vitoria and His Law of Nations. Oxford, England: Clarendon Press, 1934. A thorough discussion of Vitoria's life, putting his accomplishments in the context of the "era of discoveries" and the thinking of the Spanish School. Appendices include translations of six important *relectiones*.

Susan L. Piepke

ANTONIO VIVALDI

Born: March 4, 1678; Venice
Died: July 28, 1741; Vienna, Austria
Area of Achievement: Music
Contribution: As the most influential and original Italian composer of the early eighteenth century, Vivaldi developed the basic form of the Baroque concerto and made it the standard for instrumental music throughout much of Europe. He was a pioneer of program music, and his techniques of orchestration and lyrical violin style anticipated the Romanticism of the nineteenth century.

Early Life

Antonio Lucio Vivaldi was the eldest of six children born to Giovanni Battista Vivaldi, the son of a baker from the town of Brescia. After his father's death in 1666, Giovanni Battista was taken to Venice, where he eventually worked, at least part-time, as both a baker and a barber. In 1685, however, he was hired as a violinist at the Cathedral of St. Mark, which, like most larger churches in Europe, had its own orchestra. He achieved a certain amount of local fame as a musician, opera manager, and composer under the surname Rossi (Italian for "red"), apparently because of his red hair. Antonio Vivaldi was later to be known by the sobriquet "Il Prete Rosso" ("the red priest") for the same reason.

When Antonio was born, the midwife who delivered him performed an emergency baptism because of a *pericolo di morte*, or "risk of death." What exactly this risk was is unclear; a likely explanation is that the serious ailment which Vivaldi claimed afflicted him throughout his life had appeared at birth. The composer himself called his condition a *strettezza di petto*, or a "tightness of the chest," and various diagnoses, from asthma to angina pectoris, have been offered by historians.

Very little else is known about Vivaldi's childhood. He was probably taught to play the violin by his father. By age ten, he is reputed to have played in the cathedral orchestra whenever his father was occupied elsewhere. It was decided at some point that Vivaldi would be trained for the priesthood, since this was the only way for a commoner to achieve upward social mobility. Thus, in 1693, Vivaldi was tonsured and took minor orders. He received his instruction from the clergy of two local churches, and he was allowed to live at home, either because of his illness or to allow him to continue studying the violin. He was ordained, after ten years of training, in 1703.

Within months of becoming a priest, Vivaldi received his first professional appointment, as *maestro di violino* (violin instructor) at the Pio Ospedale della Pietà, one of four Venetian orphanages which specialized in the musical training of abandoned or indigent girls. He thereupon ceased to say masses, though he always remained outwardly pious and wrote a large quantity of splendid religious music. He later defended his decision by claiming that his chest ailment made him unable to perform the ceremony. It is equally likely that he simply preferred not to be distracted from his musical activities. Until the nineteenth century, it was not at all unusual for priests to engage in secular professions, especially in Italy.

Life's Work

In eighteenth century Venice, the four musical orphanages, and especially the Pietà, were so renowned for the quality of their instrumental and vocal instruction that their religious services had become great social affairs, much more like public concerts, with a wide variety of secular and religious music being performed. A visit to at least one of these services was considered essential by tourists, and the Pietà's chapel was always filled to capacity.

Vivaldi's position was therefore extremely important. He was required not only to provide competent instruction, to rehearse the orchestra, and to purchase and maintain its stringed instruments but also to compose a constant supply of new music for its performances. In fact, his first published works, a set of twelve trio sonatas (Op. 1), were completed in his first year on the job. Within a few more years, he wrote a set of violin sonatas (Op. 2) and a variety of concerti for various solo instruments and strings.

These concerti, and those which followed, had an immediate and dramatic impact on the European music scene. In Germany, especially, they achieved great popularity. In 1711, Vivaldi's most influential work, *L'estro armonico* (Op. 3), was published, and Johann Sebastian Bach transcribed several of its twelve violin concerti for harpsichord and strings. Other composers also copied Vivaldi's style, and several, such as Gottfried Stölzel, went to Venice to seek him out. Vivaldi is credited with having reformed the concerto by standardizing a three-movement, fast-slow-fast structure and creating thematically distinct solo parts alternating with full-ensemble ritornellos (refrains in different keys).

Vivaldi continued to compose instrumental works throughout his life; ultimately, these totaled more than five hundred inventive, deftly orchestrated concerti and sinfonias, and more than ninety sonatas. Perhaps the most famous of his works, *Il cimento dell'armonia e dell'inventione* (twelve concerti, Op. 8), appeared in about 1725. Its first four concerti, which have been immortalized as *The Four Seasons*, contain probably the most clearly articulated program music of the Baroque era. The listener can easily visualize the bubbling brook of "Spring," the hot sun of "Summer," and other images these concerti evoke.

Long before this, however, Vivaldi had already embarked upon a career in opera. His first known stage work was produced in May, 1713, and several more were performed in Venice in the years following. From 1718 to 1726, he was usually on the road in Mantua and Rome, producing and directing new operas. While in Rome, he also performed twice for the pope, and, in 1719, received a new appointment (in addition to his position at the Pietà) as court composer to the Governor of Mantua. In 1727, he dedicated a set of twelve concerti, *La cetra* (Op. 9), to the Holy Roman Emperor Charles VI, who was said to have given Vivaldi a considerable amount of money, a golden chain and medallion, and a knighthood.

As his reputation spread far and wide, so also did Vivaldi's travels. In 1729, he visited Vienna, where his father, who had accompanied him, is believed to have died. In 1730, he may also have gone to Prague, where an Italian company staged two of his new operas. Vivaldi always preferred to oversee productions of his works himself, and he often blamed his few failures on changes made by others. In 1733, he returned temporarily to Venice, but after 1735 he chose to produce new operas in other cities of Italy, especially Ferrara.

While at Ferrara, Vivaldi got into a dispute over a singer's contract and his choice of operas for performance. This may have reflected a decline in his popularity there. Three of his works were box-office failures, but Vivaldi nevertheless insisted upon receiving the maximum payment stipulated in his agreement with the theater managers. These problems evidently led the cardinal of Ferrara (which was a papal domain), in 1737, to censure Vivaldi and forbid him to enter the city. The composer was accused of having illicit relations with Anna Giraud, a famous contralto who was a member of his entourage, in addition to refusing to say Mass. Vivaldi vehemently denied the first accusation, and he blamed his failure to conduct masses on his disease. Nevertheless, his last opera written for Ferrara was performed without his supervision and was a conspicuous flop. Vivaldi, however, turned the situation to good account: He was now free to journey to Amsterdam to conduct several performances of his instrumental music.

Naturally, all of this traveling affected his work for the Pietà, and his relations with the board of governors were occasionally stormy. In 1716, he had been promoted to *maestro de' concerti*, but his travels prevented him from sustained teaching, and he often had to send new compositions to the Pietà by mail. Even so, he was promoted to *maestro di cappella* in 1735, only to be fired three years later. He continued to supply the Pietà with occasional concerti, and even directed performances there, as late as 1740.

In that year, or possibly early in 1741, Vivaldi undertook a mysterious journey to Vienna, the purpose of which is still unclear. It is known that he sold a group of concerti manuscripts there and that he was in dire financial straits. When he died, on July 28, 1741, of what was called an "internal inflammation," he was living in the house of a saddler's widow. Like Wolfgang Amadeus Mozart fifty years later, he was given a pauper's funeral.

Summary

Few known portraits of Antonio Vivaldi exist, and these differ vastly from one another. A famous caricature, sketched by Pier Leone Ghezzi in 1723, gives him a long nose, a jutting chin, and a look of avidity, while a contemporary anonymous painting makes him appear fragile and pensive. These conflicting images reflect the difficulty in evaluating his personality. His lifestyle was extravagant, flamboyant, and unconventional, and he had many enemies. He was notorious for his vanity and sensitivity to criticism, and was more highly regarded by his Italian contemporaries for his skills as a violinist than for his originality as a composer. He also had a reputation as a hard bargainer, and his concern with money may have been excessive. Some of the personal pettiness and greed which Vivaldi occasionally displayed may have been a reaction to the fact that his disease made him an invalid. Moreover, traveling with a large entourage, including a nurse, was very expensive. None of his critics, however, questioned Vivaldi's tremendous, almost fanatic, dedication to music, nor the virtuosity of his violin technique. Though the fame of his operas evaporated almost immediately after his death, the emotional force and energy of his instrumental works continued to be acknowledged for several decades.

Oddly enough, it was probably these very qualities which led to Vivaldi's subsequent oblivion. The classical period had little use, on the one hand, for what was characterized as the "wild and irregular" emotionalism of his concerti, while, on the other, he was reproached for churning out too many routine works pandering to mediocre public tastes. Like many Baroque composers, he fell into obscurity until the Bach revival that took place in the 1840's. Even then, however, he was simply regarded as one of Bach's precursors. His contributions to the development of the concerto form, and Bach's imitation of it, were not acknowledged until the beginning of the twentieth century.

Studies of Vivaldi were given a great boost by the discovery of his personal collection of manuscripts in the 1920's, but it was not until the Turin musicologist Alberto Gentili obtained a vast, previously unknown collection of his works in 1930 that Vivaldi's importance began to be truly realized. His reputation was fully rehabilitated by the first publication of his collected works in 1947 and by a famous study of the composer by the French musicologist Marc Pincherle. In the years since, enthusiasm for the music of Vivaldi has continued to grow: Thousands of Vivaldi recordings have been issued, especially of *The Four Seasons*, and these concerti and others have provided background music for many popular films. Millions of people who would otherwise have no interest in, or awareness of, Baroque music thus have been attracted to its beauties. Beyond Vivaldi's contributions to the development of the concerto form and his innovations in orchestration and violin technique, this is perhaps his most important achievement.

Bibliography

Arnold, Denis. "Vivaldi." In *The New Grove Italian Baroque Masters*, by Denis Arnold et al. New York: W. W. Norton, 1984. An excellent concise biography, one of seven included in this volume, all by noted musical scholars. Discusses Vivaldi's life, music, and influence on other composers. Contains an up-to-date catalog of Vivaldi's works, as well as a comprehensive bibliography.

Borroff, Edith. *The Music of the Baroque*. Dubuque, Iowa: William C. Brown, 1970. A brief introduction to Baroque music for students with little musical background. Provides many musical examples which are explained sufficiently to allow beginning students to learn a substantial amount of music theory relatively painlessly. Profusely illustrated. An outstanding feature is the inclusion of brief discographies for each type and area of music discussed.

Kolneder, Walter. *Antonio Vivaldi: His Life and Work*. Translated by Bill Hopkins. Berkeley: University of California Press, 1970. Kolneder has replaced Pincherle as the standard full-length biography of Vivaldi. Extremely well written, but difficult for those without a solid background in music theory. In addition to an extensive, but unclassified, bibliography, Kolneder provides many musical examples.

Palisca, Claude V. *Baroque Music*. Edited by Wiley Hitchcock. Englewood Cliffs, N.J.: Prentice-Hall, 1968. A well-known textbook by an established scholar from Yale University. Useful for understanding the Italian context of Vivaldi's concerti, sinfonias, and sonatas, comparing them to the work of his predecessors and contemporaries. Recommended mainly for music students.

Pincherle, Marc. *Vivaldi, Genius of the Baroque*. Translated by Christopher Hatch. New York: W. W. Norton, 1957. Pincherle was the scholar primarily responsible for the post-World War II Vivaldi revival. In addition to this seminal study, Pincherle also published the first comprehensive catalog of Vivaldi's works. While Pincherle's work has been superseded by later research, it is still excellent reading and a good source for the nonspecialist.

Selfridge-Field, Eleonor. *Venetian Instrumental Music from Gabrieli to Vivaldi*. Edited by F. W. Sternfield. Oxford, England: Basil Blackwell, 1975. An outstanding study of the Venetian Baroque, including a full analysis of many of Vivaldi's works, as well as those of his Venetian contemporaries. Suggests that Vivaldi's legacy to later composers may have been greater than is generally acknowledged. Surveys the history of Venetian musical practice and organizations and includes an excellent glossary of Baroque musical terms and instruments.

Talbot, Michael. *Vivaldi*. London: J. M. Dent & Sons, 1978. The best all-around discussion of Vivaldi's life, works, and impact. Among other features, it includes a complete list of Vivaldi's works, a concordance chart of the major catalogs, a chronological outline, and an extensive bibliography. Though an extremely scholarly work with abundant evidence of original research (including excerpts from many of Vivaldi's extant letters), it is nevertheless a well-written and entertaining study. Highly recommended for anyone with an interest in Vivaldi.

Thomas C. Schunk

ALESSANDRO VOLTA

Born: February 18, 1745; Como, Duchy of Milan
Died: March 5, 1827; Como, Duchy of Milan
Areas of Achievement: Physics and chemistry
Contribution: Volta contributed to the development of concepts and techniques in electrostatics, including the inventions of the electrophorus and the condensing electrometer. His most important contributions were the discovery of contact electricity and the invention of the electric battery.

Early Life

Alessandro Giuseppe Antonio Anastasio Volta was the youngest of nine children born to Filippo and Maddalena Volta in the ancient Roman town of Como, on Lake Como in what is now northern Italy. His father was a member of the Jesuit Order for eleven years before withdrawing to wed Maddalena dei Conti Inzaghi, who was twenty-two years younger than he. Although Volta's family was from the local nobility, his father had spent the family fortune and gone into debt before Alessandro's birth. Three of his brothers became priests, and two of his sisters became nuns. Throughout his life, he was active in the Catholic religion.

Although Volta did not talk until he was four, he began to excel early in school and showed special ability in foreign languages. When Volta was about seven years old, his father died, but with the aid of his two uncles he attended the local Jesuit college, where attempts were made to recruit him to the priesthood. After completing the classical course of education at the age of sixteen, Volta continued his education until 1765 at the Seminario Benzi, where he was attracted to the natural sciences. There he wrote a long Latin poem of some five hundred verses, mostly celebrating the work of the English chemist Joseph Priestley, who later wrote a two-volume history of electricity.

By the age of eighteen, Volta had decided to devote himself to the study of electricity. In 1763, he began a correspondence with the eminent French electrical scientist l'Abbé Jean-Antoine Nollet. In these letters, he supported Roger Joseph Boscovich in suggesting that electrical attraction followed the Newtonian concept of action at a distance instead of the direct emission and absorption of electrical effluvia as taught by Nollet. He also began an experimental study of electricity, with equipment and laboratory facilities provided by his friend and benefactor Giulio Gattoni. After learning of Benjamin Franklin's work, Volta and Gattoni constructed the first lightning rod in Como and studied the electricity collected by it. Volta's concentration on his work was so great that he often missed meals, slept little, and was unaware of the condition of his clothing. He soon developed a genius for inventing inexpensive but effective apparatuses, which led to a successful career.

Life's Work

Volta's research in static electricity was the foundation for his later invention of the electric battery. The first results of his work were sent in 1765 to Giovanni Beccaria, professor of physics at the University of Turin and the leading Italian electrical scientist. In a series of letters, Volta described his design of a machine to produce electrostatic effects and reported on which materials would become positive and which negative when rubbed together. Volta's correspondence with Beccaria led to Volta's first publication, *De vi attractiva ignis electrici* (1769; on the attractive force of electric fire). This seventy-two-page treatise boldly reinterpreted Beccaria's experiments and Franklin's theory of a self-repulsive electrical fluid in terms of a consistent principle of attraction. In this book and a second book in 1771, Volta remained faithful to Franklin's theory of a single electric fluid but suggested that all materials are in electrical equilibrium until disturbed by frictional activity.

Volta was appointed to his first academic post in 1774 as principal of the state school in Como, previously under Jesuit control. He was a large and vigorous man, with wide social contacts. In 1775, he sent a letter to Priestley, announcing the invention of his electrophorus, which he viewed as a kind of perpetual source of electrical fluid. This device consisted of a flat insulating cake made of three parts turpentine, two parts resin, and one part wax, hardened in a metal dish and covered by a metal plate with an insulated handle. After the cake has been rubbed, the plate can be set on it and briefly touched to transfer electrical fluid by induction. The plate thus charged can be lifted and discharged into a Leyden jar to store it; the operation can be repeated many times. The device became very popular, and its induction process reinforced Volta's emphasis on action at a distance and the similar ideas of Franz Aepinus. With his increasing fame, Volta was able to shift from administrator to professor of experimental physics without the usual examination.

Volta's interests expanded into chemistry in 1778, with his discovery of inflammable marsh gas, now called methane, in Lake Maggiore. He collected this gas from bubbles rising to the surface, especially in shallow, marshy locations. He used his electrophorus to ignite the gas from the discharge of a spark in what he called an electric pistol and correctly explained its source as decaying animal and vegetable matter. Similar experiments with hydrogen led to measurements of the contraction of air when exploded with an equal volume of hydrogen in his eudiometer, giving a total reduction of $\frac{3}{5}$. This corresponds to a $\frac{1}{5}$ contraction of air, consistent with later measurements of the oxygen content.

In a famous letter written in 1777, Volta proposed an electric signal line from Como to Milan, on which a Leyden jar could be discharged at one end, causing the detonation of an electric pistol at the other end. His increasing fame led to a state-supported trip to some of the chief science centers of Europe and a new position in 1778 as professor of experimental physics at the University of Pavia. During nearly forty years in this position, Volta was able to obtain an excellent collection of instruments at state expense. On a second tour of Europe in 1782, he met the astronomer Pierre-Simon Laplace, the chemist Antoine-Laurent Lavoisier, and most important, Franklin and Priestley. On his return, he introduced the American potato to Italian farmers. He continued his work on gases at Pavia, accurately measuring the thermal expansion of gases twenty years before Joseph-Louis Gay-Lussac.

During this time, Volta perfected his condensing electrometer, a more sensitive and less expensive form of the contemporaneous gold-leaf electrometer. In place of gold leaves, he suspended two fine straws in a square glass bottle, with a protractor scale on one face to give the degree of their divergence. The straws were suspended from a metal cover forming the base of a small electrophorus, with a thin slab of marble on top for the insulating cake. A movable upper plate had an increased capacity for storing charge because of the thinner cake, making it extremely sensitive to even minute charges. Lifting the upper plate increased the divergence of the electrometer straws. Following Henry Cavendish, Volta referred to this effect as increased tension resulting from decreased capacity and proposed a unit of tension (later called electric potential or voltage) in which a 1-degree spread of the straws corresponds to about 40 volts in modern measure. He also showed that electrical attraction on the upper plate follows the force law discovered by Charles-Augustin de Coulomb.

In 1792, Volta repeated Luigi Galvani's experiments, published in Bologna in 1791, in which a metal attached to a frog's crural nerve was brought in contact with a different metal attached to its leg muscle, causing it to contract. Characteristically, Volta tried to measure the effect and found a tension of only a fraction of a degree on his condensing electrometer. At first, he accepted Galvani's idea that this was a unique form of animal electricity, but by the end of the year he concluded that the electricity was from the metals rather than the muscles. To illustrate the function of the metals, Volta joined a piece of tin on the tip of his tongue to a silver spoon touching farther back and experienced a sour taste. Early in 1793, he announced his conclusions in an open letter to Galvani's nephew and defender, Giovanni Aldini, beginning a long debate. Volta's position was strengthened by measurements of what he called the electromotive force of different combinations of conductors with his condensing electrometer, ranking them in what is now called the electrochemical series.

In 1794, Volta married Teresa Peregrina and quickly added three sons to his new family. In the same year, he became the first foreigner to win the Copley Medal from the Royal Society of London for his contributions to physics and chemistry. By 1796, he had shown the identity of galvanic and common electricity by stimulating his electrometer with only metals in contact. After trying various combinations of metals and moist conductors, he finally obtained a sustained galvanic current by placing a moist cardboard between two different metals. He increased this effect by stacking such pairs of silver and zinc disks to form an electric pile to multiply the flow of galvanic electricity. These results were made public in 1800 in a letter to Sir Joseph Banks, president of the Royal Society, and first published in its *Philosophical Transactions* in French under the English title "On the Electricity Excited by the Mere Contact of Conducting Substances of Different Kinds" (1800). The letter also described his "crown of cups," consisting of a ring of cups filled with brine and connected by bimetallic arcs dipping into the liquid.

Volta might have published his work earlier had it not been for the distraction of the French invasion of Italy in 1796, which caused some damage to his laboratory and the closing of the university in 1799 for a year. In 1801, he demonstrated his work at the Paris Academy, where Napoleon I proposed that he be awarded a gold medal. Napoleon was so impressed with Volta's discoveries that he gave him a pension and later made him a count and senator of the kingdom of Lombardy. He continued with a reduced schedule at the university until after the Austrians returned in 1814, and retired to Como in 1819, where he died after a long illness in 1827, on the same day as Laplace. During the last twenty years of his life, he enjoyed a large income from his pension and senatorial salaries but published only two minor scientific papers.

Summary

Alessandro Volta is a good example of a devoted scientist whose concentration and effort led to important discoveries and inventions. He was a deeply religious man, who saw science and Christianity as allies, even seeking to defend religion from scientism with a confession of faith written in 1815. His many years of painstaking research in electrostatics and chemistry prepared him to capitalize on Galvani's discovery of electricity in frogs. His prior inventions of the electrophorus and condensing electrometer helped him to explore the effects of galvanic electricity and demonstrate its equivalence with common electricity. His tireless efforts and hard-earned experience led to his crowning achievement in the invention of the voltaic pile.

Volta's electric battery was one of the most important inventions of all time, providing the first useful form of electricity. The electrical revolution of the nineteenth century began with this one creation. In 1800, the year of its announcement, the English chemists William Nicholson and Anthony Carlisle used it to decompose water. Sir Humphry Davy built a powerful battery of 500 plates at London's Royal Institution and by 1808 had discovered potassium, sodium, calcium, magnesium, barium, strontium, and chlorine by electrolytic decomposition. Applications of discoveries that stem from Volta's research have changed the world. Among the many honors paid to the founder of this revolution, perhaps the greatest was the international agreement in 1881 to name the unit of electromotive force the volt, recognizing the means of producing constant electric current that Volta gave to mankind.

Bibliography

Dibner, Bern. *Alessandro Volta and the Electric Battery*. New York: Franklin Watts, 1964. This biography of Volta includes historical background on the development of electricity, his early life and work, Galvani's discovery and the resulting controversy, and the invention of the battery and its resulting influence. An appendix gives the English version of his letter to Banks, announcing his invention.

_____. *Galvani-Volta: A Controversy That Led to the Discovery of Useful Electricity*. Norwalk, Conn.: Burndy Library, 1952. This brief volume describes the work of Galvani, the defense of his ideas by Aldini, the work of Volta, the controversy that followed, and the results of Volta's work. A supplement gives a facsimile of Volta's letter to Banks in English translation as it appeared in *The Philosophical Magazine* in 1800.

Gill, Sydney. "A voltaic Enigma and a Possible Solution to It." *Annals of Science* 33 (1976): 351-370. This article analyzes Volta's work on contact electricity and attempts to explain the delay in his development of the battery and subsequent announcement of the invention. The analysis is based on several of Volta's letters.

Heilbron, J. L. *Electricity in the Seventeenth and Eighteenth Centuries: A Study of Early Modern Physics*. Berkeley: University of California Press, 1979. This volume is an exhaustive study of the history of electricity up to the time of Volta. It includes a detailed analysis of his work in electrostatics but only a brief epilogue on the voltaic pile. Bibliography includes ten entries on the works of Volta.

Potamian, Michael, and James Walsh. *Makers of Electricity*. Bronx, N.Y.: Fordham University Press, 1909. Chapter 5 in this volume, entitled "Volta the Founder of Electrical Science," gives a somewhat outdated but interesting and readable account of Volta's life and work.

Still, Alfred. *Soul of Amber*. New York: Murray Hill Books, 1944. Chapter 6 in this history of electrical science, entitled "Electrical Science Becomes Methodical," includes a description of Volta's work on electrostatics. Chapter 8, entitled "Electricity in Motion," includes a discussion of the invention of the voltaic pile. Each chapter contains about thirty bibliographic references.

Joseph L. Spradley

VOLTAIRE
François-Marie Arouet

Born: November 21, 1694; Paris, France
Died: May 30, 1778; Paris, France
Areas of Achievement: Literature and philosophy
Contribution: Voltaire encompasses in his work the extremes of rationalism during the Enlightenment. Until he was middle-aged, he was an optimist, but in his sixties, he rejected this philosophy in disgust and brilliantly argued the limitations of reason. He wrote prolifically in all literary forms during his lifetime, making critical commentary on prevailing social conditions and conventions.

Early Life

Voltaire was born François-Marie Arouet on November 21, 1694, in Paris. His father had migrated to the capital from Poitou and prospered there. He held a minor post in the treasury. Voltaire was educated at the Jesuit Collège Louis-le-Grand, and many years later the Jesuits were to be the objects of savage satire in his masterpiece *Candide: Ou, L'Optimisme* (1759; *Candide: Or, All for the Best*, 1759). Voltaire was trained in the law, which he abandoned. As a young man, during the first quarter of the century, Voltaire already exhibited strongly two traits which have come to be associated with the Enlightenment: wit and skepticism. Louis XIV ruled France until 1715, and the insouciant Voltaire (not yet known by that name) and his circle of friends delighted in poking fun at the pretentious backwardness of the Sun King's court.

In 1716, when Voltaire was twenty-two, his political satires prompted the first of his several exiles, in this instance to Sully-sur-Loire. He was, however, unrepentant; in 1717, more satirical verses on the aristocracy caused his imprisonment by *lettre de cachet* (without trial). During his eleven months in the Bastille, Voltaire, like so many imprisoned writers before him, practiced his craft. He wrote *Œdipe* (1718; *Oedipus*, 1761), a tragedy which was a great success upon the stage following his release. A year later, when *Oedipus* came out in print, the author took the name Voltaire, an approximate anagram of Arouet. Such was his fame, however, that the pseudonym afforded him little chance of anonymity. He came eventually to be known as François-Marie Arouet de Voltaire.

Life's Work

By the age of thirty, Voltaire was well established as a man of letters. For the next fifty years, he produced an enormous and varied body of work; he wrote tragic plays, satires in prose and verse, histories, philosophical tales, essays, pamphlets, encyclopedia entries, and letters by the thousands. Also by the age of thirty, he was a wealthy man. He speculated in the Compagnie des Indes with great success, and his fortune grew over the years. Voltaire's personal wealth afforded him an independence of which few writers of the period could boast.

Still, his penchant for religious and political controversy had him in trouble again by 1726. The Chevalier de Rohan caused him to be beaten and incarcerated in the Bastille for a second time. He was subsequently exiled to England, where he spent most of the period from 1726 to 1729. There, he learned the English language, read widely in the literature, and became the companion of Alexander Pope and other Queen Anne wits. *La Henriade* (1728; *Henriad*, 1732), his epic of Henry IV, was published during this period, and his sojourn in Britain would eventually produce *Lettres philosophiques* (1734; published earlier as *Letters Concerning the English Nation*, 1733). Voltaire's great achievement during the years immediately following his return to France was his *Histoire de Charles XII* (1731; *The History of Charles XII*, 1732). This account of the Swedish monarch is often characterized as the first modern history.

Letters Concerning the English Nation implicitly attacked French institutions through its approbation of English institutions. For example, Voltaire wittily suggests therein that, despite the manifest benefits of inoculation against smallpox, the French reject the practice because the English have adopted it first. Again, Voltaire angered powerful enemies. His book was burned, he barely escaped imprisonment, and he was forced to flee Paris for a third time. He settled at Cirey in Lorraine, first as the guest and eventually as the companion of the brilliant Madame du Châtelet. There, for the next fifteen years, he continued to write in all genres, but, having become acquainted with the works of John Locke and David Hume, he turned increasingly to philosophical and scientific subjects. As revealed in his *Discours en vers sur l'homme* (1738-1752; *Discourses in Verse on Man*, 1764), Voltaire embraced the philosophy of optimism during these years, believing that reason alone could lead man out of the darkness and into the millennium. Gradually, his reputation was rehabilitated within court circles. He had been given permission to return to Paris in 1735, he was named official historiographer of France in 1743, and he was elected to the French Academy in 1746. In 1748, he published his first philosophical tale, *Zadig: Ou, La Destinée, histoire orientale* (*Zadig: Or, The Book of Fate*, 1749).

Madame du Châtelet died in 1749. The next year, believing that Louis XV had offered him insufficient patronage, Voltaire joined the court of Frederick the Great of Prussia at Potsdam. For three years, Voltaire lived in great comfort and luxury, completing during this period *Le Siècle de Louis XIV* (1751; *The Age of Louis XIV*, 1752). He and the Prussian king, however, were not well suited temperamentally. They quarreled, and the inevitable breach occurred in 1753. Shortly thereafter, Voltaire purchased Les Délices (the delights), a château in Switzerland, near Geneva. He stayed in the good graces of the Swiss for exactly as long as he had managed in Prussia—three years. There, his encyclopedia entry for Geneva was perceived as having a contemptuous tone. The national pride of his hosts was wounded, and he left the country. He bought the great estate Ferney, on French soil but just across the Swiss frontier. This was the perfect retreat for a controversialist with Voltaire's volatile history; if the French authorities decided to act against him again, he could simply slip across the border. For the last twenty years of his life, Voltaire used the Ferney estate as the base from which he tirelessly launched his literary attacks upon superstition, error, and ignorance. He employed a variety of pseudonyms but made no effort to disguise his inimitable style and manner. This transparent device gave the authorities, by then indulgent and weary of attempting to muzzle him, an excuse not to prosecute.

The decade of the 1750's wrought a change in the middle-aged Voltaire's attitude far greater than any change he had undergone previously. He was deeply affected by the Lisbon earthquake of November 1, 1755. In this horrendous tragedy, perhaps as many as fifty thousand people died, many while worshiping in packed churches on All Saints' Day. Voltaire began to reexamine his concept of a rational universe that functioned according to fixed laws which man could apprehend and to which he could adapt himself. He was now repulsed by the optimists' theory that (to overstate it only slightly) this is the best of all possible worlds, and, therefore, any natural occurrence must be ultimately for the best. His first bitter attack on optimism was *Poème sur le désastre de Lisbonne* (1756; *Poem on the Lisbon Earthquake*, 1764). His rebuttal of this smug philosophy culminated in his masterpiece of dark comedy, *Candide*.

Voltaire claimed to have written this wildly improbable picaresque novel in three days during 1758. It was published in 1759 and was immensely popular; it averaged two new editions a year for the next twenty years. Pangloss, tutor to the incredibly callow hero, is a caricature of the optimistic philosophers Gottfried Wilhelm Leibniz and Christian von Wolff, although Voltaire's temperamental archenemy, Jean-Jacques Rousseau, fancied himself the model for Pangloss. *Candide*'s satire is by no means limited to optimism, and the novel reveals the best and worst of its author's traits of character. Voltaire lashes out at his lifelong enemies: superstition, bigotry, extremism, hypocrisy, and (despite the fact that it accounted for most of his personal wealth) colonialism. Also readily apparent are his anti-Semitism, his anti-Catholicism, and his sexism.

The major work of Voltaire's later years was *Dictionnaire philosophique portatif* (1764; *A Philosophical Dictionary for the Pocket*, 1765). He also involved himself deeply in the day-to-day operations of Ferney, and he maintained his voluminous correspondence with virtually all the eminent persons of Europe. For the first time in almost three decades, Voltaire returned to Paris in 1778. He was afforded a tumultuous hero's welcome, but he was eighty-three and ill; the celebration was too much for him in his fragile state of health. He died on May 30, within weeks of his triumphal return to the city of his birth.

Summary

Despite the Church's opposition to Voltaire's burial in sanctified ground, he was secretly—and inappropriately, some have suggested—interred at a convent outside the city. A decade later came the Revolution, and Voltaire's enemies had ostensibly become the French people's as well. He was exhumed and made a second grand entrance into Paris. He was reburied in the Panthéon next to Rousseau, an irony he might have enjoyed.

Voltaire's work is extremely varied, sometimes self-contradictory. His sentiments are often more personal than universal. He had had bad experiences with Jesuit priests, Protestant enthusiasts, and Jewish businessmen; hence, Jesuits, Calvinists, and Jews are mercilessly lampooned in *Candide*. He apparently had good experiences with Anabaptists, and the generous and selfless Anabaptist Jacques, in his brief appearance, is one of the few admirable characters in the novel. Voltaire had been cured of optimism by the horror of the Lisbon earthquake, the savagery of the Seven Years' War, and the reversals in his personal life. Yet he did not completely give way to pessimism. His philosophy in his later years seems to have been a qualified meliorism, as characterized by his famous injunction that every man should tend his own garden.

The famous and spurious quotation, "I disagree with everything you say, but I shall fight to the death for your right to say it," will be forever associated with Voltaire's memory. Although he probably never uttered these precise words, they are an admirable summation of the way he lived his intellectual life. The surviving pictures of Voltaire, most in old age, represent him as thin, sharp-featured, and sardonic. He is the very embodiment of one aspect of the neoclassical period—skeptical, irreverent, and valuing personal freedom above all other things.

Bibliography

Aldington, Richard. *Voltaire*. London: Routledge & Kegan Paul, 1925. One of the standard biographical-critical works. Part 1 (chapters 1-10) treats the life of Voltaire. Part 2 (chapters 11-19) examines Voltaire as poet, dramatist, literary critic, historian, biographer, philosopher, pamphleteer, and correspondent. Contains a chronological listing of Voltaire's works by genre, followed by a list of the English translations (up to that time) and a selected bibliography.

Gay, Peter. *Voltaire's Politics: The Poet as Realist*. Princeton, N.J.: Princeton University Press, 1959. A work of intellectual history which attempts to trace the psychological, social, and intellectual origins of Voltaire's ideas. The author portrays Voltaire's politics as realistic and humanely relativistic; he argues that Voltaire's humane sympathies failed him only in the case of his anti-Semitism.

Lanson, Gustave. *Voltaire.* Translated by Robert A. Wagoner with an introduction by Peter Gay. New York: John Wiley & Sons, 1966. This brief survey of Voltaire's life and work by a famous French literary historian was originally published in 1906 but was unavailable in English until sixty years later. It is an excellent introductory volume, which distinguishes between Voltaire's deeply held convictions and his more casual and whimsical arguments.

Mason, Haydn. *Voltaire: A Biography.* Baltimore: Johns Hopkins University Press, 1981. Organized according to seven periods in Voltaire's life. The author states that he has not attempted a comprehensive treatment of the life, because that would easily require ten volumes. Instead, he has attempted to capture the essence of the man as revealed under the pressure of circumstances. Contains a helpful chronology and a selected bibliography.

Torrey, Norman L. *The Spirit of Voltaire.* New York: Columbia University Press, 1938. Argues for and seeks to document Voltaire's moral integrity while granting that a certain duplicity was a necessary condition of his life and work. Concludes with a long chapter on Voltaire's religion, probing whether he was a Deist, a mystic, or a Humanist.

Patrick Adcock

RICHARD WAGNER

Born: May 22, 1813; Leipzig, Saxony
Died: February 13, 1883; Venice, Italy
Areas of Achievement: Music and theater
Contribution: Wagner wrote the librettos and scores of some of the world's greatest operas, most notably *Tristan und Isolde* (1859) and the tetralogy *Der Ring des Nibelungen* (1874; the ring of the Nibelungs). A conductor, musical director, and writer as well as a composer, he raised standards for musical performances and developed the aesthetic of the *Gesamtkunstwerk* (total work of art), using compositional techniques based on chromaticism, variable meter, the leitmotif (a musical phrase with dramatic import), and an "infinite melody" of continuous expressiveness and significance.

Early Life

Richard Wagner was born in the German cultural and commercial center of Leipzig. Legally the son of police actuary Friedrich Wagner and his wife, Johanna, the young Wagner was never certain whether his father was actually Ludwig Geyer, the painter, actor, and poet whom his mother wed nine months after the death of Friedrich in November, 1813. Geyer died when Wagner was eight years old, but the child was called Richard Geyer until his middle teens.

While Wagner never mastered score-reading or an instrument, he was an autodidact with ever-expanding interests in music, theater, and culture. His initial schooling took place during his family's stay in Dresden, where he took piano lessons and explored ancient Greek mythology. He spent his late adolescence in Leipzig, beginning lessons in harmonic theory in 1828 and briefly studying violin with a member of the Gewandhaus Orchestra in 1830. The following year, he dabbled in musical studies at the University of Leipzig and became a pupil of Christian Theodor Weinlig.

A survey of Wagner's earliest successes and failures during the ensuing years indicates the wide range of his ambitions. By the end of 1833, he had composed his Polonaise in D for Piano (1832), conducted his Concert Symphony in C Major (1832) in Prague and Leipzig, started and abandoned work on an opera, and secured employment at the Würzburg city theater. In 1834, he became music director of Heinrich Bethmann's theatrical company in Magdeburg, completed his opera *Die Feen* (the fairies), published an essay for Robert Schumann's *Die Neue Zeitschrift für Musik*, made his debut as an opera conductor in Lauchstadt, and completed a libretto for *Das Liebesverbot* (1836; the ban on love). After first attempting to have this opera presented in Leipzig, Berlin, and Paris, Wagner conducted one performance of it in 1836 in Magdeburg, before the company there disbanded.

Also in 1836, Wagner wed Christine Wilhelmina ("Minna") Planer, an actress whom he first met in Lauchstadt. During the first years of this troubled marriage, Wagner experienced a decline in productivity. In 1837, he wrote an overture based on *Rule, Britannia!* (originally by Thomas Arne) and soon afterward assumed the post of music director of the city theater in Riga, where he sparked controversy (as he had in Magdeburg) by proposing numerous reforms, including plans for a subscription series.

When his contract in Riga was not renewed, Wagner traveled with Minna to Paris via the Norwegian coast, arriving in September, 1839. There he intensified his literary activity, received the support of Giacomo Meyerbeer, and became exposed to the work of Hector Berlioz. Initially occupying himself with such piecemeal work as composition for vaudevilles, he soon completed the first versions of the *Faust Overture* (1840), the grand tragic opera *Rienzi* (1840), and the Romantic opera *Der fliegende Holländer* (1841; the flying Dutchman). By early 1843, the premieres of the latter two works had established Wagner as a composer and conductor of note.

Life's Work

In February, 1843, Wagner assumed the position of royal *Kapellmeister* left vacant after the death of Francesco Morlacchi. During his stay in Dresden, Wagner again antagonized his colleagues. Rigorous rehearsal schedules, a rearrangement of the traditional seating arrangement, and the eradication of the seniority system were among the improvements suggested by Wagner, who rarely succeeded in having his ideas enacted.

Wagner's brilliant but unorthodox approach to conducting, eliciting an impressive range of dynamic nuance, called upon orchestra and audience members to follow an idiosyncratic series of tempo changes that fully indulged the maestro's subjectivism. To retain his office, Wagner was forced to promise to interpret only new operas in this manner and to conform to tradition in conducting the old ones.

His talent as a creative administrator enabled Wagner to mount spectacles such as the 1843 choral festival, for which he hastily composed *Das Liebesmahl der Apostel* (1843; the love feast of the apostles) for more than thirteen hundred performers. He was, however, dissatisfied with this performance as well as with the premiere two years later of his grand Romantic opera *Tannhäuser* (1845), which he revised extensively over the years.

Wagner, who met the Russian anarchist Mikhail Bakunin in 1848, supported the Dresden Revolution of 1849. He fled Germany in the wake of its failure, staying briefly in Weimar, the home of his friend Franz Liszt, before settling in Zurich. Following a discouraging January, 1850, excursion to Paris, Wagner wrote the anti-Semitic essay "Das Judentum in der Musik" (1850; Jewishness and music). Wagner was also frustrated with circumstances surrounding the 1850 premiere of *Lohengrin*, directed by Liszt. In this Romantic opera, Elsa of Brabant loses the mysterious knight Lohengrin after the machinations of her enemies and her own curiosity compel her to ask him forbidden questions about his origin. Wagner's distance from the production (he did not hear a complete performance of the work until 1861) prompted him to ponder the creation of a theater designed to showcase his own works.

While in exile, Wagner completed his aesthetic treatise *Oper und Drama* (1852; *Opera and Drama*, 1913) and finished *Das Rheingold* (1854; the Rhine gold) and *Die Walküre* (1856; the Valkyrie), the first half of *Der Ring des Nibelungen* cycle. Among his financial supporters in Zurich was his neighbor Otto Wesendonck, whose wife, Mathilde, was an object of Wagner's romantic interest; his settings of her poems are known as the *Wesendonck Lieder* (1858). When the tension between the Wesendoncks and the Wagners reached a point of crisis, Wagner left Zurich for Venice, where he finished the full score of the second act to *Tristan und Isolde* in 1859. Intervention of the Saxon police forced him to complete the work in Lucerne.

By the end of the year, Wagner had returned to Paris, where successful concerts in 1860 resulted in an order from Napoleon III for a production of *Tannhäuser* at the Opéra; this support from the French government helped Wagner secure a partial amnesty, allowing travel through any part of Germany except Saxony. The 1861 Opéra performances occasioned the famous anti-Austrian Jockey Club protests that forced *Tannhäuser* to close.

In 1862, a sickly Minna visited her husband in Biebrich before retiring to Dresden, where she died in 1866. Wagner, who soon received a full amnesty, dabbled in romantic affairs and conducted his own music throughout Europe, offering a profitable series of concerts in St. Petersburg and Moscow in 1863. Final relief from financial woes came in 1864 in the person of King Ludwig II of Bavaria, who provided the artist with generous political as well as monetary support. The mid-1860's also saw the intensification of Wagner's relationship with Cosima, the daughter of Liszt and the wife of conductor/pianist Hans von Bülow, for a time one of Wagner's staunchest supporters.

Supported by Ludwig, Wagner established a luxurious home in Munich, where *Tristan und Isolde* was first performed in 1865. A tragic love story colored by Wagner's relationship with Mathilde as well as his readings of Schopenhauerian and Buddhist philosophy, this opera is perhaps his most successful attempt at creating the sustained music drama that he proposed in his writings. Opening with the ambiguous "Tristan chord" (F-B-D-sharp-G-sharp), his score is characterized by an extreme chromaticism of melody and harmony that borders on atonality, and his verse is characterized by the deft employment of alliteration, rhyme, and assonance. Together with his sensuous phrasing and evocative manipulation of leitmotifs, these elements effectively evoke an atmosphere of intensifying yearning. The strenuous title roles were performed by Ludwig Schnorr von Carolsfeld (whose death three weeks after the fourth performance fueled rumors that the vocal parts were unperformable) and his wife, Malvina.

Later in 1865, local hostility toward Wagner led to his departure to Switzerland, where he and Cosima established their home, Tribschen. For the next two years, the two strenuously tried to hide their relationship from King Ludwig, who slowly awakened to what their enemies—including an unbalanced Malvina—were as strenuously trying to point out to him. Cosima and Bülow finally dissolved their marriage in July, 1870; Cosima married Wagner the following month, by which time she was already the mother of Wagner's children Isolde, Eva, and Siegfried.

In 1868, Wagner saw the successful premiere of his most comic opera, *Die Meistersinger von Nürnberg* (1867; the mastersingers of Nuremberg). The story of an untrained singer who wins his beloved by outsinging members of a conservative songster's guild was in part a scarcely concealed attack on Eduard Hanslick, one of the composer's harshest critics. At the end of the year, Wagner met Friedrich Wilhelm Nietzsche, whose move from fervid support to chilly hostility can be traced through his writings.

Dominating Wagner's musical activities through the 1860's and the 1870's was his vision of mounting a full Ring cycle in a festival theater dedicated to his works. After plans to build such a house in Munich were abandoned in 1868, Wagner's discouragement turned to outrage when Ludwig commanded that performances of *Das Rheingold* and *Die Walküre* be given in 1869 and 1870, respectively; Wagner went so far as to deceive the king to forestall a similarly decreed performance of *Siegfried* (1871), the third part of the tetralogy.

By 1872, Wagner had chosen the town of Bayreuth as the site of his festival. Leaving Tribschen, he spent the next four years supervising the construction of the Festspielhaus and engaging in fund-raising and the recruiting of personnel. He also completed the cycle's final installment, *Götterdämmerung* (1874; the twilight of the gods), and arranged the tetralogy's publication for performance.

The August, 1876, premiere of the Ring cycle in Bayreuth represented the triumphant culmination of twenty-eight years of labor. Prominent figures from around the world flocked to this four-day forerunner of modern festivals, where they were immersed in an epic of gods, Valkyries, and giants told through Wagner's alliterative *Stabreim* verse and massive orchestration. The only disappointments associated with the festival were its large deficit and Nietzsche's departure before its conclusion.

Wagner, however, was now secure enough to spend his later years riding the crest of his popularity, his operas receiving performances throughout Europe. He dedicated much of his time to writing essays on sundry topics, completing the fourth volume of his unreliable but revealing autobiography *Mein Leben* (1911; *My Life*, 1911). Months prior to his death of a heart attack, his final opera, *Parsifal* (1882), received its premiere under the direction of Hermann Levi at Bayreuth. Considered by Wagner and his followers as a sacred work, this tale of miraculous redemption is traditionally offered during the Christian holiday of Easter.

Summary

Notwithstanding his tremendous talent as a composer, conductor, and artistic manager, Richard Wagner's sheer force of will seems to have permitted him to emerge triumphant from a career haunted by scandal and indebtedness. A combination of creativity, charisma, and controversy attracted followers to him, the cultish phenomenon of Wagnerism testifying to the magnetism of his personality. In the decades after his death, Wagner's stature as a musician mushroomed. Through the end of the nineteenth century, a significant portion of the creative world was influenced to some degree by his work, and composers past the turn of the century felt compelled to refer to his works in measuring the value of their own.

Considered in tandem with his musical achievements, Wagner's nationalism and anti-Semitism made him a cultural hero of the Fascist regime of Adolf Hitler, who closely identified Wagner's thought with his own policies. As a result of this association, works by Wagner were not programmed in Israel until Zubin Mehta led the Israel Philharmonic in a 1974 concert that was disturbed by catcalls and fistfights.

Besides being performed regularly at the world's principal opera houses (Bayreuth remains a shrine for present-day Wagnerians and music lovers in general), Wagner's music has been preserved in numerous video and audio recordings. Outstanding among the latter is a 1965 recording of *Der Ring des Nibelungen*, a legendary performance by Sir Georg Solti and the Vienna Philharmonic Orchestra, featuring vocalists Dietrich Fischer-Dieskau, Kirsten Flagstad, Christa Ludwig, and Birgit Nilsson. Wagner's music has penetrated into many aspects of popular culture, most notably as the familiar melody "Here Comes the Bride," which may be heard in act 3 of *Lohengrin*. Other settings in which excerpts from Wagner's works are heard outside their original context include Bugs Bunny cartoons, films by surrealist Luis Buñuel, works by composer John Cage, and Francis Ford Coppola's film *Apocalypse Now* (1979).

Bibliography

Burbridge, Peter, and Richard Sutton, eds. *The Wagner Companion*. New York: Cambridge University Press, 1979. This collection of essays covers a broad range of Wagner-related subjects.
Deathridge, John, and Carl Dahlhaus. *The New Grove Wagner*. Edited by

Stanley Sadie. New York: W. W. Norton, 1984. Highly recommended as a supplement for serious research, this concise scholarly treatment of Wagner's life, thought, and music includes critical analyses of potentially misleading sources of information, particularly *My Life*.

Donington, Robert. *Wagner's "Ring" and Its Symbols*. New York: St. Martin's Press, 1974. An expert presents a thorough investigation of Wagner's most complex work.

Millington, Barry. *Wagner*. Reprint. New York: Vintage Books, 1987. A brief and well-organized biography including a useful chronology and bibliography. Also includes guides to Wagner's musical compositions and a biographical listing of significant personalities in his life.

Newman, Ernest. *The Life of Richard Wagner*. New York: Alfred A. Knopf, 1933-1946. This four-volume biography remains the most comprehensive English-language account of Wagner's life.

Schonberg, Harold C. "Colossus of Germany." In *The Lives of the Great Composers*. New York: W. W. Norton, 1981. In this book, the highly popular music journalist surveys Wagner's life and most lasting contributions.

_____. "Richard Wagner." In *The Great Conductors*. New York: Simon & Schuster, 1967. A major music critic of *The New York Times* engagingly outlines Wagner's contributions to the art of conducting.

Shaw, George Bernard. *The Perfect Wagnerite*. Reprint. New York: Dover, 1967. The witty dramatist discusses the Ring cycle and other aspects of Wagner's legacy.

Shelton, Geoffrey. *Richard and Cosima Wagner*. London: Victor Gollancz, 1982. The translator of Cosima's diaries explores the famous couple's love affair and marriage.

Westernhagen, Curt von. *Wagner: A Biography*. New York: Cambridge University Press, 1979. This major study supplements Newman's biography with more recent scholarship.

David Marc Fischer

ALBRECHT WENZEL VON WALLENSTEIN

Born: September 24, 1583; Heřmanice, Bohemia
Died: February 25, 1634; Eger, Bohemia
Areas of Achievement: The military and government
Contribution: A master of recruiting and logistics, Wallenstein raised and commanded the armies that saved the Catholic Habsburgs from losing the Thirty Years' War to their Protestant opponents. He was able to amass great wealth and power and may even have aspired to an independent crown of his own.

Early Life

The son of Wilhelm Wallenstein and his wife, Margarethe, Albrecht Wenzel von Wallenstein was one of seven children. His mother died when he was not quite ten years old, and his father died within two years of her death. Albrecht was sent to live with his mother's brother-in-law, Heinrich Slawata von Chlum. The Wallenstein family, although not wealthy, was fairly well connected among the Bohemian aristocracy. While he was later to convert and become an outstanding commander of the Catholic forces, Wallenstein was reared as a Protestant.

At age fifteen, Albrecht went to the Lutheran school at Goldberg, Silesia, remained there for two years, and then attended the academy at Altdorf, near Nuremberg. It was a stay of only six months, Wallenstein being noted primarily for his violent behavior: The records indicate a number of brawls in which he was involved, and he spent at least some time in the student prison at the academy.

When Wallenstein left Nuremberg, he traveled through Europe, spending the greatest amount of time at Padua, where he studied under the unusual combination of Jesuits and astrologers. By 1606, he had converted to Roman Catholicism and would remain a dutiful son of the Church for the rest of his life. At the same time, however, he developed a firm belief in astrology, especially as it controlled his destiny. He believed his life to be under the influence of Saturn, which promised great accomplishments. In 1607, he had his horoscope cast by the famed astronomer Johannes Kepler and often referred to the predictions which had been fulfilled in later years. Holding such contradictory beliefs was only one facet of Wallenstein's enigmatic personality.

In 1604, Wallenstein embarked on his first military campaign, serving as an ensign, then a captain, with the artillery of the Holy Roman Empire in a campaign in what is now Romania. In command was Johann Tserclaes, Count Tilly; along with Wallenstein, Tilly would later be one of the two outstanding imperial generals of the Thirty Years' War.

Wallenstein married in 1609. His wife, Lucretia von Landek, was a much older and very wealthy widow. According to some unconfirmed but often-repeated stories, Wallenstein nearly died from a love potion given him by his new wife, but he survived. Lucretia died on March 23, 1614, leaving her vast wealth, including many Moravian estates, to Wallenstein.

Wallenstein's appearance aptly fits the description "saturnine," for he was somber, even austere, with a long face, sallow complexion, and dark eyes and hair. He wore the neatly trimmed beard characteristic of the period. He had irregular features and high cheekbones, and he rarely displayed his emotions; when he did, he could break into sudden, deadly fury. Throughout his life, Wallenstein inspired a number of emotions, but fear, respect, and envy were inspired more often than love or affection.

Life's Work

In May, 1618, the Defenestration of Prague marked the beginning of the Thirty Years' War. Seldom has so trivial, even ludicrous, an incident been the spark for such a long and destructive conflict. The true causes for the war were more profound than Bohemian Protestant rebels throwing Catholic imperial councillors out a window. Indeed, there was a mesh of religion—Protestant Reformation against Catholic Counter-Reformation; politics—the various smaller German states against the Holy Roman Empire; and dynastic struggle—the Habsburgs of Spain and Austria against most of Europe.

The war was Wallenstein's springboard to greatness. When the Bohemian Protestants rose in revolt against the Habsburg Emperor Matthias, Wallenstein moved swiftly, removing the contents of the Moravian treasury to the safety of imperial coffers in Vienna. Welcomed into imperial service, Wallenstein began well: At the Battle of Tein, in southern Bohemia, he smashed through the lines of a rebel army that was moving to threaten Vienna. Although he was often successful in battle, it was as an organizer and recruiter that Wallenstein proved most capable and effective.

Although his Moravian estates had been seized in the uprising, Wallenstein still retained considerable wealth, and he freely loaned this to the emperor and to his successor, Ferdinand II, who was elected to the throne in 1619. On June 9, 1623, Wallenstein remarried, taking Isabella Katharina von Harrach as his bride. Isabella came from one of the wealthiest and most influential families of the empire; Emperor Ferdinand attended the wedding, and the match further swelled Wallenstein's treasury. Much of this, too, he loaned to Ferdinand.

As the imperial forces regained Bohemia and Moravia, Ferdinand repaid his debts by granting Wallenstein lands that had been confiscated from his rebellious subjects. The Wallenstein domains steadily increased, and in 1624 the emperor created him Duke of Friedland; eventually the duchy included hundreds of thousands of acres in what is modern northern Czechoslovakia. From Friedland, Wallenstein drew grain, cattle, cloth, weapons, and other supplies needed by the imperial army. These necessities returned a flow of riches to Friedland, which remained prosperous and at peace in the midst of war.

Wallenstein became increasingly important in the imperial army, rising in 1623 to the position of "Major over all infantry," but he remained basically an organizer and staff officer. In 1624, Wallenstein made a dramatic offer: He would provide an army of fifty thousand men, and put this force into the field at no cost to the emperor. Asked how the troops could be supplied and maintained, Wallenstein gave the grim but truthful answer, "War must feed war." The troops were raised, and in 1625 Wallenstein was named imperial commander. Moving northward, he swept a powerful Danish army from Silesia, and rolled it back to the Baltic Sea. In honor of Wallenstein's victories, the emperor granted him the Duchies of Mecklenburg and Pomerania on the Baltic coast. This added to the discontent and mistrust that was already felt for Wallenstein among court circles in Vienna.

In 1629, peace came briefly to Europe, and Ferdinand maneuvered Wallenstein into resigning his command. Apparently the emperor had doubts about his powerful subject as well. In July, 1630, a Swedish army under King Gustavus II Adolphus landed on the German coast and marched southward; volunteers soon swelled its ranks to forty thousand troops. Still, Ferdinand kept Wallenstein in retirement, hoping to avoid a cause for disunity in the empire, for many of the nobility and courtiers disliked Wallenstein. Wallenstein used this time well, improving and enlarging Friedland; his duchy seems to have been the sole passion of his life. In 1632, Ferdinand, hard pressed by Swedish victories, was forced to recall Wallenstein to command. He granted Wallenstein terms that made him more a viceroy than a general: Wallenstein was given virtual independence in the territories he reconquered, with no political or religious interference in his operations. Wallenstein recognized that renewed religious persecutions would only prolong the war and increase its destruction.

Wallenstein and Gustavus sparred through the spring and summer of 1632, and the imperial general gradually forced the Swedish king northward and out of Bavaria. On November 16, 1632, the two met at the Battle of Lutzen. Only the death of Gustavus at the head of his troops, and the timely arrival of imperial reinforcements saved Wallenstein from defeat. Although left in possession of the field, the Swedish army was forced to retreat, and the most dangerous threat to the imperial cause had been repulsed.

In the fall of 1633, Wallenstein began secret negotiations with members of the Protestant Party. His motives in these talks are unclear: He might have aspired to the crown of Bohemia, or perhaps he sought a general peace for Europe. Emperor Ferdinand assumed the worst, and officers were sent to arrest Wallenstein; if he resisted, force was to be used. Wallenstein attempted to flee but was caught at the fortress of Eger, in Bohemia. There, on the night of February 25, 1634, he was killed by a blow from a halberd. His body was removed in a blood-soaked rug.

Summary

As Duke of Friedland, Albrecht Wenzel von Wallenstein issued his own coinage, and the motto he chose for it was *Invita Invida*: "I invite envy." Seldom have fewer words been more aptly chosen, for Wallenstein's career excited jealousy and fear among his contemporaries, even those he served. His aims and motives were a mystery to his time and have remained so long after his death. Was he merely a grasping opportunist intent upon personal aggrandizement, or did he have some far-reaching goal for all Europe?

On the one hand, Wallenstein seized every opportunity to enlarge his lands, increase his wealth, and consolidate his power. His position rested upon two pillars: one, the army, nominally that of the emperor but raised, equipped, and led by Wallenstein; the second, his Duchy of Friedland. Add to this Wallenstein's thirst for land and titles, and it would seem that his vision was limited strictly to personal gain.

On the other, Wallenstein's policies seem to have been calculated to increase the power of the emperor and the empire by reuniting central Europe as a religiously tolerant state no longer divided by sectarian conflict. His actions in his own territories and in those conquered by his armies show a man less interested in religious disputes than in productive farms and prosperous merchants. Some historians, notably C. V. Wedgwood, contend that he aimed at a realignment of the Holy Roman Empire into one centered on Bohemia, the valley of the Elbe River, and the Baltic Sea—a sort of Slavic-Germanic empire. In another theory, Francis Watson, Wallenstein's premier English-writing biographer, believes that Wallenstein's long-range goal was the expulsion of the Turks from Europe.

As a soldier, he was a master of raising, organizing, and supplying an army, but he was less skilled at commanding it in battle. Although successful in his campaigns, Wallenstein inspired no new tactics; his strategy was traditional, if skillfully implemented. His major contribution to warfare was to demonstrate that an enormous force could be maintained in the field for prolonged periods of time.

Wallenstein's undoubted accomplishments are considerable: From 1625 to 1629, he regained northern Germany for the empire and gave the Catholic church the opportunity to retrieve lands that had been lost to the Protestants. Forced into retirement, he returned to defeat the formidable invasion by Gustavus II Adolphus and restore imperial power in central Europe. In the meantime, he established a secure and prosperous duchy in the midst of a Europe torn by war. This is the work of a man of considerable powers and abilities—perhaps even a man whose destiny was secured by the stars.

Bibliography

Cust, Sir Edward. "Wallenstein." In *Lives of the Warriors of the Thirty Years' War: Warriors of the Seventeenth Century.* Reprint. Freeport, N.Y.: Books for Libraries Press, 1972. An amusing Victorian view of Wallenstein, his career, and his times. Cust is biased in favor of the Protestant cause, but his accounts of campaigns and battles are generally straightforward and clear even for the military novice.

Dupuy, R. Ernest, and Trevor N. Dupuy. *The Encyclopedia of Military History.* Rev. ed. New York: Harper & Row, 1977. The section on the Thirty Years' War is a brief but thorough review of the events of the time and will be especially helpful to the reader with little or no background in military studies.

Liddel Hart, B. H. "Wallenstein—The Enigma of History." In *Great Captains Unveiled.* Reprint. Freeport, N.Y.: Books for Libraries Press, 1967. The outstanding and individual British military thinker, historian, and soldier provides his own unique insight into Wallenstein's career and accomplishments. Provides an excellent thumbnail biography as well.

Mann, Golo. *Wallenstein: His Life Narrated.* Translated by Charles Kessler. New York: Holt, Rinehart and Winston, 1976. A thorough, massive, and imaginative rendering of Wallenstein's life and career. An excellent, if sometimes poetic, study of Wallenstein's psychology as well as his actions.

Watson, Francis. *Wallenstein: Soldier Under Saturn.* New York: D. Appleton-Century, 1938. An essential English-language biography of Wallenstein, this work provides considerable background on the times and milieu of its subject; a comprehensive study, written in an engaging style.

Wedgwood, C. V. *The Thirty Years' War.* New Haven, Conn.: Yale University Press, 1949. This classic work remains the best single-volume introduction to the Thirty Years' War. It contains much material on Wallenstein and his part in the struggle and is very helpful for understanding the complex military and political events of the period.

Michael Witkoski

WANG YANG-MING

Born: November 30, 1472; Yu-yao, Chekiang, China
Died: January 9, 1529; Nan-en, Kiangsi, China
Areas of Achievement: Philosophy and politics
Contribution: As a high official, holding many governmental offices from
    magistrate to governor, Wang suppressed rebellions and created a reign of
    peace in China that lasted a century. As a Neo-Confucian philosopher, he
    exercised tremendous influence in both China and Japan for 150 years.

Early Life

Wang Yang-ming was born on November 30, 1472, in Yu-yao, Chekiang
Province, the son of a minister of civil personnel in Nanking. He was re-
named Wang Yang-ming by his students, but his private name was Shou-jen
and his courtesy name was Po-an. According to legend, he could not speak
until he was given a name at the age of five. He soon began reading his
grandfather's books and reciting their contents. When he was eleven years
old, he went to live with his father at Peking. At the age of twelve, Wang
announced to a fortune-teller that the greatest occupation was that of a sage,
not that of a government official. His mother, Madame Cheng, died when he
was thirteen. At fifteen, he visited the Chu-yung Mountain passes, where he
first became interested both in archery and in the frontier.

Wang was married at the age of seventeen, but he was so absorbed in a
conversation he was having with a Taoist priest on his wedding night that he
forgot to go home until he was sent for the next morning. As he and his wife
were passing through Kuang-hsin the next year, he had another important
discussion, this time with a prominent scholar named Lou Liang. Lou was so
impressed with Wang that he predicted that Wang could become a sage if he
studied diligently. Wang, however, devoted his nineteenth year to the study
of archery and military tactics.

During the next ten years, Wang was torn between pursuing a career in the
military, in politics, in literature, and in philosophy. After receiving his civil
service degree, he delved deeply into the works of Chu Hsi. While visiting
his father in Peking, he spent seven days sitting quietly in front of some
bamboos in an attempt to discern the principles of Chu Hsi embodied within
them. The stress was too much for Wang, however, and he became very ill.
Thoroughly disillusioned with philosophy, he spent his time writing flowery
compositions instead of studying for his civil service examinations. Consequently, he failed his examinations in 1493 and again 1496, and he shifted
his interest back to military crafts and to the Taoist philosophy.

Wang finally settled on one career choice after passing his civil service
examinations in 1499, at the age of twenty-seven. He was appointed to the
Ministry of Public Works, where he impressed his superiors with a method

for defending China against invasion. Though his proposal was rejected, Wang was made minister of justice in Yunan in the following year. In 1501, Wang reversed the convictions of many prisoners after checking the prison records near Nanking. Ill health forced Wang to retreat to the Yang-ming ravine to recuperate. He built a house in the ravine and began calling himself "Philosopher of Yang-ming." Wang soon became very skeptical of some of the teachings of Taoism and Buddhism and of his literary pursuits.

Having fully recovered from his illness, Wang returned to Peking in 1504, where he was appointed director of the provincial examinations in Shantung. That same year, he became a secretary in the Ministry of War. In 1505, members of his large student following convinced him that he was better suited as a philosopher, and he began lecturing on the importance of becoming a sage. His attacks of the practice of reciting classics and writing flowery compositions alienated him from the more conservative scholars, who accused him of trying to build a reputation for himself. Only one scholar, the honored academician Chan Jo-shui, appreciated his merits. Not only did he befriend Wang but also he helped him spread the true doctrine of Confucius.

A year later, Wang's career as a lecturer was dramatically interrupted. In 1506, he came to the defense of a group of supervising censors who had been imprisoned by a corrupt eunuch, Liu Chin. Wang wrote a memorial that so angered Liu Chin that he ordered Wang to be beaten, imprisoned, and banished to Lung ch'ang, a place inhabited primarily by barbarian tribes. Wang was demoted to head of a dispatch station. He began his journey in 1507 and arrived at Lung ch'ang a year later. During his trip, he barely escaped an assassination attempt by Liu's agents.

The three years that he spent living among the aborigines were the turning point of his life. Having to scavenge for food and water for himself and his subordinates in a desolate land and to build houses for the Miao aborigines took its toll on Wang's health. Yet the isolation was beneficial, for his privations forced him to look inward. One night, he suddenly realized that one need only look into one's own mind to find the eternal principles of life instead of searching for these principles in objects. In 1509, he developed a theory that held that knowledge and action are one. Monogamy, for example, can only be fully understood when it is practiced. With these theories, Wang was revising Idealist Neo-Confucianism, as it had been pronounced by Lu Hsiang-shan. In addition, Wang was directly opposing the rationalistic Neo-Confucianism of Chu Hsi.

Life's Work

As soon as Wang's term as head of the dispatch station had ended in 1510, he was made magistrate of Lu-ling. During his seven-month stay in office, he carried out a number of reforms. As the result of an audience with the emperor, Wang was promoted to Secretary of the Ministry of Justice and

Director of the Ministry of Personnel in 1511, Vice Minister of Imperial Stables in 1512, and Minister of State Ceremonials in 1514.

Wang enjoyed his greatest military successes at Kiangsi. When he first arrived there in 1517 as the new senior censor and governor, Kiangsi was the scene of repeated insurrections by rebels and bandits. Two months after his arrival, he suppressed the rebellion and initiated the rehabilitation of the rebels. In 1518, he conducted tax reform, established schools, carried out reconstruction, and instituted the Community Compact, which improved unity as well as community morals.

Wang reached the pinnacle of his political career in 1519. On his way to suppress a rebellion in Fukien, he discovered that the Prince of Ning, Ch'en-hao, had declared himself head of state. Wang surrounded the prince's base, Nan ch'ang, and captured him. Rumors had surfaced as a result of his contact with Ch'en-hao, and Wang was accused by a jealous official of conspiring with the prince, resulting in the imprisonment of one of Wang's pupils. Nevertheless, Wang was appointed Governor of Kiangsi by the end of the year. In 1520, he instituted more reforms.

Wang's achievements were not viewed as a cause for celebration by everyone in the kingdom. The emperor tried to claim credit for the victory at Nanking by leading the expedition himself. Wang also embarrassed the emperor, first by capturing the prince and then by giving credit to the department of military affairs. Most damaging of all, though, was the fact that Wang and the prince had exchanged messengers before the rebellion took place. Wang's political enemies were so incensed by his correspondence with the prince that Wang's messenger, Chi Yuan-heng, was tortured to death.

Wang was exonerated of all charges in 1521 when the Chia-ching emperor ascended the throne. After his father died in 1522, Wang went into virtual retirement at Yu-yao for five years, where he attracted hundreds of disciples from all over China, even though his critics escalated their attacks against him. During this period, he developed his philosophy to full maturity with his doctrine of the extension of innate knowledge. With this theory, Wang turned psychology into ethics, suggesting that the human mind possesses an innate capacity for distinguishing between good and evil. Wang's conversations with his students were collected in his major work, *Ch'uan-hsi lu* (1572; *Instructions for Practical Living*, 1963).

In 1522, Wang was called upon to suppress a rebellion in Kwangsi, a feat which he accomplished in only six months. The coughing that had bothered him for years became so pronounced during the fighting that he had to conduct the battles from carriages. On his return home, he died in Nan-en, Kiangsi, on January 9, 1529. After his death, a political enemy of Wang, senior academician Kuei O, vented his anger against Wang by revoking his earldom and all of his hereditary privileges, thereby disinheriting Wang's sons. In 1567, though, a new emperor bestowed on Wang the posthumous title of Marquis of Hsin-chien. In 1584, he was accorded the highest honor of all by the offering of sacrifice to him in the Confucian temple.

Summary

Wang Yang-ming will be remembered as the scholar-official who brought a lasting peace to China. Under the leadership of such corrupt eunuchs as Liu Chin, fifteenth century China was a chaotic country, overrun with rebels and bandits. Wang rose to power through the civil service examination system, which had been the traditional avenue to fame and political authority for more than one thousand years. Although he had many political enemies, Wang used his various offices to quell the rebellions. Consequently, a large portion of China enjoyed a century of peace.

Wang's contributions to Neo-Confucian philosophy also had a tremendous effect on China. In the fifteenth century, the Confucian classics, such as the works of Chu Hsi, were being used by the rulers to restrict freedom of thought. Wang arrived at this conclusion through a three-step learning process that began with the writing of flowery compositions, proceeded to intense study of Chu Hsi's works, and culminated in his revolutionary pronouncements. His doctrine of unity of action and knowledge and his doctrine of innate knowledge invigorated the Confucian system. After his death, Wang's philosophy would become a potent force in China and Japan for 150 years, producing a number of brilliant reformers.

Bibliography

Chang Carson. "Wang Yang-ming's Philosophy." In *Philosophy East and West*, vol. 5. Honolulu: University of Hawaii Press, 1955. A short introduction to Wang's life and work. Useful primarily for its clear, concise explanation of Wang's philosophy.

Feng, Yu-lan. *A History of Chinese Philosophy.* Translated by Derk Bodde. Vol 2. Princeton, N.J.: Princeton University Press, 1953. An introduction to Wang's philosophy. Although the entry relies heavily on quotations from Wang's works, it does offer commentary at the beginning and ending of each section.

Wang Yang-ming. *Instructions for Practical Living and Other Neo-Confucian Writings.* Translated by Wing-tsit Chan. New York: Columbia University Press, 1963. The introduction is a comprehensive account of Wang's achievements as a politician and as a philosopher, based on standard Chinese sources. This text is an indispensable biography for the English-speaking reader.

_____. *The Philosophy of Wang Yang-ming.* Translated by Frederick Goodrich Henke. Chicago: Open Court Publishing, 1916. An uncritical translation, which is based largely on such legends as Wang's escape by boat from assassins. Omits some essential material, but it does provide a good overview of Wang's early life.

Zehou, Li. "Thoughts on Ming-Quing Neo-Confucianism." In *Chu Hsi and Neo-Confucianism*, edited by Wing-tsit Chan. Honolulu: University of Hawaii Press, 1986. Clarifies Wang's philosophy by contrasting it with the work of Wang's precursor, Chu Hsi.

Alan Brown

ANTOINE WATTEAU

Born: October 10, 1684; Valenciennes, France
Died: July 18, 1721; Nogent-sur-Marne, France
Area of Achievement: Art
Contribution: Watteau was one of the finest French painters of the early
   eighteenth century and was the originator and perhaps the most successful
   practitioner of the *fête galante*, the idealized, romantic representation of
   love and sexual liaison.

Early Life

Antoine Watteau was Flemish by birth, and he was born in Valenciennes,
a border town between France and the Netherlands, which had been a Flemish city until 1678. His father may have been a roofer. In any case, Watteau
came from a humble family, and there is nothing very certain about his early
years. He may have been apprenticed to a local painter, Gérin, and then to a
second, undistinguished painter, possibly named Métayer, who did some
scene painting for the Paris Opera, and may have brought Watteau to Paris.
Watteau was in Paris by 1702, living hand-to-mouth as a copyist of popular
Netherlandish genre paintings. His first professional connection was with
Claude Gillot, and he may have been apprenticed to him in the period between 1703 and 1707. Gillot had a reputation for painting theatrical subjects,
and he probably had some influence on Watteau's lifelong interest in that
subject. For some unknown reason, they parted abruptly, and Watteau joined
Claude III Audran, a popular decorative artist with a sensitive minor talent
for wall decoration, which had gained for him commissions in the royal
residences. Of importance for Watteau, given his basically provincial background, was the fact that Audran was also the curator of Luxembourg Palace, where the great collection of Marie de Médicis' Rubens was housed.
Peter Paul Rubens was to be an important influence, and the elegant park
landscape of the royal palaces was to be an ingratiating element in Watteau's
work.

Watteau was settled into steady employment by the end of the first decade
of the century, and he began to take some formal instruction at the Royal
Academy. In 1712, his career was given some legitimacy when he was
admitted as an associate member of the Academy. He was, by this time, in
demand as a painter, but he still needed to provide the Academy with a
specific painting on a specific subject in order to be considered for full
membership in the institution which set the stamp of public success on artists
at that time. Popular acceptance was one thing; his ascent to full acceptance
by his peers was to take somewhat longer.

Life's Work

The *fête galante* was not a sudden inspiration but an original variation on a kind of painting which had had long and enthusiastic popularity in the seventeenth century, particularly in the Netherlands. Genre scenes, often of vulgar peasant life, by painters such as David Teniers (1582-1649), were to have a constant market long into the eighteenth century, and Watteau may have supported himself as a painter of that kind of popular art. Certainly there is an interesting group of paintings of military camp life, painted in his early years, which can be related to that genre in their representation of the modest, day-to-day life of the military and their families as they travel through the countryside. The significant aspect of this choice of theme is its eschewing of the glory of military action in favor of the mundane conduct of a group of people living, in a sense, in the open air. This same interest in the less than glamorous aspects of certain ways of life shows up in his other paintings of the same period, in which he begins to explore the theatrical world. He seems to have had little interest in the bravura aspects of the stage, and considerable sensitivity toward actors and actresses as human beings who happen to be involved in dressing and comporting themselves in a profession which is larger than life.

There is another piece of this puzzle that is somewhat more difficult to put in place. There is a very small group of paintings which suggests that Watteau may have been one of the great erotic painters. Those that are extant suggest an implosion of sexual intensity, a kind of quiet blaze of passion, which quite transcends simple pornographic titillation, and will often show up in the *fêtes* in the flare of a nostril or a kind of glazing of an eye in something of a sexual daze.

What the *fêtes* are, in fact, seems simple when viewed as the finest examples of the French rococo theme of sexual dalliance among the upper classes. Generally that is what they are in the hands of lesser artists such as Watteau's pupil, Jean Baptiste Pater (1695-1736). Yet they are not quite so simple when Watteau is the painter. They have a Rubenesque lushness of color wedded to a Venetian influence which used color rather than line for modeling; they have, however, something more, a peculiar blending of sophisticated sexual ideality and underlying reality which reminds the viewer of Watteau's Flemish provinciality. The combination of lovers dressed in high fashion and characters dressed as players from the Parisian version of the Italian *commedia dell'arte*, portraying the ambiguities, the arabesques of sexual confrontation, creates an air of fleeting reality which transcends the obviousness of the theme. If they are rococo in shape, in color, in theme, in character, they are also larger than that, ultimately. What Watteau achieves in his *fêtes galantes* is the kind of artistic elevation which Jean-Baptiste-Siméon Chardin will later achieve in his paintings of simple servant life, and which Paul Cézanne will capture in his still lifes: a sense that the work of art has a monumentality, an aesthetic importance which defies definition, and turns the commonplace, the obvious, even the trivial theme into a symbol of the mystery of human and aesthetic endeavor. Watteau—passed by in the normal swift peregrination of the gallery visitor intent on making culture in the least amount of time—looks like any other rococo artist, pretty, but shallow. Watteau concentrated upon a much more formidable matter, a confrontation with artistic densities, symbolic connotations, and disturbing emotional depths.

These characteristics are best displayed in the painting which was to gain for Watteau full membership in the Royal Academy, the *Pilgrimage to Cythera*. There is much critical quarrel about whether the lovers are on their way to Cythera or on their way back, and whether this painting is better than a later version, but little quarrel over their greatness as paintings and the way in which the simple theme of sexual blandishments seems to say something about the fleeting nature of human desire. Gorgeous, lush, celebratory, magnificently poised in its graceful juxtaposition of elegantly dressed and beautiful people, it is also a painting which seems to carry a foreboding sense of human fragility.

What it might have meant to Watteau is impossible to say, but it is known that he was a man of some reserve, occasionally cantankerous, and given to withdrawing from society. The painting of Cythera for the Academy may have been something of a triumph in itself, but the acceptance by the institution may have been diminished by the fact that the usual categories for acceptance lay with history, landscape, or genre subjects. The Academy established a special category for Watteau as a painter of the *fête galante*. This may have been a compliment to him; some critics suggest that it was not so, but a distinction with a limiting difference, implying that Watteau was not quite up to the demands of the formally established categories. It does distinguish him, however, from other painters of the period, and he is to heighten that difference in his later paintings, in which the idealities of beauty, sexual attraction, and social position are to become even more obviously confronted with the limitations of reality.

The critical acceptance of Watteau as an early example of the Romantic artist (almost one hundred years before this type of artist was to appear formally) was fostered by the Goncourt brothers, the French men of letters of the mid-nineteenth century, who saw in Watteau's life and in his work a deep elegiac melancholy which was probably not clearly recognized during his lifetime. Certainly there was an enthusiasm for such readings of Watteau in the nineteenth century which led to a revival of his popularity, and certainly the problem of subjective imposition of tone and meaning on the arts is not uncommon, but there may be more to the idea than changing taste. Watteau was a man dying by inches in the later stages of his career, and he died very young, of tuberculosis, a wasting disease, which may give credence to the idea that he is the bagpipe player looking sadly at the dancers in *Venetian Pleasures*. In those few later years, that tender melancholy is a constant. Even paintings of the clowns of the Italian comedic world are touched with a sense of vulnerability. *Gilles*, for example, is a painting of a character in the *commedia* who is usually mischievous, stupid, and vulgar; Watteau's *Gilles* has an air of helplessness about him which is quite unnerving, and which has made the painting one of the best-known works in the history of art. This touch of reality intruding on the thin skin of his idealizations of young love and social pleasures would become stronger in his last works and would fuel the psychological reading of his career. Continually in demand, he spent almost a year in London in 1719, returning to Paris in 1720, where he continued to paint, producing one of his finest works, *Gersaint's Shopsign*, with the clear intention that it should be used as simply that, a sign to be mounted (as it was for a short time) outside the shop of his friend and dealer Edme Gersaint. It would seem that Watteau had come full circle. In the last months of his life, he rejected his fame as a painter of romantic idealities to return to the kind of work which he had probably needed to do in order to live in the early years of his career. There seems to have been little pretension in his personality; it is likely that *Gilles* was also painted for use as a poster advertising a theatrical group. In neither case did the proposed function of the work deter Watteau from painting at his very best.

Increasingly ill, Watteau retired to the outskirts of Paris in his last months, where he painted a *Crucifixion* for the local parish priest. Like so much of his work, it is missing. He died at the age of thirty-seven on July 18, 1721.

Summary

Antoine Watteau was the first, and ultimately the best, of that group of French rococo painters who were to idealize and ultimately trivialize the art of love in eighteenth century painting. Part of the reason lay in the fact that his pupils, Jean-Baptiste-Joseph Pater and Nicolas Lancret (possibly a pupil) were lesser artists; part of the reason may have been dangerously implicit in the subject itself, in its potential for excess, for sentimentalization, for emphasizing emotion at the expense of artistic integrity. He seems to have had a more salutary influence on two later painters in the genre, François Boucher, who began his career as an engraver of Watteau, and Jean-Honoré Fragonard, although Boucher had a tendency to slip into insipidity, which was never a mark of Watteau's work. Indeed, in Watteau's drawings, which are often as masterful as his best paintings, and in his finer works, there is a sense that he is the artist who leans back to the tradition of the Giorgione dreamworld and forward to the epiphanic stillnesses of Chardin. Technically dubious, sometimes downright sloppy as a painter, he is, nevertheless, an example of that peculiar kind of artist whose aesthetic vision transcends both technique and subject.

Bibliography

Brookner, Anita. *Watteau*. London: Paul Hamlyn, 1967. Short, well illustrated, and much the best introductory study of Watteau's work, written charmingly by an art historian who would later become one of Great Britain's finest novelists. Her work of eighteenth century French painters of feeling and her deep understanding of the role of the emotions in those painters makes her particularly helpful in dealing with the nuances of Watteau's work.

Gombrich, E. H. *The Story of Art*. New York: Phaidon Press, 1962, rev. ed. 1966. Watteau's greatness can be missed if he is viewed by himself. What is needed is a historical sense of Watteau: a Flemish artist, naturally inclined to a genre of considerable power in its own right, which he somehow maintains and uses to make something new, and equally valid. This book puts him in perspective within the history of art.

Levey, Michael. "The Real Theme of Watteau's *Embarkation for Cythera*." *Burlington Magazine* 103 (1961): 180-185. How Watteau's tone is to be read is a central concern for critics and lay viewers of his work. Levey argues for those who see much of Watteau's work deeply suffused with a sweet sense of the shortness of life's pleasures, using this major painting as the center of his argument.

_____. *Rococo to Revolution*. London: Thames and Hudson, 1966. Levey, a former director of the National Gallery in London, argues once again for viewing Watteau as an anticipation of Romanticism. Well written, well illustrated.

Posner, Donald. *Antoine Watteau*. Ithaca, N.Y.: Cornell University Press, 1984. This is an excellent examination of Watteau's life and career, written by the scholar who finds the "romantic" Watteau somewhat questionable and is prepared to make his interesting case to the contrary. Also very good on possible symbolic reading of Watteau paintings and very helpful on the artist's early career.

Charles Pullen

CARL MARIA VON WEBER

Born: November 18, 1786; Eutin, Oldenburg
Died: June 5, 1826; London, England
Area of Achievement: Music
Contribution: Weber was the principal founder of German Romantic music. Best known as an opera composer, he made many significant contributions to piano music and wrote some of the staples of the wind instrument player's repertoire.

Early Life

Carl Maria von Weber was born in the small town of Eutin, the son of Franz Anton Weber, who directed a touring theatrical troupe, and Genovefa Brenner, an actress and singer. Weber's earliest memories were of playing among the theatrical scenery of his father's troupe. Sickly, and with a damaged right hipbone, he did not have an active childhood, and his early education was haphazard. Weber's father was the uncle of Wolfgang Amadeus Mozart's wife and hoped that the boy would become a musician.

When the theatrical company was trapped in Salzburg in 1797 by Napoleon I's invading army, Carl was enrolled in the choir school at the cathedral and received his first systematic instruction in music from Michael Haydn, the younger brother of the famous composer Franz Joseph Haydn. His first compositions, a set of six fughettas, were published in 1798 and favorably reviewed in the *Allgemeine musikalische Zeitung*, Germany's leading music periodical, for which Weber was later to write. After more travels, Weber returned to Salzburg to revise an early mass (now lost) and his first surviving opera, *Peter Schmoll und seine Nachbarn* (1803), of which the overture is still performed.

Weber then traveled extensively, and he studied most profitably with the composer-priest Georg Joseph Vogler in Vienna in 1803 and 1804. Vogler helped him obtain an appointment as music director in Breslau (modern Wrocław, Poland), where, at the age of seventeen, he was unable to cope with the intrigues of the musicians and singers and resigned. While in Breslau, he had a near-fatal accident, drinking by mistake engraving acid, which his father had carelessly stored in a wine bottle; though Weber recovered, his fine tenor singing voice was destroyed. After his resignation from Breslau, he stayed briefly in nearby Karlsruhe, where he wrote his only two symphonies and the first version of his Concertino for French Horn for the orchestra of the Duke of Württemberg-Öls.

Life's Work

The reasons for Weber's departure from Karlsruhe are unclear, but he left Breslau hurriedly when recognized by a creditor and, after a concert tour, accepted a post as secretary to the brother of the Duke of Württemberg in Stuttgart in 1807. Weber went through a dissolute period when he was socially in great demand for his improvisations on the piano or guitar but was in disfavor with the tyrannical duke. Among his few Stuttgart works are piano pieces and his opera *Silvana* (1810).

Weber lost his position in Stuttgart in 1810. One account is that he was involved in selling a deferment from Napoleon's army; another is that the duke's brother entrusted Weber with money to buy horses but Weber's father, who was visiting at the time, used it to settle his own debts and left his son to get into financial trouble to cover the loss. In any case, Weber was imprisoned and banished from Württemberg.

Weber then embarked on a series of tours, including a visit to his teacher Vogler in Darmstadt, and resumed composing, with his first piano concerto, his first piano sonata with its perpetual-motion finale, and his sparkling one-act comic opera *Abu Hassan* (1811) as the main results. He began a fruitful association with the clarinetist Heinrich Baermann, for whom he wrote a successful clarinet concertino, which is still frequently performed. Weber later wrote a number of major works featuring the clarinet, including two concerti for that instrument and the *Grand Duo Concertant* for clarinet and piano. He also suffered several misadventures, including a string of unsuccessful love affairs and, while crossing Württemberg territory on his way to Switzerland, of being recognized, arrested, and briefly imprisoned before being allowed to proceed on his journey.

Weber's first really stable position was in Prague, where he accepted a three-year contract as director of the opera in 1813. He not only reorganized the musical establishment but also paid careful attention to the acting, to the scenic designs, and to the costumes in order to create a musical-dramatic whole. The repertoire was composed mainly of French operas of the time in German translation. One of the many new singers he engaged was Caroline Brandt, who was later to become his wife. During his stay in Prague, the first symptoms of the tuberculosis, of which he was to die, became evident. He resigned in 1816, ostensibly because of the damp winter weather, and, after visits to Berlin, accepted the post as director of the German opera in Dresden.

During the brief interval between Prague and Dresden, Weber wrote some of his most characteristic piano music, especially the second and third sonatas. Weber's piano music is quite unusual, because he had unusually long fingers and especially extended thumbs, which permitted him to execute extremely wide leaps or span large chords that are physically beyond the reach of most pianists. These characteristics account for the brilliant sonority of his piano music and for its neglect by most pianists, who lack the physical ability to do this music justice.

The capstones of Weber's piano works, the *Konzertstück* (concert piece) in F Minor (1821) and the fourth sonata (1819-1822), were written later. The freedom of form in the *Konzertstück* influenced Felix Mendelssohn and Robert Schumann in their piano concerti; the programmatic character and deep expression of the fourth sonata influenced Schumann and Franz Liszt, who were champions of Weber's music.

Weber's position in Dresden, though it became permanent after 1818, was nevertheless difficult. He was director of the newly organized German opera (part of the movement of national consciousness that swept the German states during and after the wars with Napoleon), but the principal court opera was Italian, under the direction of Francesco Morlacchi. The Italian opera was able to hire the better singers and had the larger budget. Weber sought to resign to move to Berlin, but the opera house there was destroyed by fire. Weber's patron, Count Vitzthum, was able to obtain for Weber a permanent appointment in Dresden, enabling him to marry Caroline Brandt, whom he had courted for four years.

In Dresden, Weber extended his concern about producing operas in a manner that would ensure their dramatic as well as musical effect by insisting that the singers and chorus be able to act as well as sing, by strengthening the orchestra, and by improving the set designs. His ideal was to create a whole that would be greater than the sum of its individual parts and thus paved the way for such later reformers of operatic production as Richard Wagner and Gustav Mahler. He was a pioneer in the conducting of operas; instead of directing the performance from the piano, he stood in front of the stage, conducting with a thick baton, which he held in the middle, and rearranged the seating of the orchestra so that all the players could see his gestures. In addition, he published introductory summaries of the new operas before their performance in the local press to explain the works and thus educate his audience.

The work that occupied most of Weber's free time was the opera *Der Freischütz*, which was finished in 1820 and first performed in Berlin in the following year. The title is best translated as "the charmed bullet," although it is usually literally rendered as "the free shooter"; the libretto came from a popular ghost story adapted by Weber's poet friend in Dresden, Johann Friedrich Kind. In the opera, the huntsman Max is unable to hit anything at which he shoots and thus is certain to lose the shooting contest at which the hand of his beloved Agathe is to be bestowed. In reality he is under a curse set by his colleague Caspar, who offers Max the chance to obtain charmed bullets from the devil Samiel. The climactic scene is the second act finale, laid in a desolate ravine in the forest, where Caspar and Max cast the magic bullets amid a host of various apparitions. Unknown to Max, the last bullet is Caspar's to direct; he plans to kill Agathe with it. At the shooting contest, however, the bullet kills Caspar; Max then confesses what he has done and is sentenced to temporary banishment, but Agathe will wait for him. The work's popularity in German-speaking countries is owing not as much to the plot as to the musical numbers, whether the arsenal of Romantic horror effects in the Wolf's glen scene (the finale of act 2) or the depictions of a smiling nature in the arias of the main protagonists Max and Agathe and the choruses in a popular vein.

Weber's opera was so popular so quickly that he was invited to write an opera for Vienna. He chose a medieval topic, *Euryanthe* (1823), for which Helmine von Chezy, a poet in Dresden, wrote an extremely convoluted libretto. The numerous inconsistencies of the plot and its stilted verse have been accused of having adversely affected an experimental opera with continuous music that contains some of Weber's best writing; attempts have been made to rewrite the libretto, but none has been successful.

During Weber's stay in Vienna, the symptoms of tuberculosis recurred, causing Weber to depart for Dresden. He had to abandon his writing about music (he had even drafted a semiautobiographical musical novel) and writing for piano in order to concentrate on a commission from London for a musical-dramatic work, which took shape as *Oberon* (1826), his last composition. With this work and his appearance as conductor in London, Weber hoped to amass enough money to support his wife and two sons after his death, which he sensed would be soon, since his illness was becoming worse. Weber even learned English in order to set the text appropriately.

Oberon can best be described as a multimedia work, a series of elaborate stage tableaux with vocal and instrumental music, as shown by the original playbill indicating the "order of the scenery," which includes Oberon's bower with an apparition of the Baghdad of Harun al-Rashid at the opening, and the hall of arms in the palace of Charlemagne at the end. Huon of Brabant is assigned the task of rescuing Rezia and her friends from the Emir of Tunis and bringing them before Charlemagne. Weber was thus given the opportunity to write in his chivalresque vein as well as to write exotic music for the Arabs and nature music in Rezia's grand air "Ocean, Thou Mighty Monster" and in the subsequent chorus of mermaids. Weber had planned to rewrite the work as an opera with recitatives rather than spoken dialogue upon his return to Germany, but his death in London of tuberculosis and an ulcerated windpipe on June 5 brought an end to this project. Subsequent attempts have been made, mostly in Germany, to complete Weber's project or to perform the individual numbers linked together with spoken dialogue, as in the original production.

Summary

Carl Maria von Weber is known today chiefly through the overtures to his operas, his clarinet works, and Berlioz's arrangement for orchestra of his piano piece "Invitation to the Dance," a brilliant waltz. In German-speaking countries, the opera *Der Freischütz* is a national tradition, but it has resisted translation into other repertoires. Weber's extensive use of the orchestra to underscore the drama, his freedom of form, and his occasional use of leading motives and transforming their musical contexts influenced Wagner as well as several other composers. In *Der Freischütz*, Weber had given a model of what a true national opera should be, with its use of popular idioms and with common people rather than kings and lords as principal characters. In this work and in *Oberon*, he furnished models for musically depicting both nature and the supernatural spirit world, as he provided examples for portraying the world of chivalry in *Euryanthe* and later in *Oberon*. Though Weber's reach often exceeded his grasp, and his development as a composer was cut short by an early death, he remains one of the most influential composers of the early nineteenth century.

Bibliography

Finscher, Ludwig. "Weber's *Freischütz*: Conceptions and Misconceptions." *Proceedings of the Royal Musical Association* 40 (1983/1984): 79-90. The author examines the assumptions that the first performance of Weber's *Der Freischütz* was the birthday of German Romantic opera. The libretto is based on the trivial aspects of "dark" Romanticism and has little to do with German Romantic poetry; the work's success was owing not to folk melodies but to Weber's success in composing in a popular vein.

Grout, Donald Jay, with Hermine Williams. "The Romantic Opera in Germany." In *A Short History of Opera*, 3d ed. New York: Columbia University Press, 1987. Presents the different characteristics of eighteenth and nineteenth century opera and the traits of German opera in particular before discussing Weber's last three operas. Weber was the real founder of German Romantic opera and the most important composer in that genre before Wagner.

Tusa, Michael C. "Richard Wagner and Weber's *Euryanthe*." *Nineteenth Century Music* 9 (Spring, 1986): 206-221. Many writers have commented on the strong influence and resemblances between Weber's *Euryanthe* of 1823 and Wagner's *Lohengrin* of 1847. The author identifies the various similarities between the two works in detail and shows the strong influence of Weber's opera on Wagner's *Tannhäuser* (1845).

Warrack, John. *Carl Maria von Weber*. New York: Macmillan, 1968. The standard biography of Weber in any language. The author presents careful discussion of the composer's life and music, with special attention to the operas. General readers will be grateful for the extensive plot summaries of each opera.

_____. "Carl Maria von Weber." In *The New Grove Dictionary of Music and Musicians*, edited by Stanley Sadie, vol. 20. London: Macmillan, 1980. A shorter version of the biography, with an updated bibliography, presented in a concise form but without the detail and operatic plot summaries of his full-length biography.

Weber, Carl Maria von. *Writings on Music*. Edited by John Warrack. Translated by Martin Cooper. New York: Cambridge University Press, 1981. The volume contains Weber's fragmentary autobiographical novel as well as his reviews for various papers and journals and his introductions to the operas he conducted in Prague and Dresden. Each entry is given an extensive preface and is thoroughly annotated. The introduction shows that Weber's alleged attacks on Ludwig van Beethoven's music are unfounded; rather, he generally praised Beethoven's works. Weber's reviews illustrate the immense amount of music that was performed then but is completely forgotten today.

Weber, Max Maria von. *Carl Maria von Weber: The Life of an Artist*. Translated by J. Palgrave Simpson. London: Chapman and Hall, 1865. Reprint. New York: Haskell House, 1968. 2 vols. Though this biography by Weber's son—based on the letters and documents saved by Weber's widow and the recollections of Weber's family—is extremely partisan and chauvinistic with reliance on obsolete information, it nevertheless presents a lively account of the petty intrigues and frustrations of court life, especially in Dresden, that Weber underwent.

Rey M. Longyear

AUGUST WEISMANN

Born: January 17, 1834; Frankfurt am Main
Died: November 5, 1914; Freiburg im Breisgau, Germany
Areas of Achievement: Biology, natural history, zoology, and genetics
Contribution: Weismann is most noted for his development and refinement
of the theory of the continuity of the germ plasm, for his devout support
of Darwinism and the principle of natural selection, and for his discrediting the idea of the inheritance of acquired characteristics.

Early Life

August Friedrich Leopold Weismann was born in Frankfurt am Main on
January 17, 1834, to Johann Konrad August Weismann, a classics teacher at
the *Gymnasium* in Frankfurt, and Elise Eleanore Lübbren Weismann, a musician and painter. He was the eldest of four children, and his home life was
simple and happy. As a young boy, Weismann showed an active interest in
nature. He collected butterflies, caterpillars, beetles, and plants, and he as-
sembled a herbarium. He was a lover of art, literature, and music (especially
that of Ludwig van Beethoven). These interests continued throughout his
life. He became an accomplished pianist. He attended and did well at the
Gymnasium where his father was a teacher.

Weismann was interested in chemistry and physics as a young adult and
wanted to pursue studies in that direction. His father and friends of the
family, however, suggested that he pursue medicine, since a career in medicine would be more lucrative. To this end, he entered the University of
Göttingen in 1852, where he studied with Friedrich Henle and Friedrich
Wöhler in an atmosphere that emphasized research rather than broader problems. He received his medical degree in 1856.

Life's Work

Following graduation, Weismann continued his research while working as
an assistant in the medical clinic at Rostock. In 1857, he transferred to the
Chemical Institute so that he could pursue his interest in chemistry. This was
followed by a tour of four German universities and a more extensive stay in
Vienna.

Weismann entered private medical practice in Frankfurt in 1858. His practice allowed him sufficient time to pursue studies on heart muscle fibers. His
private practice was interrupted in 1859 by the war between Austria and
Italy, at which time he entered the German army and served as a surgeon at
the field hospital in Italy. He resumed private practice in 1860.

In 1861, Weismann abandoned medicine to pursue what had become his
main interest, the biological sciences. He attended the University of Giessen
for two months in 1861 and was profoundly influenced by Rudolf Leuckart,

under whom he began his studies in insect embryology. He considered the two months he spent with Leuckart to be the most important and inspiring time of his career.

Following his stay at Giessen, Weismann became the private physician of Archduke Stephan of Austria. While in this position, from 1861 to 1863, Weismann had ample time to pursue his interest in insect development and completed his first major work, *Die Entwicklung der Dipteren* (on the development of the diptera in the egg), in 1864. He also had time to read Charles Darwin's *On the Origin of Species* (1859). Like so many scientists of the time, Weismann was profoundly influenced by Darwin's book. Along with Ernst Haeckel and Fritz Müller, Weismann became one of Germany's staunchest supporters of Darwinian theory.

In 1863, Weismann became a privatdocent at the University of Freiburg and taught zoology and comparative anatomy. In 1866, he was appointed extraordinary professor and, in 1874, professor. He was the first to occupy the chair of zoology at Freiburg. He soon became director of the Zoological Institute at the university. He was a well-respected teacher, who always attracted large numbers of students.

Weismann's first research papers examined insect histology and embryology. Several papers on these subjects were published between 1862 and 1866. One important discovery he made was that, during metamorphosis, tissues completely dedifferentiate and then redifferentiate during the formation of the adult. Weismann was also interested in the origin and fate of the germ cells of hydrozoans. The germ cells of multicellular organisms such as hydrozoans are set aside from the somatic cells early in development and provide for the continuity of the organism through the sperm and the egg. The somatic cells will eventually die, but the germ cells live on in a new individual. Only the reproductive cells have the capacity to form a complete, new individual. From these observations, Weismann developed the theory for which he is most noted, of the continuity of the germ plasm.

In 1864, Weismann's eyesight failed, and he had to cease work on the microscope. Although he turned to more general problems, his microscopic work was continued by his students, his assistants, and Marie Dorothea Gruber, whom he married in 1867. His wife read to him constantly so that he could keep abreast of the latest scientific developments. His eyesight became so poor that he took a leave of absence from his teaching position from 1869 to 1871. During that time, his eyesight improved, and he resumed lecturing in 1871 and active research in 1874. His eyesight again failed in 1884.

Work on the theory of the continuity of the germ plasm occupied the last thirty years of Weismann's life as an active scientist. The theory encompassed many areas but primarily focused on heredity and evolution. He first published on these topics in 1883. Although he was not the first to suggest the principle of the continuity of the germ plasm, he did develop the idea to its fullest. He contended that the germ plasm was to be found on the chromatin threads, the "idants" (chromosomes) in the nucleus of the cell. He hypothesized that the idants were composed of smaller units, the "ids," which in turn were composed of the "determinants," the individual hereditary units, which he correctly envisioned as being linearly arranged. The determinants, he thought, were composed of still smaller, more basic units, the "biophors."

Based only on a priori knowledge, Weismann reasoned that the chromosome number must be halved during the formation of the reproductive cells and hypothesized that a "reduction division" must occur during the process. This, he thought, was to prevent doubling of the germ plasm at each generation. This is considered by many to be his most significant and effective scientific contribution. Weismann believed that during fertilization individual ancestral germ plasms, each carrying variations, were combined. He thought that, as well as introducing new variations, this process created new combinations of variations.

Weismann's ideas on the continuity of the germ plasm put him in direct conflict with many other scientists of the time, since many had come to discredit natural selection as a mechanism of evolution and advocated Lamarckism, the inheritance of acquired traits, as an alternative. Even Charles Darwin proposed the theory of pangenesis, where each body part was thought to produce a gemmule, which could be modified by the environment and eventually passed to the germ cells. Weismann investigated many cases of reported inheritance of acquired characteristics and could find no authenticated instance of such inheritance. His own classic experiments, in which he cut off the tails of mice over several generations but found no tendency for the tail to shorten in succeeding generations, were instrumental in challenging Lamarckism. Weismann thought that the only way acquired characteristics could be passed to the offspring was if the germ cells were affected. He became more devoted to the theory of natural selection than did Darwin. Weismann did not believe that the environment in any way affected heredity.

Weismann extended Darwin's theory of natural selection to the germ cells in a new theory called germinal selection. He thought that the determinants struggled with one another for nutriment and that the stronger ones would triumph and eliminate the weaker ones. Thus, only the stronger ones would survive in the germ plasm and be passed to the offspring. This, he thought, could account for the loss of organs during evolution. Later work failed to support his idea of germinal selection. Weismann extended his germ plasm theory to development. He correctly thought that the determinants directed differentiation in individual cells but incorrectly envisioned that this was a result of the distribution of different determinants to different cells during cell division. He therefore thought that mitosis could be qualitatively unequal while being quantitatively equal.

Weismann's main works on heredity and evolution were published in *Studien zur Descendenztheorie* (1875-1876; *Studies in the Theory of Descent,* 1882), *Essays upon Heredity and Kindred Biological Problems* (1889-1892), *Das Keimplasma: Eine Theorie der Vererbung* (1892; *The Germ-Plasm: A Theory of Heredity,* 1893), *On Germinal Selection as a Source of Definite Variation* (1896), and *Vorträge über Descendenztheorie* (1902; *The Evolution Theory,* 1904). *The Evolution Theory* became an important and widely read book. It has been said that since Weismann's theoretical contributions to science were so important, his experimental and observational work was often overshadowed.

Weismann retired from the faculty of the University of Freiburg in 1912. He died peacefully at Freiburg im Breisgau, Germany, on November 5, 1914, at the age of eighty.

Summary

August Weismann was one of the most respected biologists of the latter part of the nineteenth century and the early part of the twentieth century. His ideas stimulated considerable discussion and research. His theories on heredity and development were far-reaching. He correctly recognized that the hereditary material was contained within the nucleus of the sperm and egg and that the hereditary material of the germ cells is reduced to one-half during the maturation of the sperm and egg. In a single theory, the germ plasm theory, he explained the meiotic reduction division, sexual reproduction, development, and natural selection. It has been said that Weismann's "ingenious synthesis helped prepare the way for twentieth-century genetics." Weismann was elected to the Bavarian Academy of Sciences and, as a foreign member, to the Linnean Society, the American Philosophical Society, and the Royal Society of London. He received numerous honorary degrees and medals, including the Darwin/Wallace Medal of the Linnean Society and the Darwin Medal of the Royal Society.

Bibliography

Churchill, Frederick B. "August Weismann and a Break from Tradition." *The Journal of the History of Biology* (1968): 91-112. This brief article discusses Weismann's most significant contribution, the theory of the continuity of the germ plasm. Also shows how his work related to that of Ernst Haeckel and others and how it influenced the development of modern biological thought.

Coleman, William. "The Cell, Nucleus and Inheritance: An Historical Study." *Proceedings of the American Philosophical Society* 109 (1965): 126, 149-154. Like the article by Churchill, this article analyzes the impact of the work of Weismann and others on modern biological thought. It is one of the few modern works that analyze Weismann in this light.

Conklin, Edwin. "August Weismann." *Proceedings of the American Philosophical Society* 54 (1915): iii-xii. This is a brief summary of Weismann's contribution to science, written by a friend on the occasion of Weismann's death.

Weismann, August. *Essays upon Heredity and Kindred Biological Problems.* 2 vols. Oxford, England: Clarendon Press, 1891-1892. This collection contains some of Weismann's most important theoretical contributions on heredity, the continuity of the germ plasma, sexual reproduction, and evolution.

_____. *The Germ-Plasm: A Theory of Heredity.* London: Walter Scott, 1893. This is the most significant book written by Weismann. It addresses the most important theoretical contributions Weismann was to make to science.

Charles L. Vigue

ROGIER VAN DER WEYDEN

Born: 1399 or 1400; Tournai, the Netherlands
Died: c. June 18, 1464; Brussels
Area of Achievement: Art
Contribution: One of the greatest of the fifteenth century Netherlandish painters, Rogier influenced other painters of the Christian altarpiece, stylistically and tonally, and dominated northern European painting throughout the period.

Early Life

Although Rogier van der Weyden was presumably born in the French-speaking, southern region of the Netherlands, there is no specific knowledge of his ethnic background. Indeed, scholarly controversy continues to surround his life and his work. No single painting by him is confirmed by his signature, and the documentary evidence is also very slight. It is known that one Rogier van der Weyden entered an apprenticeship with the painter Robert Campin in 1427 in Tournai and fulfilled his service, getting his patent as Master in 1432. Yet the facts are complicated by the name Rogier van der Weyden appearing on Tournai documents in 1426, already denoted a Master.

It may be that Rogier had been previously trained in another trade, perhaps sculpture, since the modeling in his paintings has distinct affinities to that art, which has led to speculation that his father might have been a sculptor. He also seems to have come to his apprenticeship as a painter relatively late in life; there is evidence that he had a son, eight years old in 1435, which suggests that he must have been married sometime in the mid-1420's.

Even his apprenticeship to Campin is conjectural. Stylistically, his work is very close to that of Campin, and it is presumed that he is the "Rogelet de le Pasture" who was taken into training by Campin. If so, he was the son of Henry de le Pasture, whose family can be traced back in Tournai as far as 1260. Whatever the truth may be concerning his early years, he was, by 1436, firmly established in Brussels, married to a Brussels native, Elisabeth Goffaerts, and employed as the official town painter.

Life's Work

The three most important Netherlandish painters of the late Gothic period are Jan van Eyck, the Master of Flémalle, and Rogier van der Weyden. Jan van Eyck has emerged in the long run as the most admired of the three, but that was not the case in the fifteenth century. In truth, Rogier had considerably more influence on other contemporary painters than either of the other two. The difficulty in speaking of his career, however, lies in the peculiar fact that there is no work clearly identified as an example of his early career as a painter. Only the great works of his maturity (although the greatest, his *Descent from the Cross*, may be fairly early) are extant, a situation which has produced one of the most interesting scholarly puzzles in art history: Where are the works of his early career?

Like van Eyck, Rogier was primarily a painter of altarpieces—that is, paintings specifically ordered to be hung above the altar used in Roman Catholic churches to celebrate the Mass. They tend, as a result, to be large and connected to a specific church, and their original function was religious rather than aesthetic. The twentieth century preference for van Eyck's works over the paintings of Rogier is directly related to the fact that van Eyck, who is often credited with developing, sometimes with inventing, oil painting, anticipated Renaissance Humanist realism in his works. There is some slight influence of his work in Rogier, but Rogier seems deliberately to eschew the splendid technical leap forward into recording the real world in favor of the more static representation of humans and nature which characterized the medieval style. Rogier refused to abandon the last stages of Gothic art; thus, Rogier's work was not only distinct from that of van Eyck but also more popular in his own century.

The painter Rogier seems to resemble most is the Master of Flémalle, the shadowy figure whose altarpieces seem to have been produced in the 1430's. Touches of van Eyckian naturalism and a close relationship to Rogier's mature works distinguish the Master's painting. The Master's identity remains a mystery, but it is often suggested that he was an associate of Rogier's Master, Robert Campin, or that he was, in fact, Campin. There is also an intriguing suggestion that the very paintings ascribed to the Master of Flémalle are Rogier's missing early work—that is, that Rogier is, in short, the Master of Flémalle, or at least the creator of some of the paintings now identified with the Master. Given the present lack of signed works and limited documentation, the question falls into the slippery area of style, technique, and connoisseurship, in which the eye of the critic dominates. Aside from the historical importance of the question, and the rather piquant nature of the problem, the arguments themselves cut to the heart of the nature of Rogier as a painter.

It is believed that much of Rogier's work has been lost. He produced a major work for the Brussels town hall, four variations on the theme of justice, but it was lost in a fire in 1695. There exist, however, several examples of his work as an altarpiece painter and some of his portraits which clearly show why he had such a long and prosperous career, not only as a painter but also as the head of a busy workshop. His best work is *The Descent from the Cross* (it is also his most popular), displayed at the Prado in Madrid. It features all those aspects of his talent which not only distinguished him from van Eyck but also established him as the most influential painter of his time in the Netherlands. The subject is the common one of the lifting of the dead Christ from the Cross; yet where other painters of van Eyckian inclination might try to portray this scene with some sense of the physical, realistic surrounding of the act of pity and awe, Rogier packs ten figures into a flat, shallow niche which reminds one of the tomb itself— with the figures spread out (though densely impinging one another) in a line across the front, similar to a sculptural frieze. The fall of the draperies and the sharply contorted poses are Gothic; yet the colors are bright and hard, almost enamelized, and the faces are charged by Rogier's greatest gift, the ability to convey a sense of spiritual suffering.

There is in Rogier not only a mannered, stylized way with composition, structures, and nature (all of which run contrary to van Eyck's warm naturalism) but also a capacity to express emotions, usually spiritual, which are quite beyond anything attempted by van Eyck. Rogier's work as a portrait painter (the lovely *Portrait of a Woman* is a good example) draws back from the particulars of realism into a kind of introverted world of religious dream.

Scholars surmise that Rogier made a trip to Italy, perhaps in 1450, and that he must have visited both Florence and Rome. His *Entombment* in the Uffizi shows that he was not entirely obdurate in his approach to his art, since it shows signs of the influence of Fra Angelico. Further, his *Madonna with Four Saints* in Frankfurt, which contains in its panels the Florentine coat of arms, contains elements of the Italian *sacra conversazione*.

Rogier's career seems to have prospered from beginning to end, and his large studio employed a group of painters who carried on in his style a type of altar painting which was to dominate during the late medieval period in the Netherlands. He died in Brussels in June of 1464.

Summary

If van Eyck is the twentieth century's painter of choice for the late Gothic period, then Rogier van der Weyden, with his stiffer, somewhat monumental seriousness and lyric, almost mystic intensity was the choice not only of the public but also of the painters who came to maturity in the same period. Rogier's way of telling the eternal story, ascetically restrained, physically desiccated (although in glowing color), was deeply admired and unabashedly imitated. It was as if Rogier read the sensibility of the age and knew that people still clung to the old imperatives, subordinating the particular, the individual, to the general, the idealized; he knew that society was not yet ready to break with the safety of the collectivized, church-centered world of religious submission to the mystery of Christianity.

The inclination today is to read Rogier's paintings through the strangely vibrant colors, the ambiguous intensities of the portrait heads, and to find his stylized draperies, his dispositions of the human body, as somewhat quaint in their Gothic awkwardness. Yet an understanding of what Rogier was doing and when he was doing it allows for a deeper appreciation of his greatness as a painter, of the imploded power, the sonority, and the graceful, dramatic timelessness of his best work.

Bibliography
Friedlaender, Max J. *Early Netherlandish Painting: From Van Eyck to Bruegel.* New York: Phaidon Press, 1956. This popular volume contains a chapter on Rogier, in addition to helpful chapters on van Eyck and the painting of the period in general.
_____. *Early Netherlandish Painting: Rogier van Weyden and the Master of Flémalle.* Translated by Heinz Norden. Brussels: Éditions de la Connaissance, 1967. Not to be confused with the previous title, this volume is a scholarly work. Yet it is so delightfully and reasonably written that it is thoroughly accessible to the lay reader. Not only does Friedlaender deal with the mystery of Rogier and the Master, but he also handles the entire career and makes pertinent assessments of Rogier's style and influence.
Fuchs, R. H. *Dutch Painting.* New York: Oxford University Press, 1978. A popular, well-illustrated history of painting in the Netherlands region. Chapter 1 is a simple and direct discussion of the period in which Rogier worked. Somewhat simplistic, but a useful introduction.
Lane, Barbara G. *The Altar and the Altarpiece: Sacramental Themes in Early Netherlandish Painting.* New York: Harper & Row, 1984. The problem of fully understanding the quality of Rogier's work, given the limited knowledge and understanding of the deeply religious sensibility, is met with care, attention, and careful argument in this short book. Rogier's work figures substantially in Lane's text.
Panofsky, E. *Early Netherlandish Paintings: Its Origins and Character.* 2 vols. New York: Harper & Row, 1971. By a master of iconography, intriguing essays on how to read the secret language of the religious painting.

Charles Pullen

WILLIAM THE SILENT

Born: April 24, 1533; Dillenburg Castle, Nassau
Died: July 10, 1584; Delft, Holland
Areas of Achievement: Government and politics
Contribution: William, Prince of Orange and Count of Nassau, led the revolt of the Netherlands against Spain despite overwhelming difficulties. His leadership proved decisive to the Dutch independence movement at its crucial beginnings in the late sixteenth century.

Early Life

William, the eldest son of Count William of Nassau-Dillenburg and his second wife, Juliana von Stolberg, was born on April 24, 1533, at Dillenburg Castle. The family was large, and the young heir's prospects not particularly remarkable until 1544, when, at the age of eleven, he inherited the titles and possessions of an elder cousin, René of Orange, who was killed during the siege of Saint Dizier. Because of the wealth and importance of his new estates, as well as the fact that William's parents had become Lutherans, the Habsburg emperor Charles V determined that the boy should be brought up at his court and educated in the Roman Catholic faith.

William's pleasant manners and appearance and genial personality soon made him a general favorite at court. The aging emperor became very fond of the young man and arranged an advantageous marriage for him with a pretty heiress, Anne of Egmond-Buren; this union would produce a son, Philip William, and a daughter. Anne died in 1558 and does not appear to have played a very important part in her husband's emotional life.

William had fulfilled a number of social and military duties at the court before the abdication of Charles V in 1555 in favor of his son Philip II. It was perhaps ironic that the emperor chose to lean upon the shoulder of the young Prince of Orange as he passed the sovereignty of Spain and his Burgundian territories to the man who would become Orange's most bitter enemy. Yet for a while the relationship between William and Philip was amicable, if not warm. Philip was godfather to Philip William, and William would be given new responsibilities. Now in his middle twenties, William's career as a loyal servant of the new monarch seemed assured.

Life's Work

There is a traditional story that Philip and William disliked each other on sight; if that were so, their mutual antagonism took time to mature. William was named a Councillor of State and a Knight of the Golden Fleece by the new king. In 1559, William was chosen to be one of three chief negotiators concluding the Treaty of Cateau-Cambrésis between France and Spain. His associates, Antoine Perrenot de Granvelle, Bishop of Arras, and Fernando

Álvarez de Toledo, Duke of Alva, would also play crucial roles in the revolt of the Netherlands. It was during this stay in France that William began to acquire his reputation for being discreet, but "taciturn" or even "sly" are better descriptive terms than the misleading nickname "silent." William was a career diplomat, fond of company and never at a loss for words.

With the conclusion of this diplomatic mission, William was appointed stadtholder (governor and military commander) in Zeeland, Utrecht, Holland, and later (1561) Franche-Comté. On the eve of Philip's departure for Spain in August, 1559, however, the nobility and people of the Netherlands were beginning to complain. Spanish troops had not been withdrawn despite the peace, Spanish courtiers were being made Councillors of State, and sterner measures were being authorized against Protestants. William and other important nobles protested, and Philip seemed willing to make concessions regarding Spanish troops and politicians—but not heretics. He appointed his half-sister Margaret, Duchess of Parma, as regent, with Granvelle (now a cardinal) as her adviser.

William was anxious to marry again, but his choice of wives was not a fortunate one. Anne of Saxony, a well-born heiress, was erratic and quarrelsome, her family had traditionally opposed the Habsburgs, and, worse, she was a Lutheran. William made vague promises about his wife's conformity when they were married in 1561, but Philip was not pleased.

As Granvelle's influence increased (he created more than a dozen new bishoprics), the nobility of the Netherlands felt their traditional leadership threatened. Snobbery also played a role in the nobility's dislike for Granvelle, who was said to be the grandson of a blacksmith. Toleration of Calvinists was initially less important than the replacement of the hated minister with one more to their liking. In letters to Philip, however, the nobles, led by William and the Counts of Egmond and Hoorne, were careful to avoid direct criticism of royal policies.

In the spring of 1564, it seemed that the anti-Granvelle faction had won; Margaret had also decided that Granvelle was a political liability, and he was withdrawn. Yet Philip, however preoccupied with the Turks and the administration of his vast empire, was unyielding in matters of faith. Catholicism was to be imposed upon the Netherlands and Protestant heresy rooted out.

William and his associates tried to support Margaret while attempting to promote a policy that would allow liberty of conscience, if not public worship, for Protestants. Efforts at a reasonable compromise were doomed to failure by both sides. A number of the lesser nobility and their supporters advocated violence to intimidate the regent and the Catholics. These men became known as the "Beggars" (*les Gueux*), from a slighting reference made about them by one of Margaret's advisers. Riots erupted in the summer of 1566. Fanatical Calvinist mobs sacked churches, even turning some of them into Protestant meetinghouses. By the end of the year, an angry Philip appointed the Duke of Alva as his general to pacify the Netherlands at any cost.

William hesitated; he refused to command the rebels, protested his loyalty to the king, and then declined to take the oath of unconditional obedience that Margaret demanded. In April, 1567, he retired to his family estates at Dillenburg. Other prudent men fled the country, but Hoorne and Egmond remained, only to be betrayed, arrested, and executed. The Duke of Alva's methods for maintaining order were so brutal that eventually Margaret resigned. A reign of terror instituted by a special commission, the Council of Troubles—soon nicknamed the Council of Blood—filled the land with fear, as thousands of victims were arrested and executed. When William refused to return, he was declared a rebel, his property in the Netherlands was sequestered, and his son, a student at the University of Louvain, was carried off to Spain, never again to see his father.

With few choices remaining save armed rebellion, William and his brothers raised an army to expel the Duke of Alva. Two invasions were launched in April, 1568, but the people did not rise; both attempts were badly defeated. William and his few supporters took refuge in France. William was entering the most difficult period of his life. Impoverished, outlawed, and peripatetic, he was made miserable by Anne of Saxony's irrational behavior. She was flagrantly unfaithful, and at last he divorced her in 1571.

Meanwhile, William continued to look for allies. Elizabeth I of England was not encouraging. The German Protestant princes had provided little support. His best hopes seemed to lie with the Calvinists, whose faith he would adopt in 1573. Another area of resistance lay with the "Sea Beggars," an irregular band of nobles, merchants, patriots, and pirates. In April, 1572, they seized the town of Brielle, which triggered a popular uprising, and soon most of Holland, Zeeland, and Friesland declared William their stadtholder.

To strengthen his advantage, William's brother Louis of Nassau launched an attack from France but was eventually blockaded at Mons. As William moved to aid him, his support among the French Huguenots was undercut by the Massacre of Saint Bartholomew's Day (August 24, 1572). Again William's forces were obliged to disband, and he retreated to Holland to lead the resistance there for four more frustrating years (1572-1576).

In June, 1575, William married his third wife, Charlotte de Bourbon, a former nun who had fled her convent, escaped to Germany, and converted to Calvinism. Catholics were outraged at this union, but it proved to be both happy and successful, as Charlotte won the trust and affection of her husband's countrymen by her devotion to their cause.

By 1576, even Philip was becoming aware of the costs of this seemingly endless war. The rebellion was not crushed, and his own troops began to mutiny for lack of pay. William's status rose with the Pacification of Ghent (November 8, 1576), in which the seventeen provinces agreed to a common cause against Spain. This was followed in January, 1577, by the short-lived Union of Brussels, in which both Catholics and Protestants joined in demanding the withdrawal of Spanish troops, the southerners reserving the right to remain Catholics. At this point, William was at the height of his power and influence, but he was unable to maintain this fragile alliance, despite his natural toleration and his talents as a diplomat.

Believing that he must have the support of another ruling dynasty against Spain, William again turned to France and proposed the unlikely candidacy of the feckless Duke of Anjou, brother of Henry III of France, as sovereign of the Netherlands. Philip riposted in March, 1581, with a ban proclaiming William a traitor and offering a considerable reward for his assassination. The first attempt on his life a year later failed, but his wife died of a fever and the strain of nursing her husband.

The Duke of Anjou's double-dealing and ambitions made him unacceptable to his new subjects, few of whom would mourn his death in June, 1583. Two months before, William had married Louise de Coligny, a daughter of the famous Huguenot leader Gaspard II de Coligny, killed on Saint Bartholomew's Day. Of his twelve children, it would be her son Frederick Henry who would leave heirs to carry on the Nassau name. With Louise, William lived simply and quietly in Delft, a father figure beloved by the people, until July 10, 1584, when he was fatally shot by a Catholic fanatic. William's dying words were a prayer for his poor country. He was given a state funeral by the city and buried in the New Church at Delft.

Summary

The sequence of events following the murder of William the Silent was a study in vengeance and intolerance by all parties. William's friends and supporters relieved their outraged feelings by torturing and slowly executing the young assassin Balthazar Gérard. When the murder became known, William's enemies, who included Philip and Granvelle, expressed triumphant satisfaction at what they considered to be divine justice. The reconquest of the entire Netherlands appeared a certainty, but such was not to be.

Philip's dream of a Catholic Netherlands as the obedient handmaiden of Spain faded before the realities of Dutch determination, his own financial mismanagement, and the defeat of his grand armada by England in 1588. Yet William's dream of a united Netherlands would not become a reality. The depths of distrust between Protestants and Catholics, middle-class merchants and the nobility, north and south were too great to be bridged. William invested his fortune, his family (three of his brothers would die on campaigns), and finally his own life for the cause in which he so strongly believed. Yet not even his personal popularity and his diplomatic skills could hold the provinces together for long. William's cause failed, but he had dared greatly and became the heart and symbol of the Dutch independence movement.

Bibliography

Geyl, Pieter. *The Revolt of the Netherlands, 1555-1609.* 2d ed. London: Ernest Benn, 1958. This is the first chronologically in a series of three books by Geyl that deal with the Netherlands from 1555 to 1715. As a Dutch historian, Geyl has a special perspective on the revolt. This book places William in his historical context. Includes maps, an extensive index, and a short bibliography.

Harrison, Frederic. *William the Silent.* Port Washington, N.Y.: Kennikat Press, 1897, reprint 1970. The style and interpretation of this biography are of necessity somewhat dated, but the lack of a standard biography of William in English makes it useful. Contains a bibliography and useful information on William's family and descendants.

Kossman, E. H., and A. F. Mellink, eds. *Texts Concerning the Revolt of the Netherlands.* New York: Cambridge University Press, 1974. This book introduces the reader to letters and documents related to the revolt. Several letters by William are included. Contains a short bibliography and an index.

Parker, Geoffrey. *The Dutch Revolt.* Ithaca, N.Y.: Cornell University Press, 1977. Parker makes the valid point that there was not one Dutch revolt but several. This study attempts to balance the majority of treatments, which are pro-Dutch, with attention to the Spanish viewpoint. Contains maps, diagrams, tables, and an extensive bibliography.

Putnam, Ruth. *William the Silent, Prince of Orange (1533-1584) and the Revolt of the Netherlands.* New York: G. P. Putnam's Sons, 1911. The character of William the Silent is at times overly idealized, but this book is a useful beginning to a study of William and his times. Pictures, maps, and facsimiles of letters make it interesting to the general reader. Includes a detailed bibliography and an index.

Swart, K. W. *William the Silent and the Revolt of the Netherlands.* London: The Historical Association, 1978. This work is one of a series on a wide range of historical topics. Though brief, it is a clear and unromantic portrait of William. Contains a useful annotated bibliography.

Wedgwood, C. V. *William the Silent, William of Nassau, Prince of Orange.* New Haven, Conn.: Yale University Press, 1944. Well written and detailed but continues the trend of older studies in idealizing William's motives and character. For the general reader.

Wilson, Charles. *Queen Elizabeth and the Revolt of the Netherlands.* London: Macmillan, 1970. The English view of the Netherlands as well as the role played by Elizabeth I is the focus of this useful study, but there is good background material on William also. Includes detailed notes on sources.

Dorothy Turner Potter

JOHANN JOACHIM WINCKELMANN

Born: December 9, 1717; Stendal, Prussia
Died: June 8, 1768; Trieste
Areas of Achievement: Aesthetics, archaeology, and historiography
Contribution: Winckelmann's studies of ancient Greek art profoundly influenced the development of the European neoclassical period in the late eighteenth century. His work helped to shape the areas of literature, the fine arts, art history, and classical archaeology.

Early Life

Johann Joachim Winckelmann was born the son of a poor shoemaker, Martin Winckelmann, in a rural village of the Mark Brandenburg, in what was then Prussia. He was an extremely intelligent and academically gifted child and was thus able to attend a formal Latin school. In 1735, he went to Berlin to study at a high school. The young Winckelmann was graduated and in 1737 registered in the department of theology at the University of Halle. His interests, however, were in the study of classical antiquity. He left after two years and worked as a private tutor until 1741, when he entered the University of Jena. After finishing at Jena, he taught school in Prussia.

Life's Work

From the early days of his childhood study of classical Greek and Latin at the local Latin school, Winckelmann was intensely dedicated to the study of ancient Greek and Roman literature, art, and civilization. In 1754, he entered the court of Augustus III, a great collector of artworks. At this time, Winckelmann wrote an essay on ancient art that would become a major influence on succeeding generations of scholars and writers, his *Gedanken über die Nachahmung der griechischen Werke in der Malerei und Bildhauerkunst* (1755; *Reflections on the Paintings and Sculpture of the Greeks,* 1765). Winckelmann was awarded a pension by the Prussian monarch because of this essay. It serves, in part, as a study leading to Winckelmann's later monumental history of classical art, *Geschichte der Kunst des Alterthums* (1764, 1776; *History of Ancient Art,* 1849-1873), and therefore deserves some detailed discussion of its major themes and insights.

Winckelmann clearly favors the art of the ancient world. The Greek sense of taste, he contends, is unparalleled, and the only path to greatness for the modern world is to imitate the artistic production of the ancients. His essay seeks to characterize the major distinctive features of Greek art. He begins his examination with a discussion of art and nature in the ancient world and sets it in comparison to the depiction of nature by modern painters. Greek artists portrayed nature in its purest and most beautiful form. This portrayal is most apparent in their representations of the human form. The human body is presented in its most ideal form, at the height of the perfection of its youth and beauty. The Greek style reflects the Greek's societal and cultural standards, their love of physical activity, and their competitive games that glorified the body. Disease and other maladies of modern society, Winckelmann claims, were not present in Greek society. He clearly prefers the artistic idealization of the human form in ancient art to the more realistic representations of the body that predominate in postclassical art.

In the second section, Winckelmann discusses the aesthetic dimension of contour, a domain in which the ancients excelled. Their figures exhibit the noblest contours, again in contrast to those found in the works of more modern artists such as Peter Paul Rubens. Winckelmann praises the sculptured figures found at Herculaneum. The brief third section deals with the artistic issue of drapery, or the way in which the human form is enveloped in garments. Again, he claims that the Greeks were far superior to the moderns in the way they depicted clothing and robes in their art.

The fourth and final section of the essay deals with the overall Greek sense of aesthetic expression. Winckelmann's characterization of ancient art in this section as exhibiting a "noble simplicity and sedate grandeur" (*edel Einfalt und stille Grösse*) was to become the most influential and frequently quoted description of the Greeks. German neoclassicist writers such as Johann Wolfgang von Goethe and Friedrich Schiller, for example, were to make this concept of aesthetic value the ideal of much of their literary production. Winckelmann discusses the Laocoön statue, one of the most famous examples of Greek (actually Hellenistic) art, which is based on a story from the legend of the siege of Troy. Laocoön and his two sons had set out to warn the Trojans of the Greek plot but were killed by a serpent sent by Apollo. The statue portrays the three figures, enveloped by the huge serpent, being crushed to death. Winckelmann notes, however, that despite their immense suffering the figures' faces are not distorted by pain—which would render the statue realistic but certainly hideous—but rather are peacefully transfigured, retaining a placid dignity and calmness that suggest the greatness of the Greek soul. This aesthetic ideal evidences the general Greek cultural vision of moderation or measure—the belief that extreme expression in any form fundamentally distorts nature and is to be avoided. Ancient art portrays not the exaggerated but the exemplary individual, whose beauty and greatness of spirit epitomize a balanced and harmonious nature.

Winckelmann's portrait of ancient Greek culture deserves some comment at this point. It should be noted that his observations were based not on actual examples of Greek sculpture but on Roman copies uncovered in Italy. Although his characterization of Greek art is for the most part accurate, his overall vision of their society and culture presents a romantic and conservative idealization of Greek civilization. For Winckelmann, the Greeks become a highly spiritual, childlike people who live in a primitive but pristine harmony with nature. They represent, in essence, a cheerful and optimistic culture. This is clearly a version of the myth of the "noble savage" found at various times in modern European thought. Winckelmann's vision of Greek culture was criticized in Friedrich Nietzsche's first philosophical work, *Die Geburt der Tragödie aus dem Geiste der Musik* (1872; *The Birth of Tragedy Out of the Spirit of Music*, 1909). Nietzsche claimed that Greek culture and art, especially the drama, sprang not from a harmony with nature but from a profound sense of the suffering inherent in human existence.

In 1756, Winckelmann traveled to Rome, where he managed the pope's collection of antiquities and also served as professor of Greek in the Vatican Library. His work there established his reputation as a world-famous authority on classical Greek art and the science of archaeology. In 1764, he published his famous and influential *History of Ancient Art*. This work was Winckelmann's magnum opus and consists of several volumes. It is divided into two major sections, one which investigates the nature of art philosophically and the other which looks at Greek art historically. In the first section, Winckelmann begins with a discussion of the origins of art in the religious traditions of various peoples. He then focuses on the development of art among the Egyptians, the Phoenicians, and the Persians. Because of certain cultural, political, and social restrictions, Egyptian art never evolved beyond a primitive stage of development, and the same holds true for the other two groups. Winckelmann also discusses the Etruscans and claims that their artistic production, although more developed than that of the Egyptians, is limited by the essentially melancholic and superstitious temperament of the people.

The longest chapter of the book discusses Greek art and reveals Winckelmann's decided bias in favor of this cultural sphere of the ancient world. Numerous factors such as climate, political organization, the development of philosophy and rhetoric, the cult of physical fitness and beauty, and the general societal esteem for artists all contributed to making the art of Greece the most sophisticated and mature of the ancient world. He goes on to describe the essential features of Greek art, its ability to capture true beauty, that is, the perfected human form which, in its perfection, reminds man of the divine. Winckelmann discusses what he sees as the four developmental periods of Greek art as well as aspects of Roman art. The brief second section of the volume elaborates on the chronological development of Greek art and presents discussions of individual statues.

In 1768, Winckelmann briefly journeyed to Germany, where, for a number of personal reasons, he suffered a severe nervous breakdown. He returned to Italy, bound for Trieste. Winckelmann had exhibited markedly homosexual tendencies for most of his adult life, and, in his depressed condition, he began a casual affair with a young man he met in Trieste. The man, who turned out to be a thief, robbed and murdered the famous scholar at the hotel in which they were staying.

Summary

Johann Joachim Winckelmann's work as an art critic and historian as well as his archaeological work in Italy served to initiate to a great degree the neoclassical art revival and the new humanistic and cosmopolitan trends of the eighteenth and early nineteenth centuries, especially in Germany from 1775 to 1832. His somewhat idealized vision of the beautiful as the spiritual harmony and balance in Greek culture profoundly influenced subsequent generations of writers, artists, and thinkers. This was the age of the great German writings of Goethe and Schiller, in which the ideals of human dignity and the perfectibility of man through progressive education became the guidelines of bourgeois culture. This was also the enlightened age of rationalism, revealed through the work of philosopher Immanuel Kant, and the development of the idea of freedom of rational choice versus the determinism of the irrational impulse. These new ideas formed, at least in part, the didactic goals of art and literature during this period. Winckelmann's portrait of Greek culture helped to shape this emergence of bourgeois humanism.

It should be remarked that Winckelmann's prescription for the modern age—the imitation of ancient Greece—represents an essentially conservative vision of history; that is, it promulgates an idealized vision of some prior "golden age" in which mankind was at one with nature and in which discord and chaos did not exist. This implicit and, at times, explicit rejection of the modern period in Winckelmann's writings is characteristic of the development of German (and European) historicism during the eighteenth and nineteenth centuries.

Bibliography

Butler, E. M. *The Tyranny of Greece over Germany.* Cambridge: Cambridge University Press, 1935. A dated but still excellent scholarly discussion of Winckelmann's promulgation of Greek art and culture in Germany. Contains notes and bibliography.

Hatfield, Henry. *Aesthetic Paganism in German Literature, from Winckelmann to the Death of Goethe.* Cambridge, Mass.: Harvard University Press, 1964. A discussion of the effects of Winckelmann's work on the development of German literature. Contains notes and bibliography.

_____. *Winckelmann and His German Critics, 1755-1781: A Prelude to the Classical Age.* New York: King's Crown Press, 1943. A dated but still useful academic work by a prominent scholar on the German reaction to Winckelmann. Contains notes and bibliography.

Honour, Hugh. *Neo-Classicism.* Harmondsworth, England: Penguin Books, 1968. A more general discussion of the artistic movement with sections on Winckelmann's work and influence. Written by an important critic. Contains notes and bibliography.

Leppmann, Wolfgang. *Winckelmann.* New York: Alfred A. Knopf, 1970.

An excellent critical biography in English. Contains notes and bibliography.

Pater, Walter. "Winckelmann." In *Studies in the History of the Renaissance*. London: Macmillan, 1873. An important and insightful essay by a prominent nineteenth century English art historian.

Rosenblum, Robert. *Transformations in Late Eighteenth Century Art*. Princeton, N.J.: Princeton University Press, 1967. Scholarly work which contains useful discussion of Winckelmann's ideas and influence. Contains notes and bibliography.

Thomas F. Barry

FRIEDRICH WÖHLER

Born: July 31, 1800; Eschersheim, near Frankfurt am Main
Died: September 23, 1882; Göttingen, Germany
Area of Achievement: Chemistry
Contribution: Wöhler synthesized urea in 1828 and thus first demonstrated that organic materials, heretofore believed to possess a vital force, need not be made exclusively within living organisms. He also isolated aluminum metal in 1827 and discovered the elements beryllium and yttrium.

Early Life

Born in the village of Eschersheim to Anton August Wöhler and his wife, Anna Katharina Schröder, Friedrich Wöhler received his early education from his father, who had been Master of the Horse to the Prince of Hesse Kassel and subsequently one of Frankfurt's leading citizens. As a child Wöhler pursued both mineralogy and chemistry as hobbies and, in addition to public school, received tutoring in Latin, French, and music. Indeed, Wöhler's early years imbued him with the Romantic spirit of the day. He studied music and poetry, and the well-known landscape painter Christopher Morgenstern encouraged him in artistic endeavors. Yet Wöhler also showed an early interest in science, as he built voltaic piles from zinc plates and some old Russian coins and experimented with the reactive elements phosphorus and chlorine. Between 1814 and 1820, Wöhler attended the *Gymnasium* to prepare himself for the University of Marburg, where he began to study medicine and won a prize for his work on the transformation of waste substances into urine. Yet it became obvious to him, at this early stage of his career, that his interests lay more in chemistry than in medicine, and thus he went to Heidelberg, where he studied under the well-known Leopold Gmelin. At Heidelberg, Wöhler earned his medical degree in 1823; rather than seek employment as a physician, however, he received permission to work in Stockholm with Jöns Jakob Berzelius, perhaps the greatest figure in chemistry of the day.

It was in Stockholm that Wöhler gained the scientific and technical skills that were crucial to his future career, as he was carefully trained in exact chemical analysis using such simple tools as a platinum crucible, a balance, and a blow pipe. This expertise, coupled with his interest in cyanic acid and the cyanates, ultimately led to investigations that transformed the fundamental nature of modern chemistry.

Life's Work

At the beginning of the nineteenth century, organic chemistry was normally associated with the extraction, isolation, and identification of animal and vegetable matter for medicinal purposes. It was thought that only in the animal and vegetable kingdom could organic molecules be synthesized and form organized bodies. The presence of a vital force was attributed to this unique chemistry found only in living systems. Organic chemistry, then, was a science concerned primarily with understanding the nature of life and creation—not merely a study of isolated reactions of carbon-containing compounds. The concept of vitalism discouraged the use of the theory of chemical affinities associated with mineral or inorganic chemistry in explanations related to the organic branch of the discipline. Thus Berzelius wrote in 1819 that his electrochemical theory could not be applied to organic matter, because, in his opinion, the influence of a vital force led to entirely different electrochemical properties. Wöhler's researches would subsequently refute this idea and thus unify the animal and mineral branches of chemistry.

Upon returning from Berzelius' laboratory in 1825, Wöhler began his teaching career at an industrial school in Berlin. He soon began communicating with University of Giessen professor Justus von Liebig, who had learned exact chemical analysis from Joseph-Louis Gay-Lussac in Paris. The two quickly formed a lifelong friendship and began collaborating on problems of mutual interest. For some time, Liebig had been working on explosive fulminates, and, during the course of these investigations, he prepared a compound that was similar in composition to silver cyanate, a compound Wöhler had prepared in 1823. Despite the fact that silver cyanate and silver fulminate had the same empirical formula, AgCNO, they had different chemical and physical properties; it remained for Berzelius in 1830 to call the new phenomenon isomerism.

Wöhler's studies on the cyanates directed him to reexamine reactions that he had initially undertaken while a student in Berzelius' laboratory, thus setting the stage for his artificial synthesis of urea, which stands as a milestone in the history of science. Wöhler prepared urea by first reacting lead cyanate with ammonia. Beautiful white crystals appeared that, when treated with nitric acid, were transformed into lustrous flakes of a substance he quickly recognized as urea. In February of 1828, Wöhler boasted to Berzelius that he had prepared urea without the kidney of man or dog. Wöhler's synthesis marked the beginning of a new chemistry in which distinctions between inorganic and organic fields were blurred. Wöhler's career was now on the rise, and in 1831 he left Berlin for Kassel, where he held a similar position. Tragedy struck amid his early scientific triumphs, however, for a year later his young wife and cousin, Franziska Wöhler, died. For consolation, Wöhler went to Liebig's laboratory, where they collaborated on an important paper dealing with oil of bitter almonds (benzaldehyde). In their investigations they demonstrated that a group of atoms remained unchanged through a series of chemical operations, and to this fundamental unit they gave the name benzoyl. This discovery played a major role in debates of the 1830's dealing with radical theory.

Liebig and Wöhler continued to work together during the 1830's, even though Wöhler returned to Kassel, where he remarried. In 1836, Wöhler succeeded Friedrich Strohmeyer at Göttingen and filled this chair for almost half a century until his death in 1882. While Wöhler worked on various problems related to organic chemistry during his first few years at Göttingen, by 1840 he increasingly turned to the study of inorganic and mineralogical chemistry. Perhaps his reorientation was the result of the frustration of working in the field of organic chemistry at that time. The field was experiencing a kind of chaos because of internal reorientation in terms of nomenclature and central concepts related to molecular structure.

Wöhler's previous background in inorganic and mineralogical chemistry had been a solid one, the result of his studies with his former mentor Berzelius on silicon, selenium, and zirconium. Indeed, in 1827 he had been the first scientist to isolate metallic aluminum by reacting a small quantity of potassium with an excess of aluminum chloride. By 1850, Wöhler was active in preparing a large number of metallic salts, and later in 1862 he was the first to synthesize calcium carbide from acetylene. Other important contributions included the preparation of silicon hydride, silicon chloroform, iodoform, and bromoform.

Unlike his close friend Liebig, Wöhler remained interested and active in chemical research until his death. Friedrich Wöhler's professional accomplishments encompassed broad areas within chemistry, and he stands out in an era in which the discipline was transformed in terms of both theoretical knowledge and technical methods.

Summary

During the past four decades, historians of science have debated the significance of Friedrich Wöhler's synthesis of urea. The importance of Wöhler's investigation lay not in his refutation of the concept of vitalism but in the development of ideas related to structural chemistry. His demonstration of the isomeric relationship between urea and ammonium cyanate further exposed previously little-known chemical complexities that could be best understood in terms of molecular structure. For chemists such as Wöhler, Berzelius, and Liebig, the vital force apparently remained a viable scientific concept even after 1828.

The experimental synthesis of acetic acid by Hermann Kolbe in 1844 and the synthesis of methane and acetylene by Marcelin Berthelot in 1855 and 1856 contributed to the decline in popularity of the vitalistic theory. More significant, however, as Timothy Lipman has suggested, is that vitalism's importance in organic chemistry declined by the mid-nineteenth century, when the life sciences became increasingly specialized. Organic chemistry dealt with compounds of carbon atoms; physiology focused on organic functions; but neither subdiscipline examined the creation of life. Thus, for the organic chemist, vitalism was no longer a necessary concept.

Bibliography

Ihde, Aaron. *The Development of Modern Chemistry.* New York: Harper & Row, 1964. This general survey in the history of chemistry includes a thorough discussion of Wöhler's chief contributions to both organic and inorganic chemistry. It is essential in placing Wöhler's work within its proper intellectual context.

Keen, Robin. "Friedrich Wöhler and His Lifelong Interest in the Platinum Metals." *Platinum Metals Review* 29 (1985): 81-85. A well-researched and clearly written article that not only provides an overview of Wöhler's life and professional career but also focuses upon his work in the isolation of aluminum and the separation of iridium and osmium. In addition, Keen links the careers of two of Wöhler's students, Wilhelm Carl Heraeus and Heinrich Rössler, to the development of the platinum industry.

Lipman, Timothy O. "Wöhler's Preparation of Urea and the Fate of Vitalism." *Journal of Chemical Education* 41 (1964): 452-458. Lipman's essay on vitalism and Wöhler provides a model of careful research and critical thinking for scholars working in the field of the history of chemistry. Lipman's purpose is to settle the issue of whether Wöhler's 1828 synthesis of urea overturned vitalistic notions in organic chemistry. In the process of demonstrating that Wöhler's experiment was one of a number of facts that accumulated during the first half of the nineteenth century that made vitalism untenable, the author thoroughly characterizes the place of vitalism in chemistry both before and after 1828.

McKie, Douglas. "Wöhler's Preparation of Urea and the Fate of Vitalism: A Chemical Legend." *Nature* 153 (1944): 608-610. This work strongly argues that Wöhler's 1828 synthesis of urea had far less influence in refuting the doctrine of vitalism than previously believed. Indeed, McKie attempts to shatter a legend that emerged long after Wöhler's early experiments, a legend perpetuated by successive generations of chemists.

Smith, Edgar F. "Some Experiences of Dr. Edgar F. Smith as a Student Under Wöhler." *Journal of Chemical Education* 5 (1928): 1554-1557. In 1928, Edgar Fah Smith of the University of Pennsylvania, one of the leading figures in the development of chemistry in nineteenth century America, reminisced to a small group of chemists, one of whom recorded the conversation. Smith's recollections are a delightful account of one student's experiences in Göttingen and provide an interesting view of Wöhler as a mentor of graduate students.

Warren, W. H. "Contemporary Reception of Wöhler's Discovery of the Synthesis of Urea." *Journal of Chemical Education* 5 (1928): 1539-1553. Although somewhat dated in terms of scholarship, this essay traces the response of several important chemists to Wöhler's 1828 synthesis of urea. By carefully examining contemporary correspondence, periodical literature, and books, the author argues that by 1840 a number of chemists were convinced of the significance of Wöhler's work in the changing views concerning vitalism and thus of the boundaries between organic and inorganic chemistry.

John A. Heitmann

SAINT FRANCIS XAVIER

Born: April 7, 1506; the Castle of Xavier, Navarre
Died: December 3, 1552; Island of Sancian, China
Area of Achievement: Religion
Contribution: Francis, who suffered many physical and mental hardships in order to bring the Christian message to countries of the Far East, was one of the first seven members of the Roman Catholic church's Jesuit Order as well as its most successful missionary.

Early Life

The youngest of a family of several children, Francis Xavier was born to a prosperous nobleman, Don Juan de Jasso of Navarre, and a mother whose connection with the Xavier family brought property into her marriage. Francis' parents focused on his education early in his life, and, since they determined he had a real love for learning, he was allowed to go to the College of Saint Barbara at the University of Paris, where, in 1530, he received a master of arts degree. After being graduated, Francis taught Aristotelian philosophy at the same institution. Francis was known to be a generous, helpful, and stirring lecturer, having a thorough knowledge of his subject. Yet, it was his sense of adventure, combined with a serious, searching, and scholarly nature, that drew students to him and made him ready to embark on daring journeys to little-known or unknown lands.

It was Ignatius Loyola (later Saint Ignatius of Loyola), a fellow student of Francis at the University of Paris, who helped Francis find his calling—that of Christian missionary work. For three years, Ignatius prodded Francis to dedicate his life to God rather than to the vain pursuits of the worldly minded; yet Francis ignored the summons. Finally, however, Francis' resistance broke down, and he decided to serve God rather than scholarship. Together, Francis and Ignatius, along with five other idealistic youths, pledged themselves to Church service at Montmartre in Paris, their group becoming the Society of Jesus (Jesuits). Six of the original seven members went on to become ordained into the priesthood at Venice, Italy.

Francis and Ignatius then went to Rome and informed Pope Paul III that they would do whatever he asked of them. The pope, impressed by their youthful vigor and intellectual gifts, eventually gave official approval to the Society of Jesus. When the time came, the young men—Ignatius, Francis, Peter Faber, Nicholas Bobadilla, Diego Laínez, Alfonso Salmeron, and Simon Rodriguez—not only took traditional monastic vows of perpetual poverty and chastity but also pledged total obedience to the pope's wishes, going wherever he might find it necessary to send them.

From inauspicious beginnings in 1534, the society would help evangelize many nations and bring countless converts to the Church, while performing humanitarian deeds for the people converted and battling any heresy, vice, and spiritual lethargy they might encounter. Francis' name would become forever intertwined with that of the society, for he came to exemplify all that was positive in it.

Life's Work

After being ordained in the priesthood in 1537, Francis, in the company of Ignatius and the other Jesuits, worked long days to make the society into a successful venture, enthusiastically spreading the news about it to potential recruits. In 1540, the Portuguese king John III instructed his Vatican emissary to petition the pope to allow Jesuits the right to propagate the Christian faith within the new Portuguese possessions overseas. An opportunity for missionary work came after a vision of Ignatius, in which God told him to ask the pope a second time for a chance to do missionary tasks. In Ignatius' vision, God said that He would make certain that the permission would be granted.

With Ignatius elected the general of the society and with orders from Paul to convert pagans in Portugal's expanding empire, Francis joined fellow priest Rodriguez in Lisbon; then, with two trusted aides, he sailed on to Goa, a Portuguese colony in India, situated on the coast. While on board the ship taking him to Goa, Francis showed characteristic love for his fellow passengers by assisting those sickened by scurvy and other diseases, by saying Mass regularly, and by arbitrating arguments among the sailors. Once in Goa, which had been a Portuguese possession for only thirty years, Francis noted with dismay that the Europeans within the colony were dissipated by debauchery of all kinds and thus provided the native people with a terrible example of Christian conduct.

Taking upon himself the same selfless activities that he had performed on ship—caring for the sick, comforting the dying, advising those in difficult situations, teaching the Catechism, and saying Masses—Francis slowly created order out of the Goan chaos, giving by precept as well as example a measure of self-discipline to the unruly inhabitants. Because he taught the residents of Goa the principles of the Catholic religion and put those principles directly into practice, Francis gained the residents' complete trust and high regard.

In 1542, having done much for Goa, Francis decided to journey to Cape Cormorin in southern India in order to teach a group of half-converted natives, called the Paravas, Christian values and beliefs; his message was well received by the poorest Paravas, who gathered in large numbers to hear him deliver his inspiring sermons. The love Francis had for the people of India was evident to almost everyone, even if his message sometimes became garbled or was incomprehensible. Once more, Francis' actions did more persuading than did his eloquent words.

After working with the Paravas, Francis decided to return to Goa in order to find new priests for the Society of Jesus. Again he was forced to deal with the immoral behavior and often outright hostility of Portuguese traders, who found his preaching an affront to a libertine way of life. This time, he worked alongside two Goanese priests and a lay catechist, helping the Goanese people by protecting them from European harassment.

At Travancore, Francis founded many churches, but at the same time he tore down the natives' ancestral places of worship and idols. He was said to have brought the dead back to life in the manner of Jesus Christ. Francis' exploits and his miracles led to his being hated by the Hindu Brahmans as well as local Muslims, who on occasion massacred Christian converts. As for his mission at Goa, Francis often wrote in letters to John III about how difficult an endeavor the mission had been for him and his followers. Fighting the immorality of the Portuguese residents at Goa demanded so much of Francis' time that he admitted to chronic weariness and, upon more than one occasion, a sense of defeat.

It may well have been his exasperation with fellow Europeans that led to Francis' departure from Goa in 1545, when he sailed to a city on the Malaysian peninsula called Malacca. There people who had previously been hostile to Christianity converted enthusiastically after Francis worked his miracles. He journeyed on to the southern Pacific Ocean, where he spent time on the Molucca Islands. There Francis once more battled the hardened, sinning Portuguese traders, some of whom would have liked to kill him.

From the Moluccas, Francis returned to Goa, this time by way of Ceylon, but wanted to journey on to the little-known secretive country of Japan. He traveled to Kagoshima on the island of Kyūshū, where he and his band were given permission to learn the Japanese language and to preach Christian doctrine to the city's inhabitants; unfortunately, this budding mission was almost destroyed when the prince who gave permission for Francis' evangelistic efforts became irate with him over the fact that Francis had dared use a base of Japanese operations other than his own city of Kagoshima.

Nevertheless, the converts that Francis had made remained faithful to the Church established in Japan. He made still more converts when he moved to the town of Hirado near Kagoshima. Other attempts at reaching the Japanese at the port city of Yamaguchi in 1549 were unsuccessful. At Kyōto, the imperial city itself, Francis found himself at another impasse, this time because he was so poorly dressed that the emperor believed that Francis could not possibly be an important Western dignitary and thus would not deign to see him. Francis, ever able to rise to a challenge, decided to purchase luxurious clothing for himself and for his fellow adventurers. Dressing as extravagantly as he could, he presented himself to Oshindono, Prince of Nagote, who, after having been impressed by the splendor of Francis' party, decided to allow him to preach the Gospel in his realm. This opening allowed Francis to baptize many in the Christian faith.

Still other missionary ventures opened at Bungo in Kyūshū province, where the ruler was friendly to Francis and his followers and friends. When Francis left Japan in 1551, he could look back on a considerable achievement: He had singlehandedly converted more than seven hundred Japanese people to the Christian faith without bloodshed or turmoil.

Francis' last major challenge was to find a way to establish a mission in the forbidding country of China, long closed to all outsiders on the pain of death. Encouraged solely by the fact that so many missions had already been established in places once thought to be totally inhospitable to Christianity, Francis believed that God wanted him to open China to his faith and gain many converts there. Yet from the outset, the venture proved impossible. Francis dreamed of being the first priest to enter China. After he had done much exhausting work for the lepers at Malacca, he asked the new governor, Don Alvaro d'Ataide, to provide him with a ship and supplies so that he might sail to China. The governor, knowing well that China remained closed to outsiders, at first refused the request but then, after reconsidering, grudgingly allowed it.

Francis' plan was to sail to Japan in company with a Christian brother and a Chinese Christian, and then to travel secretly to China in the hope of somehow gaining entry. In the late summer of 1552, he landed at the port of Shang-ch'uen, where he hired a merchant to take him by night into Canton province. At a time when he needed all the strength he could find, Francis fell ill with a raging fever and was summarily left alone by most of the Portuguese on the island, who made a precarious living trading with mainlanders. Although one ship would have taken him home to Europe, Francis could not bear the ship's motion as it made its way out to sea, and he begged the captain to take him back to Shang-ch'uen, where he died asking God's forgiveness and praising Him.

Summary

Saint Francis Xavier, canonized by Pope Gregory XV in 1622 at the same time as was his great friend Ignatius, was one of the Catholic church's most daring, astute, and productive leaders. He used his fine intellectual gifts and his ability to deliver powerful speeches and sermons to glorify God when he very well might have pursued far less arduous and far more lucrative careers than that of a missionary.

Francis was fortunate to have been born during Spain and Portugal's "Golden Age" of the sixteenth century, when empire-building was the pursuit of the Hispanic nations and their kings. Both countries, out to counter the Reformation brought on by followers of Martin Luther and to add to national coffers, needed able priests to subdue through conversion the natives of conquered lands. Thus, Francis found the kind of support he needed for his missionary efforts.

Without Francis and his fellow Jesuits, India, Japan, and other places in the Orient would have remained untouched by the Church's message and, without Francis' support, Ignatius might not have been able to found and properly organize the Jesuit Order. Today, with a debt owed to its founders, the society remains the preeminent scholarly order of the Catholic church as well as its greatest supplier of educators, who teach children in secondary schools, colleges, and universities around the world. Appropriately, Francis remains the patron saint of all involved in missionary work and the guiding influence of multitudes of priests who have served their God in foreign places.

Bibliography

Aveling, J. C. H. "The Dangerous Missions." In *The Jesuits*. Briarcliff Manor, N.Y.: Stein & Day, 1981. This superb study of the Society of Jesus and its dynamic of faith, though it chooses not to dwell for long on Francis, does a fine job of discussing the magnitude of his opening the Far East to the Christian faith.

Barthel, Manfred. "The Light of the World: The Jesuit as Missionary." In *The Jesuits: History and Legend of the Society of Jesus*. Translated by Mark Howson. New York: William Morrow, 1984. Explains Francis' contribution to the founding of the Society of Jesus and to its early mission work, and how he is to be remembered. For those readers wishing to have a grounding in the Jesuit Order's history and Francis' place in it. The general bibliography is useful.

Bartoli, Daniello, and J. P. Maffei. *The Life of St. Francis Xavier, Apostle of the Indies and Japan*. Baltimore: John Murphy Press, 1862. Bartoli's account is one of the handful of studies of the saint in English translation. Serves as a basic guide to the subject of Francis' travels.

Clarke, C. P. S. "St. Francis Xavier." In *Everyman's Book of Saints*. Milwaukee, Wis.: Morehouse, 1919. Elementary but helpful introduction to Francis' place in the canon of saints.

Foss, Michael. "Reform of the Church and the Life of Renewal." In *The Founding of the Jesuits*. New York: Weybright and Talley, 1969. Foss traces the society from its inception to the modern era. Francis is given credit for his pioneering work.

Maynard, Theodore. *The Odyssey of Francis Xavier*. Westminster, Md.: Newman Press, 1950. Compelling study of Francis and his importance to the Catholic church's missionary outreach.

John D. Raymer

GRAF VON ZINZENDORF
Nikolaus Ludwig

Born: May 26, 1700; Dresden, Saxony
Died: May 9, 1760; Herrnhut, Saxony
Areas of Achievement: Religion, theology, and church reform
Contribution: Zinzendorf revived and transformed the nearly extinct Moravian Church by infusing it with an evangelical Pietistic theology. In so doing he also became a pioneer of ecumenism among Christians and gave birth to the modern Protestant missionary movement.

Early Life

Nikolaus Ludwig von Zinzendorf was born on May 26, 1700, in Dresden, Saxony, to Charles Ludwig and Charlotte Justine von Zinzendorf. His father died from tuberculosis only six weeks later. When he was three years old, on the eve of his mother's remarriage and move to Berlin, Nikolaus was sent to live with his maternal grandmother, the Baroness Henriette Katherine von Gersdorf. Three women—his mother, his grandmother, and his mother's sister—profoundly influenced his early life. They were all devout Christians.

The atmosphere at his grandmother's estate of Gross-Hennersdorf was permeated by religion. Each day's routine included prayer, Bible study, and the singing of hymns. Like Nikolaus' parents, Baroness Gersdorf was a Lutheran Pietist. The Pietists were reacting to the Protestant Scholasticism that had transformed the insights and vibrant life of the Reformation into a dead orthodoxy of rigid formulas. In personal life they stressed the new birth, a life-style of moral purity, and a daily routine of prayer and Bible study. They also stressed service to the less fortunate and evangelism at home and abroad. These basic tenets of Pietism were to become the guiding principles of the adult Zinzendorf.

In 1710, Baroness Gersdorf enrolled her grandson in the *Pädagogium*, or boarding school, in Halle. The school was founded and run by the noted social and educational reformer August Hermann Francke. Francke was a follower of Philipp Jacob Spener, the founder of Lutheran Pietism, and was himself one of its leading promoters. At Halle, Zinzendorf joined with five other boys to found the Order of the Grain of Mustard Seed, pledging themselves to love all mankind and to spread the Gospel.

Although Zinzendorf wanted a career in the ministry, his guardian insisted that he prepare himself to fulfill his hereditary responsibilities in the state civil service. Hence, he studied law at the Universities of Wittenberg and Utrecht. As was the custom of that day for the nobility, Zinzendorf concluded his education with a grand tour of Europe in 1719-1720. While visiting an art museum in Düsseldorf, he paused before Domenico Fetti's *Ecce*

Homo, a painting of Jesus Christ with the crown of thorns. Below the painting was written, "I have done this for you; what have you done for me?" Zinzendorf was deeply moved and pledged himself to a life of Christian service. Later in life, he often pointed to that event as the turning point in his life.

In 1721, Zinzendorf moved to Dresden, where he entered the civil service of Elector August the Strong of Saxony. His apartment soon became a meeting place for informal religious services on Sunday afternoons. Also in 1721, Zinzendorf purchased the estate of Berthelsdorf from his grandmother, hoping to establish a Christian community there. On September 7, 1722, Zinzendorf married Dorothea von Reuss. From a deeply Pietistic home, she proved to be the perfect companion. She bore twelve children; only three of them survived their parents.

Life's Work

In December, 1722, a small group of ten Moravian refugees, six adults and four children, arrived at Berthelsdorf. They were a part of the surviving remnant of the Unitas Fratrum, or United Brethren Church, organized in 1457 by followers of the Bohemian religious reformer, Jan Hus. They were fleeing religious persecution, and Zinzendorf allowed them to settle on his lands. The original ten were followed by others, not only Moravians but also former Catholics, Anabaptists, Separatists, Schwenkfelders, Reformed, and even Lutherans. By 1726, their community, named Herrnhut, numbered three hundred souls and could boast a large meeting hall, academy, print shop, and apothecary. As the community prospered, there was a need to provide civil government and to define the nature and goals of Herrnhut's spiritual life.

In 1727, Zinzendorf resigned his position at court and devoted the remainder of his life to nurturing the Christian community at Herrnhut, which soon spread throughout Europe and beyond. The need to provide orderly development was met by a two-part constitution, accepted by the community in 1727. The first part recognized Zinzendorf's role as the lord of the manor and thus dealt with civic responsibilities. Perhaps of more significance was the Brotherly Agreement, which aimed at organizing the community's spiritual life.

The Brotherly Agreement emphasized practical Christian behavior and was to serve as a model for future Moravian communities. The community was divided into "choirs" determined by age, sex, and marital status. It also provided for a governing council of twelve elders, elected by the community, or, in the case of the four chief elders, chosen by lot. As if to emphasize the spiritual nature of their duties, no one of noble rank or advanced education was allowed to serve on the council.

On August 27, 1727, the Brethren at Herrnhut began an around-the-clock prayer meeting that continued unbroken for one hundred years. The year

1727 was later regarded as the birth year of the Renewed Moravian church. It also marked the point at which Zinzendorf's brand of Pietism began to diverge from the mainstream of German Pietism. Zinzendorf never desired that the Christian community at Herrnhut develop into a denomination. He believed that his mission in life, and the mission of Herrnhut, was to be an apostle of what he termed "heart religion." Zinzendorf rejected both the rationalism of the secular world and the dead orthodox Scholasticism of the churches. His concept of "heart religion" stressed the emotional and experiential side of religion. It emphasized a personal conversion to Jesus Christ, followed by a life of prayer, Bible study, and communal worship.

Zinzendorf was thoroughly ecumenical in his approach to Christianity. Indeed, many scholars regard him as the father of the modern ecumenical movement. Unlike most Christians of that era, Zinzendorf not only accepted the plurality of institutional churches but also regarded that pluralism positively. He believed that each denomination had a unique contribution to make to the spread of Christianity. All churches were a part of the one true church, the Body of Christ. Unity could be, and should be, sought on the experiential level, not on the intellectual or institutional level.

The success of Herrnhut aroused opposition from the leaders of the established Lutheran church, who feared that Zinzendorf was a sectarian. He was not, however, and he did all that he could to allay their fears. He insisted that all that was done at Herrnhut should conform to the Augsburg Confession of the Lutheran church. He invited deputations from the established church to visit the community and see for themselves that all was in line with the Augsburg Confession. The brethren at Herrnhut took communion regularly from the local Lutheran parish priest. In 1734, Zinzendorf himself was ordained as a Lutheran minister.

Zinzendorf also felt an obligation to take the gospel to the unbelieving in the farthest reaches of the globe. Through his efforts in these areas, Zinzendorf became the founder of the Protestant foreign missionary movement and a pioneer in Christian missions to the Jews. In 1731, Zinzendorf suggested sending missionaries to minister to the slaves in the West Indies. The response was enthusiastic. On August 21, 1732, the first Moravian missionaries departed Herrnhut for the West Indies. By 1735, twenty-nine missionaries had gone there, of whom only seven were still alive.

The period from 1732 to 1742 is often called the "golden decade" of Moravian missions. The Moravians were the first to believe that missionary work was the calling of the whole Christian community, laymen and clergy alike. By 1742, Moravian missionaries were serving in various parts of Africa, Asia, North America, and even Lapland and Greenland. They also sent missionaries to the Jews in Amsterdam, Holland.

As long as Zinzendorf lived, the Moravian missionaries acted almost exclusively on instructions from him. His mission philosophy had three emphases: Preach Christ, not theology; live humbly among the natives; and look for the "seekers after truth" rather than try to convert whole nations. Zinzendorf also believed that the missionaries should support themselves, thereby teaching by example the dignity of labor.

Between 1736 and 1747, Zinzendorf was banished from Saxony for his alleged sectarian activities. In 1737, he was ordained a bishop in the United Brethren church by one of its two surviving bishops. During his banishment, he traveled widely, founding Moravian communities in Europe, England, and the United States (for example, in Bethlehem, Pennsylvania). He organized a traveling executive, known as the Pilgrim Congregation, to direct the foreign missionary work and minister to the "diaspora," those cells of converts within the established churches throughout Europe. After his banishment was repealed in 1747, Zinzendorf made London the center of the Moravians' worldwide activities until 1755. One year after the death of his first wife, on June 19, 1756, Zinzendorf married Anna Nitschmann, a longtime coworker at Herrnhut. He died at Herrnhut on May 9, 1760. Anna died thirteen days later.

Summary

Graf von Zinzendorf's life had a profound impact on the history of Christianity. In an age when individual Christian sects were generally intolerant of one another, Zinzendorf labored for a unity of purpose that would overlook, but not suppress, denominational distinctions. His goal was to unite all Christians in evangelism: He was the first Christian leader to use the term "ecumenical" in its modern sense. Although he was himself a nobleman, he was perfectly at ease among the humble. While in the United States in 1741, he personally preached to Native Americans. He set an example that was followed by Moravian missionaries who ministered among slaves in the West Indies and lepers in South Africa. By 1832, there were forty-two Moravian mission stations around the world.

Stimulated by the example of the Moravians, the Baptists began foreign mission work in 1793. The annual Herrnhut Ministers Conference, inspired by Zinzendorf, led directly to the founding of both the London Missionary Society in 1795 and the British and Foreign Bible Society in 1804. Perhaps one of Zinzendorf's most far-reaching influences on church history resulted from the conversion of John Wesley, the founder of Methodism, through the influence of Moravian missionaries.

John Wesley first encountered the Moravians while on a voyage to the United States. He was greatly impressed by their humility and by their willingness to serve others. In Georgia, and later in England, Wesley frequented Moravian meetings. Then, on the evening of May 24, 1738, he experienced what he later described as his conversion experience. In August, 1738, Wesley visited Herrnhut. He summed up his impression of what he saw in his journal: "O when shall this Christianity cover the earth, as the 'waters cover the sea?'"

Christians and non-Christians alike have been generous in their praise of Zinzendorf. His zeal for spreading the Christian gospel and his deep, genuine concern for practical ministry to the poor have served as an inspiration for both Christian evangelists and secular social reformers. Perhaps the most fitting epitaph for Zinzendorf was provided by a church historian, who, referring to Jesus Christ's parable of the rich young ruler (Luke 18:18-30), characterized him as "the rich young ruler who said yes."

Bibliography

Cairns, Earle E. *An Endless Line of Splendor.* Wheaton, Ill.: Tyndale House Publishers, 1986. A noted church historian establishes the historical roots of nineteenth and twentieth century Christian revivals in the work of Zinzendorf and German Pietism.

Christian History 1 (1982). The entire issue of this popular church history magazine is devoted to Zinzendorf and the Moravians. Includes chronological charts, short biographies of leading figures associated with Zinzendorf, and numerous illustrations. "The Rich Young Ruler Who Said Yes" is an excellent biographical sketch of Zinzendorf.

Gollin, Gillian Lindt. *Moravians in Two Worlds: A Study of Changing Communities.* New York: Columbia University Press, 1967. Gollin provides an interesting history of two Moravian communities founded by Zinzendorf: Herrnhut, Germany, and Bethlehem, Pennsylvania. Using primary sources, Gollin attempts to explain the differing development of the two communities between 1722 and 1850, with respect to their religious, political, social, and economic institutions.

Langton, Edward. *History of the Moravian Church.* London: George Allen & Unwin, 1956. A popular, illustrated survey of the history of the United Brethren church from the time of Jan Hus through the death of Zinzendorf. Discusses the connections between the movement begun by followers of Hus, the revival under Zinzendorf, and the Methodist movement.

Lewis, A. J. *Zinzendorf: The Ecumenical Pioneer.* Philadelphia: Westminster Press, 1962. The author was a Moravian minister in England. The book discusses Zinzendorf's efforts to unify Christians by igniting among them an interest in missionary and evangelistic work. Zinzendorf is portrayed as a forerunner of the twentieth century ecumenical movement.

Weinlick, John R. *Count Zinzendorf.* Nashville, Tenn.: Abingdon Press, 1956. Written by a professor of historical theology at the Moravian Theological Seminary, this is the standard English-language biography of Zinzendorf. A popular biography; illustrated and very well written.

Paul R. Waibel

ÉMILE ZOLA

Born: April 2, 1840; Paris, France
Died: September 29, 1902; Paris, France
Area of Achievement: Literature
Contribution: Zola's major contributions were in three areas: literature, as a
writer of poetry, drama, novels, and essays; literary theory, as one of the
major forces in defining naturalism as a literary school; and human rights,
as a defender of Alfred Dreyfus, who was falsely accused of treason and
sentenced to Devil's Island.

Early Life

Born in Paris on April 2, 1840, Émile Zola spent his first eighteen years in
Aix-en-Provence. Zola's father, Francesco Zola, was a high-spirited Venetian, bursting with grandiose ideas for engineering projects. With a doctorate
in engineering from the University of Padua, Francesco helped plan the first
public railway in Europe, served in the French foreign legion, and, in 1839,
married Émilie-Aurélie Aubert. Twenty thousand francs in debt, he nevertheless installed Émilie in an expensive Paris apartment, where Émile,
their only child, was born.

Francesco's fortunes improved when Aix accepted his plan to build a
canal to bring water to the municipality. The family moved to Provence,
where work on the canal proceeded. During construction, Francesco caught
cold and succumbed to pneumonia, leaving his family not only destitute but
also ninety thousand francs in debt. Émilie moved with her son to smaller
quarters, bringing her parents to live with them. Émilie's parents looked after the grieving Émile while Émilie did housework for other people, supplementing that modest income by gradually selling most of her furniture.

The family tried to protect the delicate Émile. Dark-haired and dark-eyed,
he had his father's broad face and protruding brow, on which worry lines,
lines of conscience, developed early. A speech defect caused Émile's class-
mates to taunt him. His mother used her dead husband's connections to
obtain for the boy a scholarship to Collège Bourbon, where he emphasized
scientific studies but developed his passion for literature. Here began his
friendship with his classmate Paul Cézanne.

When he was eighteen, Zola moved to Paris, where his mother had relocated to increase her earnings. Isolated and lonely, he lived in squalid surroundings, first with his mother, then alone. Poverty was ever-present. Émile
enrolled in the Lycée Saint-Louis, but twice he failed the baccalaureate
examinations, partly because his use of French was judged limited and de-
fective. He took menial jobs and at twenty-four published his first collection
of stories, *Contes à Ninon* (1864; *Stories for Ninon*, 1895), which was
encouragingly reviewed but brought him little money.

Life's Work

Stories for Ninon, although a promising beginning for a young author, shows little of the combination of careful observation, practiced objectivity, and scientific method that characterized Zola's most celebrated works. The stories are modeled on medieval fables, quite a different focus from that of the naturalistic themes for which Zola is best known. Zola's first novel, *La Confession de Claude* (1865; *Claude's Confession*, 1882), failed to employ the close, objective techniques of observation Zola demanded in his naturalistic credo, *Le Roman expérimental* (1880; *The Experimental Novel*, 1893), a theoretical work that significantly changed the course of writing in Europe, Great Britain, and the United States. His second and third novels, *Thérèse Raquin* (1867; English translation, 1881) and *Madeleine Férat* (1868; English translation, 1880), moved toward the realism practiced by Honoré de Balzac, Gustave Flaubert, and the brothers Edmond and Jules de Goncourt, whose writings attracted Zola, a voracious reader.

When Zola was writing these novels, however, he had not yet been exposed to Claude Bernard's *Introduction à l'étude de la médecine expérimentale* (1865; *Introduction to the Study of Experimental Medicine*, 1927), a book from a nonliterary field on which Zola was to model his formal approach to literature, which catapulted him to the forefront of an emerging school of literature that took writing well beyond the realism then prevalent in French literature.

Almost a decade before Zola read Bernard's influential book in 1878, the year of its author's death, he had begun the daunting literary task of writing *Les Rougon-Macquart* (1871-1893; *The Rougon-Macquart Novels*, 1885-1907), designed to examine in minute detail two generations of a family, considering especially the roles that both heredity and environment played in the lives of its members. This work is an interconnected series of twenty novels. Three books of the ambitious cycle, *L'Assommoir* (1877; English translation, 1879), *Nana* (1880; English translation, 1880), and *Germinal* (1885; English translation, 1885), are considered Zola's finest.

Before Zola began work on this cycle, however, he had stirred controversy in literary circles with *Claude's Confession*, in which his forthright and nonjudgmental presentation of a prostitute created legal problems for him in a France that very strongly controlled language and the arts. If his early work was considered notorious, by the time he was writing the Rougon-Macquart cycle, the bourgeoisie viewed him as completely outrageous, a threat to public decency.

Not until *L'Assommoir*, the seventh book of the Rougon-Macquart series, was published in 1877 did Zola's writing bring him much money. He had eked out a living before that time writing essays and doing a variety of journalistic jobs. Income from *L'Assommoir*, however, enabled him to buy a summer home at Médan. He had already attracted an enthusiastic following, especially among notable writers and artists who took very seriously Zola's writing in defense of the Impressionistic artists of his day.

A significant turning point in Zola's life came in 1880, the year in which his mother died and in which *Nana* and *The Experimental Novel* were published. In this year, also, Zola's theory of literary naturalism was exemplified with the publication of the anthology *Les Soirées de Médan* (1880). This work grew out of regular weekly soirées Zola held in both Médan and Paris. In these soirées, the participants, under Zola's staunch guidance, defined literary naturalism categorically, and the regular attendees, including Guy de Maupassant, Joris-Karl Huysmans, and Henri Céard, each contributed a story to the anthology.

If *The Experimental Novel* was the handbook for literary naturalists, *Les Soirées de Médan* became their manifesto. The naturalism Zola espoused moved beyond realism in that realism attempts to present life as it really is, whereas naturalism applies a scientific method to presenting reality, with the intention of identifying social ills and, through experimentation, reaching an understanding of those ills in ways that will enable society to remedy them.

Bernard wrote of the "vital circulus," the symbiosis between the muscular and nervous activities that preserve the blood-producing organs and the blood that nourishes the organs manufacturing it. Zola transformed this concept into his "social circulus." When an organ of society becomes infected, novelists, according to Zola, must proceed scientifically as physicians do. They must discover the simple initial cause that explains the indisposition. By exposing the cause, they then make it amenable to remedy.

Naturalistic writers, then, observe, record faithfully and in detail as a laboratory scientist would, and present their findings in literary form. Naturalistic authors remain detached from their material, presenting consistently exact records of their observations rather than observations colored by personal predilections. They show how heredity and environment act upon the human organism in the social setting to create human behavior. Few literary naturalist, including Zola, remained wholly faithful to the tenets of naturalism. Nevertheless, these tenets profoundly affected the writings of future generations of authors. The positive aspects of society were treated only as they contributed to causes of social ills. Just as medicine deals with physical pathologies, so did Zola's naturalism explore social pathologies.

From his earliest days, Zola had a great zeal for reform. He sought to change a society he considered imperfect. He was fearless and, when necessary, autocratic in working to bring about social changes he deemed imperative. He was incredibly hardworking, ever planning literary projects huge in scope, not unlike the grandiose engineering projects his father had planned a generation earlier. By 1893, Zola had, quite remarkably, completed the twenty novels of the Rougon-Macquart cycle and in the same year began work on the trilogy *Les Trois Villes* (1894-1898; *The Three Cities*, 1894-

1898), consisting of *Lourdes* (1894; English translation, 1894), *Rome* (1896; English translation, 1896), and *Paris* (1898; English translation, 1898).

As his work on the trilogy neared its end, Zola, incensed at what he considered the wrongful conviction for treason and sentencing to Devil's Island of Captain Alfred Dreyfus in 1894, took a public stand in support of Dreyfus and published his stirring letter "J'accuse" (1898; "The Dreyfus Case," 1898), which led to a reopening of the case and to the eventual acquittal of the defendant. Zola, however, as a result of his stand, was found guilty on two charges of libel, fined three thousand francs, and sentenced to a year in prison.

Before the execution of his sentence, Zola fled to England, where he remained until France's president, Émile-François Loubet, pardoned him in 1899, whereupon Zola returned to France. There, he continued work on another massive project, *Les Quatre Évangiles* (1899-1903; English translation, 1900-1903), to consist of four novels, three of which, *Fécondité* (1899; *Fruitfulness*, 1900), *Travail* (1901; *Work*, 1901), and *Vérité* (1903; *Truth*, 1903), he completed before his death by coal gas asphyxiation in his Paris apartment on September 29, 1902. The death, first thought to be accidental, was likely a murder committed by elements who opposed his participation in the Dreyfus case.

Summary

Émile Zola was a man with exuberant plans, a man of enormous energy and courage. He lived a life guided by principles he arrived at consciously and intelligently. In addition to his prolific literary career, Zola's involvement in public affairs, always guided by his intellect and his immutable conscience, distinguished him throughout his life.

Zola's support of Impressionist artists in the 1860's forced him into an unpopular public stand well before his own future was assured. He supported what he believed without regard to personal consequences. He was equally stalwart in the 1870's and 1880's, as he was developing his own literary credo, which, in its final formulation as literary naturalism, became a publicly unpopular movement. Zola spent the last years of his life preoccupied with the Dreyfus affair, and on his death it was this stand that seemed best to exemplify to his countrymen his spirit of social reform, as Anatole France noted in his oration at Zola's funeral.

Zola's literary theories directly affected scores of authors, among whom some direct inheritors were Gerhart Hauptmann, Hermann Sudermann, Arthur Schnitzler, August Strindberg, Henrik Ibsen, Thomas Hardy, D. H. Lawrence, Eugene O'Neill, Frank Norris, Upton Sinclair, and Thomas Mann. Indirectly, his literary theories affected even those authors who rebelled against naturalism and went on to found such important countermovements as literary expressionism.

Bibliography

Baguley, David. *Critical Essays on Émile Zola*. Boston: G. K. Hall, 1986. The twenty essays in this book, some written especially for this volume, others drawn from previously published sources, present a balanced view of Zola criticism, ranging from such early critics as Algernon Swinburne, Henry Havelock Ellis, and Heinrich Mann to such later ones as Roland Barthes, Irving Howe, and Naomi Schor.

Knapp, Bettina L. *Émile Zola*. New York: Frederick Ungar, 1980. A brief, direct presentation, accurate and highly appropriate for those just beginning to explore Zola. The chronological table is especially useful.

Richardson, Joanna. *Zola*. New York: St. Martin's Press, 1978. Richardson succeeds in showing how what she considers Zola's contentiousness relates to the impact of his work, which overall is excellent more as a reflection of a well-defined literary credo than as an artistic contribution. Especially valuable for its clear exposition of the Dreyfus affair.

Schom, Alan. *Émile Zola: A Biography*. New York: Henry Holt, 1987. The excellence of its prose style and the carefully chosen illustrations make this book a reading delight. The research is exhaustive, and the revelations that point to Zola's death's being a well-planned assassination made to look like an accident raise fascinating questions for the modern reader.

Schor, Naomi. *Zola's Crowds*. Baltimore: Johns Hopkins University Press, 1978. Schor is concerned with Zola's remarkable ability to control the huge numbers of people who populate a work as massive as the Rougon-Macquart series, in which each novel is at once independent from but interconnected with the others. An interesting thesis in the light of Gustave Le Bon's theory of the crowd.

Walker, Philip. *Zola*. London: Routledge & Kegan Paul, 1985. This thoughtful book is meticulous in its research although somewhat pedestrian in its organization. The most valuable chapter in it is "Full Summer," which explores fruitfully Zola's necrophobia, a matter that had significant bearing on his writing.

R. Baird Shuman

HULDRYCH ZWINGLI

Born: January 1, 1484; Wildhaus, Swiss Confederation
Died: October 11, 1531; near Kappel, Swiss Confederation
Areas of Achievement: Church reform and theology
Contribution: Zwingli led the Swiss Reformation against Roman Catholic ecclesiastical abuses, sharing both the rhetoric and the theology of Germany's own reformer, Martin Luther, until the two disagreed over the nature of the Eucharist. Overshadowed in church history by both Luther and John Calvin, Zwingli's most lasting contribution to Church history is his incipient Reformed theology and his recognition of the role that secular government might play in ecclesiastical matters.

Early Life

Huldrych Zwingli was born in Wildhaus, Swiss Confederation, to wealthy, devout parents. Zwingli's father served as a village magistrate and sought early to train his son in the ways of his Catholic faith—a Catholic faith invigorated by the new Humanism, which recognized and bestowed upon mankind more human responsibility and involvement in divine affairs. His father earnestly desired that Zwingli be educated as a priest and sent the boy at age ten to a Latin school in Basel, where he excelled in grammar, music, and dialectics. In 1498, Zwingli entered college study at Berne, where he came under the tutelage of Heinrich Wölflin, an influential Humanist scholar, who planted the initial seeds of intellectual independence in Zwingli. At Berne, Zwingli, now called Ulrich, distinguished himself as a musician and singer and was urged by the Dominican Order in Berne to join their choir and study music further. Zwingli initially accepted their invitation but abruptly withdrew. He chose instead to continue his theological education and entered in 1500 the University of Vienna, where he spent two years studying Scholastic philosophy, astronomy, and physics.

In 1502, Zwingli returned to the University of Basel, where he continued his classical studies while teaching Latin in the school of Saint Martin. He completed his bachelor's degree in 1504 and his master of arts degree in 1506 and became known officially as "Master Ulrich." At Basel, he became friends with Leo Jud, who would later become a chief associate in the reformation efforts in Zurich. Both studied under the famous Thomas Wyttenbach, professor of theology at Basel, whom Zwingli credits with opening his eyes to evils and abuses of the contemporary Church, especially its trafficking in indulgences—the sale of divine favors, such as forgiveness of or license to sin, or immediate entrance into heaven upon death.

Zwingli was ordained in the priesthood by the Bishop of Constance in 1506 and appointed pastor of Glarus, the capital city of the canton of the same name. Zwingli spent ten years in Glarus, occupied by preaching and pastoral duties as well as continuing to advance his knowledge of biblical languages, Greek and Roman philosophy, and the church fathers. Unlike Martin Luther, Zwingli did not in this fallow period seek a doctor of divinity degree, content with work in local pastorates and aiming at no higher church office. In the spring of 1515, Zwingli met the great Humanist scholar Desiderius Erasmus, whose writings he had been studying, and was deeply impressed by both his learning and his moderate theological views on inherited sin and his emerging symbolic reinterpretation of the Lord's Supper. Both Wyttenbach and Erasmus had helped remove the theological naïveté from Zwingli, infusing the spirit of Humanism into his own understanding and response to traditional Catholic teaching and a spirit of skepticism in his relationship with the Church hierarchy.

During this time, Zwingli also served as chaplain to the Glarus mercenaries who served the pope—devout men who he believed were being exploited by an illegitimate foreign power. This experience fueled his Swiss patriotism and compelled him to oppose publicly the mercenary system itself so vociferously that he was forced out of his pastorate in 1516. He subsequently moved to Einsiedeln, where he served as parish priest for three years, continuing his inquiry into the Greek New Testament and the church fathers. There Zwingli crystallized his views on salvation by faith, memorizing the New Testament letters of the apostle Paul and meshing his patriotic fervor with Erasmus' radical pacifism to take both a theological and a political stance against Rome. In his preaching, Zwingli began to oppose the use of relics in worship and pilgrimages to holy shrines as acts of devotion, regarding them as needless and idolatrous concessions to a religion that had left its eternal moorings.

Life's Work

Zwingli thus emerged from his early adult life as a clergyman emancipated from blind trust in the wisdom and infallibility of the Church hierarchy and its magisterium—the accumulated body of interpretation of Scripture used as an authority in disputes over the meaning of the Bible. In his slow but inexorable independence from established Christendom, he began to place great value upon his classical learning and great emphasis upon the need for individuals to exercise their faith in God directly—without the help of intermediaries such as relics and images, priests and departed saints. This intellectual foment prepared him for the greatest task of his life: the reformation of Swiss Catholicism.

In the biographies of all the activists within the Protestant Reformation, the most important aspects of their lives rest as much on their intellectual efforts as on their dramatic deeds. This is the case with Zwingli, although his willingness to engage in armed warfare on behalf of his faith distinguishes him from some of his fellows. Nevertheless, Zwingli is most prominent for his contribution to the theological foment of his times as well as to the realignments and associations forged in his native land of Switzerland and his adopted city, Zurich. As Luther had Wittenberg and Calvin Geneva, so Zwingli had Zurich, a city in which his great ideals would find incarnation not only in its cathedrals but also in its government structures. His beliefs eventually led him into local and canton politics, as he sought to move the secular city and the City of God into a more symbiotic, merciful status with each other.

In 1518, Zwingli was nominated for the position of people's priest at the Great Minister Church in Zurich, a prestigious and powerful pastorate. His candidacy was at first opposed in view of Zwingli's admittedly broken vow of celibacy; a friend intervened, however, and Zwingli assumed his new post on January 1, 1519. His early sermons were practical and ethical rather than doctrinal and divisive. From an unassuming beginning, Zwingli's pulpit became famous and extremely popular in Zurich; his down-to-earth expositions of biblical texts—as opposed to the dense, allegorical sermons common to the time—opened up the Scriptures to his flock and made Christianity seem present and vital rather than otherworldly and detached. This fresh emphasis on the Bible as an authoritative document that could speak directly to the hearts of people became the scaffolding for the Reformation everywhere, including Switzerland.

As Luther's reform movement began to shake the Church in Germany, Zwingli could not help but take notice. The war over indulgences that Luther had valiantly won in the German church became only a minor skirmish in Zurich, as the Roman church moved quickly to rectify abuses in Switzerland in an effort to stall the wholesale revolution it feared. Zwingli would engage the war on a different front: the authority of the Bible against the authority of the papal hierarchy. Zwingli's active involvement in the reform movement may well be located in August, 1519, when a plague broke out in Zurich and swept away one-third of the population and nearly took Zwingli's life. His experience in ministry to the sick and bereaved brought him renewed faith in God and emboldened him to speak out about the responsibility of the Church to offer grace, not law, to its members. Zwingli suggested that this would be accomplished by restoring Scripture to its rightful place in the authority of the Church and by dismantling the elaborate liturgy of the Mass, replacing it with a more homely and accessible kind of personal worship that would focus on God, not man.

Zwingli also began to see the civil government as an ally in his reform effort. Actively campaigning in the city council, Zwingli persuaded its members to take action against nonbiblically centered preaching in Zurich. In December, 1520, the council ordered the priests in the city and country to preach only from the Bible—the first time a secular authority had intervened in the affairs of the Church. Zwingli himself was elected to the council in

1521, and, within a month, the council repudiated its citizens' participation in the mercenary system he had long opposed. Renouncing his papal salary, Zwingli parlayed his alliance with local government into greater dominion and influence, as his pulpit became a sharp weapon against Rome. During the season of Lent in 1522, Zwingli openly called for his parishioners to ignore prohibitions against eating meat and to practice their liberty. In addition, he called for the end of forced celibacy for clergy, having entered the same year into a secret marriage himself with Anna Reinhard, a widow with three children.

These radical demands brought on direct opposition from Rome, and the civil authorities called for two public debates on the matter. Threatened with assassination, Zwingli defended his stance vigorously both in public and in print. His *Artikel* (1523; sixty-seven conclusions)—parallel to the famous ninety-five theses that Luther nailed to the Wittenberg Cathedral door—boldly repudiated papal authority, forced celibacy, the veneration of the saints, the transubstantiation view of the Eucharist, the existence of purgatory, and the necessity of fasting. In January, 1523, the Council of Zurich declared Zwingli the victor in the disputation, and Zurich became a firm canton of the Reformation.

Most of Zwingli's writings were born of conflict, including his *De vera ac falsa religione* (commentary on true and false religion), published in 1525, which may be regarded as the first Protestant systematic theology—a thoroughgoing treatise explaining the Protestant view of key doctrines such as salvation, the nature of Christ, the authority of the Scriptures, and the role of the Church. With his co-Reformer, Leo Jud, he also translated the Scriptures into German-Swiss as the Swiss reform quickly spread to other German and Italian cantons. Zwingli's radical departure from received Catholic doctrine reached its zenith in 1525. Preceding it were months of organized purges of pictures, crucifixes, altars, candles, and any other images from the churches of the city—all on the principle that the Second Commandment forbade the making of any artistic image of God or Christ as idolatry. Then, during Holy Week of April, 1525, Zwingli formally displaced the traditional Catholic Mass with the first great Reformed communion service in the Great Minister Church, the bread and the wine celebrated as "representations" and not the "real presence" of Christ.

The reformation of Zwingli's Zurich was substantially complete by 1525, as both secular and ecclesiastical institutions united in iconoclastic spirit to create a uniquely Swiss Protestant church. Yet the controversy over the roles of each institution in the lives of Christians continued from a right flank, as a group of Reformers known as the Anabaptists, or "re-baptizers," began to oppose Zwingli's accommodations with Rome and the council. A split had occurred in 1523 during an intense debate over the Zurich city council's refusal to bring about certain religious changes called for by Anabaptist theologians. Zwingli's view that the civil authorities should be persuaded by patient preaching rather than violent social action differed from the even more radical Anabaptists, who believed that Scripture alone—not the wisdom or political machinations of a secular government—should determine the course of the Reformation. Over two years, the gap widened, as the Anabaptists pressed their opposition to the baptism of infants and to any jurisdiction of the civil government in their Church life. In spring, 1525, a complete rupture occurred when the Zurich city council, led by Zwingli, forbade the Anabaptists to assemble or to disseminate their views. Those who refused the order were tortured, incarcerated, and, in a few prominent instances, put to death by drowning. There is no indication that Zwingli opposed the latter.

From 1526 to 1531, the Reformation spread to other cantons, and intolerance of opposing views accompanied it as Protestant Switzerland was internally beset by both military and theological challenges from Rome and by doctrinal challenges from Lutheran comrades in the Reformation. In October, 1529, the Colloquy of Marburg occurred, bringing together Zwingli and Luther, and their colleagues, to reconcile their differing views on the Lord's Supper. Zwingli held firmly to his view that the transubstantiation taking place at the Lord's Supper was not in the bread and wine but in the living saints who are gathered in the congregation to celebrate it. Unable to find common ground, the Reformers and their followers went their separate ways.

Meanwhile, tensions continued to build between those cantons that had joined the Reformation, notably Basel, Berne, and Zurich, and those that remained staunchly Catholic. In 1529, a modest peace had been negotiated at Kappel that would allow for mutual toleration and the freedom of a canton to be either Catholic or Protestant. By 1531, relationships had again deteriorated as a Catholic alliance, fearing the eventual domination of Protestant Christianity over them, launched a virtual civil war, an offensive designed to bring them final relief from their aggressors. In October 9, 1531, a Catholic militia, aided by papal mercenaries, marched to the borders of Zurich at Kappel, which was unprepared. Zwingli, who had warned the city council of the impending danger that the Catholic cantons presented, accompanied the small army gathered for defense and was himself killed. His body was recovered by the victorious Catholic militia and then quartered for treason and burnt for heresy, his ashes scattered to the winds. Zwingli's mantle of leadership then fell on Heinrich Bullinger, a friend of John Calvin, who continued to fight for Zwingli's theological and political principles.

Summary

Huldrych Zwingli's legacy to history takes the form of his unique contribution to Protestantism, particularly his dissenting views on the Lord's Supper and the proper relationship between the Church and civil authority.

Zwingli had much in common with Luther and Calvin, particularly with their high view of Scriptural authority and their opposition to the legalistic theology of salvation commonly preached by contemporary Roman Catholic clerics. The Reformers, however, parted company significantly in their views of the Church, the nature of the Lord's Supper, and the relationship between the Church and civil authority. While Lutheran and Calvinistic Protestantism emphasized the Church's responsibility to preach the Word and its authority to administer the Sacraments, Zwingli understood the Church less as an institution than as a relationship called into being by Christ, a relationship resting upon the loyalty of the members of a local body of Christ to one another. What binds them together in his view is not hierarchical authority but commitment to the Bible as sole spiritual authority and to one another as functioning members of the body of Christ. Thus, Zwingli promoted the Lord's Supper as an activity to unite the Church in recognition of a common calling, not as a reenactment of the death of Christ proffered by an authoritative Church hierarchy.

Zwingli thus emerges from the sixteenth century as a much more modern, even liberal, theologian when compared with Luther and Calvin. His advocacy of an activist role in Church matters by a godly civil state sets him apart from his fellow Protestants in Germany, France, and Britain, who bitterly opposed secular intrusion into their theological and ecclesiastical dealings. Believing that God ordained the civil government as a coequal community with the Church to provide peace and order so that Christians could minister grace and salvation to the world, Zwingli offered a compromise position that established the kingdom of God in the politics of mankind. Despite the flaws of intolerance that crept into his own social and theological practice in times of tension, Zwingli's beliefs serve as a precursor to much liberation theology of the late twentieth century and certainly foreshadow the civil rights movement headed by Martin Luther King, Jr., in the United States of the 1950's and 1960's.

Bibliography
Bromiley, Geoffrey W., ed. *Zwingli and Bullinger*. Philadelphia: Westminster Press, 1953. Contains selected texts of Zwingli—and his successor Bullinger—translated into English with a good, short introduction to the life, writings, and Reformed theology of Zwingli. This is the most accessible English source for Zwingli's primary texts.
Davies, Rupert E. *The Problem of Authority in the Continental Reformers: A Study in Luther, Zwingli, and Calvin*. Westport, Conn.: Greenwood Press, 1978. This monograph has a single focus: How did the Reformers resolve issues of religious authority in their efforts to reform Roman Christianity? Davies documents with admirable clarity—in a lengthy chapter devoted entirely to Zwingli—Zwingli's attempt to place biblical authority at the

center of the Reformation, while recognizing a proper sphere for ecclesiastical authority within the life of an individual Christian. The author's comparative study of the three Reformers illuminates the answers of each to this vexing question.

Farner, Oskar. *Zwingli the Reformer: His Life and Work.* Translated by D. G. Sear. New York: Philosophical Library, 1952. A brief, very readable overview of the life, times, and theology of Zwingli by the most prominent German scholar of Zwingli in the twentieth century. Farner's main intention is to acquaint the novice reader with the broad outlines of Zwingli's thought rather than to offer an interpretive, scholarly context for understanding. In this it is primarily a helpful primer on Zwingli's contribution to the Swiss Reformation rather than a comprehensive treatise.

Furcha, E. J., and H. Wayne Pipkin, eds. *Prophet, Pastor, Protestant: The World of Huldrych Zwingli After Five Hundred Years.* Pittsburgh: Pickwick Publications, 1984. An anthology of essays by ten prominent, contemporary Zwingli scholars, who have evaluated the historical impact of Zwingli's Reformation efforts on Church history on the occasion of the five hundredth anniversary of Zwingli's birth. A compendium of wise scholarship on various aspects of Zwingli's political and theological thought, valuable for its corrective reassessment of earlier Zwingli scholarship.

Garside, Charles, Jr. *Zwingli and the Arts.* New Haven, Conn.: Yale University Press, 1966. A unique work of Zwingli scholarship that attempts to assess the nature and impact of Zwingli's views of art and creativity on sixteenth century Christian worship, particularly in the visual and musical arts. Skillfully juxtaposing Zwingli's views to those of Calvin and Luther, Garside reveals Zwingli's austere devotion to an "invisible" God who could not and should not be captured in art; thus, there was for Zwinglian Christianity no place in the Church for the Christian artist seeking an outlet for expression.

Potter, G. R. *Zwingli.* Cambridge: Cambridge University Press, 1976. This volume is the standard scholarly work on Zwingli, breathtaking in its scope and coverage of Zwingli's personality, theology, and politics. Its author, an emeritus professor of medieval history at the University of Sheffield, sets a high standard for readable scholarly biography in this work, which should be the first volume consulted for serious inquiry into Zwingli's impact on the Swiss culture and the European church history. Zwingli emerges as a man more welcome in the twentieth century than in his own.

Rilliet, Jean. *Zwingli: Third Man of the Reformation.* Translated by Harold Knight. Philadelphia: Westminster Press, 1964. Rilliet regards Zwingli as the least known and appreciated of the three famous reformers and orients his study towards rehabilitating Zwingli's place in Reformation history and bringing him out of the shadow of Calvin and Luther. Rilliet highlights both the unique emphases and truths Zwingli discovered and the errors he unwittingly promoted. The book's chief value lies in its extensive treatment of the Eucharistic controversy and of Zwingli's denial of the common Catholic and Lutheran understanding of transubstantiation.

Schaff, Philip. *History of the Christian Church*. Vol. 8, *Modern Christianity: The Swiss Reformation*. Grand Rapids, Mich.: W. B. Eerdmans, 1910. This volume focuses entirely on the Swiss Reformation and Zwingli's dominant contribution to it. The main advantage of Schaff's text, as an earlier—and formerly standard—Church history, is that it presents with its wider angle a holistic, comprehensive overview of Church history through the centuries and labors to present a less provincial treatment of the isues raised by the Swiss version of the Reformation.

Walton, Robert C. *Zwingli's Theocracy*. Toronto: University of Toronto Press, 1967. This work helpfully clarifies a long-standing controversy regarding Zwingli's conception of the role and relationship of the clergy and royalty in the governance of a Christian state. Walton argues that, when one attends to Zwingli's later writings in comparison with his more often quoted, better-known earlier works, one finds that Zwingli did not, in fact, advocate a "theocracy" but rather a state in which authority is shared in a cooperative government operated by both sacred and secular officials.

Bruce L. Edwards

INDEXES

BIOGRAPHICAL INDEX

I

BIOGRAPHICAL INDEX

III

BIOGRAPHICAL INDEX

BIOGRAPHICAL INDEX

AREAS OF ACHIEVEMENT

AREAS OF ACHIEVEMENT

AREAS OF ACHIEVEMENT

GEOGRAPHICAL INDEX

GEOGRAPHICAL INDEX

GREAT LIVES FROM HISTORY

GEOGRAPHICAL INDEX